The Role of the Father in Child Development

Fourth Edition

The Role of the Father in Child Development

Fourth Edition

EDITED BY MICHAEL E. LAMB

WILEY

John Wiley & Sons, Inc.

Library of Congress Cataloging-in-Publication Data

The role of the father in child development / edited by Michael E. Lamb. — 4th ed.
    p. cm.
   Includes bibliographical references and index.
   ISBN 0-471-23161-4 (cloth)
   1. Fathers.   2. Father and child—United States.   3. Paternal deprivation—United States.
   4. Single-parent families—United States.   I. Lamb, Michael E., 1953–

HQ756.R64 2003
306.874′2—dc21

2003053484

Printed in the United States of America
10 9 8 7 6 5 4 3 2 1

To the memory of Kathleen J. Sternberg—passionate social worker, psychologist, researcher, children's advocate, scholar, colleague, wife, mother, and friend

Contents

Contributors

Paul R. Amato
Department of Sociology
Pennsylvania State University

Ted Barker
Department of Psychology
University of Texas

Natasha J. Cabrera
Department of Human Development
University of Maryland

Marcia S. Carlson
Department of Sociology and
    Social Work
Columbia University

E. Mark Cummings
Department of Psychology
University of Notre Dame

Jessica Dennis
Department of Psychology
University of California at Riverside

Mary L. Flyr
Department of Psychology
University of California at Riverside

Cynthia Garcia-Coll
Department of Education
Brown University

Marcie C. Goeke-Morey
Department of Psychology
University of Notre Dame

Barry S. Hewlett
Department of Anthropology
Washington State University

George W. Holden
Department of Psychology
University of Texas

Carl Philip Hwang
Department of Psychology
Goteborgs Universitet

Jung-Hwan Hyun
Department of Child Care and
    Education
Seoul Theological University

Colleen Killian
Department of Psychology
University of California at Riverside

Michael E. Lamb
National Institute of Child Health
    and Human Development

Charlie Lewis
Department of Psychology
University of Lancaster

Mary M. Lutz
Department of Human and
    Community Development
University of Illinois

David J. McDowell
Department of Psychology
University of Rochester

Brent A. McBride
Department of Human and
    Community Development
University of Illinois

Sarah McLanahan
Department of Sociology
Princeton University

Brian P. Masciadrelli
Department of Human and
    Community Development
University of Illinois

Kristie L. Morris
Department of Sociology
University of California at Riverside

Jun Nakazawa
Faculty of Education
Chiba University

Maggie O'Brien
School of Social Work and
    Psychological Studies
University of East Anglia

Ross D. Parke
Department of Psychology
University of California at Riverside

Charlotte J. Patterson
Department of Psychology
University of Virginia

Elizabeth H. Pleck
Department of History
University of Illinois

Joseph H. Pleck
Department of Human and
    Community Development
University of Illinois

Jessica Raymond
Department of Psychology
University of Notre Dame

Jaipaul L. Roopnarine
Department of Community and
    Family Studies
Syracuse University

Graeme Russell
Department of Psychology
Macquarie University

David W. Shwalb
Department of Psychology
Southeastern Louisiana University

Julie M. Sobolewski
Department of Sociology
Pennsylvania State University

Catherine S. Tamis-LeMonda
Department of Applied Psychology
New York University

Margaret Wild
Department of Psychology
University of California at Riverside

Toshiya Yamamoto
Department of International
    Social Studies
Maebashi Kyoai Gakuen College

CHAPTER 1

The Role of the Father

An Introduction

MICHAEL E. LAMB and CATHERINE S. TAMIS-LEMONDA

THE FIRST TWO EDITIONS of *The Role of the Father in Child Development* (Lamb, 1976, 1981c) contained encyclopedic introductory chapters in which Lamb attempted to provide inclusive reviews of the primary and secondary literatures. Such endeavors were no longer possible by the time of the third edition, when the reference list for such a chapter would have occupied more space than any of the chapters in the book! For the same reasons, this fourth edition of the anthology instead includes an introductory chapter in which we attempt to articulate major themes in our contemporary understanding of father-child relationships and paternal influences, while referring readers to the chapters that follow for more detailed reviews of the relevant literature. In this chapter we thus discuss some defining assumptions about fatherhood and recent work on the characteristics, determinants, and effects of paternal behavior, and we then close with summaries of the chapters included in this book.

Substantial progress has clearly been made by scholars over the last 30 years. Hundreds of studies have enriched the empirical literature, while theorists have elaborated and refined the conceptual frameworks designed to elucidate fatherhood, father-child relationships, and paternal roles. When the first edition of this anthology was published in 1976, most social scientists doubted that fathers significantly shaped the experiences and development of their children, especially their daughters. As a result, contributors to the first edition all made concerted and often explicit efforts to demonstrate that fathers (a) indeed had a role to play in child development, (b) were often salient in their children's lives, and (c) affected the course of their children's development, for good as well as for ill. Although somewhat less defensive in tone, contributions to the second edition, published just five years later in 1981, not surprisingly emphasized the same conclusions. By contrast, chapters in the third volume (1997) reflected widespread acceptance of the notion that fathers are often affectively and formatively salient. The contributors' focus was thus placed on more nuanced issues and concerns.

Four prominent areas of research dominate the contributions to this volume and thus frame this chapter: (a) discourse on the nature of father involvement, (b) research on fathers' influences, (c) studies focused on the determinants of father involvement, and (d) interest in the synergy between basic research and relevant social policies. Accordingly, current appreciation of the complex, multidimensional roles that fathers play in family life today are explored in the first section. Studies that have helped researchers understand the direct and indirect influences of fathers on children's development are then discussed. In the third section we examine research on the factors that affect the nature and extent of paternal involvement. Because social constructions of fatherhood vary across historical epochs and subcultural contexts, the behaviors and experiences of fathers are viewed within nested ecological contexts in this analysis. The growing need to bridge research and policies in the fatherhood arena is then discussed in the fourth section. Now that researchers have amassed a solid body of evidence regarding the benefits of positive father involvement for children's well-being, researchers, practitioners, and policy makers are eager to link scientific findings to initiatives and programs designed to enhance and support the commitment of fathers to their young children. In the final section we outline the book and indicate how the component chapters address the broad themes introduced in the four preceding sections.

THE NATURE OF FATHER INVOLVEMENT

It seems logical to begin this anthology by examining definitions and descriptions of fathering. How available are fathers to their children? What roles do fathers play in family life today? What taxonomies might effectively characterize fathers' activities with and commitments to their children?

LEVELS OF FATHER INVOLVEMENT

Whether and how much time fathers spend with their children are questions at the heart of much research conducted over the past three decades. In the mid-1970s a number of investigators sought to describe—often by detailed observation and sometimes also through detailed maternal and paternal reports—the extent of paternal interactions with children (Pleck & Masciadrelli, this volume; Lamb & Lewis, this volume). Many of these researchers have framed their research around the three types of paternal involvement (engagement, accessibility, responsibility) described by Lamb, Pleck, Charnov, and Levine (1987). As Pleck and Masciadrelli note, researchers have consistently shown that fathers spend much less time with their children than do mothers. In two-parent families in which mothers are unemployed, fathers spend about one-fourth as much time as mothers in direct interaction or engagement with their children, and about a third as much time being accessible to their children. Many fathers assume essentially no responsibility (as defined by participation in key decisions, availability at short notice, involvement in the care of sick children, management and selection of alternative child care, etc.) for their children's care or rearing, however, and the small subgroup of fathers who assume high degrees of responsibility has not been studied extensively. Average levels of paternal responsibility have increased over time, albeit slowly, and there appear to be small but continuing increases over time in average levels of all types of paternal involvement.

In two-parent families with employed mothers, the average levels of paternal engagement and accessibility are both substantially higher than in families with unemployed mothers. In such families paternal involvement in direct interaction or engagement and accessibility average 33% and 65% of the relevant figures for mothers, respectively. Even when both mothers and fathers are employed 30 or more hours per week, however, many fathers assume little responsibility for child care. In addition, it is worth noting that fathers do not necessarily spend more time interacting with their children when mothers are unemployed; rather, the proportions increase dramatically in large part because mothers are spending less time caring for their children. Thus, fathers are *proportionally* more involved when mothers are employed, even though the extent of their involvement, in absolute terms, increases quite modestly, if at all. Over time, levels of paternal involvement in dual-earner families have increased, but the changes are much smaller than popular accounts often suggest (Pleck & Masciadrelli, this volume).

FATHERS' ROLES

Although descriptive accounts of fathers' relative accessibility to children are informative, they fall short of elucidating *what* fathers do when they are available and *why* they do what they do. In this regard, a fuller conceptualization of fathers' roles and the origins of their presumably prescribed responsibilities is warranted. Historical, cultural, and familial ideologies inform the roles fathers play and undoubtedly shape the absolute amounts of time fathers spend with their children, the activities they share with them, and perhaps even the quality of the father-child relationships.

In earlier times, fathers were viewed as all-powerful patriarchs who wielded enormous power over their families (Knibiehler, 1995), and vestiges of these notions continued until quite recently. According to Pleck and Pleck (1997), for example, White fathers were viewed primarily as moral teachers during the colonial phase of American history. By popular consensus, fathers were primarily responsible for ensuring that their children grew up with an appropriate sense of values, acquired primarily from a study of the Bible and other scriptural texts. Around the time of industrialization, however, primary focus shifted from moral leadership to breadwinning and economic support of the family. Then, perhaps as a result of the Great Depression, which revealed many men as poor providers, social scientists came to portray fathers as sex-role models, with commentators expressing concern about the failures of many men to model masculine behavior for their sons. Throughout the 20th century, fathers were urged to be involved (Griswold, 1993), and following feminist and scholarly critiques of masculinity and femininity, there emerged in the late 1970s a new concern with the new nurturant father, who played an active role in his children's lives. As Elizabeth Pleck explains in this volume, however, popular and scholarly discussions of fatherhood have long dwelled on the importance of involvement—often defined by successful bread winning—and the fear of inadequate fathering. In contrast to earlier conceptualizations of fathers' roles that often focused quite narrowly on breadwinning, researchers, theorists, and practitioners no longer cling to the simplistic belief that fathers fill a unidimensional and universal role in their families and in their children's eyes. Instead, they recognize that fathers play a number of significant roles—companions, care providers, spouses, protectors, models, moral guides, teachers, breadwinners—whose relative importance varies across historical epochs and subcultural groups. Only by considering the fathers' performance of these various roles and by taking into account their relative importance in the socioecological contexts concerned can researchers evaluate fathers' impact on child development. Unfortunately, theorists and social commentators have tended in the past to emphasize only one paternal role at a time, with different functions attracting most attention during different historical epochs.

Although fathers have typically been perceived and judged by their breadwinning or provisioning, fathers fill other roles as well. Much of the early observational and survey data suggested that mothers and fathers engaged in rather different types of interaction with their children, especially in Anglo-Saxon countries like the United States (Lamb, 1981a; Lamb & Lewis, this volume). These studies have consistently shown that fathers tend to specialize in play, whereas mothers specialize in caretaking and nurturance, especially (but not only) in relation to infants.

Although such findings seem quite reliable, the results have often been misrepresented and have led to overly stereotypic and unidimensional portrayals of fathers as play partners. Compared with mothers, fathers indeed spend a greater proportion of their time with children engaged in play, but they still spend a small proportion of their own time in play. In absolute terms, most studies suggest that mothers play with their children more than fathers do, but because play (particularly boisterous, stimulating, and emotionally arousing play) is more prominent in father-child interaction, paternal playfulness and relative novelty may help make fathers especially salient to their children (Lamb, Frodi, Hwang, & Frodi, 1983). This enhanced salience may increase fathers' influence more than would be expected based on the amount of time they spend with their children.

However, comparative studies, in which fathers' interactions are contrasted with those of mothers, typically focus on mean-level differences in parenting activities and often obscure common patterns of parent-child interaction. By highlighting the unique qualities of fathers and mothers, they may promote narrow views of fathers' and mothers' roles, thereby failing to capture similarities in the meaning or degree of influence parents exert on their children. In fact, both fathers and mothers encourage exploration during play with their infants (Power, 1985), alter their speech patterns to infants by speaking slowly and using shorter phrases (Dalton-Hummel, 1982; Golinkoff & Ames, 1979; Rondal, 1980), respond to their infants' cries and smiles (Berman, 1980), are sensitive to their 1-year-olds when preoccupied with a task (Notaro & Volling, 1999), and adjust their behaviors to accommodate developmental changes in their infants' competencies (Belsky, Gilstrap, & Rovine, 1984; Crawley & Sherrod, 1984). Sensitive fathering—responding to, talking to, scaffolding, and teaching and encouraging their children to learn—predicts children's cognitive and linguistic achievements just as sensitive mothering does (e.g., Conner, Knight, & Cross, 1997; Easterbrooks & Goldberg, 1984; Shannon, Tamis-LeMonda, London, & Cabrera, 2002). Such findings suggest that fathers can and do engage with their children in many different ways, not only as playmates, and that they are more than role models.

SUMMARY

In the last decade scholars have moved beyond unidimensional characterizations of fathers as breadwinners or as persons who are dichotomously absent or present to acknowledging the numerous roles that fathers play in their families. Multidimensional conceptions of father involvement have fostered new theoretical models and empirical testing of the relations among measures of fathering, while raising questions about how and why dimensions of fathering vary across developmental and historical time and how they jointly contribute to the life trajectories of children and families (see Day & Lamb, in press, and Tamis-LeMonda & Cabrera, 2002, for multiple examples of these trends). A broader, more inclusive conceptualization of fathers' roles recognizes the appreciable variation that exists both within and between fathers. Most individual fathers assume numerous roles in their families (including breadwinner, playmate, caregiver), while fathers differ with respect to the relative importance of these diverse roles.

FATHERS' INFLUENCES ON CHILDREN

A second line of research on fatherhood examines fathers' effects on children and the pathways through which those effects are exerted. Which aspects of child development were influenced most, at what ages, under which circumstances, and why? Three types of studies have been designed to explore this topic: correlational studies, studies of father absence and divorce, and studies of involved fathers. Here, we review these research methods and then examine direct and indirect effects of fathering on child development.

CORRELATIONAL STUDIES

Many of the earliest studies of paternal influences were designed to identify correlations between paternal and filial characteristics. The vast majority of these studies were conducted between 1940 and 1970 when the father's role as a sex-role model was considered most important; as a result, most studies were focused on sex-role development, especially in sons (for reviews, see Biller, 1971, 1993; Lamb, 1981b). The design of these early studies was quite simple: Researchers assessed masculinity in fathers and sons and then determined how strongly the two sets of scores were correlated. To the great surprise of most researchers, however, there was no consistent correlation between the two constructs, a puzzling finding because it seemed to violate a guiding assumption about the crucial function served by fathers. If fathers did not make their boys into men, what role did they really serve?

It took a while for psychologists to realize that they had failed to ask, Why should boys want to be like their fathers? Presumably they should only want to resemble fathers whom they liked and respected and with whom their relationships were warm and positive. In fact, the quality of father-son relationships proved to be a crucial mediating variable: When the relationships between masculine fathers and their sons were good, the boys were indeed more masculine. Subsequent research even suggested that the quality of the father-child relationships was more important than the masculinity of the father (Mussen & Rutherford, 1963; Payne & Mussen, 1956; Sears, Maccoby, & Levin, 1957). Boys seemed to conform to the sex-role standards of their culture when their relationships with their fathers were warm, regardless of how masculine the fathers were, even though warmth and intimacy have traditionally been seen as feminine characteristics. A similar conclusion was suggested by research on other aspects of psychosocial adjustment and on achievement: Paternal warmth or closeness appeared beneficial, whereas paternal masculinity appeared to be irrelevant (Biller, 1971; Lamb, 1981b; Radin, 1981). The same characteristics are important with regard to maternal influences, suggesting that fathers and mothers influence children in similar ways by virtue of nurturant personal and social characteristics. Research summarized in this volume by Patterson goes even further, indicating that the sexual orientation of homosexual fathers does not increase the likelihood that their children will be homosexual, effeminate, or maladjusted.

In sum, as far as influences on children are concerned, very little about the gender of the parent seems to be distinctly important. The characteristics of the father as a parent rather than the characteristics of the father as a man appear to be most significant, although it is impossible to demonstrate that the father's masculine characteristics are of no significance. Some scholars continue to underscore the crucial importance of distinctive maternal and paternal roles (Biller, 1994; Biller & Kimpton, 1997), however, and these themes are central to the claims of social commentators like Blankenhorn (1995) and Popenoe (1996) as well.

STUDIES OF FATHER ABSENCE AND DIVORCE

While this body of correlational research was burgeoning in the 1950s, another body of literature, comprising studies in which researchers tried to understand the father's role by examining families without fathers, was developing in parallel. The assumption was that by comparing the behavior and personalities of children raised with and without fathers, one could—essentially by a process of subtraction—estimate what sort of influence fathers typically had on children's development. The early father-absence and correlational studies were conducted in roughly the same era; it is not surprising, therefore, that the outcomes studied were very similar and that the implications were similar and consistent with popular assumptions as well (for reviews, see Adams, Milner, & Schrepf, 1984; Biller, 1974, 1993; Blankenhorn, 1995; Herzog & Sudia, 1973; Whitehead, 1993). As indicated by Hetherington and Stanley-Hagan (1997) children (especially boys) growing up without fathers seemed to have problems in the areas of sex-role and gender-identity development, school performance, psychosocial adjustment, and perhaps in the control of aggression.

Two related issues arising from the father-absence research must be addressed when evaluating these conclusions. First, even when researchers accept the conclusion that there are differences between children raised in families with the father present and those raised in families with the father absent, they must ask why those differences exist and how they should be interpreted. Second, it is important to remember that the existence of differences between groups of children growing up with and without fathers does not mean that every child growing up without a father has problems in the aspect of development concerned or that all children whose fathers live at home develop appropriately. One cannot reach conclusions about the status of individuals from data concerning groups simply because there is great within-group heterogeneity. This again forces us to ask why such heterogeneity exists among children in father-absent families: Why do some children appear to suffer deleterious consequences as a result of father absence, while others do not? More broadly, the question is, What is it about the context that makes for group differences between children in father-absent and father-present contexts, and what accounts for the impressive within-group variance?

Researchers and theorists first sought to explain the effects of father absence on boys by noting the absence of male sex-role models in single-parent families. In the absence of a male parental model, it was assumed that boys could not acquire strong masculine identities or sex roles and would not have models of achievement with which to identify (Biller, 1974, 1993). The validity of this interpretation is weakened by the fact that many boys without fathers seem to develop quite normally so far as sex-role development and achievement are concerned. Clearly, some factors other than the absence of a male sex-role model may be at least as important as (if not more important than) the availability of a sex-role model in mediating the effects of father absence on child development. What might these factors be?

In a conceptual and empirical extension of research on the effects of father absence, many researchers initiated studies in the early 1980s designed to explore more carefully the ways in which divorce and the transition to fatherlessness might influence children's development. The results of these studies have underscored the many ways in which paternal absence influences children (Hetherington & Kelly, 2002). First, there is the absence of a coparent—someone to help out with child care, perhaps participate in tough decisions, and take over when one parent needs a break from the incessant demands of child care. Following divorce, children consistently do better when they are able to maintain meaningful relationships with both parents unless the levels of interparental conflict remain unusually high (Kelly, 2000). Second, there is the economic stress that frequently accompanies single motherhood (Pearson & Thoennes, 1990). The median and mean incomes of single women who head households are significantly lower than in any other group of families, and the disparity is even larger when one considers per capita income rather than household income (Glick & Norton, 1979; Horn, 1995; O'Hare, 1995). Third, the tremendous economic stress experienced by single mothers is accompanied by emotional stress occasioned by a degree of social isolation and continuing (though diminished) social disapproval of single or divorced mothers and children (Hetherington et al., 1982). Fourth, children of divorce are often affected by the perceived, and frequently actual, abandonment by one of their parents (Kelly & Lamb, 2000; Lamb, 1999; Thompson & Laible, 1999). Last, there are the cancerous effects of predivorce and postdivorce marital conflict (Cummings, Goeke-Morey, & Raymond, this volume; Kelly, 2000). Because most single-parent families are produced by divorce and because divorce is often preceded and accompanied by periods of overt and covert spousal hostility, parental conflict may play a major role in explaining the problems of fatherless children.

In sum, the evidence suggests that father absence may be harmful not necessarily because a sex-role model is absent but because many paternal roles—economic, social, emotional—go unfilled or inappropriately filled in these families. Once again, the evidence suggests that recognition of the father's multiple roles as breadwinner, parent, and emotional partner is essential for understanding how fathers influence children's development.

RESEARCH ON INVOLVED FATHERS

In the 1980s several researchers sought to identify the effects of increased paternal involvement on children. In most of these studies researchers compared the status of children in more traditional families with that of children whose fathers either shared or took primary responsibility for child care (Lamb, Pleck, & Levine, 1985; Radin, 1994;

Russell, 1983, 1986); other researchers examined the correlates of varying levels of paternal engagement (Koestner, Franz, & Weinberger, 1990; Mosely & Thomson, 1995). The effects of increased paternal involvement have been addressed in several major studies, and the results have been remarkably consistent. Children with highly involved fathers were characterized by increased cognitive competence, increased empathy, less sex-stereotyped beliefs, and a more internal locus of control (Pleck, 1997; Pruett, 1983, 1985; Radin, 1982, 1994). Again the question that has to be asked is, Why do these sorts of differences occur?

Three factors are probably important in this regard (Lamb et al., 1985). First, when parents assume less sex-stereotyped roles, their children have less sex-stereotyped attitudes themselves about male and female roles. Second, particularly in the area of cognitive competence, these children may benefit from having two highly involved parents rather than just one. This ensures them the diversity of stimulation that comes from interacting with people who have different behavioral styles. A third important issue relates to the family context in which these children are raised. In each of the studies just cited, a high degree of paternal involvement made it possible for both parents to do what was rewarding and fulfilling for them. It allowed fathers to satisfy their desires for closeness to their children while permitting mothers to have adequately close relationships with their children and to pursue career goals. In other words, increased paternal involvement may have made both parents feel much more fulfilled. As a result, the relationships were probably much warmer and richer than might otherwise have been the case. One can speculate that the benefits obtained by children with highly involved fathers is largely attributable to the fact that high levels of paternal involvement created family contexts in which the parents felt good about their marriages and the child care arrangements they had been able to work out.

In all of these studies fathers were highly involved in child care because both they and their partners desired this. The effects on children appeared quite different when fathers were forced to become involved, perhaps by being laid off from work while their partners were able to obtain or maintain their employment (Johnson & Abramovitch, 1985). In such circumstances, wives may have resented the fact that their husbands could not support their families, while the husbands resented having to do "women's work" instead of providing for their families financially (Johnson & Abramovitch, 1988; Russell, 1983). It is not surprising that this constellation of factors appeared to have adverse effects on children, just as the same degree of involvement had positive effects when the circumstances were more benign. Evidently, the extent of paternal involvement may have been much less significant (so far as the effects on children are concerned) than the reasons for high involvement and the parents' evaluations thereof.

DIRECT AND INDIRECT EFFECTS

Research on paternal influences has also moved beyond correlational studies and studies of absence and divorce to explore the pathways through which fathers ultimately affect their children. Fathers affect their children directly and indirectly, and both pathways are key to a comprehensive understanding of fatherhood.

Fathers influence their children directly through their behavior and the attitudes and messages they convey. The direct effects of fathering are especially salient when fathers' and mothers' interactions differ. Because fathers typically spend less time with their children, for example, many are less familiar with their children's language competencies and thus more likely to speak in ways that challenge children's linguistic and pragmatic abilities. Specifically, when talking to their young children, fathers use more directives, requests for clarification, wh- questions, references to past events, imperatives, and contentless utterances than mothers do (e.g., Bellinger & Gleason, 1982; Fash & Madison, 1981; Kavanaugh & Jirkovsky, 1982; Leaper, Anderson, & Sanders, 1998; McLaughlin, White, McDevitt, & Raskin, 1983; Tomasello, Conti-Ramsden, & Ewert, 1990). Because these more complex forms of speech place greater linguistic demands on children, fathers are thought to serve as a bridge to the outside world (Ely, Gleason, Narasimhan, & McCabe, 1995; Gleason, 1975). Thus, fathers' unique communicative styles directly teach children about the linguistic and communicative demands of social exchanges.

Much of the research described in this book is concerned with the ways in which children are directly affected by caretaking, teaching, play, maltreatment, and neglect by their fathers, even though fathers obviously play multiple roles and affect their children's development in many ways other than via direct interaction. Fathers affect children indirectly through their effects on other people and social circumstances that bear on children's development. For example, economic support of the family constitutes an indirect but important way in which fathers contribute to the rearing and emotional health of their children. Furthermore, economic support (or the lack of it) is one of the ways in which noncustodial fathers influence their children's development (Amato & Sobolewski, this volume; Hetherington & Stanley-Hagan, 1997).

A second important, indirect source of influence stems from the father's role as a source of emotional and instrumental support to the other people, principally mothers, involved in the direct care of children (Parke, Power, & Gottman, 1979). The father's function as a source of emotional support tends to enhance the quality of mother-child relationships and thus facilitate positive adjustment by children. Conversely, when fathers are unsupportive and marital conflict is high, children may suffer (Cummings, Goeke-Morey, & Raymond, this volume; Cummings & O'Reilly, 1997). Fathers can also affect the quality of family dynamics by being involved in child-related housework, thus easing the mothers' workloads (Pleck, 1983, 1984). Paternal involvement in housework exemplifies another manner in which fathers influence children: by providing models of behavior that children can either emulate or eschew. Many of the behavior patterns acquired in childhood are the result of lessons derived from observing others and adjusting one's behavior accordingly.

Recognition that indirect patterns of influence are pervasive and perhaps more important than direct learning represents another of the major conceptual revolutions marking the 30 years of scholarship since the first edition of this anthology was prepared. Whereas some contributors to the first edition provocatively proposed that some paternal influences might be mediated indirectly (the chapter by Lewis & Weinraub, 1976, was especially noteworthy in this regard), the extraordinary importance of indirect influences is now recognized universally. Indeed, almost every contributor to this volume underscores the extent to which fathers and children must be viewed as parts of complex social systems (notably, the family) in which each person affects each other reciprocally, directly, and indirectly. From this vantage point, of course, appraising the father's impact is much more difficult, both conceptually and statistically, but the newer perspectives promise much greater validity and, ultimately, generalization.

Also of importance in the quest for understanding direct and indirect pathways is a focus on how different aspects of father involvement codetermine developmental outcomes in children. At this time, researchers have done a better job of exploring single paths of influence than of modeling interrelations among multiple aspects of fathering and child outcomes (Tamis-LeMonda & Cabrera, 2002). For example, Graham and Beller (2002) attempted to disentangle the beneficial effects of child support payments and other potential influences on children's academic achievement. They noted that child support dollars predicted child outcomes better than did other sources of income did but did not account for all of the variance, suggesting that the payment of child support does not simply have a direct impact on child development. Rather, fathers who pay child support may be more committed or dedicated to their children, may have better relationships with their children's mothers, may visit their children more often, or may have the capacity and therefore the tendency to support them. Only by exploring these potential pathways will researchers be able to explain better when, why, and how fathers matter to their children and families.

SUMMARY

Viewed together, the schools of research summarized here have all advanced our understanding of paternal influences. First, fathers and mothers seem to influence their children in similar rather than dissimilar ways. Contrary to the expectations of many developmental psychologists, the differences between mothers and fathers appear to be much less important than the similarities. Not only does the description of mothering largely resemble the description of fathering (particularly the version of involved fathering that has become increasingly prominent in the late 20th century), but the mechanisms and means by which fathers influence their children also appear very similar to those that mediate maternal influences on children. Stated differently, students of socialization have consistently found that parental warmth, nurturance, and closeness are associated with positive child outcomes regardless of whether the parent involved is a mother or a father. The important dimensions of parental influence are those that have to do with parental characteristics rather than gender-related characteristics.

Second, as research has unfolded, psychologists have been forced to conclude that the characteristics of individual fathers—such as their masculinity, intellect, and even their warmth—are much less important, formatively speaking, than are the characteristics of the relationships that they have established with their children. Children who have secure, supportive, reciprocal, and sensitive relationships with their parents are much more likely to be well adjusted psychologically than are individuals whose relationships with their parents (mothers or fathers) are less satisfying. Likewise, the amount of time that fathers and children spend together is probably much less important than what they do with that time and how fathers, mothers, children, and other important people in their lives perceive and evaluate the father-child relationship.

Third, we have come to see that the family context is often at least as important as the individual relationships within the family. Fathers must thus be viewed in the broader familial context; positive paternal influences are more likely to occur not only when there are supportive father-child relationships but when the fathers' relationships with their partners, ex-partners, and presumably other children establish a positive familial context. Marital harmony is a consistent correlate of child adjustment, whereas marital conflict is a consistent and reliable correlate of child maladjustment.

Fourth, these factors all underscore the fact that fathers play multiple roles in the family and that their success in these diverse roles influences the ways in which they affect their children's development and adjustment. Fathers have beneficial effects on their children when they have supportive and nurturant relationships with them as well as with their siblings, when they are competent and feel fulfilled as bread-winners, when they are successful and supportive partners, and so on.

Fifth, the nature of paternal influences may vary substantially depending on indi-vidual and cultural values. A classic example of this can be found in the literature on sex-role development. As a result of cultural changes, the assumed sex-role goals for boys and girls have changed, and this has produced changes in the effects of fathers' involvement on children. In the 1950s gender-appropriate masculinity or femininity was the desired goal; today, sex-role flexibility is desired. And whereas father involve-ment in the 1950s seemed to be associated with greater masculinity in boys, it is asso-ciated today with less sex-stereotyped sex-role standards in both boys and girls. Influence patterns also vary substantially depending on social factors that define the meaning of father involvement for children in particular families in particular social milieus. More generally, this underscores that the relative importance of the different paternal functions or roles varies across familial, subcultural, cultural, and historical contexts. There is no single father's role to which all fathers should aspire. Rather, a successful father, as defined in terms of his children's development, is one whose role performance matches the demands and prescriptions of his sociocultural and familial context. This means that high paternal involvement may have positive effects in some circumstances and negative effects in others. The same is true of low paternal in-volvement.

DETERMINANTS OF FATHER INVOLVEMENT

Although paternal behavior is multifaceted, embracing not only what fathers do but also how much of it they do, the existing literature on factors influencing paternal be-havior is focused primarily on variations in direct paternal involvement, ironically ig-noring much of what fathers do *for* their children by way of economic and emotional support within the family. This focus perhaps reflects the widespread assumptions that the extent of direct father-child interaction is of primary importance (for inter-ventionists as well as for researchers) and that involvement and parent-child closeness are intimately associated, even though most studies of paternal involvement ignore the emotional quality of father-child relationships or find the quality and quantity of interaction to be unrelated (Grossman, Pollack, & Golding, 1988; Radin, 1994).

Nonetheless, there is consensus that father involvement is affected by multiple interacting systems operating at different levels over the life course, including psy-chological factors (e.g., motivation, skills, self-confidence), the children's individual characteristics (e.g., temperament, gender), social support (e.g., relationships with part-ners and extended family members), community and cultural influences (e.g., socio-economic opportunity, cultural ideologies), and institutional practices and public policies (e.g., welfare support, child support enforcement). These reciprocally inter-acting levels can be viewed as a hierarchy of factors influencing paternal behavior. As explained in this section, favorable conditions must exist at each level if increased paternal involvement and broadened paternal behavior are to be possible and beneficial.

MOTIVATION

Although researchers such as the Cowans (C. P. Cowan et al., 1985; P. A. Cowan, Cowan, & Kerig, 1993) and Grossman (Grossman et al., 1988) have made careful efforts to identify psychological or individual characteristics that influence the nature and extent of paternal behavior, most researchers have implicitly assumed that variations in the definition of fatherhood are determined by subcultural and cultural factors more than individual characteristics (see also Jacobs, 1995). Many men set their goals depending on recollections of their own childhood, choosing either to compensate for their fathers' deficiencies or to emulate them. Many also express enjoyment of the time spent with children—even adolescents (Larson & Richards, 1994). Indeed, survey data long ago suggested that 40% of fathers would like to spend more time with their children than they were able (Quinn & Staines, 1979). This implies that a substantial number of men may want to be more involved in relationships with their children although there is no unanimity about the desirability of increased paternal involvement. In addition, the identification of fatherhood with breadwinning serves to limit male involvement in child care at least as much as do the constraints imposed by actual work time (Gerson, 1993). A powerful underlying assumption proposes that men are first and foremost workers and breadwinners, while women are the primary nurturers.

Changes in the level of paternal motivation have taken place in the last few decades, however, and can be attributed primarily to the women's movement and the questions it raises about traditional male and female roles. In addition, media hype about the new father has also affected motivation levels. The most impressive official program yet undertaken was initiated by the Swedish government in the early 1970s in an attempt to encourage men to become more involved in child care and overcome fears that active parenting and masculinity are incompatible (Haas, 1992; Lamb & Levine, 1983; Russell & Hwang, this volume). Continuing fears of this sort help explain why some motivational shifts have been so slow, and particularly why the number of fathers who take a major role in child care has not increased very much (nationally or internationally) despite tremendous changes in female employment patterns. It is interesting, however, that researchers have not substantiated initial predictions that the levels and types of paternal involvement would be associated with measures of the men's masculinity or androgyny (see Pleck, 1997). In addition, institutional and cultural barriers, not only personality and motivational barriers, slow the pace of change and reduce average levels of paternal involvement. One indication of this can be found in the evidence of greater flexibility regarding the types of activities in which fathers engage, despite modest changes in the amounts of time fathers spend with their children. Many fathers no longer avoid the messy child care activities they used to disparage and instead become coparents across a broad array of tasks.

SKILLS AND SELF-CONFIDENCE

Motivation alone cannot ensure increased involvement: Skills and self-confidence are also necessary. Ostensibly motivated men often complain that a lack of skills (exemplified by ignorance or clumsiness) prevents increased involvement and closeness. These complaints can constitute excuses, but they can also reflect a very real fear of incompetence and failure. The relevant skills can be obtained through participation in a growing number of formal skill-development programs (Levine & Pitt, 1995) or more informally through involvement in activities that children and fathers enjoy doing together. Such activities foster self-confidence and enjoyment, thereby promoting both further involvement and sensitivity. Sensitivity, which involves being able to evaluate a child's signals or needs and respond appropriately, is also crucial with respect to both closeness and positive impact (Kelly & Lamb, 2000; Van IJzendoorn & DeWolff, 1997). Both sensitivity and self-confidence are probably much more important than specific skills where paternal behavior and influence are concerned. Many of the studies concerned with paternal influences show that the closeness of the father-child relationship—itself a consequence of sufficiently extensive and sensitive interactions—is a crucial determinant of the fathers' impact on child development and adjustment (see Lamb & Lewis, this volume).

SOCIAL SUPPORT

Paternal behavior is undoubtedly affected by members of a father's social networks, particularly his relationships with the mother of his child. The roles that fathers play in family life and whether or not they reside with mothers or their children often depend on mothers' attitudes and expectations (Allen & Hawkins, 1999). Mothers are gatekeepers when it comes to nonresidential fathers' access to children, and they frequently constrain and define the roles and responsibilities of both residential and nonresidential fathers. Mothers communicate their expectations of their partners by handing over their babies for diapering, instead of diapering the baby themselves, for example. Likewise, subtle maternal grimaces when fathers fail to console their crying infants may lead them to "leave the nurturing to mom." In other cases, mothers may use children as bait to get what they want (money, sexual interest) from their partners.

Like paternal attitudes, women's attitudes toward paternal involvement have changed slowly over the last two decades (Pleck, 1982; Polatnick, 1973–1974). The same surveys that show a majority of men wanting to be more involved show that a majority of women do not want their husbands to be more involved than they currently are (Pleck, 1982; Quinn & Staines, 1979). This suggests that although many mothers are heavily overburdened by their responsibilities and would like their partners to do more, a substantial majority are quite satisfied with the status quo, with respect not only to the extent of paternal involvement but also to the ranges and types of activities in which fathers involve themselves (Hochschild, 1995). On the other hand, women overwhelmingly view breadwinning as a crucial role for husbands and fathers (O'Hare, 1995).

There may be many reasons for maternal hesitations about changing paternal roles. Some mothers may feel that their husbands are incompetent or fear that increased paternal involvement may threaten fundamental power dynamics within the family (Polatnick, 1973–1974). The roles of mother and manager of the household are the two roles in which women's authority has not been questioned; together they constitute the one area in which women have traditionally enjoyed real power and control. Increased paternal involvement may threaten this power and preeminence. The tradeoff has dubious value because although many women have entered the work force in the last three decades, many occupy low-paying, low-prestige positions with little prospect of advancement. Many women apparently prefer to maintain authority in the child-care arena even if that means physical and mental exhaustion. Their resistance is likely to persist until fundamental changes within society at large change the basic distribution of power. Economic conditions seem unlikely to reduce the need for both parents to obtain employment, and women continue to emphasize the need for husbands and fathers to be family breadwinners (O'Hare, 1995).

Within individual families, agreement between mothers and fathers regarding paternal roles may be of crucial importance. As mentioned earlier, family dynamics are formatively significant because fundamental conflicts between the parents have adverse effects on children's development. In this regard, it may be significant that in two longitudinal studies of high father involvement (Radin, 1994; Radin & Goldsmith, 1985; Russell, 1983), a remarkably high rate of family dissolution was evident when families were later relocated. Thus, despite initial harmony, substantial and fundamental problems concerning roles and responsibilities may arise later, particularly in times of ambivalence and confusion.

INSTITUTIONAL PRACTICES

As Russell and Hwang point out in this volume, institutional practices also affect paternal involvement, with the barriers imposed by the workplace ranking among the most important reasons given by fathers to explain low levels of paternal involvement (e.g., Haas, 1992; Yankelovich, 1974). Clearly this is an important issue for many men, and it will remain important as long as men take on and are expected to assume primary breadwinning roles. It is also true, however, that men do not trade work time for family time in a one-to-one fashion. Survey data have shown that women translate each extra hour of nonwork time into an extra 40 to 45 minutes of family work, whereas for men, each hour not spent in paid work translates into less than 20 minutes of family work (Pleck, 1983). Thus, while the pressure of work have a significant effect on parental involvement, the effects are somewhat different for men and women.

Paternity leave is the most frequently discussed means of enhancing paternal involvement, although flexible time scheduling would certainly be of greater value to employed fathers and mothers (Pleck, 1986). Two early studies showed that both mothers and fathers take advantage of flextime to spend more time with their children (Lee, 1983; Winett & Neale, 1980), but flextime remains an option open to relatively few workers. Russell and Hwang (this volume) discuss these issues more fully.

Like the workplace, institutions such as child care and educational institutions have traditionally made little effort to include fathers and have often acted in ways that exclude them or include them only in gender-typed ways (Klinman, 1986; Levine, Murphy, & Wilson, 1993).

CULTURAL ECOLOGY

Scholars are slowly (and not consistently) recognizing the diverse array of family types and sociocultural expectations and demands that shape paternal roles, family processes, and child development. In practice, this means that fathers play differing roles in different subcultural contexts and that various groups hold contrasting views of what constitutes the good father (Hochschild, 1995). For example, breadwinning (and the indirect effects of financial security) may be of paramount importance in some contexts (as when the child was conceived outside of an enduring relationship), while moral guidance may be quite unimportant. For other families and communities, financial support may be unimportant, direct care and supervision crucial, and emotional support invaluable. Such variations in the relative salience of different aspects of fatherhood further complicate attempts to conceptualize and assess paternal roles and influences, but when appropriately recognized, these promise to permit more valid and generalizable research on father-child relationships, even though the generalizability of many findings may be much narrower than researchers initially hoped.

Careful attempts to describe father-child relationships in diverse cultural contexts certainly help build the database needed for further progress in our understanding of father-child relationships. Many of the contributors to earlier editions of this anthology addressed primarily models of paternity, fatherhood, and father-child relationships that dominate White, North American, middle-class society. Reflecting the progress made to date in understanding the impact of sociocultural factors, however, several contributors to this volume discuss fathers in other cultural contexts, including African American and African Caribbean households (Roopnarine); Hispanic and Latino families (Cabrera & Garcia Coll); parts of the European Economic Union (O'Brien); Japan, Korea, and China (Schwalb, Nakazawa, Yamamoto, & Hyun); and nonindustrial cultures (Hewlett).

SUMMARY

The daunting question of why fathers do what they do lies at the heart of research on fathering. Father involvement is determined by many reciprocally interacting factors. Different configurations of predictors are likely to be more or less salient for different individuals at different stages of children's and fathers' development. To date, researchers have emphasized the centrality of motivation, skills and confidence, social supports, institutional policies, and cultural ideologies in shaping fathers' engagement with their children and their roles in family life. In the future, researchers will need to understand how these levels of influence jointly and interactively affect fathering and are themselves altered by the fathering experience.

POLICY APPLICATIONS OF RESEARCH ON FATHERS AND FATHERHOOD

Over the past two decades there has been a shift in the balance between basic and applied research goals in fatherhood studies. Earlier interest in fathers was driven by an overwhelming desire to acquire basic knowledge in a relatively new area of scientific inquiry. Currently, the quest for basic knowledge on the nature, antecedents, and consequences of father-child relationships is paralleled by growing interest in the translation of research findings into effective programs and policies that support and promote positive father-child relationships (Cabrera, Tamis-LeMonda, Bradley, Hofferth, & Lamb, 2000; Tamis-LeMonda & Cabrera, 1999, 2002). The research-to-policy link on fathers is bidirectional: Political emphasis on the importance of fathers fosters the research agenda just as evidence regarding paternal impact influences social policies and program initiatives.

PROMOTING RESEARCH ON UNDERREPRESENTED FATHERS

The growing interest of policy makers in what the experts have to say about fathers has spotlighted, in positive ways, much of what has been learned about fathers over the past three decades. Policy debates on welfare reform, child support, paternity establishment, immigration, and child custody have also unearthed alarming gaps in what is known about certain groups of fathers, however. It is not surprising that most attempts to describe and quantify the nature and extent of paternal behavior have focused on children living in two-parent families. Ironically, however, the focus on parental behavior and parent-child relationships in such families has taken place at a time when these families have become increasingly uncommon. More than half the children in the United States now spend part of their childhood in single-parent families, and similar trends are evident in other industrialized countries. Fatherlessness is particularly marked in impoverished African American communities, and considerable concern has been expressed about effects on mothers and children in these families (Blankenhorn, 1995; Popenoe, 1996; Whitehead, 1993). To date, social scientists have been remarkably unsuccessful in their efforts to understand why so many men have removed themselves or allowed themselves to be excluded from their children's lives, although the adverse effects of absent fathers on child development have been well documented (see Amato & Sobolewsky, this volume). Political concern about the growing number of fatherless families has stimulated much of the current research on fathers, which promises to advance our understanding of the factors that support sustained, positive father-child relationships.

Only recently have scholars ventured to explore the roles and influences of unmarried fathers, stepfathers, nonresidential fathers, low-income fathers, minority fathers, and immigrant fathers, although considerable information informs the chapters in this volume by Roopnarine, Cabrera and Garcia Coll, and McLanahan and Carlson. National studies of men and fathers have generally excluded homeless men, men with unstable housing, or those who do not live with their families. Until recently, little was known about nonresident fathers, for example, in part because most national household surveys did not collect information from fathers who were uncounted, incarcerated, or in the military (Hernandez & Brandon, 2002). This male undercount calls into question the accuracy of many social statistics concerning fathers (Tamis-LeMonda & Cabrera, 1999). Moreover, small-scale studies of underrepresented men have focused largely on negative aspects of behavior, such as the failure to pay child support, and on adverse effects on children. Research on potential strengths in less advantaged families is much needed and lies at the core of recent national research initiatives, including the Early Head Start evaluation, Fragile Families and Child Well-Being Study, the Early Childhood Longitudinal Study–Birth Cohort, and the welfare studies. Together, these studies promise to address many of the shortcomings of prior research by focusing on fathers from diverse ethnic and socioeconomic backgrounds while exploring how and why their roles change as their children grow up.

REACHING OUT TO FATHERS AND FAMILIES

Current demographic trends suggest that fewer fathers may be participating in their children's lives today than in any period since the United States began keeping reliable statistics. Unfortunately, researchers, policy makers, and practitioners have made limited progress in attempts to design programs that address the explicit and unspoken needs of many fathers and families (Tamis-LeMonda & Cabrera, 2002). For example, public policies focus mainly on the economic provisioning of nonresident fathers, assuming that these men are able to pay but choose not to. Indeed, some fathers refuse to pay child support despite the ability to do so and absent themselves both financially and emotionally from their children. On the other hand, many fathers who would like to support their children are unable to do so because of their circumstances (e.g., unemployment, maternal gatekeeping). Social policies do not distinguish between these groups of men and often fail to nurture the continued investment of fathers who are emotionally attached to their children yet unable to provide for them financially.

The limited impact of programs on low-income fathers cannot be blamed wholly on the lack of programs and initiatives. Indeed, the past 20 years have witnessed geometric increases in the number of programs offering services to targeted groups of fathers (Tamis-LeMonda & Cabrera, 2002), yet many of these programs have had little impact at high cost (Mincy & Pouncy, 2002). In part, these disappointing results reflect the failure to begin programs that are broad enough and reach out to fathers early enough in their parenting trajectories to affect many fathers.

Preliminary findings from the Fragile Families and Early Head Start studies indicate that initiatives aimed at fathers should begin at birth, when many fathers are highly motivated to remain involved in their infants' lives (McLanahan & Carlson, this volume). Despite their early commitment, however, many fathers in fragile families drift out of their children's lives over time. Fatherhood programs should thus take a preventive approach by providing services to new fathers well before they distance themselves from their children (Tamis-LeMonda & Cabrera, 1999, 2002).

Programs also need to address the needs of multiple family members, to expand parents' educational and employment opportunities, to support and develop parenting skills, and to intervene effectively even when there are substance abuse or mental health problems (Carlson & McLanahan, 2002; Roggmann et al., 2002). A narrow focus on motivated fathers may prompt resistance from mothers who want nothing to do with their former partners and might want to block fathers' access to their children.

Finally, the effectiveness of fatherhood programs and their components need to be evaluated systematically (McBride and Lutz, this volume). Few researchers have examined the effects of fatherhood programs on either the men's behavior or the wellbeing of their children, and even the Fathers at Work and Fragile Families projects do not include controlled, experimental evaluations (Mincy & Pouncy, 2002). As a result, researchers, practitioners, and policy makers remain unable to pinpoint whether, how, and why different types of programs affect men, families, and children.

SUMMARY

Researchers, policy makers, and practitioners alike must be mindful of the ways in which knowledge about father involvement and well-targeted policy and program initiatives together help support all family members, most notably children (Cabrera et al., 2000; Carlson & McLanahan, 2002; Tamis-LeMonda & Cabrera, 1999). Researchers should attend to constructs and variables that have theoretical relevance for policy and practice, that can be translated and incorporated readily into policy initiatives, and that might be used in evaluations of service delivery models.

Policy debates on topics relevant to fathering, such as child custody and welfare reform, have identified the narrow focus of many researchers on fathers in middle-income groups. These limitations are currently being addressed through data collection efforts involving fathers from low-income, ethnically diverse backgrounds. Findings from these studies will undoubtedly yield a better understanding of fathering in underrepresented groups.

Two heated questions remain central to work at the intersection of basic and applied research: Which current policies benefit fathers and families, and which instead lead some fathers to drift out of the lives of their children? Why, after decades of costly fatherhood programs, have we been unsuccessful in effectively supporting and enhancing fathers' commitments to their children and families? Answers to both of these questions will be possible only through the collaboration of policy makers, researchers, and practitioners.

OUTLINE OF THE VOLUME

The questions and issues articulated in the previous sections animate each of the chapters that appear in this volume. In this section we briefly introduce each of the chapters and summarize their contribution to our understanding of fatherhood, father-child relationships, patterns of paternal influence, and the effects of institutional policies and practices.

HISTORY OF FATHERHOOD

In the second chapter, Elizabeth H. Pleck presents an intriguing account of the good dad–bad dad complex, tracing its origins to colonial America and following through to the present day. Documented laws, punitive actions against men, and entries in journals, diaries, and letters are assembled to weave a story of favorable and unfavorable images of fathers, changing standards about good fathering, and acceptable roles for men. Pleck's chapter illustrates how perceptions of good and bad fathering are shaped by social change and historical events (e.g., wars and the Industrial Revolution) and their effects on men's economic circumstances. In colonial America, for example, standards of good fathering for middle-class men differed from those imposed on slaves and immigrants. Economic and educational constraints precluded slaves and immigrants from being involved fathers, much in the same way that poverty constrains opportunities for many men today. For much of history, standards of good fathering demanded that fathers promote and prolong gender asymmetry by reinforcing masculinity in sons and femininity in daughters, whereas recent social values emphasize gender equality. As a result, good fathers are now expected to be nurturant and to spend time caring for their children. Definitions of deadbeat dads, in contrast, have remained unchanged. Historically, deadbeat dads have been those who fail to fulfill their breadwinner responsibilities, and societal reactions to such fathers have consistently included moral condemnation and punishment. According to Pleck, efforts to make fathers pay reflect longstanding core beliefs about family life and the economic dependence of women and children on fathers' income. The persistence of these beliefs over three centuries of U.S. history poses a conundrum in the face of recent revolutionary changes in mothers' and fathers' family roles.

CULTURAL VARIATIONS IN THE NATURE OF FATHERHOOD

Just as some values and practices have changed over time in the United States, of course, so do perceptions and expectations of fathers vary across cultural contexts, both within the United States and around the world. The next five chapters thus explore some such facets of cross-cultural variability. Jaipaul Roopnarine's chapter on fathering by African American and African Caribbean men highlights the ways in which the economic and social histories of different ethnic groups infuse family structure and father-child relationships. Roopnarine documents parallels between African American and African Caribbean patterns of marital union, residency and caregiving arrangements, poverty, and histories of slavery and oppression, while noting the markedly different social, political, and economic contexts of life in the United States and the developing Caribbean. These differences have shaped conceptions and enactments of fathering in the two admittedly heterogeneous groups. As Roopnarine observes, there exists considerable intragroup variation in the way African American men perceive and enact their fathering roles, with many of these differences rooted in economic and educational circumstances. Although a disproportionate number of African American men do not reside with their children, their levels of social-intellectual and emotional investments in their children vary enormously. African Caribbean fathers also vary with respect to their commitments to family and children; these commitments often depend on a father's own status in the marital career process (Rodman, 1971). Progressive mating is the norm for Caribbean fathers: Fatherhood occurs in visiting, then common law, then marital unions, with marriage involving the highest levels of commitment to children. Traditional beliefs about male dominance and early sexuality as markers of manhood in African Caribbean communities combine with limited economic opportunities to impede men's participation in children's lives and to place children at increased risk of academic and social difficulties. Underscoring these historical and contemporary realities, Roopnarine invites researchers to identify the ways in which fathers from different family arrangements and economic circumstances can be positively and consistently involved in their children's lives.

Natasha Cabrera and Cynthia Garcia Coll's analysis of Latino fathers in Chapter 4 is especially timely considering that Latinos will comprise a quarter of the U.S. population only a few decades from now. Cabrera and Garcia Coll underscore the vast challenges scholars confront when attempting to describe and understand Latino fathers. Two are particularly noteworthy. First, Latinos in the United States have diverse cultural, social, and economic histories and immigration patterns. Although they share a common language as well as some cultural and family values, the impressive diversity across Latino subgroups renders generalizations about Latinos in general quite complex. Second, it is difficult to develop a model or theory of Latino fathering because so little research has been conducted. Cabrera and Garcia Coll distinguish two phases of research on Latino fathers: studies undertaken between the 1960s and 1980s and studies conducted since 1990. In the early research phase, researchers conducted small, localized studies of families living in poverty that emphasized masculine ideologies and traditional views of authoritarian and patriarchial Latino men. It is not surprising that financial provisioning was deemed important, although later changes in women's labor-force participation have transformed gender roles in Latino families much as they did in Anglo families. More recent studies, again based on relatively small samples, present a more complex picture of Latino fathers, in which middle-class Latino men appear more similar to their Anglo-American peers. This emergent model is characterized by a more egalitarian division of labor, with Latino fathers involved in child care, spending time with their children, and being sources of emotional and moral support to their children. Cabrera and Garcia Coll end with a timely plea for researchers to include Latino fathers in the sampling and design of national studies and to augment large-scale studies with ethnographic techniques that generate hypotheses about the roles and meaning of fatherhood in Latino families.

In Chapter 5, Margaret O'Brien presents a public policy perspective on fatherhood in Western Europe, where fatherhood is currently being redefined just as it is in other parts of the world. In the first half of the chapter, O'Brien interprets this transformation in light of larger social trends across the European Union, including changes to fertility patterns, partnership formations, family structures (e.g., growth in nonmarital unions), and migration and employment patterns. These recent, sweeping demographic trends have dramatically altered the face of fathering and have vital implications for the future of fathering in Europe. Less permanency in fathers' relationships with adult partners and biological children may well characterize future cohorts, posing a unique challenge for children who will have to forge relationships with a diversity of father figures within and across households. In the second half of the chapter, O'Brien describes the parental leave policies that have been adopted by European nations, where women's entry into the workforce has fostered expectations that men should actively coparent their young children. Younger cohorts of Europeans are increasingly endorsing egalitarian models of family life, and European governments have, in response, introduced legal entitlements such as paternity leave for fathers. Individual nations in the European Union have varied in their attention to fathers' issues, and families in each of these nations vary in their responses to the available entitlements. As O'Brien points out, because of the unique economic and social histories of individual nations, the same policy initiatives are realized quite differently in different locales, and similar social policies do not always have the same impact.

David Shwalb, Jun Nakazawa, Toshiya Yamamoto, and Jung-Hwan Hyun thereafter comprehensively review research on fathering in Japanese, Chinese, and Korean cultures—Asian cultures where family roles and expectations differ substantially from those that predominate in the West. The three geographically contiguous ethnic groups are characterized by low fertility rates and cultural histories shaped by Confucian principles. In comparison with their Western counterparts, fathers in these Asian societies spend less time with their children, a tradition that both reflects and shapes images of fathers as hardworking and distant figures. Japan, China, and Korea also boast unique social and economic histories, however, and these have led to intriguing divergences in family life and fathering patterns, parenting styles, gender orientations, and expectations for their children's education, as Schwalb and his colleagues reveal. In the course of describing unique fathering roles in the three societies, these scholars also document significant cultural differences in children's relationships with and perceptions of their fathers. It is interesting that the authors' descriptive accounts of fathers and children in Asian societies emphasize the impact of fathers' occupational conditions and priorities, just as in the West. Varying emphases on fathers' roles as breadwinners, the importance of work, and the practical realities of demanding work hours differentially constrain fathers' availability and their involvement in their children's everyday activities.

Of course, many fathers in the world live in nonindustrial—especially forager, farmer, and pastoral—cultures, as Barry Hewlett observes in Chapter 7. These cultures are characterized by low population density and less social and economic stratification than the industrial countries discussed in the five preceding chapters. As a result, these heterogeneous cultures offer markedly different insights into the ways in which men can do fatherhood. Such insights may be especially useful because the circumstances described by Hewlett are much more characteristic of the contexts that characterized most of human history than are analyses of global capitalistic principles that have existed for only a few hundred years. As Hewlett notes, whereas men in industrial or class-stratified cultures usually learn about children and child care when their own children are born, men in forager, farmer, and pastoral societies have regular experiences with children while growing up. Cross-cultural studies reviewed by Hewlett indicate that fathers are more involved in child care in forager and matrilineal-matriarchal societies, when parents share many activities, females contribute more to subsistence, and population densities are low, whereas they are less involved in polygamous cultures, when warfare is more common and resources are accumulated. Other ethnographic studies discussed by Hewlett provide poignant and fascinating accounts of paternal behavior in cultures that differ greatly from our own.

FATHERS IN TWO-PARENT ANGLO-SAXON FAMILIES

The next four chapters return attention to the Western industrialized and predominantly Anglo-Saxon cultures that have been the focus of most social scientists. In the first (Chapter 8), Mark Cummings, Marcia Goeke-Morey, and Jessica Raymond examine fathers in the family context, with a particular concern for the effects of marital quality and conflict. Building on the model developed by Cummings and O'Reilly (1997) for the third edition, Cummings and his colleagues propose that fathers affect children and families by way of three major pathways: by direct fathering and father-child relationships, through children's exposure to marital discord, and by virtue of fathers' psychological functioning. All of these pathways are believed to affect children's adjustment through effects on their coping processes and mechanisms, and the authors make special efforts to isolate the specific effects of fathers and fathering, a task made easier by recent methodological advances, which include reliance on multiple sources and types of data. Researchers have well documented the effects of father-child relationships and marital quality on child adjustment, Cummings and his colleagues conclude, though they have not yet explored adequately the role of fathers' psychological functioning.

Joseph Pleck and Brian Masciadrelli then comprehensively examine the nature, determinants, and consequences of father involvement (Chapter 9). They begin by defining positive father engagement, focus on the beneficial ways fathers commit to their children, and analyze the three major components of involvement (accessibility, responsibility, and engagement). Pleck and Masciadrelli discuss several conceptual and methodological issues, including challenges to the definitions of accessibility, responsibility and engagement, ways of assessing each construct, and the various sources of information about involvement. Although paternal accessibility has increased over the past several decades, fathers are available to children 50% to 65% as much as mothers, and their engagement levels are roughly 25% those of mothers. However, fathers' reports of their involvement converge with those of mothers and children, are stable over time, and exert telling influences on both children and fathers themselves. Positive paternal engagement predicts adaptive social and cognitive outcomes in children and affects men's career success and personality in positive ways. Pleck and Masciadrelli note that individual differences in involvement reflect the combined effects of fathers' motivation, skills, self-confidence, social supports, and institutional policies and practices. Unfortunately, researchers are far from understanding either the dynamics of father engagement or how its antecedents and outcomes vary depending on the family ecology.

In Chapter 10, Michael Lamb and Charlie Lewis discuss current research on the nature and meaning of father-child relationships in two-parent families with children ranging in age from infants to adolescents. Lamb and Lewis begin by describing the distinctive ways in which mothers and fathers engage their infants, noting that fathers often adopt more playful styles than mothers, particularly when there is a clear division of labor. In adolescence, mothers and fathers continue to engage their children in unique ways. Mothers spend more time overall with their adolescents, but fathers spend greater proportions of time engaged in play, recreation, and goal-related activities. These distinct engagement styles suggest that mothers and fathers may differentially affect the development of their children, and different maternal and paternal behaviors (e.g., verbal engagement as opposed to playfulness) may sometimes affect different and sometimes the same aspects of development. Of course, both mothers and fathers engage in academic and school-related activities, provide nurturance to their infants, children, and adolescents, and influence their children's and adolescents' cognitive and psychosocial adjustment, but Lamb and Lewis do more than document these main effects. They examine the antecedents and consequences of positive fathering within the broader constellation of family relationships. Paternal effects on children and adolescents are complex, often operating indirectly through unobserved or unmeasured variables, such as family harmony or maternal behavior, and are also moderated by the parents' employment patterns.

In the final chapter in the series concerned primarily with fathers in two-parent families, Ross Parke, Jessica Dennis, Mary Flyr, Kristie Morris, Colleen Killian, David McDowell, and Margaret Wild employ a systems framework to elucidate fathers' roles in shaping their children's peer relationships. Parke and his colleagues view interfamilial relationships (father-mother, father-child, mother-child), extra-familial relationships (e.g., fathers' relationships with coworkers), and children's peer relationships as interdependent, mutually influencing systems. Within this framework, the authors show that fathers influence children's peer relationships in three ways: through the quality of their relationships with children, through their direct advice and supervision, and by facilitating or limiting the children's opportunities for contact with their peers. Children's regulatory skills and cognitive representations of social relationships mediate associations between fathering and children's peer relationships. It is interesting that the authors' dynamic systems approach underscores the transactional nature of father-child relationships as well as their associations with other aspects of the social context. Specifically, children's own characteristics and behaviors shape paternal behaviors, and fathers' peer-relevant engagements unfold in the context of the marital relationship, the parents' past and present social and friendship networks, and the social capital of the community. Parke and his colleagues also articulate the need for more research, in which fathers and children are viewed in developmental and cultural contexts. How do fathers' roles in peer relationships change as children move from the dependencies of early childhood to the autonomous friendships of adolescence? To what extent does a father's own stage of development affect the way he supports his child's peer relationships? And how do paternal influences on peer relationships vary across cultures?

FATHERS IN NONTRADITIONAL CONTEXTS

The four chapters on fatherhood and father-child relationships in two-parent families are followed by four concerned with fathers with nontraditional characteristics, responsibilities, or roles. In the first of these chapters (Chapter 12), Paul Amato and Julie Sobolewski focus on nonresident fathers and stepfathers as they analyze the effects of divorce on fathers and children. Unlike the authors of many preceding chapters, Amato and Sobolewski are able to draw on an impressive and growing body of studies, many conducted using large, nationally representative samples. Many children now spend at least part of their childhoods separated from their fathers, and a significant portion of them spend some of that time living with stepfathers, so the topic has considerable significance and relevance. As Amato and Sobolewski point out, there is substantial evidence that children with divorced parents score more poorly than do children with married parents with respect to many aspects of psychosocial adjustment and well-being. For many, the crucial factor is loss of social and economic resources provided by their fathers, and these authors discuss both the transmission and withholding of these resources from nonresident and stepfathers to children. Most divorced fathers attempt to provide child support and to stay psychologically connected to their children, but many fail to do so. Even when nonresident fathers have regular contact with their children, furthermore, many do not engage in the type of authoritative parenting that promotes their children's welfare. Unfortunately, stepfathers typically do not develop authoritative relationships with children either, so most of these children are doubly disadvantaged.

Sara McLanahan and Marcia Carlson (Chapter 13) then focus more closely on the one third of children in the United States who are born to unmarried parents in fragile families and are thus at highest risk of the sorts of father absence discussed by Amato and Sobolewski. The term *fragile* reflects the fact that these unions are typically characterized by high economic, educational, and relationship instability. Despite the increasing prevalence of fragile families in the United States, little is known about these families, so McLanahan and Carlson devote their attention to data from the Fragile Families and Child Well-Being Study, a birth-cohort study of nearly 5,000 children born in 20 cities throughout the United States. When men in these families were interviewed at the time of their infants' births, they claimed to value marriage highly, but fewer than 10% were married a year later, and 20% of the men from these families rarely saw their babies. In large part, McLanahan and Carlson conclude, this is because many fatherhood programs and various tax and transfer policies designed to promote strong families instead often create disincentives for families. Accordingly, these authors recommend that social policies and programs be restructured and note that because new parents are positively oriented toward marriage and family formation, the infant's birth is an opportune time for entry into the family system. Policy makers and practitioners should thus focus their efforts early if they are to strengthen fathers' capabilities and support the stability of couples' relationships.

Although gay fathers are by no means as common as the nonresident or unmarried fathers discussed by Amato and Sobolewski or McLanahan and Carlson, they have attracted considerable attention in recent years. In Chapter 14, Charlotte Patterson shows that they constitute an extremely heterogeneous group with respect to who they are, how they became parents, and what challenges they face in raising their children. Some gay fathers come out after divorce; some are adoptive or foster parents; and others father biological children with surrogate mothers. Because the group is so heterogeneous, the study of gay fathers is challenging, and as a result the empirical literature is sparse. Children of gay fathers tend to describe their relationships as warm and supportive and are no more likely to be abused or to have difficulty in their own sexual development than are those with heterosexual fathers. In addition, gay fathers appear to have higher self-esteem than do gay men who are not fathers. Nonetheless, despite such optimistic findings, Patterson notes that these children and fathers face great challenges, including health risks such as HIV and stigmatization by educational, religious, and cultural institutions.

Unfortunately, fathers in violent families are considerably more common than gay fathers, and their impact on child development is much less likely to be benign, as George Holden and Ted Barker show in Chapter 15. However, as Sternberg (1997) reported in the third edition of this anthology, fathers have traditionally received little attention from researchers, even when they were implicitly assumed to be at the root of their families' problems! They have received considerably more attention from researchers in the ensuing years, according to Holden and Barker, with particular focus on child physical abuse and partner-spouse abuse. These authors describe some of the definitional problems that have impeded research and then discuss recent statistics documenting the incidence of family violence. Thereafter, they examine the characteristics of violent men and pay especially close attention to an issue with great significance to those making decisions regarding child custody: the degree to which fathers who are violent toward their partners are also likely to aggress against their children. As they note, partner abuse vastly increases the risk that children will also be abused, although the majority of children with abused mothers are not themselves abused, making it essential for decision makers to examine individual circumstances. In addition, it is important for researchers to recognize that fathers themselves are sometimes victims of violence. It is not surprising that all forms of family violence expose children to psychological risk, as Holden and Barker point out in the penultimate section of their chapter.

POLICIES AND PRACTICES

The last two chapters in the volume switch focus to applied issues. In the first (Chapter 16), Brent McBride and Mary Lutz document the ways in which demographic trends and changing expectations of fathers have created unprecedented demands for programs specifically designed to serve fathers, particularly those who are divorced, never married, and from low-income households. Fathers are increasingly expected to develop positive and supportive relationships with their children while sharing in the burdens of childcare, even as many families are confronting the realities of unpredictable and unstable paternal presence. McBride and Lutz observe that parenting programs vary widely with respect to their service delivery models, goals, target populations, documentation, and approaches to program evaluation. Unfortunately, programs for fathers also continue to be quite primitive: most programs are developed and implemented at a local, grassroots level without well-articulated conceptual frameworks guiding their interventions. Likewise, evaluation has been neither systematic nor comprehensive, with most program models undocumented and unexamined. This lack of evaluation and documentation impedes progress because effective strategies are not described to other practitioners interested in adopting or adapting innovative approaches. McBride and Lutz underscore the need for better communication between researchers and practitioners, with research findings used to inform the design of interventions and the findings of successful programs incorporated into the literature.

Finally, in Chapter 17 Graeme Russell and Carl Phillip Hwang draw attention to the dearth of theory and evidence linking factors in the workplace to the quality of parenting. To address this gap, they offer a framework for conceptualizing the direct and indirect effects of workplace policies and practices on father involvement. Their ecological perspective situates workplace policies within broader social, cultural, and political contexts and simultaneously addresses the ways in which individual and family factors mediate and moderate associations between workplace policies and practices on the one hand and actual parenting on the other. Russell and Hwang address three main topics: the role of workplace culture in shaping fathers' access to and utilization of initiatives that promote father involvement (e.g., leave policies and flexible working hours); links between workplace experiences and fathers' levels of engagement with their children; and the extent to which workplaces comprise contexts for education, information, and paternal support. Russell and Hwang offer a detailed description of workplace policies and practices in societies as diverse as the United States, Sweden, and Australia. Clearly, enormous cross-national variations exist with respect to workplace policies and practices, particularly in the areas of paternal leave and flexible work schedules, and many of the questions framed by Russell and Hwang's model remain to be explored empirically.

CONCLUSION

Over the last three decades, fathers have embraced much broader and more diverse definitions of their roles and have been increasingly willing to engage in a broad array of activities typically viewed as components of mothering. These changes have taken place alongside smaller changes in the extent to which fathers devote time to activities with and for their children, as well as surprising resistance to the assumption of parental responsibility. Both the observed changes and their slow pace appear attributable to secular changes, particularly in economic circumstances and maternal employment, as well as to feminist critiques of traditional social structures. In addition, these slow but significant changes in the behavior of men who live with their children have taken place against a background of dramatic increases in the number of children who have little or no contact with their fathers. Attempts to understand paternal influences on child development must thus consider the roles, functions, and impacts of father-child relationships, the effects on child development of fatherless lifestyles, and the processes that lead to these circumstances.

The multiple roles that fathers are expected to play and the roles that they are actually able to fulfill illustrate the need for researchers to explore multiple dimensions of fathering, fathers' views about aspects of fathering, family decision making and motivation, and the mechanisms through which parents exert influence on children. By elucidating associations among different aspects of fathering and recognizing how and when fathers' attention to certain areas of involvement limits their potential involvement in other ways, researchers will come closer to understanding the unique confluence of factors that affect the course of children's development, as well as the multitude of configurations that characterize positively involved fathers.

REFERENCES

Adams, P. L., Milner, J. R., & Schrepf, N. A. (1984). *Fatherless children.* New York: Wiley.

Allen, S. M., & Hawkins, A. J. (1999). Maternal gatekeeping: Mothers' beliefs and behavior that inhibit greater father involvement in family work. *Journal of Marriage and the Family, 61,* 199–212.

Bellinger, D. C., & Gleason, J. B. (1982). Sex differences in parental directives to young children. *Sex Roles, 8,* 1123–1139.

Belsky, J., Gilstrap, B., & Ravine, M. (1984). The Pennsylvania Infant and Family Development Project: 1. Stability and change in mother-infant and father-infant interaction at one, three, and nine months. *Child Development, 55,* 692–705.

Berman, P. W. (1980). Are women more responsive than men to the young? A review of developmental situational variables. *Psychological Bulletin, 88,* 668–695.

Biller, H. B. (1971). *Father, child, and sex role.* Lexington, MA: Heath.

Biller, H. B. (1974). *Paternal deprivation: Family, school, sexuality, and society.* Lexington, MA: Heath.

Biller, H. B. (1993). *Fathers and families.* Westport, CT: Auburn House.

Biller, H. B. (1994). *The father factor.* New York: Pocket Books.

Biller, H. B., & Kimpton, J. L. (1997). The father and the school-aged child. In M. E. Lamb (Ed.), *The role of the father in child development* (3rd ed., pp. 143–161, 348–352). New York: Wiley.

Blankenhorn, D. (1995). *Fatherless America.* New York: Basic Books.

Cabrera, N., Tamis-LeMonda, C. S., Bradley, R. H., Hofferth, S., & Lamb, M. E. (2000). Fatherhood in the 21st century. *Child Development, 71,* 127–136.

Carlson, M. J., & McLanahan, S. S. (2002). Fragile families, father involvement, and public policy. In C. S. Tamis-LeMonda & N. Cabrera (Eds.), *Handbook of father involvement: Multidisciplinary perspectives* (pp. 461–488). Mahwah, NJ: Erlbaum.

Conner, D. B., Knight, D. K., & Cross, D. R. (1997). Mothers' and fathers' scaffolding of their 2-year-olds during problem-solving and literacy interactions. *Journal of Developmental Psychology, 15,* 323–338.

Cowan, C. P., Cowan, P. A., Heming, G., Garrett, E., Coysh, W. S., Curtis-Boles, H., et al. (1985). Transitions to parenthood: His, hers, and theirs. *Journal of Family Issues, 6,* 451–481.

Cowan, P. A., Cowan, C. P., & Kerig, P. K. (1993). Mothers, fathers, sons, and daughters: Gender differences in family formation and parenting style. In P. A. Cowan, D. Field, D. Hansen, A.

Skolnick, & G. Swanson (Eds.), *Family, self and society: Toward a new agenda for family research* (pp. 165–195). Hillsdale, NJ: Erlbaum.

Crawley, S. B., & Sherrod, R. B. (1984). Parent-infant play during the first year of life. *Infant Behavior and Development, 7*, 65–75.

Cummings, E. M., & O'Reilly, A. W. (1997). Fathers in family context: Effects of marital quality on child adjustment. In M. E. Lamb (Ed.), *The role of the father in child development* (3rd ed., pp. 69–65, 315–325). New York: Wiley.

Dalton-Hummel, D. (1982). Syntactic and conversational characteristics of fathers' speech. *Journal of Psycholinguistic Research, 11*, 465–483.

Day, R. D., & Lamb, M. E. (Eds.). (in press). *Conceptualizing and measuring father involvement.* Mahwah, NJ: Erlbaum.

Easterbrooks, M. A., & Goldberg, W. A. (1984). Toddler development in the family: Impact of father involvement and parenting characteristics. *Child Development, 55*, 740–752.

Ely, R., Gleason, J. B., Narasimhan, B., & McCabe, A. (1995). Family talk about talk: Mothers lead the way. *Discourse Processes, 19*, 201–218.

Fash, D. S., & Madison, C. L. (1981). Parents' language interaction with young children: A comparative study of mothers and fathers. *Child Study Journal, 11*, 137–153.

Gerson, K. (1993). *No man's land: Man's changing commitment to family and work.* New York: Basic Books.

Gleason, J. B. (1975). Fathers and other strangers: Men's speech to young children. In D. P. Dato (Ed.), *Language and linguistics* (pp. 289–297). Washington, DC: Georgetown University Press.

Glick, P. C., & Norton, A. J. (1979). Marrying, divorcing, and living together in the U.S. today. *Population Bulletin, 32*(5, whole issue).

Golinkoff, R. M., & Ames, G. (1979). A comparison of fathers' and mothers' speech with their young children. *Child Development, 50*, 28–32.

Graham, J. W., & Seller, A. H. (2002). Nonresident fathers and their children: Child support and visitation from an economic perspective. In C. S. Tamis-LeMonda & N. Cabrera (Eds.), *Handbook of father involvement: Multidisciplinary perspectives* (pp. 431–453). Mahwah, NJ: Erlbaum.

Griswold, R. L. (1993). *Fatherhood in America.* New York: Basic Books.

Grossman, F. R., Pollack, W. S., & Golding, E. (1988). Fathers and children: Predicting the quality and quantity of fathering. *Developmental Psychology, 24*, 82–91.

Haas, L. (1992). *Equal parenthood and social policy.* Albany: State University of New York Press.

Hernandez, D. J., & Brandon, P. D. (2002). Who are the fathers of today? In C. S. Tamis-LeMonda & N. Cabrera (Eds.), *Handbook of father involvement: Multidisciplinary perspectives* (pp. 33–62). Mahwah, NJ: Erlbaum.

Herzog, R., & Sudia, C. E. (1973). Children in fatherless families. In B. M. Caldwell & H. N. Ricciuti (Eds.), *Review of child development research* (Vol. 3, pp. 141–232). Chicago: University of Chicago Press.

Hess, R. D., & Camara, K. A. (1979). Post-divorce family relationships as mediating factors in the consequences of divorce for children. *Journal of Social Issues, 35*, 79–96.

Hetherington, E. M., Cox, M., & Cox, R. (1982). Effects of divorce on parents and children. In M. E. Lamb (Ed.), *Nontraditional families* (pp. 233–288). Hillsdale, NJ: Erlbaum.

Hetherington, E. M., Cox, M., & Cox, R. (1985). Long-term effects of divorce and remarriage on the adjustment of children. *Journal of the American Academy of Child Psychiatry, 24*, 518–530.

Hetherington, E. M., & Kelly, J. (2002). *For better or for worse.* New York: Norton.

Hetherington, E. M., & Stanley-Hagan, M. M. (1997). The effects of divorce on fathers and their children. In M. E. Lamb (Ed.), *The role of the father in child development* (3rd ed., pp. 191–211, 360–369). New York: Wiley.

Hochschild, A. R. (1987). *The second shift: Working parents and the revolution at home.* New York: Avon Books.

Hochschild, A. R. (1995). Understanding the future of fatherhood: The "daddy hierarchy" and beyond. In M. C. P. van Dongen, G. A. B. Frinking, & M. J. G. Jacobs (Eds.), *Changing fatherhood: An interdisciplinary perspective* (pp. 219–230). Amsterdam: Thesis.

Horn, W. F. (1995). *Father facts.* Lancaster, PA: National Fatherhood Initiative.

Jacobs, M. (1995). The wish to become a father: How do men decide in favor of parenthood? In M. C. P. van Dongen, G. A. B. Frinking, & M. J. G. Jacobs (Eds.), *Changing fatherhood: An interdisciplinary perspective* (pp. 67–83). Amsterdam: Thesis.

Johnson, L. C., & Abramovitch, R. (1985). *Unemployed fathers: Parenting in a changing labour market.* Toronto: Social Planning Council.

Johnson, L. C., & Abramovitch, R. (1988). Parental unemployment and family life. In A. Pence (Ed.), *Ecological research with children and families: From concepts to methodology* (pp. 49–75). New York: Teachers College Press.

Kavanaugh, R. D., & Tirkovsky, A. M. (1982). Parental speech to young children—A longitudinal analysis. *Merrill-Palmer Quarterly, 28,* 297–311.

Kelly, J. B. (2000). Children's adjustment in conflicted marriage and divorce: A decade review of research. *Journal of the American Academy of Child and Adolescent Psychiatry, 39,* 963–973.

Kelly, J. B., & Lamb, M. E. (2000). Using child development research to make appropriate custody and access decisions for young children. *Family and Conciliation Courts Review, 38,* 297–311.

Klinman, D. (1986). Fathers and the educational system. In M. E. Lamb (Ed.), *The father's role: Applied perspectives* (pp. 413–428). New York: Wiley.

Knibiehler, Y. (1995). Fathers, patriarchy, paternity. In M. C. P. van Dongen, G. A. B. Frinking, & M. J. G. Jacobs (Eds.), *Changing fatherhood: An interdisciplinary perspective* (pp. 201–214). Amsterdam: Thesis.

Koestner, R., Franz, C., & Weinberger, J. (1990). The family origins of empathic concern: A 26 year longitudinal study. *Journal of Personality and Social Psychology, 58,* 709–717.

Lamb, M. E. (Ed.). (1976). *The role of the father in child development.* New York: Wiley.

Lamb, M. E. (1981a). The development of father-infant relationships. In M. E. Lamb (Ed.), *The role of the father in child development* (Rev. ed., pp. 459–488). New York: Wiley.

Lamb, M. E. (1981b). Fathers and child development: An integrative overview. In M. E. Lamb (Ed.), *The role of the father in child development* (Rev. ed., pp. 1–70). New York: Wiley.

Lamb, M. E. (Ed.). (1981c). *The role of the father in child development* (Third ed.). New York: Wiley.

Lamb, M. E. (1999). Non-custodial fathers and their impact on the children of divorce. In R. A. Thompson & P. R. Amato (Eds.), *The post-divorce family: Research and policy issues* (pp. 105–125). Thousand Oaks, CA: Sage.

Lamb, M. E., Frodi, M., Hwang, C. P., & Frodi, A. M. (1983). Effects of paternal involvement on infant preferences for mothers and fathers. *Child Development, 54,* 450–452.

Lamb, M. E., & Levine, J. A. (1983). The Swedish parental insurance policy: An experiment in social engineering. In M. E. Lamb & A. Sagi (Eds.), *Fatherhood and family policy* (pp. 39–51). Hillsdale, NJ: Erlbaum.

Lamb, M. E., Pleck, J. H., Charnov, E. L., & Levine, J. A. (1987). A biosocial perspective on paternal behavior and involvement. In J. B. Lancaster, J. Altmann, A. S. Rossi, & L. R. Sherrod (Eds.), *Parenting across the lifespan: Biosocial perspectives* (pp. 111–142). Hawthorne, NY: Aldine.

Lamb, M. E., Pleck, J. H., & Levine, J. A. (1985). The role of the father in child development: The effects of increased paternal involvement. In B. B. Lahey & A. E. Kazdin (Eds.), *Advances in clinical child psychology* (Vol. 8, pp. 229–266). New York: Plenum.

Larson, R., & Richards, M. (1994). *Divergent lives: The emotional lives of mothers, fathers, and adolescents.* New York: Basic Books.

Leaper, C., Anderson, K. J., & Sanders, P. (1998). Moderators of gender effects on parents' talk to their children: A meta-analysis. *Developmental Psychology, 34,* 3–27.

Lee, R. A. (1983). Flexitime and conjugal roles. *Journal of Occupational Behavior, 4,* 297–315.

Levine, J. A., Murphy, D. T., & Wilson, S. (1993). *Getting men involved.* New York: Scholastic.

Levine, J. A., & Pitt, E. (1995). *New expectations: Community strategies for responsible fatherhood.* New York: Families and Work Institute.

Lewis, M., & Weinraub, M. (1976). The father's role in the child's social network. In M. E. Lamb (Ed.), *The role of the father in child development* (pp. 157–184). New York: Wiley.

McLaughlin, B., White, D., McDewitt, T., & Raskin, R. (1983). Mothers' and fathers' speech to their young children: Similar or different? *Journal of Child Language, 10,* 245–252.

Mincy, R. B., & Pouncy, H. W. (2002). The responsible fatherhood hold: Evolution or goals. In C. S. Tamis-LeMonda & N. Cabrera (Eds.), *Handbook of father involvement: Multidisciplinary perspectives* (pp. 555–597). Mahwah, NJ: Erlbaum.

Mosely, J., & Thomson, E. (1995). Fathering behavior and child outcomes: The role of race and poverty. In W. Marsiglio (Ed.), *Fatherhood: Contemporary theory, research, and social policy* (pp. 148–165). Thousand Oaks, CA: Sage.

Mussen, P. H., & Rutherford, E. (1963). Parent-child relations and parental personality in relation to young children's sex-role preferences. *Child Development, 34,* 589–607.

Notaro, P. C., & Volling, B. L. (1999). Parental responsiveness and infant-parent attachment: A replication study with fathers and mothers. *Infant Behavior and Development, 22,* 345–352.

O'Hare, W. P. (1995). *KIDS COUNT Data Book.* New York: Annie Casie Foundation.

Parke, R. D., Power, T. G., & Gottman, J. (1979). Conceptualizing and quantifying influence patterns in the family triad. In M. E. Lamb, S. J. Suomi, & G. R. Stephenson (Eds.), *Social interaction analysis: Methodological issues* (pp. 231–252). Madison: University of Wisconsin Press.

Payne, D. E., & Mussen, P. H. (1956). Parent-child relations and father identification among adolescent boys. *Journal of Abnormal and Social Psychology, 52,* 358–362.

Pearson, J., & Thoennes, N. (1990). Custody after divorce: Demographic and attitudinal patterns. *American Journal of Orthopsychiatry, 60,* 233–249.

Pleck, E. H., & Pleck, J. H. (1997). Fatherhood ideals in the United States: Historical dimensions. In M. E. Lamb (Ed.), *The role of the father in child development* (3rd ed., pp. 33–48, 314–318). New York: Wiley.

Pleck, J. H. (1982). *Husbands' and wives' paid work, family work, and adjustment.* Wellesley, MA: Wellesley College Center for Research on Women.

Pleck, J. H. (1983). Husbands' paid work and family roles: Current research issues. In H. Lopata & J. H. Pleck (Eds.), *Research in the interweave of social roles: Vol. 3. Families and jobs* (pp. 251–333). Greenwich, CT: JAI Press.

Pleck, J. H. (1984). *Working wives and family well-being.* Beverly Hills, CA: Sage.

Pleck, J. H. (1986). Employment and fatherhood: Issues and innovative policies. In M. E. Lamb (Ed.), *The father's role: Applied perspectives* (pp. 385–412). New York: Wiley.

Pleck, J. H. (1997). Paternal involvement: Levels, sources and consequences. In M. E. Lamb (Ed.), *The role of the father in child development* (3rd ed., pp. 66–103, 325–332). New York: Wiley.

Polatnick, M. (1973–1974). Why men don't rear children: A power analysis. *Berkeley Journal of Sociology, 18,* 44–86.

Popenoe, D. (1989). The family transformed. *Family Affairs, 2*(2–3), 1–5.

Popenoe, D. (1996). *Life without father.* New York: Free Press.

Power, T. G. (1985). Mother- and father-infant play. *Child Development, 56,* 1514–1524.

Pruett, K. D. (1983). Infants of primary nurturing fathers. *Psychoanalytic Study of the Child, 38,* 257–277.

Pruett, K. D. (1985). Children of the fathermothers: Infants of primary nurturing fathers. In J. D. Call, E. Galenson, & R. L. Tyson (Eds.), *Frontiers of infant psychiatry* (Vol. 2, pp. 375–380). New York: Basic Books.

Quinn, R. P., & Staines, G. L. (1979). *The 1977 Quality of Employment survey.* Ann Arbor, MI: Survey Research Center.

Radin, N. (1981). The role of the father in cognitive, academic, and intellectual development. In M. E. Lamb (Ed.), *The role of the father in child development* (Rev. ed., pp. 379–428). New York: Wiley.

Radin, N. (1982). Primary caregiving and role-sharing fathers. In M. E. Lamb (Ed.), *Nontraditional families: Parenting and child development* (pp. 173–204). Hillsdale, NJ: Erlbaum.

Radin, N. (1994). Primary-caregiving fathers in intact families. In A. E. Gottfried & A. W. Gottfried (Eds.), *Redefining families: Implications for children's development* (pp. 11–54). New York: Plenum.

Radin, N., & Goldsmith, R. (1985). Caregiving fathers of preschoolers: Four years later. *Merrill-Palmer Quarterly, 31,* 375–383.

Rodman, H. (1971). *Lower-class families: The culture of poverty in Negro Trinidad.* New York: Oxford University Press.

Roggman, L. A., Fitzgerald, H. E., Bradley, R. H., & Rarkes, H. (2002). Methodological, measurement, and design issues in studying fathers: An interdisciplinary perspective. In C. S. Tamis-LeMonda & N. Cabrera (Eds.), *Handbook of father involvement: Multidisciplinary perspectives* (pp. 1–30). Mahwah, NJ: Erlbaum.

Rondal, J. A. (1980). Fathers' and mothers' speech in early language development. *Journal of Child Language, 7,* 353–369.

Russell, G. (1983). *The changing roles of fathers?* St. Lucia, Queensland: University of Queensland Press.

Russell, G. (1986). Primary caretaking and role-sharing fathers. In M. E. Lamb (Ed.), *The father's role: Applied perspectives* (pp. 29–57). New York: Wiley.

Sears, R. R., Maccoby, E. E., & Levin, H. (1957). *Patterns of child rearing.* Evanston, IL: Peterson.

Shannon, J., Tamis-LeMonda, C. S., London, K., & Cabrera, N. (2002). Beyond rough and tumble: Low-income fathers' interactions and children's cognitive development at 24 months. *Parenting: Science and Practice, 2,* 77–104.

Sternberg, K. S. (1997). Fathers, the missing parents in research on family violence. In M. E. Lamb (Ed.), *The role of the father in child development* (3rd ed., pp. 284–308, 392–297). New York: Wiley.

Tamis-LeMonda, C. S., & Cabrera, N. (1999). Perspectives on father involvement: Research and social policy (with commentary by Ross Thompson). *Society for Research in Child Development, Social Policy Report, 13*(2), 1–26.

Tamis-LeMonda, C. S., & Cabrera, N. (Eds.). (2002). *Handbook of father involvement: Multidisciplinary perspectives.* Mahwah, NJ: Erlbaum.

Thompson, R. A., & Laible, D. J. (1999). Noncustodial parents. In M. E. Lamb (Ed.), *Parenting and child development in "nontraditional" families* (pp. 103–123). Mahwah, NJ: Erlbaum.

Tomasello, M., Conti-Ramsden, G., & Ewert, B. (1990). Young children's conversations with their mothers and fathers: Difference in breakdown and repair. *Journal of Child Language, 17,* 115–130.

Van Ijzendoorn, M. H., & DeWolff, M. S. (1997). In search of the absent father—Meta-analyses of infant-father attachment: A rejoinder to our discussants. *Child Development, 68,* 604–609.

Whitehead, B. D. (1993). Dan Quayle was right. *Atlantic Monthly* (April), 47–84.

Winett, R. A., & Neale, M. S. (1980). Results of experimental study of flexitime and family life. *Monthly Labor Review, 113*(November), 29–32.

Yankelovich, D. (1974). The meaning of work. In J. Rosow (Ed.), *The worker and the job*. Englewood Cliffs, NJ: Prentice Hall.

CHAPTER 2

Two Dimensions of Fatherhood

A History of the Good Dad–Bad Dad Complex

ELIZABETH H. PLECK

SOCIOLOGIST FRANK F. FURSTENBERG published "Good Dads–Bad Dads: Two Faces of Fatherhood" in 1988. In what has become a highly influential article, he described two contrasting sides to contemporary fatherhood, the new father, the good dad, who was both a provider and a full and equal partner in the care of his children, and the bad dad, who denied paternity or, if he acknowledged it, refused to support his children. To Furstenberg the two faces of fatherhood arose since the 1960s, the result of "the declining division of labor in the family" and "the breakdown of the good-provider role" (Furstenberg, 1988, p. 218). Before describing the contemporary situation, he provided a thumbnail sketch of the history of American fatherhood. He emphasized that colonial fathers were both patriarchs and fully involved fathers, but that after the colonial period, the main role of the father was as a good provider. For the purposes of this chapter, the good father is what is now called the involved father. Furstenberg limited the bad dad to the deadbeat dad, although throughout American history, the American public has also defined the bad dad much more broadly to include immorality or psychological passivity. To provide a historical survey that matches Furstenberg's emphasis, the discussion of the bad dad here emphasizes the deadbeat dad.

The present chapter shows that the good dad–bad dad complex originated not in the 1960s but in the colonial era of American history and has continued ever since. Although Furstenberg (1988) alluded to the historical origins of both faces of fatherhood, his brief separate section on the history of fatherhood discussed mainly the decline in parental authority in the family and the evolution of the male breadwinner role. Furstenberg offered no historical discussion of the history of the deadbeat dad, in part because historians had written mainly about good dads and breadwinners. (Sociologists, because of their greater interest in family breakdown, have written more extensively about deadbeats.) The historian confronts a difficulty in applying present-day concepts to people in the past. In periods of American history before the contempo-

32

rary era, the concept of the good father varied by social group and changed over time. It involved some activities we would recognize as good fatherhood and might have included what social scientists regard as the three defining elements of the involved father: engagement, accessibility, and responsibility (Lamb, Pleck, Charnov, & Levine, 1985, 1987). However, such concepts existed in entirely different contexts. Leading the family in prayers, for example, was once considered involvement, which entailed engagement, accessibility, and responsibility.

Even taking into account the difficulty in applying present-day terms to the past, several additional factors make it difficult to trace fully the history of the good dad–bad dad complex. Men who were involved fathers and who were exhorted to be so came from all ranks of society, but we know the most about middle- and upper-class fathers. Such men have left the journals, diaries, and letters on which historians rely greatly. Although there is now much historical writing based on other sources about the history of the working class, immigrants, native Americans, and Blacks, the fathering of these groups tends to be characterized along dimensions of breadwinning or as bad dads, with some hard digging still to be done to learn about involved fathers in these groups (Ho, 1999; Osburn, 1998). Moreover, the writing on middle-class fatherhood assumes an existing marriage, so that single fathers, cohabiting fathers, and gay fathers are rarely discussed.

If we want to know about the diversity of family form and social background and offer a more subtle account of the entire range of family dynamics, then much more research is needed (Coltrane & Parke, 1998; Lamb, 1998). Indeed, although there are many overview essays written for nonhistorians (Coltrane & Parke, 1988; Demos, 1986; Gillis, 2000; Griswold, 1998; Mintz, 1998; J. H. Pleck, 1987; E. H. Pleck & Pleck, 1997; Rotundo, 1985; Stearns, 1991), there have been few in-depth monographs about fatherhood among specific groups and in particular regions, and the subject of the bad dad lies buried within histories of social welfare. In effect, the focus on the good father puts the emphasis on socially approved and culturally dominant fathers—men who were middle or upper class—while assembling information about the deadbeat dad places the emphasis on poor, often immigrant and Black men.

What follows then is a tentative history of what Furstenberg (1988) calls the good dad–bad dad complex. It is a study of rhetoric and behavior, which examines both the most favorable and the least favorable images of the father and their congruence with social reality. Most historical essays about fatherhood do not have this kind of focus. Rather, they tend to omit discussion of the history of the deadbeat dad and instead trace the decline in parental authority from what is perceived as its height in the colonial period. Thus, in *Life with Father* sociologist David Popenoe (1996) argued that since the Industrial Revolution, the history of fatherhood is the history of decline in the power of men—and because of the decline in their power, a decline in their responsibility as well. He wrote, "since Puritan times, one could say, it has all been downhill for fathers. They have lost power, authority, control, and status" (Popenoe, 1996, p. 90). Granted, when viewed against the legal power that White men held in colonial times, there has been a decline in (White) men's paternal power.

However, Popenoe's (1996) generalizations do not apply to all fathers. They exclude most African Americans, who as slaves gained power, even power as fathers, with emancipation. Even limiting generalizations to White men of property poses problems of interpretation. To be sure, separated or divorced White fathers by law received custody of minor children as a matter of course until the mid-19th century, and fathers had the legal right physically to punish insubordinate wives, children, servants, apprentices, or slaves. Once again, the past meaning of the modern-day concepts of engagement, accessibility, and responsibility must be considered. From the colonists' point of view, the proper exercise of authority could not be separated from engagement. They tended to regard arranging for a child's apprenticeship or a daughter's marriage as an instance of paternal authority and an act of involvement (Wilson, 1999, p. 3).

This survey of the good dad–bad dad complex is divided into two equal parts, a history of the good father and a history of the bad father. Two separate chronological surveys covering the same periods of time are necessary to make clear the timing and sources of change. Within each chronological survey, there is some attention to ethnic, class, and racial variation. The history of the good father is a history of the major figures who have advocated a new standard for fathering, the rationales they offered, and some speculation as to how much their appeals were heeded. The second half of this survey contains the history of the deadbeat dad. It is much more a history of laws and courts, with occasional exhortations for men to repent and reform. We know most about efforts to punish men who failed to assume their economic responsibilities for their children. Obviously, in numerous instances material about the good dad implies something about the bad dad, and vice versa. Even while there is opportunity to discuss the one in relationship to the other, for the purposes of understanding the evolution of the good dad or the bad dad, discussion of the opposite type of fatherhood is deferred to a separate section.

CONCEPTIONS OF THE GOOD FATHER

THE COLONIAL PERIOD

Historians have continued to push back the date when the good dad originated. They have concentrated mainly on the ideal of the good dad, but there are data, especially in recent research, on paternal behavior as well. J. H. Pleck (1987) identified the origins of the idea of the father as sex-role model. The idea emerged in developmental psychology beginning around 1940, the earliest precursor to contemporary involvement. In *Fatherhood in America* Robert L. Griswold (1993) located the sources of the contemporary good dad in the 1920s, as psychologists and sociologists claimed that fathers were needed as role models to promote healthy psychological adjustment in children. LaRossa (1997) agreed with Griswold's dating of the origins of the good father and thought that key developments were the growth of parenting guides written by men for men and the participation of men in largely female parenting organizations. Stephen Frank and Shawn Johansen, examining both fathers' own writings and advice literature directed toward fathers, traced the origins of the good father to the first half of the 19th century, revising the view of the Victorian father as distant, cold, and absent (Frank, 1998; Johansen, 2000). Looking back even further, John Gillis and Lisa Wilson heralded the ideal of the good father created by the Protestant Reformation three centuries earlier (Gillis, 1996; Wilson, 1999).

Whereas the major reason for paternal involvement in the 1970s was feminism and the ideal of gender equality, a variety of other reasons were offered in the past for why fathers should become involved with their children. The good father was thought to express religious principles and to be good for society, for fathers themselves, and for children (especially sons). In the 1970s, involvement tended to focus on equal participation with women in child care and equal involvement in the rearing of girls as well as boys. These dimensions were sometimes present earlier, but involvement also focused on the father as moral and religious guide, playmate, and confidant.

It is useful for a study of the good father to begin with Native American fathers in the colonial period since they were the first American fathers (Osburn, 1998; Perdue, 1998). The concept of the good father was not one they used, although there were elements of it in a father's role as an instructor, moral guide, and a participant in the care of infants. Native American women gave birth alone and had a month-long lying-in period. Many Indian fathers also had a lying period, although it lasted only about four days. Breastfeeding was a mother's biological function, and preparing food for a child was a task of women and girls. Moreover, the father was not thought of as a special playmate because all members of the tribe were potential playmates. The Indian father did train a boy in his gender role. He tended to take a greater interest in a son than a daughter and taught him to hunt, fish, and make war. Women and girls often accompanied men and boys on the hunt, but adult men provided the instruction for boys (Osburn, 1998; Perdue, 1998). As fundamental as the division between mothers and fathers was that between different ways of reckoning kinship. In patrilineal cultures fathers had responsibility for the education of their biological sons. By contrast, in many East Coast tribes that traced their kinship through the female line, the mother's brother often was responsible for the education of his sister's sons (Rountree, 1989).

The concept of good fatherhood was meaningful among the White Protestant population in the British colonies (Demos, 1986; Rotundo, 1985; Wilson, 1999). It was probably also the case among the miniscule Jewish population, although these concepts of fatherhood have not been studied. It has been claimed to have been less prevalent among Catholics because the good father was a celibate priest who had no biological children of his own (Gillis, 1996). The Protestant Reformation encouraged not only paternal authority but also paternal involvement. The nuclear family, with the father as moral guide, became a religious as well as an economic unit. In essence, the ideal of the celibate life and prayer in the Catholic church was replaced by the Protestant ideal of married life with prayer in the home and reading of the Bible presided over by the father. The good Protestant father was expected to teach his children their catechism and lead his family in prayers. Protestantism rejected the maternal symbol of Mary. Instead, it invoked the figure of God the father and looked on the family patriarch as God's spiritual representative in the family (Gillis, 1996). Martin Luther equated godliness with fatherhood and fatherhood with masculinity. Luther described day-to-day fatherhood as truly manly, despite criticism from those who regarded changing diapers as feminizing. He wrote, "when a father washes diapers and performs some other mean task for his child, and someone ridicules him as an effeminate fool . . . God with all his angels and creatures is smiling" (Gillis, 1996, p. 186).

A way of understanding biological functions different than the modern one also encouraged the idea of the good father. Men experienced "the husband's toothache," morning sickness so severe they could not work. In English folk culture a mother could transfer her labor pains to her husband (Gillis, 1996). Stories about pregnant men and nursing fathers circulated. Fathers were seen as generators of life and mothers as the incubators of it. Only in the 18th century were men and women seen as biologically different from each other. Women before that time were regarded as anatomically inferior versions of men; men had their genitals on the outside, whereas women had the same genitals, but on the inside (Laqueur, 1990).

Although most fathers in the colonial period did not engage in the daily care of young children, they appear to have been keen observers of child rearing. A father recorded in his journal if his wife had pain in breastfeeding. He noted when his children were weaned and measured their growth. Such men thought of breastfeeding as a joint project. A New England father in the 1660s wrote to their friends "today we began to wean ye child [emphasis added]" (Wilson, 1999, p. 123). A father also asked his friends for suggestions of how to care for infants. He carried his child to baptism and held the child during the ritual (Gillis, 1996; Wilson, 1999). Most colonial families relied on midwives and female family members at childbirth and when they were sick. Nonetheless, in all the colonies elite fathers not only decided on medical treatment but administered purges and vomits and kept track of "bowel movements, the passage of worms, the color and quantity of urine, the contents of vomit and, above all, the presence of different kinds of bile" (Brown, 1996, p. 347).

Colonial fathers were expected to be involved throughout a child's life, even into adulthood (Rotundo, 1993). Although children dressed as adults and assumed responsibilities of adult work as early as age 7, the father, even after the child reached 7, was still the child's guide, governor, disciplinarian, and protector. In colonial America it was often the case that a child could be apprenticed to another family and live with them for several years. In such situations, the head of the household, rather than the parent, had the right to discipline and the supervisory responsibility for the child. But a father was still expected to correspond with his children and, if he could, visit them. Sons were more likely to be literate than daughters. They usually corresponded directly with their father rather than addressing letters to their mother (Rotundo, 1993).

Eighteenth-century elite men, especially planter fathers in the South, were susceptible to a more romantic, even indulgent ideal of the father's role (Lewis, 1983; Smith, 1980). The romantic age valued the open expression of emotions, even for fathers. Such men did not look to religious principles and ideals as a source of inspiration, since many were Deists and, with the coming of the American Revolution, nationalists. The American Revolution affected the ideal of a father's relationship with his children. The revolutionary generation rejected not only the tyranny of the English king but also the tyranny of patriarchal fathers who dictated their children's marriage choices. At the same time, however, such fathers still wanted obedient children. A Revolutionary War militia officer and lawyer from Williamsburg, Virginia, St. George Tucker was the father of nine biological children from two marriages and five stepchildren; Tucker combined militia-like discipline with open expression of affection. Tucker wrote about his children as "sweet brats," "vagabonds," "rogues," and "my little monkies" (Colonial Williamsburg, no page). Thus, at the end of the colonial period with the rise of romanticism, the good father became a bit warmer and more playful, even as he retained his role as moral guide and supreme parental authority. Native American fathers were always allowed to be warmer and more playful than European fathers because their culture permitted more open expression of feelings and made less of a distinction between work and play.

The 19th Century

Family size was declining throughout the 19th century, from a completed family of seven or eight children around 1800 to one of about four by 1900. Fathers as well as mothers wanted smaller families, although more of the impetus for a smaller family came from mothers, who had to suffer the pain, the possible gynecological difficulties, and the threat of death that came with childbirth (Degler, 1980). At the same time, the advent of the railroad and the steam engine in the 19th century heralded the beginning of a new economic stage, the Industrial Revolution, with far-reaching consequences for mothers' and fathers' roles. In 1997 E. H. Pleck and Pleck argued that the development of a commercial economy as part of the Industrial Revolution that began in the late 1700s led to the decline in paternal involvement. The ideals of the time dictated that men and women should inhabit separate spheres. The female sphere was said to be that of home and family, and the husband's and father's that of business and politics. In general, the assumption was that as the father came to concentrate almost exclusively on earning a living, he became increasingly removed from involvement with home and family and relegated to roles of disciplinarian, financial decision maker, and occupational guide for older sons.

Since that time Frank (1998) and Johansen (2000) have revised this portrait and found that men were more involved in the female sphere of the home than had been previously thought. Moreover, detailed portraits of fathers in the 19th century describe men who would put some of today's new fathers to shame (Carroll, 1999). For example, the abolitionist William Lloyd Garrison cooked and sang to his children at bedtime. Diaries kept by physicians after the 1830s began to note the husband's presence at his wife's bedside during labor. Wives wanted the comfort and assurance of their husbands, even though female neighbors, the midwife, and perhaps a physician were usually present as well (Johansen, 1995).

The good father did do some housework and child care as well, but usually not out of a sense of equal participation in housework but because of social norms and necessity. If a wife and child were sick, a father did the nursing when a female friend or relative was unavailable. Similarly, the urban father went to the market to select butter, eggs, vegetables, and meat six days a week. He bought the groceries because the market was an unsuitable place for a woman—crowded, dirty, filled with livestock being slaughtered, and frequented by disreputable characters. However, as cities began to enact higher sanitary standards for their markets and shop owners opened neighborhood meat markets, mothers began to take over the job of shopping for the family's food. Moreover, as cooking standards rose, the job of marketing required more time and skill in selecting ingredients to make a meal pleasing to the palate and the eye (Dudden, 1983).

In 1996 it was widely believed that the 19th-century middle-class father was less involved with his children than his colonial era counterpart *because* the mother had become the primary parent (E. H. Pleck & Pleck, 1997). According to Johansen (2000), this is the zero-sum interpretation of fatherhood. If women gained power as mothers, their gain must have come at the expense of the power that fathers enjoyed. Johansen insisted that it is possible that in the middle-class both the roles of fathers and mothers increased (Johansen, 2000). One reason this happened is that the new ideal of the family emphasized companionship of the couple and sentimentality toward the child. These new ideals then encouraged fathers to be involved. Mintz (1998) wrote,

> The essential point is that the assault on patriarchal authority did not undermine men's position in the family. Although it delegitimized one particular conception of men's familial roles, it simultaneously promoted an alternative vision, emphasizing sentimentality toward children and a more companionate relationship with one's wife . . . a new romantic sensibility urged greater masculine involvement in the lives of their family. (p. 13)

Mintz added that the romantic sensibility meant allowing for more open expression of feelings. While 19th-century middle-class men were expected to play with young children, it was assumed that they would be more restrained and less frolicsome with older children (Frank, 1998; Johansen, 2000; LaRossa, 1997). Fathers gave piggyback rides, pushed children on swings, and helped them build toy houses. They bought or made wooden blocks to teach children the alphabet. Middle-class fathers saw play as good for the child and good for the man because men derived pleasure from it after a harried and frustrating day at work and were allowed to express their more affectionate, more sensitive and spontaneous sides. In Frank's (1998) view, however, the fact that fathers provided evening frolic while mothers supplied care throughout the day confirmed "father's secondary role as a caregiver" (p. 138).

The religious ideal of Christian nurture was a second reason why 19th-century middle-class fathers were called on to be involved with their children (Carroll, 1999; Frank, 1998). Evangelical religious revivals in this period inspired the ideal of the Christian father. If the pressures of breadwinning and the drive for success took men away from their families, their sense of religious mission pulled them back. Protestant ministers often wrote child rearing pamphlets and advice books on parenting for fathers, urging men to devote more time to fatherhood than to business and telling them that Christian ideals demanded no less. They encouraged fathers to educate their children, counter the dangers of immorality to which their children were exposed, and provide the necessary vocational education for sons (daughters were to receive theirs from their mothers).

Before emancipation, slave fathers were not urged to be good fathers because that would have threatened the owner's authority (Genovese, 1976). Slave fathers did not have legal guardianship over their children, and they could not prevent their children from being sold—or their own sale, for that matter. For the most part, the slave (and freed) father's idea of good fatherhood rested heavily on the idea of being able to provide for his wife and children, protect them from harm, and punish them for disobedience. Some did strive for a bit of bargaining power by working for hire or running away temporarily. Nonetheless, slavery did not demolish the male provider, protector, or disciplinary role. Slave fathers played these roles but within constraints imposed by the master. For example, they helped to provide for their families by hunting, fishing, making furniture, and, in some cases, being able to hire themselves out for pay. Providing was supplemental, however, because masters handed out allotments of food and clothing to all families, single and two parent. Single slave mothers could raise children in a manner not all that different from slave children growing up with two parents (Schwartz, 2000). Although slave mothers delivered whippings, it was customary for the father to serve as the major disciplinarian. Both slave parents played the role of moral instructor, especially as instructors in racial socialization. They taught children when they needed to accommodate to and show deference to Whites and when they could safely challenge a master's authority without being whipped or sold away (King, 1995).

The good father in the 19th century was usually not thought to be immigrant or working class, either (Griswold, 1998). This father was seen as a disciplinarian, a protector, a shadowy figure, and a dutiful or inadequate provider, depending on the particular man. In industrial labor at the end of the 19th century, full-time employees worked an average of over 60 hours per week. Many of these workers were immigrants. Because of these long hours and the exhausting nature of the work, the immigrant father was unlikely to have been a playmate to his children. If anything, fathers spent their after-hours leisure with other men at saloons, pool halls, fraternal lodges, or sometimes at brothels. As is true today, working-class men may not have subscribed to ideals of father involvement, but they may have been forced by necessity to become caretakers of young children (Hood, 1983). When working-class mothers held paying jobs outside the home, their husbands sometimes looked after the children. In New York City at this time, African American fathers often cared for children during the day while their wives did housecleaning or held other paying jobs (Mintz, 1998). Although the farm father spent a lot of time with his children, supervising their work and eating his meals with the family, the middle-class concept of the father as playmate was at war with an older concept that viewed play as a sign of idleness.

Frank (1998) argued that as society became more secular in the late 19th century, the religious argument for paternal involvement began to diminish. Instead, physicians, scientists, and health reformers began to argue that fatherhood was proof of male virility. As Frank points out, "this biological celebration of paternity had little to say about the tasks of fatherhood but its logic was to reinvest the parental role with masculine meaning" (p. 52). A cult of masculine toughness, inspired by Teddy Roosevelt and further encouraged by the Spanish-Cuban-Philippines War and quest for empire, led to the manly father's effort to make his son more masculine. Mother-dominated child rearing was seen as bad for sons because it made them too soft. Therefore, father involvement was needed to toughen up a son. Distrust of mothers, created by the fear that men were not manly enough, spurred interest in fatherhood. Fathers were needed precisely because mothers had too much power, and fathers needed to gain some back. Mothers no longer enjoyed the unqualified esteem in which they were held in the mid-19th century (Marsh, 1990; J. H. Pleck, 1987). Thus, as the century came to an end, American imperialism combined with anxiety about women's changing roles seemed to require fathers to spend more time with their sons.

THE 20TH CENTURY

In the early 20th century, however, there was a countervailing trend. Experts called on men to cook, participate in housework, and be present at childbirth (Marsh, 1990). The growth of suburban single-family homes, with their new play spaces (the den and the backyard), and a backlash against the men's clubs (e.g., the Elks and the Freemasons), which reached their heyday in the 1890s, led to the expectation that men should spend more time with their children (Carnes, 1989; Marsh, 1990). The advocates of this new father were Ennis Richmond, Carl Werner, Bernard MacFadden, and other authors of advice books on how to raise boys, as well as home economists, such as Martha and Robert Bruere (Marsh, 1990). The main justification these authors gave for paternal involvement was that fathers could prevent sons from falling into evil ways.

By the 1920s the rationale for father involvement was a complex mixture of companionship and an antidote to maternal overprotection (Griswold, 1993; LaRossa, 1997). The newer version of the companionate ideal popular in the 1920s reflected the belief that marriage should be a sexual and emotional companionship between the husband and the wife. Because it included sexual compatibility of the couple as well as the use of contraception, fathers had a new role to play—they were to educate their sons about sex. The 1920s dad was called on to be a companion for his children as well as for his wife. Unlike in the 19th century, the father was expected to play with his older children as well as with his younger ones. While the term *dad* was used in the middle of the 19th century, the term *daddy* was invented in the 1920s and indicated a rising level of affection for a father. It may have been more of a girls' than a boys' term, since on the whole it was a daughter more than a son who regarded her father as the more affectionate parent. Daddy was supposed to be his daughter's companion so that she could learn about the world of men and learn from her father how to pick out the right man to marry.

Another way that the 1920s daddy differed from his 19th-century counterpart was in the expectation that he teach his son sports and participate with him in outdoor activities, joining organizations that included fathers and sons, and taking his children on trips. The 19th-century dad took his son fishing, but since that time several sports had developed that required instruction and equipment, such as baseball and basketball. The Boy Scouts, 4-H clubs, and, by the late 1930s, Little League were all examples of organizations that invited the participation of fathers with their sons (Mechling, 2001).

The 1920s father also had to be involved in order to be a proper gender-role model for his son (J. H. Pleck, 1987). This rationale originated with Freudian psychology, which gained in popularity in this decade. Psychologists registered concern with effeminacy in boys and, by implication, with the fear that the effeminate boy would become a homosexual. The son who had the greatest problem becoming a man in the psychiatric view was the sissy who was, by definition, effeminate. A child psychiatrist, E. S. Rademacher, said he rarely saw fathers in his practice except when the father was concerned that his son might become a sissy. Rademacher advised fathers to teach sissies how to play baseball because sports or outdoor activities were seen as helping to make boys manly (Rademacher, 1933, p. 6).

In the 1930s and 1940s, while the nation was in crisis, the psychiatric fear of the effeminate boy was still the dominant rationale for father involvement (Griswold, 1993; LaRossa, 1997). Angelo Patri, a New York City junior high school principal, published a nationally syndicated advice column for 40 years and was on the radio for 15 (LaRossa, 1997). Fathers' letters to Patri revealed that they had picked up on the cues in the psychiatric literature. They were worried about sons who were insufficiently masculine, and they were also concerned about teaching children about sex and about poor school performance. However, records of child guidance clinics from the 1930s indicate that even though fathers participated in treatment, they usually attended only one interview. Even in the rare case where the father was defined as the source of his child's problem, the social worker, usually female, provided counseling to the mother (Jones, 1999).

The failure of many young men to pass army physicals during World War II led to charges that overly solicitous mothers and absent fathers made sons soft, weak, or too cowardly to fight (Blankenhorn, 1995; Griswold, 1993). Edward Strecker, a wartime military psychiatrist, was alarmed by the high number of draftees who had to be rejected because of mental illness. He concluded that in the vast majority of cases the reason these men had to be turned away was "mom and her wiles" (Buhle, 1998, p. 149). Philip Wylie in *Generation of Vipers* (1942) and David Levy in *Maternal Overprotection* (1943) argued that mothers protected too many boys from the inevitable struggle with fathers, the elemental struggle that would make a boy manly and independent. Mothers were overprotective, said Wylie, but what he really believed was that mothers had too much power in the family and fathers had too little (Buhle, 1998). *Vipers* hit the bestseller list and became required reading in college journalism and English classes. Fathers were needed to make decisions, punish their children, act with authority, and teach sons the facts of life. This kind of good dad could prevent his son from becoming a homosexual. In *Their Mother's Sons* Strecker (1946) emphasized how mothers might turn sons into homosexuals. In *Their Mother's Daughters,* however, Strecker (1956) also claimed that daughters could be so traumatized by so-called demonic mothers that they would become lesbians (Terry, 1998). Although Strecker advocated classes to prepare boys for fatherhood and girls for motherhood, unlike Wylie, he was much more concerned about lowering mothers' levels of involvement rather than raising men's.

As early as the debate about drafting fathers into the military during World War II, it was clear that fathers were thought necessary to stem the psychological problems that children and adolescents might face (Griswold, 1993). Opponents of drafting fathers during World War II argued that working mothers and absent fathers would result in an epidemic of juvenile delinquency. The war was a time of adolescent rebellion—fathers were away from home, families were migrating in search of wartime employment, and many teenagers had jobs. During the war young boys were smoking marijuana, stealing cars, and getting arrested, and young girls (called V-girls, for victory-girls) were running away from home and becoming prostitutes.

After the war ended, psychological experts such as Strecker regarded paternal involvement as a solution to the problems the war caused. As Griswold (1993) explained, postwar experts called on fathers to become involved with their children in order to offset "the new dangers of the age, authoritarianism, juvenile delinquency, schizophrenia, and homosexuality" (p. 186). Mothers who had raised their sons alone now had to allow the father returned home from the war to take over (Buhle, 1998). In the 1950s hypermasculinity (i.e., exaggerated masculine behavior), interpreted as a defense against unconscious feminine identification, began to be seen as a problem that was evident especially in juvenile delinquency. The experts were concerned about juvenile delinquency in daughters as well as in sons. The psychoanalytic explanation for juvenile delinquency in girls was that a father was unavailable and therefore unable to help his daughter work through her Oedipal desires (Devlin, 1998, p. 104).

Mothers in the 1950s often demanded that fathers become more involved with their children. American husbands and fathers as well as their wives embraced domesticity from the backyard barbecue to the repair workshop in the basement of the home (Rutherdale, 1999). Experts of the 1950s, such as psychologists, home economists, pediatricians, journalists, and family living experts, called on a father to be more involved with his children from infancy onward so that he would have a good relationship with his grown children (Weiss, 1998, 1999, 2000). Because the 1950s was an era of outward conformity to social rules, the advice of the decade repeated the emphasis dating back to the 1920s that a father's role was to promote proper gender roles in both his son and his daughter. He was to help turn his son into a healthy (heterosexual and marriage-inclined) man and make his daughter feel feminine and provide her with a model of the kind of good husband she should marry. Because a father was assumed to be a breadwinner who was unavailable to his children during the day, he was expected to spend quality time with his children in the evenings, on the weekends, and during holidays and family vacations. As historian Jessica Weiss (2000, p. 92) pointed out, "what family experts envisioned was the injection of male presence into the family, not a fundamental reassessment of male and female gender roles."

Wives and mothers also wanted fathers to be involved for more practical reasons.

The main reason for this greater demand from women was the changing nature of marriage in the 1950s. Age at first marriage fell to an all-time low, and during the baby boom there were more children spaced more closely together. Mothers wanted some assistance in caring for several young children (Weiss, 2000). What mothers had in mind was not equality in tasks or a fair-minded division of responsibility but accessibility—that is, greater participation in the tasks mothers delegated. Fathers were urged to change diapers, read children bedtime stories, and give their baby a midnight bottle. These reasons disappeared as the baby boomers became adolescents and young adults. But children of the baby boom came of age in the 1960s, a time of social protest, war, and unprecedented questioning of established institutions. Fathers were then called on to be involved to counteract the effects of the 1960s. Thus, parent's magazines wanted fathers to impose rules and advocate traditional morality when so many young adults were challenging all aspects of authority.

Feminists in the 1970s insisted that fathers participate equally in child rearing as part of an egalitarian relationship between husbands and wives (E. H. Pleck, 1987; J. H. Pleck, 1987; Rotundo, 1985). This particular new father—the coparent father—made central the father's coequal responsibility for parenting. The coparent was a caregiver to the infant, the preschooler, the youngster, and the teen. The main rationale for the coparent was to share equally in the care of the child. To some, mothers and fathers were even seen as interchangeable. A father was expected to carry his share of the load because it was the fair thing to do. Therefore, fathering was work, not simply play. A popular term for this way of defining fatherhood was the *new father*. In the event of divorce, the best option for the fully involved father was sole custody or the newly available joint custody. Because of the rise of gay liberation in the 1970s as well, gay fathers were also claiming a presence as involved fathers after a divorce.

This new father of the 1970s was expected not only to be involved but also to be an equal participant with his wife in the physical care of the child, even a labor coach and attendant at childbirth (Rotundo, 1985). When childbirth had moved out of the home into the hospital (a majority experience by the late 1930s), the father was relegated to the hospital waiting room. The presence of fathers at childbirth began in the 1970s with the impact of Lamaze and the women's health movement on birth practices in hospitals (Ruzek, 1979).

Between 1984 and 1987 several social scientists constructed the concept of father involvement (Lamb et al., 1985, 1987). They divided father involvement into three measurable components (engagement, accessibility, and responsibility) and expected that fathers should be held to a high standard in all three, especially responsibility, which many men had abdicated to women. It was an academic response to feminist demands that husbands and father share equally in the responsibilities of child raising and do so especially if the mother was employed. Scholars picked up these issues, measuring the extent of the inequity in the division of housework and of child care (Berk, 1980; Polatnick, 1973–1974). There were other family trends prompting the social scientific response. With rising levels of divorce, there was more concern about father absence. Many in the public worried about whether children were getting *enough* fathering. It is important to note that these worries extended from the father living apart from his children to the resident father who spent too little time with his children. In addition, writings of men calling for more involved fathers expressed regret about fathers who had been too little involved with them due to absence or preoccupation with work (Griswold, 1993).

Television commercials in the 1980s also conveyed the image of the new father. More fathers than mothers were shown holding a baby or pushing a stroller (Coltrane & Allan, 1994), and in order to counter racial stereotypes of the absent Black father, photos in textbooks often portrayed the new father as African American. Many social scientists argued that representation had changed but not the reality of fathering. In a highly influential ethnographic study of housework, *The Second Shift,* sociologist Arlie Hochschild (1989) insisted that employed mothers returned home from full-time paid work only to take on almost another full-time job of attending to the responsibilities of home and children. Fathers, she claimed, did not similarly have a second shift, and because they did not have one, there was a "stalled revolution" in housework and childcare. Necessary changes in work and family roles arising out of feminist demands and increased maternal employment had reached a kind of plateau, she concluded, from which additional changes would be extremely unlikely to occur (Hochschild, 1989). Sociologist Ralph LaRossa (1988) added that the image of the new father gave the impression that men had changed more than they had. Still others claimed that the ideal of the new father was mainly one of the upper middle class, who were allowed to see men beneath them as culturally inferior because such men had failed to adopt this new ideal (Griswold, 1993; Hondagneu-Sotelo & Messner, 1994).

However, J. H. Pleck (1997) showed that Hochschild's summary of time diary research about men's housework and child care used data from 1965, when more recent data were easily accessible, and that she used only part of the available data from 1965. He also showed that there was consistent evidence of a modest increase in men's housework and child care between the 1960s and the 1990s. Hochschild's error in reporting the actual time men spent in housework and child care seemed quite similar to Lenore Weitzman's (1985) overestimate of the decrease in income women suffered after divorce. Both were widely reported studies by feminist sociologists in the 1980s, and both tended to overestimate the barriers women faced, apparently in order to make the case for continued feminist pressure for change. Thus, sociologists were contributing to the image of the lazy dad even as father involvement in housework and child care continued to increase.

CONCEPTIONS OF THE BAD FATHER

THE COLONIAL PERIOD

Just as many people mistakenly assume that the idea that fathers should be involved with their children is a new demand, so, too, do they assume, as Furstenberg did, that the deadbeat dad is a relatively recent phenomenon, the product of high divorce rates, single motherhood, and moral declines in family commitment since the 1960s. In fact, not only have there always been deadbeat dads, but they have always been a source of social concern and condemnation as well. Public policy has focused on recognizing paternity as a means of providing support for a man's biological children, regardless of whether he continued to reside with them. If men failed to support their families, charities, religious institutions, and governments provided aid, especially when the numbers of children were large and women's wages were low. The goal of public and private policy was to reduce welfare costs by forcing fathers to support their families.

Whereas the good father had some limited salience for Native American culture, the concept of the bad dad was entirely alien. Determining the biological paternity of a child was not significant because a child was not the property of the father but instead belonged to either his mother or father's clan, depending on the tribe's kinship structure. It was easy for a husband and wife to divorce without any legal process. Native Americans had self-divorce: A woman who wanted a divorce had merely to put a husband's moccasins outside the tepee or wigwam. Land was not individually held. Because a mother and her children could depend on their kin for housing, food, and nursing when sick, a mother was not left destitute or disadvantaged if her marriage dissolved (Osburn, 1998).

After the European encounter with Native Americans, however, Native Americans acquired the concept of the lazy and idle dad. Some acculturated Indian women wanted to marry a White or Black husband because he would be more industrious (Anderson, 1991; Devens, 1992). White observers of Native American life, beginning with explorers and Christian missionaries, viewed Native American men as lazy because they were not farmers. They tended to visit villages where men were at rest after a hunt, and women and girls were preoccupied with farming, using hoes and working in groups. Europeans regarded hunting and fishing as leisure pursuits. Christian missionaries and later agents of the U.S. government sought to turn so-called lazy Indian fathers into industrious ones through productive pursuits. They wanted Native American fathers to become farmers of individual homesteads and Indian mothers to become homemakers and farmers' wives. Since the 1600s, missionaries and then government agents had only limited success in such efforts. Many Indian men did not want to farm, and the land on which Native Americans were supposed to become farmers was often arid or more suitable for grazing (Perdue, 1998).

In the British colonies two of the fundamental attributes of the bad dad were that he did not acknowledge paternity and did not support the children he fathered (Dayton, 1991). These attributes were based on an English common law conception of the responsibilities and duties of the husband in marriage. A wife was supposed to provide service, sex at her husband's command, deference, and assurance of the legitimacy of a husband's heirs; a husband was expected to provide protection and economic support. Although in theory a bad father could be the one who failed to protect his children from harm, in practice, such a father was regarded as weak or cowardly, not deficient. Even though colonial families could be defined as economic partnerships in which wives and older children contributed to the enterprise, it was nonetheless the case that the father was seen as having breadwinning responsibility, which he might delegate to others in his absence. These views of the marriage bargain were ultimately derived from the colonist's views about gender. Men were seen as the stronger, more reasonable sex and thus properly had responsibility for the care and protection of their dependents.

Most colonists did not include physical or sexual abuse or drunkenness in their definitions of a bad father (Dayton, 1991). The bad father was the one who did *not* whip his children when it was needed. Exactly where the line was drawn between necessary discipline and excessive whipping is unclear; court actions against physically abusive fathers in colonial times were extremely rare (E. H. Pleck, 1987). A truly wicked father committed incest and could be hanged if convicted. There were only a handful of convictions, but ever since colonial times, incest was assumed to be aberrant and uncommon (Barnett, 2000). A certain amount of drunkenness was accepted. Men who failed to assume the responsibilities of paternity were both sinners and criminals. Many colonies whipped both parties found guilty of the crime of bastardy. However, the

New England colonies took more seriously the religious ideals of family stability. They were more likely than the Southern colonies of Maryland and Virginia to impose whipping as a punishment for nonmarital births (Norton, 1996). As religious norms receded in the 18th century, even in New England, most courts were content with ensuring support rather than exacting a whipping.

Colonial women provided the crucial evidence regarding the paternity of their children. The unmarried mother was questioned as to the paternity of the father; it was believed that a woman in the pains of childbirth would not lie about such matters (Ulrich, 1990). The man she named was considered the reputed father and was required to pay child support. A warrant was then sworn against him, and he was made to appear in court. A woman often dropped charges if the father promised to marry her. Men who married the mother of the child tended to come from established families. Those who fled were usually transients, seamen, or lumbermen (Ulrich, 1990). Cornelia Dayton (1991) argued that in the 18th century, the norm of the responsible man who married a girl he got pregnant was beginning to give way to a denial of responsibility as religious and communal norms began to fade. Such men denied paternity, forced the woman they impregnated to get an abortion, or moved to another town.

In the British colonies the husband who deserted his wife was morally condemned as a wastrel. There were two main legal mechanisms to make men pay. The first was an action brought by a merchant or shop owner, the second, by the wife herself. Under English common law, a wife had no separate legal identity. Any debts she incurred were those of her husband, not hers. A father was thus responsible legally for the debts of his wife and children. If the husband could be found, and if he had money to pay his debts, he could be sued for failure to pay his wife's debts.

A wife could also try to make a husband support her and her children. Full divorce with the right to remarry was permitted only in the New England colonies; in most of the other colonies, the alternative was separate maintenance, a legal action that permitted a wife to live separately from her husband but required the separated husband to support his family (Riley, 1991). Desertion in most colonies was a cause for a legal separation. However, many couples entered into private and informal agreements in addition to those with full legal sanction (Basch, 1999). Thus, while colonial governments were involved in enforcing child support, the other mechanisms for doing so were moral suasion and individual agreements between the separating parties in a couple.

THE 19TH CENTURY

After the founding of the republic, states enacted additional laws to make men pay. Vagrancy laws, passed beginning in the early 19th century, were also the way that states punished deadbeat dads—as well as wife beaters (Cole, 1999). Presumably, the reason for passing these laws was that geographic mobility was on the increase and, accordingly, that desertion was rising as well. Under these statutes, the complaint was brought by the county prosecutor, not by the wife. Like many other punishments of deadbeat dads, this was designed to reduce the relief rolls. A vagrant father could be required by the court to post a bond and remain with his family. If that did not work, the local sheriff could hire the man out (in 19th-century Illinois, for nine months), and use the man's earnings to support his wife and children. If no jobs were available, the man could be flogged. Although Southern states continued to rely on chain gangs for cheap labor, Northern states became reluctant to do so because unfree labor violated principles on which the Civil War had been fought. Thus, in the 1870s the Illinois Supreme Court ruled that forcibly hiring out vagrants was a form of involuntary slavery (Willrich, 2000).

American racism, combined with racial taboos, shaped the unstated norms about who was a deadbeat and how he was punished. White men who fathered slave children were never required to acknowledge paternity. Interracial marriage was forbidden by law, and the law regarded the child of a slave mother as a slave. The issue of support did not arise because the slave child by about age 7 performed lifetime unremunerated work, for which he or she received food and lodging. Southern White men during slavery were expected not to acknowledge such children because doing so meant admitting that interracial sex had occurred. Southern gentlemen were thought to adhere to a code of conduct that forbade sex with their slaves. For example, Thomas Jefferson, who fathered children by his slave Sally Hemmings, did not educate them, provide for them in his will, or emancipate them. He did allow one of his sons to escape from Monticello. Even though Jefferson's relationship with Hemmings was a matter of gossip in the Washington newspapers, his economic and educational responsibilities for his children were never raised (Rothman, 1999). After emancipation, these unstated rules remained in effect. White men who fathered interracial children rarely acknowledged them, and Black mothers of interracial children were unable to secure child support. Such children were rarely left any money or property in their father's will (Ball, 1998; Schwalm, 1997). The father was subject to gossip, but he did not lose his standing in the White community and was never characterized as a deadbeat for failing to support his biracial children.

The temperance movement, which arose along the East Coast as early as the 1810s, greatly expanded public discussion of the bad dad (Epstein, 1981). Temperance advocates argued that drunkenness explained why such fathers failed to support their families. Originally, the alcoholic was portrayed as familyless—a single man who caused fires or property damage when drunk. With the sentimentalization of the home in the 1840s, he was more often presented as a miscreant who spent his wages on drink, depriving his family of coal, food, and clothing, or as physically abusive to his wife and children (E. H. Pleck, 1987). Women's rights advocates favored divorce as the solution for the "drunkard's wife." Most advocates of temperance, however, believed in the moral reformation of the father, who was urged to sign a pledge of temperance and join a self-help group consisting of formerly alcoholic men. Daughters were often portrayed as being able to redeem their father from drunkenness and thus save and preserve the family. Temperance stories written for children had one theme: a drunken father climbing into bed with his innocent young daughter. The father did not rape his daughter, however. Instead, he was saved from addiction by his innocent daughter's love (Sanchez-Eppler, 1995).

As long as a man left home but continued to send money to his wife and children, he was not a wastrel, a deserter, or a deadbeat because he was fulfilling his role as a good provider. This was true even if the husband absented himself for years on end. Sailors were the second largest occupational group in the 19th century, second only to farmers. Men on whaling ships around the time of the American Revolution were absent for months; by the 19th century they could be away from their families for as much as five years at a time (Norling, 2000). Migrant laborers, often male, spent months away from home. In the 19th century most of the immigrants who came to the

United States were men—that is, single men attracted by jobs as menial laborers. When married men migrated, they left their families behind temporarily—and, in the case of Chinese men, permanently because they were not allowed by law to bring their families to the United States between 1882 when the Chinese Exclusion Act was passed and 1943 when it was lifted. Immigrant men who resided in the United States often moved back home or established a beachhead in the United States and then sent for their families. When men sent home remittances to their family, they were fulfilling their breadwinner role. Their lack of involvement in child rearing—even much knowledge of the child—was both common and accepted (Piore, 1979).

Because there were already many civil and criminal punishments for desertion and nonsupport on the books, what is remarkable is how many states between 1890 and 1915 made failure to pay child support a crime (Willrich, 2000). Moreover, several cities also established courts of domestic relations. The main purpose of these courts was to serve as collection agencies for court-ordered support. (Previously, societies for the prevention of cruelty to children acted as collection agents for child support.) In most cases, nonsupport was punished with probation, but some fathers were sent to jail for as much as year because of failure to comply with these laws. There were other indicators of the rising interest in the problem of the so-called home slacker. Beginning around 1904, social investigators published books on the problem of desertion (Baldwin, 1904; Brandt, 1905).

The National Council of Jewish Charities also established the National Desertion Bureau (NDB) in 1902. The NDB was eager to pursue Jewish deadbeats so as to stave off popular demand for immigration restriction. Their research determined that in a typical case a lonely Jewish husband who immigrated to America without his family took a mistress. When his wife and children arrived, he had already transferred his affections. Some Jewish deserted wives turned to prostitution to support themselves and their children (Fridkis, 1981; Friedman, 1982). Social agencies other than the NDB also tried to determine circumstances behind desertion. They learned that some of the men were welfare cheats who colluded with their wives so that the family would qualify for relief. Others left temporarily but returned home from time to time. Some were not deserters at all but lived with their families and failed to provide adequate support (Gordon, 1988).

Michael Willrich (2000) provided several explanations for the rising interest in the problem of the home slacker during the Progressive era. Making men pay was a way to reduce relief rolls, which were rising during the depression of the 1890s. Officials wanted to eliminate deserted wives from the relief rolls and force them to find their husbands and make men provide support. Thus, *desertion* was defined not by a husband's absence but by his wife's application for relief. As the desire to reduce relief costs rose, the range of parties that could prosecute the errant father increased. In addition to public officials, court rulings, beginning in the 1880s, also gave poor relief officials the power to bring suit, soon followed by charity workers, county welfare officials, the police, and neighbors. Willrich argued that such expansion of the interested parties able to bring prosecutions reflected rising moral concerns about desertion. The public was worried about a crisis of the family—not merely rising desertion rates, but also rising rates of divorce, falling birth rates (among well-to-do, native-born Protestants), and the growth of women's employment. Part of the solution to these problems was to compel men to shoulder their breadwinning responsibilities and, in doing so, to make it unnecessary for mothers to have to look for paid work outside the home in order to support their children. Nonetheless, Willrich pointed out that many deadbeats could not afford to pay. Very few employers at the time paid a family wage—a union-initiated demand dating from the 1830s that a breadwinning father receive a wage sufficient for the support of a dependent wife and children (May, 1988).

How effective were these efforts to make fathers pay? Willrich (2000) claimed that court orders contributed to wife and child abuse, since after some of the men were hauled into court, they retaliated against their wives and children. A study of New York City's family courts between 1910 and 1936 found that most of the men who were brought to court to pay child support subsequently skipped town. The system also depended on the investigative work of deserted wives who helped the courts to track down deadbeat dads. The courts asked the wives to stake out their husband's place of unemployment, café, or saloon and notify the police of his whereabouts so that the police could serve the man with a warrant. Women spent many hours in such activities and also had to devote time each week to appearing at the alimony bureau to collect their check for support (Igra, 2000). Although there was increased awareness of the problem of the home slacker, the main solution—enforcement of child support through the family courts—was a cumbersome and even unfair means for collecting the payments.

GROWING CONSCIOUSNESS ABOUT DEADBEAT DADS SINCE THE 1930S

Because of the widespread nature of unemployment during the Great Depression, the unemployed man was portrayed with more sympathy than he was during the Progressive era (Igra, 2000). Family courts continued to impose the same requirements for deadbeat dads, but judges tended to believe a nonsupporting father when he said he could not help his family because he was unemployed. New Deal programs of the 1930s were the federal government's response to the problem of the "forgotten man" and his family. The aim was to provide him with a job, a pension in old age, and assurance that his home would not be foreclosed by a bank.

Buried within significant New Deal legislation for Social Security was a small program begun during the Progressive era that would eventually shape public policy toward deadbeat dads. Mother's pensions consisted of aid from individual states for widowed mothers and their children. Initially, the pensions were made available to widows and children. Deserted wives were omitted because of the possibility that wives might collude with husbands in order to seek public aid. By the 1920s, however, such women were included in these state-administered programs. Mothers' pensions programs were folded into a federal law under a provision of the Social Security Act of 1935 that established a small program called Aid to Dependent Children (ADC).

ADC was established by federal law but was administered by states that also had responsibility for enforcing child support. Although the original ADC was intended to aid deserving widows and their dependent children, after the war an increasing number of its recipients were single and deserted mothers. States enacted "suitable home provisions" that eliminated mothers from welfare for engaging in "immoral behavior," such as cohabitation. By the late 1940s, critics were arguing that such provisions were used as a means of eliminating African American mothers and their children from the welfare rolls. Under pressure from the Truman administration, some states abolished their suitable home provisions, while many others, especially Southern states with large Black populations, retained them. However, Congress wanted to increase child support enforcement. Mothers who failed to cooperate in pursuit of these men could be denied aid. Welfare workers staged unannounced midnight raids to make sure a man was not living with a mother on welfare. In the 1960s, activism, inspired by the civil rights movement, grew among welfare recipients, who protested welfare restrictions and surveillance and regarded welfare as a right of a citizen. Antipoverty lawyers, acting in concert with organizations of welfare recipients, successfully challenged the constitutionality of many rules for welfare eligibility (Davis, 1993).

In *King vs. Smith* (1968) the U.S. Supreme Court overturned ADC's so-called man-in-the-house rules. According to these rules, called suitable father rules, a woman could be eliminated from welfare if she had a sexual relationship with a man who could support her and her children. In an effort to cut their relief rolls, state welfare departments had adopted these provisions. Such departments also wanted to deny welfare to Black families, as their numbers increased on the relief rolls. From the very beginning, pension programs for mothers were racially discriminatory. Widowed mothers were given aid, and Black women, deserted or widowed, were seen as able to work and told they must do so (Goodwin, 1997). The deadbeat in *King vs. Smith* was Mr. Williams, a married African American man in Dallas County, Alabama. He was employed and lived with his wife and supported her and their nine children. He was also having an affair with a welfare mother, a widowed mother of four. He had sex with her on the weekends and stayed over Saturday nights. The mother and children were cut off welfare because Mr. Williams was declared a substitute father: able bodied and thus able to support his mistress and her four children. The U.S. Supreme Court struck down man-in-the-house rules as a denial of equal protection under the 14th Amendment and by implication decided that Mr. Williams did not qualify as a deadbeat (Davis, 1993).

It was not simply an accident that Mr. Williams was an African American father or that discourse about Black father absence appeared at the same time as urban riots and a major increase in Blacks on the welfare rolls in Northern cities. Although discussion about father absence had been a staple of sociological writing about the Black family since W. E. B. DuBois wrote *The Negro American Family* (1908), the Moynihan report (1965) repackaged the worry about father absence as part of social policy in the 1960s. Moynihan argued that the internal dynamics of the Black family lay at the heart of the problem of Black poverty. The problem, according to Moynihan, was the matriarchal family structure common among Blacks. In this family structure, fathers were absent. As a result, Black sons grew up with a frustrated sense of masculinity and low self-esteem, which they overcompensated for in violence or crime. One solution was for Black sons to learn appropriate manly roles by going into the military. Another was for the government to provide job training for Black men as a means of encouraging marriage and family stability.

The Moynihan report touched off a firestorm of protest because it castigated the Black family as the source of Black social problems and disadvantage. Civil rights leaders feared that the report encouraged the White public to blame Black poverty and other social problems on the Black family rather than on the legacy of racial, economic, political, and educational inequality (Rainwater & Yancey, 1967). Social experts, still interested in the deadbeat dad, turned toward more race-neutral ways of discussing Black father absence without the strong moral condemnation Moynihan used.

One of the aims of Jimmy Carter when he ran for the presidency in 1976, was to bring national attention to the social problem of teen pregnancy (Skolnick, 1991). Although his main focus was on the teen mothers, the teen father emerged as a new type of deadbeat dad. The partners of most teen mothers were men over 20, but they were not substantially older than that (Landry & Forest, 1995). To be sure, teen fathers had a high rate of denying paternity. Furstenberg defined one aspect of the deadbeat dad in such terms, but he did not explicitly single out teen fathers. The reason that the teen mother—and the teen father—had become social issues was not the teen birth rate, which was actually higher in the 1950s than in the 1970s, but the fact that more teen mothers were deciding to raise their children, rather than marry the father or give the children up for adoption. Some of these mothers then applied for welfare, once again raising the issue of welfare dependency and denial of paternal support (Luker, 1995).

In Ronald Reagan's presidential campaign in 1980 and in his presidency, the focus turned back to women, either the so-called welfare queens or the teen mothers, who, it was feared, were dependent on welfare (Stacey, 1996). Reagan believed that welfare resulted from family breakdown and a general decline in morality. Fear about negative changes in the family was mainly focused on mothers, not fathers. Mothers tended to be blamed for problems of poverty and immorality. In the public's mind these mothers were also assumed to be Black, although in reality the majority of teen mothers and welfare mothers at the time were White.

Even before Reagan's presidential campaign, the welfare rolls were rising, and legislators and the public were looking for additional ways to reduce the costs of welfare. Although Reagan's presidential election rhetoric identified welfare queens as symbols of a system out of control and in need of reform, in truth, there had been a variety of earlier efforts, some from liberals as well as conservatives, interested in reforming welfare by encouraging child support enforcement. In the 1970s feminist groups joined a coalition with social conservatives in demanding increased enforcement of child support. For feminists, child support enforcement represented a way to reduce the stigma of welfare dependency and place the responsibility on men. Meanwhile, conservatives sought to decrease government subsidy of the poor and thereby cut taxes needed to pay for these programs. In 1974 Congress responded by creating a Federal Office of Child Support, thus making child support enforcement a federal as well as a state and local matter. States were required to establish departments devoted to child support enforcement within welfare agencies. Congress passed additional legislation in the 1980s that created uniform standards for payments, rules for enforcement of payments, and increased efforts to establish paternity. A new term was invented, reflecting increased public concern. Newspapers and magazines first began to refer to the *deadbeat dad* in the early 1980s (Blankenhorn, 1995). The demand for changes in federal policy entered presidential campaigns, with George Bush Sr. and Bill Clinton in 1992 agreeing that making deadbeat dads pay was important social policy. In Clinton's presidency new child support legislation was passed, and child support enforcement became an important component of welfare reform, passed in 1996 (Katz, 2002).

Steven Mintz (1998) noted that to an unprecedented degree, men's roles as fathers and husbands have become highly politicized in the 1980s and in the 1990s (p. 22). Revitalization movements promised to turn deadbeats into good fathers without state interference. Christian revivalism led to the Promise Keepers, founded in 1990. By the mid-1990s Promise Keepers were filling football stadiums with Christian men who pledged to take on the full authority of benevolent patriarchs in their households (Lundskow, 2002). Black nationalists, under the leadership of Nation of Islam minister Louis Farrakhan, sponsored a Million Man March in Washington, D.C., in 1995 as a means of encouraging greater paternal involvement of African American men (Messner, 1997). Of course, there were other men's movements that focused on fathers' rights, rather than their involvement, or on the emotional deficits of the traditional male role. Fathers' rights movements were concerned with greater legal power for fathers in custody disputes, in challenging daughter's claims of incest, and in protesting laws against spousal and child abuse (Gavanas, 2002). The mythopoetic men's movement, associated with poet Robert Bly and Sam Keen, encouraged male retreats to the wilderness and masculine rituals of drumming and male bonding. These rituals were seen as solutions to "overdominant motherhood and absent fatherhood" (Kimmel, 1996, pp. 317–318).

In the mid-1990s two influential books, David Blankenhorn's *Fatherless America* (1995) and David Popenoe's *Life with Father* (1996), argued that fatherlessness was the underlying social problem of the age. Both authors, with funding from conservative foundations, were making the case for moral reform and a return to male exercise of authority in the family. Both echoed Bruno Bettelheim's views from the 1950s that fathers should not try to be mothers. These analyses reflected the increasing influence of conservative authors on social policy. In addition, the intellectual interest in fatherlessness can be attributed to receptivity to biological arguments about gender difference, the volume of research linking poverty to father absence, public fears about the declining significance of marriage, and the rising number of children growing up without a biological father present in the household (Stacey, 1998). Thus, the century ended with great concern about the social problems engendered by deadbeat dads.

CONCLUSION

The ideal of the good father has a long history, reaching as far back as the Protestant Reformation. Except in more recent times, the standard for the good father has been different from that for mothers. Mothers, especially in the 20th century, were more often blamed for the failings of children than fathers and were more often praised for children's success. They were also assumed to be more responsible for the physical care of children, especially young children, than were fathers. Because mothers were seen as having primary responsibility for child rearing, except in certain areas, they were the parent to praise or condemn. Being more removed from responsibility, fathers were simply regarded as less critical.

Until recently, the good father was also a teacher of the gender roles that his society upheld. He was supposed to teach the rules, not teach his children to disobey them, although there were the occasional fathers who encouraged their daughters to be tomboys or their sons to play the violin. Again, except for the new father, the good father was expected to raise and treat his daughter differently than his son. For most of American history, the good father was supposed to support gender asymmetry, not gender equality. Because of fears of maternal overprotection and the influence of psychologists, fatherhood has been seen as a means of ensuring the masculinity of sons and making daughters womanly.

Even though less has been expected of fathers, the lower standard does not appear to have been self-reinforcing. Instead, there have been periodic efforts to raise the standard for what should be expected of good fathers precisely because it was believed that not enough was demanded of fathers. The main advocates of the new fatherhood throughout American history have been men, not women. What is striking is how many and various are the claims about why fathers should be involved. These rationales reflect the prevailing beliefs and anxieties of the age; they extended from the religious to the secular and from the instinctual and biological to the nationalist and even imperialist. For much of the 20th century, the public was especially anxious about homosexuality and juvenile delinquency in boys (Griswold, 1998). Fathers were seen as providing either the role model of heterosexuality or the proper discipline and authority to punish a son intent on crime. Father involvement was valued not only for its impact on children, especially sons, but for the fun and frolic it brought to father's lives.

Did such exhortations to fathers to become more involved actually lead to fathers' spending more time with their children? There was at least some congruence between exhortation and actual practice, although a gap between the ideal and the real was always present. Rising standards were likely to raise the time fathers spent with their children among some and guilt among others who believed in the new standards but failed to achieve them. Rising standards also brought to the fore class distinctions because the new father served as one feature among many of the more privileged class's conception of its enlightenment (Griswold, 1993).

David Blankenhorn (1995), who also noticed the periodic discovery of the good father, asked what function the rediscovery served. He argued that the main function of the good father is to press for paternal tenderness. Advisors must insist on paternal tenderness, he argued, because this quality does not come naturally to men. He contrasted such advice with that given to women, who did not have to be told to be tender because tenderness did come naturally to them. Statements about what is natural for each sex are ideological claims that originated with the beginnings of scientific thinking in the 18th century. The evaluation of these claims is not the issue here. What we have observed, however, is that for much of American history, maternal tenderness has been held in low regard and fathers have been urged to be involved to compensate for the deficiencies caused by it (Blankenhorn, 1995). Moreover, those advisors who did insist on paternal tenderness often argued that they favored it because it might be combined with fun for the father rather than because it was necessary for the child.

The long history of concern about the deadbeat dad is an indirect way of revealing the centrality of the breadwinner role to American fatherhood. The most important aspect of the father's role throughout American history has been his role as provider and protector. Not only was a father seen as having this responsibility, but the government also staked out a role to play in requiring a father to fulfill his breadwinner responsibility. (The protector role, while valued, is seen as something other men or the authorities might provide, whereas the breadwinner role is regarded as unique to the father.) The deadbeat dad has always elicited moral condemnation and highly punitive measures to punish desertion. Penalizing deadbeat dads represents a significant strand in the development of the American welfare state. American social provision has been concerned not only with providing for the needy but also with ensuring that individual husbands and fathers bear their fair share of their responsibilities (Willrich, 2000). The long-running theme in this strand of welfare thinking is on detection and punishment, rather than on what we might call prevention. Rarely are the difficulties fathers face in securing employment sufficient to pay a family wage discussed. In a society that places so much value on the work ethic and on individual responsibility, the deadbeat is the fatherly face of a man deficient in both those respects. Since colonial times efforts have centered mainly on securing child support from a man not residing with his family, as well as on encouraging a biological father to live with his family and provide support. We have noted, however, that at particular times, the search for support has widened to include men who were not the biological fathers of dependent children. The persistence of efforts to make fathers pay reveals something about the long-standing core beliefs about marriage and family in American society. Anna R. Igra (2000) wrote concerning Progressive era reform, "antidesertion reformers believed that protecting dependent women and children within the conventional heterosexual family form was sound economic policy" (p. 59). One hundred years later, despite enormous economic and technological change and a virtual revolution in family life, contemporary family policy echoes the beliefs of a previous generation of reformers. Whether the results of their efforts will prove as disappointing as those in the past remains to be seen.

REFERENCES

Anderson, K. (1991). *Chain her by one foot: The subjugation of native women in seventeenth-century New France.* New York: Routledge.

Baldwin, W. H. (1904). *Family desertion and non-support laws.* Washington, DC: Kempster.

Ball, E. (1998). *Slaves in the family.* New York: Ballantine.

Barnett, L. (2000). *Ungentlemanly acts: The army's notorious incest trial.* New York: Hill & Wang.

Basch, N. (1999). *Framing American divorce: From the revolutionary generation to the Victorians.* Berkeley: University of California Press.

Berk, S. F. (Ed.). (1980). *Women and household labor.* Beverly Hills: Sage.

Blankenhorn, D. (1995). *Fatherless America: Confronting our most urgent social problem.* New York: Basic Books.

Brandt, L. (1905). *Five hundred and seventy-four deserters and their families: A descriptive study of their characteristics and circumstances.* New York: Charity Organization Society.

Brown, K. M. (1996). *Good wives, nasty wenches, and anxious patriarchs: Gender, race, and power in colonial Virginia.* Chapel Hill: University of North Carolina Press.

Buhle, M. J. (1998). *Feminism and its discontents: A century of struggle with psychoanalysis.* Cambridge: Harvard University Press.

Caines, M. (1989). *Secret ritual and manhood.* New Haven, CT: Yale University Press.

Carroll, B. C. (1999). "I must have my house in order": The Victorian fatherhood of John Shoebridge Williams. *Journal of Family History, 24*(3), 275–305.

Cole, S. (1999). Keeping the peace: Domestic assault and private prosecution in antebellum Baltimore. In C. Daniels & M. V. Kennedy (Eds.), *Over the threshold: Intimate violence in early America* (pp. 148–172). New York: Routledge.

The Colonial Williamsburg Foundation. (2003, June 25). Redefining the family. http://www.history.org/Almanack/life/family/essay.cfm

Coltrane, S., & Allan, K. (1994). "New" fathers and old stereotypes: Representations of masculinity in 1980s television advertising. *Masculinities, 2,* 1–25.

Coltrane, S., & Parke, R. D. (1998). *Reinventing fatherhood: Toward an historical understanding of continuity and change in men's family lives.* Unpublished paper commissioned by the National Center on Fathers and Families.

Davis, M. F. (1993). *Brutal need: Lawyers and the welfare rights movement, 1960–1973.* New Haven, CT: Yale University Press.

Dayton, C. (1991). Taking the trade: Abortion and gender relations in an eighteenth-century New England village. *William and Mary Quarterly, 48*(January), 19–49.

Degler, C. (1980). *At odds: Women and the family in America from the Revolution to the present.* New York: Oxford University Press.

Demos, J. (1986). The changing faces of fatherhood. In J. Demos (Ed.), *Past, present and future* (pp. 41–67). New York: Oxford University Press.

Devens, C. (1992). *Countering colonization: Native American women and Great Lakes Mission, 1630–1900.* Berkeley: University of California.

Devlin, R. (1998). Juvenile delinquency and the problem of paternal authority. In S. A. Inness (Ed.), *Delinquents and debutantes: Twentieth-century American girls' culture* (pp. 83–106). New York: New York University Press.

DuBois, W. E. B. (1908). *The Negro American family.* Atlanta: Atlanta University Publications.

Dudden, F. E. (1983). *Serving women: Household service in nineteenth-century America.* Middletown, CT: Wesleyan University Press.

Epstein, B. L. (1981). *The politics of domesticity: Women, evangelism, and temperance.* Middletown, CT: Wesleyan University Press.

Frank, S. M. (1998). *Life with father: Parenthood and masculinity in the nineteenth-century American North.* Baltimore: Johns Hopkins University Press.

Fridkis, A. L. (1981). Desertion in the American Jewish immigrant family: The work of the National Desertion Bureau in cooperation with the Industrial Removal Office. *American Jewish History, 71*(2), 285–299.

Friedman, R. S. (1982). "Send me my husband who is in New York City": Husband desertion in the American Jewish immigrant community, 1900–1926. *Jewish Social Studies, 44,* 1–18.

Furstenberg, F. F., Jr. (1988). Good dads–bad dads: Two faces of fatherhood. In A. Cherlin (Ed.), *The changing American family and public policy* (pp. 193–218). Washington, DC: Urban Institute.

Gavanas, A. (2002). The fatherhood responsibility movement: The centrality of marriage, work and male sexuality in reconstructions of masculinity and fatherhood. In B. Hobson (Ed.), *Making men into fathers: Men, masculinities and the social politics of fatherhood* (pp. 213–244). Cambridge, England: Cambridge University Press.

Genovese, E. D. (1976). *Roll, Jordan, roll: The world the slaves made.* New York: Random House.

Gillis, J. R. (1996). *A world of their own making: Myth, ritual, and the quest for family values.* New York: Basic Books.

Gillis, J. R. (2000). Marginalization of fatherhood in Western countries. *Childhood: A Global Journal of Child Research, 3*(May), 225–238.

Gordon, L. (1988). *Heroes of their own lives: The politics and history of family violence, 1880–1960.* New York: Viking.

Goodwin, J. (1997). *Gender and the politics of welfare reform: Mother's pensions in Chicago, 1911–1929.* Chicago: University of Chicago Press.

Griswold, R. (1993). *Fatherhood in America: A history.* New York: Basic Books.

Griswold, R. (1998). The history and politics of fatherlessness. In C. R. Daniels (Ed.), *Lost fathers* (pp. 11–32). New York: St. Martin's Press.

Ho, W. (1999). *In her mother's house: The politics of Asian American mother-daughter writing.* Walnut Creek, CA: AltaMira Press.

Hochschild, A. (1989). *The second shift: Working parents and the revolution at home.* New York: Viking.

Hondagenu-Sotelo, P., & Messner, M. A. (1994). Gender displays and men's power: The "New Man" and the Mexican immigrant man. In H. Brod & M. Kaufman (Eds.), *Theorizing masculinities* (pp. 200–218). Thousand Oaks, CA: Sage.

Hood, J. C. (1983). *Becoming a two-job family: Role bargaining in dual worker households.* New York: Praeger.

Igra, A. R. (2000). Likely to become a public charge: Deserted women and the family law of the poor in New York City, 1910–1936. *Journal of Women's History, 11*(4), 59–81.

Johansen, S. (1995). Before the waiting room: Northern middle-class men, pregnancy and birth in antebellum America. *Gender and History, 7*(2), 183–200.

Johansen, S. (2000). *Family man: Middle-class fatherhood in early industrializing America.* New York: Routledge.

Jones, K. W. (1999). *Taming the troublesome child: American families, child guidance, and the limits of psychiatric authority.* Cambridge, MA: Harvard University Press.

Katz, M. B. (2002). *The price of citizenship: Redefining the American welfare state.* New York: Holt.

Kimmel, M. (1996). *Manhood in America: A cultural history.* New York: Free Press.

King, W. (1995). *Stolen childhood: Slave youth in nineteenth-century America.* Bloomington: Indiana University Press.

Lamb, M. E. (1998). Fatherhood then and now. In A. Booth & A. C. Crouter (Eds.), *Men in families: When do they get involved? What difference does it make?* (pp. 47–52). Mahwah, NJ: Erlbaum.

Lamb, M. E., Pleck, J. H., Charnov, E. L., & Levine, J. A. (1985). Paternal behavior in humans. *American Zoologist, 25,* 883–894.

Lamb, M. E., Pleck, J. H., Charnov, E. L., & Levine, J. A. (1987). A biosocial perspective on paternal behavior and involvement. In J. B. Lancaster, J. Altman, & A. Rossi (Eds.), *Parenting across the lifespan: Biosocial perspectives* (pp. 111–142). New York: Academic Press.

Landry, D. J., & Forrest, J. D. (1995). How old are U.S. fathers? *Family Planning Perspectives, 27,* 159–165.

LaRossa, R. C. (1988). Fatherhood and social change. *Family Relations, 37,* 451–457.

LaRossa, R. (1997). *The modernization of fatherhood: A social and political history.* Chicago: University of Chicago Press.

Laqueur, T. W. (1990). *Making sex: Body and gender from the Greeks to Freud.* Cambridge, MA: Harvard University Press.

Levy, D. M. (1943). *Maternal overprotection.* New York: Columbia University Press.

Lewis, J. (1983). *The pursuit of happiness: Family and values in Jefferson's Virginia.* Cambridge, England: Cambridge University Press.

Luker, K. (1995). *Dubious conceptions: The politics of the teenage pregnancy crisis.* Cambridge, MA: Harvard University Press.

Lundskow, G. N. (2002). *Awakening to an uncertain future: A case study of the Promise Keepers.* New York: Peter Lang.

Marsh, M. (1990). *Suburban lives.* New Brunswick: Rutgers University.

May, M. (1988). The "problem of duty": Family desertion in the Progressive Era. *Social Service Review, 62*(1), 40–60.

Mechling, J. (2001). *On my honor: The Boy Scouts and American culture.* Chicago: University of Chicago Press.

Messner, M. A. (1997). *Politics of masculinities: Men in movements.* Thousand Oaks, CA: Sage.

Mintz, S. (1998). From patriarchy to androgyny and other myths: Placing men's family roles in historical perspective. In A. Booth & A. C. Crouter (Eds.), *Men in families: Why do they get involved: What difference does it make?* (pp. 3–30). Mahwah, NJ: Erlbaum.

Norling, L. (2000). *Captain Ahab had a wife: New England women and the whalefisher, 1720–1870.* Chapel Hill: University of North Carolina Press.

Norton, M. B. (1996). *Founding mothers and fathers.* New York: Knopf.

Office of Policy Planning and Research, United States Department of Labor. (1965). *The Negro family: The case for national action.* Washington, DC: U.S. Government Printing Office.

Osburn, K. M. (1998). "I am going to write to you": Nurturing fathers and the Office of Indian Affairs on the Southern Ute reservation, 1895–1934. In L. McCall & D. Yacovone (Eds.), *A shared experience: Men, women, and the history of gender* (pp. 245–270). New York: New York University Press.

Perdue, T. (1998). *Cherokee women: Gender and culture change, 1700–1835.* Lincoln: University of Nebraska Press.

Piore, M. J. (1979). *Birds of passage: Migrant labor and industrial societies.* Cambridge, MA: Cambridge University Press.

Pleck, E. H. (1987). *Domestic tyranny: The making of American social policy against family violence from colonial times to the present.* New York: Oxford University Press.

Pleck, E. H., & Pleck, J. H. (1997). Fatherhood ideals in the United States: Historical dimensions. In M. Lamb (Ed.), *The role of the father in child development* (3rd ed., pp. 33–48). New York: Wiley.

Pleck, J. H. (1987). American fathering in historical perspective. In M. Kimmel (Ed.), *Changing men: New directions in research on men and masculinity* (pp. 83–97). Newbury Park, CA: Sage.

Pleck, J. H. (1997). Paternal involvement: Levels, sources, and consequences. In M. Lamb (Ed.), *The role of the father in child development* (3rd ed., pp. 66–103). New York: Wiley.

Polatnick, N. (1973–1974). Why men don't rear children: A power analysis. *Berkeley Journal of Sociology, 18,* 45–86.

Popenoe, D. (1996). *Life with father: Compelling new evidence that fatherhood and marriage are indispensable for the good of children and society.* New York: Kessler Books.

Rademacher, E. S. (1933). For fathers only. *Parents magazine* (August), 6.

Rainwater, L., & Yancey, W. (1967). *The Moynihan Report and the politics of controversy: A transaction social policy report.* Cambridge, MA: MIT Press.

Riley, G. (1991). *Divorce: An American tradition.* New York: Oxford University Press.

Rothman, J. D. (1999). James Callender and social knowledge of interracial sex in antebellum Virginia. In J. Lewis & P. Onuf (Eds.), *Sally Hemmings and Thomas Jefferson: History, memory, and civic culture* (pp. 127–161). Charlottesville: University Press of Virginia.

Rotundo, E. A. (1985). American fatherhood: An historical perspective. *American Behavioral Scientist, 29,* 7–25.

Rotundo, E. A. (1993). *American manhood: Transformations in masculinity form the revolution to the modern era.* New York: Basic Books.

Rountree, H. (1989). *Powhatan Indians of Virginia: Their traditional culture.* Norman: University of Oklahoma Press.

Rutherdale, R. (1999). Fatherhood, masculinity, and the good life during Canada's baby boom, 1945–1965. *Journal of Family History, 24*(3), 351–374.

Ruzek, S. B. (1979). *The women's health movement: Feminist alternatives to medical control.* Westport, CT: Praeger.

Sanchez-Eppler, K. (1995). Temperance in the bed of a child: Incest and social order in nineteenth-century America. *American Quarterly, 47*(1), 1–33.

Schwalm, L. A. (1997). *A hard fight for we: Women's transition from slavery to freedom in South Carolina.* Urbana: University of Illinois Press.

Schwartz, M. J. (2000). *Born in bondage: Growing up enslaved in the antebellum South.* Cambridge, MA: Harvard University Press.

Skolnick, A. (1991). *Embattled paradise: The American family in an age of uncertainty.* New York: Basic Books.

Stacey, J. (1996). *In the name of the family: Rethinking family values in the postmodern age.* Boston: Beacon Press.

Stacey, J. (1998). Dada-ism in the 1990s: Getting past baby talk about fatherlessness. In C. R. Daniels (Ed.), *Lost fathers: The politics of fatherlessness in America* (pp. 51–84). New York: St. Martin's Press.

Stearns, P. N. (1991). Fatherhood in historical perspective: The role of social change. In F. W. Bozett & S. M. H. Hanson (Eds.), *Fatherhood and families in cultural context* (pp. 28–52). New York: Springer.

Strecker, E. A. (1946). *Their mother's sons: The psychiatrist examines an American problem.* Philadelphia: Lippincott.

Strecker, E. A. (1956). *Their mothers' daughters.* Philadelphia: Lippincott.

Terry, J. (1998). "Momism" and the making of treasonous homosexuals. In M. Ladd-Taylor & L. Umansky (Eds.), *"Bad" others: The politics of blame in twentieth-century America* (pp. 169–190). New York: New York University Press.

Ulrich, L. (1990). *A midwife's tale: The life of Martha Ballard, based on her diary, 1785–1812.* New York: Knopf.

Weiss, J. (1998). Making room for fathers: Men, women, and parenthood, 1945–1980. In D. Yacavone & L. McCall (Eds.), *A shared experience: Men, women, and parenthood, 1945–1980* (pp. 349–368). New York: New York University Press.

Weiss, J. (1999). "A drop in catering job": Middle-class women and fatherhood, 1950–1980. *Journal of Family History, 24*(3), 374–390.

Weiss, J. (2000). *To have and to hold: Marriage, the baby boom, and social change.* Chicago: University of Chicago Press.

Weitzman, L. (1985). *The divorce revolution: The unexpected social and economic consequences for women and children in America.* New York: Free Press.

Willrich, M. (2000). Home slackers: Men, the state, and welfare in modern America. *Journal of American History, 87*(2), 460–489.

Wilson, L. (1999). *Ye heart of a man: The domestic life of men in colonial New England.* New Haven, CT: Yale University Press.

Wylie, P. (1942). *Generation of vipers.* New York: Farrar and Rinehart.

CHAPTER 3

African American and African Caribbean Fathers

Level, Quality, and Meaning of Involvement

JAIPAUL L. ROOPNARINE

IT IS HIGHLY DOUBTFUL that any singular characterization can capture the ethos of African American and African Caribbean fathers' levels of investment in the welfare of the family. From Edith Clarke's (1957) accounts of Jamaican families in *My Mother Who Fathered Me* and Elliott Liebow's (1967) rich descriptions of African American men in *Tally's Corner*, to more contemporary excursions into African American (Ahmeduzzaman & Roopnarine, 1992; W. D. Allen & Doherty, 1996; Hamer, 2001; Hamer & Marchioro, 2002; Hans, Ray, & Bernstein, 1997; Jarrett, Roy, & Burton, 2002; McAdoo, 1993; McLoyd, Cauce, Takeuchi, & Wilson, 2000) and African Caribbean family life (Barrow, 2002; Chevannes, 1999, 2001; Mohammed, 2002; Roopnarine, 2002), it is clear that there is considerable variability in the family contexts within which African American and African Caribbean men become fathers and develop relationships with their children (Coley, 2001; Hamer & Marchioro, 2002; Roy, 1999). On a multivariate continuum, some men show unflagging commitment in provisioning for family members and face up to the responsibilities of caring for and nurturing their offspring, while others provide little or no economic support for their children, may abandon them, or abrogate caregiving responsibilities altogether.

Taking note of conceptual advances in our understanding of the confluence of multiple and extended child-rearing alliances and nonmarital-nonresidential fatherhood in families from different cultural-ethnic backgrounds (Barrow, 2001, 2002; Chase-Lansdale, Gordon, Coley, Wakschlag, & Brooks-Gunn, 1999; Coley, 2001; Hans, Ray, & Bernstein, 1997; Jarrett et al., 2002; Lamb, 2002), the goal of this chapter is to chronicle the levels and meaning of African American and African Caribbean fathers' involvement with their children. To this end, the focus centers on family arrangements within which fatherhood is realized and father-child relationships are grounded, beliefs about manhood and fatherhood, paternal beliefs and practices in child rearing, the nature and quality of paternal involvement, and the links between paternal involvement and children's intellectual and socioemotional development. For the present discussion, fatherhood and fathering are conceived in broad terms to include levels of engagement, accessibility, and responsibility toward children (Lamb, Pleck, Charnov, & Levine, 1987; Palkovitz, 1997, 2002); fathers' social capital (cultural and behavioral skills, personal acumen about everyday life, schooling, understanding of developmental progression in children, and ability to expose and inculcate models of successful behavioral and intellectual outcomes that are required for life in specific cultural settings; Becker, 1991; Coley, 2001); ethnotheories about fatherhood and manhood (Roopnarine, 2002; Super & Harkness, 1997); and other contextual factors that affect the dynamics of fathering (McLoyd et al., 2000).

Noteworthy parallels can be drawn between African American and African Caribbean families in the domains of children born in nonmarital unions and nonresidential fatherhood, multiple caregiving arrangements and multigenerational families, children raised in poverty, and histories of slavery and prolonged oppression. The impact of slavery, racism, and economic oppression on family organization and child-rearing patterns in both groups has been discussed in great detail (see Blassingame, 1979; Frazier, 1951; Guttman, 1976; W. J. Wilson, 1987). There are enough divergences in sociocultural beliefs, family experiences, and child-rearing practices to dissuade any thoughts of establishing cultural equivalence between the two groups of families. To begin with, political, social, and economic life in the United States is markedly different from that in developing, postcolonial Caribbean societies. In addition, as is obvious, the progressive mating and child-shifting patterns, beliefs about manhood and fatherhood, and austere methods employed in the socialization of children are more firmly planted in African Caribbean than in African American family life. Furthermore, there is the likelihood of greater within-culture variability in the lifestyles, educational attainment, and socioeconomic status of African American than in that of African Caribbean families. What is known about African American and African Caribbean fathers is presented sequentially.

AFRICAN AMERICAN FATHERS

After decades of persistent warnings by prominent scholars about the practice of stereotyping African American men as distant and uninvolved (e.g., Billingsley, 1968, 1992; McAdoo, 1993; McLoyd et al., 2000; Stack, 1974; Staples, 1999) and the preoccupation with framing African American family life in a principally social-problems perspective (Cochran, 1997; Taylor, Jackson, & Chatters, 1997), there is a shift toward greater acknowledgement of the range of family contexts within which fatherhood is realized and father-child relationships are shaped. Along these lines, some social scientists have shown restraint in equating nonresidential fatherhood with the overall lack of paternal involvement and are reticent in declaring family forms that deviate from the traditional nuclear norm as automatically treacherous to healthy childhood outcomes (see Black, Dubowitz, & Starr, 1999; Coll et al., 1996; Danziger & Radin, 1990). Put differently, there is increasing recognition that in some cultural groups other kinship and nonkinship members assume important roles in the socialization of children when biological fathers are not present or when nonresident fathers flow in and out of children's lives during their formative years (Chase-Lansdale et al., 1999; Hans et al., 1997; Jarrett et al., 2002; Kiernan, 2002; Stack & Burton, 1993; M. N. Wilson & Tolson, 1990). To date, the contributions of these other caregivers–kin givers to childhood development have not been adequately studied (see DeLeire & Kalil, 2002).

Progress in documenting father-child relationships in African American families has been steady but slow (Cochran, 1997; McAdoo, 1993; McLoyd et al., 2000; Roy, 1999). From what exists, there is a bias toward studying young, unmarried fathers who are primarily from low socioeconomic backgrounds. Understandably, while this may be due to concerns over the disproportionate number of African American families and children who live in poverty, over the risks to children attendant with being raised under extreme economic hardship without fathers (Berrick, 1995; Carlson & McLana-han, 2002; McLoyd, 1989, 1990, 2002a; Sigle-Rushton & McLanahan, 2002; McLanahan & Sandefur, 1994), and over family welfare policies in the United States (see Kelly & Colburn, 1995; Roy, 1999; Seccombe, 2000), little is known about father-child relation-ships in married families or about older fathers with better economic resources. Re-member that in 1999, of the 8.4 million African American families, 47% were married couples (U.S. Bureau of the Census, 2000), and births to adolescents make up a portion of all nonmarital births (Taylor et al., 1997). In the same vein, there are few normative observations of the day-to-day interactions of African American fathers and children longitudinally (McLoyd et al., 2000) and of father figures who often act as surrogates in fulfilling the parenting role vacated by nonresidential biological fathers. Unfortu-nately, the social science literature on African American fathers remains unbalanced and incomplete. Before proceeding into a discussion of beliefs about fatherhood and levels of involvement, it is first necessary to provide a sociocultural basis for under-standing African American fathers.

SOCIAL CONTEXTS OF FATHERHOOD

It is not simply that African American men experience fatherhood in diverse family contexts—marital and nonmarital, residential and nonresidential, custodial and non-custodial; they tap into the emotional and financial resources of interdependent family and nonfamily systems with viable child-rearing networks (Billingsley, 1968; Hans et al., 1997; Jarrett et al., 2002; Jayakody, Chatters, & Taylor, 1993; Stack, 1974). Data obtained from national representative samples (e.g., National Survey of Black Americans, NSBA; N = 2,107 households; Hunter, 1997b), community samples (Wil-liams, Auslander, Houston, Krebill, & Haire-Joshu, 2000), and smaller, qualitative studies (Ray & Hans, 1997, 2001) confirm the diverse living arrangements of African American families. By distinguishing family (related by blood, marriage, of adoption and sometimes containing nonrelatives) from nonfamily households (individuals liv-ing alone or with unrelated adults), Hunter (1997b) categorized African American families into seven prototypes: nonfamily (23.2%), married-couple/nuclear (37.6%; 47% in 1999), single-parent/nuclear (19.9%), married-couple/extended (7.7%), single-head/extended (9.8%), and cohabiting family (1.8%). Other researchers (Billingsley, 1968; Carlson & McLanahan, 2002; Chase-Lansdale et al., 1999; Ray & Hans, 2001; Sigle-Rushton & McLanahan, 2002b; Stack, 1974; M. N. Wilson & Tolson, 1987) also have documented the different circumstances (i.e., visiting, cohabiting, "friending") under which African American families engage in childbearing and child rearing. As men and women move through the life cycle, membership in the different family arrangements, personal well-being, economic resources, and parental availability to children and parenting skills may change markedly (Bowman & Forman, 1997; Hunter, 1997a).

Despite the inclination toward diverse family systems and their nonstative nature among African Americans, fatherhood is still largely premised within the confines of marriage and the two-parent mother-father dyad (Silverstein, 1993; Silverstein & Auerbach, 1999). Unwittingly, paternal involvement in other family arrangements is held against the traditional two-parent norm (Silverstein & Auerbach, 1999, in press). Debates being waged about the inherent parochialism encompassed in these definitions (Coley, 2001) have called into question the appropriateness of such a narrow conceptualization for examining fathering in other cultural groups. It has been aptly demonstrated that social fathering—in which stepfathers, maternal partners, and other men serve as father figures and form invisible triangles to assume instrumental and expressive roles in child rearing—is an accepted phenomenon in African American families (Coley, 2001; Hamer, 1997; Rasheed, 1998). For instance, in assessments of low-income African American men who assumed the paternal role, 59% were the child's biological father, 26% were the mother's partner, 7% were other relatives, and 7% were friends (Black, Dubowitz, & Starr, 1999; Dubowitz, Black, Kerr, Starr, & Harrington, 2000). Comparable rates of father figures were seen in samples of children enrolled in Head Start (Fagan & Iglesias, 1999); maternal partners were identified as sharing care in raising toddlers (Hans et al., 1997) or being in visiting relationships (Carlson & McLanahan, 2002); and children readily named nonbiological father figures as important in their lives (Coley, 1998; Coley & Chase-Lansdale, 2002; Hunter, Pearson, Ialongo, & Kellam, 1998).

In the argot of nonresidential fatherhood, the general impression is one of irresponsibility—men who provide little economic support for their children and have no emotional connection to them (see Hamer, 1997). The barrage of statistics are alarming: the proportion of African American children living with a never married mother rose to 72% by 2000 (see Sigle-Rushton & McLanahan, 2002a); 47% of African American males in their late 20s and early 30s have fathered children outside of marriage, with some having several children in nonmarital relationships (Lerman & Sorenson, 2000); and many nonresident fathers provide little formal financial support for their families (Coley, 2001). On the other hand, nonresidential fathering is not a static practice and could evolve into marriage, cohabitation, or other living arrangements as men age and become more economically secure. Data from the National Longitudinal Study of Youth indicate that 6 to 10 years after the first nonmarital birth, 20.6% of Black men were married and lived with the child and mother (Lerman & Sorenson, 2000). The point is that not all nonresident fathers show minimal interest in their children, and some may show greater interest than others and provide in-kind support and money to their partners (Carlson & McLanahan, 2002; Coley & Chase-Lansdale, 1999; Jarrett et al., 2002). Nevertheless, other nonresident African American fathers become custodial dads by default and must accept the primary caregiving role and financial responsibility for their children in a hurry (Hamer & Marchioro, 2002). Until recently, nonresident African American fathers have been treated as a homogeneous group (Lerman & Sorenson, 2000). The probability of underestimating their contributions to children's development at different stages in the life cycle looms large (see Jarrett et al., 2002; Mott, 1990).

In seeking to comprehend fathering among African American men, it is necessary to break away from restricted definitions of fatherhood and move toward an acceptance of the family milieus within which children are raised by multiple caregivers who may include mothers and other maternal figures, biological and nonbiological fathers and males, and other kinship and nonkinship family members (Hofferth, Stueve, Pleck, Bianchi, & Sayer, 2002; Hunter, 1997a; Jarrett et al., 2002; Silverstein & Auerbach, in press). Considering the economic realities of life for African American families in the United States, this interdependent, extended caregiver perspective holds tremendous promise for teasing out the areas in which men complement, supplant, or rely on other caregivers (kin givers) within different family systems to meet the responsibilities of parenthood (see Chase-Lansdale et al., 1999; Hans et al., 1997). If there is a single issue that has plagued our overall understanding of African American fathers, it is the persistent focus on low-income young men who father children in nonmarital relationships.

BELIEFS ABOUT THE PROVIDER ROLE AND FATHERHOOD

Developmental and cultural psychologists propose that in different societies, fathers' and mothers' culture-specific ideas or ethnotheories about paternal roles may guide the assumption of child-care responsibilities (Sigel & McGillicuddy-DeLisi, 2002) and the structuring of daily cognitive and social routines (Harkness & Super, 1996; Super & Harkness, 1997). Role identity theorists (see Coltrane, 1995; LaRossa & Reitzes, 1993) have also emphasized the importance of parental cognitions in deriving meaning out of child rearing. Paternal beliefs about child-rearing responsibilities are likely molded by political, social, economic, and moral forces within the culture itself (Sigel & McGillicuddy-DeLisi, 2002; Super & Harkness, 1997). Thus, understanding men's ethnotheories about manhood, fatherhood, and parental responsibilities can prove fruitful in interpreting what drives their levels of involvement with children. This is particularly so for nonresidential and noncustodial fathers, given the importance assigned by social service agencies and society at large to common residence and the economic support of children as key to responsible fatherhood (see Hamer, 1998; Kelly & Colburn, 1995; Roy, 1999; Sigle-Rushton & Garfinkel, 2002), as well as to the associations between economic status and paternal involvement (Bowman & Sanders, 1998; Bryan & Ajo, 1992; Carlson & McLanahan, 2002; McLoyd, 1989, 1990; Wade, 1994; W. J. Wilson, 1987).

How do African American men define manhood and fatherhood? Answers to this question are divergent, and interpretations about manhood and fatherhood must be understood within the context of harsh economic conditions and role strain, educational attainment, folk theories and self-knowledge, family experiences, religiosity, age, and area of residence (Bowman & Forman, 1997; McLoyd et al., 2000; Sullivan, 1993). The complex interplay of provider-caregiver-husband role scripts imposed by society and kin scripts and the factors that facilitate their evolution also should not be overlooked. The image of African American men as providers and fathers historically has been laid out in sufficient detail elsewhere (Franklin, 1984; Frazier, 1939; Hunter & Davis, 1992; Madhubuti, 1990; Staples, 1971a, 1971b) and is beyond the scope of the present chapter. To be sure, it would be an oversimplification to present African American men's beliefs about manhood and fatherhood in monolithic, unidimensional terms. Like men in other cultural groups in the United States, African American men's views about manhood and fatherhood are probably in a state of transformation (see

Furstenberg, 1995). Perceptions about the meaning of manhood and fatherhood from different periods appear to signal precisely this possibility.

It is generally accepted that the role perceptions of African American men are inextricably tied to socioeconomic factors (Brown, 1983; Bryan & Ajo, 1992; Hendricks, 1981). Traditional, conservative views about being head of the household and the major economic provider are more characteristic of men who live in urban areas with larger concentrations of African Americans living below poverty, who battle constant financial difficulties, and who tend to be more religious (Bowman, 1989; Bowman & Forman, 1997; Cazenave, 1979; McLoyd, 1993; McLoyd et al., 2000). Small sample studies of married, working-class African American men (Brown, 1983; Cazenave, 1979; Hendricks, 1981) and larger national data sets speak to the salience of the provider role as most important in being a man and father (Lerman, 1993). Endorsing the provider role as central to manhood and fatherhood is not that straightforward for African American men, however. Joblessness seem to impart severe instrumental role difficulties for men (Bowman & Forman, 1997; Bowman & Sanders, 1998), may assuage definitions of manhood among the poor in urban areas (Hunter & Davis, 1992), and may alienate men from their families and children (Bowman & Sanders, 1998; W. J. Wilson, 1987).

Opinions echoed by African American men from different economic standings seem to challenge the centrality of the provider role in influencing male identity. Representing a departure from more traditional definitions of manhood, middle-class African American men place being a husband ahead of the provider role (Cazenave, 1984). Yet other African American men hint of fathers as coproviders when economic conditions are unfavorable and advocate sharing the provider and child-care roles with mothers (Bowman & Forman, 1997). When noncustodial fathers were interviewed about how they perceived the meaning of fatherhood as men and as Black Americans, they placed the caregiving role (time spent with children and emotional support) as the most important followed by discipline and being a role model or teacher-guide. The economic provider role was perceived as secondary to their interest in child rearing (Hamer, 1997, 2001). Likewise, when asked, "What do you think it means to be a man?" African American men rated family relations, pride, spirituality, and humanism as being more important than the traditional masculine traits of manliness, power, sexuality, and ownership (Hunter & Davis, 1992). Unwed adolescent fathers also expressed responsibility toward children as a salient ingredient of fatherhood (W. D. Allen & Doherty, 1996; Dallas & Chen, 1998; Jarrett et al., 2002), and inner city adults drew a distinction between "fathers" and "daddies" and recognized that fatherhood entails much more than providing financial support to children (Furstenberg, 1992). Young men referred to "doing for your children," invoking a sense of responsibility in being accessible and involved with their offspring (Furstenberg, 1995; Nelson, Clampet-Lundquist, & Edin, 2002).

It may be useful to view conceptions of manhood and fatherhood among African American men as situated in "multiple arenas and contexts both within and beyond traditional notions of masculinity and male role" (Hunter & Davis, 1992, p. 475). In other words, depending on economic circumstances, oppression, personal psychological characteristics, stage in the life cycle, and their own relationships with their fathers, African American men may vacillate in their attempts to define the self within the boundaries of intra- and interculture expectations of manhood and fatherhood (see Ray & Hans, 2001).

Parental Practices and Beliefs

As already mentioned, understanding beliefs and practices about child rearing can offer solidity in interpreting the male parenting roles and behaviors of African Americans. Several recent papers and volumes (e.g., Coll et al., 1996; H. McAdoo, 1997; Staples, 1999; Staples & Johnson, 1993; Taylor et al., 1997) have covered some of the research on African American parents' beliefs about child rearing and socialization practices. A bulk of this work has concentrated on parenting styles and discipline (McLoyd et al., 2000). A common theme that emerges is that African American families assume a more authoritarian and punitive posture in child rearing (Deater-Deckard & Dodge, 1997; Deater-Deckard, Dodge, Bates, & Pettit, 1996; Portes, Dunham, & Williams, 1986). Perhaps because African American families emphasize obedience to adults, African American fathers (Staples & Johnson, 1993) and mothers from low-income backgrounds preferred to use more physical than verbal disciplinary techniques (Durrett, Shirley, & Pennabaker, 1975; Kelly, Power, & Wimbush, 1992). Note that fathers rarely withdrew love when they used physical discipline (Staples, 1971a, b; Staples & Johnson, 1993).

Parent-centered, harsher approaches to child rearing among African American families may not be that pervasive, though. In middle- and lower-income families physical punishment was the least used, and reasoning, a trait of authoritative parenting, was the most used technique in disciplining young children (Bluestone & Tamis-LeMonda, 1999). Similarly, associations among sociodemographic variables (education in particular) and more sensitive and flexible approaches to parenting (Kelly, Sanchez-Hucles, & Walker, 1993; M. N. Wilson, Kohn, Curry-El, & Hinton, 1995), potential biases in observer perceptions of parental interactions in minority families (Gonzales, Cauce, & Mason, 1996), and the meaning of parenting styles for non–European American families (Chao, 1994) raise additional uneasiness about the generalizability of designating African American families as less child centered and more family centered in their approach to child rearing.

Evolving out of African family traditions of coresidential family patterns, multigenerational families and extended networks have been repeatedly hailed as core vectors of African American family life (Sudarkasa, 1999). African American families emphasize harmony, affect, and communalism (Boykin & Toms, 1985). Family boundaries are flexible, permitting social interactions between individual members and across households; families provide mutual assistance to one another; and religion helps to cement social relationships and is a source of strength for families. Women were more likely to maintain contact with and receive aid from kinship members, and individuals at higher (not lower) socioeconomic levels have greater interactions with kinship members (Hatchett & Jackson, 1999). These general patterns of family life and functions have been substantiated (see Aschenbrenner, 1975; Ellison, 1997; Hatchett & Jackson, 1999; Hunter, 1997a; Stack, 1974; Taylor, Hardison, & Chatters, 1996) and with increasing educational attainment and better economic standing are likely to be modified.

Another issue that deserves attention here is racial socialization. Born out of the necessity to protect or insulate children from racism and discrimination and to instill a sense of ethnic pride, African American parents from all socioeconomic levels embrace racial socialization as important in child rearing (Thornton, 1997). A general goal of racial socialization is to equip children with coping strategies through love and felt security and lay the foundation for the development of ethnic identity and self-respect (Peters, 1985; Thornton, 1997). Parents adopt a range of socialization approaches to achieve these objectives. For instance, some focus on mainstream experiences (achievement and hard work), whereas others focus on the minority experience (acceptance of one's color, racial barriers, etc.) and cultural experiences (e.g., heritage and cultural traditions). These modes of socialization are influenced by age and gender, marital status, educational attainment, and region of residence in the United States. It appears that males engage in racial socialization far less than females, and single-parent households are less likely to do so than are marital households (Thornton, 1997).

AFRICAN AMERICAN FATHER INVOLVEMENT

Over 35 years ago, Liebow (1967) wrote, "The spectrum of father-child relationships is a broad one, ranging from complete ignorance of the child's existence to continuous day to day contact between father and child" (p. 73). Despite the infrequent and short bouts of contact between fathers and children, Liebow observed that African American street-corner men were very sensitive and affectionate toward their own and others' children. In a central way, Liebow's perceptive comments epitomize the levels and qualities of paternal involvement that are at play in African American father-child relationships today. Fathers' time investment with children extends from intermittent visits to no visits in nonresidential father arrangements, to daily contacts with appreciable time investment in coresidential nonmarital and marital households (Ahmeduzzaman & Roopnarine, 1992; Carlson & McLanahan, 2002; Lerman & Sorenson, 2000; Zimmerman, Salem, & Maton, 1995). At the same time, paternal sensitivity and participation in cognitive and social activities with children are likely to vary in different family arrangements based on quality of parenting skills, relationship with the child's mother, stage in the life cycle, and formal and informal economic provisions for the child, among a host of other factors (Marsiglio, Amato, Day, & Lamb, 2000).

Time, Frequency of Contact, and Quality of Involvement

As intimated earlier, there is a paucity of data on the amount of time African American fathers spend with children in married and two-parent households. Roopnarine and his colleagues (Ahmeduzzaman & Roopnarine, 1992; Hossain & Roopnarine, 1994) estimated that among middle- to lower-middle income, married families with stable jobs and in households where the mother worked full-time outside of the home, fathers spent 1.13 hours feeding, .89 hours cleaning, and 2.19 hours per day playing with infants (average age 13.75 months), and in households in which mothers worked part-time (less than 25 hours per week), fathers spent 1.39 hours feeding, .96 hours cleaning, and 2.80 hours playing with infants. The number of hours mothers worked outside of the home did not affect fathers' time spent with children. In married, two-parent families with preschool-aged children, both fathers and mothers estimated that fathers spent on average 2.8 hours per day in primary caregiving. During infancy, father's time investment constituted 42% that of mothers', and 33% that of mothers' during the preschool years. In a study of African American and Puerto Rican fathers whose children were enrolled in Head Start (84% were biological fathers, and all resided with the child's mother), Fagan (1998) found that over two weekdays and one weekend day, on average fathers spent 4.5 hours per day with children, 1.38 hours in direct interaction with children, and .40 hours playing with children. Older children who live with both biological parents spent about 19.52 hours per week with their fathers (Zimmerman, Salem, & Maton, 1995).

In a rather comprehensive study of time investment with infants among African American teenage fathers, Rivara, Sweeny, and Henderson (1986) examined paternal involvement and residential status through the transition to fatherhood. Mothers remained the head of the household through the prenatal (54%) and postpartum (55%) periods, but fathers were more likely postpartum to establish a household themselves than were controls (19% vs. 7%). A third of the fathers joined partners in prenatal visits, and about 15% attended birth classes. Whereas 61% of men were present with the mother for an hour or more during labor, only 27% were in the delivery room. Eighty-eight percent of fathers visited the infant in the nursery, and 53% of children were given the father's surname. A small number (11%) of fathers lived with their children, and between 25% and 36% had daily contacts with children at 9 and 18 months, respectively. During visits, 44% of fathers spent all day with the child, and 31% spent between 4 to 7 hours per day; 57% had spent a night with the child at least once when the child was around 18 months old.

Similar levels of social contacts were evident among young and older unwed African American men (W. D. Allen & Doherty, 1996; Dallas & Chen, 1998; Gadsden & Smith, 1994; Ray & Hans, 1997, 2001; Roy, 1999), fathers and father figures of children enrolled in Head Start programs (Fagan, Newash, & Schloesser, 2000; Lue, Smalley, Smith, & Seaton, 1998), and toward preschoolers in low-income, mostly unmarried families living in an urban area. Among the latter, 72% of fathers had daily contacts with children, and 61% lived with the child at least four days a week (Black et al., 1999; see also Jarrett et al., 2002, for a review of qualitative research). In other investigations, it was determined that 31.4% of nonresidential African American fathers had daily visits, and 32.8% had monthly visits with children (Stier & Tienda, 1993); about 50% had frequent contacts with children (Gavin et al., 2002; Mott, 1990); 81% of noncustodial fathers saw their children on a weekly (26%), biweekly (29%), or daily basis (26%; Hamer, 1997); and visits occurred from two times a week to holidays with teenagers (Rodney & Mupier, 1999). Contrary to popular claims, for some African American fathers, involvement with nonmarital children seems to persist through the early childhood period: 30% visited at least once a week, and close to 30% lived with the child and mother two to six years after the first nonmarital birth. The rates of contacts and coresident status dropped slightly when the same assessments were made 6 to 10 years later (Lerman & Sorenson, 2000).

But not all nonresident fathers demonstrate sustained time investment with children. In a large sample of unwed young fathers (N = 6,009; 68% Black) from urban areas in the Northeast and Midwest, only 7% of fathers were living with their children, and 49% had no contacts with their children at all, 20% had contacts less than once a week, and 31% had contacts once a week or more. Seventy-three percent of fathers had not spent the night with their child during the three-month period prior to the interviews (Rangarajan & Gleason, 1998). Sporadic contacts between single fathers and nonmarital children were noted by other researchers as well. For example, Greene and Moore (2000) calculated that 22% of fathers had visited their children at least once a week, 33% had no contact at all during the past year, and 21.3% visited between 2 and 11 times during the past year. Decreased contacts with children are governed in part by economic circumstances, relationships with the child's mother, and area of residence (W. D. Allen & Doherty, 1996; Coley, 2001; McLoyd, 1989, 1990).

Does the frequency of father-child contacts vary by household structure? It appears that time spent with older children was asymmetrical across family structural living arrangements in two reports. Those who resided with both biological parents spent on average 19.52 hours per week with their fathers—a figure that is at least three times that spent by fathers in households with single mothers, stepparents, mothers with extended family, and extended families (Zimmerman et al., 1995). Subsequently, it was shown that 45% of children who lived with two biological parents spent 7 hours a week with their fathers, compared with 29% who lived with the mother and an extended family member, 23% with the mother and stepfather, 20% with an extended family member only, and 9% with a single-mother. Only 9% of children who lived with two biological parents, as opposed to 57% who lived with a single mother, did not spend any time with their fathers each week. In family arrangements in which the father or stepfather was present, children had convincingly more favorable attitudes about the importance of fathers and the father as a role model than in families in which a father figure was not present (Salem, Zimmerman, & Notaro, 1998).

So far, the focus has been on the amount of time devoted to and the frequency of contacts between African American fathers and children. Heeding the suggestion that this may present a limited perspective of father involvement and given conceptual frameworks that stress the qualitative aspects of father-child relationships—emotional involvement, the types and nature of activities fathers engage in with children, responsibility, and commitment to the fathering role (Coley, 2001; Coley & Chase-Lansdale, 1999)—an attempt is made to examine the modes of care and interactions between fathers and children more closely. In the main, involvement in basic caregiving, educational, and social activities; guidance and nurturance offered in the course of child rearing; discipline; parent-child communication; expectations about the development of the child; decision making that involves the welfare of the child; emotional support to mother and child; and formal and informal financial support all represent more detailed investment in children. Accordingly, paternal involvement in these domains is laid out in broad terms.

Regardless of family structural arrangement, age, or socioeconomic status, what is abundantly clear is that African American fathers showed interest in and cared for their children in sensitive ways (Hossain & Roopnarine, 1994; Kelly & Colburn, 1995). In married, working families, 40% of fathers reported changing diapers, 77% played with the baby, 68% disciplined children, 49% helped children with homework, and 49% frequently took children to the doctor and dentist (Cazenave, 1979). These trends in basic caregiving were detected among men in married households of middle- and lower-middle income during the infancy period (Hossain, Field, Pickens, Malphurs, & Del Valle, 1997; Hossian & Roopnarine, 1994) and in social and educational activities during the preschool years (Ahmeduzzaman & Roopnarine, 1992). Paternal involvement in basic caregiving was equally as apparent among unwed, noncustodial fathers. Seventy-three percent fed the child, 39% changed their diapers, 82% stayed alone with the child, 64% took the child out, 19% bathed the child, and 97% played with the child at 18 months (Rivara et al., 1986). Sixty-five percent reported being very involved with their infant, feeding and holding them, and changing their diapers (Gavin et al., 2002). Unwed fathers spoke of being there for their children to develop loving supportive relationships, to teach and guide them morally, to protect them

(W. D. Allen & Doherty, 1996; Ray & Hans, 2001), and to bond with them (Dallas & Chen, 1998). In multigenerational families, 53% of fathers showed consistent involvement in caring for and being emotionally involved with their preschool-aged child (Chase-Lansdale et al., 1999).

Other indicators of the texture of African American fathers' involvement with children can be gleaned from research on childhood socialization and parent-child interactions. Observations, telephone and face-to-face interviews, qualitative descriptions, narratives, and responses on surveys suggest that fathers from various socioeconomic backgrounds and residential statuses were warm and nurturant to their preschool-aged children (Kelly, Smith, Green, Berndt, & Rogers, 1998; J. McAdoo, 1979), emotionally responsive and attuned to their children (Chase-Lansdale et al., 1999; Gavin et al., 2003; Shannon, Tamis-LeMonda, London, & Cabrera, 2002), provided a supportive teaching environment that may enhance the communication and social skills of their children in Head Start (Fagan & Iglesias, 1999, 2000; see also Pfannensteil & Honig, 1991), and served as playmates to children (Gavin et al., 2002; Hossain & Roopnarine, 1994; Kelly et al., 1998).

In the area of child rearing, African American fathers were controlling, supportive, strict, expected earlier autonomy, spurned wasted time, and encouraged equalitarian family roles (Bartz & Levine, 1978; Grief, Hrabowski, & Maton, 1998). They were actively involved in the racial socialization of children (Bright & Williams, 1996; Thornton, Chatters, Taylor, & Allen, 1990) and in setting rules, teaching moral values, disciplining children (Hyde & Texidor, 1988; McAdoo, 1981), and reading to children and assisting them with schoolwork (Bright & Williams, 1996; Cooksey & Fondell, 1996). Participation in general decision making regarding their children (Jackson, 1974; Lerman, 1993; Seltzer, 1991), the pregnancy (D. B. Miller, 1994), and whether to keep and breastfeed or bottle feed the infant were also indicated by fathers (Gavin et al., 2002). In related findings, African American fathers provided equipment such as strollers, cribs, clothes and shoes for the child, and money to the mother (Gavin et al., 2002); kept close tabs on the domestic life and functioning of the mothers of their children; were willing to assume full-time responsibility for caring for their children (Rasheed, 1998); and established a system whereby offspring from different mothers connected with each other through emerging ties with their fathers (Roy, 1999). In one survey, a majority (75%) of African American fathers reported performing very well in the parental role (Taylor & Johnson, 1997).

On the whole, these findings suggest that African American residential and nonresidential fathers from different socioeconomic backgrounds who are in marital and nonmarital relationships show levels and qualities of involvement with children that are quite variable but similar to men in other ethnic groups in the United States (see Hofferth et al., 2002; Pleck, 1997). Much of the work in this area is based on self-reports of how often men visit or have social contacts with their offspring in low-income, unwed families who are in the early stages of the life cycle. There is little cross-validation of what men actually do when they are around their children. Nor are there detailed analyses of patterns of father engagement and disengagement in children's lives over time (Jarrett et al., 2002). Moreover, African American men are often undercounted in household surveys (as many as 20–40% in the 20–39 age group in some estimates; Hernandez & Brandon, 2002), and those in jail, prison, and the military are not well represented in research studies. Nevertheless, a few things emerge about African American fathers: There are multiple contexts for fatherhood in African American families;

men's commitment to and investment in their children appear more stable in economically better-off, two-parent families than in other living arrangements where economic resources are scarce; fathers from different socioeconomic and family living arrangements engaged in a range of social, caregiving, and educational activities with children; and nonresidential fathers are distinctly heterogeneous in terms of their social-intellectual and economic investment in their children.

Looking ahead, examining the personal characteristics of African American men and the sociodemographic, educational, and other factors that abet or impede father involvement might usher in a far better understanding of their commitments to their children. Positive self-image (Christmon, 1990), dedication to and communication within the family (Ahmeduzzaman & Roopnarine, 1992), support networks within and across households (Hamer, 2001; Hossain et al., 1997; Ray & Hans, 2001), geographic proximity to child (McKenry & Price, 1992), relationship with the child's mother (W. D. Allen & Doherty, 1996; Furstenberg, 1995), children from prior unions and new maternal unions (Coley & Chase-Lansdale, 1999), relationship history with own father (W. D. Allen & Doherty, 1996; Hamer, 1997, 2001), parenting skills and knowledge about childhood development (Lamb, 1997), income and education (Ahmeduzzaman & Roopnarine, 1992; Bowman & Forman, 1997; Hamer, 1998; McAdoo, 1993; McLoyd, 1989, 1990; Price-Bonham & Skeen, 1979; W. J. Wilson, 1987), and social and economic policies (Roy, 1999; Sigle-Rushton & Garfinkel, 2002) are all at the root of effective parenting among African American men.

SIGNIFICANCE OF PATERNAL INVOLVEMENT

Family structure alone may prove inadequate in predicting the psychological well-being of children (see Sigle-Rushton & McLanahan, 2002a). The nurturance and love, appropriate family management techniques, stability and sense of personal control over affairs within and external to the family, understanding and respect for the child's pace of development, family cohesion, economic resources, and support from extended family members are all associated with positive outcomes in childhood development (Coll et al., 1996; Lamb, 1997; Sigle-Rushton & McLanahan, 2002a; Silverstein & Auerbach, 1999). Bearing this in mind, let us explore the interrelationships between paternal involvement in African American men and girls' and boys' social and intellectual development jointly. For the most part, the findings fall in line with two major perspectives: family structure and family functioning.

Social-Behavioral Outcomes

Children who indicated a father figure as instrumental in their lives had better perceived competence and social acceptance than did children who did not do so (Dubowitz et al., 2000, 2001). Households that contained a father were more child centered, and there were fewer behavior problems in children (Black et al., 1999); and children whose fathers lived with them displayed higher adaptive functioning (Dunn & Tucker, 1993) and fewer behavioral problems (Teachman, Day, Carver, Call, & Paasch, 1998), had better self-esteem (Alston & Williams, 1982), and were less likely to run away from home and get into trouble with the law (Rodney & Mupier, 1999). Family structure and organization predicted parents' and teachers' ratings of social competence, communication effectiveness, and child behavior problems in kindergarten children (E. P. Smith, Prinz, Dumas, & Laughlin, 2001). There is a lower risk for early sexual intercourse among girls in married than in single-mother households (Moore & Chase-Lansdale, 2001), and African American boys in unmarried households had lower self-control, feelings of personal power, self-competence, and perceptions of body functioning than did their counterparts in married households (Mandara & Murray, 2000). By contrast, a few studies have failed to show child functioning differences due to family structure (Austin, 1992; Ensminger, 1990; Fanworth, 1984; Salem et al., 1998; Zimmerman et al., 1995).

Several statistically significant associations have been obtained between family functioning variables and childhood behaviors. Among a group of mostly unmarried men whose children were enrolled in Head Start, father communication was correlated with children's communication skills and in turn was linked to childhood behavior problems (Fagan & Iglesias, 2000). In similar work relationships were found between time spent with children and positive perceptions of parent-child communication (Strom et al., 2000a, 2000b), and between duration of paternal involvement and parenting effectiveness, and decreased propensity toward child neglect (Dubowitz et al., 2000); paternal sensitivity was positively related to socialization whereas restrictiveness was negatively related to childhood communication, socialization (interpersonal relationships, play and leisure and coping skills), and daily living skills (Kelley et al., 1998); paternal warmth was associated with prosocial behaviors while control and discipline from fathers and father figures led to better school behaviors among 3rd- and 4th-grade children (Coley, 1998); and close relationships and support from fathers were related to self-esteem and lower depressive symptoms in adolescence (Furstenberg & Harris, 1993; Zimmerman et al., 1995), whereas the lack of a close relationship with fathers did result in greater depressive symptoms in African American girls (Coley & Chase-Lansdale, 2002).

Cognitive Outcomes and School Functioning

Family structure differences have been ascertained in the areas of cognitive performance and other school-related variables. A general trend is that African American children who live in father-present homes do better in school and have more supportive home environments than do those from father-absent homes. For example, African American children in two-parent households had better mathematics and reading scores (Teachman et al., 1998), were exposed to more positive attitudes about school and had more resources to pursue educational opportunities (Savage, Adair, & Friedman, 1978), and judged that their homes were more achievement oriented (Mandara & Murray, 2000), whereas those from father-absent homes were significantly more likely to repeat a grade, to have poorer grades than other children in the class, to be suspended from school, and to cut classes than were children from father-present homes (Rodney & Mupier, 1999). In addition, they were less likely to be in school during the late teenage years (McLanahan, 1985). However, some studies did not find associations between family structure and cognitive functioning (e.g., Luster & McAdoo, 1994), and two (DeLeire & Kalil, 2002; Entwisle & Alexander, 1996) point to the possible benefits of other adult figures in multigenerational households in boosting educational outcomes.

As far as interpersonal and intrapersonal functioning is concerned, support from fathers or father figures, nurturance during play, and satisfaction in the parenting role were associated with better cognitive and receptive language scores in children (Black et al., 1999; Dubowitz et al., 2001), and paternal sensitivity was associated with motor skills as measured by the Bayley scales (Kelley et al., 1998). High-achieving African American boys enrolled in the Meyerhoff Project in Baltimore came from homes where fathers strongly encouraged achievement through education, set clear goals for grades, were demanding but supportive, and were more involved in monitoring their children's homework and where expectations and rules were clear, there was open, consistent, and clear communication, and families drew on the resources of the community (e.g., extended family, church) to raise their children (Grief et al., 1998). Furthermore, informal child support was correlated with the level of cognitive stimulation at home (Greene & Moore, 2000).

Although the differences in childhood development and school achievement attributed to family structure appear fairly robust and favor being raised in two-parent, married families, they should be interpreted cautiously. First, few studies on the impact of father involvement on the well-being of African American children have controlled for the mediating or moderating effects of economic resources provided by biological fathers or nonbiological parental figures, parental interpersonal and intrapersonal functioning both before and after the birth of children (e.g., couple relationship, depression, interpersonal conflicts, parenting skills), preexisting differences that may relate to social capital deficits, processes and changes that are associated with familial living arrangements (see Sigle-Rushton & McLanahan, 2002a, for a discussion), psychological presence of the father, and support from other adults in multigenerational families in buffering the impact of not having a biological father around consistently (DeLeire & Kalil, 2002). It may well be that these factors are more reliable predictors of child development outcomes than are marital and residential status per se. Second, the findings are rather mixed and assembled from reports that employ different methodological, measurement, and data analytic approaches, thereby obscuring meaningful comparisons of outcomes. Third, in spite of general assertions that African American boys suffer more than girls from father absence and minimal involvement, there are few well-designed studies that have actually assessed this issue.

AFRICAN CARIBBEAN FATHERS

The multiple ethnic groups in the Caribbean (e.g., African Caribbean, Indo-Caribbean, Amerindians, Black Caribs, people of European ancestry) have variously been affected by slavery, indentured servitude, the imposition of religious ideology by their European conquerors, intermarriages, economic exploitation and discrimination, and internal and external migration during different periods of their history. To avoid making global inferences about their family organization patterns and methods of child rearing, the focus herein is on African Caribbean men from the Anglophone Caribbean islands of Trinidad and Tobago, Jamaica, Grenada, Barbados, Dominica, St. Kitts, St. Lucia, St. Vincent, and Nevis and from the continental countries of Guyana and Belize. Though controversial, the argument has been advanced that, within and between social classes, at the base of these English-speaking societies are shared beliefs and values regarding socialization and child rearing (see Young, 1991). Accepting that this may be so, an overview is presented of men's involvement with children in the different countries of the English-speaking Caribbean. In this regard, attention is paid to socioeconomic and between-country variability in men's level and quality of involvement.

Quite a bit has been written about the matrix of family life in the English-speaking Caribbean (e.g., Barrow, 1998, 2002; Chevannes, 2001; Rodman, 1971; Roopnarine & Brown, 1997; Senior, 1991; R. T. Smith, 1996). It would be a mistake to discuss parent-child relationships among Caribbean families without mentioning the pervasive burden of poverty. Throughout their existence, sizable numbers of Caribbean families have lived at or below poverty (43.2% in Guyana, 21% in Trinidad, 18.7% in Jamaica; World Bank Development Indicators Data Base, World Bank, 2000) and have been at the whims of the constantly fluctuating economic conditions in the region. Consequently, families struggle daily to feed, clothe, and educate their children (mortality rates for children under 5 are 73.2/1,000 for Guyana, 18.9/1,000 for Trinidad, and 23.5/1,000 for Jamaica; World Bank Development Indicators Data Base, World Bank, 2000). A prominent obstacle in the ability to execute parenting roles and employ effective child-rearing strategies (McLoyd, 1989; McLoyd, Jayaratne, Ceballo, & Borquez, 1994), poverty can profoundly alter how parents prioritize child-rearing goals (LeVine, 1974, in press). This being the case, the impact of economic conditions on family organization patterns and father-child relationships is integrated into the discussion that follows.

Social Contexts of Fatherhood

Like African Americans, African Caribbean families have high rates of nonmarital births, nonresidential fatherhood, and female-headed households. For a majority of African Caribbean families, childbearing begins in nonmarital unions—visiting and common-law—where mate shifting is a common cultural practice. Nearly 70% of children in the Caribbean are born in nonlegal unions (Powell, 1986; see also Barrow, 2001, for a discussion of teenage births in Barbados; Bernard, 1998). This phenomenon has been in existence for over 150 years (Roberts & Sinclair, 1978) and may have its origins in slavery but is perpetuated by societal adaptations to poor economic conditions and low educational attainment (Brown, Newland, Anderson, & Chevannes, 1997). With high frequencies of nonmarital unions is the increased probability of mother-headed households and nonresidential fatherhood. In separate assessments of family structures across the Caribbean, female-headed households ranged from 22.4% in Guyana to 45.3% in Grenada (Brown, 2002; Massiah, 1982; Powell, 1986), and 35.5% of families in Antigua, 29.2% in St. Kitts, 45% in St. Lucia, 37.9% in St. Vincent, 49.2% in Barbados, and 58% in Jamaica did not have fathers residing with children (Leo-Rhynie, 1997). Needless to say, these structural arrangements combined with the mating patterns of mothers and fathers add greater complexity to the dynamics of fatherhood and the nature of paternal involvement with children.

Through progressive mating, biological and social fatherhood may occur first in visiting unions, then common-law unions, and eventually in marital relationships. It is suggested that visiting unions make up about 25% of mating relationships in the Caribbean (between 19% and 34% in four different samples of men in Jamaica) and are more prevalent among low-income, younger men (Brown et al., 1997; Senior, 1991). Mating couples reside with their families of origin and meet at a prearranged location to engage in sexual and social relationships. A significant percentage of women in these relationships see themselves as the head of the household. Of the total number of women recruited for the Women in the Caribbean Project (WICP), 39.2% in Barbados, 43% in Antigua, and 33.7% in St. Vincent alleged that they were the head of their households (Powell, 1986), and 57% of women (24.4% of male partners) in St. Vincent, 63.8% (26.2% of male partners) in Barbados, and 64.7% (19.5% of male partners) in Antigua were the main source of income for the family. Decision-making in these relationships is purportedly female dominated, as few women report sharing the head of the household with their partners (under 6%; Powell, 1986). Both men and women rely heavily on kinship and nonkinship members for assistance with child care. The assumption of roles and responsibilities by men in these unions remains sketchy.

Normally, after spending time in visiting unions, men and women may enter common-law relationships. About 20% of mating relationships are considered common-law, although they could be considerably higher in some countries (between 12% and 48% in different samples of men in Jamaica; Ramkissoon, 2002; Roopnarine, 2002; Senior, 1991). In these unions, there is the appearance of greater commitment to the relationship as couples share a common residence and resources. Although men may view themselves as assuming the dominant position in the relationship, their partners may not necessarily agree; in the WICP, 27.1% of the sample women in Barbados, 28.3% in Antigua, and 21.1% in Grenada regarded themselves as the head of their households. Across these three countries, about 64.5% of men (range 59.7–67.8%) in common-law unions were the chief wage earner in the family. This level of financial support exceeds that furnished by men in marital unions, where 57.6% were the primary wage earner (Powell, 1986). There is legal uncertainty surrounding common-law unions even though most countries in the region have some form of legislation that mandates the support of children after paternity is established (Senior, 1991).

Probably reflecting life-stage developmental processes, after engaging in progressive mating (mate shifting) and attaining a measure of economic security, older men may marry. In four different groups of Caribbean men, on average, 9.35% of fathers under 30 years were married, 41.3% were in common-law unions, and 44.9% were in visiting relationships. By contrast, for men over 50 years of age, the marriage rate was 54.3% with only 8.9% still in visiting relationships (Brown et al., 1997) and was higher (62.5%) among men in the middle and upper socioeconomic classes (Ramkissoon, 2002). These trends are supported by data from surveys of the familial experiences of women: in the 45–54 age group, 48.8% of women in Barbados, 52.9% in Antigua, and 48.6% in St. Vincent were married, and only 12%, 14.7%, and 14.7% in each country, respectively, were in visiting relationships. Female headship drops precipitously in married households (13% across the three countries), where slightly over 25% of women were the main source of income for the family. Fewer than 5% of children were raised by fathers only (Dann, 1987; Powell, 1986), a figure noted by Clarke (1957) three decades earlier. By the time a man marries, it is not unusual for him to have borne children from between three and five partners. Data gathered from different samples of men recruited for the Contributions of Caribbean Men to the Family (CCMF) Project (Brown, Anderson, & Chevannes, 1993; Chevannes, 2001) indicated that a little over half of the men (54.4%) had one "baby mother," over a third (37.5%) had between two and three baby mothers, and 8.1% had four or more baby mothers. About 24% of the men recruited for the study had outside children (Brown et al., 1997), and as many as 50% did in a more privileged group (Ramkissoon, 2002).

In summary, African Caribbean men's relationships with and obligation to their children and mating partners or spouses must be viewed within the parameters of multiple unions and the flow of activities throughout the marital career (Rodman, 1971). The presence of men in households does not mean that they are the head of their families, since Caribbean women are the main wage earners and raise families in the absence of men (see Barrow, 1998). Be this as it may, increasing financial standing does not necessarily bring greater power to women, as resource theory suggests. Within the patriarchal strictures of Caribbean society, women must battle with the duality of designating family headship to men while shouldering a lion's share of child rearing and the responsibility of providing economic support for family members.

In the different family configurations just outlined, some men abdicate responsibility to care for their children to previous or concurrent partners; others receive emotional and instrumental support for child rearing from an expansive network of female and sometimes male caregivers (Barrow, 1996, 1998; Brodber, 1975; Russell-Brown, Norville, & Griffith, 1997). As African Caribbean men move on to new relationships, children may be shifted to other households or lose contact with their biological fathers. In several analyses of this practice, it has been calculated that about 24% of children born to young mothers in Barbados, 15% of Jamaicans under age 14, and 50% of children in 1,600 households in three eastern Caribbean countries were shifted to other residences (Dann, 1987; Roberts & Sinclair, 1978; Russell-Brown et al., 1997). Fathers may be involved in the decision making to shift children to other residences, but it is unclear to what extent they provide direct care for these children. By virtue of residential patterns, children must contend with the possibility of forming social relationships with nonbiological fathers or their mother's new romantic partner and with occasional visits from their biological fathers. This scenario can be perplexing to children and place severe demands on men's resources and human capital.

BELIEFS ABOUT MANHOOD AND FATHERHOOD

As discussed previously, men's beliefs about the concepts of manhood and fatherhood may be linked directly to their investment and their accessibility to children. Ethnographic and survey studies indicate that for African Caribbean men, conceptions of manhood and fatherhood are tightly woven together (Brown et al., 1993, 1997; Chevannes, 1999). Beliefs or ethnotheories about manhood and fatherhood are grounded in varied interpretations of the tenets of religious doctrines embodied in Christian, Rastafari, and Orisha practices and cultural scripts about male dominance and sexual prowess. How, then, do African Caribbean men view their roles as men and fathers?

Manhood

For most African Caribbean men there are three essential components to manhood: rampant heterosexual activity, provisioning for the family economically, and being the head of the family (Brown et al., 1997; Chevannes, 1999, 2001). Early and frequent heterosexual activity with several partners either serially or concurrently in several relationships is seen as a strong reflection of manhood and a sign of maturity. The number of offspring that results from the sexual relationships, both within and external to the union or family, is tangible proof of the man's virility. Accomplishing this first and foremost, men must then provide for and fiercely protect family members. There is the suggestion that across Caribbean countries both men and women attribute the provider role to men (Brown et al., 1997; Roopnarine et al., 1995), but traditional beliefs may be changing (Bernard, 1998). Thus, regardless of whether or not it is carried out, baby fathers are expected to provide for their offspring and maintain a family. But manhood also entails being the scriptural authority over women and children. Such authority is seen as ordained by God, inherited from ancestors in Africa and, at least in sentiment, accepted by women even when they are the heads of their households (Brown et al., 1997; Chevannes, 2001). In Orisha and Rastafari religious rituals, women are assigned secondary roles (see Chevannes, 1998).

Fatherhood

As is the case in several other cultures around the world (Suppal, Roopnarine, Buesig, & Bennett, 1996; Sun & Roopnarine, 1994; see Roopnarine & Gielen, in press), a predominant cultural belief of both men and women throughout the Caribbean is that the primary role of fathers is to provide economic support to "mind" or provide economic support for family members. When asked what they thought the role of the father was, 96% of low-income single-earner and 74% of low-income dual-earner Jamaican fathers in common-law unions reported that fathers should be breadwinners and the head of the household (94% and 72%, respectively, for mothers). None of the 88 men interviewed mentioned that fathers should assume the nurturing or primary caregiving role (Roopnarine et al., 1995). Similar opinions were expressed by men in 10 communities in Jamaica, Guyana, and Dominica (Brown et al., 1997), as well as by men in Barbados (Dann, 1986), though not among younger, unmarried people without children in Trinidad and Tobago (Bernard, 1998). Providing for the family economically is so central to the definition of being a father that men who are unable to achieve this goal in the face of limited economic opportunities in the Caribbean are often seen as not being men.

Do African Caribbean men accept and understand other dimensions of fatherhood? Invariably, African Caribbean men report that they find a great deal of satisfaction in biological fatherhood because this bestows on them a sense of self-definition and provides an avenue toward personal maturity. Offspring from early sexual relationships increase men's status in the community (Brown et al., 1997). These deep-seated beliefs may not bode well for understanding the emotional and intellectual responsibilities of fathers toward children, however. In as much as some African Caribbean men seem to be aware of the psychological aspects of fatherhood (e.g., being a good role model, teaching moral values, counseling and guiding children), others have a less firm grasp of their social and intellectual responsibilities toward children (Brown et al., 1997, 2002). Nevertheless, there is the sense that African Caribbean men are coming to grips with the idea that responsible fatherhood extends beyond merely providing economic support for children.

Not unlike so many other aspects of fathering, it is not clear how economic and educational factors intersect with cultural practices to shape internal working models about manhood and fatherhood in African Caribbean men. Difficult economic conditions in the Caribbean do not permit men the luxury to contemplate the human capital aspects of fatherhood as fully as do their counterparts in the more developed areas of the world. The reality is, African Caribbean men must expend considerable energies in garnering economic resources. This, coupled with traditional beliefs about male dominance in household and mating relationships, early sexual activity to prove manhood, and men as protectors of family members, could work to limit African Caribbean men's participation in their children's lives. As a result, defining and working in the direction of achieving optimal fatherhood remains challenging for African Caribbean men (see Brown, 2002).

The Cultural Contexts of Fathering

Child-Rearing Beliefs and Practices

Generally speaking, African Caribbean fathers' knowledge about parenting and normative patterns of childhood development is not well-defined and delineated (Arnold, 1982; Leo-Rhynie, 1997; Roopnarine, Bynoe, Singh, & Simon, in press; Wint & Brown, 1988). From perusing the parenting literature, it can be said that ethnotheories about child care and development and accompanying child-rearing practices among low-income Caribbean families are hierarchically arranged and lean toward harsher forms of discipline that are situated in more autocratic parenting styles (Leo-Rhynie, 1997), where parents have unreasonable developmental expectations of children and are less likely to support their intellectual curiosity (Brown & Wint, 1988; Payne & Furnham, 1992). Families with better economic resources and educational attainment appear more flexible and less restrictive in their approach to parenting than do those with less education and incomes (see Morrison, Ispa, & Milner, 1998; Ramkissoon, 2002; Ricketts, 2000). Findings from a large-scale survey of Barbadian parents from different occupations provide support for this contention: Both mothers and fathers in nonmanual occupations indicated greater physical involvement with children and higher levels of intellectual nurturance, whereas those in manual occupations and those who were unemployed reported being more restrictive (e.g., controlling through guilt and suppression of child's feelings; Payne & Furnham, 1992). Regardless of socioeconomic background, mothers and fathers focus on the disapproval of inappropriate behaviors at the expense of not praising children for their academic efforts and the display of desirable behaviors. The open expression of affection is problematic for African Caribbean parents (Leo-Rhynie, 1997) and is avoided by fathers, particularly toward daughters (Brown et al., 1997).

Emerging out of ignorance about appropriate child-rearing techniques and frustrations encountered in daily life, a more insidious practice that works in tandem with these parental beliefs involves the enforcement of physical punishment to bring children in line with adults' ideas about behavioral conduct. The prevalence and cultural tolerance of physical punishment is adequately documented (Anderson & Payne, 1994; Arnold, 1982; Payne, 1989; Roopnarine & Jung, 2002; Wint & Brown, 1988). Across Caribbean countries, men and women from varied socioeconomic backgrounds believe in firm discipline and subscribe to the Biblical injunction "Spare the rod and spoil the child." In conjunction with obedience, respect for parents and elders is expected (Grant, Leo-Rhynie, & Alexander, 1983), and it is believed that physical punishment dispensed with warmth and attention is quite appropriate in child rearing. Because of the marginal position that fathers may assume in the family and dreading the likelihood of losing respect from children, they are only too willing to administer a beating to demonstrate their authority in the household (Arnold, 1982).

It would be unfair and misleading to leave the general impression that all African Caribbean families are harsh disciplinarians. After all, physical punishment is under great scrutiny and on the decline with countrywide efforts to improve parenting skills (e.g., Jamaica; Brown, 2002; Payne & Furnham, 1992), and recent studies (e.g., Ramkissoon, 2002) have revealed that 58.6% of middle- and upper-class Jamaican families utilized authoritative parenting behaviors in child rearing. Because of the proclivity toward nonmarital unions, children are cared for by numerous adults in multigeneration and extended family units through what Brodber (1975) termed a system of emotional expansiveness. Adults approach child rearing with determination to meet children's social and economic needs. The positive inner- and outward-directed qualities that mothers and fathers muster to achieve child-rearing goals have been articulated in different reports (see Dann, 1987; Morrison et al., 1998; Ramkissoon, 2002; Roopnarine et al., in press). It is not surprising that parents with better economic resources and educational attainment are better able to influence their children's development in a positive manner (Brown et al., 1997; Payne & Furnham, 1992; Ramkissoon, 2002).

AFRICAN CARIBBEAN FATHER INVOLVEMENT

It has been widely demonstrated that Caribbean women assume most of the responsibility for early child care (see Bailey, 1998; Roopnarine & Brown, 1997; Senior, 1991); and, as stated before, they draw on other women and children in the community at large for child-care help and support (Brodber, 1975; Leo-Rhynie, 1997). On the other hand, conjecture still outweighs research information on African Caribbean fathers. From the views voiced in the pulpits of churches, through call-in radio programs, and community-based fatherhood projects (see Barrow, 2001; Brown 2002, for a discussion), there is the general view that English-speaking Caribbean men are not living up to the scripted image of responsible fatherhood. Adding to the public fervor are concerns raised by mental health specialists about the inherent barriers posed by mate shifting and child shifting in thwarting father-child contacts, which then slight children of the opportunity to acquire valuable skills and knowledge and emotional support from their fathers (Sharpe, 1997). As with African American men, when emphasis moves away from equating nonresidential status with noninvolvement with children, a more accurate picture emerges about African Caribbean men as fathers.

Time, Frequency, and Quality of Involvement

Research on the frequency and amount of time African Caribbean fathers spend with children in different social and cognitive activities is rather sparse. Using Clarke's seminal work on Jamaican families as a starting point, early sociological and anthropological accounts revealed that paternal interest in children was greater in married than in nonlegal-union households. It was nevertheless surmised that in total, "paternal devotion and kindness were far outweighed" by irresponsibility where Jamaican men "had only fathered the idea" of children and left them in the care of mothers "who really fathered" them (Clarke, 1957, p. 161) or that Guyanese men were not centrally involved in the socialization of children but remained accessible to them as a father figure (R. T. Smith, 1956). At the time, these sentiments reverberated throughout the academic and literary communities and aided in the pathologizing of Caribbean families for decades to come (Barrow, 1998, 2001). Pitted against nuclear family norms and held against legal marriages, nonresidential father households and common-law unions were deemed deficient, and fathers were readily personified as physically and emotionally absent from children's lives. Apart from a few feeble attempts in the 1960s and 1970s to estimate men's time investment with children in nonmarital unions (roughly 14.5 hours per week; Roberts & Sinclair, 1978) and to suggest that most Jamaican children grow up with their fathers or other adult male figures around (Schlesinger, 1968), it was not until the 1990s that the focus of research drifted away from matrifocality and dysfunctional family structure toward recording men's participation in children's lives.

Inspired by conceptual frameworks and methodological approaches employed by researchers in North America and Europe (see Lamb, 1997; Marsiglio et al., 2000), observational and interview studies provided much-needed insights into men's time investment and the nature of the care they provided to children. Fathers' time investments in feeding, cleaning, and playing with 1-year-old infants were assessed in common-law, low-income, single- and dual-earner Jamaican families living in the Whitfield township area of Kingston, Jamaica (Roopnarine et al., 1995). Although mothers and fathers believed that both parents should care for infants jointly, mothers were more likely to feed, soothe, clean, sing, and display affection toward infants than were fathers. In the two groups combined, fathers spent on average each day .94 hours feeding infants, .52 hours cleaning and bathing infants, and 2.75 hours playing with them in stimulating ways. Fathers' time investments in play versus other activities lend support to Lamb's thesis about the primacy of fathers' availability as play partners to children (Lamb, 1997). Women's employment status did not seem to influence fathers' time investment with children.

By comparison, extremely low levels of involvement were observed among Black Carib fathers in Belize. Fathers were present in the social environment of 3- to 18-month-old infants 11% of the time, engaged in no caregiving activity, and did not hold the infant during that time. They were present in the social environments of 3- to 9-year-olds only 3% of the time. Patterns of investment were not affected by the residential status of the father. A similar profile emerged among Carib men in Dominica who spent little time with their wives and children. The mother and her sister, female siblings or half-siblings, and the maternal grandmother were the chief caregivers (Layang, 1983). The time estimates and physical distance from children are within the range of father availability (3–14%; Munroe & Munroe, 1992; Pleck, 1997; Whiting & Whiting, 1975) and the cooperative care offered by female offspring and adult females in other societies (e.g., Marquesan, Nso, and Efe; see Hewlett, 1992; Martini & Kirkpatrick, 1992).

Turning to frequency of involvement with children, a sociological survey assessed paternal involvement in basic caregiving activities in families in Georgetown, Guyana (L. C. Wilson, 1989; L. C. Wilson & Kposowa, 1994; L. C. Wilson, Williams, & Wilkins, 1992). Roughly 72% of fathers reported changing diapers and bathing the infant, 70% prepared food or fed the baby, and 64% got up at night to attend to the baby "sometimes" to "very often." This level of investment was also seen in how often fathers played with and cuddled the infant (only 2.9% of fathers reported not ever cuddling or playing with the infant; L. C. Wilson, 1989). Separate analysis performed on men who were living with a spouse and had older children showed that 61% played with children, 40% took children for walks or to places of amusement, 62.2% talked to children about things that were important to them, and 42.3% spent time helping children with school work "often" or "very often." Levels of paternal involvement were affected by income and family structure. Fathers in low-income households showed greater involvement with young children than did their peers at higher income levels, whereas the reverse was the case for involvement with older children. Perhaps because of child-care support from others, fathers in extended households were less involved with children than were those in other family arrangements, and men were less involved with children if their spouses were employed. Mastery, as a measure of self-efficacy, had a strong, direct relationship with paternal involvement.

Basically, similar levels of involvement were obtained in two projects conducted at the Caribbean Child Development Centre at the University of the West Indies in Jamaica. Relying on interview and ethnographic methodologies to examine male parenting in primarily low-income, working-class men in four communities in the Kingston, Jamaica, area and in six communities in Jamaica, Guyana, and Dominica, Brown and her colleagues (Brown et al., 1993, 1997) found that a majority of the 700 Caribbean men surveyed in four communities around Kingston (Woodside, Mavis Bank, Seivright Gardens, and Braeton) showed active involvement with children. Thirty-one percent reported tidying children daily (18.9% once or twice weekly); 66.7% played with children daily; 42.5% helped children with homework daily (19.4% once or twice weekly); 60.2% reasoned with children daily; and 44.3% stayed with children daily (24.4% once or twice weekly). Concerning outside offspring, 13.7% fathers played with and 9% reasoned with children daily. Fathers in the other countries indicated heavy investment in domestic labor, but their levels of involvement with children were unclear. Dissatisfaction with the role as father was largely due to the inability to provide for children economically and with having outside children.

In observing paternal care among inhabitants in the northern coast of Trinidad, Flinn (1992) was able to document the quality and distribution of child-care responsibility among diverse kinship and nonkinship members. During the infancy and early childhood periods, mothers engaged in 44.2%, fathers 10.3%, siblings 16.3%, grandparents 17.6%, aunts and uncles 4.5%, and distant kin and nonrelatives 7.2% of the care interactions directed at children. In corresponding kinship and age categories, males appear less central to caregiving than females (e.g., mothers more than fathers; aunts more than uncles, grandmothers more than grandfathers, etc.). Fathers were observed to engage in direct care of infants: holding, feeding, cleaning, playing, teaching, changing diapers, and other caregiving activities. Genetic parent-offspring interactions accounted for 35.6% of observed care overtures, with mothers assuming more responsibility for care during infancy (average for coresident mothers = 31.9%, range 14–67%; average for fathers = 3.3%, range 0–9%) and early childhood (average for coresident mothers = 22.9%, range 8–36%; average for fathers = 4.2%, range 0–17%).

Beyond infancy, mother-daughter interactions are highest in the early childhood years, whereas mother-son interactions show a steady decline into the adolescent years. Fathers interact less with infants and preadolescents than with older children, with father-daughter interactions intensifying during the adolescent years. Overall, fathers interact more with sons than with daughters. Care interactions were more prevalent across caregivers in resident-father households than in nonresident father households, with far fewer interactions occurring between nonbiological fathers and children than between biological fathers and children. The interactions between non-biological fathers and children were more agonistic than those between biological fathers and children. Due to jealousy and issues attached to child support, fathers' interactions with their children were severely curtailed if they or their ex-spouses entered new mating relationships.

By focusing on child-rearing practices in an island-wide sample of males and females in Barbados, Payne and Furnham (1992) provided some of the first indications of men's level of nurturance and restrictiveness with school-age children. Making use of a modified version of the Block Child Rearing Practices Report, these researchers were able to show that positive parent-child contact, encouragement of intellectual curiosity and reflection, approval of emotional expression, and behavioral control through positive expression were part of the child-rearing agenda for men who had at least one school-age child living in the household. Restrictive and punitive approaches to parenting were embraced equally by fathers and mothers but less so for better educated and more financially stable families. In a like manner, patterns of authoritative parenting practices were determined among middle- and upper-class Jamaican fathers with school-aged children (Ramkissoon, 2002).

Admittedly, it is too risky to draw strong conclusions from this relatively small group of studies. However, these findings help to debunk general myths about male marginality in Caribbean families. Relegating *all* Caribbean men to paternal irresponsibility is rather farfetched. Granted, paternal involvement is not uniform across countries or groups. But under poor socioeconomic conditions and in different conjugal arrangements and socioeconomic levels, African Caribbean fathers exhibit different levels of involvement in caregiving, as well as in educational and play activities with young children. However, fathers in the middle and upper classes are more inclined to use an authoritative mode of parenting than are those who are less economically endowed. There is a good chance that during caregiving overtures and social-cognitive activities, fathers provide emotional support for children. It is less clear how much economic support Caribbean children receive from biological and nonbiological fathers in nonmarital households and to what degree mothers convey, directly or indirectly, negative images of men as fathers and providers (see Coley, in press, for a discussion of this issue).

CARIBBEAN IMMIGRANT FATHERS

Despite significant waves of population movements from the Caribbean to the United States, Canada, and Europe over the last three decades of the previous century (see Foner, 2001; Roopnarine et al., in press, for a profile), there is virtually no research on English-speaking African Caribbean immigrant fathers. A bulk of the research on English-speaking Caribbean immigrant families has been on childhood psychopathology (Goupal-McNicol, 1993; Rambally, 1995; Rutter, Yule, Berger, Morton, & Bagley, 1974), psychosocial adjustment and educational experiences of children (Rong & Brown, 2001; Roopnarine et al., in press; White-Davis, 1996), and stresses and strains in couple and parent-child relationships (Arnold, 1997; Millette, 1998). Thus, what is known about African Caribbean immigrant fathers must be inferred from a handful of child-rearing studies.

Because African Caribbean immigrant fathers enter postindustrialized societies with diverse job-related and educational skills, commitments to the family, child-rearing belief systems, and economic resources, patterns of adaptation to and integration into family life are not uniform (see Zhou, 1997). Some (e.g., Alba & Nee, 1997; Vickerman, 2001) add that skin color figures prominently in interacting with neighborhood factors (e.g., access to quality housing, schools, and businesses; ethnic density), ethnic identity, class (education and income), gender, and social networks to influence parenting and child development outcomes. For African Caribbean immigrant fathers, then, ethnicity and class may work in concert with natal cultural practices to determine parental investment in their offspring (Vickerman, 2001; Waters, 1999).

In large measure, the child-rearing beliefs and practices of Caribbean immigrant men and fathers in North America and Europe mirror those evident in the countries of origin. For instance, men and fathers in the northeastern United States held traditional views about husband-wife (Millette, 1998) and child-rearing roles (Roopnarine, 2002), and mothers and fathers in the United States and Great Britain used more punitive and authoritarian control combined with indulgence and protectiveness (Arnold, 1997; Roopnarine, 2002) and showed a propensity toward harsher forms of discipline (Deyoung & Zigler, 1994; Foner, 1997; Roopnarine, 1999). In a mixed-ethnic sample (African Caribbean and Indo-Caribbean residents in the New York City area), fathers spent on average roughly 4 hours per weekday in caregiving and under 8 hours per week in educational activities with preschoolers and kindergartners (Roopnarine, 2002). This level of involvement with children far exceeds those of men in the Caribbean (see Roopnarine et al., 2001).

Finally, there are issues closer to the immigration process itself that may undermine paternal involvement with children. Separation from and reunification with parents during serial migration may mean multiple disruptions to the attachment bonds children establish initially with parents and later, in their absence, with nonparental caregivers (Arnold, 1997). Transitional difficulties may also emerge from intergenerational conflicts stemming from challenges to extreme paternal authority to discipline children, parent-child communication, the assimilation of dominant culture values by children that run counter to those in the Caribbean, and confusion regarding immigrant identity (Roopnarine & Shin, 2003; Waters, 1999).

POTENTIAL MEANING OF PATERNAL INVOLVEMENT OR LACK OF INVOLVEMENT

The dearth of systematic long-term studies on the associations between paternal involvement and childhood development in African Caribbean families makes it difficult to forecast the social and cognitive outcomes of being raised in different family configurations in the Caribbean. As indicated, the mating and family patterns in the Caribbean have raised considerable speculations about the impact of unstable male figures and family structural arrangements on children's psychological development. Researchers who approach father absence (or minimal presence) from an evolutionary biology perspective (e.g., Draper & Harpending, 1982) suggest that in societies such as the Caribbean, where father absence is normative, unstable paternalism may influence competitive behavior and dominance in males and encourage early sexual activity and weaken pair-bond stability in females. The findings on the associations between paternal behaviors among Caribbean men and child development indicators are mixed and thus provide only partial support for this hypothesis. Even so, due to the specious nature of some associations and the lack of control of factors endemic to effective parenting (e.g., education, income, skills and confidence, knowledge of development), most outcomes should be taken as suggestive at best.

Piecing together information from disparate sources, a few things surface regarding paternal absence and behavioral and nutritional outcomes in Caribbean children. Not entirely unique to Caribbean families, children in homes without fathers are at greater risk for poor nutrition (E. Miller, 1991), developmental delays, running away from home, engaging in petty crime, and experiencing physical and sexual abuse (Sharpe, 1997); face more obstacles in negotiating family relationships with permanent and transient members (Bailey, Branche, McGarrity, & Stuart, 1998; Samms-Vaughn, 2000); have a lower level of trust in their fathers; and are exposed to less psychological presence and input from fathers on decisions about their lives (Ramkissoon, 2002). There is the claim that early sexual activity and male dominance among Jamaican youth are linked to weak father-child relationships. Here the evidence is more indirect and inferred from the high percentage of Jamaican males who are sexually active before age 14 (McKenzie, 1992) and from the fact that most births in the Caribbean occur during the teenage years. It is necessary to point out that teenage pregnancy is an accepted practice in the Caribbean and that young mothers receive support for early parenthood (see Garcia Coll & Garcia, 1996). While this might attenuate some of the negative consequences of teenage childbearing, in the absence of material and emotional support from fathers, the life conditions of young mothers and children in the poorer nations of the Caribbean can be extremely difficult.

The proposition that father absence in Caribbean families is harmful to children was further explicated in attempts to look at problem behaviors in young adults and adolescents and examine dimensions of their childhood histories and home life. Suffice it to say, these efforts did not clarify the structural-deficit argument further. What was revealed suggested that young adults who displayed passive dependency had unsatisfactory relationships with their parents and were more likely to have one or both parents absent during childhood than were adults without this clinical condition (A. Allen, 1985; Dann, 1987) and that adolescents with conduct disorder had fewer contacts with their mothers, greater exposure to poor paternal role models, and more unstable living arrangements than did those without conduct disorder. It is interesting that rates of father absence were almost identical for adolescents with and without conduct disorder (53% vs. 49%; Crawford-Brown, 1997). The aforementioned findings certainly create a condition of redress regarding father absence as a predictor of problem behaviors in children.

Directing energy away from assessing family structural variables and childhood development, Flinn (1995; Geary & Flinn, 2001) sought to explore the impact of temporary parental absence and stress in young children as measured by cortisol levels in their saliva. In the Caribbean, parents routinely migrate internally and externally in search of better economic opportunities (Roopnarine & Shin, 2003). During parental absences children are cared for by other relatives. Apparently, even short, predictable absences can cause the cortisol levels in Domincan children to rise. Girls between the ages of 9 and 16 seem particularly susceptible to maternal absences, whereas infant boys were more distressed at paternal absences (Geary & Flinn, 2001; Small, 2000). Showing the same pattern of response every time their parents leave them, children may be telling us that adjusting to parental absences can be extremely difficult, a trend observed among other Caribbean children whose parents leave them behind during migration to North America and Europe (Arnold, 1997; Suarez-Orozco & Todorova, 2001). Because of mate shifting, child shifting, and the intermittent contacts children have with fathers in the Caribbean, these results may provide a window for viewing the stress that children may experience when their biological parents place them in the care of others during prolonged absences.

In one of the first attempts to assess psychological presence and its impact on child well-being in Caribbean families, Ramkissoon (2002) solicited the perceptions of Jamaican children about the importance of their fathers in their lives (e.g., How often do you think about your father? How often do you look forward to seeing your father?) and assessed various components of parents' functioning within the family (e.g., parenting styles, trust between partners, parent-child relationship). Although psychological presence was toward the high end in this predominantly middle-class group of families, children with high scores found their fathers to be more companionable, involved in their lives, and emotionally supportive than did those with moderate scores. Notably, the physical presence of the father had similar positive benefits (i.e., greater trust and involvement in decisions about the child), suggesting that physical and psychological paternal presence in concert underlie childhood well being.

Let us now discuss educational outcomes and father involvement. A few Caribbean scholars (e.g., E. Miller, 1991) have argued that father absence may not be linked to the poor school performance of children. This proposal is backed by a lack of significant differences in the school performance of children who are raised in two-parent and single-parent households. However, boys seem to have more difficulties in school (e.g., higher drop out rates, poorer attendance records) and are outperformed academically by girls throughout the educational system in the Caribbean. Some studies (e.g., Ramkissoon, 2002) do indicate better psychological well-being for boys than girls from primarily married families with good economic resources, but this is not representative of most families in the Caribbean.

Are boys more prone than girls to academic failure due to father absence? Do boys receive less guidance and emotional input from mothers when fathers are absent or minimally present? Answers to these deceptively simple questions are not available at the moment. In the mean time, there are some insights as to why girls may fare better than boys in Caribbean societies where paternal absence is high. Brown et al. (1993, 1997) stated that Caribbean girls are offered more protection and monitored more closely, restricted from moving about the neighborhood, encouraged to engage in domestic and school activities, and are perceived to be easier to raise than boys. Quite the opposite is true for boys. They are given more freedom to roam about and to gain societal and economic skills on the road and in the company of men in the neighborhood (Bailey, 1998; Branche, 1998; Brown et al., 1997). The quality of these social contacts may not serve young boys well because they are void of the necessary protection and guidance that are essential to inoculating children from illicit, noneducational risk-taking activities, early sexual encounters, and symbols of irresponsible fatherhood. Under many circumstances, some of these behaviors are encouraged by the male subculture in order for boys to prove early manhood.

All that can be said at this point is that research on the impact of father involvement on African Caribbean children's intellectual and social functioning is in its neonatal stages. Data on family processes and childhood development are now emerging. Just as with African American families, much is inferred from the structural dynamics of families with little or no consideration for the nature and quality of parent-child contacts, paternal figures or nonbiological father-child relationships, and childhood characteristics. From a thin research base, it appears that the increased risk for educational and social difficulties due to paternal physical and psychological absence is somewhat similar to that outlined for children in the more industrialized countries of the world (see Biller, 1993; Biller & Kimpton, 1997). It is worth repeating that father absence is a normative phenomenon in the English-speaking Caribbean and that women have utilized the assistance of kinship and nonkinship caregivers to raise their children, perhaps insulating them from the negative effects of paternal absence and weak, ineffective male parents. The role of these additional caregivers in mitigating the full impact of father absence or minimal presence requires additional consideration, as is greater emphasis on psychological presence.

CONCLUSION

African American and African Caribbean fathers share common characteristics and processes in their approaches to fathering in certain areas but diverge in others. African American and African Caribbean men become fathers in diverse familial arrangements, through different marital-relationship processes (e.g., visiting, cohabiting) in which biological and nonbiological fathers and father figures may join other familial and nonfamilial agents in providing care for and socializing children in multigenerational units. In both cultural milieus, a large number of children are born in low-income, nonmarital unions, and men have children from multiple partners (baby mothers). Some of these relationships become more stable over time with marriage and cohabitation (coresidence with child and mother) and better economic resources. Perhaps not different from men in other developing and postindustrialized societies (see Lamb, 1987, 1997), the frequency and quality of paternal involvement in African American and African Caribbean men vary tremendously, with social contacts and sensitive, caring involvement occurring between fathers and children in diverse familial arrangements and under diverse socioeconomic circumstances. However, there is modest support for the claim that levels of involvement appear more consistent and the cognitive and social outcomes more positive when children live with two biological parents rather than in other living arrangements (see Sigle-Rushton & McLanahan, 2002a). Given that few studies have controlled for inequities in human capital and economic resources and the array of intra- and interpersonal factors that may affect the level and quality of paternal involvement across living arrangements in African American and African Caribbean families and inconsistency in results (see Salem et al., 1998), such broad statements need further verification.

Apart from these similarities are male parenting practices and beliefs that differentiate African American from African Caribbean fathers. Beliefs about fatherhood are more strongly immersed in traditional conceptions of manhood and male identity in African Caribbean than in African American men. Increasingly, African American men are reporting more flexible role conceptions that place caregiving and responsibility for children above sex-typed views of masculinity (e.g., provider, head of household; Hunter & Davis, 1992). Parenting practices also appear less rigid among African American than among African Caribbean men. Though influenced by education and income, most Caribbean men believe in and dispense harsh discipline toward children and expect total obedience from them. The prevalence of authoritarian parenting styles in African American families has been challenged (Bluestone & Tamis-LeMonda, 1999).

The diversity of family patterns within which African American and African Caribbean men become fathers and establish or fail to establish relationships with their children begs for newer conceptual frameworks that are more culturally based and more refined analysis of the multitude of factors that may influence the level and quality of paternal involvement. It is high time we accept that child rearing in nonmarital relationships is normative in African Caribbean families and, with declining marriage rates, is becoming so among African Americans. Instead of zeroing in on the deficiencies of African American and African Caribbean fathers and the litany of reasons for their failures during the early stages of their life cycle, it might be more informative to highlight the areas in which representative samples of men from different socioeconomic backgrounds and familial arrangements (married, cohabiting, single-parent, father figures, etc.) mature and succeed as parents in raising socially and intellectually competent children and what factors are responsible for such triumphs. Additionally, more controlled studies that take into account cultural beliefs and practices, processes and changes in paternal involvement (e.g., parenting practices, economic resources) at different stages of the life cycle with different age children, quality of the partner-spousal relationship, extrafamilial support and provisioning of resources, social and cognitive deficits in familial arrangements that are linked to education and income, and psychological presence would further assist us in teasing out the indirect and direct influences of African American and African Caribbean fathers on childhood development and well-being.

REFERENCES

Ahmeduzzaman, M., & Roopnarine, J. L. (1992). Sociodemographic factors, functioning style, social support, and fathers' involvement with preschoolers in African-American families. *Journal of Marriage and the Family, 54,* 699–707.

Alba, R. D., & Nee, V. (1997). Rethinking assimilation theory for a new era of immigration. *International Migration Review, 31,* 826–874.

Allen, A. (1985). Psychological dependency among students in a "cross-roads" culture. *West Indian Medical Journal, 34,* 123–127.

Allen, W. D., & Doherty, W. J. (1996). The responsibilities of fatherhood as perceived by African American teenage fathers. *Families in Society: The Journal of Contemporary Human Services, 77,* 142–155.

Alston, D., & Williams, N. (1982). Relationship between father absence and self-concept of Black adolescent boys. *Journal of Negro Education, 51,* 134–138.

Anderson, S., & Payne, M. A. (1994). Corporal punishment in elementary education: Views of Barbadian school children. *Child Abuse and Neglect, 18,* 377–386.

Arnold, E. (1982). The use of corporal punishment in childrearing in the West Indies. *Child Abuse and Neglect, 6,* 141–145.

Arnold, E. (1997). Issues in re-unification of migrant West Indian children in the United Kingdom. In J. L. Roopnarine & J. Brown (Eds.), *Caribbean families: Diversity among ethnic groups* (pp. 243–258). Norwood, NJ: Ablex.

Aschenbrenner, J. (1975). *Lifelines: Black families in Chicago.* New York: Holt Rinehart & Winston.

Austin, R. L. (1992). Race, female headship, and delinquency: A longitudinal analysis. *Justice Quarterly, 9,* 585–607.

Bailey, W. (Ed.). (1998). *Gender and the family in the Caribbean.* Mona, Jamaica: ISER, University of the West Indies.

Bailey, W., Branche, C., McGarrity, G., & Stuart, S. (1998). *Family and the quality of gender relations in the Caribbean.* Mona, Jamaica: ISER, University of the West Indies.

Barrow, C. (1996). *Family in the Caribbean: Themes and perspectives.* Kingston, Jamaica: Ian Randle.

Barrow, C. (Ed.). (1998). *Portraits of a nearer Caribbean: Essays on gender ideologies and identities.* Kingston, Jamaica: Ian Randle.

Barrow, C. (2001). Contesting the rhetoric of "Black Family Breakdown" from Barbados. *Journal of Comparative Family Studies, 32,* 419–441.

Barrow, C. (Ed.). (2002). *Children's rights: Caribbean realities*. Kingston, Jamaica: Ian Randle.

Bartz, K. W., & Levine, B. S. (1978). Child rearing by Black parents: A description and comparison to Anglo and Chicano parents. *Journal of Marriage and the Family, 40,* 709–720.

Becker, G. S. (1991). *A treatise on the family* (Rev. ed.). Cambridge, MA: Harvard University Press.

Bernard, G. S. (1998). Aspects of family life, gender relations and ethnic background: An empirical evaluation of multi-ethnicity and youth in Trinidad and Tobago. In W. Bailey (Ed.), *Gender and the family in the Caribbean* (pp. 147–184). Mona, Jamaica: ISER, University of the West Indies.

Berrick, J. D. (1995). *Faces of poverty: Portraits of women and children on welfare*. New York: Oxford University Press.

Biller, H., & Kimpton, J. (1997). The father and the school-aged child. In M. E. Lamb (Ed.), *The role of the father in child development* (3rd ed., pp. 143–161). New York: Wiley.

Billingsley, A. (1968). *Black families in White America*. Englewood Cliffs, NJ: Prentice Hall.

Billingsley, A. (1992). *Climbing Jacob's ladder: The enduring legacy of African American families*. New York: Simon & Schuster.

Black, M., Dubowitz, H., & Starr, R. H. (1999). African American fathers in low income, urban families: Development, behavior, and home environment of their three-year-old children. *Child Development, 70,* 967–978.

Blassingame, J. W. (1979). *The slave community: Plantation life in the ante-bellum South*. New York: Oxford University Press.

Bluestone, C., & Tamis-LeMonda, C. S. (1999). Correlates of parenting styles in predominantly working- and middle-class African American mothers. *Journal of Marriage and the Family, 61,* 881–893.

Bowman, P. J. (1990). Coping with provider role strain: Adaptive cultural resources among Black husbands-fathers. *Journal of Black Psychology, 16,* 1–21.

Bowman, P. J., & Forman, T. A. (1997). Instrumental and expressive family roles among African American fathers. In R. J. Taylor, J. Jackson, & L. M. Chatters (Eds.), *Family life in Black America* (pp. 216–247). Thousand Oaks, CA: Sage.

Bowman, P. J., & Sanders, R. (1998). Unmarried African American fathers: A comparative life span analysis. *Journal of Comparative Family Studies, 29,* 39–56.

Boykin, A. W., & Toms, F. D. (1985). Black child socialization: A conceptual framework. In H. McAdoo & J. McAdoo (Eds.), *Black children* (pp. 33–51). Beverly Hills, CA: Sage.

Branche, C. (1998). Boys in conflict. In W. Bailey (Ed.), *Gender and the family in the Caribbean* (pp. 185–201). Mona, Jamaica: ISER, University of the West Indies.

Bright, J. A., & Williams, C. (1996). Childrearing and education in urban environments: Black fathers' perspectives. *Urban Education, 31,* 245–260.

Brodber, E. (1975). *A study of yards in the city of Kingston*. Mona, Jamaica: Institute for Social and Economic Research, UWI.

Brown, J. (2002). *Fatherwork in the Caribbean*. Unpublished manuscript, Caribbean Child Development Centre, University of the West Indies, Mona, Jamaica.

Brown, J., Anderson, P., & Chevannes, B. (1993). *The contribution of Caribbean men to the family*. Report for the International Development Centre, Canada, Caribbean Child Development Centre, Mona, Jamaica: University of the West Indies.

Brown, J., Newland, A., Anderson, P., & Chevannes, B. (1997). In J. L. Roopnarine & J. Brown (Eds.), *Caribbean families: Diversity among ethnic groups* (pp. 85–113). Norwood, NJ: Ablex.

Brown, S. (1983). The commitment and concerns of Black adolescent parents. *Social Work Research and Abstracts, 19,* 27–34.

Bryan, D. L., & Ajo, A. A. (1992). The role perceptions of African American fathers. *Social Work Research and Abstracts, 28,* 19–21.

Carlson, M., & McLanahan, S. S. (2002). Fragile families, father involvement, and public policy. In C. S. Tamis-LeMonda & N. Cabrera (Eds.), *Handbook on father involvement: Multidisciplinary perspectives* (pp. 211–248). Mahwah, NJ: Erlbaum.

Cazenave, N. A. (1979). Middle-income Black fathers: An analysis of the provider role. *Family Coordinator, 28,* 583–593.

Cazenave, N. A. (1984). Race, socioeconomic status, and age: The social context of American masculinity. *Sex Roles, 11,* 639–656.

Chao, R. (1994). Beyond parental control: Authoritarian parenting style. Understanding Chinese parenting through the cultural notion of training. *Child Development, 45,* 1111–1119.

Chase-Lansdale, P. L., Gordon, R. A., Coley, R. L., Wakschlag, L. S., & Brooks-Gunn, J. (1999). Young African American multigenerational families in poverty: The contexts, exchanges, and processes of their lives. In E. M. Hetherington (Ed.), *Coping with divorce, single parenting, and remarriage: A risk and resiliency perspective* (pp. 165–191). Mahwah, NJ: Erlbaum.

Chevannes, B. (1985). *Jamaican men: Sexual attitudes and beliefs.* Unpublished report, National Planning Board, Kingston, Jamaica.

Chevannes, B. (1998). Introducing the native religions of the region of Jamaica. In B. Chevannes (Ed.), *Rastafari and other African-Caribbean worldviews* (pp. 20–42). New Brunswick, NJ: Rutgers University Press.

Chevannes, B. (1993). *Stresses and strains: Situation analysis of the Caribbean family.* Regional meeting preparatory to International Year of the Family, United Nations Economic Commission for Latin America and the Caribbean, Cartagena, Colombia.

Chevannes, B. (1999). *What we sow and what we reap: Problems in the cultivation of male identity in Jamaica.* Jamaica, Grace Kennedy Foundation Lecture Series.

Chevannes, B. (2001). *Learning to be a man.* Kingston, Jamaica: University of the West Indies Press.

Christmon, K. (1990). The unwed father's perceptions of his family and of himself as a father. *Child and Adolescent Social Work Journal, 7,* 275–283.

Clarke, E. (1957). *My mother who fathered me: A study of family in three selected communities in Jamaica.* London: George Allen & Unwin.

Cochran, D. L. (1997). African American fathers: A decade review of the literature. *Families in Society: The Journal of Contemporary Human Services, 78,* 340–351.

Coley, R. (1998). Children's socialization experiences and functioning in single-mother households: The importance of fathers and other men. *Child Development, 69,* 219–230.

Coley, R. (2001). (In)visible men: Emerging research on low-income, unmarried, and minority fathers. *American Psychologist, 56,* 1–11.

Coley, R. (in press). What mothers teach, what daughters learn: Gender mistrust and self-sufficiency among low-income women. In A. C. Grouter & A. Booth (Eds.), *Just living together: Implications of cohabitation on families, children, and social policy.* Mahwah, NJ: Erlbaum.

Coley, R., & Chase-Lansdale, L. P. (1999). Stability and change in paternal involvement among urban African-American fathers. *Journal of Family Psychology, 13,* 1–20.

Coley, R., & Chase-Lansdale, L. P. (2002). *The sting of disappointment: Father-daughter relationships in low-income African American families.* Manuscript submitted for publication.

Coll, C. G., Lamberty, G., Jenkins, R., McAdoo, H. P., Crnic, K., Wasik, B. H., et al. (1996). An integrative model for the study of developmental competencies in minority children. *Child Development, 67,* 1891–1914.

Coltrane, S. (1995). The future of fatherhood: Social, demographic, and economic influences on men's family involvements. In W. Marsiglio (Ed.), *Fatherhood: Contemporary theory, research, and social policy* (pp. 255–274). Thousand Oaks, CA: Sage.

Cooksey, E. C., & Fondell, M. M. (1996). Spending time with the kids: Effects of family structure on fathers' and children's lives. *Journal of Marriage and the Family, 58,* 693–707.

Crawford-Brown, C. (1997). The impact of parent-child socialization on the development of conduct disorder in Jamaican male adolescents. In J. L. Roopnarine & J. Brown (Eds.), *Caribbean families: Diversity among ethnic groups* (pp. 205–222). Norwood, NJ: Ablex.

Dallas, C. M., & Chen, S. C. (1998). Experiences of African American adolescent fathers. *Western Journal of Nursing Research, 20,* 210–222.

Dann, G. (1986). *Getting outta hand: Men's view of women in Barbados.* Paper presented to the ISER/UNESCO seminar on "Changing family patterns and women's role in the Caribbean," University of the West Indies, Cave Hill, Barbados.

Dann, G. (1987). *The Barbadian male: Sexual beliefs and attitudes.* London: Macmillan.

Danziger, S., & Radin, N. (1990). Absent does not equal uninvolved: Predictors of fathering in teen mother families. *Journal of Marriage and the Family, 52,* 636–642.

Deater-Deckard, K., & Dodge, K. A. (1997). Externalizing behavior problems and discipline revisited: Nonlinear effects and variation by culture, context, and gender. *Psychological Inquiry, 8,* 230–235.

Deater-Deckard, K., Dodge, K. A., Bates, J. E., & Pettit, G. S. (1996). Physical discipline among African American and European American mothers: Links to children's externalizing behaviors. *Developmental Psychology, 32,* 1065–1072.

DeLeire, T., & Kalil, A. (2002). Good things come in threes: Single-parent multigenerational family structure and adolescent adjustment. *Demography, 39,* 393–413.

Deyoung, Y., & Zigler, E. (1994). Machismo in two cultures: Relation to punitive childrearing practices. *American Journal of Orthopsychiatry, 64,* 386–395.

Draper, P., & Harpending, H. (1982). Father absence and reproductive strategy: An evolutionary perspective. *Journal of Anthropological Research, 38,* 255–273.

Dubowitz, H., Black, M., Cox, C. E., Kerr, M. A., Litrownik, A. J., Radhakrishna, A., et al. (2001). Father involvement and children's functioning at age 6 years: A multisite study. *Child Maltreatment, 6,* 300–309.

Dubowitz, H., Black, M. M., Kerr, M. A., Starr, R. H., & Harrington, D. (2000). Fathers and child neglect. *Archives of Pediatric Adolescent Medicine, 154,* 135–141.

Dunn, C., & Tucker, C. (1993). Black children's adaptive functioning and maladaptive behavior associated with quality of family support. *Journal of Multicultural Counseling and Development, 21,* 79–87.

Durrett, M. E., Shirley, O., & Pennabaker, J. W. (1975). Childrearing reports of White, Black, and Mexican-American families. *Developmental Psychology, 11,* 871.

Ellison, C. G. (1997). Religious involvement and the subjective quality of family life among African Americans. In R. J. Taylor, J. Jackson, & L. M. Chatters (Eds.), *Family life in Black America* (pp. 117–131). Thousand Oaks, CA: Sage.

Ensminger, M. E. (1990). Sexual activity and problem behaviors among Black urban adolescents. *Child Development, 61,* 2032–2046.

Entwisle, D. R., & Alexander, K. L. (1996). Family type and children's growth in reading and math over the primary grades. *Journal of Marriage and the Family, 58,* 341–355.

Fagan, J. (1998). Correlates of low-income African American and Puerto Rican fathers' involvement with their children. *Journal of Black Psychology, 24,* 351–367.

Fagan, J. (2000). African-American and Puerto Rican American parenting styles, paternal involvement, and Head Start children's social competence. *Merrill-Palmer Quarterly, 46,* 592–612.

Fagan, J., & Iglesias, A. (1999). Father involvement program effects on fathers, father figures, and their Head Start children: A quasi-experimental study. *Early Childhood Research Quarterly, 14,* 243–269.

Fagan, J., & Iglesias, A. (2000). The relationship between fathers' and children's communication skills and children's behavior problems: A study of Head Start children. *Early Education and Development, 11,* 307–320.

Fagan, J., Newash, N., & Schloesser, A. (2000). Female caregivers' perceptions of fathers' and significant adult males' involvement with their Head Start children. *Families in Society: Journal of Contemporary Human Services, 81,* 186–196.

Fanworth, M. (1984). Family structure, family attributes, and delinquency in a sample of low-income, minority males and females. *Journal of Youth and Adolescence, 13,* 349–364.

Flinn, M. (1992). Paternal care in a Caribbean village. In B. Hewlett (Ed.), *Father-child relations: Cultural and biosocial contexts* (pp. 57–84). New York: de Gruyter.

Flinn, M. (1995). Childhood stress and family environment. *Current Anthropology, 36,* 854–866.

Foner, N. (1997). The immigrant family: Cultural legacies and cultural changes. *International Migration Review, 31,* 961–974.

Foner, N. (Ed.). (2001). *Islands in the city: West Indian migration to New York.* Berkeley: University of California Press.

Franklin, C. W. (1984). *The changing definition of masculinity.* New York: Plenum.

Frazier, E. F. (1939). *The Negro family in the United States.* Chicago: University of Chicago Press.

Furstenberg, F. F., Jr. (1992). Daddies and fathers: Men who do for their children and men who don't. In F. F. Furstenberg Jr., K. E. Sherwood, & M. L. Sullivan (Eds.), *Caring and paying: What mothers and fathers say about child support* (pp. 34–56). New York: Manpower Demonstration Research Corporation.

Furstenberg, F. F., Jr. (1995). Fathering in the inner city: Paternal participation and public policy. In W. Marsiglio (Ed.), *Fatherhood: Contemporary theory, research, and social policy* (pp. 119–147). Thousand Oaks, CA: Sage.

Furstenberg, F. F., Jr., & Harris, K. (1993). When and why fathers matter: Impacts of father involvement on the children of adolescent mothers. In R. Lerman & T. Ooms (Eds.), *Young unwed fathers: Changing roles and emerging policies* (pp. 117–138). Philadelphia: Temple University Press.

Gadsden, V. L., & Smith, R. R. (1994). African American males and fatherhood: Issues in research and practice. *Journal of Negro Education, 63,* 634–648.

Garcia Coll, C. T., & Garcia, H. A. (1996). Definition of competence in adolesence: Lessons from Puerto Rican adolescent mothers. In D. Cicchetti & S. L. Toth (Eds.), *Adolescence: Opportunities and challenges. Rochester Symposium on developmental psychopathology* (Vol. 7, pp. 283–308). Rochester, NY: University of Rochester Press.

Gavin, L. E., Black, M. M., Minor, S., Abel, Y., Papas, M. A., & Bently, M. E. (2003). Young, disadvantaged fathers' involvement with their infants: An ecological perspective. *Journal of Adolescent Health, 31,* 266–276.

Geary, D. C., & Flinn, M. V. (2001). Sex differences and behavioral and hormonal responses to social threat. *Psychological Review, 109,* 745–750.

Gonzales, N. A., Cauce, A. M., & Mason, C. A. (1996). Interobserver agreement in the assessment of parental behavior and parent-adolescent conflict: African American mothers, daughters, and independent observers. *Child Development, 67,* 1483–1498.

Goupal-McNicol, S. (1993). *Working with West Indian families*. New York: Guilford Press.

Grant, D. B. R., Leo-Rhynie, E., & Alexander, G. (1983). *Life style study: Children of the lesser world in the English speaking Caribbean: Vol. 5. Household structures and settings*. Kingston, Jamaica: Bernard Van Leer Foundation–Centre for Early Childhood Education.

Greene, A. D., & Moore, K. A. (2000). Nonresident father involvement and child well-being among young children in families on welfare. *Marriage and Family Review, 29,* 159–180.

Grief, G. L., Hrabowski, F. A., & Maton, K. I. (1998). African American fathers of high-achieving sons: Using outstanding members of an at risk population to guide intervention. *Families in Society: Journal of Contemporary Human Services, 79,* 45–52.

Guttman, H. (1976). *The Black family in slavery and in freedom: 1750–1925*. New York: Random House.

Hamer, J. F. (1997). The fathers of "fatherless" Black children. *Families in Society: Journal of Contemporary Human Services, 78,* 564–578.

Hamer, J. F. (1998). What African American noncustodial fathers say inhibits and enhances their involvement with children. *Western Journal of Black Studies, 22,* 117–127.

Hamer, J. F. (2001). *What it means to be a daddy: Fatherhood for Black men living away from their children*. New York: Columbia University Press.

Hamer, J. F., & Marchioro, K. (2002). Becoming custodial dads: Exploring parenting among low-income and working-class African American fathers. *Journal of Marriage and the Family, 64,* 116–129.

Hans, S., Ray, I., & Bernstein, V. (1997). *Caregiving in the inner city*. Final report to the Carnegie Corporation of New York and The Charles Stewart Mott Foundation. Units for Development in Child Psychiatry and Development, University of Chicago, and the Erikson Institute.

Harkness, S., & Super, S. (Eds.). (1996). *Parental cultural belief systems: Their origins, expressions, and consequences*. New York: Guilford Press.

Hatchett, S. J., & Jackson, J. S. (1999). African American extended kin systems: An empirical assessment in the National Survey of Black Americans. In H. P. McAdoo (Ed.), *Family ethnicity: Strengths in diversity* (pp. 171–190). Thousand Oaks, CA: Sage.

Hendricks, L. E. (1981). Black unwed adolescent fathers. In L. E. Lawrence (Ed.), *Black men* (pp. 131–138). Beverly Hills, CA: Sage.

Hernandez, D. J., & Brandon, P. D. (2002). Who are the fathers of today? In C. S. Tamis-LeMonda & N. Cabrera (Eds.), *Handbook on father involvement: Multidisciplinary perspectives* (pp. 33–62). Mahwah, NJ: Erlbaum.

Hewlett, B. S. (1992). Husband-wife reciprocity and the father-infant relationship among Aka Pygmies. In B. S. Hewlett (Ed.), *Father-child relations: Cultural and biosocial contexts* (pp. 153–176). New York: Aldine de Gruyter.

Hofferth, S. L., Stueve, J. L., Pleck, J., Bianchi, S., & Sayer, L. (2002). The demography of fathers: What fathers do. In C. S. Tamis-LeMonda & N. Cabrera (Eds.), *Handbook on father involvement: Multidisciplinary perspectives* (pp. 63–90). Mahwah, NJ: Erlbaum.

Hossain, Z., Field, T. M., Pickens, J., Malphurs, J., & Del Valle, C. (1997). Fathers' caregiving in low-income African-American and Hispanic-American families. *Early Development and Parenting, 6,* 73–82.

Hossain, Z., & Roopnarine, J. L. (1994). African-American fathers' involvement with infants: Relationship to their functioning style, support, education, and income. *Infant Behavior and Development, 17,* 175–184.

Hunter, A. G. (1997a). Counting on grandmothers: Black mothers' and fathers' reliance on grandmothers for parenting support. *Journal of Family Issues, 18,* 251–269.

Hunter, A. G. (1997b). Living arrangements of African American adults: Variations by age, gender, and family status. In R. J. Taylor, J. Jackson, & L. M. Chatters (Eds.), *Family life in Black America* (pp. 262–276). Thousand Oaks, CA: Sage.

Hunter, A. G., & Davis, E. D. (1992). Constructing gender: An exploration of Afro-American men's conceptualization of manhood. *Gender and Society, 6, 464–479.*

Hunter, A. G., Pearson, J. L., Ialongo, N. S., & Kellam, S. G. (1998). Parenting alone to multiple caregivers: Child care and parenting arrangements in Black and White urban families. *Family Relations, 47, 343–353.*

Hyde, B. L., & Texidor, M. S. (1988). A description of the fathering experience among Black fathers. *Journal of Black Nurses Association, 2, 67–78.*

Jackson, J. J. (1974). Ordinary Black husbands: The truly hidden men. *Journal of Social and Behavioral Science, 20, 19–27.*

Jarrett, R. L., Roy, K., & Burton, L. M. (2002). Fathers in the "hood": Insights from qualitative research on low-income African American men. In C. S. Tamis-LeMonda & N. Cabrera (Eds.), *Handbook on father involvement: Multidisciplinary perspectives* (pp. 211–248). Mahwah, NJ: Erlbaum.

Jayakody, R., Chatters, L. M., & Taylor, R. J. (1993). Family support to single and married African American mothers: The provision of financial, emotional, and child care assistance. *Journal of Marriage and the Family, 55, 261–276.*

Kelly, M. L. (1997). The division of family work among low-income African Americans. *Journal of African-American Men, 3, 87–102.*

Kelly, M. L., & Colburn, C. B. (1995). Economically disadvantaged African American fathers: Social policy and fathering. *Journal of African-American Men, 1, 63–74.*

Kelly, M. L., Power, T. G., & Wimbush, D. D. (1992). Determinants of disciplinary practices in low-income Black mothers. *Child Development, 63, 573–582.*

Kelly, M., Sanchez-Hucles, J., & Walker, R. R. (1993). Correlates of disciplinary practices in working- to middle-class mothers. *Merrill-Palmer Quarterly, 39, 252–264.*

Kelly, M. L., Smith, T. S., Green, A. P., Berndt, A. E., & Rogers, M. C. (1998). Importance of fathers' parenting to African-American toddlers' social and cognitive development. *Infant Behavior and Development, 21, 733–744.*

Kiernan, K. (2002). *Unmarried cohabitation and parenthood: Here to stay? European perspectives.* Paper presented at the Conference on Public Policy and the Future of the Family, Maxwell School, Syracuse University, October 25.

Lamb, M. E. (Ed.). (1987). *The father's role: Cross-cultural perspectives.* Hillsdale, NJ: Erlbaum.

Lamb, M. E. (Ed.). (1997). *The role of the father in child development* (3rd ed.). New York: Wiley.

Lamb, M. E. (2002). Nonresidential fathers and their children. In C. S. Tamis-LeMonda & N. Cabrera (Eds.), *Handbook on father involvement: Multidisciplinary perspectives* (pp. 169–184). Mahwah, NJ: Erlbaum.

Lamb, M. E., Pleck, J. H., Charnov, E. L., & Levine, J. A. (1987). A biosocial perspective on paternal behavior and involvement. In J. B. Lancaster, J. Altman, A. Rossi, & L. R. Sherrod (Eds.), *Parenting across the lifespan: Biosocial perspectives* (pp. 111–142). New York: Academic.

LaRossa, R., & Reitzes, D. C. (1993). Symbolic interactionism and family studies. In P. G. Boss, W. J. Doherty, R. LaRossa, W. R. Shumm, & S. K. Steinmetz (Eds.), *Sourcebook of family theories and methods: A contextual approach* (pp. 135–166). New York: Plenum Press.

Layang, A. (1983). *The Carib reserve: Identity and security in the West Indies.* Washington, DC: University Press of America.

Leo-Rhynie, E. (1997). Class, race, and gender issues in child rearing in the Caribbean. In J. L. Roopnarine & J. Brown (Eds.), *Caribbean families: Diversity among ethnic groups* (pp. 25–55). Norwood, NJ: Ablex.

Lerman, R. (1993). A national profile of young unwed fathers. In R. Lerman & T. Ooms (Eds.), *Young unwed fathers: Changing roles and emerging policies* (pp. 27–51). Philadelphia: Temple University Press.

Lerman, R., & Sorenson, E. (2000). Father involvement with their nonmarital children: Patterns, determinants, and effects on their earnings. *Marriage and Family Review, 29,* 137–158.

LeVine, R. (1974). Parental goals: A cross-cultural view. *Teachers College Record, 76,* 226–239.

LeVine, R. (in press). Challenging expert knowledge: Findings from an African study of infant care and development. In U. Gielen & J. L. Roopnarine (Eds.), *Childhood and adolescence in cross-cultural perspective.* Westport, CT: Praeger.

Liebow, E. (1967). *Tally's corner: A study of Negro streetcorner men.* Boston: Little, Brown and Company.

Lue, M. S., Smalley, S. Y., Smith, B., & Seaton, G. (1998). African American fathers with their preschool children. *Educational Forum, 62,* 300–305.

Luster, T., & McAdoo, H. P. (1994). Factors related to the achievement and adjustment of young African American children. *Child Development, 65,* 1080–1094.

Madhubuti, H. (1990). *Black men: Obsolete, single, dangerous?* Chicago: Third World Press.

Mandara, J., & Murray, C. B. (2000). Effects of parental marital status, income, and family functioning on African American adolescent self-esteem. *Journal of Family Psychology, 14,* 475–490.

Marsiglio, W., Amato, P., Day, R. D., & Lamb, M. (2000). Scholarships on fatherhood in the 1990s and beyond. *Journal of Marriage and the Family, 62,* 1173–1191.

Massiah, J. (1982). *Women who head households.* WICP, Institute of Social and Economic Research, UWI, Barbados.

McAdoo, H. P. (Ed.). (1997). *Black families.* Thousand Oaks, CA: Sage.

McAdoo, J. L. (1979). A study of father-child interaction patterns and self-esteem in Black preschool children. *Young Children, 34,* 46–53.

McAdoo, J. L. (1981). Black fathers and child interaction. In L. Gray (Ed.), *Black men* (pp. 115–130). Newbury Park, CA: Sage.

McAdoo, J. L. (1993). The roles of African-American fathers: An ecological perspective. *Families in Society: Journal of Contemporary Human Services, 74,* 28–35.

McKenry, P. C., & Price, S. J. (1992). Predictors of single, noncustodial fathers' physical involvement with children. *Journal of Genetic Psychology, 153,* 305–320.

McKenzie, H. (1992). Paper presented at the Commonwealth Medical Association International Symposium, October 31–November 3. Reported in the *Daily Gleaner,* October 9.

McLanahan, S. S. (1985). Family structure and the reproduction of poverty. *American Journal of Sociology, 90,* 873–901.

McLanahan, S., & Sandefur, G. (1994). *Growing up with a single parent: What hurts, what helps.* Cambridge, MA: Harvard University Press.

McLoyd, V. (1989). Socialization and development in a changing economy: The effects of paternal job and income loss on children. *American Psychologist, 44,* 293–302.

McLoyd, V. (1990). The declining fortunes of Black children: Psychological distress, parenting and socioemotional development in the context of economic hardship. *Child Development, 61,* 311–346.

McLoyd, V., Cauce, A. M., Takeuchi, D., & Wison, L. (2000). Marital processes and parental socialization in families of color: A decade review of research. *Journal of Marriage and the Family, 62,* 1070–1093.

McLoyd, V., Jayaratne, T. E., Ceballo, R., & Borquez, J. (1994). Unemployment and work interruption among African American single mothers: Effects on parenting and adolescent socioemotional functioning. *Child Development, 65,* 562–589.

Miller, D. B. (1994). Influences on paternal involvement of African American adolescent fathers. *Child and Adolescent Social Work Journal, 11*, 363–378.

Miller, E. (1991). *Men at risk.* Kingston: Jamaica Publishing House.

Millette, R. (1998). West Indian families in the United States. In R. Taylor (Ed.), *Minority families in the United States: A multicultural perspective* (2nd ed.). Upper Saddle River, NJ: Prentice Hall.

Mohammed, P. (Ed.). (2002). *Gendered realities: Essays in Caribbean feminist thought.* Kingston, Jamaica: University of West Indies Press.

More, M. R., & Chase-Lansdale, L. (2001). Sexual intercourse and pregnancy among African American girls in high-poverty neighborhoods: The role of family and perceived community environment. *Journal of Marriage and the Family, 63*, 1146–1157.

Morrisson, J., Ispa, J., & Milner, V. (1998). Ideas about childrearing among Jamaican mothers and early childhood education teachers. *Journal of Research in Childhood Education, 12*, 166–175.

Mott, F. L. (1990). When is a father really gone? Parental-child contact in father-absent homes. *Demography, 27*, 499–517.

Munroe, R., & Munroe, R. (1992). Fathers in children's environments: A four-culture study. In B. Hewlett (Ed.), *Father-child relations: Cultural and biosocial contexts* (pp. 213–229). New York: de Gruyter.

Nelson, T. J., Clampet-Lundquist, S., & Edin, K. (2002). Sustaining fragile fatherhood: Father involvement among low-income, noncustodial African-American fathers in Philadelphia. In C. S. Tamis-LeMonda & N. Cabrera (Eds.), *Handbook on father involvement: Multidisciplinary perspectives* (pp. 525–553). Mahwah, NJ: Erlbaum.

Palkovitz, R. (1997). Reconstructing "involvement": Expanding conceptualizations of men's caring in contemporary families. In A. J. Hawkins & D. C. Dollahite (Eds.), *Generative fathering: Beyond deficit perspectives* (pp. 200–216). Thousand Oaks, CA: Sage.

Palkovitz, R. (2002). Involved fathering and child development: Advancing our understanding of good fathering. In C. S. Tamis-LeMonda & N. Cabrera (Eds.), *Handbook on father involvement: Multidisciplinary perspectives* (pp. 119–140). Mahwah, NJ: Erlbaum.

Payne, M. (1989). Use and abuse of corporal punishment: A Caribbean view. *Child Abuse and Neglect, 13*, 389–401.

Payne, M., & Furnham, A. (1992). Parental self-reports of childrearing practices in the Caribbean. *Journal of Black Psychology, 18*, 19–36.

Peters, M. (1985). Racial socialization of young Black children. In H. McAdoo & J. McAdoo (Eds.), *Black children* (pp. 159–173). Beverly Hills, CA: Sage.

Pfannensteil, A. E., & Honig, A. S. (1991). Prenatal intervention and support for low-income fathers. *Infant Mental Health Journal, 12*, 103–115.

Pleck, J. (1997). Paternal involvement: Levels, sources, and consequences. In M. E. Lamb (Ed.), *The role of the father in child development* (3rd ed., pp. 66–103). New York: Wiley.

U.S. Census Bureau & U.S. Department of Commerce, Economics, and Statistics Administration. (2000, September). *Population characteristics: The Black population in the United States* (pp. 20–530). Washington, DC: U.S. Government Printing Office.

Portes, P. R., Dunham, R. M., & Williams, S. (1986). Assessing childrearing style in ecological settings: Its relation to culture, social class, early age intervention, and scholastic achievement. *Adolescence, 21*, 723–735.

Powell, D. (1986). Caribbean women and their responses to familial experience. *Social and Economic Studies, 35*, 83–130.

Price-Bonham, S., & Skeen, P. (1979). A comparison of Black and White fathers with implications for parents' education. *The Family Coordinator, 28*, 53–59.

Rambally, R. T. (1995). The overrepresentation of Black youth in the Quebec social service system. *Canadian Social Work Review, 12,* 85–97.

Ramkissoon, M. W. (2002). *The psychology of fathering in the Caribbean: An investigation of the physical and psychological presence of the Jamaican father.* Unpublished doctoral dissertation, University of West Indies, Mona, Jamaica.

Rangarajan, A., & Gleason, P. (1998). Young unwed fathers of AFDC children: Do they provide support? *Demography, 35,* 175–186.

Rasheed, J. M. (1998). The adult life cycle of poor African American fathers. *Journal of Human Behavior in the Social Environment, 1,* 265–280.

Ray, A., & Hans, S. (1997). *Contributions to African-American mothers' views of their children's fathers' caregiving: Fathers past and present.* Paper presented at the meeting of the National Council on Family Relations, Arlington, VA.

Ray, A., & Hans, S. (2001). *"Being there for my child": Inner city African American fathers' perspectives on fathering and sources of stress.* Paper presented at the Biennial meetings of the Society for Research in Child Development, Minneapolis, MN.

Ricketts, H. (2000). *An assessment and analysis of parenting in Jamaica.* United Nations Report. Kingston, Jamaica.

Rivara, F. P., Sweeny, P. J., & Henderson, B. F. (1986). Black teenage fathers: What happens when the child is born? *Pediatrics, 78,* 151–158.

Roberts, G., & Sinclair, S. (1978). *Women in Jamaica.* New York: KTO Press.

Rodman, H. (1971). *Lower-class families: The culture of poverty in Negro Trinidad.* New York: Oxford University Press.

Rodney, H. E., & Mupier, R. (1999). Behavioral differences between African American male adolescents with biological fathers and those without biological fathers in the home. *Journal of Black Studies, 30,* 45–61.

Rong, X. L., & Brown, F. (2001). The effects of immigrant generation and ethnicity on educational attainment among young African and Caribbean Blacks in the United States. *Harvard Educational Review, 70,* 537–565.

Roopnarine, J. L. (1997). Fathers in the English-speaking Caribbean: Not so marginal. *World Psychology, 3,* 191–210.

Roopnarine, J. L. (1999). *Father involvement and parental styles in Caribbean immigrant families.* Paper presented at the American Educational Research Association conference, Montreal, Canada, April.

Roopnarine, J. L. (2002). Father involvement in English-speaking Caribbean families. In C. S. Tamis-LeMonda & N. Cabrera (Eds.), *Handbook on father involvement: Multidisciplinary perspectives* (pp. 279–302). Mahwah, NJ: Erlbaum.

Roopnarine, J. L., & Brown, J. (Eds.). (1997). *Caribbean families: Diversity among ethnic groups.* Norwood, NJ: Ablex.

Roopnarine, J. L., Brown, J., Snell-White, P., Riegraf, N. B., Crossley, D., Hossain, Z., et al. (1995). Father involvement in child care and household work in common-law dual-earner and single-earner families. *Journal of Applied Developmental Psychology, 16,* 35–52.

Roopnarine, J. L., Bynoe, P. F., Singh, R., & Simon, R. (in press). Caribbean families: A rather complex mosaic. In J. L. Roopnarine & U. Gielen (Eds.), *Families in global perspective.* Boston: Allyn & Bacon.

Roopnarine, J. L., & Gielen, U. (Eds.). (in press). *Families in global perspectives.* Boston: Allyn & Bacon.

Roopnarine, J. L., & Jung, K. (2002). *The propensity toward physical punishment in Caribbean and Caribbean immigrant families: Consequences for child well-being.* Unpublished manuscript.

Roopnarine, J. L., & Shin, M. (2003). Caribbean immigrants from English-speaking countries: Sociohistorical forces, migratory patterns, and psychological issues in family functioning. In L. L. Adler & U. P. Gielen (Eds.), *Migration, immigration, and emigration in international perspective* (pp. 123–142). Westport, CT: Praeger.

Roy, K. (1999). Low-income single fathers in an African American community and the requirements of welfare reform. *Journal of Family Issues, 20,* 432–457.

Russell-Brown, P., Norville, B., & Griffith, C. (1997). Child shifting: A survival strategy for teenage mothers. In J. L. Roopnarine & J. Brown (Eds.), *Caribbean families: Diversity among ethnic groups* (pp. 223–242). Norwood, NJ: Ablex.

Rutter, M., Yule, W., Berger, M., Morton, J., & Bagley, C. (1974). Children of West Indian immigrants: I. Rates of behavioral deviance and psychiatric disorder. *Journal of Child Psychiatry, 15,* 241–262.

Salem, D. A., Zimmerman, M., & Notaro, P. C. (1998). Effects of family structure, family process, and father involvement on psychosocial outcomes among African American adolescents. *Family Relations, 47,* 331–341.

Samms-Vaughn, M. (2000). *Cognition, educational attainment and behavior in a cohort of Jamaican children.* Working Paper no. 5, Planning Institute of Jamaica.

Savage, J. E., Adair, A. V., & Friedman, P. (1978). Community-social variables related to Black parent-absent families. *Journal of Marriage and the Family, 40,* 779–785.

Schlesinger, B. (1968). Family patterns in Jamaica: Review and commentary. *Journal of Marriage and the Family, 30,* 136–148.

Seccombe, K. (2000). Families in poverty in the 1990s: Trends, causes, consequences, and lessons learned. *Journal of Marriage and the Family, 62,* 1094–1113.

Seltzer, J. (1991). Relationships between fathers and children who live apart: The father's role after separation. *Journal of Marriage and the Family, 53,* 79–101.

Senior, O. (1991). *Working miracles: Women's lives in the English-speaking Caribbean.* Bloomington: Indiana University Press.

Shannon, J. D., Tamis-LeMonda, C. S., London, K., & Cabrera, N. (2002). *Beyond rough and tumble: Low-income fathers' interactions and children's cognitive development at 24 months.* Unpublished manuscript, New York University.

Sharpe, J. (1997). Mental health issues and family socialization in the Caribbean. In J. L. Roopnarine & J. Brown (Eds.), *Caribbean families: Diversity among ethnic groups* (pp. 259–273). Norwood, NJ: Ablex.

Sigel, I., & McGillicuddy-DeLisi, A. (2002). Parental beliefs are cognitions: The dynamic belief systems model. In M. H. Bornstein (Ed.), *Handbook on parenting* (Vol. 3, 2nd ed., pp. 485–508). Mahwah, NJ: Erlbaum.

Sigle-Rushton, W., & Garfinkel, I. (2002). The effects of welfare, child support, and labor markets on father involvement. In C. S. Tamis-LeMonda & N. Cabrera (Eds.), *Handbook on father involvement: Multidisciplinary perspectives* (pp. 409–429). Mahwah, NJ: Erlbaum.

Sigle-Rushton, W., & McLanahan, S. (2002a). *Father absence and child well-being: A critical review.* Paper presented in the Maxwell School, Syracuse University, October 25.

Sigle-Rushton, W., & McLanahan, S. (2002b). The living arrangements of new, unmarried mothers. *Demography, 39,* 415–433.

Silverstein, L. (1993). Primate research, family politics, and social policy: Transforming "CADS" into "DADS." *Journal of Family Psychology, 7,* 267–282.

Silverstein, L., & Auerbach, C. F. (1999). Deconstructing the essential father. *American Psychologist, 54,* 397–407.

Silverstein, L., & Auerbach, C. F. (in press). (Post)modern families. In J. L. Roopnarine & U. Gielen (Eds.), *Families in global perspective.* Boston: Allyn & Bacon.

Small, M. F. (2000). Trouble in paradise. *New Scientist, 168,* 34–38.

Smith, E. P., Prinz, R. J., Dumas, J. E., & Laughlin, J. (2001). Latent models of family process in African American families: Relationships to child competence, achievement, and problem behavior. *Journal of Marriage and the Family, 63,* 967–970.

Smith, R. T. (1956). *The Negro family in British Guiana.* London: Rutledge & Kegan Paul.

Smith, R. T. (1988). *Kinship and class in the West Indies.* Cambridge, England: Cambridge University Press.

Smith, R. T. (1996). *The matrifocal family: Power, pluralism, and politics.* London: Routledge.

Stack, C. (1974). *All our kin: Strategies for survival in a Black community.* New York: Harper & Row.

Stack, C., & Burton, L. (1993). Kinscripts. *Journal of Comparative Family Studies, 24,* 157–170.

Staples, R. (1971a). The myth of the impotent Black male. *Black Scholar, 2,* 2–9.

Staples, R. (1971b). Toward a sociology of the Black family. *Journal of Marriage and the Family, 33,* 119–138.

Staples, R. (Ed.). (1999). *The Black family: Essays and studies.* Belmont, CA: Wadsworth.

Staples, R., & Johnson, L. B. (1993). *Black families at the crossroads.* San Francisco: Jossey-Bass.

Stier, H., & Tienda, M. (1993). Are men marginal to the family? Insights from Chicago's inner city. In J. Hood (Ed.), *Men, work, and family* (pp. 23–44). Thousand Oaks, CA: Sage.

Strom, R. D., Amukamara, H., Strom, S. K., Bekert, T. E., Moore, E. G., Strom, P. S., et al. (2000a). African American fathers: Perceptions of two generations. *Journal of Adolescence, 23,* 513–516.

Strom, R. D., Amukamara, H., Strom, S. K., Bekert, T. E., Moore, E. G., Strom, P. S., et al. (2000b). Parenting success of African American fathers. *Journal of Research and Development in Education, 33,* 257–267.

Suarez-Orozco, C., & Todorova, I. (2001). *The transnationalization of families: Immigrant separations and reunifications.* Paper presented to the American Family Therapy Academy, Miami, FL.

Sudarkasa, N. (1999). African American females as primary caregivers. In H. P. McAdoo (Ed.), *Family ethnicity: Strengths in diversity* (pp. 191–200). Thousand Oaks, CA: Sage.

Sullivan, M. (1993). Young fathers and parenting in two inner-city neighborhoods. In R. Lerman & T. Ooms (Eds.), *Young unwed fathers: Changing roles and emerging policies* (pp. 52–73). Philadelphia: Temple University Press.

Sun, L., & Roopnarine, J. L. (1996). Mother-infant, father-infant interaction and involvement and household labor among Taiwanese families. *Infant Behavior and Development, 19,* 121–129.

Super, C., & Harkness, S. (1997). The cultural structuring of child development. In J. Berry, P. Dasen, & T. S. Saraswathi (Eds.), *Handbook of cross-cultural psychology: Basic processes and human development* (pp. 1–39). Needham, MA: Allyn & Bacon.

Suppal, P., Roopnarine, J. L., Buesig, T., & Bennett, A. (1996). Ideological beliefs about family practices: Contemporary perspectives among north Indian families. *International Journal of Psychology, 31,* 29–37.

Taylor, R. J., Hardison, C. B., & Chatters, L. M. (1996). Kin and nonkin as sources of informal assistance. In H. W. Neighbors & J. S. Jackson (Eds.), *Mental health in Black America* (pp. 130–145). Newbury Park, CA: Sage.

Taylor, R. J., Jackson, J. S., & Chatters, L. M. (Eds.). (1997). *Family life in Black America.* Thousand Oaks, CA: Sage.

Taylor, R. J., & Johnson, W. E. (1997). Family roles and family satisfaction among Black men. In R. J. Taylor, J. Jackson, & L. M. Chatters (Eds.), *Family life in Black America* (pp. 248–261). Thousand Oaks, CA: Sage.

Teachman, J., Day, R., Carver, K., Call, V., & Paasch, K. (1998). Sibling resemblance in behavioral and cognitive outcomes: The role of father presence. *Journal of Marriage and the Family, 60,* 835–848.

Thornton, M. C. (1997). Strategies of racial socialization among Black parents: Mainstream, minority and cultural messages. In R. J. Taylor, J. Jackson, & L. M. Chatters (Eds.), *Family life in Black America* (pp. 201–215). Thousand Oaks, CA: Sage.

Thornton, M. C., Chatters, L., Taylor, R. J., & Allen, W. R. (1990). Sociodemographic and environmental influences on racial socialization by black parents. *Child Development, 61,* 401–409.

Vickerman, M. (2001). Jamaicans: Balancing race and ethnicity. In N. Foner (Ed.), *New immigrants in New York* (pp. 201–228). New York: Columbia University Press.

Wade, J. C. (1994). African American fathers and sons: Social, historical, and psychological considerations. *Families in Society: Journal of Contemporary Human Services, 74,* 561–570.

Waters, M. (1999). *Black identities: West Indian immigrant dreams and American realities.* Cambridge, MA: Harvard University Press.

White-Davis, G. (1996). Recommendations for enhancing the education of English-speaking students in the New York public schools. In G. Irish (Ed.), *Caribbean students in New York* (Occasional Papers No. 1, pp. 133–143). New York: Caribbean Diaspora Press.

Whiting, B. B., & Whiting, J. W. M. (1975). *Children of six cultures: A psycho-cultural analysis.* Cambridge, MA: Harvard University Press.

Williams, J. H., Auslander, W. F., Houston, C. A., Krebill, H., & Haire-Joshu, D. (2000). African American family structure: Are there differences in social, psychological, and economic well-being? *Journal of Family Issues, 21,* 838–857.

Wilson, L. C. (1989). *Family and structure and dynamics in the Caribbean: An examination of residential and relational matrifocality in Guyana.* Unpublished doctoral dissertation, University of Michigan.

Wilson, L. C., & Kposowa, A. J. (1994). Paternal involvement with children: Evidence from Guyana. *International Journal of Sociology of the Family, 24,* 23–42.

Wilson, L. C., Williams, D., & Williams, K. (1992). Family structure and mental health in urban Guyana. *Anthropology, 10,* 117–126.

Wilson, M. N., Kohn, L. P., Curry-El, J., & Hinton, I. (1995). The influence of family structure characteristics on the childrearing behaviors of African American mothers. *Journal of Black Psychology, 21,* 450–462.

Wilson, M. N., & Tolson, T. F. J. (1987). Familial support in the Black community. *Journal of Clinical Child Psychology, 19,* 347–355.

Wilson, W. J. (1987). *The truly disadvantaged: The inner city, the underclass, and public policy.* Chicago: University of Chicago Press.

Wint, E., & Brown, J. (1988). The knowledge and practice of effective parenting. *Social and Economic Studies, 37,* 253–277.

World Bank Development Indicators database. (2000). *Annual reports.* Washington, DC: World Bank.

Young, V. H. (1991). Vincentian domestic culture: Continued debate. *Social and Economic Studies, 40,* 155–167.

Zhou, M. (1997). Segmented assimilation: Issues, controversies, and recent research on the second generation. *International Migration Review, 31,* 975–1008.

Zimmerman, M. A., Salem, D. A., & Maton, K. I. (1995). Family structure and psychosocial correlates among urban African American adolescent males. *Child Development, 66,* 1598–1613.

CHAPTER 4

Latino Fathers

Uncharted Territory in Need of Much Exploration

NATASHA J. CABRERA and CYNTHIA GARCIA COLL

IN WRITING THIS CHAPTER, we have come face to face with the lack of research on this important topic. Latino fathers: Who are they? How do they conceptualize their roles? How are they involved with their children? What obstacles get in the way of their involvement? What impact do they have on their children? These questions merit theoretically pertinent and empirically sound answers, yet we have less than a handful of studies that attempt to shed light on them.

Why is this the case? Perhaps the problematic nature of the category *Latino* gets in the way. The Latino population in the United States is a highly heterogeneous group. Latinos can be of mestizo or Indian heritage, but they can also be considered White, Black, or Asian. In the United States, the Latino category encompasses Mexican Americans whose families have been in this country for eight generations, Cuban refugees who arrived in the late 1960s, recently arrived undocumented workers from various countries in Central America, and Puerto Ricans who are American citizens at birth whether they are born on the island of Puerto Rico or on the mainland. Third-generation upper-class Cubans may share little with Mayan-speaking recent immigrants from Guatemala or Mexico or with Puerto Ricans who can move freely between the island and the mainland as U.S. citizens.

It follows that as a group, Latinos in the United States have varied histories and cultural and socioeconomic backgrounds, very different immigration patterns and generational statuses, and that they end up in very different niches in our society. There are also important intraethnic differences in terms of education, income, and English proficiency. For example, in the United States, Mexican-descendant Americans include those people born in Mexico, those born in the United States of Mexican-born parents, and those born in the United States of U.S.-born parents (Buriel, Mercado, Rodriguez, & Chavez, 1991). Racial features, gender, socioeconomic status, language, immigration status, and reason and mode of immigration shape and define their experiences in this country. Ancestry to a Latin American country—initially colonized by Spain and having Spanish as the dominant language—is sometimes the only common thread among these very different sociodemographic groups. These interethnic and intraethnic differences have created some unique challenges and opportunities for researchers, policy makers, and educators interested in understanding the processes of fathering among Latinos and in identifying points of intervention. Acknowledging diversity within this population also has important implications for translation of research from small location-specific samples to the broader Latino population.

Although there are many ethnic and sociodemographic differences among Latinos in the United States, there are also some striking similarities. Latinos share a language as well as many cultural and family values and configurations. These similarities facilitate the study of Latinos within broad parameters and highlight the value of looking at general processes without negating the interethnic variation. Moreover, although the use of ethnic categories has many analytic limitations, such as the negation of intergroup variability, membership in these categories has powerful impacts on developmental processes and outcomes (Garcia Coll & Vazquez Garcia, 1996). Therefore, it is imperative that at the same time that we recognize the limitations of broad characterizations of Latinos, we study both the commonalities and differences among Latinos and between Latinos and other demographic groups.

The study of Latino families has grown steadily since the 1970s (e.g., Mirande, 1991; Vega, 1990), and the recent surge of interest in these families (e.g., Zambrana, 1995) parallels the research on the transformation and stability of the family in mainstream American culture (Casper & Bianchi, 2002). Although these literatures are not connected, they have generally neglected men and fathers. In recent decades, however, a steady effort to include fathers in research, practice, and policy has yielded important information about fathers. Unfortunately, progress in understanding minority men, especially Latino fathers, has lagged behind (Erkut, Szalacha, & Garcia Coll, in press). In essence, studies examining the processes of Latino fatherhood, the antecedents and consequences of their involvement, and how their cultural-ethnic-minority characteristics shape their behavior are sparse.

Given the scarcity of research in this area, the aim of our chapter is more modest than we anticipated. Our goals are to (a) provide a demographic description of Latino fathers, (b) outline theoretical frameworks to study Latino fathers, (c) pose questions about universal processes of fatherhood, (d) describe unique fatherhood processes for Latino men, (e) describe the ways that Latino men are actually involved with their children, and (f) conclude with a set of recommendations of directions for research.

SETTING THE STAGE: WHO ARE LATINO FATHERS?

In order to understand how Latino men behave as fathers, the challenges and barriers they face, and how their ethnicity affects their role as fathers, it is helpful to outline a more specific demographic profile of who Latino fathers are in the United States. A word of caution about the official statistics we use: These come from national surveys that tend to underrepresent minority men, nonresidential men, and illegal immigrants. Hence these data provide only a crude portrayal of Latinos in the United States.

A closer demographic examination of the population in the United States reveals that in the new millennium, more than a quarter of the U.S. population is composed of members of ethnic minorities, including African Americans, Latinos, and Asian Americans. The 35 million Latinos (note that official census data use the term *Hispanic* instead of *Latino*) in the United States make up about 12.5% of the total population. This is the same proportion as the African American population. However, it is estimated that due to both immigration and higher fertility rates (Bean & Tienda, 1987), by the year 2050 a quarter (about 100 million people) of the U.S. population will be of Hispanic origin (U.S. Bureau of the Census, 2000). Latinos will be the largest minority group in the country. These statistics point to the role that the present and projected Latino population growth plays in the demographic transformation of American society.

The breakdown of the Latino population into ethnic subgroups reveals some interesting demographic differences that are pertinent to our characterization of Latino fathers because they serve as proxies to immigration and other socioeconomic differences. Two thirds of all Latinos in the United States come from Central and South America. This group grew by over 100% between 1990 and 2000 (U.S. Census Bureau, 2000). Using country of origin, the 1999 Current Population Survey reports that individuals of Mexican origin constitute two thirds or 66.1% of the entire Latino population in the United States. Latinos of Puerto Rican origin make up 9%; 14.5% are from Central and South American; 4% are Cuban; and 6.4% are identified as Other Latinos (Ramirez, 2000).

For the population aged 15 years and older, Latinos were more likely to have never been married than were non-Latino Whites (33.2% vs. 24.5%). Among Latinos, Cubans were least likely to have never been married (20.4%). In terms of residential status, the majority of Latino fathers reside with their children. Regardless of marital status, in 2001, 78% of White, non-Latino children lived with two parents, compared with 38% of Black children and 65% of children of Latino origin. Although one third of all births in the United States are nonmarital, among poor and minority populations, the proportions are higher. Forty percent of births among Latinos and 70% among Blacks occur outside of marriage (Ventura et al., 1995). Nonmarried parents who either live with the child or visit weekly are similar across ethnic groups. Seventy-two percent of African American children, 75% of Latino children, and 72% of White children have fathers who either live with or visit them (Casper & Bianchi, 2002; also see McLanahan et al., 1998). These findings question the image of minority fathers as being absent from their children's lives, even though many of them might not be legally married. That is, regardless of residency status, most minority fathers are in constant contact with their children.

It is also noteworthy that African American children are much more likely to have a visiting relationship with their fathers, whereas Latino and White children are more likely to be living with their fathers (Casper & Bianchi, 2002). At the other extreme, 19% of White children never see their fathers as compared with 13% of Hispanic and African American children. The reasons why Hispanic fathers never see their children are speculative at this point. This group may include fathers who live abroad or those who have started a second family while waiting for the first family to immigrate to the United States. White children who are born outside marriage are about 1.5 times more likely than Black and Hispanic children never to see their fathers.

In terms of the stability of father-child relationships (not changing status), there are some interesting ethnic differences. White children have the most stable arrangements, especially among parents who cohabit or never see each other. Black children have less stable relationships with their fathers than do White children, but those in a visiting relationship have more stability. Although based on small samples, recent analysis suggests that Latino children appear to have the least stable arrangements; stability in the relationship with the child is evident only when parents cohabit. Nearly 70% of Hispanic children who live with cohabiting parents during their first year of life are still living with their fathers two years later (McLanahan et al., 1998).

As just noted, single parenting is much more common among Blacks and Hispanics than among Whites, but the likelihood that a single-parent family is maintained by a father rather than a mother is actually greater among Whites (Casper & Bianchi, 2002). Among Whites in 1998, 22% of the single-parent families were father-only families (Casper & Bianchi, 2002). The comparable estimates for Black and Hispanics were 8% and 6%, respectively.

In terms of age at which Latino men father, given the substantial personal and social costs of teen pregnancy, a lot of attention has been placed on teen births. Although the rate for the general population is abating, rates have not decreased across all subgroups (Goodyear, Newcomb, & Allison, 2000). In the early 1990s, the national teen pregnancy rate rose more than 30% for Latinos (Goodyear et al., 2000). In general, teen fathers complete fewer years of education, are less likely to finish high school and use social services (Pirog-Good, 1996), and are more likely to have a history of antisocial behavior problems (Elster, Lamb, & Tavare, 1987). However, some studies have found the tendency to engage in risky behaviors to be higher for Caucasian fathers than for African American or Latino fathers (Lerman, 1993; Pirog-Good, 1995). These findings suggest that different pathways may be conducive to early parenthood in different ethnic populations (Erkut et al., in press; Garcia Coll & Vazquez Garcia, 1996).

Other characteristics of Latino families can have an impact on fathers. In general, Latinos (30.6%) live in family households that are larger (five or more people) than those of non-Hispanic Whites (11.8%). Educational attainment and economic self-sufficiency also vary among Latinos. The Latino population age 25 and older was less likely to have at least graduated from high school than was that of non-Hispanic Whites (57% and 88%, respectively). However, substantial variability is observed within: Cubans and other Hispanics are most likely to have graduated from high school (73% and 72%, respectively) compared with Mexicans (5%). Latinos are also more likely than non-Latino Whites to be unemployed and to live in poverty. Almost 23% of Latinos live below the poverty level; again, Cubans and Central and South American are least likely to be poor (17%; Therrien & Ramirez, 2000). The implication of these statistics for fathers is that, intraethnic differences notwithstanding, Latino men in general are overrepresented among the poor and unemployed and may be responsible not only for their own immediate families but also for extended family members. As a collective group, however, Latino men are most likely to live with their children, less likely to have children outside of marriage, and more likely to have stable relationships with their children than are African American men. Although these interethnic differences do not speak to the quality of Latino or African American men's involvement with their children, they underlie different intraethnic cultural, historical, and economic experiences.

In addition, the heterogeneity of the Latino population in the United States presents challenges for our understanding of fathering processes in this population. The heterogeneity stems from pre- and postmigration issues as well as from historical processes that impinge in their adaptations to current circumstances (Garcia Coll et al., 1996). Although the dominant demographic profile of Latino fathers is that of Mexican ancestry, poor, with little formal education, living in the household and perhaps still involved if living elsewhere and at risk for other psychosocial stresses associated with poverty and their minority status, this profile does not fit many Latino fathers in the United States. Affluent third-generation Mexican Americans, highly educated recent immigrants from South America, and middle-class Puerto Ricans have very little in common with this description. However, they might share some strong cultural definitions of fatherhood and family functioning. This complexity pleads for the use of complex theoretical models that will include the many contextual influences that we need to consider in order to achieve a satisfactory understanding of Latino fathers.

THEORETICAL FRAMEWORK

In general, the area of fatherhood and fathering has been highly atheoretical. While various researchers have utilized different theoretical frameworks to frame their studies, the parsimony and power of these theories to explain the range of fathering behaviors are unknown. In terms of models that conceptualize and measure father involvement, the existing models are based largely on Anglo-European middle-class samples (Cabrera, Tamis-LeMonda, Bradley, Hofferth, & Lamb, 2000; Erkut et al., in press). It is unclear how and whether these models capture Latino fathers' involvement with their families mainly because they have been conceptualized using the Anglo-European family as the template. Emerging ethnographic data suggest that these models might not be appropriate for groups other than the ones for which they were developed. For example, in a small study of low-income men whose children were enrolled in Early Head Start that was based on Lamb and his colleagues' (1987) model of father involvement, a Latino man expressed his frustration after answering a lengthy questionnaire on how often he sings to, dances with, and bathes his child and changes his child's diaper (Shannon, Tamis-LaMonda, London, & Cabrera, 2002). Later in the interview, the man asked the researcher when she would ask him about how he breaks his back to support his child. The issues of trade-off—if low-income men have to work long hours to support their families—may be more relevant for fathers with fewer resources than for those who are better off.

However, in another study, Toth and Xu (1999) used Palkovitz's (1997) concept of father involvement to explore racial and ethnic cultural variations in American fathers' involvement with their children. Toth and Xu hypothesized that the type of parental involvement varies by race and ethnicity, and using the National Survey of Families and Households (NSFH), the authors found that ethnicity, socialization patterns, parenting role beliefs, and child-rearing values play an important role in how African American, Hispanic, and White fathers interact with their children. However, these findings might not generalize to all Latino fathers because national data sets such as the NSFH tend to exclude from their sample designs men who are nonmarried, nonresidential, incarcerated, or in the military. Nevertheless, Palkovitz's model can be used with Latino samples to draw meaningful conclusions about their parental experiences.

One way of thinking about fathers' involvement in general is in terms of resources available to the family that support, undermine, and help define the father's role and involvement with his children. Drawing from psychology, economics, sociology, and education, these resources can be divided into social, human, and physical (or financial) capital (Becker, 1981; Coleman, 1988; Lee, 1993). Each of these forms of capital has dimensions that can describe the resources of the family and the assets of the community in which the family operates. Given the unique demographic characteristics of Latino fathers and the unique circumstances of Latino families, this framework seems to be useful to study them.

Social capital includes the quality of the relationships within the family, the way that parents interact with their children and each other, the educational aspirations parents have for their children, the home environment (rules, routines, order, harmony of household), and even the time that family members have to devote to each other. Parental involvement itself, whether in the home or in the school, is a form of social capital (Lee, 1993). Other individuals and institutions outside the household such as neighbors, religious institutions, and schools facilitate it. It also includes the extent of social capital within each of these institutions. For example, school policies and teacher practices that encourage parental involvement may be viewed as a form of social capital.

In respect to social capital, Latino families have been described as highly familistic. The value of familism has been used behaviorally as involvement with family members through visits and exchange of services representing feelings of loyalty, solidarity, and reciprocity among family members (Vega, 1990). Familism represents ideals that influence behavioral outcomes, and hence Latino groups are seen as more family oriented than Whites (Baca Zinn, 1982–1983; Kane, 1993). Although Mexican Americans may place greater emphasis on family and children than do Puerto Ricans or Cuban Americans, all three groups rank family as more important than do Whites (Sabogal, Marin, & Otero-Sabogal, 1987). We would expect Latino fathers to be involved in a rich, extended network that could encompass not only blood relatives but also fictive kin such as *compadres* and *comadres* (their children's godparents). The question would be, How do these relationships define and support fathers' definitions of their roles and their involvement? What happens to these *comadres* when the family immigrates? Do new sources of support arise? How much continuity and discontinuity exist in the definition and supports between mainstream American ideals and Latino families of diverse backgrounds?

Human capital within the family includes parental education levels and the skills and abilities that parents and other family members have. Within the community, it includes the education, skills, and abilities of those in the community and of those who work in important institutions, such as schools. As we know from our demographic profile of Latino fathers in the United States, these men are mostly young, poor, and with low educational attainment. The implications of these characteristics for Latino fathers are yet to be understood. Although education is an important characteristic of successful parenting in non-Latino groups (Davis-Kean, Eccles, & Schnabel, 2002), at least one study suggests that the process for Latino families might be different. Harwood, Miller, Carlson, and Leyendecker (2002) found that even in middle-class populations, Puerto Rican mothers view *respeto* as an integral value of their child rearing. Roopnarine and Ahmeduzzaman (1993) found that for a small sample of mainland middle-class Puerto Rican fathers, family income, rather than father's education and income per se, was positively associated with length of marriage and a general commitment to the family, including high levels of paternal involvement. These Latino families have high aspirations for their children's academic success and display a strong investment in the well-being of their family. Despite having formal education, they still differ in values and interactions with their White, middle-class, female counterparts. However, stability of marriage and employment may be distant goals for other Latino men who might not have the psychological, educational, and economic resources to have a stable marriage and employment.

Physical capital includes such things as family income, the assets in the home including computers and books, and the resources of the local community, including community institutions such as schools, libraries, parks, and recreation centers. Again, the demographic profile of Latino fathers is relevant here. Taking level of poverty as proxy for physical capital, the average Latino family is poor and hence would have diminished physical capital and also lack the tools to accumulate wealth. We would posit that as income increases, it allows a family to live in a better neighborhood, to send their children to better schools, and to provide educational materials in the home. At the same time, if that income derives from long working hours, it may actually reduce some of the social capital available in the household even as it increases the physical capital.

Other researchers (e.g., Roopnarine & Ahmeduzzaman, 1993) have used cultural-ecological models because they allow families to be studied in their cultural contexts by focusing on their strengths and unique attributes (Ogbu, 1983; Slaughter-Defoe, Nakagawa, Takanishi, & Johnson, 1990) and the human ecology model, which emphasizes contextual markers that may be linked to the process of development (cf. Bronfenbrenner, 1986). These models may adapt themselves better to understand how men father not only in the context of poverty, unemployment, and lack of support but also within the parameters of culture, linguistic diversity, and ethnicity.

Finally, other conceptual models have been proposed more recently to add issues of racism, segregation, and discrimination as other centrally relevant variables to the study of minority populations, inclusive of Latino fathers (Erkut et al., in press; Garcia Coll & Vazquez Garcia, 1996). For example, many Latinos live in highly segregated environments that create limited access to certain social and physical capital. Specifically, residential segregation and racial-ethnic discrimination have been found to play a role in the rates of unemployment of Latino men (Tienda & Wilson, 1992). A pertinent question that derives from these theoretical frameworks and these findings is, How does perceived and actual discrimination in the job market affect a father's view and enactment of his own role in his children's life?

In sum, although these theoretical approaches and models have been used in various studies of Latino families, there are no qualitative studies that can inform how to measure different constructs (e.g., education) in a meaningful way or guide the design and development of survey questionnaires for Latino families. It is uncertain how culture affects the social and human capital and the behavior of Latino men. For example, in the Early Head Start National Evaluation study, field-workers reported that Latino fathers, especially those of low income, felt uncomfortable answering questions about economic contribution to the family (C. Tamis-LeMonda, personal communication, June 2002). Similarly, using mainstream models of father involvement with minority populations may yield misleading information. For example, questionnaires such as those used in the Early Head Start National Evaluation emphasize parental involvement by breaking it down into different domains of involvement. One of these domains includes activities related to the care of children (e.g., bathing, changing diapers, putting them to bed, etc.). Latino men who view this aspect of care as a mother's job but are very involved with other aspects of child rearing (e.g., taking the children to games, outdoors activities, etc.) may score low on this questionnaire, suggesting noninvolvement when in fact they are quite involved.

IS THERE A UNIVERSAL PROCESS OF FATHERHOOD?

Aside from the heterogeneity of Latinos in the United States, their unique demographic characteristics, and the multiple theoretical considerations that need to be taken into account in the study of Latino fathers, another challenge needs to be faced as we propose a research agenda in this topic: the definition of a good father that is meaningful across ethnic and cultural groups. The general question of whether there are universals of father involvement that cut across cultures and ethnic groups has not been thoroughly addressed in the larger area of father research. The issue of threshold—how much fathering is enough to make a positive impact on child development—is also underexplored. This is especially challenging given that the main problem with research on this area is the exclusion of race and culture from it. There are very few analyses of the interplay between culture and race and its impact on men's participation in the fathering role.

This issue is further complicated by the recognition that the definitions of family and good parenting have evolved over time. There is evidence that even in mainstream American culture the concept of the ideal father has drastically changed (Pleck, this volume; Pleck & Pleck, 1997). Recent social, economic, and other demographic changes partly explain this historical change. Mothers' increased participation in the workforce, the increasing use of reproductive technology, increasing rates of divorce and cohabitation, increased residential mobility, and uncertain economic conditions have forever altered the social, political, and economic fabric of this country. These profound changes have brought about challenges to some basic and fundamental assumptions about the meaning of families, parental roles and expectations, and how children function within families and society.

These changes provide evidence that the definition of quality of fathering is intimately tied to the evolving role of fathers in a particular ecology. Although acknowledgement of paternity and economic provision have always been a fundamental—and perhaps universal—component of fathering, there exists a new middle-class American idea of the coparent, in which the gender division of labor in domestic and breadwinning responsibilities is diminished (Pleck & Pleck, 1997). A fundamental question that needs to be addressed is, How do Latino fathers measure against this new ideal? Is this the ideal that they strive for? How does this ideal combine with other Latino cultural values and assumptions? These questions can form the basis for a future research agenda.

As a variety of family structures have evolved even within ethnic groups that are considered traditionalist, different expectations and beliefs about the roles of fathers have followed, and the scientific study of fathers has changed accordingly. For example, as mother's participation in the labor force increased, the focus shifted to whether fathers were doing enough child rearing to alleviate the perceived absence of employed mothers. As a consequence, the social concern during the 1980s focused on whether children were getting enough fathering. The emphasis was on the amount of fathering rather than on the kind and quality of fathering. Were Latino men aware of this quality versus quantity debate? Given that Latino men in the United States participate in social institutions that prescribe these expectations, it is reasonable to assume that they have experienced similar concerns. The question is to what extent. Did it affect their behaviors toward their children, family, and work? Research on Euro-American middle-class families and other groups suggests that although mothers are the primary caregivers to young children in diverse cultures around the world (Lamb 1987; Roopnarine & Carter, 1992), fathers are increasingly spending more of their non-work time with children (Hofferth, 1999). However, it is unclear whether increases in paternal involvement are universal. Father involvement in many cultures is different in nature, type, and frequency. In the new millennium we have established that fathers are more involved (spend more time with their children; Bond, Galinksy, & Swanberg, 1998), so the focus is on the quality of fathering: What impact does positive father involvement have on children's development? For a Latino-father research agenda, a more fundamental question is whether there are universals on how families define and enact good father involvement and how contextual factors (e.g., varieties of capital, cultural constructions of fatherhood, and experience or perception of racism and discrimination) mediate or moderate such processes.

Recent studies suggest that there might be some commonalities across fathers of diverse ethnic backgrounds in their perceptions of fatherhood. For example, new ethnographic data of studies that include Latino men (Nelson, Clampet-Lundquist, & Edin, 2002; Summers, Raikes, & Butler, 1999) suggest that for fathers, "being there" for their children is paramount. Although some fathers report being more cautious with their personal safety and vowing to take fewer risks once their children are born, others are willing to do anything to keep connected to their children (Nelson, Edin, & Torres, 2001), including selling drugs, which might take them farther away from their children. These data suggest some universals definitions of good fathering (i.e., being there), but they also attest to the fact that these perceptions may have different meanings for different fathers and that minority men, including Latinos, face many challenges and barriers that must be overcome at the personal, social, and community levels if they are to be there for their children. These studies have yet to unpack what *being there* means or to give insights into how low-income men navigate fatherhood from a disadvantaged position (i.e., having little bargaining power in the home, having been the target of racism and discrimination in various settings, and having little social and human capital).

Other evidence of fatherhood processes that can cut across ethnic groups comes from studies of secondary analysis. Using Palkovitz's (1997) three dimensions of fathering (cognitive, behavioral, and affective), Toth and Xu (1999) showed that "regardless of racial or ethnic origin, American fathers are almost equally likely to be expressive, affectionate, and encouraging while rearing their children aged between 5 and 18 years of age" (p. 92). In addition to general commonalities, there are also intergroup differences. Toth and Xu also reported that across race and ethnicity, fathers who hold nontraditional gender-roles and who are committed to fatherhood and value or demand the child's obedience are much more involved fathers than are those who are not (Palkovitz, 1997). However, these authors also reported that patterns of father involvement vary by ethnicity and ethnic background. For example, African American men are more likely than White men to monitor and supervise their children's activities (cognitive domain). The authors attributed this finding to the African American men's experience with racism. Similarly, Latino fathers are more likely to monitor their children and spend time with them than are their White counterparts. Although both Hispanic and African American men display similar levels of monitoring, Hispanic men interact more with their children than do African American men.

In sum, we can argue that there are certain aspects of fatherhood (the provider role, the feeling of being there for the children) that might be universal across cultures. However, the form and meaning of these processes are culturally dependent and have not been explored in the literature. Although sociodemographic changes across ethnic and cultural groups in family life in the United States have given way to a new definition of father involvement and impetus for the recent wave of research on fatherhood (Cabrera et al., 2000; Lamb, 1987; Palkovitz, 2002), the emerging fatherhood research continues to be more representative of White middle-class fathers than other minorities, including Latinos. Recent research on fatherhood has made many important contributions on many fronts—conceptual, methodological, and analytical—but we are still grappling with issues related to how to define a good father given the contextual realities of poor minority men. The lack of basic research is especially true for Latino and Asian fathers, as some important research is being conducted with African American samples (Coley, 2001; Jayakody & Kalil, 2002; McAdoo, 1993; Nelson et al., 2002). The fact remains that fundamental questions such as cultural variations in the father role, especially interethnic variations in fatherhood, are virtually unexplored in the literature, with some exceptions (Mirande, 1991; Roopnarine & Ahmeduzzaman, 1993). Hence, the universality of fatherhood processes is difficult to ascertain.

UNIQUE PROCESSES FOR LATINO FATHERS

The literature on Latino fathers consists of small studies based on clinical populations or on ethnographic accounts of certain ethnic groups (Suarez-Orozco & Paez, 2000), overemphasizing the psychosocial stress related to the immigration process (Salgado de Snyder, Cervantes, & Padilla, 1990) and focusing on parenting in general with an emphasis on mothers. National data on Latino families is scant (Buriel, 1993; Toth & Xu, 1999). Although there have been some efforts to include Latino fathers in ongoing large-scale surveys (see Cabrera et al., 2002), these studies include in-depth data on Latino families and children as a group but will not produce nationally representative samples of subgroups of Latinos. This problem does not exist only for Latinos: Most minority-group young men's transitions to fatherhood remain unexplored (Erkut et al., in press). The process of becoming a father or being a father in a cultural context different from one's own or in an environment depleted of resources to support the role is virtually unknown.

In general, research on Latino families supports two views of Latino fatherhood, a traditional and an emergent view.

THE TRADITIONAL CONSTRUCTION OF LATINO FATHERHOOD

As with studies on other minority families, including African Americans, early scholarship on Latino families used the Euro-American family as the template for measuring the behavior of Latinos (Slaughter-Defoe et al., 1990) and was conducted in convenient, small sample sizes primarily living in poverty. In spite of these methodological limitations, these early findings were generalized to all Latinos and used to develop stereotypical and rigid views of these families.

Unlike the traditional view of African American men as absent or marginal figures in their families, the view that emerged from the early studies of Latino fathers portrayed them as being distant, avoiding intimacy, being obsessed with machismo, discipline, and honor, and inspiring fear in their children (Mirande, 1991; Ortiz-Achilla, 1992). In fact, the traditional view of the Latino father (Mirande, 1991) was intimately attached to a mythical and stereotyped understanding of machismo. A *macho* is an aggressive, tyrannical ruler of a household (Mayo, 1997; Mirande, 1991; Powell, 1995) where "the woman is a quiet, submissive, and servile figure" (Mirande, 1991, pp. 59–60). This completely negative stereotype ignores any positive qualities of machismo—being a caring protector and provider (Mayo, 1997).

In general, Latino mother-father relationships are described as being strongly gender differentiated and marked by male dominance and female subservience. Mothers are responsible for caregiving and domestic work, and fathers are the breadwinners, responsible for all matters linking the family to the outside world (e.g., work, participation in school activities). Based on ethnographic work on both rural and urban populations living in poverty in the early 1960s, Latino men were seen as tyrannical rulers, instilling fear in their wives, domineering, demanding respect for elders, and womanizing (Mirande, 1991). Given the different roles that mothers and fathers played in the household, they had different styles of parenting. Whereas fathers punished severely, mothers punished more frequently (Madsen, 1973). The father was seen strictly as the provider and disciplinarian (Borrás, 1989). In the extreme stereotype of Latino families, Latino fathers' relationships with their children were inspired by fear and respect but hardly love (Mirande, 1991).

As observed in other populations, fatherhood among Latinos is viewed here as intrinsically tied to what Thompson and Pleck (1995) call *masculine ideology:* the socially constructed nature of masculinity and the stereotyped, internalized form that accompanies it. The masculine ideology invoked by early researchers of Latino fathers is one in which procreation, but not necessary involvement with the progeny, is integral. There is some evidence suggesting that this might be the case for some Latino male adolescents who father a child under the belief that causing a pregnancy is a marker of manhood (Goodyear et al., 2000; Resnick, Chambliss, & Blum, 1993). However, the generalizability of these findings to any other subgroup of Latino fathers is questionable.

Finally, the early view of minority families in general and Latino families in particular stressed definitions of families and fatherhood based on modernization ideals and classified minority families as "traditional," clinging to outdated norms that would disappear as they would become more modern (i.e., more Anglo-American). The point was that once acculturated and assimilated, Latino families would evolve from traditional ways to the more egalitarian modes of American families (V. Ortiz, 1995, p. 20).

THE EMERGENT CONSTRUCTION OF LATINO FATHERHOOD

Since the early 1990s there has been a growing recognition of the inherent problem in using the Euro-American family to judge the parent-child relationships of Latino families (Roopnarine & Ahmeduzzaman, 1993; Slaughter-Defoe et al., 1990), and this is leading to a new view of Latino fathers and families. While this new work has yet to document how healthy Latino families function given their cultural milieu and minority status, it is moving the field from portraying all Latinos as rigid traditionalists waiting to be acculturated and liberated to a more emergent and diverse view of Latino families.

First, researchers have begun to question the view that all Latino families conform to this authoritarian-traditionalist view. They have challenged the view of the Latino patriarchal family and shown that Latino households in the United States are more egalitarian than the traditional view would lead us to believe (Toth & Xu, 1999). Studies of conjugal decision making and ethnographies have shown that families are more flexible in their division of labor and less rigidly structured along age and gender lines (Mirande, 1991). Women may share some of the decision making and appear to have more visible roles in the household, but they still carry most of the household burden. Latino men may show more nurturance and willingness to take care of their children, but they are not expected to run the household. More important, this emerging research rejects the perception that, in view of what we know about Anglo-American families, racially diverse or ethnic families, such as Latinos, are somehow deviant or defective.

Second, studies of the role of acculturation on Latino families have painted a more complicated and individualistic picture than the universal, linear, positive assimilation processes suggested in the literature. For example, Buriel and his colleagues (1993) have shown that as Mexican American families assimilate, some aspects of family functioning remain the same whereas others change (Sabogal et al., 1987). The work on acculturation in general presents some findings contradictory to the notion that families are better off as they assimilate into mainstream American culture. Data from immigrant studies suggest that Latinos who are recent immigrants have better outcomes (i.e., nutrition, pregnancy, academic achievement, etc.) than do those who have lived here longer and are actually more acculturated (Fuligni, 1998). However, the mechanism of how this happens is unknown (Fuligni & Yoshikawa, 2002). This paradoxical outcome is attributed to a host of variables including the loss of immigrant values of family obligation, the loss of support from extended families, and the adoption of high-risk lifestyles associated with poverty. We can also postulate that as acculturation increases, there is also an increased perception of barriers and discrimination, and as a consequence, individuals might lose motivation to strive for better outcomes. Acculturation and the stress associated with immigration are correlated with decreased family cohesion, problems related to adapting to a changed environment, diminished coping capacity, and lack of satisfaction with family interactions (Weiss, Page, Wilson, & Warda, 1999). The consequences of these processes for parenting among Latino families who vary in human and social capital need to be studied.

An additional consequence of the process of acculturation is the alteration of the link between masculinity and fatherhood. Because many Latino fathers are recent immigrants, the process of fathering in the United States may involve drawing on cultural-ethnic expectations and roles of what fathers do "back home" and at the same time incorporate into these schemata the expectations and values of American culture. How do Latino fathers navigate these two opposing, perhaps even contradictory, systems?

Third, cross-ethnic comparisons of mother and father roles among middle-class respondents suggest that Latino families share commonalities with Anglo-American families. Researchers have argued that Mexican American and Anglo-American parental roles may be more similar than dissimilar (Mejia, 1975; Toth & Xu, 1999). Anglo-American mothers seemed more permissive and Chicano mothers more restrictive, but fathers across both groups did not differ in permissiveness. Although it is difficult to generalize from these small studies to the whole population, it is reasonable to use these data to question and challenge views and perceptions that can explore new ways of understanding Latino families and fathers in particular.

Fourth, Latino men, just as mainstream men, have shown flexibility in adaptation in response to drastic alterations in the traditional role of males due to feminism or demographic changes such as the increased participation of women in the labor force. For example, Chavez (1984) showed that Latino men whose wives were defined as main breadwinners adjusted to their roles of househusbands even when teased by other males. They seemed to accept their new role, maintained a positive masculine self-concept, and saw this status as temporary and emanating from economic necessity (Chavez, 1984). Their wives, however, continued to perform housework. Sanchez (1997) reported egalitarian family patterns among Mexican American families where wife and husband share household responsibilities, child rearing, and decision making. As with trends in the general culture, this is evidence that broader sociodemographic shifts and other cultural changes are transforming gender roles among Latino families as well. In addition to experiencing unique ethnic and cultural continuities and changes, Latino families are experiencing similar changes in gender roles and division of labor as are their counterparts in the mainstream culture.

Finally, there is also evidence that the evolution from traditional to emergent Latino fathers is also taking place in Latin American countries and is more complicated than was previously believed. Guttman (1996) challenged the stereotypical portrayals in his ethnographic study of the meaning of machismo in Mexico City. He found that being a father is tied to the various cultural definitions of masculinity in Mexico, and hence there are diverse fathering practices among Mexicans according to socioeconomic status, generation, ethnicity, and region. Regardless of these differences, however, most fathers believe that the most important role they play in their children's lives is that of provider. Moreover, although there are differences between rich and poor men, there is also tremendous within-group variation. Contrary to other findings, on average, low-income men may spend more time with their children than do middle- and upper-class men (who can hire a *muchacha*—a nanny—to take care of their children).

One of Guttman's (1996) most important findings was that among poor and working-class men, masculinity was defined in part in terms of their active role in parenting: "the practice of fatherhood is central to the notions of many men and women about what it means to be a (good) man" (Guttman, 1996, p. 248). These men define masculinity in part in terms of their active role in parenting. The question that this research poses for Latino fathers in the United States is whether in a different context these men would consider being a father to be part of their masculinity. How will this definition change as acculturation proceeds?

These are critical questions because one important aspect of how cultural context shapes behavior is the set of rewards and incentives that either promote or hinder certain behaviors. Nieto (1983) conducted a small study of Latino fathers in the United States who had assumed sole custody of their children. These men willingly took both parental roles and vowed not to be cold and distant as their own fathers were to them.

Nieto reported that these men were amply rewarded by the Latino family who mobilized resources on their behalf. Cultural constructions of fatherhood can be redefined to adapt to new circumstances as existing resources support new behavioral repertoires that are seen as adaptations to new circumstances yet congruent with other highly valued cultural values (i.e., the importance of child rearing in a highly familistic context).

In sum, earlier studies of Latino families and fathers portrayed a rather distorted view based on small, locality-specific samples and a deficit-modernity framework. Thus the traditional machista-authoritarian, distant, harsh disciplinarian view of the father is in flux. Studies show that this view is being replaced by a more flexible, adaptable, and caring view of Latino men. It is clear that studies conducted in mainstream populations have contributed to the emerging view of the Latino father by showing that men can make significant contributions to the positive development of their children (i.e., Bronstein, 1988). In fact, one of the biggest barriers that Latino men must overcome is the negative stereotype that surrounds them. But the end result is that there are now two images of Latino fathers—traditional and emergent (Mirande, 1991).

FATHER INVOLVEMENT: ARE LATINO FATHERS REALLY INVOLVED?

As we noted before, the paucity of research with Latino fathers and the diversity of the Latino population in the United States make it difficult to formulate generalizations about parenting experiences and practices across and within Latino groups. However, we will draw from the extant, locality-specific studies tentative generalizations of the amount and nature of father involvement in these families.

Consistent with the emergent view of Latinos, recent research supports the view that Chicano fathers are more actively involved than stereotypes predict, even though they do less family work than mothers (R. Ortiz, 1996). In one study that looked at shared and divided parental tasks in school-related and learning experiences in the homes of Mexican American families, researchers found that Latino fathers who shared child-care tasks with their wives were also more likely to read to their children and engage in other learning activities with them than were fathers who divided parental tasks with their wives (R. Ortiz, 1996). There is also a wide range of literacy activities in the home, which is indirectly related to the type of paternal employment. Reese, Gallimore, and Goldenburg (1999) reported that fathers who had jobs where they used literacy also had homes that were coded as "literacy environments," and their children performed higher on a reading task than did children of fathers who were manual laborers.

Using Palkovitz's (1997) three dimensions of father involvement, Toth and Xu (1999) showed that Latino fathers are more likely than White fathers to monitor their children (cognitive) and interact and spend time with them (behavioral). As the authors pointed out, this finding is consistent with the notion of familism that is reflected in strong beliefs about family, child rearing, and family cohesion (Baca Zinn, 1982–1983; Carrasquillo, 1997; Vega, 1990). Like African American parents, Latino fathers emphasize family closeness, respect, and obedience to authority to their children (Carrasquillo, 1997). These attitudes are reflected in how they show affection to their children. Strict Hispanic fathers who emphasize obedience, regardless of socioeconomic factors, seem to be less affectionate toward their children than are their White counterparts. However, these authors report an interaction between race or ethnicity and cultural ideology and values. Although all American fathers who hold traditional family-role ideology are generally more detached from child rearing across the three domains of involvement, this is more so for White than for Hispanic fathers. Fathers who hold nonegalitarian family beliefs show decreases in all three dimensions of father involvement. This finding is greater for White than for Latinos, supporting the emergent view of the Latino father as more egalitarian than was expected.

Moreover, the contemporary or emergent view of Latino families suggests that parents' relationships with their children are more flexible. For example, Zapato and Jaramillo (1981) reported in a small-sample study of Chicano families that parents apportioned responsibilities to children regardless of gender and fathers engaged with their children in a nonauthoritarian way. They also found that children did not categorize what parents did in the house along gender lines; for example, they did not see mothers as being solely responsible for household chores.

A challenge to understanding and conceptualizing parental involvement in the schools among Latino families is defining what education means for them. Education has a different meaning from its Spanish counterpart of *educación*. For Latino families, childrearing values of *educación* include values of respect, obedience, and display of good manners (Reese et al., 1999). These values of *educación* tend to be implemented more when the father is actively involved in domestic routines (Reese, Balzano, Gallimore, & Goldenburg, 1995). Latino parents who want *educación* for their children are generally asking for more than academics. They expect their children to be obedient, respect authority, and generally conform to social norms. This set of expectations and beliefs makes parent's involvement in school and their advocacy on behalf of their children different from what one would expect from Anglo-European families.

Another consideration is that parental involvement in children's education is found to be higher if parents are confident that they can be of assistance to the child, if they believe that the child is capable of doing well in school, and if they have high educational aspirations for the child (Eccles & Harold, 1996). A recent nationally representative study of the educational needs of Latinos revealed that the high school graduation rate for Latinas is lower than for girls in any other racial or ethnic group and that Latinas are the least likely of any group of women to complete a bachelor's degree (Ginorio & Huston, 2000). Latinos fare worse than Latinas. Ginorio and Huston wrote that although Latinos value education, family needs and peer pressure clash with school expectations. Latinas feel pressure from their peers and boyfriends not to be "too educated" and hesitate going away to college because their families will be disrupted.

School policies and teacher practices also have a strong influence on the level of Latino parents' involvement in their children's schools (Delgado-Gaitan, 1991). For Latino parents, the language barrier as well as inflexible work hours might prevent them from participating in school activities. Parental involvement varies by other characteristics of the schools; for example, it tends to be higher in smaller as opposed to larger schools and in private as opposed to public schools (Zill & Nord, 1994). Given the socioeconomic circumstances of most Latino families, Latino parents might not be as involved with their children's schools as their middle-class counterparts. This might be due not only to cultural differences but also to both perceived and actual barriers due to long hours of work, beliefs about schools, other family responsibilities, or school characteristics (Garcia Coll et al., 2002).

It is easier for parents who have high levels of education, engage in literacy activities at home, and have confidence in their ability as parents to guide and motivate their children to get involved in school activities than it is for parents with fewer economic and social resources (Reese, Gallimore, & Goldenburg, 1999). Nonetheless, the evidence suggests that even with those limitations, Latino fathers do get involved in their children's *educación*. There is evidence suggesting that Latino fathers are involved in school activities but that they do it differently than Whites. Latino men report high aspirations for children's academic success and strongly held beliefs of *educación* (Reese et al., 1995). They work hard to support these values and motivate their children to succeed. Reese et al. (1999) used qualitative and quantitative data from a nine-year study of second-generation immigrant Latino youth in low-income, urban California settings that looked at the different contributions of Latino mothers and fathers to their children's school success. Reese et al. found that both mothers and fathers contribute in significant but different ways to children's school performance. Mothers are involved in child care and primarily oversee or are involved in learning activities in the home, whereas fathers provide emotional and moral support. Although these fathers may not engage in specific learning activities with their children, perhaps due to low levels of education, they show support through talking; purchasing clothing, toys, and so on and rewarding performance; and periodically participating in school activities and events.

Other studies suggest that Latino fathers might be involved with their children even before school starts and in other areas of *educación*. In a study that looks at mainland Puerto Rican fathers' involvement with young children in intact middle-class families, Roopnarine and Ahmeduzzaman (1993) hypothesized that personal functioning (warm, helpful, accepting style) and support from others influences parent-child relationships and may also be linked to fathers' involvement in the care of their young children, including child-care settings. These researchers found that Puerto Rican men in their sample spent about 2.7 hours per day as primary caregivers, which was in agreement with mothers' perceptions of paternal involvement. Although wives were the primary caregivers, fathers spent on average about 37% of the time mothers estimated they spent as primary caregivers. Inconsistent with previous research, these men were nurturing and companionable to their children. Moreover, these men showed no preferential involvement in caregiving based on gender of their children. It is interesting that commitment to the family unit was positively correlated with involvement with children. Although fathers' education and income were not associated with paternal involvement, family income was positively correlated with the length of marriage. With greater economic security, fathers' functional styles with the family may have a strong influence on paternal involvement above that of education and income (Roopnarine & Ahmeduzzaman, 1993).

Similarly, Gutmann (1996) observed in urban Mexico how the gender and age of the child and the generation and socioeconomic background of the family had a significant impact on the level and nature of a father's involvement in the children's life. Within low socioeconomic groups, fathers were less involved with younger children, although spot observations showed that carrying infants and toddlers in public places was more the function of the father than of the mother. As children got older, their fathers became sources of guidance—even nurturance in some cases—and spent more time in direct child care. Even in older generations, boys (primarily) were taken by their fathers to their workplace or to visit friends. Fathers were also involved in their children's lives across the life span: Some father-adult son dyads were described as rather close regarding important instances of decision making. This contrasted with the more aloof position of upper-class Mexican fathers, whose children were raised primarily by their wives and nannies.

The process of parenting and becoming an effective parent is fraught with rewards, challenges, and frustrations even under the best of circumstances. In addition to the normal stress of being a parent, Latino fathers face additional challenges, including economic hardship, a language barrier, low education attainment, discrimination, racism, other stresses endemic to all minorities in the United States, and the fact that there is a gap between themselves and their children in terms of how they become acculturated and assimilated into U.S. culture. There is little understanding of how the barriers and challenges that Latino fathers face affect the parenting process over time.

In sum, the studies carried out so far in this area point out a view of father involvement that is congruent with the emerging view of Latino fathers and families in general. Fathers are involved in areas that reflect the cultural construction of their role as providers, primarily, who are also involved in other aspects of their children's lives. It is clear that as in other populations, Latino mothers are in charge of child care and that parents get involved when they are around. But Latino fathers' involvement goes beyond the monetary contribution to the family well-being. Latino fathers can be sources of support and inspiration throughout the life span.

In addition, the role of the mother as a gatekeeper of the father's involvement needs to be ascertained. Leadbeater, Way, and Raden (1996) found that some Puerto Rican mothers wished to limit their children's contact with their nonresident fathers. This was because the mothers perceived the fathers as undermining the limits mothers set and getting the children emotionally upset (depressed or hyper) during their visits. In fact, the findings corroborated the mother's perceptions: More father involvement was associated with more externalizing behaviors in the child. It is our prediction that as we move to measure the quality rather than just the quantity of fathers' involvement, the role of culture and other relational and contextual variables will become even more evident.

The research agenda for this field of inquiry is therefore extensive. It takes considerable resources to change public discourse and research frameworks and alter images that are generally perpetuated in the broader sociocultural context. One such effort, sponsored by the Department of Human Health and Services, occurred about three years ago. The workshop and report were titled "Hispanic Fathers and Family Literacy" (Bernal et al., 2000). The effort included community providers of services for Hispanic fathers, national Hispanic organizations, and literacy programs for advocates for fatherhood. The main purpose of the meeting was to provide information to service providers to help them design and implement programs that promote Hispanic fathers' involvement in their children's lives and to encourage links among various groups interested in strengthening the roles of Hispanic fathers in their children's lives. This was an important effort that provided a forum for the exchange of information. However, it did not link providers with researchers, perhaps because there is little research to draw from.

CONCLUSIONS AND RECOMMENDATIONS

The field of fatherhood research among Latinos is almost nonexistent and lags considerably behind the monumental effort of recent years designed to understand, conceptualize, and measure father involvement in mainstream populations. Whatever research there is on Latino fathers is generally conducted with small, convenient samples and, with few exceptions, lacks the rigor and depth that this type of inquiry merits (e.g., Mirande, 1991). The lack of research is particularly striking given that in less than 50 years, a quarter of the U.S. population is projected to be of Hispanic origin. Given the diversity within Latinos, their unique demographic characteristics, and their relative role in the stratification system of our society, the lack of data on Latino families challenges the theoretical relevance of research on American families so far and questions its applicability to understand and design interventions for this particular population.

The existing research on Latino fathers points to an interesting evolution on how Latino men have been portrayed and researched. The traditional view of Latino fathers is one of a cold, distant, authoritarian father (Mirande, 1991). This fits the traditional portrayal of the Latino family as an "authoritarian, patriarchal unit where the 'macho' (i.e., the father) is lord and master of the household and the woman is a quiet, submissive, servile figure" (Mirande, 1991, p. 59). As discussed earlier, many argue not only that this is inaccurate but also that its perpetuation leads to negative stereotypes and faulty research paradigms and policies (Bernal et al., 2000; Mayo, 1997; Mirande, 1991). The traditional model of Latino families—where mothers take care of home and children and fathers work—is not as universal as was believed. An emergent model (Mirande, 1988) describes the Latino family as more egalitarian and the power of the man as less absolute. Fathers are allowed and expected to be more nurturing, and women can work outside the home. In this respect, Latino fathers and families might be more similar to mainstream populations than was expected; on the other hand, culturally specific adaptations can come about to structural changes in families. These continuities and discontinuities, however, need empirical verification.

In order to have a deep cultural understanding of Latino fathers, we need to look at the roles and functions that men play within their families and the structures that are in place to support them in this important role. Cross-cultural studies in other populations have shown that there is wide cultural variation in terms of who plays the role of fathers. While in some cultures men play this role for all their biological kin (Townsend, 2002), in others this role is played by men who may or may not be biologically related to the children. The role of *compadres*—uncles and other adult males in single, nuclear, or extended families—needs to be ascertained. Similarly, the roles of the child's mother and other family members in supporting or undermining the father's role need to be explored. Finally, the role of unemployment, perceived and actual racism, and other sources of oppression on fathers need to be simultaneously considered because mainstream and many Latino groups differ not only culturally but also in minority status. Unlike with White families, the experience that Latinos, African Americans, and other minority families have with racism—both historically and its contemporary manifestations—is reflected in their approach to parenting. Parents are aware that their children will encounter racism and discrimination and hence prepare their children to deal with it (LeMasters & Defrain, 1983). Purging culture—language, beliefs, expectations, roles, and aspirations—and other contextual influences from research lead us to information that is inaccurate and uninformative. Research needs to move us away from an Anglo-American view of parenting to encompass a more ecological understanding of what specific groups of Latino fathers do as fathers.

In addition, Latino fathers may fulfill their parental roles in ways that are different from Anglo-American families. For example, storytelling is a rich tradition among Latino families. A father may spend time telling stories to his children but not reading. If our research emphasizes reading to the child (many fathers may be illiterate) but does not include telling stories, Latino fathers may look less involved or supportive (Bernal et al., 2000). Qualitative or more exploratory quantitative studies might inform us of what Latino fathers and families can do rather that what they do not do based on a middle-class Anglo-American framework.

We close this chapter making the same plea we made at the beginning of this chapter. There is an urgent need to improve our database on Latino families. There is a great need for studies with nationally representative samples that include large numbers of various Latino subgroups so that analyses within and across groups are possible. These studies need to employ theoretical paradigms and methodologies that capture not only the cultural context but also the consequences of being a member of a minority group in the United States (Erkut et al., in press; Garcia Coll et al., 1996). This plea does not in any way diminish the need for rigorous qualitative and ethnographic studies that can generate hypotheses and provide flesh for the statistics. The plea for national data, however, is critical if we are to understand how Latino men father, how they make a difference in their children's lives, what types of barriers and challenges they face as they develop into their roles as men and as fathers, and how we can link research-generated data to appropriate policies and interventions. We are in urgent need of small- and large-scale studies if we are to make progress in this field.

REFERENCES

Baca Zinn, M. (1982–1983). Familism among Chicanos: A theoretical review. *Humboldt Journal of Social Relations, 10,* 224–238.

Bean, F., & Tienda, M. (1987). *The Hispanic population of the United States.* New York: Russell Sage Foundation.

Becker, G. S. (1981, February). Altruism in the family and selfishness in the market place. *Economica, 48,* 1–15.

Bernal, V., Gilmore, L. A., Mellgren, L., Melendez, J., Seleme-McDermott, C., & Vazquez, L. (2000, December). Hispanic fathers and family literacy: Strengthening achievement in Hispanic communities. U.S. Department of Health and Human Services. Hispanic Association of Colleges and Universities. National Practitioners Network for Fathers and Families. Washington, DC: U.S. Department of Health and Human Services.

Bond, J. T., Galinski, E., & Swanberg, J. E. (1998). *1997 study of a changing workforce.* Washington, DC: Family and Work Institute.

Borrás, V. A. (1989). Dual discipline role of the single Puerto Rican women head of household. In C. T. Garcia Coll & M. de Lourdes Mattei (Eds.), *The psychological development of Puerto Rican women* (pp. 200–213). New York: Praeger.

Bronfenbrenner, U. (1986). Ecology of the family as a context for human development: Research perspectives. *Developmental Psychology, 20,* 1074–1081.

Bronstein, P. (1988). Father-child interaction: Implications for gender-role socialization. In P. Bronstein & C. P. Cowan (Eds.), *Fatherhood today: Men's changing role in the family* (pp. 107–124). New York: Wiley.

Buriel, R. (1993). Childrearing orientations in Mexican American families: The influence of generation and sociocultural factors. *Journal of Marriage and the Family, 55*, 987–1000.

Buriel, R., Mercado, R., Rodriguez, J., & Chavez, J. M. (1991). Mexican American disciplinary practices and attitudes toward child maltreatment: A comparison of foreign- and native-born mothers. *Hispanic Journal of Behavioral Sciences, 13*, 78–94.

Cabrera, N., Tamis-LeMonda, C., Bradley, B., Hofferth, S., & Lamb, M. E. (2000). Fatherhood in the twenty-first century. *Child Development, 71*, 127–136.

Cabrera, N., Brooks-Gunn, J., Moore, K., West, J., Boller, K., & Tamis-LaMonda, C. S. (2002). Bridging research and policy: Including fathers of young children in national studies. In C. S. Tamis-LaMonda & N. Cabrera (Eds.), *Handbook of father involvement: Multidisciplinary perspectives* (pp. 489–524). Mahwah, NJ: Erlbaum.

Carrasquillo, H. (1997). Puerto Rican families in America. In M. K. DeGenova (Ed.), *Families in cultural context* (pp. 155–172). Mountain View, CA: Mayfield.

Casper, L. M., & Bianchi, S. M. (2002). *Continuity and change in the American family.* Thousand Oaks, CA: Sage.

Chavez, V. (1984). *Hispanic househusbands.* Unpublished manuscript.

Coleman, J. (1988). Social capital in the creation of human capital. *American Journal of Sociology, 94*, 95–120.

Coley, R. L. (2001, September). (In)visible men: Emerging research on low-income, unmarried, and minority fathers. *American Psychologist, 56*(9), 743–753.

Davis-Kean, P. E., Eccles, J. S., & Schnabel, K. U. (2002, August). *How the home environment socializes a child: The influence of SES on child outcomes.* Paper presented at the International Society for the Study of Behavioral Development, Ottawa, Canada.

Delgado-Gaitan, C. (1991). Involving parents in the schools: A process of empowerment. *American Journal of Education, 100*, 20–46.

Eccles, J. S., & Harold, R. D. (1996). In A. Booth & J. F. Dunn (Eds.), *Family-school links: How do they affect educational outcomes?* (pp. 3–34). Hillsdale, NJ: Erlbaum.

Elster, A. B., Lamb, M. E., & Tavaré, J. (1987). Association between behavioral and school problems and fatherhood in a national sample of adolescent youths. *Journal of Pediatrics, 111*, 932–936.

Erkut, S., Szalacha, L. A., & Garcia Coll, C. (in press). A framework for studying minority youth's transitions to fatherhood: The case of Puerto Rican young men. *Adolescence.*

Fuligni, A. J. (1998, August). The adjustment of children from immigrant families. *Current Directions in Psychological Science, 7*, 121–140.

Fuligni, A. J., & Yoshikawa, H. (2002). *Investments in children among immigrant families.* Conference draft for the Joint Center for Poverty Research Summer Institute. Chicago, IL.

Garcia Coll, C. T., & Vazquez Garcia, H. (1996). Definitions of competence during adolescence: Lessons from Puerto Rican adolescent mothers. In D. Cicchetti & S. Toth (Eds.), *Adolescence: Opportunities and challenges* (Vol. 7, pp. 283–308). Rochester, NY: University of Rochester Press.

Garcia Coll, C. T., Lamberty, G., Jenkins, R., McAdoo, H. M., Crnic, K., Wasik, B., et al. (1996). An integrative model for the study of developmental competencies in minority children. *Child Development, 67*, 1891–1914.

Ginorio, A. B., & Huston, M. (2000). *!Si, se puede! Yes, we can: Latinas in school.* Washington, DC: American Association of University Women.

Goodyear, R. K., Newcomb, M. D., & Allison, R. D. (2000). Predictors of Latino men's paternity in teen pregnancy: Test of a mediational model of childhood experiences, gender role attitudes, and behaviors. *Journal of Counseling Psychology, 47,* 116–128.

Guttman, M. C. (1996). Imaginary fathers, genuine fathers. In M. C. Guttman (Ed.), *The meaning of being macho: Being a man in Mexico City* (pp. 50–88). Thousand Oaks, CA: Sage.

Harwood, R. L., Miller, A. J. M., Carlson, V. J., & Leyendecker, B. (2002). Parenting beliefs and practices among middle-class Puerto Rican mother-infant pairs. In J. M. Contreras, K. A. Kerns, & A. M. Neal-Barnett (Eds.), *Latino children and families in the United States* (pp. 133–154). Westport, CT: Praeger.

Hofferth, S. L. (1999). Receipt of public assistance by Mexican American and Cuban American children in native and immigrant families. In D. Hernandez (Ed.), *Children of immigrants: Health, adjustment, and public assistance* (pp. 546–583). Washington, DC: National Academy Press.

Jayakody, R., & Kalil, A. (2002, May). Social fathering in low-income, African-American families with preschool. *Journal of Marriage and Family, 64,* 504–516.

Kane, N. (Ed.). (1993). *The Hispanic-American almanac: A reference work on Hispanics in the United States.* Detroit, MI: Gale Research.

Lamb, M. E. (Ed.). (1987). *The father's role: Cross-cultural perspectives.* Hillsdale, NJ: Erlbaum.

Lamb, M. E., Pleck, J. H., Charnov, E. L., & Levine, J. A. (1985). A biosocial perspective on paternal behavior and involvement. In J. B. Lancaster, J. Altaman, A. Rossi, & R. L. Sherrod (Eds.), *Parenting across the lifespan: Biosocial perspectives* (pp. 11–42). New York: Academic.

Leadbeater, B. J., Way, N., & Raden, A. (1996). Why not marry your baby's father? Answers from African American and Hispanic adolescent mothers. In B. J. Leadbeater & N. Way (Eds.), *Urban girls: Resisting stereotypes, creating identities* (pp. 193–209). New York: New York University Press.

Lee, S. M. (1993). Racial classification in the U.S. census: 1890–1990. *Ethnic and Racial Studies, 16,* 85–95.

LeMasters, E. E., & Defrain, J. (1983). *Parents in contemporary America: A sympathetic view* (4th ed.). Homewood, IL: Dorsey.

Lerman, R. I. (1993). A national profile of young unwed fathers. In R. I. Lermans & T. J. Ooms (Eds.), *Young unwed fathers: Changing roles and emerging prospects* (pp. 27–51). Philadelphia: Temple University Press.

Madsen, W. (1973). *The Mexican-American of South Texas.* New York: Holt, Reinhart, & Winston.

Mayo, Y. (1997). Machismo, fatherhood, and the Latino family: Understanding the concept. *Journal of Multicultural Social Work, 5*(1/2), 46–91.

McAdoo, J. L. (1993). The roles of African American fathers: An ecological perspective. *Families in Society, 74,* 28–35.

McLanahan, S., Garfinkel, I., Brooks-Gunn, J., Zhao, H., Johnson, W., & Rich, L. (1998). *Unwed fathers and fragile families.* (Working Paper No. 98-12). Center on Research on Child Wellbeing.

Mejia, D. P. (1975). *Cross-ethnic father roles: Perceptions of middle class Anglo-American and Mexican-American parents.* Unpublished doctoral dissertation, University of California, Irvine.

Mirande, A. (1988). Chicano fathers: Traditional perceptions and current realities. In P. Bronstein & C. P. Cowan (Eds.), *Fatherhood today: Men's changing role in the family* (pp. 93–106). New York: Wiley.

Mirande, A. (1991). Ethnicity and fatherhood. In F. W. Bozett & S. M. H. Hanson (Eds.), *Fatherhood and families in cultural context* (pp. 53–81). New York: Springer.

Nelson, T. J., Clampet-Lundquist, S., & Edin, K. (2002). Sustaining fragile fatherhood: Father involvement among low-income, noncustodial African-American fathers in Philadelphia. In

C. S. Tamis-LeMonda & N. Cabrera (Eds.), *Handbook of father involvement: Multidisciplinary perspectives* (pp. 525–553). Mahwah, NJ: Erlbaum.

Nelson, T. J., Edin, K., & Torres, K. (2001, March). *Unplanned but not accidental: Low-income, non-custodial fathers' participation in childbearing decisions.* Paper presented at the annual meeting of the Population Association of America, Washington, DC.

Nieto, D. S. (1983). Hispanic fathers: The growing phenomena of single fathers keeping their children. *National Hispanic Journal, 1,* 15–19.

Ogbu, J. (1983). Minority status and schooling in plural societies. *Comparative Education Review, 27,* 168–190.

Ortiz, R. (1996). Father's contribution to children's early literacy development: The relationship of marital role functions. *Journal of Educational Issues of Language Minority Students, 16,* 131–148.

Ortiz, V. (1995). The diversity of Latino families. In R. E. Zambrana (Ed.), *Latino families: Scholarship, policy, and practice* (pp. 18–39). Thousand Oaks, CA: Sage.

Ortiz-Achilla, S. (1992). Families in Puerto Rico: An analysis of the socialization process from a macrostructural perspective. In J. L. Roopnarine & B. Carter (Eds.), *Parent-child socialization in diverse cultures* (pp. 159–171). Norwood, NJ: Ablex.

Palkovitz, R. (1997). Reconstructing "involvement": Expanding conceptualizations of men's caring in contemporary families. In A. J. Hawkins & D. C. Dollahite (Eds.), *Generative fathering: Beyond deficit perspectives* (pp. 200–216). Thousand Oaks, CA: Sage.

Palkovitz, R. (2002). *Involved fathering and men's adult development.* Mahwah, NJ: Erlbaum.

Pirog-Good, M. A. (1995). The family background and attitudes of teen fathers. *Youth and Society, 26,* 351–376.

Pirog-Good, M. A. (1996). The education and labor market outcomes of adolescent fathers. *Youth and Society, 28,* 236–262.

Pleck, E. H., & Pleck, J. H. (1997). Fatherhood ideals in the United States: Historical dimensions. In M. E. Lamb (Ed.), *The role of the father in child development* (3rd ed., pp. 33–48). New York: Wiley.

Powell, D. R. (1995). Including Latino fathers in parent education and support programs: Development of a program model. In R. E. Zambrana (Ed.), *Understanding Latino families: Scholarship, policy, and practice* (pp. 85–106). Thousand Oaks, CA: Sage.

Ramirez, R. (2000). *The Hispanic population in the United States (P20-527).* Washington, DC: Census Bureau, Department of Commerce.

Reese, L., Balzano, S., Gallimore, R., & Goldenburg, C. (1995). The concept of educación: Latino family values and American schooling. *International Journal of Educational Research, 23,* 57–81.

Reese, L., Gallimore, R., & Goldenburg, C. (1999). *Job required literacy, home literacy environments, and school reading: Early literacy experiences of immigrant Latino children.* Manuscript submitted for publication.

Resnick, M. D., Chambliss, S. A., & Blum, R. W. (1993). Health and risk behaviors of urban adolescent males involved in pregnancy. *Families in Society, 74,* 366–374.

Roopnarine, J. L., & Ahmeduzzaman, M. (1993, February). Puerto Rican fathers' involvement with their preschool-age children. *Hispanic Journal of Behavioral Sciences, 15,* 96–107.

Roopnarine, J. L., & Carter, B. (Eds.). (1992). *Parent-child socialization in diverse cultures.* Norwood, NJ: Ablex.

Sabogal, F., Marin, C., & Otero-Sabogal, R. (1987). Hispanic familism and acculturation: What changes and what doesn't. *Hispanic Journal of Behavioral Sciences, 9,* 397–412.

Salgado de Snyder, V. N., Cervantes, R. C., & Padilla, A. M. (1990). Gender and ethnic differences in psychosocial stress and generalized distress among Hispanics. *Sex Roles, 22,* 441–453.

Sanchez, Y. M. (1997). Families of Mexican origin. In M. K. DeGenova (Ed.), *Families in cultural context* (pp. 61–83). Mountain View, CA: Mayfield.

Slaughter-Defoe, D. T., Nakagawa, K., Takanishi, R., & Johnson, D. J. (1990). Toward cultural/ecological perspectives on schooling and achievement in African- and Asian-American children. *Child Development, 61,* 363–383.

Shannon, J. D., Tamis-LeMonda, C. S., London, K., & Cabrera, N. (2002, April–June). Beyond rough and tumble: Low-income fathers' interactions and children's cognitive development at 24 months. *Parenting: Science and Practice, 2,* 77–104.

Suarez-Orozco, M. M., & Paez, M. (Eds.). (2002). *Latinos: Remaking America.* Berkeley: University of California Press.

Summers, J. A., Raikes, H., & Butler, J. (1999). Low-income fathers' and mothers' perceptions of the father role: A qualitative study in four Early Head Start communities. *Infant Mental Health Journal, 20,* 291–304.

Therrien, M., & Ramirez, R. (2000). *The Hispanic population in the United States (P20-527).* Washington, DC: Census Bureau, Department of Commerce.

Thompson, E. H., & Pleck, J. H. (1995). Masculinity ideology: A review of research instrumentation on men and masculinities. In R. F. Levant & W. S. Pollack (Eds.), *A new psychology of men* (pp. 129–163). New York: Basic Books.

Tienda, M., & Wilson, F. D. (1992). Nativity, gender, and earnings discrimination. *Hispanic Journal of Behavioral Sciences, 14,* 134–143.

Toth, J. F., & Xu, X. (1999, September). Ethnic and cultural diversity in fathers' involvement: A racial/ethnic comparison of African American, Hispanic American, and White fathers. *Youth and Society, 31,* 76–99.

Townsend, N. W. (2002). *The package deal: Marriage, work, and fatherhood in men's lives.* Philadelphia: Temple University Press.

U.S. Bureau of the Census. (2000, March). *The Hispanic population in the United States: Current Population Reports (P20-535).* Washington, DC: U.S. Department of Commerce.

Vega, W. A. (1990). Hispanic families in the 1980s: A decade of research. *Journal of Marriage and the Family, 52,* 1015–1024.

Ventura, S. J., Bachrach, C. A., Hill, L., Kaye, K., Holcomb, P., & Koff, E. (1995). *The demography of out-of-wedlock childbearing: Report to Congress on out-of-wedlock childbearing.* Washington, DC: Department of Health and Human Services.

Weiss, S. J., Page, A., Wilson, P., & Warda, M. (1999). The impact of cultural and familial context on behavioral and emotional problems of preschool Latino children. *Child Psychiatry and Human Development, 29,* 287–301.

Zambrana, R. E. (Ed.). (1995). *Understanding Latino families.* Thousand Oaks, CA: Sage.

Zapato, J. T., & Jaramillo, P. T. (1981). The Mexican American family: An Adlerian perspective. *Hispanic Journal of Behavioral Sciences, 3,* 275–290.

Zill, N., & Nord, C. W. (1994). *Running in place: How American families are faring in a changing economy and an individualistic society.* Washington, DC: NCES.

CHAPTER 5

Social Science and Public Policy Perspectives on Fatherhood in the European Union

MARGARET O'BRIEN

AMONG SOCIAL SCIENCE and public policy makers in Europe, there is increasing awareness of the complex and contradictory nature of contemporary fatherhood. Although some commentators portray a model of fatherhood in transition through the erosion of patriarchal fatherhood and an emergent caring father ideal (Björnberg, 1992), others focus on the idea of fatherhood in crisis, a state where men are unable either to care or provide cash for their families (Hobson, 2002). The rights and wrongs of this European fatherhood debate are hampered somewhat by the relative lack of comparative empirical studies of fatherhood across Europe and by the continued tendency of official European statistical sources to omit analysis by men's parental status. Nevertheless, changes in employment and family structure and the growing multiethnic and multifaith character of contemporary Europe are creating new socioeconomic and cultural contexts for negotiating what it means to be a father. In everyday life, traditional dimensions of the good father, such as providing for the material welfare of the family, take place alongside practices that were previously considered solely maternal, such as bathing infants. European fatherhood is therefore in the process of reconstruction and transformation.

Just as the negotiation of tradition and change is at the heart of contemporary fatherhood in Europe, so too the nature of Europe itself is in transition. This nation of nations, as it were, has experienced significant political changes in its landscape since the disruption of the Second World War, from the formation of the European Economic Community (EEC; now European Union, EU) in 1956, to the transformation of Eastern European states in the post-Communist era of the late 1980s and early 1990s. Originally consisting of six Western European nations, the EU has expanded to 15 member states with 10 further candidate countries, mainly from Central and Eastern Europe, joining in 2004. The growing scale and size of Europe with its diverse set of languages and cultural traditions should make any scholar wary of assuming a homogeneous European father. However, increased democratization of the father's position in the family, through the decline in patriarchal sociological structures and processes, and an increasing marginalization of fathers from family life, particularly through the rise in lone motherhood, have been dominant trends in Europe during the last century.

In the first section of this chapter the demographic context of fatherhood is reviewed to examine how changing patterns of fertility, partnership formation and breakdown, family structure, migration, and employment in Europe have influenced men's parenting roles. This demographic framework highlights the general importance of understanding the increasingly complex and diverse contexts in which men negotiate fatherhood over their life courses. The second section of the chapter reviews current European theoretical models of fathering and their link with empirical inquiry. Social science research into fatherhood still remains at a low critical mass in Europe although there are signs of a reawakening of interest. The chapter ends with a focus on how European parental-leave policies have developed to help fathers manage their work and family lives. Whereas fatherhood has rarely been a central plank of European family policy, it will be shown how the range of parental-leave schemes developed within Europe since the mid-1970s reveal implicit assumptions about the role of the father in family life.

FATHERS AND THE EUROPEAN DEMOGRAPHIC CONTEXT

Any discussion of fatherhood in Europe must place men's family roles and responsibilities in the context of the more general demographic trends in Europe. At the turn of the 21st century, the key European demographic trends in which fatherhood is embedded are creating a complex set of family contexts.

DECLINE IN FERTILITY

Since the 1970s, the tendency in the more affluent and industrialized areas of Europe has been to have fewer children. The present EU fertility rate is 1.4 children per female (Eurostat, 2002a). Many EU countries now have a fertility rate below replacement level. The general decline in fertility has occurred for a range of reasons as men and women are either deciding not to have children, are delaying the arrival of children in their lives, or are having only one child. As more men are not having children either by choice or circumstance, one consequence will be the decreasing stock of fathers across Europe.

Comparative analysis has shown that in some European nations, living without children has become normative for significant parts of the adult life course. For example, couples living without children make up more than half of all couples in Denmark, Sweden, and the Netherlands (*Women and Men in Europe and North America*, 2000). The proportion of childless individuals has also increased for younger generations (*Women and Men in Europe and North America*, 2000). However, unlike women, men of course can continue to father children later in life, and in several European countries 7% to 10% of births occur to fathers who are over 40 years of age (*Women and Men in Europe and North America*, 2000).

Aging of the Population

Recent analysis (Eurostat, 2000) shows that the EU population continues to age. In 2000 there were 61 million people aged 65 and over in the EU compared with only 34 million in 1960. In fact, elderly people make up 16% of the total EU population, and this proportion is expected to rise to 27% in 2010. On the economic front, this aging trend could cause future contraction of the working adult population with potential negative economic consequences unless retirement ages are changed. As far as European fathers are concerned, one consequence is likely to be a growing pressure to work more hours for longer periods in order to support families economically, a pattern already apparent in the United States (Polatnick, 2000). This structural factor of an ageing population may inhibit any movement toward reducing fathers' working hours, which has become an important dimension in the new caring-father ideal. A further aspect of the ageing process may be that as the life course expands for men, there is less time pressure to embark on significant life stages such as leaving home and getting married or partnered at a young age. Again there is evidence that in some European countries, particularly in the south, young men are living with parents longer (e.g., in Spain, Greece, and Italy the proportions of men aged 25–29 years living with parents increased from 51% to 65% between 1986 and 1994; Deven, Inglis, Moss, & Petrie, 1998), and, as will be seen shortly, men are getting married at a later age.

Patterns of Marriage, Cohabitation, and Divorce

In the latter part of the 20th century, marriage rates, particularly first marriage rates, have declined while cohabitation rates have increased across Europe. Although a majority of Europeans marry at least once in their lives, the proportion of the population that is married has reduced (*Women and Men in Europe and North America*, 2000). For instance, in the United Kingdom the percentage of married men declined from 71% of all adults over 16 in 1971 to 53% in 2000 (*Social Trends*, 2002). Across Europe the average age at first marriage for men and women has increased.

In some Nordic countries, notably Denmark, Norway, and Sweden, cohabitation is becoming an alternative to marriage. In the United Kingdom, where cohabitation is not at the high level of Nordic countries, the proportion of men cohabiting has more than doubled between 1986 and 1998/9 from 11% of men aged 16 to 59 years to 26% (Matheson & Summerfield, 2001). The increase in consensual unions has led to a growth in extramarital childbirth across Europe, with particularly high rates in the Nordic countries and lower rates in the southern European countries of Italy, Spain, and Greece (*Social Trends*, 2002).

Clearly, for increasing numbers of European men, marriage is no longer the prerequisite for parenthood; fatherhood is taking place in an increasing diversity of partnership settings. One consequence is that the differentiation of the partnership context can influence the timing and onset of fatherhood. For instance, in many European countries, men who get married are more likely to have children at an older age than are men who cohabit, although this difference will tend to reduce as cohabitation rates becomes more normative. In addition, not all children conceived in nonmarital unions live in couple-headed households; some are children born to lone mothers or mothers with nonresident partners. The growth of nonmarital childbearing indicates a further movement toward the marginalization of biological fathers from the lives of their children. Indeed, Clarke and Cooksey (1999) found that in both the United Kingdom and the United States, being unmarried and having children under 25 years were two key risk factors associated with fathers living apart from their children.

The increase in divorce and repartnering toward the end of the last century in Europe is a further demographic change shaping contemporary fatherhood. Although divorce rates have stabilized, and even declined, in several European countries linked to the decline in marriage rates (*Women and Men in Europe and North America*, 2000), divorce, separation of consensual unions, and repartnering have changed the nature of fathers' families. Throughout their life course, fathers are now more likely than in previous generations to experience more than one family type (*serial fathering*), and in the process fathers typically cease to reside with the children of their first relationship, which increases the potential for marginalization. For some fathers, however, there is also the potential for a diversification of fathering roles as they develop new ways of relating to children across different households and networks of family relationships.

Household and Family Structure

One implication of the demographic changes described so far is that European fatherhood is less likely to take place within the traditional nuclear family household. In comparison to previous cohorts of fathers, future cohorts will experience less time with a married partner and biological children and more transitions into and out of household types. Across Europe the proportion of households composed of couples and dependent children has declined (Eurostat, 2000), although rates vary from Denmark, where this household form constitutes 40.1% of couple households, to Ireland, where it makes up 74.3% (*Women and Men in Europe and North America*, 2000). Clearly, there is and will continue to be more diversity in fathers' lifetime family experiences.

Migration and Mobility

A further demographic feature of Europe in recent times has been the growth in migration across national frontiers. These movements in population increased after the political transformation in Eastern Europe in the late 1980s and more recently have intensified following political and economic upheavals in Africa and Asia. Recent analysis indicates that in the last five years, 70% of the growth in the EU population has been generated by international in-migration as fertility rates tend to be higher among minority ethnic groups (Eurostat, 2000). As Halsey (2000, p. 18), a British sociologist, has commented, when these cohorts age, the "Britain of the twenty-first century will be multiethnic," as will be the case for wider Europe. As far as fatherhood is concerned, social scientists and public policy makers will need to be aware of diverse models of fatherhood aspired to by different ethnic and faith groups. An increased visibility of distinctive religious philosophies, in particular Islam in Europe, has shown the continuing relevance of a more patriarchal model of fatherhood for many contemporary communities (Pels, 2000), which complicates linear theories of modernization. This migration context stresses the importance of sensitivity to cultural variation in fathering behaviors in future research activity. Furthermore, the extent to which parental behavior in these new cultural groups converges with preexisting demographic tendencies, such as the rise in maternal employment, is an issue for future investigation.

THE EMPLOYMENT CONTEXT FOR FATHERS IN EUROPE

As is the case for fathers across most advanced economies globally, a major change for European fathers has been the increased labor participation of their partners. The employment activity rates of European women have continually increased since the 1970s. As indicated in the Eurostat (2000a), after a dip for men in the early 1990s, employment rates have in fact increased for both men and women over the last five years: The proportion of women aged 15 to 64 in employment increased from 49.5% in 1994 to 52.5% in 1999, and the respective proportions for men were 70.5% to 71.5%. Accordingly, the proportion of dual-earner families has expanded throughout Europe with higher rates in the Nordic countries, France, the Netherlands, Austria, Portugal, and the United Kingdom and lower rates in Greece, Spain, and Italy (Eurostat, 2002a; see Table 5.1). Therefore, across Europe the couple family is now most likely to be a two-earner family with the traditional male full-time breadwinner accounting for a decreasing proportion of cases.

More women are having shorter gaps away from work after the arrival of children when compared to previous cohorts of women, and across Europe more mothers are working full-time (Rubery, Smith, & Fagan, 1999). These changes in maternal employment occurred earlier in the Nordic countries so that by the late 1990s Sweden, Finland, and Denmark had the smallest differences in economic activity between

Table 5.1
Employment Patterns in Couples with Children in the European Union
(% of couples with at least one partner working)

Country		One Earner		Two Earner	
		Male PT, Female PT	Male PT, Female FT	Male FT, Female PT	Male FT, Female FT
Belgium	27.3	1.9	1.7	28.3	40.8
Germany	39.7	0.6	0.7	32.9	26.1
Spain	56.3	0.2	0.4	7.5	35.6
France	36.0	1.2	1.1	16.3	45.4
Ireland	55.5	1.1	—	16.2	27.1
Italy	53.6	1.3	0.9	13.0	31.2
Luxembourg	51.2	—	—	23.2	25.7
Netherlands	32.7	2.3	1.3	52.9	10.8
Austria	32.6	—	0.9	27.7	38.8
Portugal	26.5	—	—	7.0	66.5
United Kingdom	29.8	0.7	0.9	40.0	28.6

Note: Full-time is defined as 30 hours or more worked per week. Data are from 2000, with the following exceptions: 1997 for Ireland and 1999 for the United Kingdom and Luxembourg.
Source: Adapted from Eurostat (2002b).

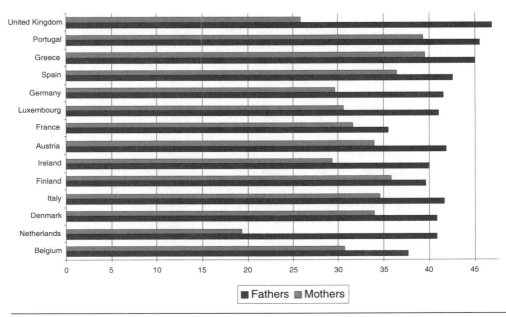

Figure 5.1   Average hours of paid work per week for fathers and mothers with children under 17 years in 15 EU nations in 1995, excluding Sweden.

Note: Denmark = parents with child under 10 years.

Source: Adapted from Deven et al. (1998).

parents. The majority of employed Finnish and Danish mothers of young children under 11 work full-time, as do about 50% of Swedish and Norwegian mothers with children under 7 years (Deven et al., 1998; Leira, 1999). As Hantrais and Letablier (1996, p. 176) commented, "the Nordic countries, like North America, have been setting trends which are subsequently followed by the member states in the centre of the Union and then by the south European countries."

Fathers' employment behavior across Europe has been rarely analyzed with the notable exception of the innovative work of the EC Childcare Network (European Commission Network on Childcare, 1996). The most recent analysis of the 1997 data set shows that fatherhood tends to increase men's economic activity in that fathers' employment is usually at a higher level than that of nonfathers in each European nation (Deven et al., 1998). Similarly, nearly all fathers work full-time rather than part-time. The average weekly working hours vary between fathers in different European countries; the longest hours were worked in the United Kingdom (46.9 hours per week), which was about 15% longer than the average working week for Belgian and Danish fathers (Figure 5.1). More recent analyses suggest that by 2001 the average number of hours worked by British fathers had remained high (46.1 hours a week) and the average hours worked by British mothers had increased to 27.8 hours a week from 25.8 hours a week in 1995 (O'Brien & Shemilt, 2003). These working hours are not as high as are those in the United States, where fathers and mothers work on average 50.9 hours and 41.4 hours a week, respectively, including commuter time (Polatnik, 2000). This increase in parental working hours for fathers and mothers combined and its impact on family relationships has become a key public policy issue in Europe. The increased participation of women in the European labour market alongside continually high paternal working hours has added impetus to policies promoting the reconciliation of work and family life—in particular, the wish to reduce working hours. In France during the late 1990s the socialist government responded to these anxieties about work intensification and introduced the 35-hour working week, hoping also that the measure would help reduce high levels of unemployment. Thirty-five hours became the legal standard working week on January 1, 2000, but the law was rescinded in 2002 with the arrival of a new government. While there were many media accounts of increased family and leisure time, dissatisfaction with the measure from blue-collar workers reliant on overtime was also reported. A systematic evaluation of the impact of the French working hours experiment on family life has yet to be written.

However, recent analysis of work satisfaction in 15 EU member states and Norway (Fagan, 2000) showed that 61% of men with children under 6 years want to work fewer hours, a higher level than men in general (54% of men with no young children in the household also wished to reduce their working hours). For all respondents, male and female, as working hours increased, so did the desire to reduce working hours. For those men and women working 50 hours or more, 79% and 82% of men and women respectively wished to decrease their time at work.

Summary

In conclusion, this review of the demographic context of fatherhood in Europe has revealed that patterns of change and continuity coexist. The increase in nonmarital child bearing, relationship breakdown, and repartnering over the last 30 years means that there is less permanency in fathers' relationships to their adult partners and biological children. In comparison to previous cohorts, future cohorts of European fathers will experience less time in the lifelong marriage form of the nuclear family. However, the extent of demographic change in the family life of European fathers should not be exaggerated, as most children still spend their childhood in a stable relationship setting (Clarke, 1996). This section also highlighted that the growth in maternal participation in the labor market and in particular the increase in maternal working hours has created new challenges for contemporary fathers and mothers across Europe. A key issue for parents is how to balance economic provision with caring responsibilities for children. Public policy makers in Europe are no longer approaching work-family balance as purely a mother's issue, and as a consequence the dilemmas of the working father are receiving more attention. This trend toward father-sensitive family policies in Europe is reviewed in the next section.

STUDIES OF FATHERS IN EUROPE

Empirical studies of fathers and their family relationships remain at a low critical mass in Europe, and comparative studies of European fathers are even rarer (Edwards, Back-Wiklund, Bak, & Ribben, 2002). As in the United States, early interest in European fatherhood research dates back to the late 1970s and early 1980s, particularly though not exclusively from British scholars (e.g., Hwang, 1987; Lewis & O'Brien, 1986; McKee & O'Brien, 1982; Sandqvist, 1987), but it did not expand as quickly or as deeply as did U.S. scholarship. This first wave of fatherhood research from psychologists and sociologists was embedded primarily in a discovery mode and was subsequently influenced by the lively new father–new man debate, prominent in both Europe and the United States during the 1980s (Lamb, 1987). Social science commentaries and empirical studies represented a behavioral and academic exploration of the widening range of family lifestyle options newly available to fathers (Delaisi de Parseval & Hurstel, 1987; New & Benigni, 1987; Nickel & Kocher, 1987; Nugent, 1987). Firsthand accounts of men's family life or life course transitions, such as becoming a father or caring for children alone, indicated that men could experience these events in an emotionally intense manner, showing behaviors that did not fit into the stereotype of the distant, disengaged father. A common theme in this early European work was to uncover more about the *meaning* of being a father—in particular, how men were responding to new expectations about their parenting (Clarke & O'Brien, 2003). As Bertaux and Delcroix (1992, p. 185), commenting on French family life, suggested, "The children of today grope for a relationship with their daddy as a human being not as an authoritative figure. 'The father of duty' (*pere de devoir*) leaves the scene; enter the 'loving father' (*pere de coeur*)." The so-called detraditionalization of fatherhood has been an implicit strand in European social policy and family analysis, where fathers are conceptualized as moving from an ascribed to an achieved status (Jensen, 1999). European writers such as Beck and Beck-Gernsheim (2001) have argued that in modern societies individuals are less likely to adopt prescribed roles governed by collective historical traditions but now have more cultural and personal freedom to construct personal identities (the process of individualization). It is suggested that the declining influence of paternal models of provision and power has confronted fathers with a "complex diversity of choices" about how to conduct their personal relationships (Giddens, 1991, p. 80). In Europe theoretical models of fathering, usually implicit in more general theories of family and societal change, have been generated in advance of detailed empirical inquiry. The next section explores the extent to which the theoretical models of fathering are borne out by empirical indicators.

Fatherhood in Europe: Juggling Diversity?

Despite a dominant gender equity agenda in Europe focused on how much time men contribute to child care, there is surprisingly little comparative analysis at a European level. A new resource, provided by the European Community Household Panel (ECHP) data set, is showing some potential for more detailed cross-national examination of the extent of father's involvement in child care. Using this data set, Smith (2002) found evidence for an upward trend in male child caring across most EU countries between 1994 and 1996 (Table 5.2). Her indicator of male child caring, the proportion of men who were engaged in 14 or more hours per week of unpaid child care, showed an increase in most countries although there were wide differences. Levels were consistently high in Denmark, where 41.3% of men were involved in at least 14 hours of unpaid child care per week (1996) in contrast to the lowest ranked country, Portugal, where the proportion was 13.3% for the same year. These general trends are in line with other time-use surveys across Europe and the United States (e.g., Bianchi, 2000; Gershuny, 2001). For instance, using international time budget diary comparisons, Gershuny showed increased child-care time spent by British fathers since the mid-1970s, with increases especially sharp since 1985 and in particular for those fathers

Table 5.2
Percentage of Male Child Caregivers (14 or more hours/week unpaid)

Country	1994	1995	1996	Average	Rank
Denmark	39.35	42	41.26	40.87	1
Finland	n.a.	n.a.	38.98	38.98	2
Netherlands	30.56	37.67	39.1	35.77	3
UK	30.01	33.3	28.6	30.63	4
Luxembourg	22.42	31.92	33.74	29.36	5
Germany	26.58	30.58	30.78	29.31	6
Belgium	27.19	30.92	29.56	29.22	7
Italy	26.96	28.89	29.61	28.49	8
Spain	27.29	29.88	26.44	27.87	9
Ireland	23.87	32.57	25.25	27.23	10
France	23.83	23.54	24.72	24.03	11
Austria	n.a.	19.86	20.42	20.14	12
Greece	18.58	17.32	22.03	19.31	13
Portugal	11.65	14.2	13.31	13.05	14

Source: Smith (2002), using European Community Household Panel (ECHP) data set.

with children under age 5 years, indicating similar trends in father child care as in the United States. Although men still do less child care than women, Gershuny (p. 198) suggests that men's involvement in child care gradually rises as the stock of employed women increase in the pattern of a "lagged adaptation." However, the slow rate of change toward gender equity in child care and housework continues to preoccupy European social scientists (Hobson, 2002).

Recent qualitative studies of fathers suggest that contemporary European fathers are juggling diverse models of fatherhood. Brannen's (2001) in-depth study of fatherhood models in 12 four-generation English families shows the continuing power of breadwinning even when it is transformed into its contemporary equivalent of careerism:

> Current fathers sought to achieve a complex of staggered life course transitions before they embarked on fatherhood. In contrast for the generation of fathers born around the Second World War, life course transitions fell thick and fast so that marriage, parenthood and labour-market transitions all occurred within a very few years. Yet despite these structural shifts, fatherhood remains tied to breadwinning. . . . New emergent forms of fatherhood are evident in the current father generation. The most transformative version of fatherhood—the "hands on father"—involved a "young father" who embraced an active caring identity but resisted a worker identity. (Brannen, 2001, pp. 18–19)

The continuity of breadwinning in shaping contemporary fatherhood models is also apparent in studies of cultural images of fathers. An analysis of newspaper coverage of men as carers in seven EU countries (Deven, 1994) portrayed an ambivalent and even negative set of media images surrounding fathers, particularly those not performing their traditional duties of financial provision. Ten newspapers in each country were monitored for a four-week period in June 1994. Articles examining fathers' caring responsibilities were less common than were features describing men's failure to provide for the family, particularly after marital separation. Human interest stories on fatherhood tended to focus on celebrities (e.g., sportsmen fathers), heroes, and villains. As Deven (1994, p. 23) argued, "Newspapers offered little in the way of role models, guidance or support for men seeking a new and more equal place in the family." It appeared that European newspapers of the time were marking and sustaining the boundaries of more conventional fathering models. Warin, Solomon, Lewis, and Langford (1999, p. 19) pointed to the growth of consumerism among teenagers to explain the continued power of fathers' economic-provision role, suggesting that "fathers' relationships with their teenage children were frequently mediated through the provision of material goods, and this was intensified in families where fathers had low incomes."

The continuing relevance of traditional fathering ideals is shown also in a rare study of fathering in an Islamic community in Europe. In Pels's (2000, p. 89) study of Moroccan migrant fathers in the Netherlands, she describes how "fathers are discouraged by traditional sectors of the community from 'becoming a woman' and from allowing an altered power and role division within the family. Male honour may also be threatened through social control and gossip and Moroccan law or Islamist movements may offer an important counterbalance to pressure for changing family relations."

Despite the growth of secularism in Europe, religion, especially Islam, remains a powerful source of values about the conduct of family relationships. However, Pels's (2000) study suggests that immigration and settlement can have an impact on traditional Muslim family values so that family duties and gender roles do not remain fixed. Although many of the tensions in Muslim families have tended to concentrate on girls and women's actions, future clashes between Western and Islamic values may begin to include men's family roles.

The qualitative studies reviewed in this section suggest that there is no unitary father model in Europe but instead that the caring father ideal juggles with the economic father ideal. In addition to these sociologically oriented studies, Europe continues to have a strong tradition of developmental psychology research into fatherhood, particularly influenced by attachment theory (see Lamb & Lewis, this volume). During the 1990s more developmental projects have been incorporating fathers into their research designs (e.g., Dunn, Davies, & O'Connor, 2000). Researchers have found that gathering knowledge about early father-child relationships to supplement the traditional focus on early mother-child relationships is helpful in predicting children's psychological outcomes (Steele & Steele, 1996). Similarly, psychodynamic writers using observational methods are reassessing the more positive dimensions of fathering in contemporary families (Trowell & Etchegoyen, 2002). The strength of psychological theory and research on fathers is that it uses more fine-grain concepts and measures of fathering that can complement studies adopting more macrosocial and global units of analysis (Clarke & O'Brien, 2003).

Although empirical studies of father-child relationships are still rather low in volume in Europe, there is a growing body of analysis of fatherhood in the family policy field. The European Union's policy push to help workers reconcile their family and employment responsibilities has provided fertile ground for an examination of the treatment of fathers. In the next section the development of father-sensitive family policies in Europe is traced. Attention is given to the implicit assumptions that specific policies reveal about the role of fathers in family life, and the research evidence on the impact of these policies on paternal behavior is reviewed.

THE EUROPEAN FATHERHOOD DEBATE: RECONCILIATION OF WORK AND FAMILY

The attention given to fathers by national family policies can be seen as a signifier of the importance placed by any one nation on the involvement of men in the care of children and of their spousal or partnership role in the household. At a very basic level, a family policy that makes reference to fathers allows for the possibility that they may have child-care and home-related responsibilities. Family policy provisions for fathers can also implicitly and explicitly prescribe the actual expectations of male caring, particularly concerning the minimal amounts of time they should spend with children both routinely and on more special family life transitions such as childbirth.

Early Father-Sensitive Family Policy

The early 1970s saw the beginnings of father-sensitive family policies in the modern industrial societies. Sweden, with its advanced social welfare system, was the first country to introduce a paid parental leave scheme that included an option for fathers to take paternity leave after the birth of children. This scheme was in place in 1974. The philosophy behind the Swedish innovation and much of the Nordic parental support developments since has been an equal opportunities one: the wish to create a social environment where women and men have the same access to vocational, familial, and personal fulfillment.

The idea of *paternity leave* marked the social obligation or right that a father could be absent from work for a period of time when a child is born. The inclusion of fathers in subsequent leave, after the initial early maternity and paternity leave, typically called *parental leave,* indicated that fathering and partner support were also significant during the early years of a child's life. Before 1974 any form of employment leave in Europe to look after babies and older children had been awarded only to mothers.

Sweden, not a member of the EU until 1995, has always been a pioneer in father-sensitive family policy innovation, through its inclusion of fathers as well as mothers in its interventions to support work-family balance. Similarly, implicit in Sweden's parental leave legislation has always been a child's perspective, with leave arrangements designed to meet children's well-being and children's relationships with both fathers and mothers. It should be noted that Sweden's holistic perspective toward family policy is still lacking in the highly employment-driven agenda at the supranational EU level.

Among subgroups within the EU, a discourse about the importance of sharing family duties was publicly articulated from the early 1980s (Crawley, 1990) and was influential in setting up the EEC Equal Opportunities unit in that period. By the early 1990s, the role of men as parents and carers moved forward on the unit's agenda, in fact becoming a prioritized policy theme. An important early EU development was a public statement by the Council of Ministers on child care, which included a commitment to encourage more male participation in the rearing of children in their respective countries:

> It is recommended that Member States should promote and encourage, with due respect for freedom of the individual, increased participation by men, in order to achieve a more equal sharing of parental responsibilities between men and women and to enable women to have a more effective role in the labour market. (Article 6, Council of Ministers Recommendation on Child Care, 1992 in EC Network Childcare, 1996, p. 37)

Some EU countries reacted positively to the challenge posed by the 1992 Council of Europe's Ministers Recommendation. For instance, the Danish government hosted several national conferences and encouraged a public debate on fatherhood (Carlsen & Larsen, 1993; *Fathers in Families of Tomorrow*, 1993; Moss, 1993). This debate fed directly into policy change: In 1994 Denmark's 10-week paid parental leave was increased to a 6-month paid leave for each parent, with a second sixth month dependent on employers' endorsement. By contrast, the UK government at the time was not enthusiastic about implementing any further EU-driven employment regulation on its workforce. Thus the UK remained the only EU country not to have any parental leave provision, apart from maternity leave around the time of childbirth, until a change of policy was initiated by the arrival of the Labour Government in 1997.

The Nordic example, when compared to the situation in the United Kingdom, illustrates the diversity of family policy practices with regard to fathers in the European Union. The comparison shows the need to take each nation's cultural and political history into account when examining its response to EU initiatives. European governments develop their parental leave policies in the context of national issues with their own historical legacies and welfare state models regulating the relationship between the market and family. Writers have characterized Britain and Ireland as examples of strong male breadwinner welfare systems with governments historically emphasizing private rather than public responsibility for dependents (e.g., Lewis, 1992). There has been a tendency in these liberal welfare countries (Esping-Anderson, 1999), as opposed to the Nordic social democratic regimes, to encourage private, individual solutions to child-care problems except for the poor and dispossessed. By contrast, the welfare benefits of Nordic countries have tended to be offered to all members of society and perceived as citizens' entitlements, not just as a safety net, thus minimizing the risk of citizens to market vagaries. One consequence of the latter approach is high taxation; parental leave provision is funded out of taxes on employers' income and in Sweden accounted for 43% of Swedish governmental support for children and families in 1997 (Haas & Hwang, 1999).

CURRENT PATERNITY AND PARENTAL LEAVE FOR EMPLOYED FATHERS IN EUROPE

By the late 1990s most EU member states provided statutory parental leave, including paternity leave for some, and the adoption in 1996 of the EU Directive on Parental Leave made parental entitlement universal in the EU by the end of 1999 (see Table 5.1 for a summary of current provision, including Norway). Currently, 8 of the 15 EU nations have a paternity leave entitlement ranging from two days in Spain to three weeks in France (Deven & Moss, 2002). In most countries paternity leave is paid at a relatively high proportion of earnings. As far as parental leave is concerned, there is great variety in leave entitlements from 6 months in Belgium, Greece, and the United Kingdom to 3 years per family in Germany and France (see Table 5.3; Deven & Moss, 2002; Moss & Deven, 1999). Although most countries have some provision for economic compensation, again this varies considerably from flat rates, often at a lower-than-average salary compensation level, to earnings-related entitlements, generally compensating at a higher level than the flat-rate approach. However, parental leave remains unpaid in the Netherlands, Portugal, Greece, Spain, the United Kingdom, and Ireland.

A recent trend in Nordic countries has been to mark a proportion of paid parental leave to be devoted *exclusively* to fathers (first implemented in Norway in 1993, Sweden in 1995, and Denmark in 1999). These designated "daddy periods," occurring after early paternity leave when a child is born, have been developed to strengthen fathers' caring role with their infants and also to encourage more fathers to take leave (Björnberg, 1994).

In Norway this father-sensitive measure, a special father's quota of four weeks, has been very popular (Leira, 1999). As is the case in Denmark and Sweden, the period of leave is lost to the family if not taken up by fathers. Up until this change, only 2% to 3% of Norwegian fathers took any share in parental leave on a voluntary basis. However, nearly 70% of eligible fathers took the father's quota in 1997, rising to 85% in 2000 (Rostgaard, 2003). The direct policy intervention into paternal participation in family life was greeted as a great success (Leira, 1999):

> Any fear that fathers might reject being "forced" into fatherhood have, so far, been proved wrong. . . . The legislation clearly states that the family loses four weeks of parental leave if the father does not use it. This reduces parental bargaining concerning the use of these weeks, and greatly improves the fathers' position negotiating with reluctant employers. (pp. 278–279)

Moreover, the policy was introduced in a gender-collaborative context, as the father quota was an extension of parental leave and was not subtracted from maternal leave.

The introduction of a similar scheme in Sweden in 1999 called *daddy month* had a less dramatic impact as the levels of father usage were already quite high. Evidence from Swedish cohorts of children born in the early 1990s showed that by 30 months, parental leave had been shared by 50% of parents, with 49% of the remaining leave days being used by mothers only and 1% by fathers only (Haas & Hwang, 1999). On average, fathers had taken around 2 months leave in all (an average of about 59 days), making up about one fifth of the possible available time. As Björnberg (1994, pp. 64–65) commented, "there is a clear tendency over the years for more and more fathers to exercise their right to take parental leave, and the number of days taken is increasing. . . . In public discourse there is a high degree of agreement about the necessity for fathers to share parental responsibility."

Data from other non–Nordic European countries, particularly those without father targeting, show lower levels of parental-leave usage by men. In those countries where there is no reservation of leave for the father, data from the early 1990s showed that only about 5% of eligible fathers made use of a parental leave provision (OECD, 1995). However, paternity leave rates are generally high. Father targeting is in part a general process of allocating parental leave as an individual, nontransferable entitlement rather than as a family, gender-neutral entitlement, but some countries such as Swe-

Table 5.3

Paternity Leave and Parental Leave Provision in Europe

Country	Paternity Leave and Parental Leave Provision
Austria	No paternity leave. Maternity leave: 8 weeks. Parental leave available as family entitlement (can be shared by father and mother) until child is 24 months. Paid at a flat-rate allowance.
Belgium	Paternity leave: 2 weeks, earnings-related allowance (100%). Maternity leave: 8–14 weeks. Parental leave available as an individual entitlement until child is 6 months (3 months for father, 3 months for mother). Paid at a flat-rate allowance.
Denmark	Paternity leave: 2 weeks, earnings-related up to a low maximum. Maternity leave: 14 weeks. Parental leave available as a family entitlement until child is 7.4. Paid at an earnings-related allowance up to a low maximum.
Finland	Paternity leave: 1 week, to below 70% of earnings. Maternity leave: 9.5–12.5 weeks. Parental leave available as a family entitlement until child is 26 weeks (with an additional care leave up to 36 months). Paid at an earnings-related, part flat pay.
France	Paternity leave: 3 weeks, earnings-related allowance (100%). Maternity leave: 10–12 weeks. Parental leave available as a family entitlement until child is 36 months (flat-rate dependent on number of children).
Germany	No paternity leave. Maternity leave: 8 weeks. Parental leave available as a family entitlement until child is 36 months (flat-rate and flexible income related).
Greece	No paternity leave. Maternity leave: 7–11 weeks. Parental leave is available as an individual entitlement until child is 6 months (no payment).
Ireland	No paternity leave. Maternity leave: 4–14 weeks. Parental leave is available as an individual entitlement until child is 6.5 months (no payment).
Italy	No paternity leave. Maternity leave: 13 weeks. Parental leave is available as a family individual entitlement until child is 11 months (if father takes 3 months, otherwise 10 months). Paid to below 70% of earnings.
Luxembourg	No paternity leave. Maternity leave: 8 weeks. Parental leave is available as an individual entitlement until child is 12 months (flat-rate payment).
Netherlands	No paternity leave. Maternity leave: 10–12 weeks. Parental leave is available as an individual entitlement until child is 12 months (must be taken part-time). No payment.
Norway	Paternity leave: 2 weeks, no payment. Maternity leave: none (6 weeks of parental leave must be taken by mother). Parental leave available as part-family and part-individual entitlement until child is 12 months. Paid at part earnings-related and part flat rate. Further 12 months unpaid parental leave available.
Portugal	Paternity leave: 1 weeks, earnings-related allowance (100%). Maternity leave: 8.5–13 weeks. Parental leave available as an individual entitlement until child is 12–48 months (no payment).
Spain	Paternity leave: 2 days, earnings-related allowance (100%). Maternity leave: 6–16 weeks. Parental leave available as an individual entitlement until child is 36 months (no payment).

(*continued*)

Table 5.3
Continued

Country	Paternity Leave and Parental Leave Provision
Sweden	Paternity leave: 2 weeks, earnings-related up to more than 70% of earnings. Maternity leave: only available before birth for unwell women. Parental leave available as part family and part individual entitlement until child is 16 months. Paid at part earnings-related and part flat rate (13 months at 80% of earnings up to a maximum and flat rate for 3 months). Further 18 months unpaid parental leave available.
United Kingdom	Paternity leave: 2 weeks, universal flat rate. Maternity leave: up to 52 weeks, part earnings-related, part flat rate, and part unpaid. Parental leave available as an individual entitlement until child is 6 months (no payment).

Source: Adapted from Deven and Moss (2002).

den have developed mixed-model approaches (Table 5.4; Deven & Moss, 2002). In their analysis, Bruning and Plantenga (1999) showed that when parental leave is a family entitlement, mothers generally tend to use it. For instance, in Belgium, where parental leave was only introduced in 1998 following the implementation of the EU Directive, 95% of leave takers are mothers (Deven & Nuelant, 1999). Similarly, recent figures for 1998 show that 2% of eligible German fathers took up parental leave (Rost, 1999).

In a recent EU-wide analysis, Smith (2002) examined national and institutional factors that operated to promote fathers' use of parental leave and male caretaking between 1994 and 1996. Smith concluded that male parenting was greatest in countries when parental leave was an individual nontransferable entitlement, where there was high wage compensation, where there was flexibility in the way leave could be used by couples, and where the advantages of fathers taking parental leave were marketed through government awareness campaigns. Sweden was ranked as the country with the most father-friendly parental leave provision. Since the inception of paternity leave in 1974 there has been sustained cultural support and campaigning on active fatherhood at all levels in the political and administrative process. Interventions have included advertising and educational campaigns and modeling by political leaders, many of whom have taken parental leave themselves. An influential cross-political party, Fathers' Group of leading national men, was set up in 1992 and has also been credited as promoting fathers' taking parental leave (Rostgaard, 2002).

Fathers' Use of Parental Leave

An early important Danish study of a nationally representative sample of parents with children born between 1984 and 1989 examined why fathers did not use paid parental leave when it was available to either themselves or their partner during their child's third to sixth month (Christoffersen, 1990). Christoffersen (1990) identified four main reasons: First, respondents reported that leave was not possible because the mother was still breastfeeding regularly; second, respondents felt it would not have been economically viable for the family if the father rather than the mother took time out from paid work (because the economic compensation did not fully cover average paternal income); third, respondents felt that the father's work did not allow him to be

Table 5.4

Reasons Given by Fathers and Mothers When Mothers Took All of the Parental Leave
(children born 1984–1989, in %)

	Fathers	Mothers	Total
Mother was still breastfeeding the child	16	25	21
It would have been an economic burden for the family	22	16	19
Father's work did not allow him to be on parental leave	20	22	21
Family had not considered the possibility of letting the father be on leave	23	19	21
Father believed that he was not able to take care of the child	1	1	1
Mother was better taking care of the newborn baby	10	6	8
Father was not interested	5	5	5
Other/no answer	3	4	4
Number	358	383	741

Note: Includes only families with both parents economically active at the time of the child's birth.
Source: Christoffersen (1990).

on parental leave; and finally, respondents reported that the family had not even considered the possibility of letting the father rather than the mother take leave (see Table 5.4). One strong dimension of this study was that both mothers and fathers were questioned independently. Christoffersen found that mothers were more likely than fathers to mention the issue of breastfeeding and economic problems and that fathers were more likely than mothers to highlight that the family had not considered the option of the father's taking parental leave.

Christoffersen was able to examine more closely the minority of cases where fathers had taken part of the parental leave and compare these parents to the rest of the sample. As with other studies (e.g., Carlsen, 1993), maternal rather than paternal factors were more predictive of fathers' use of parental leave. High maternal education levels and high maternal attachment to employment increased the probability of fathers' taking parental leave. In addition, workplace factors were important: Paternal leave was more common when fathers worked in the public sector and in predominately female workplaces, suggesting a more economically and culturally supportive milieu in these working environments.

Unfortunately, the study did not clarify patterns of breastfeeding between the groups and whether breastfeeding rates varied for infants in predominately maternal or paternal leave contexts. Sensitivity to breastfeeding in the first year of life and more general health needs of the child may be underlying factors influencing the timing of men's use of male parental leave. In Denmark, the proportions of men taking parental leave are highest when children are in the 3- to 5-year-old age group and lowest for infants under 1 year (Rostgaard et al., 1999). Similarly, in Sweden the most common time for fathers to take parental leave is when their child is between 11 and 15 months and not younger (Rostgaard, 2002).

Couple negotiation about who should take leave has been subject to some recent investigation in Sweden and Norway (Brandth & Kvande, 2001, 2002; Haas & Hwang, 1999). Haas and Hwang (1999, p. 60), reporting on an untranslated Swedish qualitative study on couples in the process of making a decision about parental leave, suggested that "men get the solution they want: their wishes and arguments tend to hold sway over those of women, who adapt themselves to men's values." They argued that fathers working in organizations with long work hours and insensitive family-life policies will have a strong negotiating position to withdraw from leave taking. However, little detail is given about the nature of the samples used in this research, and clearly more work is required.

In a more comprehensive Norwegian study Brandth and Kvande (2002) found a complex process of couple negotiation and bargaining. The study involved a survey of 2,194 men becoming new fathers between May 1994 and April 1995 in central Norway (response rate 62%) and interviews with 30 couples from the sample who had used the parental leave system. The researchers found different motivations for taking parental leave among fathers. Wishing to spend more time with the child was a dominant motivation, although some fathers cited a legal-right motivation. This latter group of fathers was characterized by initially taking the leave only because it was available but nonetheless using the time for the intended purpose of child care and child bonding. The study shows the importance of couples' parenting values and preferences as well as workplace factors in influencing fathers' use of parental leave.

Other studies have shown the relevance of the *parental pay gap,* both perceived and actual, when calculations are made about who should take leave. The higher the father's salary in comparison to the mother's, the less likely he is to take parental leave (e.g., Haas & Hwang, 1999). In most European countries it appears that a family's immediate loss of income is less if mothers rather than fathers use parental leave. This structural factor may operate to create a barrier to fathers' leave taking, although the Swedish government has challenged the income-loss argument by showing that continued engagement of mothers in the labor market after parental leave will tend to offset short-term costs linked to men's taking leave (Haas & Hwang, 1999). The importance of high income replacement compensation benefits, in addition to the imperative to couples to take a longer term view on family income assets, has been timely but is less compelling to households where fathers are absolute and relative high earners. It is also notable that although the gender pay gap has been reduced in Sweden, it still exists (Ginsburg, 2001).

Workplace factors also need to be examined in order to understand fully fathers' use of parental leave (see also Russell and Hwang, this volume).

MANAGERIAL ATTITUDES TO FATHERS IN THE WORKPLACE

Most of the European research on fathers in the workplace has been conducted in Nordic countries (Haas, Hwang, & Russell, 2000). In the Danish context, private sector managers were found to be less accepting of fathers' taking parental leave; and in general across public and private sectors, employees report male managers to be less sympathetic than female managers to paternal leave taking (Anderson, Appledorn, & Weise, 1996). Den Dulk (1999), in a cross-national study of employers' attitudes to providing parental leave in the Netherlands, Sweden, United Kingdom, and Italy, found that family-friendly provisions are more likely to develop in large public sector organizations with some female employees. He suggested that employers with female employees might be more sensitized to the issue of retaining valuable female employees. Moreover, he argued that large public sector organizations are vulnerable to media attention, so it is in their interest to offer work-life balance support to employees.

Swedish research (Haas & Hwang, 1999) suggests also that there are few systems in place to help fathers negotiate their workload and tasks during periods of leave and that some fathers are left to make their own arrangements. Replacements can be found if appropriate planning is in place, and in some cases fathers can keep in touch and even remain working at home, albeit at a slower pace, through the use of fax, e-mail, and telephone.

Haas and Hwang (1999) argued that more positive workplace attitudes toward men's taking parental leave are essential if usage rates are to be improved. In particular, there should be a move from *encouraging* men to become more engaged in child care toward an *expectation* that they be involved fathers. However, workplace attitudes cannot shift in isolation; the interaction of the feelings, attitudes, and behaviors of the parental couple in interaction with the workplace is a crucial dynamic to be considered in future research.

In some countries parental leave had very negative associations for employers. In Germany, for instance, the literal meaning of parental leave is "vacation for raising children." For a number of the employers in Rost's (1999) German study, men's access to parental leave implied a licence to be idle.

Employer surveys in Sweden in the early 1990s have also shown that between 40% and 70% reported that parental leave schemes had caused problems for their organization. Large public sector organizations, presumably with the greater number of individuals wanting leave, had higher levels of reported problems, but also arguably more economies of scale. However, there have been no systematic economic cost-benefit analyses calculating the financial impact of maternal or paternal leave policies on organizations, although regular claims are made by individual employers for financial losses and benefits alike. In terms of losses, Nasman's (1997) study reported that only one tenth of private-sector and one third of public-sector employers reported long-term economic productivity gains, and in small private firms (under 50 employees), more employers anticipated a reluctance to take on mothers with young children. In terms of benefits, some Swedish firms have begun to use extra financial incentives for fathers taking leave as part of their recruitment strategy, claiming enhanced retention and loyalty, although these are rare (Haas & Hwang, 1999). In addition, as Haas and Hwang (1999, p. 51) noted, the recent Swedish Government approach has linked taking parental leave as a labor market asset for fathers: "Benefits that are often mentioned include the development of interpersonal and communication skills, enhanced ability to do multiple tasks simultaneously and the chance to become a 'whole human being.'" In general, Swedish research has shown that leave does not appear to have a negative impact on fathers' work prospects in the longer term (they are rarely replaced on return or loose significant income; Haas, 1992).

IMPACT OF PATERNAL AND PARENTAL LEAVE ON FATHER INVOLVEMENT

In a national evaluation of parental leave in Denmark, parents reported overwhelming benefits, notably more time with family—particularly when the child is young—and a less stressful family environment overall (Anderson et al., 1996). Swedish and British research on fathers' perceptions of paternity and parental leave benefits points to similar findings, with the majority reporting satisfaction and enjoyment (Bell, Mc-Kee, & Priestly, 1983; Haas, 1992).

Swedish fathers who use a higher proportion of leave than average (20% or more of all potential leave days) at least in the short term appear to sustain a more engaged family commitment, working fewer hours and being more involved in child-care tasks and household work (Haas, 1992). Similarly Huttunen's (1996) survey of Finnish fathers who had taken parental leave found that the opportunity it gave to develop a closer relationship with infants was valued most by the fathers. However, when fathers on parental leave were asked directly about the problems they experience, about a quarter described feeling lonely, missing work, and feeling stress associated with home life at slightly higher levels than did mothers (Haas, 1992).

Aside from Haas's and Huttunen's studies, there are few further outcome studies examining the evidence base as to whether parental leave makes a difference to the quality of family relationships, in particular paternal involvement, beyond retrospective self-reports. However, an important 15-year longitudinal study of paternal involvement in Sweden has been able to illuminate the relationship between fathers taking leave and later paternal involvement in child care (Chuang, Lamb, & Hwang, 2003; Hwang & Lamb, 1997). This study followed 116 children born in the early 1980s, tracing links between absolute time-based and relative estimates of maternal and paternal involvement over time. At the beginning of the children's second year (average age 1.3 years), higher levels of father involvement and responsibility were found for fathers who had taken more than two weeks paternity leave, and by the beginning of the third year (average age 2.3 years), taking paternity leave was associated with greater accessibility to children during weekdays. However, maternal and paternal overall working hours were more powerful correlates of father involvement at 3.3 years than was the short period of paternity leave itself. As parental leave tends to be longer and more sustained than paternity leave, it could be predicted that paternity leave would have less impact on father involvement, as suggested by Salmi and Lammi-Taskula (1999, p. 114):

> The short (6–18 days) paternity leave, which the majority of fathers use, does help the mother in the first days after birth. But it is a short period for the mother to recover, especially if there are other children in the family, and it is far too short for a strong caring relationship to develop between the father and child. During this period, the father is not alone with the child, and thus not taking responsibility for his care.

However, paternity and parental leave cannot be seen either in isolation or in purely quantitative terms, as both are embedded in a complex web of parenting styles, parental motivation, infant behavior, and wide-ranging socioeconomic factors.

SUMMARY

This section examined the treatment of fathers in European family policies developed to help parents reconcile employment and family commitments. The analysis illuminated the changing and varied expectations of male caring across Europe over the last 30 years. There is increasing appreciation of men's emotional commitments and responsibilities to children. As expectations for active fatherhood have become more heightened, the compatibility of fathers' working and family lives has come under increasing scrutiny. From the late 1990s onward there has been a rapid expansion of paternity leave and parental leave provision targeted at fathers, particularly in the Nordic countries. These developments suggest that a strong policy focus on fatherhood has emerged in recent years across the main nations of Europe. As Deven and Moss (2002, p. 240) commented in their systematic review of changes in parental leave, "If we consider the developments since 1998, the most striking trend is a growing emphasis on fatherhood." Empirical inquiry into the impact of paternity leave and men's taking parental leave on family life is still relatively undeveloped, but the evidence to date indicates emotional benefits for parents and a limited short-term increase in father involvement in child care. Because paid leave has been in Sweden as far back as the 1970s, the Swedish experience, alongside that of other Nordic countries, points to the optimal conditions for fathers' responsiveness and use. Deven and Moss's (2002) review suggests that income replacement levels of up to 80% to 100% of earnings may be necessary for high levels of use. As well as structural barriers, fathers face personal and familial constraints in using these new entitlements. Within the home context, breastfeeding may impact the appropriate timing of parental leave for fathers, and within the workplace, employers' attitudes toward men taking family-related leave appear to be a crucial factor.

CONCLUSION

The demographic portrait of European fathers has shown a trend toward less predictability and permanency in their family relationships. Although a majority of European families still remain stable over time, divorce and repartnering trends have shown an upward rise since the 1970s, creating a growing minority of households without resident fathers. More European fathers will experience an increased number of transitions into and out of household types during their life course. Little is known about the experience of European fathers who do not reside with their biological children, and clearly more research is required. It appears that the diversification of fathers' family and kinship networks has created more complexity in the codification of men's obligations and responsibilities to children of different families. Similarly, the impact of the growth in nonmarital unions across Europe needs further examination, as initial research indicates that the relationships between cohabiting fathers and their children may be more fragile than that of married fathers. However, the meaning of cohabitation varies significantly across European countries from the Nordic countries, some of which (notably Sweden) have a tradition of stable cohabitation, to the south, where cohabitation is still relatively rare and not as socially accepted.

Although fertility rates have been declining across Europe, the higher fertility rates among minority ethnic groups in many European nations suggest an increasing ethnic and religious diversity in future fatherhood. Moreover, this diversity will result in variable fathering behavior within individual countries. For instance, in the British context, recent analysis has shown different residential patterns between minority ethnic fathers (Berthoud, 2000): Black British fathers are less likely to live with their children than are White British fathers, and Asian fathers are the most likely to be living in the married-couple family context with their children. Clearly, growing cultural and religious diversity in Europe will generate a rich mix of fathering models, the meaning and significance of which will again require further research. For example, the general movement away from paternal authority as a major organizing principle in family life in most European societies may lie uneasily with religious models of fathering that stress the importance of male elders.

However, with the rapid growth of maternal employment across Europe since the

1970s, a caring dimension has become more central to the social construction of fathering. There are greater expectations on men to be active in the upbringing of children and supportive coparents to their partners, and younger cohorts of Europeans are endorsing a more egalitarian model of family life (Scott, Brown, & Alwin, 1998). The spousal exchange of male instrumental provision for female expressive care may no longer match the requirements of contemporary families with dependent children.

The parental leave entitlements, with their increased targeting of fathers, go some way to help employed parents. However, the family policies do not resolve the wider dilemma of work-family balance for fathers, and indeed mothers, beyond the early period of parenthood. As was shown in this chapter, fathers continue to work long hours, and the economic dimension of fathering is still an important aspect of European men's identity as parents. Full sharing of the breadwinning will remain constrained by the continuation of gender differences in income across Europe. European parents are making employment and child-care decisions in the context of fathers' greater earning power and an uneven quality of child-care provision. Clearly, future policy makers and researchers into European fatherhood will need to examine the contradictory underlying models of fatherhood embedded in the diversity of peoples and families that make up an expanding Europe.

REFERENCES

Anderson, D., Appleldorn, A., & Weise, H. (1996). Orlov-evaluering af orlovsord-ningerne. København: Socialforskningsinstituttet. In T. Rostgaard, N. Christoffersen, & H. Weise (1999), Parental leave in Denmark. In P. Moss & F. Deven (Eds.) *Parental leave: Progress or pitfall? Research and policy issues in Europe* (Vol. 35). The Hague and Brussels: NIDI/CGBS Publications.

Beck, U., & Beck-Gernsheim, E. (2001). *The chaos of love.* London: Sage.

Bell, C., McKee, L., & Priestly, K. (1983). *Fathers, childbirth, and work.* Manchester, England: Equal Opportunities Commission.

Bertaux, D., & Delcroix, C. (1992). Where have all the daddies gone? In U. Björnberg (Ed.), *European parents in the 1990s* (pp. 181–196). New Brunswick, NJ: Transaction.

Berthoud, R. (2000). *Family formation in multi-cultural Britain: Three patterns of diversity.* Institute for Social and Economic Research Working Paper No. 2000-34. Colchester, University of Essex.

Bianchi, S. M. (2000). Maternal employment and time with children: Dramatic change or surprising continuity? *Demography, 37,* 401–414.

Björnberg, U. (1992). Parenting in transition. In U. Björnberg (Ed.), *European parents in the 1990s* (pp. 1–41). New Brunswick, NJ: Transaction.

Björnberg, U. (1994). Reconciling family and employment in Sweden. *Cross National Research Papers, 4,* 59–67.

Brandth, B., & Kvande, E. (2001). Flexible work and flexible fathers. *Work, Employment and Society, 15,* 251–267.

Brandth, B., & Kvande, E. (2002). Reflexive fathers: Negotiating parental leave and working life gender. *Work and Organisation, 9,* 186–203.

Brannen, J. (2001, September). *Changing family and generational patterns: A comparative assessment of fatherhood.* Paper presented at the European Observatory on the Social Situation, Demography and Family Seminar, Vienna, Austria.

Bruning, G., & Plantenga, J. (1999). Parental leave and equal opportunities in eight European countries. *Journal of European Social Policy, 19,* 195–209.

Carlsen, S. (1993). Men's utilization of paternity leave and parental leave schemes. In S. Carlsen & J. E. Larsen (Eds.), *The equality dilemma: Reconciling working life and family life, viewed in an equality perspective—The Danish example.* Copenhagen, Denmark: Danish Equal Status Council.

Carlsen, S., & Larsen, J. E. (Eds.). (1993). *The equality dilemma: Reconciling working life and family life, viewed in an equality perspective—The Danish example* (pp. 79–90). Copenhagen, Denmark: Danish Equal Status Council.

Christoffersen, M. N. (1990). Barselsorlov-maends og kvinders erhvervsmaessige baggrund for at tage orlov. Rapport 90: 18. København: Socialforskningsinstituttet. In T. Rostgaard, N. Christoffersen & H. Weise (1999), Parental leave in Denmark. In P. Moss & F. Deven (Eds.). *Parental leave: Progress or pitfall? Research and policy issues in Europe* (Vol. 35, pp. 25–44). The Hague and Brussels: NIDI/CGBS Publications.

Chuang, S., Lamb, M. E., & Hwang, C. P. (2003). Internal reliability, temporal stability and correlates of individual differences in paternal involvement: A 15-year longitudinal study in Sweden. In R. Day & M. E. Lamb (Eds.), *Reconceptualizing and measuring fatherhood* (pp. 129–148). Mahwah, NJ: Erlbaum.

Clarke, L. (1996). Demographic change and the family situation of children. In J. Brannen & M. O'Brien (Eds.), *Children in families: Research and policy.* London: Falmer Press.

Clarke, L., & Cooksey, E. (1999). Fathers and absent fathers: Sociodemographic similarities in Britain and the United States. *Demography, 35,* 217–228.

Clarke, L., & O'Brien, M. (2003). Father involvement in Britain: The research and policy evidence. In R. Day & M. Lamb (Eds.), *Reconceptualizing and measuring fatherhood* (pp. 35–59). Mahwah, NJ: Erlbaum.

Crawley, L. (1990). The European Parliament Committee on Women's Rights. In M. O'Brien, L. Hantrais, & S. Mangen (Eds.), *Women, equal opportunities and welfare.* Loughborough, England: Loughborough University.

Den Dulk, L. (1999). Employers and parental leave: A comparative analysis. In P. Moss & F. Deven (Eds.), *Parental leave: Progress or pitfall? Research and policy issues in Europe* (Vol. 35, pp. 227–247). The Hague, Netherlands: NIDI/CGBS.

Deven, F. (1994). *Men, media, and childcare.* Luxembourg: Office for Official Publication of the European Communities.

Deven, F., & Moss, P. (2002). Leave arrangements for parents: Overview and future outlook. *Community, Work and Family, 5,* 237–255.

Deven, F., & Nuelant, T. (1999). Parental leave and career breaks in Belgium. In P. Moss & F. Deven (Eds.), *Parental leave: Progress or pitfall? Research and policy issues in Europe* (Vol. 35, pp. 141–154). The Hague, Netherlands: NIDI/CGBS.

Deven, F., Inglis, S., Moss, P., & Petrie, P. (1998). *State of the art review on the reconciliation of work and family life for men and women and the quality of care services.* Research Report 44. London: Department for Education and Employment.

Ditch, J., Barnes, H., & Bradshaw, J. (1997). *European Observatory on National Family Policies 1996 Report.* York, England: Social Policy Research Unit.

Dunn, J., Davies, L., & O'Connor, T. (2000). Parents' and partners' life course and family experiences: Links with parent-child relationships in different family settings. *Journal of Child Psychology and Psychiatry, 41,* 955–968.

Edwards, R., Back-Wiklund, M., Bak, M., & Ribben, J. (2002). Step-fathering: Comparing policy and everyday experience in Britain and Sweden. *Sociological Research Online, 7,* 1.

Esping-Anderson, G. (1999). *Social foundations of post-industrial economics.* New York: Oxford University Press.

European Commission Network on Childcare. (1996). *The EC Childcare Network 1986–1996: A decade of achievements.* Luxembourg: Office for Official Publications of the European Communities.

Eurostat. (2000). *Employment in Europe.* Luxembourg: Office for Official Publications of the European Communities.

Eurostat. (2002a). *The Social Situation Report.* Luxembourg: Office for Official Publications of the European Communities.

Eurostat (2002b). *Statistics in focus.* Population and Social Condition, report no. 9. Luxembourg: Office for Official Publications of the European Communities.

Fagan, C. (2000, April). *Who works long hours and why?* Paper presented at BSA Annual Conference, Manchester, England.

Fathers in Families of Tomorrow. (1993). Report from the Conference. Copenhagen, Denmark: Ministry of Social Affairs.

Gershuny, J. (2001). *Changing times.* New York: Oxford University Press.

Giddens, A. (1991). *Modernity and self identity.* Cambridge, England: Polity Press.

Ginsburg, N. (2001). Sweden: The Social Democratic case. In A. Cochrane, J. Clarke, and S. Gewirtz (Eds.), *Comparing welfare states* (pp. 195–222). London: Sage.

Haas, L. (1992). *Equal parenthood and social policy: A study of parental leave in Sweden.* New York: State University of New York Press.

Haas, L., & Hwang, P. (1999). Parental leave in Sweden. In P. Moss & F. Deven (Eds.), *Parental leave: Progress or pitfall? Research and policy issues in Europe* (Vol. 35, pp. 45–68). The Hague, Netherlands: NIDI/CGBS.

Haas, L., Hwang, D., & Russell, S. (2000). *Organizational change and gender equity: International perspectives on fathers and mothers at the workplace.* Thousand Oaks, CA: Sage.

Halsey, A. J. (2000). *Social trends.* London: Stationary Office.

Hantrais, L., & Letablier, M. T. (1996). *Families and family policies in Europe.* London: Longman.

Hobson, B. (Ed.). (2002). *Making men into fathers: Men, masculinities and the social politics of fatherhood.* Cambridge, England: Cambridge University Press.

Huttunen, J. (1996). Full-time fathers and their parental leave experiences. In U. Björnberg & A. K. Kollind (Eds.), *Men's family relations* (pp. 79–90). Göteborg, Sweden: Göteborg University.

Hwang, C. P. (1987). The changing role of Swedish fathers. In M. E. Lamb (Ed.), *The father's role: Cross-cultural perspectives* (pp. 115–138). Mahwah, NJ: Erlbaum.

Hwang, C. P., & Lamb, M. E. (1997). Father involvement in Sweden: A longitudinal study of its stability and correlates. *International Journal of Behavioural Development, 21,* 621–632.

Jensen, A.-M. (1999). Partners and parents in Europe: A gender divide. *Comparative Social Research, 18,* 1–29.

Lamb, M. E. (1987). Introduction. In M. E. Lamb (Ed.), *The father's role: Cross-cultural perspectives* (pp. 3–25). Mahwah, NJ: Erlbaum.

Leira, A. (1999). Cash-for-child care and daddy leave. In P. Moss & F. Deven (Eds.), *Parental leave: Progress or pitfall? Research and policy issues in Europe* (Vol. 35, pp. 267–291). The Hague, Netherlands: NIDI/CGBS.

Lewis, C., & O'Brien, M. (Eds.). (1986). *Reassessing fatherhood.* London: Sage.

Lewis, J. (1992). Gender and the development of welfare regimes. *Journal of European Social Policy, 2,* 159–173.

Matheson, J., & Summerfield, C. (Eds.). (2001). *Social focus on men.* London: Stationery Office.

McKee, L., & O'Brien, M. (Eds.). (1982). *The father figure.* London: Tavistock.

Moss, P. (1993). Strategies to promote fathers' involvement in the care and upbringing of their children: Placing leave arrangements in a wider context. In S. Carlsen & J. E. Larsen (Eds.), *The equality dilemma: Reconciling working life and family life, viewed in an equality perspective— The Danish example.* Copenhagen, Denmark: Danish Equal Status Council.

Moss, P., & Deven, F. (Eds.). (1999). *Parental leave: Progress or pitfall? Research and policy issues in Europe* (Vol. 35). The Hague, Netherlands: NIDI/CGBS.

Nasman, E. (1997). Work-family arrangements in Sweden: Family strategies. In L. Den Dulk, J. van Doorne-Huiskes, & J. Schippers (Eds.), *Work-family arrangements in Europe* (pp. 45–63). Amsterdam: Thela-Thesis.

New, R., & Benigni, L. (1987). Italian fathers and infants: Cultural constraints on paternal behavior. In M. E. Lamb (Ed.), *The father's role: Cross-cultural perspectives* (pp. 139–167). Mahwah, NJ: Erlbaum.

Nickel, H., & Kocher, E. (1987). West Germany and the German-speaking countries. In M. E. Lamb (Ed.), *The father's role: Cross-cultural perspectives* (pp. 89–114). Mahwah, NJ: Erlbaum.

Nugent, K. (1987). The father's role in early Irish socialization: Historical and empirical perspectives. In M. E. Lamb (Ed.), *The father's role: Cross-cultural perspectives* (pp. 169–193). Mahwah, NJ: Erlbaum.

O'Brien, M., & Shemilt, I. (2003). *Working fathers: Earning and caring.* Manchester, England: Equal Opportunities Commission.

OECD. (1995). Long-term leave for parents in OECD countries. In OECD (Ed.), *Employment Outlook 1995* (pp. 171–196). Paris: Author.

Pels, T. (2000). Muslim families from Morocco in the Netherlands: Gender dynamics and fathers' roles in a context of change. *Current Sociology, 48*(4), 75–93.

Polatnick, M. (2000). Working parents: Issues for the next decades. *Phi Kappa Phi Journal, 30* (Summer), 1–4.

Relaisi de Parseval, G., & Hurstel, F. (1987). Paternity "a la francaise." In M. E. Lamb (Ed.), *The father's role: Cross-cultural perspectives* (pp. 59–87). Mahwah, NJ: Erlbaum.

Rost, H. (1999). Fathers and parental leave in Germany. In P. Moss & F. Deven (Eds.), *Parental leave: Progress or pitfall? Research and policy issues in Europe* (Vol. 35, pp. 249–266). The Hague, Netherlands: NIDI/CGBS.

Rostgaard, T. (2003). Setting time aside for the father: Father leave in the Scandinavian countries [Special issue]. *Community, Work and Family, 5,* 343–364.

Rostgaard, T., Christoffersen, N., & Weise, H. (1999). Parental leave in Denmark. In P. Moss & F. Deven (Eds.), *Parental leave: Progress or pitfall? Research and policy issues in Europe* (Vol. 35, pp. 25–44). The Hague, Netherlands: NIDI/CGBS.

Rubery, J., Smith, M., & Fagan, C. (1999). *Women's employment in Europe: Trends and prospects.* London: Routledge.

Salmi, M., & Lammi-Taskula, J. (1999). Parental leave in Finland. In P. Moss & F. Deven (Eds.), *Parental leave: Progress or pitfall? Research and policy issues in Europe* (Vol. 35, pp. 85–121). The Hague, Netherlands: NIDI/CGBS.

Sandqvist, K. (1987). *Fathers and family work in two cultures.* Stockholm: Almqvist and Wiksell.

Scott, J., Brown, M., & Alwin, D. (1998). Partner, parent, worker: Family and gender roles. In R. Jowell, J. Curtice, A. Park, J. Brook, K. Thomson, & C. Bryson (Eds.), *British and European social attitudes: How Britain differs* (pp. 29–37). Aldershot, England: Ashgate.

Smith, A. (2002). *The role of the state in encouraging male parenting: Lessons from Europe.* Paper presented at Women in Politics Conference, Birkbeck College, London.

Social trends. (2002). London: The Stationery Office.

Steele, H., Steele, M., & Fonagy, P. (1996). Associations among attachment classifications of mothers, fathers, and their infants. *Child Development, 69,* 592–594.

Trowell, J., & Etchegoyen, A. (2002). The importance of fathers: A psychoanalytic re-evaluation.

Warin, J., Solomon, Y., Lewis, C., & Langford, W. (1999). *Fathers, work and family life.* London: Family Policy Studies Centre.

Women and men in Europe and North America. (2000). Luxembourg: Office for Official Publications of the European Communities.

CHAPTER 6

Fathering in Japanese, Chinese, and Korean Cultures

A Review of the Research Literature

DAVID W. SHWALB, JUN NAKAZAWA, TOSHIYA YAMAMOTO, and JUNG-HWAN HYUN

PSYCHOLOGICAL RESEARCH and theories on fathering have been dominated by a Western viewpoint (Lamb, 1997), and one purpose of this paper is to redress that imbalance by introducing the literature on fathering in three Asian societies. Most research on fathers in Asia has been conducted on three East Asian cultures: Japanese (approximate population = 126 million), Chinese (population over 1.28 billion in the People's Republic of China, or PRC, including 7 million in Hong Kong, which was incorporated into the PRC in 1997; and 22 million in Taiwan) and Korean (47 million in South Korea and 22 million in North Korea). These cultural groups are geographical neighbors, share a long history of interaction, and have a common cultural heritage. For instance, both Japan and Korea were profoundly influenced by Chinese culture, importing and transforming aspects of Chinese religion, philosophy, politics, science, language, and literature. Confucianism is relevant to our consideration of the contemporary paternal role because its basic concepts such as "koh" (孝, filial piety), which gave children a sense of duty to their parents, still have some influence in all three cultures. Yet each culture has also been subject to a unique combination of influences from modernization, economic growth, and globalization. Because of their different histories, Japan, China, and Korea saw a divergence in their patterns of fathering, family relations, and even Confucianism, long before the onset of modernization. In this chapter we look at social science research on fathering in three related yet distinct cultural groups.

This chapter was prepared with the support of the Southeastern Louisiana University Psychology Department (Al Burstein, head) and the Brigham Young University Psychology Department (Erin Bigler and Gawain Wells, chairpersons) and is dedicated to Harry Shwalb, Solomon Greenwald, Shirou Nakazawa, Mari Yamamoto, and Mar-Sun Yi.

QUALITY AND QUANTITY OF RESEARCH

A direct comparison of fathers in Japan, China, and Korea would be desirable, but it is difficult to make conclusive comparisons based on the current literature. The first reason for this difficulty is that there has been little research on fathering in China and Korea. Social science research on parenting in Japan, China, and Korea has centered on mothers rather than fathers (Ho, Spinks, & Yeung, 1989; U. Kim & Choi, 1994; Rothbaum, Pott, Azuma, Miyake, & Weisz, 2000; Shwalb & Shwalb, 1996) because affective relationships between mothers and children are considered more important than father-child relationships in these cultures. Second, very few of the research reports described in this chapter were comparative in design. Indeed, researchers have used such a wide variety of methods to study East Asian fathering that it is problematic to synthesize research even for one culture. Third, because almost all fathering studies in East Asia used nonprobability convenience sampling, and because samples usually represent specific regions or social classes, integration of the literature is complicated by the questionable generalization of most research. Fourth, the work of Shek, Yang, Zhang, and others (e.g., Shek, 2000; J. A. Yang, 1999b; Zhang, 1997) on adolescents reminds us of the paucity of Chinese and Korean research on father-adolescent relations. Research on fathers of adult children is even rarer.

Research would ideally report objective evidence of paternal involvement, motivation, and influence. Looking at individual studies, however, we are reminded of anthropologist Hiroshi Wagatsuma's distinction between "what fathers think they *should* do, what they *think* they do, and what they *actually* do" (Wagatsuma, 1977, p. 204). Most data on East Asian fathering consist of self-reports by fathers or perceptions by their wives and children, providing subjective judgments rather than measures of what fathers actually do. Psychologist Hiroshi Azuma (1986) provided a second cautionary note by distinguishing in Japan between the *official* authority of the father and the *reality* of informal maternal power. According to Azuma, when Japanese fill out a questionnaire, they tend to give the proper public stance, called the *tatemae* (建前), which is often contrasted with the private reality, or *honne* (本音). In Japan, reality often consists of maternal responsibility, as contrasted with the proper and artificial facade of paternal leadership in the home (Vogel, 1996). This distinction between public ideology and reality may also be relevant in reviewing research on Chinese and Korean fathers.

QUANTITY

Japan

Fathering research is far more active in Japan than in either China or Korea, and research on Japanese fathers has flourished since the 1980s. A search of a National Diet Library electronic database of 9,000 Japanese journals ("Index of Journal Articles"; Nichigai Web, 2002) showed that the quantity of Japanese articles with *father* as a keyword increased dramatically from 1975 (see Table 6.1), just as fathering research mushroomed in the West (Lamb, 1976). Publication of reports on fathering began in the late 1970s, increased in the 1980s (Saitoh, 1984), and grew exponentially since the mid-1990s (Kashiwagi, 1993; Makino, Nakano, & Kashiwagi, 1996; Takahashi et al., 1994). The impetus for research in the 1980s was a suspicion of fathers' partial culpa-

Table 6.1
Quantity of East Asian Publications about Fathering

	1975–1979	1980–1984	1985–1989	1990–1991	1995–1999	2000–August 2002
Japan	78	146	115	81	372	284
China	2	12	17	16	46	46
Korea	11	32	54	87	99	31

bility for increases in childhood psychopathology (Shwalb, Imaizumi, & Nakazawa, 1987). In that era, acts of violence by some adolescents toward their parents were associated with ineffectual fathering. In the 1990s, public attention focused on bullying in schools, murders by terrorist cults in 1995, and the killing of an elementary school child by a 14 year-old boy in 1997. As before, the public pointed the finger at lack of paternal guidance. In addition, government policies in the 1990s encouraged fathers to become more involved with child development. Researchers want to know the effects of policy and social changes, and whether fathers might be responsible for the various social ills. In recent years, increasing numbers of mothers (and fathers) have shown either apathy or disgust toward children, and child abuse has become more noticeable, all of which has spawned interest in studies of parental cognition.

China

In the social science literature on the Chinese family between 1970 and 1985, fewer than 0.1% of citations referenced fathers (Ho et al., 1989), reflecting the peripheral place of fathering in Chinese research. A 2002 search of an electronic database of psychological research at the National Library in Beijing produced several references to fathering (see Table 6.1), but most citations were novels or children's biographies of celebrity fathers. The quantity of Chinese fathering citations increased gradually since the 1980s, especially since 2000, yet it is still a far smaller and less data-driven literature than is that in Japan.

Korea

As shown in Table 6.1, publications referring to Korean fathers began in the 1970s and increased in quantity over the past generation, based on our informal count. From about 1985, reflecting increased public awareness of the impact of social change and the paternal role on child development, the number of Korean researchers interested in fathering increased. Most Korean fathering research has been on paternal influences, variability according to paternal characteristics, changes in the paternal role, and cross-cultural comparisons. But with few social scientists in Korea, quality research on Korean fathers is very sparse.

SUMMARY AND COMMENTARY

Until about 1975, research on fathers was nearly nonexistent in Japan, China, and Korea, mainly because mother-child relations were considered more important than father-child relations, but also because of the relatively small number of social science researchers in China and Korea. The quantity of research has grown since the 1980s, for various reasons, but perhaps most often because of a suspicion that fathers had some responsibility for various types of child psychopathologies, but also because Western research on fathering (Lamb, 1976) made East Asian researchers more aware of the viability of fathering as a research topic. Research in Japan, China, and Korea is improving but has been characterized by five main deficiencies: (a) reliance on convenience sampling and subjective self-report measures, (b) lack of comparable measures between research studies, (c) lack of cross-national designs or comparability of measures used in the three cultures, (d) lack of a distinction between paternal ideology and paternal behavior, and (e) a replicative approach that has imitated choices of topics and methods in Western research on fathering. Fathering research has mushroomed in Japan in the past decade but still lags behind in both quality and quantity in both China and Korea.

THE CONTEXTS OF FATHERING

HISTORICAL AND CULTURAL CONTEXT

Japan: "Once Confucian, Now Fatherless?"

As described by Shwalb et al. (1987), the Japanese father was the head of the traditional family system, or *ie* (家), and the legal, social, moral, and economic leader of the family. One of the father's primary duties was to train his heir (i.e., eldest son) in the occupational, financial, and moral domains. But paternal authority began to diminish in the latter half of the 19th century as compulsory schools took away the traditional functions of families and fathers. Following World War II, the 1945–1952 American occupation of Japan (Kawai, 1960) introduced democratic values to the family, and fathers' authority declined further as they were reduced in legal status to equals with their wives and grown children. The modal Japanese family evolved in the half-century since the occupation to become democratic, individualistic, and achievement-oriented, with fathers as primary wage earners and mothers as domestic authorities, although there may be a growing level of diversity even in the relatively homogenous Japanese population.

China: Diversity and Fluidity

Chinese society (in the PRC) can be divided into at least 56 major ethnic groups, and contemporary China has major cultural divisions between rural (64% of the PRC population) and urban areas, as well as between various ethnic and geographical divisions. The Han (漢) race accounts for 98% of the PRC (Chinese National Bureau of Statistics [CNBS], 2001), yet even the Han race is very diverse. Despite power shifts, ethnic group migrations, and fluctuations between poverty and affluence among subcultures (Chu, 1985), China maintained (with notable exceptions) a united historical identity and Confucian heritage of philosophical, ethical, and political beliefs.

Researchers have long been aware of within-culture variation in Chinese fathering (Ho, 1987, 1996), parenting (Wu, 1996), and families (Stevenson, Chen, & Lee, 1992; Strom, Xie, & Strom, 1993). We cannot overemphasize this diversity—it is the dynamic that energizes Chinese society yet makes generalization about Chinese fathers difficult. Even within each geographical region in modern China there are urban-rural, social class, and ethnic variations that influence fathering. Despite Chinese diversity, the stereotypical image of the Han Chinese father has been exemplified by the motto *yan-fu-ci-mu* (嚴父慈母, "strict father, kind mother"; Ho, 1987) and has been a unifying cultural concept for centuries. In addition, the Confucian principle of respect for elders has been basic to Chinese relationships, particularly between fathers and sons (Ho, 1994).

The research literature on Chinese fathering includes data from various subcultures, and in these different locations fathers experience a variety of social and economic realities. For instance, Taiwan and Hong Kong have differed from the mainland of China in their political and economic systems and ideologies, from 1898 through 1997 in Hong Kong, and since 1949 in Taiwan. Taiwanese fathers live in a context of a capitalist economy and a political system in which democratization began in 1986, replacing the one-party system that followed Chiang's arrival. Hong Kong fathers live in a cultural setting with a 100-year history of British colonialism that brought a Western influence to its government and capitalist economy.

Korea: Two Versions of Patriarchy

Korea has undergone cycles of social upheaval from the time of the introduction of Confucianism in the 3rd and 4th centuries A.D., during the Japanese colonial period and Korean War, and up through the current period of economic development (K. B. Lee, 1984). As in China, however, traditional values have persisted because of Korea's Confucian heritage. In Korean society, traditional social norms were also founded on Confucian ideals, including the three bonds (三綱, *Samkang*) and the five moral principles of human relations (五倫, *Oryun*; Yoo, 1999). These ideals influenced paternal values and behavior, first because the Korean father was the patriarch and had absolute power over his wife and children. He also controlled the family's resources and was responsible for children's education, while children were bound to the father through filial piety and a sense of obligation. As in China, only a son could extend the family blood line, so a preference for male children developed over Korean history. Even today there is a preference for male children, and Korea has the world's highest sex-ratio imbalance at birth. In 2000, 114.6 Korean boys were born for every 100 girls, well above the natural ratio of 106:100 births of girls to boys (*DongA Ilbo*, 2002). As in China and Japan, the slogan "strict father, kind mother" is well known in Korea (J. S. Ryu, 1994).

North Korea.   In 1945, at the time of liberation from Japan, Korea divided into North and South, with different political systems and ideologies. Except for Yi et al.'s 1999 survey and papers by H. J. Jang (1996) and M. E. Lee (1996), research on fathering in North Korea is believed to be otherwise nonexistent, and all other Korean papers reviewed here were about the two thirds of Koreans living in South Korea. Yi et al. surveyed 158 individuals who had left North Korea after 1990 about childhood education and child rearing. They found that North Korea was under the strict control of a patriarchal leadership and that paternalism had a pervading influence on fathering and families. According to M. E. Lee (1996), devotion to the leader of society as a father figure was even more important than filial piety, even though Confucianism taught the primacy of the father-son relationship. H. J. Jang (1996) also observed that decision making and authority over finances among North Koreans were held jointly by husbands and wives, and the role of the father in the family was strictly prescribed as part of the wider national ideology.

Summary and Commentary

Fathering must be viewed in a historical context. For example, in Japan the paternal role has changed in response to modern and postmodern societal conditions, and it underwent perhaps its most important redefinition during the American occupation, as discussed later. Chinese fathering has an even longer history, and its most notable characteristic may be that it evolved in various subcultures, although Chinese fathers retained a common identity because their subcultures share an overall history and the legacy of Confucianism. Less has been written about historical influences on Korean fathering (especially for North Korea), which like its Japanese and Chinese counterparts has been influenced by Confucianism and numerous periods of social upheaval. Because of their unique histories, we are not surprised that fathering evolved differently in each culture. Yet Japanese, Chinese, and Korean fathers probably have similar features, too, because of the proximity and history of interaction between their cultures.

EMPLOYMENT AND WORK-ROLE CONTEXTS

Japan

Japanese corporate culture changed significantly in the 1990s as the economy soured and employee attitudes became more family oriented. Unemployment rose from 2.1% in 1991 to 5.0% in 2001 (Somusho, 2002b), and whereas Japan approached full employment in the 1980s, it exceeded the American unemployment rate in 1999. In addition, workers' average annual labor hours fell below 2,000 hours in 1995 (down from 2,269 in 1970), and the proportion of workers who took two full work days off weekly rose from 39% in 1990 to 60% in 1996 (Rodosho, 2000). One impetus for this change was the belief that fathers spent too much time at work. Coincident to the trend toward a five-day work week, all public schools moved to a five-day school week in 2002.

Japanese fathers who are involved in child rearing often face a conflict between their jobs and the paternal role. Fuyuki and Motomura (1998) found that fathers who returned home from work after 8 P.M. on weekdays and were more committed to their companies had a role conflict between work and fathering, and that fathers with the greatest conflict were highly committed to both their companies and to child rearing. Fukumaru (2000) interviewed 42 fathers and mothers of preschool children about this role conflict. Over 60% of fathers agreed with the statement, "I cannot spend enough time with my family because of my job." A majority also indicated that work had a negative effect on home life. Many fathers (24%) reported that the stress of child rearing hurt their job performance, as in "When I'm tired from child rearing, work does not go well, and I get impatient more than other men." Many fathers were resigned to the priority of work over fathering. At the same time, 48% of respondents indicated that their paternal role positively influenced their worker role, or vice versa. Therefore, the incidence of negative spillover (negative effect of a role on performance of another role) is greater than that of positive spillover, although a plurality of fathers believed the fathering and work roles were complementary rather than in conflict. At the same time, Shwalb, Kawai, Shoji, and Tsunetsugu (1995) found that Japanese fathers had very little in the way of personal networks, or contact with other people who knew their children.

Variability in Paternal Involvement. Fukumaru, Muto, and Iinaga (1999) further investigated the connection between men's attitudes toward work and children and involvement in child rearing of preschoolers and infants. Their regression analysis showed that participation in child rearing was negatively correlated with men's weekly work hours and the attitude that "work is of utmost importance to me." Fukumaru et al. also found that fathers who worked in companies with demanding promotion systems were relatively more job centered than family oriented.

Chiba (1996) analyzed data on fathering in Japan, South Korea, Thailand, Sweden, the United States, and the United Kingdom. Compared to fathers in other cultures, Japanese fathers varied more in levels of child-rearing involvement according to their job categories (e.g., salaried company workers vs. self-employed). Although Japanese company workers as a cultural group were less active in child rearing than were any other national group in the study, self-employed Japanese fathers were moderately involved in child rearing relative to other national groups.

Transfer Isolation: Japanese-Style Father Absence. Transfer isolation (単身赴任, *tanshin funin*) occurs when a Japanese father's job transfer separates him from his family. For various reasons (children's schooling, home mortgages, need to care for elderly parents), it is difficult for wives and children to change residences along with the fathers. In a study of families of children between 5th and 12th grade, transfer isolation had an especially strong effect on maternal stress when mothers had sole responsibility for child rearing (Tanaka, Nakazawa, & Nakazawa, 1996). This group also conducted a 5-year follow-up study when children were in college or employed. Grown children's stress was higher when the transfer isolation continued, compared with when the father had returned to his family or when mothers and children had accompanied fathers on the transfer (Nakazawa, Tanaka, & Nakazawa, 1998). Long-term transfer isolation also generally seems to contribute to maternal stress and anxiety about child rearing because it removes the daily communication and support mechanisms that families normally provide (Tanaka, Nakazawa, & Nakazawa, 2000).

China

The CNBS's (2001) survey of 19,512 men and women between the ages of 18 and 64 found that in 2000, 87% of women had paid jobs, compared with 94% of men. However, the percentages were lower in urban areas, where reportedly only 64% of women and 81% of men were employed. This suggests some difficulty for women to gain employment in urban areas, given that four out of five wives wanted to work. In agricultural regions it is normal for both men and women to perform fieldwork. Urban work conditions differ for Chinese males and females. The gender gap for income is widening in the PRC, and employment turnover of women is especially high in urban centers, where men earn 43% more than women. This gap and the amount of female turnover are related to the transition from an egalitarian socialist employment system to the market economy in which businesses are free to treat male and female employees differentially (CNBS, 2001).

Korea

As in Japan, the Korean government has instated a five-day work week, reducing the work week from 44 to 40 hours and eliminating Saturday work. Most Koreans (77.8%) favor this reform, which makes it likely that it will become effective despite resistance from some companies. This reform will have an important effect on the paternal role by giving men two days at home, because long hours at work may be the biggest barrier to fuller expression of the paternal role (S. H. Lee & Han, 1998). S. H. Lee and Han studied the images of 30- to 50-year-old fathers among children between preschool and middle school ($N = 270$) and noted that although many fathers in their 30s and 40s strived to become more active with their children, the biggest obstacle to paternal involvement with children was being too busy at work. These fathers have a stressful responsibility as breadwinners because investment and sacrifice are necessary to provide for children's education (N. J. Han, 1989).

In the era of the small Korean family, the father is usually the primary wage earner, and maternal income typically supplements the husband's wages (N. J. Han, 1989). Families are particularly vulnerable if fathers lose their jobs or take a pay cut. M. S. Choi (1998) found that when fathers face economic hardship, their stress leads to greater tension and anxiety in the father-child relationship. In a study of paternal anxiety and stress, K. H. Kim (1998) surveyed fathers ($N = 669$) about their infants. He found that the biggest predictor of paternal child-rearing stress was satisfaction with one's employment. The second predictor of stress was marital satisfaction, followed by fathers' degree of self-esteem.

Summary and Commentary

Fathering in all three cultures must be seen in relation to the occupational conditions of men and women. The primary role of both Japanese and Korean fathers has been as breadwinner, and many researchers have been interested in how their work role constrained their paternal role. For instance, studies of transfer isolates, spillover, and personal networks in Japan indicated that fathers were unable to be actively involved with their children when work duties took priority over parenting. Both Japanese and Korean governments have taken some steps to reduce men's hours at work, and this reform suggests that public opinion prefers that men spend more time at home. Less is known about the relationship between employment and parenting roles in Chinese culture, although it is apparent that urban-rural differences are particularly relevant in the PRC. In addition, the ideology of equal employment opportunity, as well as maternal employment, may be more firmly established in China than in Japan or Korea, where most men are still breadwinners.

FAMILY CONTEXTS

Japan

Japanese mean family size has decreased to a record low of 2.67, down from 2.99 in 1990 (Somusho, 2002a). In small nuclear families with modern conveniences, it became feasible for Japanese mothers to handle child rearing and housework by themselves, so many fathers lost their sense of purpose at home. At the same time, some young fathers became increasingly interested in child rearing as family size decreased, perhaps because it was easier to lavish attention on individual children in a small family than when one's children were numerous. Finally, spousal decision making in the post–World War II era became more egalitarian, and mothers have become intensely involved with their children as education-centered mothers (教育ママ, *kyoiku-mama*). The bursting of the economic bubble in the early 1990s, followed by the current decade-long recession, increased the stress on fathers, who still have to support the high expectations for children's education and high standards of living.

In our opinion, changes in the family have impacted the parenting styles (Baumrind, 1971) of Japanese fathers. Specifically, we consider the effects of the American occupation of Japan following World War II to be one cause of weakness in many of today's Japanese fathers. The occupation ostensibly promoted democracy, equality, and individualism, and although its goal of democratization succeeded in overturning the traditional patriarchy, for some Japanese it replaced authoritarian fathering with permissive rather than authoritative fathering. This may have happened because some Japanese took the antiauthoritarian American ideology to mean antiauthoritative and thus expressed democracy and individualism in the form of permissiveness (which is compatible with Japanese-style relationships). We also believe that as a result of this historical influence, Japanese fathers generally have become weaker than Chinese or Korean fathers. Objective research, however, is needed to test this thesis.

China

Family size has changed throughout Chinese history and decreased over the past century. The number of individuals per household was 4.87 about 2,000 years ago, rose to 6.57 in A.D. 280, and fluctuated between 4 and 7 members through the end of the Qing Dynasty in 1912 (G. Chen, 2000). Average family size was 5.17 at the time of the 1911 revolution and, following a slight increase after the founding of the PRC, decreased to 3.96 in 1990 and 3.70 in 1995. Mean family sizes in 1995 were even smaller in Shanghai (3.02) and Beijing (3.04; G. Chen, 2000).

Since 1979 the PRC instituted a one-child policy (独生子女政策, *De Sheng Zi Nu Zheng Ci*). One concern is that limited to only one child, fathers may spoil their children, which would change the nature of father-child relations. The policy has limited most urban families to one child, but it has not been enforced as strictly in rural areas and among minority groups. Despite the trend toward nuclear families, child rearing in China retains a traditional kinship-based quality, especially in rural China. For example, Zhou, Liao, and Wang (1999) found in a rural town in northern China that while parents and their adult children lived in separate dwellings, homes were built close by, and child rearing was based on mutual assistance between households. Another trend that influences Chinese fathering is an increase in divorces. According to the State Family Planning Commission (2001), the number of divorces in the PRC increased from 800,000 in 1990 to 1.2 million in 2000, an increase of 50% in just one decade.

Korea

In 2000 the average number of children born to Korean mothers was only 1.30, and the average household size was 3.12 persons (Korean National Statistical Office, 2000). At the same time, women have been gaining increased access to higher education. In this context, the role of the father as family patriarch has changed. The top priority in the Korean family is the family unit rather than the individual (Lee, 1975; Ok, 1989; Y. J. Ryu, 1993). Although traditional thinking may have declined in Korea, familism retains a strong cultural value (Yi, 1996). Over the past three decades, educational standards also have risen dramatically, and fathers have become increasingly conscious of education. It is academic achievement that now unites the Korean family, and the family invests all its energy in children's education.

Because of the breakdown of the South Korean economy since 1997, many fathers have lost their jobs. Unemployment rose in 1998 alone by 250%, and in 1998 the annual inflation rate was 8.1%, damaging the finances of many families. The stress, anxiety, and tension faced by parents in this context have impacted children and have been associated in the Korean media with increases in homelessness, paternal suicide, child abuse, and family violence and dissolution (JoongAng Ilbo, 1998). In addition, the Korean divorce rate in 2000 was seven times the rate of divorce of 1970 (*DongA Ilbo,* 2002).

Summary and Commentary

The mean sizes of families in Japan, China, and Korea have become very small. It is possible that the reasons for small families have changed historically. Whereas population control began in each society in an era of scarce resources (and in the case of China, controlling its megapopulation remains a necessity), in this new millennium small families have become necessary so that families can concentrate their resources on the very high costs of education. Small families have been associated with different phenomena in each culture (e.g., the Japanese education-centered mothers, the Chinese one-child policy, and familism in Korea). However, fathers in all three cultures have one thing in common: a small number of children.

Contexts of Husband-Wife Relationships and Women's Roles

Japan

Maternal employment, family demographics, and husband-wife relations all affect the paternal role (Ishii-Kuntz & Maryanski, in press; Shwalb, Shwalb, Sukemune, & Tatsumoto, 1992). In 2000, 46% of Japanese mothers of preschoolers were employed (up from 39% in 1996; Kosei Rodosho, 2001), which affects paternal responsibilities. For instance, 37% of women and 52% of men in a 1987 survey agreed that "Husbands work outside and wives take care of the household," but this number fell to only 21% of women and 30% of men in 2000 (Sorifu, 2000).

A recent study by Onishi and Gjerde (2002) suggested another way that the husband-wife relationship may influence fathering. Their multimethod research on 40 Japanese couples revealed asymmetry in the marital relationship; that is, fathers appeared to be care receivers while mothers were care providers to their husbands (pp. 436–438). In a sense, the nurturing function of the Japanese mother extended to her marriage relationship. This raises interesting research questions: Are Japanese fathers being parented by their wives, and how does being nurtured by their wives affect fathers' nurturing of children?

Maternal and Paternal Anxiety and Stress.   Maternal anxiety and stress about child rearing tend to be strongest in nuclear families where mothers have sole responsibility for child rearing and feel neglected emotionally by their job-centered husbands. In one study of fathers and mothers of infants and preschoolers (Ino, 1994), mothers felt more stressed and repressed when fathers regarded child rearing as exclusively female work, compared with wives whose husbands thought child rearing was both parents' responsibility. In addition, a study of parents of infants revealed that fathers' family-centered attitudes correlated with maternal satisfaction about child rearing, sharing of housekeeping and child rearing, and a positive husband-wife relationship (Oyabu & Maeda, 1997). Similarly, Ogata and Miyashita (2000) found that when fathers had more communication with their wives and preschool children, wives had less stress or feelings of distraction and isolation, and Fukumaru et al. (1999) showed a positive correlation between paternal involvement with infants and preschoolers and harmonious husband-wife relations.

China

It is usually the case that PRC fathers do more than provide economic support, while mothers are active both in the family and at work. It is rare for a father to be only a wage earner, and the ideology of gender equality has affected the thinking and behavior of PRC fathers. Yet there is also evidence of differences between the functions of fathers and mothers, in both the PRC and Taiwan. This was suggested by a content analysis of several child-rearing manuals. Up to the present, most manuals have advocated strict parental authority by both fathers and mothers, and no gender differences can be seen between them (e.g., Ye et al., 1981). In the 1990s, however, some manuals began to address mother-specific (e.g., attachment relationships) and father-specific (e.g., sons' masculinity) topics, and another PRC child-rearing manual even advocated the revival of some aspects of traditional fathering and mothering (Lin, 1999).

Some publications have reported behavior that contradicted the "strict father, kind mother" motto. For example, a Hong Kong report found that mothers were more coercive toward their children than were fathers (Tang, 1998), and a PRC magazine article titled "Role Reversal: The Kind Father and Stern Mother" (Zhai, 1994) questioned the motto altogether. But these case studies did not provide objective evidence of changes in fathers. We emphasize the distinction between actual behavior and the "strict father, kind mother" ideology. Men more likely blend strictness and kindness in their behavior, just as they may blend paternal love based on dignity and respect with maternal love based on benevolence and affection (L. Zhongde, personal communication, August 18, 2002).

Korea

The percentage of women in the Korean work force rose from 42.3% in 1980 to 48.8% in 2001. Research on the relationship between maternal employment and paternal behavior has produced contradictory results. Three studies have shown, respectively, that fathers become more active when mothers are employed (S. Y. Yoon & Chung, 1999), less active (Jeung & Park, 1996), or do not differ in activity according to maternal employment (Ko & Ok, 1994). Because it is common in Korea for an employed mother to rely on her own mother or on the husband's mother for child care, paternal involvement can remain constant even when mothers are employed.

Summary and Commentary

The expression "strict father, kind mother" is used throughout East Asia, and research is necessary to ascertain whether parents' behavior actually coincides with this motto. For instance, some research has shown a distinction in both Japan and China between fathers' attitudes and behavior with regard to their responsibility for child rearing and housework. The nature of husband-wife relations and women's roles has differed between cultures. Maternal employment increased in Japan and Korea in recent years, whereas in China women traditionally performed both farm work and child-rearing functions. Japanese research has also shown that the quality of the husband-wife relationship influences men's relationships with their children, as well as how much stress fathers and mothers experience as parents. Finally, an important aspect of the paternal role in all three cultures has been as an emotional support to the mother.

PSYCHOLOGICAL STUDIES OF FATHERS

FATHER-CHILD RELATIONSHIPS

Japan

Japanese fathers between ages 25 and 29 years reported in 1996 that they only spent 12 minutes per day with their children, compared with 11 minutes per day for fathers aged 30 to 39 years. The comparable amounts of time with children reported for mothers were 2 hours 2 minutes for ages 25 to 29 years and 1 hour 22 minutes for women ages 30 to 39 years. The average daily time performing domestic tasks were 3.8 hours for mothers and 0.5 hours for fathers (Sorifu, 1997).

In a survey of 1,160 fathers (Shwalb, Kawai, Shoji, & Tsunetsugu, 1997), the following percentages of men described their functions in the family: "economic provider" (74%), "support for child to go out into society" (71%), "emotional support to my wife" (68%), "protect the family" (53%), "family leader and decision maker" (35%), "support wife's child rearing and housekeeping" (34%), "supportive of mother-child relations" (33%), and "participate in housekeeping" (30%). Asked why they get involved with their children, fathers' most common reason was "I like my child" (81%), followed by "I want to teach my child many things" (65%) and "I worry about my child" (33%). Among fathers who were uninvolved at home, the most common reasons for inactivity were "I am too busy at work" (59%), "It is better to just leave my child to the mother" (35%), and "It is too tiring to do things with my child" (21%).

Toda (2001) related Japanese fathering styles to men's own childhood experiences. She found that authoritative fathers reported having parents who also had authoritative attitudes, a more extroverted and active personality of their own, and (in their current families) a harmonious atmosphere and children with sociable temperaments. Authoritarian fathers reported that their own parents were authoritarian and favored corporal punishment, were more anxious or depressed themselves, and currently had a hostile family atmosphere and children with impulsive and emotional temperaments. Finally, permissive fathers tended to have parents with a combination of permissive and authoritarian attitudes, their own anxious or depressed personality, a self-centered and isolated family atmosphere, and impulsive or stubborn children.

Some Japanese fathers experience stress and anxiety about child rearing, and this affects their participation in child care. In one investigation of fathers of infants (Iwata & Matsuo, 2001), men who actively participated in child rearing had less stress about child rearing. However, a second study of fathers of infants showed that paternal anxiety about children's development was higher among fathers who shared child-rearing responsibility at home, compared with fathers who left child rearing exclusively to their wives (Sumida & Fujii, 1998). Together, these two studies showed that *stress* as a parent is lower among involved and interested fathers who know their children better, whereas *anxiety* regarding the child can be greater among the same stressed fathers because they are more concerned and worried about their children.

China

PRC fathers appear to be more involved with housework than are Japanese fathers. For example, 77% of the men in the CNBS (2001) survey agreed that "Men should perform half of domestic housework." This view of responsibility was different from their attitudes toward division of labor, as 54% of men and 50% of women agreed that "Men are chiefly responsible for activity in society while women are responsible for the home." This result was about the same as in the 1990 CNBS survey, when 52% of men and 48% of women agreed with the same statement. In addition, evidence of the difference between attitudes toward division of labor and actual time use was seen when mothers reported an average of 4.0 hours of daily housework compared to 1.3 hours for fathers, and 85% of Chinese reported that women were primarily responsible for kitchen and cleaning work.

Based on Western theory, we might predict that authoritarian parenting would be associated with cold relations rather than empathic or warm Chinese father-child relations. However, in a study of fathering in the PRC, Taiwan, and Hong Kong, daughters perceived fathers as warmer whereas sons perceived them as more controlling (Berndt, Cheung, Lau, Hau, & Lew, 1993). Additionally, Jose, Huntsinger, Huntsinger, and Liaw (2000) observed Taiwanese, Taiwanese American, and European American parents of preschool children, noting that while Taiwanese fathers had more traditional parenting values and were more controlling, their relationships with children were just as warm as were those of European American fathers. Apparently, individual Chinese fathers balance and blend authoritarian and authoritative parenting styles, as has also been observed in Zhejiang Province (Wo, Ma, & Liu, 2002), and in Beijing and Shanghai (X. Chen et al., 1998).

Various people besides fathers and mothers, especially grandmothers, are involved in Chinese child rearing. Multiple caretakers, seen throughout the PRC in multigenerational child rearing and in urban China in the hiring of caretakers and residential day care facilities (G. Chen, 2000), reduce the need for paternal involvement with their children. For example, Zhou et al. (1999) found in rural Hebei Province that most fathers worked outside the home, had little contact with children, and had minimal involvement in child rearing. Similarly, in urban Fuyang, mothers had far more influence on the development of elementary school children than did fathers (Wo, Ma, & Liu, 2002).

In contrast to Zhou et al.'s (1999) report of minimal paternal involvement, Jankowiak (1992) observed active fathering in a longitudinal study in Huhhot, the Inner Mongolian capitol. According to Jankowiak's data, men were considered incompetent with babies and therefore were not involved with infants for about the first half-year of life, but after early infancy fathers became involved, taking walks or going shopping with children. Jankowiak also noted that fathers' style of holding and playing and communicating with children differed from the style of most mothers. In another study of parents of 1-year-olds (Sun & Roopnarine, 1996), urban Taiwanese fathers' interactions with infants had a more rough and playful quality than did that of mothers, as in some Western societies.

Korea

Research findings suggest that the Korean paternal role sometimes has differed for sons and daughters. In the past Korean fathers concentrated on their sons whereas mothers attended more to their daughters (K. W. Kim & Lee, 1998; S. H. Lee & Han, 1998; J. A. Yang, 1999a), and recent data indicate that some Korean fathers are more involved with taking care of sons than with taking care of daughters. However, many contemporary fathers are equally involved with children whether they are girls or boys. The main reason children of both genders now receive ample attention is small family size (S. Y. Yoon & Chung, 1999).

As Korean maternal employment has increased, expectations for paternal involvement with children and domestic tasks have risen (Oh & Ohm, 1997; Wui, 1983). In addition, it has become desirable for fathers to be companions to their children (K. H. Han, 1995). As a result, fathers in their 30s are more actively involved in child rearing than are fathers in their 40s and 50s (O. Y. Kim & Ok, 2000; S. H. Lee & Han, 1998; C. H. Yoon & Lee, 1993). Younger Korean fathers feed, bathe, and diaper their young children (K. H. Han, 1997) more than did their own fathers. These young fathers did not experience the rapid changes in the Korean economy, culture, and society and tend to be nontraditional and gentle (Ahn, 1990; K. H. Han, 1995). In contrast, however, a newspaper article (JoongAng Ilbo, 1997) reported that fathers in their 40s and 50s were like "boarders in their own families," and 55% of this cohort did not even see their children on a daily basis.

Paternal Characteristics.   Several other factors have been related by researchers to Korean paternal influence on child development. The longer the hours men spend at the workplace, the smaller their role is at home (S. H. Lee & Han, 1998). This may be because long working hours make it difficult for most Korean fathers to establish a place for themselves in the family other than as breadwinners. Those fathers who are more satisfied with their marriages or jobs tend to be more emotionally stable and have more interest in family life (H. J. Lee, 1995; S. H. Lee & Han, 1998). Fathers who are more highly educated tend to have more of a domestic role (S. H. Lee & Han, 1998; S. Y. Yoon & Chung, 1999), and those in professional fields and with greater incomes have been reported to be more actively involved with their children (K. S. Choi, 1991; Park, 1996; S. Y. Yoon & Chung, 1999). Finally, fathers who have better defined value systems and clearer concepts of childhood and development are more active (Kang, 2000; E. J. Kim & Park, 2002).

Comparative Research

Although there have been a few comparative studies of fathers, the research reviewed in the following sections included no *direct* comparisons of fathers in all three national groups. A three-culture comparative study is at the top of the agenda for future research in this region.

Japanese versus Chinese Fathers.   Very few studies have compared fathers in Japan and the PRC, although some researchers have written that Chinese fathers were more controlling than Japanese fathers (Ho, 1987; Yamamoto, 1997) and have been more strict about education for several centuries (Emori, 1989). Fukaya (1995) compared perceptions, evaluations, and frequency of contact with fathers, as reported by Japanese (Tokyo) and Taiwanese junior high school pupils. She noted that fewer Japanese fathers than Taiwanese fathers had frequent contact with their children. In addition, adolescents described fathers differently in the two cultures, as more "reliable," "egocentric," and "stubborn" in Japan, and as more "gentle," "respected," "dignified," and "interested in education" in Taiwan. More Taiwanese rated fathers as important for "family support" (82%, vs. 65% in Japan), "making important family decisions" (73%, vs. 51% in Japan), and "creating a positive family atmosphere" (76%, vs. 42% in Japan). Fukaya concluded that Japanese fathers were perceived as more traditional and alienated from family life, whereas Taiwanese fathers were seen as more involved, respected, and gentle.

Japanese versus Korean Fathers.   Nihon Joshi Shakai Kyoiku Kai (1995) reported on parents of newborn to 12-year-old children in Japan, South Korea, Thailand, the United States, the United Kingdom, and Sweden. Relative to the other national samples, self-reports by Japanese and South Korean fathers were quite similar. First, Korea had the lowest maternal employment rate, and Japan's was second lowest. Both Korean and Japanese mothers tended to have primary responsibility for child rearing. Japanese fathers reported the least amount of contact with children, and Koreans had the next least. Respondents also rated whether various activities were performed by the mother, father, or both. Japanese and Korean fathers reported less involvement than fathers in the other four cultures in preparing meals, advising children about the future, disciplining children, and helping children with problems and studies. On the other hand, Korean fathers rated their importance as breadwinners higher than did any other cultural group, followed by the Japanese. Japanese and Korean fathers were different only on one item: Japanese fathers ranked third highest and Korean fathers ranked lowest among the cultures as children's "playmate."

Kang (1997) compared fathers' reports of relationships with elementary school children in Japan and Korea. She found two dimensions of fathering in a factor analysis: (a) quality of relationship (i.e., affective communication, listening, and encouragement) and (b) quantity of activity (i.e., degree of involvement, knowing child's teachers and friends, and watching television together). Japanese fathers rated themselves as emotionally closer to children, on the qualitative dimension, than did Korean fathers. On the quantitative dimension, however, Korean fathers rated themselves as more involved with children than Japanese fathers. In both Japan and Korea, relationship quality was correlated with paternal educational attainment. In addition, Japanese rated themselves as more active with daughters than sons on the quantitative dimension, whereas Korean fathers favored their daughters also, but only on the qualitative dimension.

Summary and Commentary

Comparative studies have shown that Chinese and Korean fathers differed in their time use, attitudes, and functions from their Western counterparts, and that Japanese and Korean fathers were relatively uninvolved with their children. Time-use data suggest that Chinese fathers may be somewhat more involved than Japanese fathers, but even Chinese fathers' contributions to child rearing and housework tasks were secondary to those of their wives. In terms of parenting styles, research has suggested that parenting styles in both Japan and China may differ from those of Western fathers, and values and cognitions about children may be related to different fathering styles both between and within the three cultures. As a topic area, the father-child relationship is perhaps the most popular area of research on fathering in Japan, China, and Korea. However, it was noticeable that measures are not comparable between studies in each culture, making it difficult to draw conclusions about paternal functions, style, and even time use.

IMAGES OF FATHERS

Japan

The traditional Japanese paternal image was Confucian (Wagatsuma, 1977, p. 181). For example, the saying "earthquake, thunder, fire, and father" (地,雷,火事,親父, *jishin, kaminari, kaji, oyaji*) idealized fathers as strong and fearsome. In contrast, the stereotype of fathers in post–World War II Japan changed from that of a strong family leader to an ineffectual figure who was absent either physically or psychologically. This negative image was reinforced by expressions like *dame oyaji* (dumb dads) and *sodai gomi* (couch potatoes akin to heavy trash objects awaiting curbside hauling; Ohgiya, 1983). Another common post–World War II image of the Japanese father was of a hardworking breadwinner (Shwalb et al., 1987). Wagatsuma (1977) cautioned that the behavior of pre- and postwar Japanese fathers may not differ as much as these images imply; because there are no behavioral measures of past generations of Japanese fathers, we cannot directly compare fathers across generations. In our opinion, many prewar Japanese fathers were relatively gentle and even permissive, compared with Chinese fathers.

Research findings also suggest that Japanese men value domestic roles as much as or more than they value their work roles. Shwalb et al. (1997) asked 1,150 fathers of preschoolers to prioritize their roles, and men ranked the paternal role as their highest priority, followed in order by the roles of husband, person, worker, and male; that is, their self-image was child centered. However, perceptions depend on the individual father's behavior and the child's age and gender. Ishii-Kuntz (1999) compared Japanese and American children's perceptions of their fathers and found that girls, younger children, and children who spent more time with their fathers expressed more affection toward their fathers.

Fukaya and Morikawa (1990) conducted a factor analysis of 78 items from a survey on the paternal image (N = 3,132 fathers and 783 high school students). Fathers evaluated both their own fathers and themselves, and the students evaluated only their fathers. Men evaluated their own fathers using descriptors like "leadership" and "seriousness," and current fathers saw themselves (as confirmed by their children) as having qualities such as "maternal-like warmth" and "brightness." These data indicate that the Japanese paternal image evolved into a balance of instrumental and expressive characteristics.

Finally, Shwalb (1996) conducted a retrospective survey about the paternal images of college women and their parents (N = 150 families), as respondents recalled how the fathering role changed across childhood and adolescence. Fathers, mothers, and daughters agreed that men spent the most *time* with their daughters as preschoolers (followed about equally by the periods of infancy and lower elementary school) and the least amount of time with them from the upper elementary school years and on. High school was recalled as the time of peak paternal *responsibility* for their daughters. Significantly fewer daughters than fathers or mothers recalled middle school as a time of paternal responsibility, and more mothers than fathers or daughters saw the college years as an important time of paternal responsibility. The periods of least paternal *influence* were infancy and college age; influence was about equal throughout childhood and adolescence. *Closeness* of the father-daughter relationship was associated most often with the preschool and college years and least often for infancy and upper elementary school. Lastly, the period chosen by daughters, fathers, and mothers as the most *important* for father-daughter relations was the middle school years. These data indicated that the images held by fathers, mothers, and their children are both similar and distinct, depending on whether the issue was involvement, responsibility, influence, closeness, or importance.

China

Research on images of Chinese parents has mainly concerned parenting styles. One study that shed light on urban-rural differences in perceptions of Chinese fathers took place in both rural and urban sections of Xiandong Province (Zhang, 1997). This study replicated Perris, Jacobsson, Lindstrom, von Knorring, and Perris' (1980) questionnaire survey of middle school students (N = 895; Han Chinese n = 858; one-child family n = 455). Zhang noted a strong similarity in adolescents' perceptions of the parenting styles in the urban and rural samples. There were also group differences; for example, fathers reported different expectations for their adolescents in rural and urban areas. Because urban families were more affluent and had higher financial aspirations, urban fathers had higher expectations for children's education. These expectations were associated with a demanding and controlling style among both urban fathers and mothers. Children of urban fathers also reported a warmer father-adolescent relationship than did their rural counterparts. This suggested to Zhang that urban fathers are more maternal yet also more demanding because they have higher expectations for their children. Zhang's data point to an important aspect of Chinese modern life that influences fathering: high expectations for children's education. Expectations are expressed as both warmth and strictness, helping to explain why previous studies (e.g., Chao, 1994) found a blend of authoritarian and authoritative parenting in Chinese populations.

Korea

A content analysis of elementary school textbooks in 1996 showed that fathers were portrayed in family activities (e.g., at home having supper with children, riding on a train together, or playing at the beach). Korean children generally perceived fathers as breadwinners (Chung & Kim, 1996). In their analysis of poems about fathers written by 2nd- and 5th-grade elementary school pupils ($N = 69$), they found many images of fathers as being busy and tired, coming home late, and doing little at home other than sleeping or watching television. Korean children defined fathers as providers who have to work extremely hard and do not seem to mind if fathers lacked the time to play with them or be companions. Many Korean children also reportedly felt obligated to study hard to express appreciation to their hard-working fathers.

Other studies have shown that fathers are perceived as gentle friends toward their children (Ahn, 1990; K. H. Han, 1995, 1997). In addition, in a study of 130 boys and girls at a middle school and high school (Kwak & Choi, 1997), 83.6% of children thought of the father as "close." However, of those who felt close to their fathers, half reported that they spent less than 30 minutes together every day, and only 16.2% said they talked to their fathers about problems (compared with 60.1% who talked with their mothers). Most children (87.7%) also responded that the role of fathers in the home should be actively to build close, egalitarian, and mutual family relationships rather than to be authorities.

Summary and Commentary

Studies of paternal images have used different measures and looked at different age groups and populations, making it difficult to compare the Japanese, Chinese, and Korean data. Some aspects of the Japanese and Korean paternal image included a hardworking yet distant figure with little responsibility or involvement at home. There have been few studies on images of Chinese or Korean fathers, but the most important findings on Chinese fathers were that they were seen as very concerned about education and that images differed between rural and urban fathers. Finally, one retrospective study showed that images and men's roles may vary among children of different ages. It appears to us that there were generally more similarities than differences in the images of Japanese, Chinese, and Korean fathers.

THE INFLUENCE OF FATHERS ON CHILD DEVELOPMENT

Cognitive Development and Learning

Japan.   Nakano (1992a) found that teacher ratings of 2- to 3-year-old children in day care correlated with reported frequency of father-child interactions and with paternal attitudes. The amount of time fathers spent at play and in direct contact with children, as well as fathers' favorable ratings of their interactions with children, was correlated with teacher ratings of children as advanced in development of emotions, self-expression, language, cognition, and sociability.

Satoh and Miyake (1978) observed interactions between fathers and 5-year-old preschool children on problem-solving tasks. Paternal sensitivity and responsiveness correlated positively with children's achievement motivation, sociability, and curiosity. In addition, there was a positive correlation between paternal sensitivity and children's IQ at age 4 and 5 and a negative correlation between IQ and fathers' intrusiveness with children during problem-solving tasks.

China.   The modernized Chinese educational system began in the 19th century, and a new system instituted in 1912 included early childhood education (He, 1990). The literacy rate of Chinese boys and girls is over 95% (Ministry of Education, PRC, 2002). The influence of both fathers and mothers on education may be indirect in providing financial support or helping with homework. Abbott, Zheng, and Meredith (1992) reported that PRC fathers helped more with children's homework than mothers, but Ho (1987) reported the opposite for Hong Kong parents (Hong Kong YMCA & Hong Kong Shue Yan College, 1982). Paternal influence on education was also studied over a two-year period in the PRC, where Chen, Liu, and Li (2000) found that paternal warmth (for 12-year-olds) predicted school achievement and maternal warmth predicted emotional adjustment.

Korea.   According to Roh and Park (1999), who surveyed 649 fathers of 4- to 5-year-old children, fathers provided logical guidance and gave rational explanations when disciplining their children. Fathers' awareness of their children's capabilities enabled them to have an important influence on children's cognitive and personality development. The authors also noted that fathers who were more involved with their children tended to have a stronger influence on the cooperativeness, emotional expressiveness, and cognitive resourcefulness of their children.

Social Development

Japan.   Most East Asian research on fathers' impact on social development has focused on Japanese preschoolers. For instance, Mera (1997) studied how mothers and fathers of preschoolers discipline or control children (e.g., for refusing to eat, not brushing teeth, misbehaving at a supermarket, writing on walls). In her survey, fathers reported that they confronted and disciplined children directly, whereas mothers used persuasion or ignored their children's misbehavior. Specifically, fathers gave orders to children without offering explanations, whereas mothers used rules, logic, or appeals to children's feelings. Mera also found that "flexible" fathers were more involved with their children than were "one-pattern fathers" who used the same imperative-directive style in every possible situation. This latter finding suggested to Mera that fathers who take care of their children develop a more flexible and adaptive parenting style.

In a 1993 study that they replicated in 1998, Katoh, Ishii-Kuntz, Makino, and Tsuchiya (2002) also found correlations between paternal involvement and ratings of children's social skills by preschool teachers. Similarly, a questionnaire survey by Ogata (1995) showed that paternal involvement in child rearing was associated with development of social skills among preschool children. In a follow-up study, Ogata and Miyashita (2000) observed that children's social skills were higher when fathers had frequent communication with their children and wives.

Nakano (1992b) investigated fathers' attitudes and behaviors toward 2- and 3-year-old children in relation to children's ability to separate from their mothers. At a day care center, mothers and children were observed working together for 30 minutes and then after they separated. Fathers of children who separated smoothly from mothers reported that they played with their children more, had more direct contact with and understanding of their children, and participated more in child care. Fathers expressed more devotion to and responded more positively to those children who were better at temporary separations. These data showed that children's ability to separate in a stable manner from mothers was related to paternal attitudes and behavior.

Finally, Ohtani and Kida (1993) surveyed junior high school pupils and their fathers about social orientations such as individuality, sociability, and interrelatedness. Their results showed that the more young adolescents reported contact with fathers, the greater the convergence was in the interpersonal values of the teenagers and fathers.

Korea.   A study of Korean fathers and their 1st- through 6th-grade elementary school children ($N = 407$) showed that fathers influenced the social adaptability of their children (Yoon & Chung, 1999). The more time fathers spent with their children, the more adaptive and emotionally stable were their children. In addition, K. W. Kim and Lee's (1998) study found that paternal involvement and cooperativeness with 4- to 5-year-old children was correlated with children's self-control, activeness in peer groups, and curiosity. Jeong and Choi (1992, 1995) associated paternal involvement in child rearing with preschoolers' social adaptability, emotional responsiveness, and prosocial orientation. Finally, E. J. Kim and Park (2002) surveyed the teachers of 3- to 6-year-old preschoolers ($N = 194$) about their social behavior and fathers' beliefs about socialization and concluded that fathers have an important influence on children's social cognitive development in the formation of children's goals and value systems.

Gender Role Development

Katoh (1992) studied Japanese fathers' behavior in relation to gender role orientations and socialization. Fathers who were more conscious of masculine roles tended to have more overall contact with and played more with their preschool-age sons than with their daughters, and they also took care of their daughters less. The sons of these son-oriented masculine fathers played more with action-figure toys, and their daughters played more feminine games in preschool. Katoh concluded that paternal gender role orientations are an important aspect of fathers' interactions with sons and daughters.

Childhood Psychopathology

Japan.   School refusal and adolescent aggression toward their parents were among the notable problems in the 1980s (Shwalb et al., 1987), and in the 1990s bullying in school and child abuse by parents joined school refusal as highly publicized problems (Shoji, in press; Yoneyama, 1999). Media accounts of violence by children and adolescents increased in the 1990s, for example in nationwide attention focused on a murder committed by a junior high school boy in 1997 (Kaneko Shobo, 1997) and on how students who had been outstanding achievers in secondary school took part as young adults in the Aum Shinrikyo cult murders of 1995 (Furuhata, 1998). Psychologists have also begun to observe a problem called shutting-in (*hikikomori*), when adolescents refuse to come out of their bedrooms to eat or attend school. In fact, some Japanese in their early 20s who live with their parents exhibit shutting-in by refusing to go to their company jobs. Shwalb et al. (1987) noted that Japanese clinicians and media experts commonly blame father absence or weakness for many problems, but only a few commentators (e.g., Hirayama, 2001) support their conjecture with objective evidence.

China.   Shek (1998) examined the relationships between parent-adolescent conflict and adolescent psychological well-being, based on reports by a sample of Chinese adolescents and their parents ($N = 378$ families). The results indicated that parent-adolescent conflict based on their ratings was concurrently related to adolescents' hopelessness, life satisfaction, self-esteem, life purpose, and morbidity, at two times of measurement. Longitudinal analyses showed that the relationship between parent-adolescent conflict and adolescent psychological well-being was bidirectional. Although the strengths of these associations were similar for male and female adolescents, father-adolescent conflict was found to exert a stronger influence than did mother-adolescent conflict, on well-being. Another study found a correlation between problem behavior of 1st-grade primary school children ($N = 92$) and conflicting parenting styles of fathers and mothers (Wo, Ma, & Liu, 2002).

Korea.   The impetus for research on Korean paternal influence on children's problem behavior was the economic downturn that began around 1997. During this period of massive layoffs and corporate restructuring, families have suffered in terms of stress, anger, and disintegration. For instance, M. S. Choi (1998) found that stress and anxiety among fathers has an important influence on their children. Finally, Heo (1998) showed how financial stress increased disunity within families, as well as depression and withdrawal among children. Unfortunately, clinical and applied research on child psychopathology is deficient in South Korea, and is entirely lacking in North Korea, where poverty and family dislocation are huge social issues.

Summary and Commentary

A variety of research on paternal influences on children has been conducted, mainly in Japan, focusing on cognitive, social and gender role development, education, and childhood psychopathology. In Japan, data show important paternal influence throughout these domains, mainly among preschool-age children, but research is needed to address the widespread social concern that poor fathering is a root of childhood psychopathologies. Korean research is beginning to emerge on the effects of fathers on children's cognitive, social, and personality development, although the quantity of Korean studies is still limited. Overall, the data showed consistently that fathers influenced various aspects of child development, although comparative research is needed to clarify the relative levels of influence across cultures.

The Development of Fathers

Most research in this area is on Japanese fathers, although one relevant study has been conducted in Korea.

Transition to Fatherhood

Onodera and Kashiwagi (1997) conducted a longitudinal survey beginning a month before respondents became fathers, and when their children were 7 to 8 months old and 2 years of age. Men ranked the roles of father, worker, and husband, in order of importance for their identities. In addition, compared to their responses before becoming fathers, men reported an increased sense of responsibility and restriction on their lives, and less worry or annoyance about taking care of a baby, at 7 to 8 months following the birth of their children. When their children were 2 years old, fathers reported that they understood their children better, were adapted to the paternal role, but were also more annoyed about taking care of a child, felt more irritable and restricted by the child, and were less confident about supporting their families.

In an experimental study, Kamiya (2002) compared fathers of infants with men who were expecting their first child and with newlywed men. He found that fathers of infants responded more positively to infant cries than did men in the other groups and that paternal experience with child rearing was related to a better ability to differentiate the different causes of crying. Besides confirming that fatherhood changes men, Kamiya's study was notable because reports of experimental research are extremely rare in the Asian literature on fathering.

Witnessing Childbirth

The father's appearance at the birth of his child has gradually become more common since the 1980s, and current local estimates of such appearance range from 18% to 25% (Igarashi & Iijima, 2001; Sasaki, 2001). Chiga et al. (1990) compared father-infant interactions between fathers who had versus had not witnessed the birth, over the first year of life. They found that fathers who were present at birth played with and took care of their children more often, had more positive feelings toward the babies, and communicated better with their wives. We cannot be certain from these data whether paternal interest in children increased because of the experience of witnessing a birth or whether fathers who chose to witness a birth were predisposed to be involved fathers.

Personality Changes in Fathers

There is growing interest in Japan about how fathering affects men's personality and thinking. In the first study on this topic, Makino and Nakahara (1990) elicited free responses from 163 husband-wife couples about their changes as parents, and the authors found different kinds of changes between mothers and fathers. Mothers most often reported changes in "personality or psychological characteristics" (38%), followed in frequency by "no longer self-centered" (20%), "social world has widened" (8%), and "became more responsible" (8%). In contrast, the largest number of fathers (26%) reported "no change," followed by "became more responsible" (23%).

Shintani, Muramatsu, and Makino (1993) surveyed over 1,200 mothers and fathers of children attending preschools, elementary schools, and middle schools, and their factor analysis revealed three dimensions of change: self-awareness as being a parent, maturity as a human being, and stress about child rearing. Fathers who were more involved tended to emphasize changes in self-awareness and maturity, while stress was not related to reported involvement with children.

Kashiwagi and Wakamatsu (1994) also conducted a factor analysis of paternal and maternal self-reports ($N = 346$ husband-wife couples), and they derived six dimensions of change in parents: (a) flexibility, (b) self-control, (c) acceptance of fate and faith, (d) widening perspective, (e) sense of worthwhile existence, and (f) strength of self. Mothers reported more change than fathers on all six dimensions as a result of raising children. Fathers who were more involved with their children reported more change on all six dimensions than did fathers who were less involved. This suggests that degree of involvement rather than merely becoming fathers influences men's development. Kashiwagi and Wakamatsu also reported that the greatest changes were among fathers who had higher educational degrees and employed wives. In a similar study of fathers of preschoolers and adolescents, Mera (2001) added another dimension (self-assertion) to the six dimensions reported by Kashiwagi and Wakamatsu. She replicated their finding that mothers reported more change than did fathers on every dimension.

Korea

S. H. Lee and Han (1998) studied changes in fathers in their 30s and 40s ($N = 270$). Many fathers agreed that they "felt great responsibility" (92.6%), "obligation to provide financially has increased" (53.3%), and "my life is centered around my children" (48.5%). Fewer agreed that "having children has improved my relations with my own father" (34.4%) or "having children has improved my marital relationship" (38.9%). Some fathers also reported that becoming a father enabled them to understand better their own fathers' experience, and that sharing the joy of childbirth had given them the opportunity to join with their wives in raising children.

Summary and Commentary

Research on the development of fathers in Japan (and one Korean study) showed important changes in men after they became fathers. Increasing numbers of Japanese fathers are witnessing childbirth. Personality changes in the transition to fatherhood were not as profound as those for mothers, but longitudinal studies have shown that Japanese fathers reassess their roles and change significantly, particularly those who were actively involved with their children.

Public Policies and Fathering

Japan

The Japanese government has implemented many new policies to encourage the increased involvement of fathers in child rearing and housekeeping. For example, the Child Care Leave Law was instituted in 1992 to promote both paternity and maternity leave (Ishii-Kuntz, 2001; Ota, 1999); paternity leave is for eight weeks if the mother is at home and for up to one year if the mother is working at least three days a week. In 1999 the Ministry of Health and Welfare conducted a public relations campaign to promote paternal involvement, and the campaign poster read, "A man who does not participate in child rearing is not a father" (see Figure 6.1). From 2001, this law was extended to apply to fathers until their children enter elementary school, giving fa-

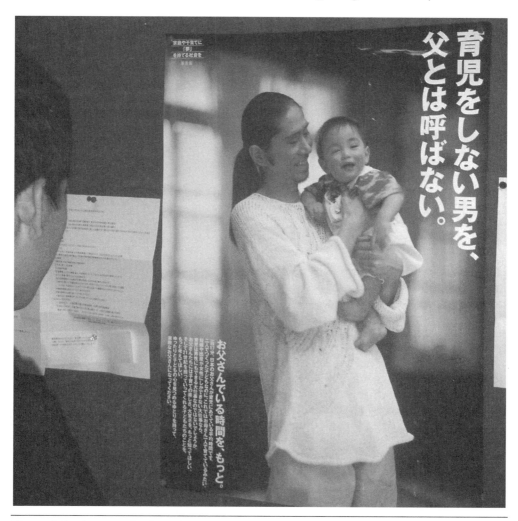

Figure 6.1 A poster distributed by the Japanese government stated that "A man who does not participate in child rearing is not a father." Photo courtesy of Keito Nakamichi and Naoko Sugimoto.

thers the same legal protection as mothers to take time off to care for children. However, many believe that the corporate mentality still discourages active fathering (Wijers-Hasegawa, 2002) and view these policies with skepticism. In this context, advocacy groups such as Ikujiren (育時連) promoted paternity leave, sharing of child rearing, job sharing, and attracted considerable attention (Ishii-Kuntz, 2001).

China

The PRC's one child policy, which became a law effective September 1, 2002, rather than just a decree, was formulated to stabilize the huge size of the Chinese population (see Figure 6.2). This campaign succeeded in halting the population explosion, but it

Figure 6.2 A sign on the concourse of Beijing International Airport in 2001 proclaimed, "If we reduce the population, everyone will feel relief." Photo courtesy of Toshiya Yamamoto.

continues to be promoted by the government. For instance, a sign was prominently placed at Beijing International Airport proclaiming "If we reduce the population, everyone will feel relief." The vast majority of urban families now have only one child, and the first cohort of these children is now college aged. In rural China, however, there has been strong resistance to the program because children are needed as laborers and eventually to look after their parents in old age. In addition, the traditional importance of the father-son relationship made it necessary for a son to perpetuate the family bloodline (Lin, 2000). It was also assumed that a wife had a duty to give birth to a male heir. Parents use abortion and other measures to increase the probability of having a son, creating disproportionate birthrates for males and females. In fact, one research team has warned that in the coming generation there may be a surplus of 30 million unmarriageable Chinese males (Hudson & Den Boer, 2002). The one child policy continues to evolve and is controversial; in rural China, for example, many people resisted the policy because of the traditional preference for sons. In some cases, parents avoid registering the child until they have a son, which is known as the *heihaizi* (黑孩子, literally, "black children") problem of unregistered children. Under such circumstances, the government has had no choice but to allow a second child if the first child was female or handicapped. Some experts believe that the one child policy will lead to the gradual erosion of Chinese paternal authority as families become more concerned with affection toward children and exert less control and authority (L. Zhongde, personal communication, August 18, 2002).

Summary and Commentary

Government policies have been concerned with fathering throughout East Asia, although research on the effects of policies has been lacking, especially in Korea. In Japan, the national government has promoted maternal employment, paternal involvement in child rearing, equal employment opportunity, and, most recently, increasing the size of the family. These measures are all new, and we expect the effects of these policies to be seen in the next generation of fathers. In China, the one child policy has restricted most urban families to a single child, whereas more exceptions to the policy are the case in rural China. This policy conflicts with traditional Chinese values placed on large families and the father-son relationship and is likely to have a profound impact on the nature of the Chinese paternal role.

THE FUTURE OF FATHERING

JAPAN

There seem to be at least two current patterns of Japanese fathering (Ishii-Kuntz, 2001), the first of which describes the minority of fathers who are becoming increasingly involved with their children. The large majority of fathers, however, are uninvolved with their children and families mainly because of job demands that discourage participation in child rearing and housework. Despite legal measures that ostensibly promote gender equality, we predict that role conflict between work and family will continue. Even though companies increasingly promote family-oriented *attitudes,* we believe that only when companies prioritize family life over work-group harmony will these fathers become more involved on the *behavioral* level.

CHINA

PRC membership in the World Trade Organization will bring its people more deeply into the world marketplace, and this transformation will promote globalization and higher living standards. But despite changes in the structure of society and families, and in attitudes, we predict continuity in some aspects of traditional Chinese fathering behavior. We anticipate the type of combined change and continuity that was observed by Abbott et al. (1992). They found in a sample of southern Chinese fathers an increase in active involvement with child rearing coexisting with traditional functions of the father as an authority figure and teacher.

We also predict that Chinese interpersonal relationships will continue to differ from the Japanese emphasis on group harmony or *wa* (和) that inhibits Japanese self-expression, and from the individualism of American-style relationships. Just as the Japanese preserved their style of interpersonal relationships after becoming a global economic power, the Chinese will probably maintain their own approach, including their unique fathering styles.

The ideology of the PRC has emphasized equality between the sexes, but we do not believe that equality between the sexes has been achieved as in the vision of the socialist revolution, although it has influenced paternal involvement in housework and child rearing. Present-day China is not characterized by true male-female equality, but rather by a growing gender inequality in economic terms. We anticipate a redistribution of power and affection in the family, as Chinese values continue to change. Whether the movement toward the market economy will lead to equality between fathers and mothers, or greater paternal involvement in domestic matters, is a subject for future research on Chinese fathers and families. At the same time, authority is very important in Chinese culture, and we do not expect Chinese fathers simply to concede such authority as the economy changes.

KOREA

On September 13, 2002, an anonymous poem titled "Who Is Father?" appeared in the nationwide newspaper, *DongA Ilbo* (see Figure 6.3). The poem caused a sensation and was viewed by 5.4 million people on the newspaper's Web site (www.donga.com), its most Web hits ever, second only to the aftermath of the September 11 terrorism at-

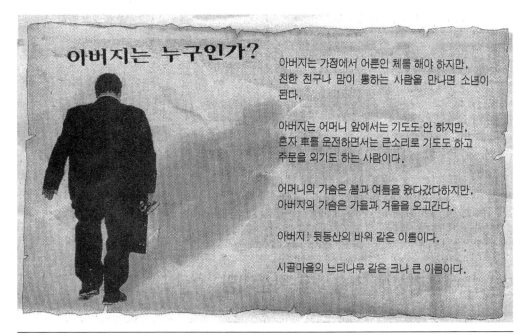

아버지는 누구인가?

아버지는 가정에서 어른인 체를 해야 하지만,
친한 친구나 맘이 통하는 사람을 만나면 소년이
된다.

아버지는 어머니 앞에서는 기도도 안 하지만,
혼자 차를 운전하면서는 큰소리로 기도도 하고
주문을 외기도 하는 사람이다.

어머니의 가슴은 봄과 여름을 왔다갔다하지만,
아버지의 가슴은 가을과 겨울을 오고간다.

아버지! 뒷동산의 바위 같은 이름이다.

시골마을의 느티나무 같은 크나 큰 이름이다.

Figure 6.3   An anonymous poem (abridged here) titled "Who Is Father?" was published in the Korean Newspaper *DongA Ilbo,* September 13, 2002, and caused a public sensation.

tacks. The newspaper also reported an unprecedented flood of e-mails about fathering and requests for faxed copies of the poem. We believe the reaction to this poem reflected a growing concern with fathering in Korea.

Many Korean fathers are developing a new role in which they are like friends to children and foster children's autonomy through an emotional relationship. They are also joining support groups and other organizations and using the Internet to exchange information and receive advice about fathering and child development. Some fathers are now invited to visit some elementary schools and middle schools on their days off, an activity that was previously the exclusive domain of mothers (Y. S. Yoon, 1996). Research is already showing that fathers have a significant influence on children when they become involved with children's school activities (S. Y. Yoon & Chung, 1999). We predict that such activities will become more common as the benefits of paternal involvement become clear to the Korean public.

CONCLUSIONS

RESEARCH QUALITY AND QUANTITY

The quality of fathering research in Japan, China, and Korea is improving but remains deficient because it has relied on convenience sampling and self-report measures, seldom used comparable measures across studies or made cross-cultural comparisons, and often failed to distinguish between paternal ideology, perceptions of fathers, and actual behavior. The quantity of fathering research has mushroomed in Japan but still lags behind in China and Korea.

CONTEXTS

Fathering is affected by the contexts of history, changing families, work roles, and marital relationships. We have observed that a unique set of societal transitions affected the evolution of fathering in each of the three cultures. In Japan, the most notable transformation took place after World War II under the American occupation in an era of democratization. The Chinese, who have experienced social upheavals for thousands of years and yet have remained unified by their history and Confucianism, now face dramatic changes and continue to adapt their culture to new realities. Korea, too, has retained its identity despite numerous societal transitions including the Japanese occupation and rapid modernization.

In recent decades, Japanese and Korean fathers have been under great pressure to support a high standard of living, and men have forfeited their roles in home life in order to provide financially for their families. Japanese "transfer isolation" is a good example of how work life has taken priority over family life and affected children's development and family relationships. Perhaps to a greater extent than in Japan and Korea, the socialist ideology of the PRC (despite regional variations) promotes gender equality at work and encourages both men and women to be active in child rearing.

Japanese, Chinese, and Korean families have become increasingly nuclear in structure and small in size. Childhood socialization in the three cultures promotes a high level of achievement motivation, and mothers generally have primary responsibility for housekeeping, child rearing, and monitoring their children's education. Research in Japan indicates that fathers spend very little time with children or domestic tasks, although their attitudes are becoming more family centered. In contrast, Chinese fathers appear to be somewhat more involved than Japanese fathers, and they blend a combination of warmth, control, authority, and authoritativeness in their parenting styles. Korean fathers have historically tended to focus on their sons, but they spend more time with each child nowadays because of the drastic reduction in the size of Korean families in recent decades. Finally, a small number of cross-cultural studies showed that Japanese and Korean fathers are not very involved with their children, compared with Western fathers.

PSYCHOLOGICAL RESEARCH

A clear distinction was evident in research in both Japan and China between fathers' attitudes and their actual responsibility for child rearing and housework. In addition, the quality of marital relationships influenced fathers' relationships with their children. For instance, research showed in Japan that an important aspect of the paternal role is as an emotional support to the mother, and one study also indicated that the maternal role includes nurturing of husbands. The Confucian expression "strict father, kind mother" remains an important phenomenon in all three cultures, although men's behavior is not always consistent with the slogan.

Children's images of Japanese and Korean fathers were very similar and combined negative and positive aspects. Chinese paternal images differed between urban and rural areas, and economic standards of living appeared to have an impact on paternal expectations for their children's education. Most research on men's influence on their children has been conducted in Japan, focusing on cognitive, social, and gender role development; Korean fathers appeared to influence several domains of child development, although there is a paucity of such research in Korea. One area of influence that is common in Japan, China, and Korea, yet is seldom the subject of research, is paternal influence on childhood psychopathology.

Aspects of social policies in each society can be seen as reflecting the culture's perceptions of the paternal role and the society's agenda for families. For example, policies and laws in Japan have promoted maternal employment, paternal involvement in child rearing, equal employment opportunity, and, recently, increasing the size of the family. In the PRC, the goal of population control has led to the promotion of a one child policy that restricts most urban families to a single child, although more exceptions to the rule are the case in rural China. This policy conflicts with Chinese traditions emphasizing large families and father-son relationships.

RESEARCH AGENDA

The coverage of research reviewed in this chapter was broad but shallow, and many research questions remain unanswered. For example, in Japan research is necessary to assess the impact of the laws and social policies intended to increase paternal involvement and promote maternal employment. Future research on Chinese fathering should include the study of diversity among fathers and the meaning of broad cultural images or stereotypes (e.g., "strict father, kind mother") for Chinese fathers. In Korea, higher quality research is needed to clarify how fathers adapt to changing social and economic conditions.

Comparative studies within and among Japan, China, and Korea are perhaps our highest priority; comparisons drawn between the three cultures in this section are partially speculative because of the lack of comparative data. It will be interesting to discover how modernization and globalization affect fathers and fathering in the three cultures, given their similarities and differences in values, economic systems, gender roles, and exposure to the West. Finally, inspection of the choice of topics in research reviewed shows that fathering research in East Asia has clearly been derived from Western research and theory up until now. It will serve the interests of psychology as an international science to look more closely at fathering in China, Japan, and Korea for indigenous constructs and phenomena that may challenge Western theory.

In future research, we hope to see more use of direct measures (e.g., face-to-face interviews and both naturalistic and controlled observations). These methods, as well as the inclusion of qualitative methods such as participant observation and ethnography, would be an improvement over the current reliance on questionnaires and maternal reports. In addition, longitudinal designs and experimental methods are necessary to understand developmental and causal variables. The paternal role in East Asia is evolving rapidly and must be studied as a dynamically changing phenomenon. Finally, research is needed not only on fathers' direct influence on their children, but also on how they influence children indirectly through the husband-wife relationship.

LOOKING AHEAD

Our predictions for the future of fathering in East Asia have included aspects of both continuity and change. Traditional values and philosophies will continue to exert a strong influence. Yet we also expect that changes in societies, families, educational systems, economic systems, technology, and children themselves will change the nature of fathering. As globalization, modernization, capitalism, and other forces continue to change the nature of the paternal role in Japan, China, and Korea, public access to research on fathering is likely to increase men's awareness of their potential as fathers.

REFERENCES

Abbott, D., Zheng, F. M., & Meredith, W. (1992). An evolving redefinition of the fatherhood role in the People's Republic of China. *International Journal of Sociology of the Family, 29,* 45–54.

Ahn, B. C. (1990). The role of Korean males in the family: Correlates with participation. *Journal of Social Science, 9,* 231–251.

Azuma, H. (1986). Why study child development in Japan? In H. Stevenson, H. Azuma, & K. Hakuta (Eds.), *Child development and education in Japan* (pp. 3–12). New York: Freeman.

Baumrind, D. (1971). Current patterns of parental authority. *Developmental Psychology Monographs, 4*(1, Pt. 2).

Berndt, T. J., Cheung, P. C., Lau, S., Hau, K., & Lew, W. J. F. (1993). Perceptions of parenting in Mainland China, Taiwan, and Hong Kong: Sex differences and societal differences. *Developmental Psychology, 29,* 156–164.

Chao, R. (1994). Beyond parental control and authoritarian parenting style: Understanding Chinese parenting through the cultural notion of training. *Child Development, 64,* 1111–1119.

Chen, G. (2000). *Revolution of the family.* Beijing: Chinese Social Science Press.

Chen, X., Hastings, P., Rubin, K., Chen, H., Cen, G., & Stewart, S. (1998). Child-rearing attitudes and behavioral inhibition in Chinese and Canadian toddlers: A cross-cultural study. *Developmental Psychology, 34,* 677–686.

Chen, X., Liu, M., & Li, D. (2000). Parental warmth, control, and indulgence and their relations to adjustment in Chinese children: A longitudinal study. *Journal of Family Psychology, 14,* 401–419.

Chiba, A. (1996). Characteristics and problems of fathers raising children in contemporary Japan: From international comparative research on "home education." *Annual Report of the Faculty of Education, Bunkyo University, 30,* 139–150.

Chiga, Y., Horiguchi, S., Mizuno, K., Mochizuki, T., Sone, H., Sato, R., et al. (1990). Study on the perinatal care and parents education care of their infants with or without attending wife's births (3). *Report of the Studies of Nippon Aiiku Research Institute for Maternal Child Health and Welfare, 27,* 63–73.

Chinese National Bureau of Statistics. (2001). Fifth bulletin of national population census (No. 1). Retrieved from http://stats.gov.cn/tjgb/rkpcgb/qgrkpcgb/200203310083.htm on March 31, 2002.

Choi, K. S. (1991). Children's perceptions of paternal involvement in childrearing. *Journal of Pusan Women's College, 31,* 247–270.

Choi, K. S. (1992). *Paternal childrearing behavior in relation to children's social skills.* Doctoral thesis, Korea University, Seoul.

Choi, M. S. (1998). *A structural analysis of factors related to the influence of stress on children in time of economic trouble.* Master's thesis, Sookmyung Women's University, Seoul.

Chu, G. C. (1985). The emergence of the new Chinese culture. In W.-S. Tseng & D. Y. H. Wu (Eds.), *Chinese culture and mental health* (pp. 15–28). New York: Academic Press.

Chung, S. H., & Kim, S. H. (1996). Fathers in children's poems. *Journal of Child Studies, 17,* 79–105.

DongA Ilbo. (2002, July 26). A statistical view of female births (p. 29).

Emori, I. (1989). *The history of corporal punishment.* Tokyo: Shincho-sha.

Fukaya, N. (1995). A comparative study of fathers in Tokyo and Taipei. *Journal of Child Study, 1,* 54–66.

Fukaya, K., & Morikawa, H. (1990). A study of factor analysis about fathers. *Journal of Home Economics of Japan, 41*, 487–495.

Fukumaru, Y. (2000). Relationships between multiple roles and depression of parents with young children: The data of interview by fathers. *Journal of the Graduate School of Humanities and Sciences, Ochanomizu University, 3*, 133–143.

Fukumaru, Y., Muto, T., & Iinaga, K. (1999). Concepts of work and children among parents of young children in relation to paternal involvement in child care. *Japanese Journal of Developmental Psychology, 10*, 189–198.

Furuhata, K. (1998). *The Aum trial.* Tokyo: Asahi Shinbunsha.

Fuyuki, H., & Motomura, H. (1998). The effect of social and psychological factors on fathers' role conflict. *Annals of Family Studies, 23*, 56–70.

Han, K. H. (1995). *Middle age: Men's work and family life.* Seoul: Korean Family Research Institute.

Han, K. H. (1997). Changes in images of fathers. *Sociocultural Research Center Reports, 8*, 33–52.

Han, K. H. (1998). *Middle age: Men's work and family life.* Seoul: Korean Family Research Institute.

Han, N. J. (1989). *Research on the contemporary Korean family.* Seoul: Lijisa.

He, X. (1990). *A brief history of Chinese education.* Beijing: BNU Press.

Heo, S. Y. (1998). *Changes in the childrearing behavior of mothers and fathers and family changes in the era of economic turmoil: Influences on children's distress.* Master's thesis, Sookmyung Women's University, Seoul.

Hirayama, S. (2001). Adolescent mental health and paternal involvement in families: Incongruent ratings of fathers and mothers. *Japanese Journal of Developmental Psychology, 12*, 99–109.

Ho, D. Y. F. (1987). Fatherhood in Chinese culture. In M. E. Lamb (Ed.), *The father's role: Cross-cultural perspectives* (pp. 227–245). Hillsdale, NJ: Erlbaum.

Ho, D. Y. F. (1989). Continuity and variation in Chinese patterns of socialization. *Journal of Marriage and the Family, 51*, 149–163.

Ho, D. Y. F. (1994). Cognitive socialization in Confucian heritage cultures. In P. Greenfield & R. Cocking (Eds.), *Cross-cultural roots of minority child development* (pp. 285–313). Hillsdale, NJ: Erlbaum.

Ho, D. Y. F. (1995). Selfhood and identity in Confucianism, Taoism, Buddhism, and Hinduism: Contrasts with the West. *Journal for the Theory of Social Behaviour, 25*(2), 115–139.

Ho, D. Y. F. (1996). Filial piety and its psychological consequences. In M. Bond (Ed.), *The handbook of Chinese psychology* (pp. 155–165). Hong Kong: Oxford University Press.

Ho, D. Y. F., Spinks, J., & Yeung, C. S. H. (1989). *Chinese patterns of behavior.* New York: Praeger.

Hong Kong YMCA & Hong Kong Shue Yan College. (1982). *Report on working mothers in family function.* Hong Kong: Author.

Hudson, V., & Den Boer, A. (2002). A surplus of men, a deficit of peace. *International Security, 26*, 5–38.

Igarashi, H., & Iijima, S. (2001). Fathers' modes of thinking and behavior in child care. *Yamanasi Idai Kiyou, 18*, 89–93.

Ikujiren. (2003). Equal childrearing time for women and men. www.eqg.org/index-e.html

Ino, I. (1994). A study of feelings and attitudes of a married couple in child care: I. Husband's lack of recognition of wife's feelings in child care. *Journal of Home Economics of Japan, 45*, 999–1004.

Ishii-Kuntz, M. (1999). Children's affection toward fathers: A comparison between Japan and the United States. *International Journal of Japanese Sociology, 8*, 35–50.

Ishii-Kuntz, M. (2001). Balancing fatherhood and work: Emergence of diverse masculinities in contemporary Japan. In J. Roberson & N. Suzuki (Eds.), *Men and masculinities in contemporary Japan* (pp. 198–216). New York: Routledge.

Ishii-Kuntz, M., & Maryanski, A. (in press). Conjugal roles and social networks in Japanese families. *Journal of Family Issues.*

Iwata, M., & Matsuo, Y. (2001). A study of relation between infants' fathers' participation in housework and in child care and their parenting stress as well as their marital quality. *Bulletin of Fukuoka University of Education, 50,* 239–246.

Jang, H. J. (1996). *The family systems of South and North Korea and women's roles.* Seoul: Institute for Far Eastern Studies, Kyungman University.

Jang, K. Y. (1989). *Paternal childrearing behavior in relation to children's social abilities.* Master's thesis, Myongji University, Seoul.

Jankowiak, W. (1992). Father-child relations in urban China. In B. Hewlett (Ed.), *Father-child relations: Cultural and biosocial contexts* (pp. 345–363). New York: Aldine de Gruyter.

Jeong, H. H., & Choi, K. S. (1992). Fathers' childrearing behavior and children's prosocial moral judgments. *Journal of Child Studies, 13,* 38–51.

Jeong, H. H., & Choi, K. S. (1995). Fathers' child-rearing behaviors, children's sex-role taking, children's emotion responses and children's prosocial behavior. *Korean Journal of Child Studies, 16,* 33–48.

Jeung, C. A., & Park, S. Y. (1996). The effect of parenting stress and social support on marriage satisfaction. *Journal of the Korean Home Economic Association, 34,* 115–128.

JoongAng Ilbo. (1997, May 19). Fathers are boarders in their own families (p. 1).

JoongAng Ilbo. (1998, April 27). The impoverishment of loss of family ethics (pp. 1–2).

Jose, P., Huntsinger, C., Huntsinger, P., & Liaw, F.-R. (2000). Parental values and practices relevant to young children's social development in Taiwan and the United States. *Journal of Cross-Cultural Psychology, 31,* 677–702.

Kamiya, T. (2002). Paternal cognition of infant crying. *Japanese Journal of Developmental Psychology, 13,* 284–294.

Kaneko Shobo. (1997). The Kobe primary school murder: Background of the incident and implications for education [Special issue]. *Jidoshinri, 51.*

Kang, R. H. (1997). Children's gender-role trait and fathers' child-rearing behavior: A comparison between Japan and Korea. *Human Developmental Research, CODER Annual Report, 12,* 79–87.

Kang, R. H. (2000). Career vs. child: Differences in the child-rearing practices of Korea and Japanese fathers. *Journal of Korean Child Studies, 21,* 119–133.

Kashiwagi, K. (Ed.). (1993). *The developmental psychology of fathers.* Tokyo: Kawashima Shoten.

Kashiwagi, K., & Wakamatsu, S. (1994). Personality development in relation to "becoming a parent." *Japanese Journal of Developmental Psychology, 5,* 72–83.

Katoh, K. (1992). Father-child relationship in the first three years of life: Masculinity and father-child relationships. *Journal of Family Education Research Center, 14,* 117–123.

Katoh, K., Ishii-Kuntz, M., Makino, K., & Tsuchiya, M. (2002). The impact of paternal involvement and maternal childcare anxiety on sociability of three-year-olds: Two cohort comparison. *Japanese Journal of Developmental Psychology, 13,* 30–41.

Kawai, K. (1960). *Japan's American interlude.* Chicago: University of Chicago Press.

Kim, E. J., & Park, S. Y. (2002). Father's socialization beliefs as related to child social behaviors. *Korean Journal of Child Studies, 23,* 187–203.

Kim, H. S. (1993). *The relationships between academic achievement and parents' childrearing methods and interest in learning.* Master's thesis, Hongik University, Seoul.

Kim, K. H. (1998). A study on the parenting stress of fathers. *Journal of the Korean Home Management Association, 36,* 49–62.

Kim, K. W., & Lee, I. S. (1998). The relationship between the childrearing investment of fathers and children's social-economic competence. *Korean Journal of Child Studies, 19,* 65–75.

Kim, O. Y., & Ok, S. W. (2000). Patterns of commitment to work role and fathering and the level of life satisfaction among married men. *Journal of the Korean Home Management Association, 18,* 125–139.

Kim, U., & Choi, S. H. (1994). Individualism, collectivism, and child development: A Korean perspective. In P. Greenfield & R. Cocking (Eds.), *Cross-cultural roots of minority child development* (pp. 227–257). Hillsdale, NJ: Erlbaum.

Ko, S. J., & Ok, S. W. (1994). Transition to parenthood: III. Parental strain satisfaction division of child-care task. *Journal of the Korean Home Economic Association, 32,* 83–95.

Korea National Statistical Office. (2002). *A national survey of population and residence.* Seoul: Author.

Kosei Rodosho. (2001). *Basic survey of people's lives.* Tokyo: Ministry of Health, Labor and Welfare.

Kwak, B. H., & Choi, E. J. (1997). A study of the father in relation to the family. Symposium of Korea Legal Aid Center for Family Relations: Changing society and changing fathers (pp. 26–53). Seoul: Korea Legal Aid Center for Family Relations.

Lamb, M. E. (Ed.). (1976). *The role of the father in child development.* New York: Wiley.

Lamb, M. E. (Ed.). (1997). *The role of the father in child development* (3rd ed.). New York: Wiley.

Lee, H. J. (1995). *Research on the paternal role: Satisfaction with marriage and work.* Master's thesis, Ewha Women's College, Seoul.

Lee, K. B. (1984). *A new history of Korea.* Cambridge, MA: Harvard University Press.

Lee, K. K. (1975). *Analysis of the structure of Korean families.* Seoul: Lijisa.

Lee, L. (1992). Day care in the People's Republic of China. In M. Lamb, K. Sternberg, C.-P. Hwang, & A. Broberg (Eds.), *Child care in context* (pp. 355–392). Hillsdale, NJ: Erlbaum.

Lee, M. E. (1996). *Changing South and North Korean societies and the culture of traditional Confucianism: Families and extended families.* Seoul: Institute for Far Eastern Studies, Kyungnam University.

Lee, S. H. (1995). The great work of men and the mutual efforts of families: Company workers of major corporations. *Journal of Korean Sociological Association, 29,* 271–289.

Lee, S. H., & Han, E. J. (1998). A study on paternal role-behavior of married men. *Journal of the Korean Home Management Association, 16,* 49–62.

Lin, G. (2000). *Revolution of child rearing.* Beijing: ET Press.

Makino, N., & Nakahara, Y. (1990). Research on changing process of parents' consciousness in child-rearing. *Journal of Family Education Research Center, 12,* 11–19.

Makino, K., Nakano, Y., & Kashiwagi, K. (1996). *Child development and the role of the father.* Kyoto: Minerva.

Mera, A. (1997). The father and mother's control strategy: The relationship with parental feeling and cognition about children and child-care, and father's involvement with child-care. *Human Developmental Research, CODER Annual Report, 12,* 51–58.

Mera, A. (2001). Personality development of fathers and mothers by child-care. *Human Developmental Research, CODER Annual Report, 16,* 87–98.

Ministry of Education, PRC. (2002). Brief report of anti-literacy policies in the PRC since 1990. Retrieved on September 3, 2002 from http://www.moe.edu.cn/news/2002_9/3.htm

Nakano, Y. (1992a). Father-child relationship in the first three years of life: Child development and father-child development. *Journal of Family Education Research Center, 14,* 124–129.

Nakano, Y. (1992b). Father-child relations in the first three years of life: Mother-child separation and father-child relationships. *Journal of Family Education Research Center, 14,* 130–134.

Nakazawa, J., Tanaka, Y., & Nakazawa, S. (1998). Effects of father absence on children's socioemotional development. *Research and Clinical Center for Child Development Annual Report, 22,* 69–77.

Nichigai Web. (2002). *Search for journal articles.* Tokyo: National Diet Library.

Nodong.org (2002). Public favors five-day work week. http://5days.nodong.org/pol/hangil-1 .htm

Nihon Josi Shakai Kyoiku Kai. (1995). *International comparative research on "home education": Survey on children and family life.* Tokyo: Society of Japanese Women's Social Education.

Ogata, K. (1995). The father's care of pre-school children and their social adaptability: A comparison of single income families and double income families. *Japanese Journal of Educational Psychology, 3,* 335–342.

Ogata, K., & Miyashita, K. (2000). Father and family: Exploring links between husband-wife relations, wife's mental stress, infant social adaptability and father's own personality development. *Bulletin of Faculty of Education, Chiba University, 48,* 1–14.

Oh, Y. H., & Ohm, J. A. (1997). *Parents and child.* Seoul: Dong Hyun.

Ohgiya, S. (1983). The Society of Thunderous Fathers. In *Basic information on current expressions.* Tokyo: Jiyukokuminsha.

Ohtani, N., & Kida, J. (1993). The relationship between fathers and junior high school children and child's developing value consciousness. *Bulletin of Osaka Kyoiku University* (Series II), *4,* 57–72.

Ok, S. W. (1989). *Research on the value of "familism" in contemporary Korea.* Doctoral thesis, Seoul National University, Seoul.

Onishi, M., & Gjerde, P. (2002). Attachment strategies in Japanese urban middle-class couples: A cultural theme analysis of asymmetry in marital relationships. *Personal Relationships, 9,* 435–455.

Onodera, A., & Kashiwagi, K. (1997). Longitudinal study on the process of becoming a parent. *Human Developmental Research, CODER Annual Report, 12,* 59–78.

Ota, M. (1999). Dad takes child-care leave. *Japan Quarterly, 46*(1), 83–89.

Oyabu, Y., & Maeda, T. (1997). Effects influencing maternal satisfaction with infant rearing: III. Effects of fathers' work-centeredness and home-centeredness. *Journal of Child Health, 56,* 54–60.

Park, M. S. (1996). The quality of life among middle-aged men and women. *Journal of the Korean Home Management Association, 14,* 19–33.

Perris, C., Jacobsson, L., Lindstrom, H., von Knorring, L., & Perris, H. (1980). Development of a new inventory for assessing memories of parental rearing behavior. *Acta Psychiatric Scandinavia, 61,* 265–274.

Rodosho. (2000). *Survey of work time system in 1999.* Tokyo: Ministry of Labor.

Roh, H. M., & Park, I. J. (1999). Relationship between fathers' childrearing behavior and competencies of young children. *Korean Journal of Child Studies, 20,* 231–245.

Rothbaum, F., Pott, M., Azuma, H., Miyake, K., & Weisz, J. (2000). The development of close relationships in Japan and the United States: Paths of symbiotic harmony and generative tension. *Child Development, 71,* 1121–1142.

Ryu, J. S. (1994). *Traditional society and children's education.* Daegu, South Korea: Joogmunsa.

Ryu, Y. J. (1993). *Research on the mechanisms of Korean families.* Seoul: Gyonmoonsa.

Saitoh, H. (1984). The role and influence of the father. In *Annual Review of Japanese Child Psychology 1984* (pp. 103–135). Tokyo: Kaneko Shobo.

Sasaki, K. (2001). A report of investigation on recognition of obstetrics staff on the "child birth accompanied by the husband." *Iryo: Japanese Journal of National Medical Service, 55,* 419–423.

Satoh, K., & Miyake, K. (1978). What aspects of parental behavior lead to the child's positive cognitive development during years prior to and soon after school entrance? *Research and Clinical Center for Child Development Annual Report, 2,* 15–30.

Shek, D. T. L. (1998). A longitudinal study of the relations between parent-adolescent conflict and adolescent psychological well-being. *Journal of Genetic Psychology, 159*(1), 53–67.

Shek, D. T. L. (2000). Parental marital quality and well-being, parent-child relational quality, and Chinese adolescent adjustment. *American Journal of Family Therapy, 28,* 147–162.

Shintani, Y., Muramatsu, M., & Makino, N. (1993). A study on the transition of parenthood and its determinants. *Journal of Family Education Research Center, 15,* 129–140.

Shoji, J. (in press). Child abuse in Japan: Culture, causes, and treatment. In D. Shwalb, J. Nakazawa, & B. Shwalb (Eds.), *Child development in cultural context: Applied research on Japanese children.* Greenwich, CT: Greenwood Press.

Shwalb, D. W. (1996). The Japanese father role, as viewed across life stages by junior college women. *Cross Culture: The Bulletin of Koryo Women's College, 14,* 231–250.

Shwalb, D. W., Imaizumi, N., & Nakazawa, J. (1987). The modern Japanese father: Roles and problems in a changing society. In M. E. Lamb (Ed.), *The father's role: Cross-cultural perspectives* (pp. 247–269). Hillsdale, NJ: Erlbaum.

Shwalb, D. W., Kawai, H., Shoji, J., & Tsunetsugu, K. (1995). The place of advice: Japanese parents' sources of information about child health and development. *Journal of Applied Developmental Psychology, 16,* 645–660.

Shwalb, D. W., Kawai, H., Shoji, J., & Tsunetsugu, K. (1997). The middle class Japanese father: A survey of parents of preschoolers. *Journal of Applied Developmental Psychology, 18,* 497–511.

Shwalb, D. W., & Shwalb, B. J. (Eds.). (1996). *Japanese childrearing: Two generations of scholarship.* New York: Guilford Press.

Shwalb, D. W., Shwalb, B. J., Sukemune, S., & Tatsumoto, S. (1992). Japanese non-maternal childcare: Past, present and future. In M. E. Lamb, K. Sternberg, C.-P. Hwang, & A. Broberg (Eds.), *Childcare in context* (pp. 331–353). Hillsdale, NJ: Erlbaum.

Somusho. (2002a). *Labor force survey: Ministry of Public management.* Tokyo: Home Affairs, Post and Telecommunications, Statistical Bureau and Statistic Center.

Somusho. (2002b). *System of social and demographic statistics.* Tokyo: Ministry of Public Management, Home Affairs and Telecommunications, Statistical Bureau and Statistic Center.

Sorifu. (1997). *Time use and leisure activity in 1996.* Tokyo: Prime Minister's Office.

Sorifu. (2000). *Survey on the gender-equal society.* Tokyo: Prime Minister's Office.

Stevenson, H., Chen, C.-S., & Lee, S.-Y. (1992). Chinese families. In J. Roopnarine & D. Carter (Eds.), *Parent-child socialization in diverse cultures: Advances in applied developmental psychology* (Vol. 5, pp. 17–33). Norwood, NJ: Ablex.

Strom, R., Xie, Q., & Strom, S. (1993). Family changes in the People's Republic of China. *Journal of Instructional Psychology, 22,* 286–292.

Sumida, M., & Fujii, M. (1998). A study on child-rearing anxiety of fathers. *Research Bulletin, Graduate School of Human Environment Studies, Kyusyu University, 1,* 79–98.

Sun, L., & Roopnarine, J. L. (1996). Mother-infant, father-infant interaction and involvement in child care and household labor among Taiwanese families. *Infant Behavior and Development, 19,* 121–129.

Takahashi, T., Takano, A., Komiyama, K., Ohohinata, M., Shindou, Y., & Kubo, R. (1994). *Development of paternality.* Tokyo: Kaseikyoikusya.

Tanaka, Y., Nakazawa, J., & Nakazawa, S. (1996). Women's psychological stress as caused by men's job transfers: A comparative study between men who are dislocated with vs. without their families. *Japanese Journal of Educational Psychology, 44,* 156–165.

Tanaka, Y., Nakazawa, J., & Nakazawa, S. (2000). The effects of long-term husband absence on wives' stress: A cross-sectional and longitudinal study. *Japanese Journal of Psychology, 71,* 370–378.

Tang, C. S.-K. (1998). Frequency of parental violence against children in Chinese families: Impact of age and gender. *Journal of Family Violence, 13,* 113–130.

Toda, S. (2001). The influential factors and structure in fathers' parenting practice. *Journal of Hokkaido University of Education, 51,* 33–43.

Vogel, S. (1996). Urban middle-class Japanese family life, 1958–1996. In D. Shwalb & B. Shwalb (Eds.), *Japanese childrearing: Two generations of scholarship* (pp. 177–200). New York: Guilford Press.

Wagatsuma, H. (1977). Some aspects of the contemporary Japanese family: Once Confucian, now fatherless? *Daedalus, 106,* 181–210.

Wijers-Hasegawa, Y. (2002, January 4). Dads take child-care leave at own risk: Revision to law enabling time off unlikely to make up for stigma. *Japan Times,* 2–3.

Wo, Ma, & Liu (2002). A study of correlations between problem behaviors of first graders and their parents' ideas and methods of education. In J. Wo, H. Ma, & J. Liu (Eds.), *The development of mental health.* Beijing: Sino-Culture Press.

Wu, D. Y. H. (1996). Chinese childhood socialization. In M. Bond (Ed.), *The handbook of Chinese psychology* (pp. 142–167). Hong Kong: Oxford University Press.

Wui, Y. H. (1983). A theoretical consideration of father-child relations: The paternal role and father-child mutuality. *Korean Journal of Child Studies, 4,* 23–31.

Yamamoto, T. (1997). The origin of Japanese naturalistic childrearing. *Bulletin of the Faculty of Social Welfare, Hanazono University, 5,* 93–98.

Yang, J. A. (1999a). An exploratory study of Korean fathering: Paternal involvement and children's social-emotional competence. *Korean Journal of Child Studies, 20,* 135–145.

Yang, J. A. (1999b). An exploratory study of Korean fathering of adolescent children. *Journal of Genetic Psychology, 160,* 55–69.

Ye, G., Zhu, Z., Lin, Q., Cai, Y., & Xue, X. (Eds.). (1981). *Encyclopedia of childrearing.* Beijing: Beijing Publishing House.

Yi, S. H. (1996). Familism, collectivism, and the relationship between childrearing values and guiding maturity. *Journal of Korean Sociological Association, 30,* 545–573.

Yi, S. H., Rhee, K. C., Lee, K. Y., Rhee, E. Y., Kim, D. N., Park, Y. S., et al. (1999). Ideological characteristics and child-rearing practices of North Korea. *Korean Journal of Child Studies, 20,* 43–59.

Yoneyama, S. (1999). *Japanese high school: Silence and resistance.* New York: Routledge.

Yoo, A. J. (1999). *Traditional methods of Korean childrearing.* Seoul: Seoul National University.

Yoon, C. H., & Lee, I. S. (1993). Degree of fathers participation of child-rearing in relation to demographic variables parents' sex-role stereotypes and conjugal power structure. *Journal of the Korean Home Management Association, 11,* 191–202.

Yoon, S. Y., & Chung, O. B. (1999). The relationship between fathering practices and children's social adjustment. *Korean Journal of Child Studies, 20,* 101–122.

Yoon, Y. S. (1996, January 11). Gentle Korean fathers are increasing in number. *DongA Ilbo,* 19.

Zhai, L. (1994, January 17–23). Role reversal: The kind father and stern mother. *Beijing Review,* 22–23.

Zhang, W. (1997). A comparison of parenting styles in urban and rural areas. *Psychological Development and Education, 13,* 44–49.

Zhou, Y., Liao, Y., & Wang, C. (1999). *Childrearing in Hubai Village, China.* Working Papers in Early Childhood Development (No. 25).

CHAPTER 7

Fathers in Forager, Farmer, and Pastoral Cultures

BARRY S. HEWLETT

T HIS CHAPTER summarizes and evaluates recent research on the roles of fathers in child development in hunting-gathering (also known as foraging), simple farming, and pastoral (i.e., heavy reliance on cattle, camels, goats, etc.) communities around the world. In the past, these societies were referred to as "preindustrial," "preliterate," or "traditional" societies, but these terms are somewhat derogatory or imply that the people were in some way or another less intelligent or complex than peoples in modern, literate, and industrial societies. These cultures are characterized by their relatively low population densities and minimal amounts of social and economic stratification. Anthropologists have conducted most of the research in these communities, but some developmental psychologists have also contributed to the literature (e.g., Harkness & Super, 1992; Morelli & Tronick, 1992; Nsamenang, 1992).

In this chapter, I review three types of studies conducted on fathers in foraging, farming, and pastoral cultures: (a) evolutionary studies from human behavior ecology, (b) large (i.e., more than 100 cultures) cross-cultural studies of father involvement, and (c) detailed ethnographic case studies of fathers. Evolutionary studies are considered first because they examine some of the biological or reproductive bases of father involvement. Evolutionary and ethnographic research with foragers, farmers, and pastoralists are similar in that they are usually long-term field-based studies of one or a few cultures. Ethnographers are more eclectic in their theories and methods, using qualitative and quantitative methods, whereas human behavioral ecologists use evolutionary theory and rely almost exclusively on systematic behavioral observations (i.e., they are interested in what fathers do rather than what they say).

This chapter also emphasizes two general theoretical orientations: *adaptationist* and *cultural*. Adaptationist studies assume that fathers' roles are functional in that they are adapting to particular social, economic, reproductive, or demographic conditions or contexts. By contrast, researchers who utilize a cultural orientation assume that symbols, such as language, schema, ideology, or culture cores (i.e., configurations of beliefs and practices that are maintained by conservative mechanisms of cultural transmission), dramatically influence fathers' roles. Most researchers who utilize this theoretical orientation study the parental or cultural ideologies regarding fathers. Only a few researchers have emphasized the culture core and cultural transmission approach. This latter approach assumes that the distribution of cultural beliefs and practices (in this case, those regarding fathers' roles) are influenced by demic diffusion—people taking their beliefs and practices with them when they move or expand to a new area. For instance, English and French peoples expanded during the period of colonialism and took their beliefs and practices regarding fathers with them even when they moved to dramatically different natural and social environments. Their beliefs and practices were maintained through conservative cultural transmission. From this perspective, fathers' roles may or may not be adaptive. This is a simple theoretical dichotomy, and probably no researcher feels that fathers' roles are influenced by only one suite of factors. The fact is, however, that researchers usually have a limited time to conduct their research and thus tend to emphasize one or the other theoretical orientation.

ISSUES, CONCEPTS, AND TERMS

Why should we care about fathers in these cultures? We cannot understand fathers' roles in every ethnic group, so why not concentrate on large cultures, such as the Chinese or Danes, with millions of members rather than on cultures with a few thousand members?

First, most studies of fathers described in this volume were conducted in cultures with complex levels of hierarchy, inequality, and capitalism (i.e., fathers living in global economic cash economies). Some studies are cross-cultural, but the fathers in these groups are similar to middle-class Anglo-American families in that socioeconomic inequality and the material accumulation of wealth characterize and permeate their daily lives. Differences certainly exist between stratified cultures (e.g., some are much more sociocentric than others), but they share inequality in daily life. Second and along the same lines, most class-stratified societies are governed by strong nation-states. This means that fathers in most of the studies in this volume live in situations where their roles as protectors and educators of their children are diminished because the state provides a police or military force as well as some level of formal education. Consequently, research on fathers in stratified cultures focuses on their economic and caregiving roles. This emphasis on fathers as caregivers and providers also exists in studies of foragers and farmers, in part because research questions emerge from studies of fathers in urban-industrial cultures and researchers working with foragers and farmers are influenced by concerns in their own culture. The cultures described in this chapter live in nation-states and may be affected by laws in their respective countries, but in general they receive little protection or formal education from the nation-state. This does not mean that studies of contemporary stratified cultures are not relevant to understanding fathers' roles, but that there are limitations and important contexts to keep in mind, especially when universal or general features of fathers' roles are proposed.

Third, theoretically and conceptually, it seems that if we want to understand the nature of fathers' roles, we should consider fathers' roles in contexts that characterized most of human history. Global capitalism has been around for about 200 years, class stratification (chiefdoms and states) about 5,000 years, simple farming and pastoralism about 10,000 years, and hunting-gathering at least hundreds of thousands of years (at least 90% of human history). An understanding of fathers' roles in hunting and gathering societies seems to be especially important for understanding the nature of fathers' roles; consequently, several of the studies reviewed in this chapter focus on foragers.

Finally, males in class-stratified cultures usually do not learn about child caregiving until they have their own children. They acquire their knowledge from specialists (e.g., pediatricians, school counselors), how-to books, friends (because they seldom live near family members), or imagined others, such as images of men on TV whom they want to emulate. By contrast, men in the studies described in this chapter were frequently around, if not caring for, children while they were growing up (i.e., men's parenting knowledge is based on regular observations or experiences with children).

Before the three types of studies and two theoretical orientations are examined, the nature of *culture* is discussed because it is used often in this chapter and volume. Minimally, culture is defined as shared knowledge and practices that are transmitted nonbiologically generation to generation. It is symbolic, historic, and integrated and dramatically influences how we perceive and feel about the world around us. Regular interactions with others with similar schemas and styles of interaction (called *internal working models* by Bowlby, 1969) contribute to the emotional basis of culture. The emotional basis of culture often leads us to feel that our own ways are natural, universal, and usually better than are those of others. In regard to understanding fathers' roles, it means we are likely to have ethnocentric views of what is a good or bad father or to have strong feelings about the kinds of father research that should be conducted. Most middle-class parents, developmental psychologists, and policy agencies in contemporary urban, industrial cultures feel very strongly that regular and frequent father caregiving is important for healthy child development. National programs give the impression that regular direct care by fathers is natural and "good for all." Several positive benefits for active fathers in contemporary middle-class U.S. families may exist (i.e., families are more isolated from other families, so fathers' assistance may be important for several reasons), but cross-cultural studies indicate dramatic variability in the importance of direct father care. In some cultures, such as the Aka foragers of central Africa, father care is pervasive and sensitive, while in most African farming communities fathers provide almost no direct care to infants and young children. Children in both groups grow up to viable, competent, and self-assured individuals.

A classic example of how feelings impact our expectations of fathers comes from U.S. childbirth practices, in which fathers are expected to have an active role in so-called natural childbirth. This active role is far from natural and universal, as cross-cultural studies indicate that fathers seldom have an active role in childbirth, and in no culture do fathers direct the birthing process (Hewlett & Hannon, 1989). It may be important in middle-class U.S. families, where fathers are seldom around the child after the birth, but in most forager and farmer cultures, fathers are frequently around their children even though they may not be active caregivers.

EVOLUTIONARY STUDIES OF FATHERS

Evolutionary studies evaluate how a father's or a child's reproductive fitness influences his or her interactions. For instance, one hypothesis, discussed later, is that if a man knows he is the biological father of a child, he is more likely to invest time and energy in his children than if he is not the biological father. It is not in his reproductive interests to invest in nonbiologically related children. Evolutionary research is briefly reviewed because researchers have conducted several studies with foragers and simple farmers, and these provide one example of an adaptationist approach to explaining fathers' roles.

One consistent finding in evolutionary studies of men during the past 10 years of research is that by comparison to mothers, a good part of fathers' time and energy in direct care or providing of children may be mating effort rather than parenting effort. It was long thought that fathers were important providers and caregivers to their own biological children and that paternity certainly was a key factor for understanding father involvement (Lancaster, Altmann, Rossi, & Sherrod, 1987). Fathers would not be acting in their best reproductive interests if they cared for or provided food for children who were not their own. Biological fathers were hypothesized to be important providers, protectors, and caregivers. Evolutionists started to question this hypothesis when nonhuman primate studies indicated that males in species with low paternity certainty (e.g., multimale species where most adult males have sex with females in estrus) were more likely to provide direct care to infants than were males in species where paternity certainty was much higher (dominant male with harem, such as gorillas; Smuts & Gubernick, 1992; Van Schaik & Paul, 1996), child survival was not linked to having a father in several hunting-gathering cultures (Marlowe, 2000), and males in hunting-gathering communities were found to give most of the game they captured to other families rather than their own (Hawkes, O'Connel, & Blurton Jones, 2001). The evolutionary idea is that fathers are interested in showing off or signaling their abilities to parent to potential future mates. Fathers may also invest highly in stepchildren, but only as long as they are with the mothers (Kaplan, Lancaster, Bock, & Johnson, 1995).

The emphasis on mating rather than parenting effort is consistent with developmental psychology and sociological studies that demonstrate that fathers extrinsically value parenting whereas mothers intrinsically value parenting (LaRossa & LaRossa, 1981) and fathers are more likely to engage in direct caregiving in public places (e.g., playgrounds and grocery stores; Mackey & Day, 1979) rather than in the privacy of their home. But this does not mean that paternity certainty does not influence father-child relations. Marlowe (1999) indicated that Hadza hunter-gatherer fathers provided more direct care to genetically related children than to step-children, but that fathers provide even less care to biological children when their mating opportunities increase, such as when the number of reproductive women in camp increases.

Summary

Human behavioral ecological studies of foragers and farmers suggest that men and women have different reproductive interests and that what may appear to be father involvement in part functions to attract new mates or keep an existing one. Human behavioral ecology is one example of an adaptationist approach to father involvement.

CROSS-CULTURAL STUDIES OF FATHER INVOLVEMENT

Several cross-cultural studies have been conducted to identify factors that influence the level of father involvement. Many researchers utilize precoded father involvement data on hundreds of cultures. Anthropologists who write general ethnographies, which are detailed descriptions of one culture, often describe a few things about fathers' roles. Anthropologists, such as Barry and Paxson (1971), have reviewed hundreds of these ethnographies and qualitatively coded the level of father involvement and a variety of other aspects of infant and child development. Coded ethnographic samples include the Ethnographic Atlas (EA; over 1,000 cultures), the Human Relations Area Files (HRAF; over 300 cultures), and the Standard Cross-Cultural Sample (SCCS; 186 cultures). Most studies of fathers utilized the SCCS. The majority of cultures in these samples are hunter-gatherers, simple farmers, and pastoralists. An advantage of the cross-cultural studies is that father involvement in many societies can be systematically compared and analyzed. Comparing father involvement in only two or three cultures can be problematic because of the potential bias is the selection of cultures. One problem with these large studies is that the coding of father involvement is often based on a few descriptive sentences about fathers in a particular culture. The coding also masks all of the variability that often exists *within* a culture.

Given these limitations, the research has identified factors associated with high father involvement: lack of material accumulation, such as land, cattle, or money (Goody, 1973; Hewlett, 1988); high female contribution to the family diet (Katz & Konner, 1981); regular cooperation and participation of husband and wife in economic, domestic, and leisure activities (Hewlett, 1992); low population density (Alcorta, 1982); infrequent warfare (Katz & Konner, 1981); and infrequent polygyny (Katz & Konner, 1981).

All of these factors are more likely to occur in hunting and gathering societies rather than among farmers and pastoralists. Hunter-gatherers are mobile, often moving 5 to 20 times a year. They can accumulate only so much material wealth because they must carry it with them. Hunter-gatherers also tend to practice prestige avoidance, that is, doing anything not to draw attention to themselves. They have a variety of other cultural mechanisms, such as rough joking and demand sharing, that prevent accumulation, inequality, and drawing attention to oneself (Hewlett, 1991). Hunter-gatherers also share food and child care more extensively than farmers or pastoralists, as they often give away 50% to 80% of the foods they collect during the day. Population densities are lower in part because of their reliance on wild food. Warfare is less common because there are fewer material resources to defend.

Farmers and pastoralists, on the other hand, generally do what they can to accumulate more wealth (e.g., land or cattle). Generally, it is the males who accumulate the wealth, and this limits female access to resources necessary for survival and reproduction. The accumulated resources, such as crops or cattle, also need to be defended, so lineages and clan structures develop to defend resources. Both of these factors lead to greater male control ideologies and higher frequencies of polygynous marriages, even though women may contribute the majority of the calories to the diet. This is especially true in simple farming communities. Many women may be interested in marrying the same man because he controls many resources important to her and her children's survival. By comparison to foragers, population densities are somewhat higher, warfare is more common, and husband and wife do fewer activities together.

Marlowe (2000) conducted a cross-cultural study of paternal investment and confirmed many of the findings just described above. Table 7.1 summarizes his results. The study provides actual cross-cultural coding scores and tests of significance, but Table 7.1 lists results only. His study is consistent with the previous cross-cultural studies of fathers, but it is more detailed than were previous studies. For instance, he

Table 7.1
Modes of Production and Subsistence and Fathers' Roles

Mode of Production	Wealth Variation	Residence	Father's Direct Care	Father's Contributions to Family Diet	Marriage System
Hunter-gatherers	None	Multilocal	High	Moderate/high	Monogamy
Horticulturalists	Low to moderate	Patri- or matrilocal	Moderate	Low	Polygyny
Pastoralists	High	Patrilocal	Low	Very high	Polygyny
Agriculturalists	Very high	Patrilocal	Low	High	Polygyny
Industrial states	Very high	Neolocal	Moderate	Moderate	Monogamy

Note: Horticulture involves simple hoe farming, and agriculture refers to intensive irrigation or plow farming.
Source: Modified from Marlowe (2000, p. 49).

demonstrates that fathers' direct care is lowest in pastoral and agricultural (intensive farming) cultures rather than in horticultural (simple farming) cultures.

The studies mentioned thus far emphasize functional or adaptationist explanations (e.g., related to cultures' modes of production) for father involvement. Most research tests functional hypotheses, but it is important to point out that father involvement is influenced also by a culture's demic diffusion and the nature of cultural transmission and acquisition. Cultures connected by history are more likely to have similar levels of father involvement. For instance, Table 7.2 summarizes the average father involvement scores from various regions of the world. Regional grouping is based on Burton, Moore, Whiting, and Romney's (1996) analysis. Father involvement is lowest in African cultures, while it is highest in Southeast Asian and Pacific Island cultures. Cultures are generally within a particular region because they share a particular history and demic diffusion (i.e., a particular culture expanded and differentiated to new cultures within the region, such as the expansion of Bantu-speaking peoples in Africa). Cultures that share an expansionist history (diaspora) often share a *culture core*—a set of values, schemas, and behaviors—that is conservatively transmitted generation to generation. Recent studies have shown that many aspects of kinship and family life are more related to demic diffusion than to cultural diffusion (i.e., acquiring cultural beliefs or practices from neighbors) or natural ecology (Hewlett, de Silverti, & Gugliemino, 2002). The implication is that fathers' roles are part of a culture core in a particular region. One must be cautious with the data in Table 7.2 because the cultures placed within a region may have divergent histories. For instance, African cultures have the lowest average father involvement, but African hunter-gatherer groups, such as the !Kung and Aka, have very separate histories from that of the Bantu groups and are very involved fathers. The average score in Table 7.2 includes hunter-gatherers, and if omitted, the average involvement score in Africa and other regions with hunter-gatherers would decline.

The previous discussion of father involvement in various regions of the world points out that culture history, demic diffusion in particular, is an important factor for understanding cultural beliefs and practices regarding fathers' interactions with children. Culture cores are often maintained by conservative mechanisms of cultural transmission and acquisition. That is, these aspects of culture are transmitted early

Table 7.2
Father Involvement with Infants in Various Regions of the World

Region of the World	Number of Cultures Evaluated	Mean Score	Proportion of 4–5 Scores in the Region
Sub-Saharan Africa	22	2.40	0.09
Middle Old World	12	2.87	0.33
North Eurasia and Circumpolar	12	3.17	0.25
Southeast Asia and Pacific Islands	22	3.60	0.55
Australia, New Guinea, Melanesia	12	3.42	0.50
Northwest Coast	7	3.29	0.43
Northern and Western North America	7	2.71	0.00
Eastern Americas (includes North and South America)	16	3.05	0.44
Mesoamerica, Central America, and Andes	9	3.22	0.33

Note: The mean score is the average from Barry and Paxson's (1971) coding, where a 1–3 score means the father is never, seldom, or occasionally proximal to the infant and 4–5 means a father is in regular or frequent proximity.

within the family and immediate community. Before mass media such as radios, TVs, and the Internet were available, most beliefs and practices regarding child care were transmitted and acquired within the family. This form of transmission leads to highly conserved elements of culture. As a group of people migrates and expands, many elements of culture are conserved even though the natural and social environment may have changed. On the other hand, once the mass media are in place, cultures can change quite quickly.

SUMMARY

An analysis of cross-cultural studies on fathers indicates that the level of father involvement is influenced primarily by two general forces: (a) a web of factors associated with mode of production and subsistence (Hewlett, 1991; Katz & Konner, 1981; Marlowe, 2000) and (b) common culture ancestry and diaspora (i.e., via demic diffusion and conservative cultural transmission). The first assortment of factors suggests that paternal roles are adaptive to particular social, economic, reproductive, and demographic settings, whereas the second configuration of factors suggests that fathers' roles with children have more to do with the history-diaspora and transmission of a particular culture and that fathers' roles may or may not be adaptive.

ETHNOGRAPHIC STUDIES OF FATHERS

Fathers are seldom the focus of ethnographic studies, but in some cases ethnographers have emphasized the study of fathers in order to investigate particular hypotheses. Few detailed ethnographic studies of fathers exist, but by comparison to the cross-cultural studies, they are better able to evaluate the complex web of relationships related to fathers' roles. They can also be limiting (e.g., they focus on father involvement and neglect fathers' roles as protector or provider) because they evaluate a limited number of hypotheses. Ethnographic studies examined include my own study of Aka hunter-gatherer fathers of central Africa (Hewlett, 1991), Beckerman and Valentine's (2002) study of farming-fishing fathers among the Bari and other cultures of South America, and Harkness and Super's (1992) study of agropastoral Kipsigis fathers of East Africa. The Aka are known for the high level of father involvement, Kipsigis for their lack of father involvement, and the Bari and other South American cultures for their beliefs and practices regarding multiple fathers.

INTIMATE FATHERS

My work (Hewlett, 1991) with infants (3–18 months) among Aka foragers of Central Africa evaluated Lamb's (1981) hypothesis regarding the role of rough-and-tumble play in an infant's attachment to his or her father. The prevailing hypothesis was, and often still is, that infants become attached to their fathers in part due to their vigorous play and interactions. Infants become attached to mothers via their regular and sensitive care, whereas fathers, who are around less frequently, develop attachment with the infant through vigorous rough-and-tumble play. Studies in urban industrial societies around the world indicated that vigorous play was a distinctive feature of fathers' versus mothers' style of interaction with infants (see chapter by Lamb & Lewis, this volume, for further details). Unlike fathers in urban-industrial cultures, Aka fathers were frequently with their infants (i.e., holding or within an arm's reach of their infants 47% of the day) and rarely engaged in vigorous play with their infants. Aka fathers engaged in physical play only once in 264 hours of systematic naturalistic father and infant focal observations. Aka fathers were also more likely to show affection (i.e., kiss, hug) an infant while holding than were mothers.

I suggested that Aka fathers were not vigorous because they intimately knew their infants through their extensive care. Because Aka fathers knew their infants so well, they did not have to use vigorous play to initiate communication or interaction with their infants. They could initiate communication and show their love in other ways. Infants often initiated communication, and Aka fathers knew how to read and understand their infants' verbal and nonverbal (e.g., via touch) communication. Fathers (or mothers) who are not around their infants are less likely to be able to read and understand infant communication and therefore more likely to initiate communication, often with the use of physical stimulation and play. Aka fathers are often around their infants because men, women, and children participate together in net hunting. Women are active in and important to net hunting (Noss & Hewlett, 2001), and husband-wife communication and cooperation are key to hunting success. Net hunting contributed to regular husband-wife cooperation and fathers' intimate knowledge of their infants.

Although Aka are generally very involved fathers, there is remarkable intracultural variability. Some Aka fathers held their infants 2% of the time, whereas others held their infants about 20% of daylight hours. Also, not all "pygmies" or hunter-gatherers of the African rainforest have highly involved fathers. Efe hunter-gatherer fathers of the Democratic Republic of the Congo held their infants 2.6% of the time in the camp setting in comparison with 22.0% of the time among the Aka fathers (S. Winn, 1989, personal communication). Bailey (1991, p. 171) found that Efe men actively engaged in child care only 0.7% (about 5 minutes per day) of daylight hours and indicated that "strong father-child attachments among the Efe were uncommon." Efe fathers were also not the secondary or even tertiary caregivers of their infants; several other females (older siblings, grandmother, mother's sister) provided more care than did fathers. Efe differ from Aka in several ways: Efe do not cooperatively net hunt (men hunt with bows and arrows or small traps), Efe spend less time in the forest, and very high infertility rates exist, so there are many other adult women without children available to help with child care.

DISTANT FATHERS

Harkness and Super (1992) conducted a comparative study of East African Kipsigis and Anglo-American middle- to upper-class fathers and their infants and young children (0–4 years). Kipsigis fathers were somewhat more likely to be present with their infants during the day than were U.S. fathers (35% vs. 24%), but Kipsigis fathers never engaged in direct caregiving during the first four years of the child's life, whereas U.S. fathers provided 13% to 17% of the child's direct care. Kipsigis fathers never fed, dressed, bathed, or carried the infant outside the house. Kipsigis believe that the infant can be damaged by the strength of the father's gaze and that the father's masculinity can be compromised by the dirtiness of the infant. When fathers were present with their infants, Kipsigis and U.S. fathers' activities were quite different. When present, U.S. fathers were actively involved with their children 24% to 46% of the time (e.g., bed and bath routines, storytelling, playing, etc.), whereas Kipsigis fathers were more likely to be watching the child or talking with others.

Harkness and Super (1992) also described parental ideologies in the two cultures and suggested that the different ideologies motivated and explained the observed differences in Kipsigis and U.S. father-child interactions. Kipsigis fathers viewed their roles as primarily economic—to provide school fees and cover expenses when their children were sick. Fathers also felt that they were responsible for disciplining their children and making sure their children were obedient (especially regarding chores and being deferent and respectful of others, especially those older than them). American fathers, on the other hand, emphasized the importance of developing a close emotional relationship with their children as well as stimulating their cognitive development. They felt that bedtime and playtime were good times to develop this emotional relationship and also to provide educational stimulation.

MULTIPLE FATHERS

The research and descriptions of intimate and distant fathers just provided assumed that each infant had one father. Research methods, be they behavioral observations of infants with fathers or informal interviews with fathers, assumed that each child had one father. Most Euro-Americans, including researchers, assume that each child has a single, generally biological, father. In order to further illustrate the diverse ways in which fatherhood can be culturally constructed, the next section briefly describes cultures in which it is common for a child to have more than one father.

Beckerman and Valentine (2002) described multiple fatherhood in foraging and farming communities in several lowland South American cultures. Beckerman et al.

conducted research with South American groups in which women had sexual relations with one or more men other than their husband and each of these men became a social father and contributed to the child in a variety of ways (e.g., feeding, holding, training). A common belief is that it takes a regular amount of sperm for a fetus to grow and that it is not unusual that more than one man to contribute to the growth of the fetus. Beckerman and Valentine called this *partible paternity.* Hill and Hurtado (1996) described partible paternity among the Ache of Paraguay:

> A man (or men) who was frequently having intercourse with a woman at the time when "her blood ceased to be found" is considered to be the real father of the child. . . . These primary fathers are most likely to be the ones who take on a serious parenting role. . . . Secondary fathers are also generally acknowledged and can play an important role in the subsequent care of a child. . . . Secondary father include all those men who had sexual intercourse with a woman during the year prior to giving birth (including during pregnancy) and the man who is married to a woman when her child is born. (pp. 249–250)

Beckerman and Valentine (2002) reanalyzed Hill and Hurtado's (1996) Ache data on multiple fathers and found that 70% of children with only one father survived to age 10, whereas 85% of children with primary and secondary fathers survived to age 10. Kinship terms also reflected the belief in secondary fathers, as the Matis use the term *ebutamute* for fathers, which translates to "he with whom I procreate" (Erikson, 2002). Beckerman and Valentine also conducted detailed reproductive interviews with the Bari, a culture they had worked with for several years, and found that having a secondary father did not increase child survival after birth, but it did increase the probability that a woman with an identified secondary father before childbirth was more likely to produce a child and that that child was more likely to survive to age 15. Secondary fathers among the Bari provided meat, fish, and other food items to the pregnant woman, and this in turn increased child survival.

Beckerman (2002) utilized multiple fathers' data to question or reject paternity certainty theory, as discussed earlier in the evolutionary section. Paternity certainty is low in these cultures, but several fathers invest in the same child. Hrdy (1999) pointed out that females may use males' concern over paternity certainty to increase support for them and their children from several men. If a few men are led to believe that they are potentially the fathers of the child, they are likely to make some investment in the child. The South American cultures with the highest frequencies of multiple fatherhood are matrilocal with weak male-control ideologies. In other words, where patriarchy is weak, multiple fatherhood is more common. Where patriarchy is strong, it is more difficult for women to have or acknowledge sexual relations with someone other than the husband.

SUMMARY

The three ethnographic examples described in this section provide more examples of the two general theoretical orientations. The South American multiple fathers and the Kipsigis distant fathers illustrate cultural explanations for father-child relations. Beliefs and practices in multiple fatherhood exist in Lowland South America, but seldom, if ever, in other parts of the world. This suggests demic diffusion of this belief and practice in Lowland South America. It may have been adaptive when it was initiated in a particular group, but it demically diffused and may or may not be adaptive. Harkness and Super (1992) emphasized cultural ideology to explain why Kipsigis fathers are distant. Their distant fathering style is also common to several sub-Saharan cultures described in the cross-cultural section of this chapter and is consistent with an emphasis on culture rather than adaptation. Certainly local and individual variations and adaptations exist within these cultures, but the nature of father-child interactions in these groups is affected by culture history and transmission.

By contrast, the research on the Aka provides an example of an adaptationist explanation for father-child relations. Aka fathers are frequently around their infants, in part because of net hunting, which in turn contributes to higher (by comparison to foraging communities, where men go out and hunt and women go gathering) levels of husband-wife reciprocity in a wide range of activities, including child care. Aka fathers are more intimate with their infants than are other hunter-gatherer groups because of particular adaptations to local conditions (i.e., active women's role in net hunting, close husband-wife relations).

CONCLUSION

This chapter described cross-cultural variability in fathers' roles. Aka fathers held or were within an arm's reach of their infants about half of the day, whereas Kipsigis fathers generally did not provide direct care to children until the fourth or fifth year of the child's life. Part of this variability was explained by factors associated with mode of production (accumulation of wealth, women's role in subsistence, frequency of warfare, husband-wife relations) or cultural ancestry and diaspora (demic diffusion and conservative mechanisms of cultural transmission and acquisition). Hunter-gatherer fathers were more likely to be involved with children than were fathers in any other mode of production. In terms of cultural diaspora and demic diffusion, fathers with African (in particular, Bantu) cultural ancestry were the least likely to be involved fathers, whereas cultures with Southeast Asian and Pacific Island ancestry were most likely to have involved fathers.

Although data were presented to support these generalizations, these data demonstrated enormous variability among hunter-gatherers groups (e.g., Efe fathers were not very involved) and variability within cultures (e.g., Aka father holding ranged from 2% to 20% of daylight hours). Regional, local, and individual contexts and histories influenced this diversity.

In terms of styles of father-child interactions, fathers' physical rough-and-tumble play, characteristic of many urban industrial cultures, was infrequent among Aka fathers, suggesting that vigorous play was not necessary, biological, or the universal way by which infants became attached to fathers. Aka infant attachment to fathers seems to occur through regular and sensitive caregiving.

Finally, human behavioral ecological studies suggested that at least some aspects of father involvement were mating effort rather than parenting effort. Partible paternity, active stepfathers, and men's extensive giving of food items to nonbiological children in foraging cultures indicated that fathers (and men in general) may enhance their reproductive fitness by providing food, care, defense, and other forms of investment to children who are not biologically related to them. Men may invest in children in these contexts to attract new mates or keep an existing mate.

There are several limitations to existing studies of forager, farmer, and pastoral fathers. None of the studies conducted with foragers or farmers systematically evaluated how these different levels of involvement affect the child's social, emotional, cognitive, or moral development. Obviously, systematic research in these cultures is desperately needed. My research and observations of children in a diversity of African cultures, as well as statements from forager and farmer ethnographers from around the world, suggest that most children in foraging, farming, and pastoral cultures are socially, emotionally, cognitively, and morally competent regardless of whether fathers are intimate or distant. For instance, I have lived with intimate Aka forager fathers and distant Ngandu farmer fathers for 30 years, and children in both groups appear to be more self-assured, secure, and competent than are children of comparable ages in the United States. Why do so many child development studies in the United States and elsewhere indicate that father presence and involvement are so important to a child's development?

Research in contemporary stratified capitalistic cultures has focused on fathers, in part because the family and social-economic contexts are so dramatically different from the cultures that characterized most of human history. Individuals in capitalistic systems move away from extended family in search of higher education and higher paying jobs, but in so doing they isolate themselves from extended family and close friends. As mothers and fathers seek to move up the economic ladder, they are likely to move away from family. They tend to have fewer children, in part because they no longer live with extended family, where they can obtain regular, economically reasonable, quality care. Less time is also spent around children because men's and women's workplaces do not permit children. Forager and farmer children, on the other hand, grow up with a wide range of caregivers (e.g., grandmothers and grandfathers, aunts and uncles, siblings, clan members, etc.) who know the child well. Aka fathers are very involved in direct care, but so are many other caregivers because infants and young children are held most of the day. Father involvement in contemporary urban-industrial cultures may be especially important to healthy social, emotional, cognitive, and moral development of children, but this may be due to a relatively unusual (by cross-cultural standards) family context—isolation from family and long-term friends.

Another feature of contemporary urban-industrial cultures is that parents can be very involved and sensitive caregivers and develop their child's sense of trust with self and others, but once the child moves into formal schooling and starts to make a living in the cultural system, he or she must deal with inequality on a daily basis. Students are ranked from higher and lower and must learn to respond to social-economic inequality, such as being deferent to those who have higher rank or more resources. Those who succeed in the system tend to feel better than others and expect more from others. Those who have difficulty may feel unsure about themselves and others. One learns to be deferent toward those who have more resources or success. By comparison, forager children move into a system where ranking is actively discouraged and trust of self and others continues throughout childhood. Farmers and pastoralists rank by age and gender, but it is within a familiar context throughout childhood.

Context also influences how fathers acquire their parenting skills and helps to explain why Aka father caregiving lacks the vigorous play found in urban-industrial cultures. As mentioned earlier, urban-industrial fathers learn to parent from specialists and trial and error. By comparison, a characteristic feature of hunter-gatherers is that their population density is low, but their living density is high. A group of 25 hunter-gatherers often live within a 400 to 800 square foot area. This means that everyone sees how to care for children, and someone is quickly informed if he or she holds, cleans, or feeds a child in an inappropriate way. This leads to consistency of care from a large range of individuals, including fathers.

The limited data presented in this chapter suggest that father involvement must be viewed in context and that high father involvement is not natural or universal or even important in some contexts. Policy makers, in particular, need to consider context, diversity, and flexibility in fathers' roles.

Finally, this discussion makes generalizations about forager and farmer fathers often to make points about the nature of fathers' roles in urban-industrial cultures. A problem with this approach is that it can make forager and farmer fathers sound exotic, near the limits of humanity, in that they represent the unfamiliar "other." Aka fathers are more involved than fathers in most parts of the world; Bari have multiple fathers; and Kipsigis fathers do not provide direct care to infants, but fathers in all these cultures are similar in many way to fathers in any other part of the world. They love their children, are concerned about their children's health and well-being, provide less care than the mother, and generally spend considerable (if not most of their) time talking to or being with other men rather than their wives or groups of women. Like fathers and men in the United States or elsewhere, forager, farmer, and pastoral fathers are trying to do the best they can in their particular cultural, ecological, economic, and demographic contexts.

REFERENCES

Alcorta, C. (1982). Paternal behavior and group competition. *Behavior Science Research, 17*, 3–23.

Bailey, R. C. (1991). *The socioecology of Efe pygmy men in the Ituri forest, Zaire.* Ann Arbor: University of Michigan.

Barry, H., & Paxson, L. M. (1971). Infancy and early childhood: Cross-cultural codes 2. *Ethnology, 10*, 466–508.

Beckerman, S., & Valentine, P. (Eds.). (2002). *Cultures of multiple fathers: The theory and practice of partible paternity in Lowland South America.* Gainesville: University Press of Florida.

Bowlby, J. (1969). *Attachment.* New York: Basic Books.

Burton, M. L., Moore, C. C., Whiting, J. W. M., & Romney, A. K. (1996). Regions based on social structure. *Current Anthropology, 37*, 87–123.

Erikson, P. (2002). Several fathers in one's cap: Polyandras conception among the Panoan Matis (Amazonia, Brazil). In S. Beckerman & P. Valentine (Eds.), *Cultures of multiple fathers: The theory and practice of partible paternity in Lowland South America* (pp. 123–136). Gainesville: University Press of Florida.

Goody, J., & Tambiah, S. J. (Eds.). (1973). *Bridewealth and dowry.* Cambridge, England: Cambridge University Press.

Harkness, S., & Super, C. M. (1992). The cultural foundations of father's roles: Evidence from Kenya and the United States. In B. S. Hewlett (Ed.), *Father-child relations: Cultural and biosocial perspectives* (pp. 191–212). New York: de Gruyter.

Hawkes, K., O'Connell, J. F., & Blurton Jones, N. G. (2001). Hadza meat sharing. *Evolution and Human Behavior, 22*, 113–142.

Hewlett, B. (1988a). *Dad and cad strategies: Father's role in human evolution.* Paper presented at Evolution and Human Behavior Program, University of Michigan, Ann Arbor.

Hewlett, B. S. (1988b). Sexual selection and paternal investment among Aka pygmies. In L. Betzig, P. Turke, & M. Borgerhoff Mulder (Eds.), *Human reproductive behaviour: A Darwinian perspective* (pp. 187–205). Cambridge, England: Cambridge University Press.

Hewlett, B. S. (1991). *Intimate fathers.* Ann Arbor: University of Michigan Press.

Hewlett, B. S. (1992). Husband-wife reciprocity and the father-infant relationship among Aka pygmies. In B. S. Hewlett (Ed.), *Father-child relations: Cultural and biosocial perspectives* (pp. 153–176). New York: de Gruyter.

Hewlett, B. S., & Hannon, N. (1989). *Myths about "natural" childbirth.* Paper delivered at annual meeting of the Society for Cross-Cultural Research, New Haven, CT.

Hewlett, B. S., de Silvestri, A., & Guglielmino, R. (2002). Semes and genes in Africa. *Current Anthropology, 43,* 313–321.

Hill, K., & Hurtado, M. (1996). *Ache life history: The ecology and demography of a foraging people.* New York: de Gruyter.

Hrdy, S. (1999). *Mother nature.* New York: Pantheon.

Kaplan, H. S., Lancaster, J. B., Bock, J. A., & Johnson, S. E. (1995). Does observed fertility maximize fitness among New Mexican men? A test of an optimality model and a new theory of parental investment in the embodied capital of off-spring. *Human Nature, 6,* 325–360.

Katz, M. M., & Konner, M. L. (1981). The role of father: An anthropological perspective. In M. E. Lamb (Ed.), *The role of the father in child development* (2nd ed., pp. 155–181). New York: Wiley.

Lamb, M. E. (Ed.). (1981). *The role of the father in child development* (2nd ed.). New York: Wiley.

Lancaster, J. B., Altmann, J., Rossi, A., & Sherrod, L. (1987). *Parenting across the lifespan: Biosocial perspectives.* New York: Aldine.

LaRossa, R., & LaRossa, M. M. (1981). *Transition to parenthood: How infants change families.* Beverly Hills, CA: Sage.

Mackey, W. C., & Day, R. (1979). Some indicators of fathering behaviors in the United States: A cross-cultural examination of adult male-child interaction. *Journal of Marriage and the Family, 41,* 287–299.

Marlowe, F. (1999). Showoffs or providers? The parenting effort of Hadza men. *Evolution and Human Behavior, 20,* 391–404.

Marlowe, F. (2000). Paternal investment and the human mating system. *Behavioural Processes, 51,* 45–61.

Morelli, G. A., & Tronick, E. Z. (1992). Male care among Efe foragers and Lese farmers. In B. S. Hewlett (Ed.), *Father-child relations: Cultural and biosocial perspectives* (pp. 231–262). New York: de Gruyter.

Noss, A., & Hewlett, B. S. (2001). The contexts of female hunting in Central Africa. *American Anthropologist, 103,* 1024–1040.

Nsamenang, B. A. (1992). Perceptions of parenting among the Nso of Cameroon. In B. S. Hewlett (Ed.), *Father-child relations: Cultural and biosocial perspectives* (pp. 321–344). New York: de Gruyter.

Smuts, B. B., & Gubernick, D. J. (1992). Male-infant relationships in nonhuman primates: Paternal investment or mating effort? In B. S. Hewlett (Ed.), *Father-child relations: Cultural and biosocial perspectives* (pp. 1–30). New York: de Gruyter.

Van Schaik, C. P., & Paul, A. (1996). Male care in primates: Does it ever reflect paternity? *Evolutionary Anthropology, 5,* 152–156.

CHAPTER 8

Fathers in Family Context

Effects of Marital Quality and Marital Conflict

E. MARK CUMMINGS, MARCIE C. GOEKE-MOREY, and JESSICA RAYMOND

M ARITAL QUALITY and conflict are related to children's functioning and adjustment (e.g., Cummings, Davies, & Campbell, 2000; Grych & Fincham, 2001). The influence of marital processes on children has typically been viewed from a dyadic level of analysis, that is, the marital relationship considered as a single unit, without explicit examination of the particular role of fathers. In fact, the characteristics of marital relations, including marital dissolution (Coiro & Emery, 1998), reflect an important category of influence of fathers in their children's lives. The effects of marital quality on children illustrate the pertinence of a broader perspective on fathering than simply father-child interactions. That is, the importance of a family-wide perspective on fathering is indicated (Parke, 2002).

This chapter examines paternal influences on child development in the context of this broader family-wide conceptualization of fathering, emphasizing the context provided by marital relationships. Cummings and O'Reilly (1997) proposed a framework for multiple influences of fathers on children and families, calling attention to the pivotal role of the marital relationship (see also Marsiglio, Amato, Day, & Lamb, 2000). As shown in Figure 8.1, which is a revision of the Cummings and O'Reilly model, fathers in the context of marital relationships affect children and families through three major pathways: (a) fathering and father-child relationships, (b) children's exposure to fathers' marital discord, and (c) fathers' psychological functioning. Moreover, the personal characteristics of the father (Papp, Goeke-Morey, & Cummings, 2003) or child (Davies & Lindsay, 2001) may moderate these effects. Furthermore, each pathway is assumed ultimately to relate to children's adjustment via influences on children's coping processes and mechanisms (Cummings & Davies, 2002). Finally, the model calls

Preparation of this paper was supported in part by a grant from the National Institute of Child Health and Human Development (HD 36261) to E. Mark Cummings.

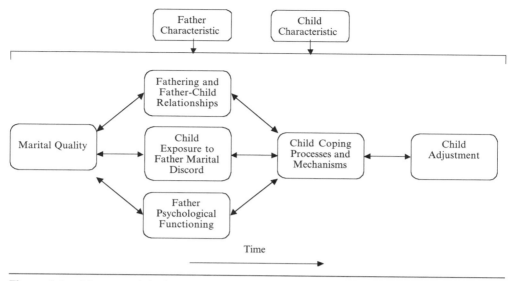

Figure 8.1 A framework for fathers in the context of marital quality (adapted from Cummings & O'Reilly, 1997).

attention to the significance of examining effects over time (Cummings & Davies, 2000; Cummings et al., 2000).

This chapter updates the analysis of fathers' influence in the marital context, reviewing very recent studies relevant to this topic. In addition, a particular focus is on *isolating* fathers' particular effects. That is, effects on fathering or due to fathers' behavior are identified, a step beyond considering fathers' effects only at the level of the marital dyad. This next step in understanding fathering in the marital context is made possible in part by recent advances in the methodological quality and sophistication of research, allowing more definitive inferences about these questions than was possible at the time of the Cummings and O'Reilly (1997) review. In particular, there is increasing inclusion of fathers as reporters and participants, so research does not rely solely on mothers' accounts. Finally, reflecting another advance of the present report over the Cummings and O'Reilly review, explicit hypotheses about each of the three pathways (see Figure 8.1) are examined.

As shown in Figure 8.1, one pathway concerns interrelations between marital quality and fathering, and father-child relationships (Cabrera, Tamis-LeMonda, Bradley, Hofferth, & Lamb, 2000; Cox, Paley, & Harter, 2001). The accumulation of evidence to support this pathway (i.e., marital functioning affects parenting) is impressive (Erel & Burman, 1995). The present discussion focuses on the relative effects on fathers' in comparison with mothers' parenting and parent-child relationships. With regard to theory, a *fathering vulnerability hypothesis* is examined for this pathway (e.g., Belsky, Gilstrap, & Rovine, 1984). That is, we consider evidence for the notion that fathering and father-child relationships are more vulnerable to negative effects of marital discord than are mothering and mother-child relationships, with differentially more negative implications for children's adjustment.

The second pathway reviewed concerns influences of fathers on children through exposure to father marital discord (Cummings, Goeke-Morey, Papp, & Dukewich, 2002).

Although effects on children of exposure to destructive marital conflict at a dyadic level of analysis are well documented (Cummings & Davies, 2002), until recently, remarkably few studies compared children's reactions to exposure to fathers' in comparison with mothers' marital conflict behaviors. Concerning theory, a *differential reactivity hypothesis* is examined. We consider the proposition that children are more reactive and distressed by fathers' than mothers' expressions of discord in marital disputes; that is, in comparison to mothers' conflict expression, children have more negative responses to the same negative conflict expressions exhibited by fathers. Recent work has called attention to the prevalence of constructive behaviors during everyday marital conflict, noting children's generally positive reactions to such conflict expressions by parents (Cummings et al., 2002). Accordingly, it is pertinent to consider whether a differential reactivity hypothesis holds also for children's reactions to constructive conflict behaviors.

The third pathway concerns interrelations among marital quality, fathers' psychological functioning, and children's functioning and adjustment. Marital conflict and parental depression are causally related (e.g., Fincham, Beach, Harold, & Osborne, 1997; see the review in Whisman, 2000), with children of depressed parents at elevated risk for adjustment problems (e.g., Weissman, Warner, Wickramaratne, Moreau, & Olfson, 1997). Moreover, marital conflict and parental depression are interrelated as predictors of children's adjustment problems (e.g., Davies, Dumenci, & Windle, 1999; see the review in Downey & Coyne, 1990). However, maternal depression has been studied in this regard much more often than has paternal depression (Cummings & Davies, 1994b). Relatively little is know about relations between marital conflict and fathers' depressive symptomatology or, more broadly, fathers' psychological functioning, with regard to implications for child development (Cummings et al., 2000). Questions include the extent to which discordant marital conflict behaviors are related to fathers' in comparison to mothers' depressive or other psychopathological symptoms, and the implication of fathers' symptomatology for children's adjustment. Another, related, issue is whether fathers' supportive behaviors toward their wives decrease the risk for children associated with maternal psychopathological symptoms (e.g., Lamb, 2000). A *paternal mental health hypothesis* is proposed. This hypothesis calls attention to the role of *fathers' psychological functioning* in the impact of marital conflict, either as another pathway for risk or as a protection.

The organization of the paper is to consider, in turn, recent evidence for each of the three pathways, including evaluation of the hypotheses associated with each pathway, that is, the fathering vulnerability hypothesis, the differential reactivity hypothesis, and the paternal mental health hypothesis, respectively. In addition, evidence toward completing the process-oriented model for fathers in family context outlined in Figure 8.1 is examined, including (a) relations between fathering across these multiple pathways, (b) the role of children's characteristics and coping processes and mechanisms, and (c) relations with changes in children's adjustment over time.

EFFECTS OF MARITAL CONFLICT ON FATHERING AND FATHER-CHILD RELATIONSHIPS: THE FATHERING VULNERABILITY HYPOTHESIS

Evidence for the fathering vulnerability hypothesis has a relatively long history. Based on studies from the 1980s and early 1990s, Cummings and O'Reilly (1997) concluded that differences between mother-child and father-child relationships increased as marital quality declined, with father-child relationships being more vulnerable to low marital satisfaction and high marital conflict than mother-child relationships (see Frosch, Mangelsdorf, & McHale, 1998). More recently, Coiro and Emery (1998) concluded that when there were significant differences, greater effects were found for fathering than for mothering. Similarly, Krishnakumar and Buehler's (2000) meta-analysis of relations between interparental conflict and parenting provided support for a fathering vulnerability hypothesis, including relations with parenting control, acceptance, harsh discipline, and overall quality of parenting. Owen and Cox (1997) reported negative effects of marital conflict on attachments to both mothers and fathers but more pervasive negative effects of marital conflict on father-child attachments than on mother-child attachments. Relatedly, Frosch, Mangelsdorf, and McHale (2000) found that marital conflict was negatively related to insecure attachment to both mothers and fathers, with warm and engaged marital interactions associated with the security of father-child attachment relationships but not with the security of mother-child attachments.

On the other hand, the need for qualifications for a fathering vulnerability hypothesis is also apparent. *Parenting* vulnerability is the most consistent finding. Even when fathering is found to be relatively more affected than mothering, the impact of marital discord on both mothering and fathering is often indicated. Moreover, when differences are reported (e.g., differences in the size of correlations), they are often not directly tested statistically. Thus, the pattern of supportive evidence may not be as persuasive as it may seem at first glance (Coiro & Emery, 1998). Contextual factors may also be important. For example, Clements, Lim, and Chaplin (2002) reported that lower marital quality was more *consistently* related to greater parental negativity for fathers than for mothers. That is, for fathers, lower marital quality was associated with poorer parenting both in the presence of the spouse (i.e., triadic context) and in the spouse's absence (i.e., dyadic context), whereas lower marital quality was linked with poorer parenting for mothers only in the triadic context. On the other hand, there is scant support for the counternotion of a *mothering vulnerability hypothesis*. That is, studies either have reported findings consistent with accentuated fathering vulnerability or found no differences between effects on mothering and fathering (e.g., Erel & Burman, 1995). As we will see later, recent studies have continued to provide qualified support for a fathering vulnerability hypothesis.

THE ROLE OF CHILD GENDER

An intriguing possible corollary to the fathering vulnerability hypothesis is that fathers' relationships with children are differentially affected by marital discord as a function of child gender. As shown in Figure 8.1, the characteristics of the child, including gender, may factor into the way in which mothering and fathering are affected by marital quality and conflict. Some studies have failed to report differences as a function of child gender. For example, Osborne and Fincham (1996) found that marital conflict was similarly linked with negative mother-child and father-child relationships for both boys and girls. Other studies report more problems in some parent-child dyads than others. This issue is sometimes framed in terms of greater threat to the father-son relationship; alternatively, however, vulnerability with regard to the father-daughter relationship has also been emphasized.

Father-Son Relations

Some studies suggest that marital discord results in greater vulnerability in terms of fathering of boys than fathering of girls. Experimental studies examining the influences of marital conflict on parenting are particularly cogent with regard to the fathering hypothesis and differential effects as a function of child gender, since effects are immediately observable. Jouriles and Farris (1992) examined fathers' and mothers' immediate interactions with children following situations requiring marital conflict resolution. Although both parents showed lower rates of conversation with their sons following marital conflict than following nonconflictual situations, fathers used significantly vaguer and more confusing commands with their sons, and sons displayed relatively higher rates of noncompliance with their fathers. Employing a similar experimental design, Kitzmann (2000) reported that parents showed disrupted parenting after conflictual exchanges, which contrasted with democratic parenting shown after pleasant marital interactions. Marital conflict predicted more disruptions in father-son than in mother-son interactions. Moreover, Neighbors, Forehand, and Bau (1997) found that exposure to marital conflict in middle adolescence had long-term negative effects on sons' relationships with their fathers, but such links were not found with regard to daughters' relationships with fathers. Based on these studies, one might conclude that fathering of boys was especially vulnerable to heightened marital conflict.

Father-Daughter Relations

On the other hand, some studies have reported greater vulnerability for fathering of girls than boys. For example, Cowan, Cowan, and Kerig (1993) reported findings suggesting that when marital conflict increased, mothers treated their sons and daughters similarly. However, fathers used more authoritarian parenting with their daughters than with their sons, particularly if their parenting styles differed from their wives'. Similarly, Kerig, Cowan, and Cowan (1993) found that as marital conflict increased, fathers were more globally negative toward their daughters than toward their sons. McHale (1995) reported that discrepancies between fathering and mothering increased as marital conflict worsened, but primarily in families with girls. Finally, maritally distressed fathers were more likely than maritally distressed mothers to show low levels of engagement with their daughters. Thus, one would infer from this series of studies that fathering vulnerability was more closely tied with father-daughter than with father-son relationships.

In summary, relations between marital conflict and fathering of sons and daughters vary across studies, suggesting that effects may be complexly determined (Snyder, 1998). Little evidence has emerged to indicate that quality of attachment to fathers varies as a function of child gender (Cassidy & Shaver, 1999), but other parenting processes, such as parental engagement with children or discipline during play, may be more influenced by the interaction between parent and child gender. It may be the case that parent gender and parent-child gender interactions are important for some aspects of parenting but not for others (Russell & Saebel, 1997). On the other hand, a general lack of consistency has characterized child gender effects in the literature on marital conflict and children (Davies & Lindsay, 2001). Furthermore, there has been frequent failure to find effects, or a relative paucity of findings in comparison to the number of statistical tests conducted (Russell & Saebel). Notably, there may be far more variability in responding within than between genders, so that child gender or parent-child gender interactions may be no more than modest (i.e., weak and unreliable) factors relating to fathering vulnerability.

SPILLOVER EFFECTS: DAILY REPORT METHODOLOGIES

Studies based on parents' daily reports fill an important methodological gap between the study of immediate (e.g., Kitzmann, 2000) and long-term (e.g., Neighbors et al., 1997) effects in the analysis of family processes. Using this methodology, relations between family processes can be examined intensively over a period of days or weeks (Larson & Almeida, 1999). Studies utilizing daily report methodologies have shown greater spillover from marital tensions to tensions in the parent-child and sibling relationships for distressed than nondistressed families (Margolin, Christensen, & John, 1996). Based on mothers' and fathers' completion of short diary questionnaires over 42 consecutive days, Almeida, Wethington, and Chandler (1999) reported "overwhelming" support for negative effects of marital tensions on tensions in the parent-child dyad for both mothers and fathers. That is, both mothers and fathers were more likely to have tense interactions with children on days following marital tensions than following maritally stress-free days. Notably, certain contextual factors further increased the likelihood of spillover, but only for fathering. That is, on days when fathers experienced work or home stressors, tension spillover was more than twice as likely as on stress-free days. More spillover was also found for fathers when wives worked full-time. Furthermore, tension spillover for mothers was unidirectional, that is, from marital to mother-child dyads, whereas fathers' tension was bidirectional, so that father-*child* tension on the previous day also increased the likelihood of *marital* tension. This study thus adds another wrinkle to the examination of fathering vulnerability, suggesting the greater vulnerability of fathering than mothering to challenging family and work contexts.

EXPLANATIONS FOR FATHERING VULNERABILITY

Another set of questions concerns *why* fathering is more vulnerable to effects of marital discord and conflict than mothering. Most often, variations of the notion that motherhood is a more fundamental role for women than fatherhood is for men are proposed (Belsky, 1979). Thus, mothers may be more prone to shielding their parenting role from marital problems, resulting in less carryover from problems in marital relations to parenting for mothers than for fathers. One possible explanation is that mothers develop relations with children regardless of fathers' presence, whereas fathers primarily develop relations with children when mothers are present (Clements et al., 2002). For fathers, parental and husband roles may be more fused, so that quality of relations with children is more affected by quality of relations with spouses (Belsky et al., 1984). Relatedly, for fathers, parenthood may be a smaller portion of their identity, and less well defined, than it is for mothers (Cowan et al., 1993) and therefore more affected by other family relationships than the maternal role (Belsky, Youngblade, Rovine, & Volling, 1991).

POSITIVE PARENTING

Parenting is a multidimensional construct, so various aspects of parenting may be differentially related to marital functioning. Another intriguing direction concerns relations between marital quality and positive parenting. Russell (1997) examined marital satisfaction as a predictor of positive parenting. He found that for mothers, greater marital satisfaction related to more warmth and affection, positive involvement, and overall positive parenting during an observational task, but for fathers, marital satisfaction did not relate to positive parenting. At one level, it is striking how much research has focused on the ways in which marital problems can increase parenting problems and how little has examined the potentially positive outcomes for parenting of happy and satisfied marriages. One might expect that happy marriages will lead to more positive parenting outcomes, as well as fewer negative outcomes, but we know little about these potentially beneficial effects. At another level, the Russell (1997) results considered in the context of the broader literature on marital functioning and parenting suggest the unfortunate possibility that in addition to being more disturbed than mothering by negative marital relations, fathering also benefits less in a positive parenting sense from happy and secure marital relations. However, much more research is needed on positive parenting before any conclusions can be drawn.

TESTS OF DIRECT AND INDIRECT EFFECTS ON CHILDREN'S ADJUSTMENT

As shown in Figure 8.1, marital conflict is hypothesized to affect children's adjustment through exposure to marital discord between the parents (i.e., direct effects) and by influencing parent-child interactions or parenting practices (i.e., indirect effects; Cummings & Davies, 1994a). Pertinent to the broader process-oriented model outlined in Figure 8.1, several recent studies have examined evidence for direct and indirect pathways of marital conflict to child adjustment. The evidence regarding indirect effects has implications for the fathering vulnerability hypothesis. Webster-Stratton and Hammond (1999) found direct and indirect effects of marital conflict on children's conduct problems for both fathers and mothers. However, no support was found for a fathering vulnerability hypothesis; that is, the parenting of both mothers (i.e., low emotional responsivity) and fathers (i.e., low emotional responsivity, critical parenting) was negatively associated with marital conflict, in each case with negative implications for children's adjustment.

Harold, Fincham, Osborne, and Conger (Study 1, 1997) reported evidence for direct and indirect effects of marital conflict on adolescents' adjustment. Pathways through both mother-child and father-child hostility were significant for the prediction of both internalizing and externalizing problems. The data were inconclusive with regard to a fathering vulnerability hypothesis because tests of the size of pathways through mothering in comparison with fathering were not conducted. However, it is notable that path coefficients were consistently larger for fathering than mothering in models relating to children's externalizing and internalizing problems.

Buehler and Gerard (2002) also reported evidence for direct and indirect pathways of marital conflict on children's adjustment. With regard to children, indirect effects of marital conflict through parenting were identified for harsh discipline and low involvement. For adolescents, parent-child conflict also served as a mediating parenting factor in relations between marital conflict and child adjustment. These results were consistent based on the reports of fathers and mothers and held for both boys and girls. However, an effect consistent with a fathering vulnerability hypothesis was that the pathway from marital conflict to low parental involvement to child adjustment was significant for fathers but not for mothers.

COPARENTING

Moreover, additional conceptualizations of marital functioning and parenting further reinforce the notion of relations between marital quality and parenting for both fathers and mothers. For example, Margolin, Gordis, and John (2001) recently reported that for both husbands and wives, coparenting mediated relations between marital conflict and parenting, although statistical tests of effects for fathers in comparison with mothers were not conducted. Coparenting was defined in terms of the parents' cooperation, triangulation, and conflict around child-rearing issues. Notably, with regard to the interest in relations between coparenting and marital conflict, recent work suggests that marital conflicts occurring in front of children are more intense and more often about child-rearing issues than are other conflicts (Papp, Cummings, & Goeke-Morey, 2002).

SIBLING RELATIONS

Other family relationship systems may also be affected by interrelations between marital conflict and parenting. For example, Noller, Feeney, Sheehan, and Peterson (2000) examined relations between parents' perceptions of marital conflict and their ratings of twins' behavior. For fathers, negative marital conflict patterns were associated with more negative ratings of their adolescents, whereas for mothers no consistent relations between marital conflict and twins' behavior toward one another were found. These findings suggest possible relations between fathering and sibling relationships that merit further investigation.

RACE AND ETHNICITY

Finally, another important direction with regard to the fathering vulnerability hypothesis is to examine possible differences as a function of race and ethnicity. For example, marital quality may be lower, and the incidence of marital violence higher, in African American than European American families (McLoyd, Cauce, Takeuchi, & Wilson, 2000). On the other hand, the increased incidence of African American children's involvement in extended families may reduce the psychosocial impact of marital discord. Based on the 1988 National Survey of Families and Households, Buehler and Gerard (2002) found similar patterns of effects for marital conflict, fathers' and mothers' parenting, and child adjustment for families with various ethnic backgrounds.

SUMMARY AND INTERPRETATION

Findings in support of the notion that fathering is more affected than mothering have continued to accumulate since the Cummings and O'Reilly (1997) review. That is, when differences between fathering and mothering are found, the direction is consistently suggestive of more negative effects on fathering, although nonsignificant differences are frequently reported. Systematic tests of various explanations for fathering vulnerability are needed, and new directions for examining fathering vulnerability are emerging (e.g., positive parenting, implications for sibling relationships). Parent gender differences may have both biologically based and sociocultural foundations. However, in the context of this argument, it is important to acknowledge that the evidence suggests more similarities than differences in marital influences on mothering and fathering. As with child gender differences related to marital discord (Davies & Lindsay, 2001), the variability among fathers observed in fathering effects are likely greater than the mean differences between effects on fathering and mothering.

CHILDREN'S EXPOSURE TO FATHERS' IN COMPARISON WITH MOTHERS' MARITAL DISCORD: THE DIFFERENTIAL REACTIVITY HYPOTHESIS

As shown in Figure 8.1, children's exposure to marital discord is another pathway of the impact on children of fathers' behavior in the marital context. Given that extensive investigation has documented that children are negatively affected by exposure to destructive marital conflict (Cummings et al., 2000), it is significant to articulate the role of fathers in the marital context in order to determine whether fathers' conflict expressions have effects on children that are similar, or different, from the same expressions by mothers. As noted earlier, the differential reactivity hypothesis considers whether, given the same behaviors, children are more reactive to these behaviors when expressed by fathers than by mothers.

At the time of the Cummings and O'Reilly (1997) review, few studies had attempted to differentiate the effects on children of exposure to fathers' in comparison with mothers' discord. Thus, there was little basis for evaluating a differential reactivity hypothesis. A notable exception was Crockenberg and Forgays's (1996) finding that in response to videotapes of couples' conflict resolution, girls judged their fathers to be angrier than did boys, despite the absence of differences according to the reports of independent observers. In the period since the Cummings and O'Reilly (1997) review, more evidence pertinent to this hypothesis has accumulated.

CHILDREN'S EMOTIONAL RESPONDING TO MARITAL AGGRESSION

With regard to the issue of differential reactivity to marital conflict, Crockenberg and Langrock (2001) recently examined relations between marital aggression and children's emotional reactions to conflict between parents. Fathers' marital aggression correlated with girls' anger, sadness, and fear responses, but no significant correlations were found between mothers' marital aggression and children's emotional responses. These results are thus consistent with the notion of differential reactivity to fathers' discord, at least with regard to daughters. However, a limitation of these results is that specific forms of marital discord were not distinguished, and reactions to comparable incidents of marital conflict expressions were not examined for fathers and mothers. Thus, alternative explanations are possible, including that fathers' discordant behaviors were more hostile in front of girls than were mothers' conflict expressions, thus eliciting more extreme reactions due to their differential negativity. Another possibility is that children are more reactive to aggression by fathers, but not necessarily more reactive to other everyday marital conflict behaviors (e.g., nonverbal anger).

CHILDREN'S RESPONDING TO CONSTRUCTIVE AND DESTRUCTIVE CONFLICT EXPRESSIONS

Analog Methodology in the Lab

Recently, tests have been conducted of children's immediate reactions to fathers' and mothers' expressions of marital conflict, including tests of children's reactions to multiple forms of constructive as well as destructive marital conflict strategies. Based on the responses of 175 8- to 16-year-old U.S. children and 327 11- to 12-year-old Welsh children, Goeke-Morey, Cummings, Harold, and Shelton (in press) examined children's responses to analog presentations of a series of everyday marital conflict tactics enacted by mothers and fathers, respectively, in separately taped scenarios. Consistent with the differential reactivity hypothesis, for both the U.S. and Welsh samples, children showed a pattern of more negative reactions to physical aggression against the spouse when enacted by fathers than when enacted by mothers. The results are similar to those reported by Crockenberg and Forgays (1996) and Crockenberg and Langrock (2001) in indicating children's greater reactivity to fathers' than mothers' marital aggression, although there was no evidence that girls were more sensitive than boys to these forms of marital conflict behaviors by fathers.

On the other hand, a different pattern emerged for other conflict behaviors that was less supportive of a hypothesis of differential reactivity to father discord. In addition to interparental aggression, children's reactions to other marital conflict tactics classified as destructive were examined. Behaviors were classified as destructive if they elicited more negative than positive emotional reactions from children (see Goeke-Morey, 1999). For these additional destructive marital conflict behaviors, differences as a function of parent gender were inconsistent for the U.S. sample. That is, in the U.S. sample, threats to the intactness of the family, nonverbal hostility, and pursuit of conflict topics elicited more negative reactions when used by mothers than when used by fathers, whereas verbal hostility and physical aggression against objects were more distressing when used by fathers than by mothers. One interpretation is that the more physically threatening behaviors (i.e., physical aggression against the spouse, physical aggression against objects, and verbal hostility) were judged more distressing when enacted by fathers than mothers, whereas less extreme destructive behaviors reflective of dissatisfaction with family relationships raised greater concerns when used by mothers than fathers.

It is interesting that for the Welsh sample, more negative reactions by children to nonphysically aggressive but nonetheless destructive conflict tactics were consistently found in reaction to mothers' enactments. Specifically, for the Welsh sample all of the following were judged more distressing when shown by mothers than fathers: physical aggression against objects, threats to the intactness of the family, verbal hostility, nonverbal hostility, and pursuit. In other words, for destructive behaviors less intense than interpersonal aggression between the parents, children never reported more negativity to fathers' than mothers' conflict expressions. To account for these cultural variations, Goeke-Morey et al. (in press) speculated that Welsh children may view communication of the mothers' dissatisfaction and distress more pessimistically because they perceive more negative implications of the mothers' than the fathers' distress for the day-to-day management and emotional harmony of family life. That is, given that mothers are often primary caregivers in more traditional family structures, children in Welsh families may be more sensitive to mothers' than fathers' particular expressions of conflict and the implications for children's own emotional security in the family context.

An interesting and quite different pattern of results emerged, consistent across both the U.S. and Welsh samples, with regard to children's reactions to behaviors classified as *constructive* conflict tactics during marital discord. Behaviors were classified as constructive if they elicited more positive than negative emotional reactions from children (see Goeke-Morey, 1999). For the U.S. sample, problem solving, support, and affection each elicited more positive reactions when enacted by fathers than mothers. For the Welsh sample, fathers' affection resulted in more positive responses than mothers' affection. Thus, across both cultures, children were more reactive to fathers' than mothers' constructive conflict tactics, but in a positive, rather than negative, way. Thus, the findings overall indicate that fathers' conflict behaviors may be especially influential in relations between marital conflict and children's functioning when they reflect relatively extreme behaviors, including marital aggression, on the one hand, and constructive conflict behaviors, on the other. For more moderate but nonetheless destructive conflict expressions, children's reactions may be less predictable as a function of parent gender, with contextual factors also being influential (e.g., culture).

Two important qualifications should be noted, however. First, *classifications* of marital conflict behaviors as constructive as opposed to destructive were unaffected by parent gender. Physical aggression against spouse, physical aggression against objects, threat to intactness of the family, verbal hostility, nonverbal hostility, and pursuit were classified as destructive whether enacted by mothers or fathers in both samples. Moreover, problem solving, support, and affection were classified as constructive conflict tactics when evidenced by either mothers or fathers in both cultures. Thus, the fundamental impact of exposure to these behaviors was not altered by whether the parent engaging in the behaviors was the mother or the father.

Second, statistical effects sizes for classification of these conflict tactics were far greater than for parent gender. Thus, the median effect sizes for classification were .76 for the U.S. sample and .70 for the Welsh sample. By contrast, median effects sizes for the significant parent gender comparisons were much smaller, only .09 for the U.S. sample and .02 for the Welsh sample. An exception was the relatively large effect size for U.S. children's emotional reactions to fathers' in comparison with mothers' physical aggression against the spouse (i.e., .31). Thus, the meaning of marital discord from the children's perspective with regard to their own sense of emotional security appears to be more closely tied to parents' expressions of marital conflict behaviors than the gender of the parent engaging in the conflict behaviors (Davies, Harold, Goeke-Morey, & Cummings, 2002).

Diary Methodology in the Home

Given that the Goeke-Morey et al. (in press) results were based on analog tests, the generalizability of these findings to naturally occurring marital conflict in the home merits consideration. Pertinent to this issue, Cummings et al. (in press) recently investigated children's reactions to marital conflict expressions in the home based on parents' (fathers' and mothers') diary reports of conflict incidents and children's responses. Parental negative emotionality and destructive conflict tactics were each linked with children's insecure emotional (e.g., mad, sad, fearful) and behavioral (i.e., attempts to regulate parental conflict) responses in the home. By contrast, parental positive emotionality and constructive conflict tactics were associated with children's secure (i.e., positive emotionality) responding. Similar patterns of results emerged based on fathers' and mothers' diary reports.

These results provide a level of ecological support for the results based on Goeke-Morey et al.'s (in press) analog study and are consistent with their conclusion that responding to fundamental categories of constructive and destructive conflict tactics enacted by mothers or fathers are similar. Little support was found for differences in children's reactions as a function of parent gender. On the other hand, reflecting, in part, differences in the strengths and weaknesses of the different methodologies, the Cummings et al. (in press) diary study was not able to go as far in determining children's reactions to specific marital conflict behaviors as was the Goeke-Morey et al. investigation; that is, only composites of constructive and destructive conflict tactics, and negative and positive emotional expressions, were distinguished. Notably, based on the Goeke-Morey report, reactions to *specific* expressions of marital conflict may be the level of analysis at which differential reactivity to mother and father discord is apparent. This question thus needs to be tested in future research in the home.

MARITAL AGGRESSION AND CHILDREN'S ADJUSTMENT

With regard to interparental aggression, McDonald, Jouriles, Norwood, Ware, and Ezell (2000) recently reported that fathers' interparental aggression, based on a combination of mothers' and fathers' reports, was linked with fathers' reports of child internalizing problems, even after accounting for parental aggression toward children, general marital discord, and mothers' interparental aggression. Davies, Hops, Alpert, and Sheeber (1998) found that aggressive responding by children (girls and boys) was sequentially related to interparental conflict. Indexing a type of differential reactivity, when evidencing aggression following parents' conflict, both boys and girls were more likely to aggress against the mother than the father. However, boys' aggression tended to be in response to an attack by the mother on the father, whereas girls' aggression predominantly followed an attack by the father on the mother. Thus, mothers may be more victimized by children when children are aroused to hostility following marital conflict, but a variety of other explanations are certainly possible (e.g., see Davies et al.). At the least, these findings indicate another pattern of responding to interparental discord as a function of parent gender that merits further investigation.

CHILDREN'S ATTRIBUTIONS OF BLAME

Another important class of reactions to marital conflict concerns children's attributions of blame for the conflict. Children's cognitive understanding of conflict may be a mediating factor in the impact of marital conflict on children (Grych & Fincham, 1990, 1993). Pertinent to this issue, Weston, Boxer, and Hetherington (1998) interviewed children (5 to 12 years old) concerning their beliefs about the causes of the arguments. Across all ages, children made somewhat different attributions about fathers in comparison with mothers in marital arguments. That is, they were more likely to attribute mothers' behavior to state (e.g., "the mom had a bad day") than to trait (e.g., "its because of the kind of person the dad is") causes, with fewer trait attributions for the mother than for the father. One interpretation is that fathers are viewed more often as angry due to trait causes than situational provocations.

Summary and Interpretation

The research reviewed suggests that both a positive and a negative version of the differential reactivity hypothesis may hold for fathers. That is, children are more negatively reactive to interparental violence by fathers than mothers (negative version) and also more positively responsive to constructive conflict behaviors by fathers than mothers (positive version). One possible explanation is that children read more meaning into relatively dramatic expressions by fathers, perhaps reflecting that fathers typically are either highly engaged or withdrawn from everyday marital disputes (Christensen & Heavey, 1990), perhaps due to differences between fathers and mothers in capacities to regulate arousal (e.g., see Cummings & Davies, 1994a). Thus, children may learn that focused engagement (constructive behaviors) or extreme hostility (interparental aggression) by fathers each reflects their heightened investment in marital disputes, and thus their behavior has especially meaningful implications from the perspective of the children. On the other hand, children may read more meaning into moderately negative, nonviolent behaviors by mothers than fathers because this level of pursuit of conflict issues is more typical of mothers and may be more possible from an arousal regulation perspective (see Cummings & Davies, 1994a). Therefore, from the children's perspective, moderately negative behaviors are more salient, and credible, forms of conflict expression when evidenced by mothers than fathers. However, there may be cultural variations with regard to the purview of credible maternal conflict behaviors (see Goeke-Morey et al., in press).

With regard to this pathway, it is also important to put the question of father in comparison with mother effects in perspective. The great majority of conflict behaviors are classified as destructive or constructive (depending on the behavior) *regardless* of the gender of the parent engaging in the behavior. Moreover, effect sizes due to the way in which conflict is expressed are much greater than are effect sizes due to parent gender (see previous discussion of Goeke-Morey et al., in press). In other words, the specific marital conflict expressions exhibited by either fathers or mothers would appear to matter a great deal to children's reactions, with the gender of the parent only an accent on the fundamental direction of children's responses.

Tests for replication of patterns of findings are needed. Future studies might also examine additional forms of conflict tactics or dimensions of conflict expressions. Moreover, it will be important to examine further the role of child age and gender, as well as other child characteristics, as factors influencing the impact of direct exposure to fathers' as opposed to mothers' marital discord.

MARITAL QUALITY AND PARENTAL PSYCHOLOGICAL FUNCTIONING: PATERNAL MENTAL HEALTH HYPOTHESIS

As discussed earlier (see Figure 8.1), adjustment problems in parents and problems in marital relationships have been linked, and both factors together have been shown to relate to children's adjustment (Cummings et al., 2000; Downey & Coyne, 1990). Associations among marital conflict, parental depressive symptomatology, and children's adjustment have been further examined and articulated since the Cummings and O'Reilly (1997) review. In a longitudinal investigation of adolescent adjustment, Davies and Windle (1997) found that family discord mediated the effects of maternal depressive symptoms on girls' social and emotional adjustment. Moreover, Davies et al. (1999) showed that for both adolescent boys and girls, marital distress mediated the effects of maternal depressive symptoms on externalizing problems, and maternal depressive symptomatology mediated the impact of marital distress on depressive symptoms.

However, important gaps remain in understanding these relations. Fathers' depressive symptomatology in the marital context is rarely examined, although the limited literature suggests relations with marital conflict (e.g., McElwain & Volling, 1999). Moreover, marital discord is typically treated as a global, negative construct in this literature, although the broader literature on marital conflict and children indicates that children's reactions are highly affected by variations in marital conflict styles (Cummings & Davies, 2002). Finally, consideration of parents' psychological functioning is typically limited to depressive symptomatology, whereas multiple dimensions of parents' psychological functioning may potentially be affected by marital quality and conflict.

FATHERS' MARITAL CONFLICT BEHAVIORS AND FATHERS' DEPRESSIVE SYMPTOMATOLOGY

Accordingly, a next step for research is to examine the links between marital quality and conflict expressions, and both maternal and paternal depressive symptoms. It is also important to determine which maternal and paternal patterns of marital conflict behavior associated with parental depression are particularly linked with children's adjustment problems. Based on observations of 267 couples' interactions during marital conflict resolution tasks, Du Rocher Schulich and Cummings (in press) found that parental dysphoria was negatively related to constructive conflict styles (humor, support, physical affection, calm discussion, problem solving, resolution, positivity) and positively related to destructive (verbal and nonverbal hostility, defensiveness, pursuit, personal insult, physical aggression, anger) and depressive (physical distress, withdrawal, sadness, fear) conflict styles for both mothers and fathers. Moreover, structural equation modeling demonstrated that marital discord, in particular depressive conflict styles, mediated the relationship between parental dysphoria and internalizing problems reported for the 8- to 16-year-old children of these couples. Furthermore, whereas for mothers, depressive conflict styles partially mediated links between dysphoria and child internalizing problems, for fathers, depressive conflict styles fully mediated this link.

These results thus indicate that, for fathers as well as mothers, marital conflict styles factor in relations between parental dysphoria and child adjustment, with depressive conflict expressions particularly implicated in the impact of parental depression. Moreover, depressive conflict style was an even more powerful mediator of children's internalizing problems for fathers than for mothers. With regard to possible explanations, these authors speculated that depressive marital conflict behaviors may be especially disturbing for children because the parents are presented as vulnerable and fragile (e.g., they may appear scared, sad, or distressed during the conflict). Observation of these parental expressions during marital conflict thus may pose a particular threat to children's sense of emotional security. It may be especially disturbing for children when fathers behave in this way because such behaviors particularly contradict possible expectations about fathers as strong or invulnerable parental authority figures, although the evidence also suggests that such behaviors by either parent add to the negative impact of parental depressive symptomatology.

FATHERS' SUPPORT AND HOSTILITY AND MOTHERS' DEPRESSIVE MARITAL CONFLICT

Additional questions concerning the impact of parental depression and marital conflict include whether (a) parental depressive behavior during marital conflict adds to the negative impact of general interparental hostility from the children's perspective and (b) partners' supportive responses to spouses' depressive marital conflict behavior reduces or mitigates the negative impact for children of observing marital conflict that includes depressive conflict expressions. With regard to these issues, Huffman and Cummings (2002) recently investigated the responses of 7- to 12-year-olds to analog representations of marital conflict involving mutual hostility, mothers' depressive behavior with fathers' hostility, mothers' depressive behavior with fathers' support, or conflict resolution. Even though mutual hostility was rated by children as the most intensely angry of the four classes of conflict scenarios, mothers' depressive behavior with fathers' hostility actually induced the most pervasive negative reactions from children, including significantly elevated sadness and withdrawal, in relation to reactions to the other conflict scenarios. By contrast, fathers' supportive behavior in the context of marital conflict involving mothers' depressive conflict styles resulted in substantially reduced negative reactions from children, with children's behavioral distress, in particular, being no greater than the responses found in reaction to resolved conflict. Although caution should be exercised in generalizing results from tests based on analog procedures, these findings intriguingly suggest both that mothers' depressive affect may exacerbate marital conflict expressions from the perspective of bystanding children and that the observed presence of an understanding, supportive father substantially reduces the negative impact for children of the mix of conflict and depressive behavior associated with parental dysphoria.

BROADER PSYCHOLOGICAL SYMPTOMS

Finally, although research has focused primarily on parental depression and children's adjustment, a variety of forms of psychopathological symptoms, in addition to depressive symptomatology, may in fact be related to children's adjustment. Moreover, marital conflict may also factor in the effects of other forms of parental psychopathology. However, there has been scant investigation of these questions, especially for fathers' symptomatology. With regard to these questions, for a community sample of 53 4- to 11-year-old children and their families, Papp et al. (2003) found that psychological symptoms of both mothers and fathers related to marital discord and child adjustment, with more direct relations evident for fathers than for mothers. Moreover, for both mothers and fathers, marital functioning moderated relations between dimensions of parental psychological functioning and child adjustment. The quality of the marital relationship moderated the effect of multiple dimensions of maternal psychological functioning (e.g., somatization, anxiety, depression, phobic anxiety, interpersonal sensitivity, paranoid ideation) on children's internalizing and externalizing symptoms, including protective relations linked with marital satisfaction, and increased risk associated with negative marital conflict strategies. By contrast, for fathers, moderational results were limited to increased risk for children's externalizing problems associated with negative marital conflict strategies and parental depressive symptomatology. Thus, for mothers, the marital relationship and psychological symptoms were more pervasively linked with children's adjustment problems than for fathers (see also McElwain & Volling, 1999). For fathers, depression may function differently than other psychological symptoms, calling for further investigation on multiple dimensions of psychological functioning as they relate to marital conflict and children.

SUMMARY AND INTERPRETATION

Recent studies identify promising directions toward better articulation of relations between fathers' marital functioning, fathers' as well as mothers' psychopathology, and children's adjustment. Consistent themes are that (a) these relations depend on how, specifically, marital functioning is assessed, including how parents engage in marital conflict, and (b) fathers' as well as mothers' marital quality and conflict expressions factor in children's functioning as a correlate of parental psychopathology. It will be important to extend the range of parental psychopathology examined in future research. For example, parents' problem drinking may be considered another category of parental adjustment problems, with interrelations between marital conflict and parental alcohol abuse implicated in the prediction of children's adjustment problems (El-Sheikh & Cummings, 1997; El-Sheikh & Flanagan, 2001). Thus, investigators should consider these and other issues further in future studies, as research moves to the next step of examining relationships in the context of prospective longitudinal research designs with the aim of more cogently specifying causal relations between these parental, marital, and child outcome variables (see Figure 8.1).

COMPLETING THE PROCESS-ORIENTED MODEL FOR FATHERS IN FAMILY CONTEXT

As shown in Figure 8.1, completing the process-oriented model for the effects of fathers in the family context requires assessing (a) relations between fathering across these multiple pathways, (b) the role of children's characteristics and coping processes and mechanisms, and (c) relations with changes in children's adjustment over time. To this point, no single study has satisfied all of these requirements for a family-wide model for the particular relations between fathers' functioning in family contexts and children's adjustment.

Methodological characteristics often sharply limit interpretation. For example, only global assessments of marital quality and conflict based on retrospective questionnaire data are often used. Furthermore, fathers' and mothers' conflict expressions may not be differentiated, or the records of marital discord employed may be based only on the reports of mothers. Even when data are collected for mothers and fathers and models are tested separately for each parent, these models may not be directly compared, limiting conclusions about effects for fathers as compared to mothers.

Moreover, even when data are collected longitudinally, change analyses that refine the articulation of causal processes cannot be conducted when only two time points are examined (Cummings et al., 2000). Nonetheless, since the Cummings and O'Reilly (1997) review, progress has been made toward articulating various elements and aspects of this model. Next we provide a selective review of contributions toward a broader, process-oriented model of relations between marital and child adjustment, emphasizing the role of fathers.

LONG-TERM EFFECTS

Neighbors et al. (1997) examined long-term effects associated with marital conflict as a predictor of children's adjustment, with the initial assessment occurring when children were in early to middle adolescence and reassessment occurring 6 years later, when the children were young adults. Multiple regression analyses based on questionnaires completed by children and their mothers (but not fathers) were used to examine links between interparental conflict and children's functioning at the two time points. For boys, current interparental conflict predicted both antisocial behavior and general psychopathology ($p < .06$) in young adulthood. In addition, interparental conflict during adolescence predicted boys' reports of problems in their relationships with their fathers in young adulthood. No relations were found between interparental conflict and girls' outcomes.

CHILDREN'S EMOTIONAL REACTIONS AS COPING PROCESSES AND MECHANISMS

Crockenberg and Langrock (2001) reported that mothers' marital aggression and avoidance predicted both internalizing and externalizing problems for girls only. Fathers' marital aggression predicted boys' and girls' externalizing problems, as well as internalizing problems for boys. Reflecting an apparent cumulative effect, girls who had two maritally aggressive parents had more pronounced externalizing problems than did girls with only an aggressive mother. It is notable that direct effects remained significant even after parenting factors were considered. Advancing the study of the role of children's coping processes and mechanisms, evidence was uncovered for children's emotional reactions to interparental conflict as mediating or moderating children's adjustment. That is, in association with fathers' marital aggression, girls' fear and a fear-anger interaction related to their internalizing problems. For boys, fathers' marital conflict behaviors interacted with boys' angry reactions to relate to boys' externalizing problems, and interacted with boys' fear to relate to boys' internalizing difficulties.

Jenkins (2000) examined associations between parents' anger-based marital conflict (based on mothers' reports) and children's angry and aggressive functioning in home and school contexts. Indexes of mothers' and fathers' anger-based marital conflict were related to children's anger and aggression in relationships with others, as reported by peers, teachers, and parents. Evidence was found for the relative coherency in anger organization in children across multiple measures and contexts. Moreover, children's greater exposure to more anger-based marital conflict was linked with children's greater tendencies toward their own anger-based emotional organization, with no evidence of similar effects for a sadness-based emotional organization. Notably, in contrast to Crockenberg and Langrock (2001), the authors concluded that fathers' aggression was *not* more influential than mothers' in fostering child anger and aggression. Referring to Figure 8.1, these results thus highlight relations between parents' organizations of marital conflict expressions (i.e., parents' anger-based expressions of conflict) and children's coping processes and adjustment outcomes (i.e., children's problems with the regulation of angry emotions and aggression).

Exposure to Marital Conflict Behaviors in the Home

Extending the study of the effects of parents' *specific* conflict tactics on children's functioning based on analog methodologies (e.g., Goeke-Morey et al., in press), Cummings, Goeke-Morey, and Papp (in press) examined children's reactions to specific marital conflict behaviors in the home based on parental diary reports. Mothers and fathers reported on naturally occurring incidents of marital conflict in the home, with 1,638 records of conflict incidents obtained from mothers and 1,281 obtained from fathers, including reports of conflict occurring in front of the children. Participants were 116 families with 8- to 16-year-old children, with parents providing records over a 15-day period after obtaining laboratory-based training in the use of daily report procedures. Analyses were conducted using hierarchical generalized linear modeling (HGLM), appropriate to the characteristics of parental diary data (e.g., dependent measurements, varying numbers of reports from participants over the reporting period). Consistent with Goeke-Morey et al.'s (in press) classifications, parental tactics of threat, personal insult, verbal hostility, defensiveness, nonverbal hostility, marital withdrawal, and physical distress occurring during everyday marital conflict were linked with children's negative emotional and behavioral reactions, whereas parental support and affection elicited positive reactions. Thus, classifications of specific marital conflict expressions as destructive and constructive based on analog procedures generalized to children's reactions to naturally occurring incidents of marital conflict occurring in the home. Consistencies in findings across the reports of mothers and fathers increased confidence in the pattern of results.

In another investigation based on daily home diaries kept by mothers and fathers, O'Hearn, Margolin, and John (1997) reported that children from homes with marital physical aggression were more likely than children from homes characterized by low or nonphysical conflict to appear highly distressed by marital conflict, including misbehaving or appearing angry, leaving the room, or appearing sad or frightened. In terms of Figure 8.1, these findings further support a pathway from exposure to marital discord to children's coping processes of sensitized emotional and behavioral dysregulation.

Children's Coping Processes and Mechanisms and the Emotional Security Hypothesis

Cummings and O'Reilly (1997) specified the *emotional security hypothesis* (Cummings & Davies, 1996; Davies & Cummings, 1994) as providing a promising theoretical model for children's coping processes and mechanisms. In a recent monograph for the Society for Research in Child Development, Davies et al. (2002) reported a series of studies pertinent to the viability of this process-oriented model of the effects of interparental conflict on children's adjustment over time. Pertinent to Figure 8.1, the aim was to examine critically the coping processes and mechanisms mediating and moderating effects of marital conflict on children, with a focus on testing the emotional security hypothesis against other theories (e.g., social learning theory).

In Study 1, for a sample of 327 Welsh children, a series of tests was conducted examining the relative viability of the predictions of the emotional security and social learning hypotheses regarding children's coping processes and mechanisms. Findings indicated the prominence of processes implicated by the emotional security hypothesis, including children's fear, avoidance, and involvement, with little support found for processes implicated by modeling hypotheses, including imitation. In particular, there was weak to negligible support for the notion that children were more likely to model the same-sex parent. Girls were significantly more likely to model mothers' than fathers' aggressive behaviors in only one of the eight analyses conducted on this question (13%). Moreover, no evidence indicated that boys modeled fathers' aggression more than mothers' aggression.

Providing one of the few longitudinal tests of process-oriented theories in this area, a second study reported in Davies et al. (2002) examined the relative roles of child emotional security and social-cognitive appraisals (Grych & Fincham, 1990) in accounting for relations between marital conflict and children's adjustment for a sample of 285 Welsh children and their parents. Child emotional security emerged from these analyses as a robust intervening process in prospective links between marital conflict and children's internalizing and externalizing problems across the two-year span between initial and follow-up assessments, even when processes implicated in social-cognitive models (Grych, Seid, & Fincham, 1992) were included in the analyses. Notably, data for ratings of marital conflict were based on the reports of both mothers and fathers.

A third study specified the existence of separate pathways of relations among interparental conflict, child emotional insecurity, and child maladjustment, on the one hand, and parenting difficulties, child emotional insecurity, and child maladjustment, on the other. That is, children's emotional security in the context of interparental conflict and child-parent attachment security were shown to constitute distinct pathways mediating the effects of interparental conflict and parenting, respectively, in predicting children's adjustment. Thus, emotional security theory was specifically implicated as a promising direction for articulating mediators of pathways of multiple family influences, including marital quality and parenting. On the other hand, future research should explore other possible mechanisms and processes, given that additional processes may possibly underlie effects on children (Jenkins, 2002).

CHILD CHARACTERISTICS

Finally, pertinent to conceptualizations of child characteristics as moderators of child adjustment outcomes, Davies and Windle (2001) examined temperament, childhood behavior problems, and perceived family support as possible moderators of relations between marital discord and adolescent depressive symptoms and delinquency for a sample of 360 adolescent-mother dyads (see also Davies et al., 2002, Study 4). The negative effects of marital conflict were potentiated by difficult temperament, and adolescents were protected from adverse effects of marital conflict by heightened perceptions of family support. Childhood behavior problems were associated with the persistence of high levels of depressive symptoms over time under conditions of high levels of marital conflict.

Another promising direction for the analysis of child characteristics and coping responses is to examine higher order organizations of children's emotional and social responses to marital and family discord. Directions in person-oriented characterizations of coping patterns are promising. For example, Maughan and Cicchetti (2002) found that person-oriented emotion regulation patterns in children were linked with both family discord histories and child adjustment outcomes. In particular, dysregulated emotional response patterns were highly associated with maltreatment in preschoolers, with undercontrolled or ambivalent emotion regulation patterns especially linked with child behavior problems and anxious or depressed symptoms (see also Davies & Forman, 2002).

CONCLUSIONS

Studies emerging since the Cummings and O'Reilly (1997) review thus further substantiate that fathers exert multiple influences on children's development as a function of marital quality and conflict (see Figure 8.1). That is, marital relationships are related to fathering and father-child relationships and also affect children due to exposure to marital discord (e.g., Owen & Cox, 1997). Moreover, marital relationships are a factor in the association between fathers' psychological functioning and children's adjustment. Finally, recent work advances understanding of child characteristics and children's coping processes as elements in process-oriented models.

Turning to the *Fathering and Father-Child Relationship* variable in Figure 8.1, this review underscores that researchers should include data based on father reports, as well as consideration of father-child interactions. Investigators should test separate pathways for fathering and mothering and also compare the size of the effects on fathering in comparison with mothering due to marital discord. This last test has typically been neglected, even in instances in which such analyses would have been possible.

Recent work underscores *Child Exposure to Father Marital Discord* as a pathway for the effects of fathers in the marital context. Several directions for future research are pertinent to further understanding of this pathway: (a) investigation of direct effects of fathers' marital discord on children's adjustment (e.g., Harold et al., 1997), (b) further identifying the coping processes and mechanisms mediating effects of fathers' discord on children's adjustment (e.g., Davies et al., 2002), and (c) documenting further children's reactions to exposure to fathers' and mothers' *specific* conflict expressions (e.g., Goeke-Morey et al., in press). With regard to this last direction, global assessment of marital discord cannot distinguish between the possibilities that one parent typically engages in more intense conflict expressions in the home than the other parent, or that specific expressions differentially effect children due simply to the gender of the parent expressing the behaviors.

It remains that the pathway through *Father Psychological Functioning* (see Figure 8.1) is little examined. It may be the case, in fact, that mothers' psychological functioning is more generally tied to marital processes than fathers' psychological functioning, with a wider range of psychological problems moderated by marital quality in affecting children's adjustment for mothers than fathers (McElwain & Volling, 1999; Papp et al., 2003). An exception may be fathers' depressive symptomatology, which Papp et al. (2003) found was tied to negative marital conflict behaviors in effects on children. Moreover, fathers' supportive behavior or, alternatively, hostility may moderate the impact of mothers' marital distress associated with depressive symptomatology from the children's perspective (Huffman & Cummings, 2002). Moreover, fathers' expressions of conflict in the context of depressive behavior may carry more weight than mothers' in influencing children's reactions to parental depression (Du Rocher Schud-lich & Cummings, 2002).

With regard to *Child Characteristics* and *Child Coping Processes and Mechanisms* (see Figure 8.1), child gender may be a factor (e.g., Crockenberg & Langrock, 2001; Neigh-bors et al., 1997), but findings are inconsistent (e.g., Jenkins, 2000). An important di-rection for future research will be to examine age-gender changes over time as a function of fathers' and mothers' marital conflict expressions. Differences between boys and girls in reaction to marital conflict may change with time, with the possibil-ity that relative dispositions toward sadness and anger may switch at the onset of ado-lescence (Cummings, Ballard, & El-Sheikh, 1991; Cummings, Ballard, El-Sheikh, & Lake, 1991). Thus, sensitivity to detecting parent gender–child gender effects is lim-ited in current research when responding is assessed across broad age periods. Given that individual children mature at different times, prospective longitudinal studies may be especially necessary to detect individual differences in changes during im-portant developmental transitions, including possible parent gender–child gender ef-fects during the transition to adolescence.

Recent work further advances the cogency of the emotional security hypothesis in relation to other theoretical models. This model was advanced in the Cummings and O'Reilly (1997) review on fathers in the marital context, but little direct work pertinent to that theory had accumulated at that time. Recent work argues for the promise of this account for children's coping processes and mechanisms. In particular, findings argue against the cogency of the modeling account (e.g., see also Cummings, Zahn-Waxler, & Radke-Yarrow, 1981). Moreover, support is accumulating for the emotional security hypothesis based on prospective longitudinal tests of children's coping processes and mechanisms. On the other hand, cognitive theories and attachment theory also con-tribute meaningfully to explanatory accounts, and it must be recognized that other processes, as yet untested, may be operational.

A gap is the paucity of accounts of the role of *Father Characteristics* (see Figure 8.1). In this regard, little is know about the role of culture and ethnicity as these pertain to fathers in the marital context (McLoyd et al., 2000). Additional issues for future study of the moderating role of fathers' characteristics include fathers' relations with their own parents, their own parents' marital relationship, personality characteristics, sex-ual preference, intelligence-cognitive abilities, age (adolescent fathers, older fathers), and biological-genetic factors.

Finally, it is important for future research to incorporate more inclusive research de-signs and more reliance on naturalistic observational methodologies in order to im-prove the cogency of process-oriented explanations (Cummings, Goeke-Morey, & Dukewich, 2001). Relatedly, cogent model testing requires the use of prospective lon-gitudinal research designs, which are a limitation in the broader literature on marital conflict and children (Fincham & Grych, 2001). Improvements in methodology are perhaps as important as other advances for the next review of literature on this ques-tion to be able to draw more informative conclusions about these issues.

REFERENCES

Almeida, D. M., Wethington, E., & Chandler, A. L. (1999). Daily transmission of tensions be-tween marital dyads and parent-child dyads. *Journal of Marriage and the Family, 61,* 49–61.

Belsky, J. (1979). The interrelation of parental and spousal behavior during infancy in traditional nuclear families: An exploratory analysis. *Journal of Marriage and the Family, 41,* 749–755.

Belsky, J., Gilstrap, B., & Rovine, M. (1984). The Pennsylvania infant and family development project: I. Stability and change in mother-infant and father-infant interactions in a family setting at one, three, and nine months. *Child Development, 55,* 692–705.

Belsky, J., Youngblade, L., Rovine, M., & Volling, B. (1991). Patterns of marital change and parent-child interaction. *Journal of Marriage and the Family, 53,* 487–498.

Buehler, C., & Gerard, J. M. (2002). Marital conflict, ineffective parenting, and children's and adolescents' maladjustment. *Journal of Marriage and Family, 64,* 78–92.

Cabrera, N. J., Tamis-LeMonda, C. S., Bradley, R. H., Hofferth, S., & Lamb, M. E. (2000). Fatherhood in the twenty-first century. *Child Development, 71,* 127–136.

Cassidy, J., & Shaver, P. R. (Eds.). (1999). *Handbook of attachment: Theory, research, and clinical applications.* New York: Guilford Press.

Christensen, A., & Heavey, C. L. (1990). Gender and social structure in the demand/withdraw pattern of marital conflict. *Journal of Personality and Social Psychology, 59,* 73–81.

Clements, M. L., Lim, K. G., & Chaplin, T. M. (2002, November). Marriage, parenting, and co-parenting: Effects of context, parent gender, and child gender on interactions. In F. M. Hughes (Chair), *Bridging the marital dyad and the family triad: A process-oriented approach.* Symposium conducted at the 36th Annual Convention of the Association for Advancement of Behavior Therapy, Reno, NV.

Coiro, M. J., & Emery, R. E. (1998). Do marriage problems affect fathering more than mothering? A quantitative and qualitative review. *Clinical Child and Family Psychology Review, 1,* 23–40.

Cowan, P. A., Cowan, C. P., & Kerig, P. K. (1993). Mothers, fathers, sons, and daughters: Gender differences in family formation and parenting style. In P. A. Cowan, D. A. Field, A. Skolnich, & G. Swanson (Eds.), *Family, self, and society: Toward a new agenda for family research* (pp. 165–195). Hillsdale, NJ: Erlbaum.

Cox, M. J., Paley, B., & Harter, K. (2001). Interparental conflict and parent-child relationships. In J. Grych & F. Fincham (Eds.), *Child development and interparental conflict* (pp. 249–272). New York: Cambridge University Press.

Crockenberg, S., & Forgays, D. K. (1996). The role of emotion in children's understanding and emotional reactions to marital conflict. *Merrill-Palmer Quarterly, 42,* 22–47.

Crockenberg, S., & Langrock, A. (2001). The role of specific emotions in children's responses to interparental conflict: A test of the model. *Journal of Family Psychology, 15,* 13–182.

Cummings, E. M., Ballard, M., & El-Sheikh, M. (1991). Responses of children and adolescents to interadult anger as a function of gender, age, and mode of expression. *Merrill-Palmer Quarterly, 37,* 543–560.

Cummings, E. M., Ballard, M., El-Sheikh, M., & Lake, M. (1991). Resolution and children's responses to interadult anger. *Developmental Psychology, 27,* 462–470.

Cummings, E. M., & Davies, P. T. (1994a). *Children and marital conflict: The impact of family dispute and resolution.* New York: Guilford Press.

Cummings, E. M., & Davies, P. T. (1994b). Maternal depression and child development [Annual Research Review]. *Journal of Child Psychology and Psychiatry, 35,* 73–112.

Cummings, E. M., & Davies, P. T. (1996). Emotional security as a regulatory process in normal development and the development of psychopathology. *Development and Psychopathology, 8,* 123–139.

Cummings, E. M., & Davies, P. T. (2002). Effects of marital conflict on children: Recent advances and emerging themes in process-oriented research. *Journal of Child Psychology and Psychiatry, 43,* 31–63.

Cummings, E. M., Davies, P. T., & Campbell, S. (2000). *Developmental psychopathology and family process.* New York: Guilford Press.

Cummings, E. M., Goeke-Morey, M. C., & Dukewich, T. L. (2001). The study of relations between marital conflict and child adjustment: Challenges and new directions for methodology. In J. H. Grych & F. D. Fincham (Eds.), *Interparental conflict and child development: Theory, research, and applications* (pp. 39–63). New York: Cambridge University Press.

Cummings, E. M., Goeke-Morey, M. C., & Papp, L. M. (in press). Children's responses to everyday marital conflict tactics in the home. *Child Development*.

Cummings, E. M., Goeke-Morey, M. C., Papp, L. M., & Dukewich, T. L. (2002). Children's responses to mothers' and fathers' emotional behavior and conflict tactics during marital conflict in the home. *Journal of Family Psychology, 16*, 478–492.

Cummings, E. M., & O'Reilly, A. W. (1997). Fathers in family context: Effects of marital quality on child adjustment. In M. E. Lamb (Ed.), *The role of the father in child development* (3rd ed., pp. 49–65). New York: Wiley.

Cummings, E. M., Zahn-Waxler, C., & Radke-Yarrow, M. (1981). Young children's responses to expressions of anger and affection by others in the family. *Child Development, 52*, 1274–1282.

Davies, P. T., & Cummings, E. M. (1994). Marital conflict and child adjustment: An emotional security hypothesis. *Psychological Bulletin, 116*, 387–411.

Davies, P. T., Dumenci, L., & Windle, M. (1999). The interplay between maternal depressive symptoms and marital distress in the prediction of adolescent adjustment. *Journal of Marriage and the Family, 61*, 238–254.

Davies, P. T., & Forman, E. M. (2002). Children's patterns of preserving emotional security in the interparental subsystem. *Child Development, 73*, 1880–1903.

Davies, P. T., Harold, G. T., Goeke-Morey, M. C., & Cummings, E. M. (2002). Child emotional security and interparental conflict. *Monographs of the Society for Research in Child Development, 67*(3, Serial No. 270).

Davies, P. T., Hops, H., Alpert, A., & Sheeber, L. (1998). Child responses to parental conflict and their effect on adjustment: A study of triadic relations. *Journal of Family Psychology, 12*, 163–177.

Davies, P. T., & Lindsay, L. L. (2001). Does gender moderate the effects of marital conflict on children? In J. Grych & F. Fincham (Eds.), *Interparental conflict and child development* (pp. 64–97). Cambridge, England: Cambridge University Press.

Davies, P. T., & Windle, M. (1997). Gender-specific pathways between maternal depressive symptoms, family discord, and adolescent adjustment. *Developmental Psychology, 33*, 657–668.

Davies, P. T., & Windle, M. (2001). Interparental discord and adolescent adjustment trajectories: The potentiating and protective roles of intrapersonal attributes. *Child Development, 72*, 1163–1178.

Downey, G., & Coyne, J. C. (1990). Children of depressed parents: An integrative review. *Psychological Bulletin, 108*, 50–76.

Du Rocher Schulich, T. D., & Cummings, E. M. (in press). Parental dysphoria and children's internalizing symptoms: Marital conflict styles as mediators of risk. *Child Development*.

El-Sheikh, M., & Cummings, E. M. (1997). Marital conflict, emotional regulation, and the adjustment of children of alcoholics. In K. Barrett (Ed.), *New directions in child development: Emotion and communication* (pp. 25–44). San Francisco: Jossey-Bass.

El-Sheikh, M., & Flanagan, E. (2001). Parental problem drinking and children's adjustment: Family conflict and parental depression as mediators and moderators of risk. *Journal of Abnormal Child Psychology, 29*, 417–432.

Erel, O., & Burman, B. (1995). Interrelatedness of marital relations and parent-child relations: A meta-analytic review. *Psychological Bulletin, 118*, 108–132.

Fincham, F. D., Beach, S. R. H., Harold, G. T., & Osborne, L. N. (1997). Marital satisfaction and depression: Different causal relationships for men and women? *Psychological Science, 8,* 351–357.

Fincham, F. D., & Grych, J. H. (2001). Advancing understanding of the association between interparental conflict and child development. In J. H. Grych & F. D. Fincham (Eds.), *Interparental conflict and child development: Theory, research, and applications* (pp. 443–451). New York: Cambridge University Press.

Frosch, C. A., Mangelsdorf, S. C., & McHale, J. L.(1998). Correlates of marital behavior at 6 months postpartum. *Developmental Psychology, 34,* 1438–1449.

Frosch, C. A., Manglesdorf, S. C., & McHale, J. L. (2000). Marital behavior and the security of preschooler-parent attachment relationships. *Journal of Family Psychology, 14,* 144–161.

Goeke-Morey, M. C. (1999). *Children and marital conflict: Exploring the distinction between constructive and destructive marital conflict behaviors.* Unpublished doctoral dissertation, University of Notre Dame, Notre Dame, IN.

Goeke-Morey, M. C., Cummings, E. M., Harold, G. T., & Shelton, K. H. (in press). Categories and continua of destructive and constructive marital conflict tactics from the perspective of U.S. and Welsh children. *Journal of Family Psychology.*

Grych, J. H., & Fincham, F. D. (1990). Marital conflict and children's adjustment: A cognitive-contextual framework. *Psychological Bulletin, 108,* 267–290.

Grych, J. H., & Fincham, F. D. (1993). Children's appraisals of marital conflict: Initial investigations of the cognitive-contextual framework. *Child Development, 64,* 215–230.

Grych, J. H., & Fincham, F. D. (Eds.). (2001). *Child development and interparental conflict.* New York: Cambridge University Press.

Grych, J. H., Seid, M., & Fincham, F. D. (1992). Assessing marital conflict from the child's perspective. *Child Development, 63,* 558–572.

Harold, G. T., Fincham, F. D., Osborne, L. N., & Conger, R. D. (1997). Mom and dad are at it again: Adolescent perceptions of marital conflict and adolescent psychological distress. *Developmental Psychology, 33,* 333–350.

Huffman, D. G., & Cummings, E. M. (2002). *Children's reactions to marital conflict simulations featuring mutual hostility and parental depression.* Manuscript submitted for publication.

Jenkins, J. M. (2000). Marital conflict and children's emotions: The development of an anger organization. *Journal of Marriage and Family, 62,* 723–736.

Jenkins, J. M. (2002). Mechanisms in the development of emotional organization. Commentary on P. T. Davies, G. T. Harold, M. C. Goeke-Morey, & E. M. Cummings, Child emotional security and interparental conflict. *Monographs of the Society for Research in Child Development, 67*(3, Serial No. 270), 116–127.

Jouriles, E. N., & Farris, A. M. (1992). Effects of marital conflict on subsequent parent-son interactions. *Behavior Therapy, 23,* 355–374.

Kerig, P. K., Cowan, P. A., & Cowan, C. P. (1993). Marital quality and gender differences in parent-child interaction. *Developmental Psychology, 29,* 931–939.

Kitzmann, K. M. (2000). Effects of marital conflict on subsequent triadic family interactions and parenting. *Developmental Psychology, 36,* 3–13.

Krishnakumar, A., & Buehler, C. (2000). Interparental conflict and parenting behaviors: A meta-analytic review. *Family Relations, 49,* 25–44.

Lamb, M. E. (2000). The history of research on father involvement: An overview. *Marriage and Family Review, 29,* 23–42.

Larson, R. W., & Almeida, D. M. (1999). Emotional transmission in the daily lives of families: A new paradigm for studying family process. *Journal of Marriage and the Family, 61,* 5–20.

Margolin, G., Christensen, A., & John, R. S. (1996). The continuance and spillover of everyday tensions in distressed and nondistressed families. *Journal of Family Psychology, 10,* 304–321.

Margolin, G., Gordis, E. B., & John, R. S. (2001). Coparenting: A link between marital conflict and parenting in two-parent families. *Journal of Family Psychology, 15,* 3–21.

Marsiglio, W., Amato, P., Day, R. D., & Lamb, M. E. (2000). Scholarship on fatherhood in the 1990s and beyond. *Journal of Marriage and the Family, 62,* 1173–1191.

Maughan, A., & Cicchetti, D. (2002). Impact of child maltreatment and interadult violence on children's emotion regulation abilities and socioemotional adjustment. *Child Development, 73,* 1525–1542.

McDonald, R., Jouriles, E. N., Norwood, W., Ware, H. S., & Ezell, E. (2000). Husbands' marital violence and the adjustment problems of clinic-referred children. *Behavior Therapy, 31,* 649–665.

McElwain, N. L., & Volling, B. L. (1999). Depressed mood and marital conflict: Relations to maternal and paternal intrusiveness with one-year-old infants. *Journal of Applied Developmental Psychology, 20,* 63–83.

McHale, J. P. (1995). Coparenting and triadic interactions during infancy: The roles of marital distress and child gender. *Developmental Psychology, 31,* 985–996.

McLoyd, V. C., Cauce, A. M., Takeuchi, D., & Wilson, L. (2000). Marital processes and parental socialization in families of color: A decade review of research. *Journal of Marriage and Family, 62,* 1070–1094.

Neighbors, B. D., Forehand, R., & Bau, J. (1997). Interparental conflict and relations with parents as predictors of young adult functioning. *Development and Psychopathology, 9,* 169–187.

Noller, P., Feeney, J. A., Sheehan, G., & Peterson, C. (2000). Marital conflict patterns: Links with family conflict and family members' perceptions of one another. *Personal Relationships, 7,* 79–94.

O'Hearn, H. G., Margolin, G., & John, R. S. (1997). Mothers' and fathers' reports of children's reactions to naturalistic marital conflict. *Journal of the American Academy of Child and Adolescent Psychiatry, 36,* 1366–1373.

Osborne, L. N., & Fincham, F. D. (1996). Marital conflict, parent-child relationships, and child adjustment: Does gender matter? *Merrill-Palmer Quarterly, 42,* 48–75.

Owen, M. T., & Cox, M. J. (1997). Marital conflict and the development of infant-parent attachment relationships. *Journal of Family Psychology, 11,* 152–164.

Papp, L. M., Cummings, E. M., & Goeke-Morey, M. C. (2002). Marital conflicts in the home when children are present in comparison with absent. *Developmental Psychology, 38,* 774–783.

Papp, L. M., Goeke-Morey, M. C., & Cummings, E. M. (2003). *Psychological symptoms, marital functioning, and child adjustment.* Manuscript submitted for publication.

Parke, R. D. (2002). Fathers and families. In M. Bornstein (Ed.), *Handbook of parenting: Vol. 3. Being and becoming a parent* (2nd ed., pp. 27–74). Mahwah, NJ: Erlbaum.

Russell, A. (1997). Individual and family factors contributing to mothers' and fathers' positive parenting. *International Journal of Behavioral Development, 21,* 111–132.

Russell, A., & Saebel, J. (1997). Mother-son, mother-daughter, father-son, and father-daughter: Are they distinct relationships? *Developmental Review, 17,* 111–147.

Snyder, J. R. (1998). Marital conflict and child adjustment: What about gender? *Developmental Review, 18,* 390–420.

Webster-Stratton, C., & Hammond, M. (1999). Marital conflict management skills, parenting style, and early-onset conduct problems: Processes and pathways. *Journal of Child Psychology and Psychiatry, 40,* 917–927.

Weissman, M. M., Warner, V., Wickramaratne, P., Moreau, D., & Olfson, M. (1997). Offspring of depressed parents: 10 years later. *Archives of General Psychiatry, 54,* 932–940.

Weston, H. E., Boxer, P., & Heatherington, L. (1998). Children's attributions about family arguments: Implications for family therapy. *Family Process, 37,* 35–49.

Whisman, M. (2000). The association between depression and marital dissatisfaction. In S. R. Beach (Ed.), *Marital and family processes in depression: A scientific foundation for clinical practice* (pp. 3–24). Washington, DC: American Psychological Association.

CHAPTER 9

Paternal Involvement
by U.S. Residential Fathers

Levels, Sources, and Consequences

JOSEPH H. PLECK and BRIAN P. MASCIADRELLI

BEFORE THE FORMULATION of the involvement construct in the mid-1980s, the paternal variable studied most frequently, by far, was father absence. During the 1950s and 1960s, the study of fathering within father-present families was limited, and the research available focused especially on the father's role in children's development of gender identity (Pleck, 1981). In the 1970s and early 1980s, many additional aspects of paternal behavior and children's relationships with their fathers began to be studied (see Lamb, 1976, 1981), such as fathers' role in children's cognitive, social, and moral development, fathers' interaction style, and infant attachment to fathers. However, no formal construct had yet been developed that addressed how large a part fathers play in the care and socialization of their children—in simple terms, how much fathers *do* as parents.

Lamb, Pleck, Charnov, and Levine (1985, 1987; Pleck, Lamb, & Levine, 1985) proposed that paternal involvement had three components: (a) paternal engagement (direct interaction with the child, in the form of caretaking or play or leisure), (b) accessibility (availability) to the child, and (c) responsibility, making sure that the child is taken care of and arranging resources for the child. The emergence of the construct of paternal involvement during the 1980s reflected both social developments during the preceding decades. Apprehensions developed during the 1960s and 1970s about whether children were getting *enough* fathering. One expression of this increasing disquiet was the growing attention to the problem of father absence (Moynihan,

The work reported here was supported in part by the Cooperative State Research, Education and Extension Service, U.S. Department of Agriculture, under Project No. ILLU-45-0329 to Joseph H. Pleck.

1965). This concern now expanded to include not only the father living apart from his child, but also the resident father who spent too little time with him or her. In addition, a new literature on men's roles gave voice to some men's regret about fathers who had been too little involved with them due to absence, preoccupation with work, or other factors, and their regret about not spending enough time with their own children (Fein, 1974).

The second social concern contributing to the construct of paternal involvement focused on whether fathers were doing enough to reduce the child-rearing burden of employed mothers. This second issue derived from the resurgence of feminism beginning in the late 1960s and was reflected in new feminist analyses in family studies that identified marital inequity in the division of housework and especially child care as a social problem (Berk, 1980; Polatnick, 1973–1974). Outside academic circles, Levine (1976, p. xvii) noted among some women "absolute outrage at the fact that men have not been involved more in the daily tasks of caring for children." These interrelated concerns reflected an emerging "gender politics of family time" (Daly, 1996; for further analyses of the historical development of the involvement construct, see Lamb, 2000; Pleck, 1997; Pleck & Stueve, 2001).

In this chapter we review recent research concerning the levels and sources of paternal involvement and its consequences for children, for mothers and marriage, and for fathers themselves. We restrict our focus to adult fathers in heterosexual two-parent families, as other important paternal groups are considered elsewhere (this volume; Day & Lamb, in press; Lamb, 1997; Tamis-Lemonda & Cabrera, 2002). Investigations conducted in the United States provide most of the data discussed here, although some research from other industrialized countries is included.

The concept of paternal involvement has received considerable critical scrutiny in the last decade. We thus begin by analyzing methodological and conceptual issues in each component of paternal involvement: paternal engagement (direct interaction with the child, in the form of caretaking or play or leisure), accessibility (availability) to the child, and responsibility (making sure that the child is taken care of and arranging resources for the child; Lamb et al., 1985, 1987; Pleck et al., 1985). Later researchers have studied engagement far more than accessibility or responsibility, and engagement is sometimes treated as synonymous with involvement (e.g., Hawkins & Palkovitz, 1999; Palkovitz, 1997). Engagement thus receives disproportionate attention here. The next section summarizes recent data concerning average levels of these components and the extent to which they may have increased in recent decades. We then turn to research findings on selected hypothetical sources of paternal involvement and conclude with a discussion of its consequences for children, mothers, and fathers.

MEASUREMENT AND CONCEPTUAL ISSUES

Assessment of Engagement and Accessibility

Lamb et al. (1985, p. 884) defined engagement as "the father's direct contact with his child, through caretaking and shared activities," and accessibility as "the father's potential availability for interaction, by virtue of being present or accessible to the child whether or not direct interaction is occurring." We first review the four approaches most commonly used to assess paternal engagement and/or accessibility: time diaries, time estimates, activity frequency measures, and relative engagement measures. We then consider how recent research has implicitly, and often explicitly, redefined paternal engagement to mean *positive* paternal engagement (i.e., activities likely to promote child development). We then address methodological issues such as the validity and stability of engagement over time and conclude with analysis of methodological and conceptual issues in paternal responsibility.

Time Diaries

Time diary methodology played an important part in the development of the concept of paternal involvement. It is useful to consider an example of a father's time diary entries and review how variables coded from diaries came to be interpreted as engagement and accessibility. In this methodology, respondents are asked to describe in their own words their activities for the preceding day, from midnight to midnight. Table 9.1 presents an excerpt from Robinson's (1977a) sample of 20 diaries from a 1965–1966 U.S. national study, the only published diary transcripts available. This excerpt shows what a 31 year-old male salesman, married with four children, reported for the period from 5:30 P.M. to 9:00 P.M. the preceding day. Entries in the first column ("What did you do?") are termed primary activities. Entries in the last column ("Doing anything else?") are secondary activities. All time in activities during which a child was noted as being present ("With whom?"), including primary activities, is termed "child contact" (Robinson, 1977b).

Pleck (1983, 1985) conducted secondary analyses of the 1975–1976 Study of Time Use (STU), a national time diary survey conducted by Juster and Stafford (1985). Following procedures used in earlier time use research, Pleck calculated fathers' "child

Table 9.1

Excerpt from a Sample Time Diary: 31-Year-Old Male Salesman, Married with Four Children

What did you do? (Primary Activities)	Time Began	Time Ended	Where?	With whom? (Used for Child Contact)	Doing anything else? (Secondary Activities)
Drove home	5:30 P.M.	6:15 P.M.	Transit	0	Radio
Washed and changed clothes	6:15	6:30	Home	0	No
Drove to grocery store	6:30	6:45	Transit	Wife and 4 children	Talking
Shopped for groceries	6:45	7:10	Store	Family	Talking
Eat at a drive-in	7:10	7:45	Drive-in	Family	Talking
Drove home	7:45	8:10	Transit	Family	No
Kids ready for bed	8:10	8:30	Home	Family	Talking and TV
Washed and cleaned up	8:30	9:00	Home	0	No

Source: Robinson (1977a), pp. 128–129.

care" as the sum of their primary activity time in eight activity categories (previously coded in the data set by Juster and Stafford): baby care, child care, medical care–kids, helping/teaching children, reading/talking with children, indoor playing with children, outdoor playing with children, babysitting/other, and travel–child care. In Table 9.1's sample diary, for example, the father is coded as doing 20 minutes of child care: getting his children ready for bed, from 8:10 P.M. to 8:30 P.M.

In formulating the construct of paternal involvement, Lamb et al. (1985) reconceptualized fathers' child care time as engagement. They supplemented the 1975–1976 STU data with results from several smaller developmental studies that assessed the time fathers spent interacting with their children via observation or other methods. Then, Lamb et al. interpreted Robinson's diary measure of "child contact" (all activities in which a child was noted as present) as accessibility. Because data on child contact were not available in the 1975–1976 STU, Lamb et al. instead used the child contact figures from an earlier 1965–1966 national study (Robinson, 1977b) as the principal data.

A particular advantage of these time diary data is their derivation from large probability samples of known generalizability. Many studies also had sampling frames, making it possible to characterize fathers of different educational levels and ethnicities. Further, the fathers completing time diaries have no reason to think that their time with children might be a focus of data analysis, making it unlikely that social desirability bias would lead fathers to overreport it. Researchers have adapted the diary method for use in smaller scale studies in a variety of ways (Almeida, Wethington, & McDonald, 2001; Bailey, 1995; Fagan, 1998; Hwang & Lamb, 1997; Lamb, Chuang, & Hwang, in press; McBride & Mills, 1993; McBride et al., 2002). One such related approach is the *experience sampling method,* in which parents or children wear pagers and are beeped at random times during the day, and they record what they were doing when beeped and other variables of interest to the researcher (Larson, 1993). These episodes are interpreted as a random sample of the individual's daily experiences, and proportions of daily time in various activities can be extrapolated from them.

Time diary methodology also has disadvantages. For engagement, the primary activities combined together can differ considerably in the nature and degree of the father-child interaction actually occurring. Even a single activity description such as "children ready for bed" in Table 9.1's diary excerpt can refer to a wide range of interactions. Another limitation is that for fathers who have more than one child, engagement is generally calculated from their time diaries as their time with all their children combined (i.e., not on a per-child basis).

For accessibility, time diary measures of child contact are problematic. This variable does not actually match Lamb et al.'s (1985, p. 884) formal definition of the concept as "the father's potential availability for interaction, by virtue of being present or accessible to the child whether or not direct interaction is occurring" in two ways. Robinson coded child contact to include primary activity time (i.e., engagement). More important, though, fathers' child contact time does not actually include all time when they are accessible to their children. A father whose children are elsewhere in the house when he is doing an activity may not list his children as present, but he may nonetheless be available to them. The data in Table 9.1 suggest that most of the child contact time in which fathers are not engaged in primary activities with their children is secondary activity time (e.g., "talking" from 6:30 to 7:45). Child contact may serve as a proxy for total engagement time (primary and secondary activities combined) and thus actually reflect engagement more than accessibility.

A recent major development in time diary methodology is the reintroduction of diary methods with children. Although such diaries had been obtained in a 1981 national study, analyses of those data were limited (Timmer, Eccles, & O'Brien, 1985). In 1997, the Child Development Supplement of the Panel Study of Income Dynamics (PSID) collected time diaries for children under 13 in a nationally representative sample of households, including diaries for 1,172 children living in two-parent families (Hofferth, 2003; Yeung, Sandberg, Davis-Kean, & Hofferth, 2001). In this study, primary caregivers (almost always mothers) completed time diaries for a target child aged 0 to 12 years in their family. For each activity, the caregiver reported "who was doing the activity with the child," "who (else) was there but not directly involved in the activity," and "what else was the child doing at the same time." Paternal engagement is coded as children's time in activities in which the father is listed as doing the child's activity with the child. Paternal accessibility is coded as children's time in activities in which the father is noted as present but not directly involved in the child's activity. In the diary protocol, the father's presence is operationalized more broadly than in earlier adult studies and in a way corresponding more closely to Lamb et al.'s (1985) definition. For example, if the child is in a particular room at home, the father is considered present if he is in another room or in the yard. The PSID children's time diaries are especially valuable because they provide data about paternal engagement per individual child (rather than for all his children combined, as in fathers' time diaries). In addition, mothers are the informants about paternal engagement, eliminating the potential social desirability bias in fathers' own reports. A third party, the researcher, codes mothers' reports into specific activity categories, which may have disadvantages as well as advantages.

Like adults' time diaries, children's diaries have the limitation that the nature and intensity of the activities coded as engagement can vary widely. Partially responding to this limitation, PSID analyses give more attention to subcategories of engagement time (e.g., play) than did earlier diary studies (Yeung et al., 2001), and the study supplements diaries with other kinds of engagement measures and assessment of qualitative dimensions such as warmth and monitoring (Hofferth, 2003).

Time Estimates

This approach simply asks fathers to estimate how much time they spend in child-related tasks or activities. For example, the 1987–1988 National Survey of Families and Households (NSFH) asked parents with children under 5 "about how many hours in a typical day do you spend taking care of (child's) needs, including feeding, bathing, dressing, and putting him/her to bed?" (Blair & Hardesty, 1994). Time estimate measures produce considerably higher figures for engagement time than do diary measures. (Because fathers' average estimates of the time they spent "taking care of and doing things with their children" in the 1977 Quality of Employment Survey were so high and were comparable to levels of child contact in Robinson's, 1977b, diary study, Lamb et al. interpreted this measure as assessing accessibility rather than engagement.) Most researchers today regard time estimate measures as imprecise measurements of the amount of time an individual parent spends with his or her children (Pleck, 1985; Sandberg & Hofferth, 2001). However, others report relatively high correlations between time diary and time estimate measures of engagement (e.g., .62 in Canada's 1988 General Social Survey, higher than the parallel diary-estimate correlations for work and housework; Zuzanek, 2000). Engagement time estimates are often converted to proportional measures (e.g., father's proportion of the total reported for both parents). Because the exact wording may vary in time estimate questions, converting the results to proportions makes it possible to compare results across studies. Respondents could be asked to estimate their accessibility time, but existing research has rarely done this.

Activity Frequency Measures

Here, fathers are asked to report how frequently they engage in specific activities. For example, in the 1987–1988 NSFH, fathers with preschool children were asked about the frequency of three activities with their child or children—outings away from home (e.g., parks, zoos, museums), playing at home, and reading—with six response categories ranging from never to almost every day. Men with school-aged (5 to 18 years) children reported the frequency of leisure activities, working on projects or playing at home, private talks, and helping with reading and doing homework (Marsiglio, 1991). Other examples include the caregiving subscale of Bruce and Fox's (1997; Fox & Bruce, 2001) Paternal Involvement Scale and the 13-item parental activity scale in the 1997 PSID (Hofferth, Pleck, Stueve, Bianchi, & Sayer, 2002). It is important to realize that the specific activities included in these measures are not necessarily intended to represent engagement activities relative to their frequency of occurrence. As suggested by the previous examples, items focus on more interactive or "quality" engagement (i.e., forms of engagement likely to promote development). Finally, Radin's (1994) Paternal Index of Child Care Involvement (PICCI) includes an accessibility subscale in frequency format (sample item: being away from home days at a time [reverse coded]). However, because this subscale also contains several items concerning engagement (e.g., has breakfast during the week with children and family), using it to assess accessibility requires excluding these items.

Relative Engagement Measures

These measures ask fathers (or mothers) how engagement activities with the child are divided with the child's other parent. Common response categories are father entirely, father more than mother, equal, mother more than father, and mother entirely. Examples include the subscales assessing child care and child socialization engagement in Radin's (1994) PICCI, which involves multiplying the fathers' percentage of the performance of the task by a three-point rating of how frequently the task is performed in the family. Although Radin labels these subscales as child care *responsibility* and socialization *responsibility*, these subscales concern how various child care and socialization activities are actually divided between mother and fathers ("what percentage of these tasks are actually done by . . ."), thus assessing engagement rather than responsibility in Lamb et al.'s (1995) sense. Like activity frequency measures, these relative engagement measures tend to focus on "quality" engagement activities.

Summary

Thus, four general strategies have been used to assess paternal engagement. Activity frequency and relative engagement measures have been used far more often than time diaries and time estimates. Recent research employing time use measures generally supplements them with activity measures. Each strategy has advantages and disadvantages. The first two time-oriented engagement measures may be more appropriate in research concerning time trends in engagement and accessibility and concerning the parental division of labor and its consequences for wives and marital dynamics. The latter activity frequency and relative engagement measures focus on more interactive forms of engagement and thus may have greater value in research on the consequences of paternal engagement for children and for fathers themselves. Both sets of measures may have value in the exploration of sources of involvement. Of the four assessment strategies, time diaries and activity frequency measures have been used to assess paternal accessibility, but currently available measures do not closely match the concept of accessibility.

THE CONCEPTUAL SHIFT TO POSITIVE PATERNAL ENGAGEMENT

Since its early formulation, paternal engagement has in practice come to be interpreted as *positive* paternal engagement. From a developmental perspective, the primary reason for studying paternal involvement is its potential impact on children. As Cabrera, Tamis-LeMonda, Bradley, Hofferth, and Lamb (2000, p. 130) observed, there is little evidence linking "parental involvement per se (i.e., amount) with desirable outcomes." Furthermore, there is little conceptual basis for such a link. (In a parallel literature, Bianchi, 2000, pointed out that economists have traditionally assumed that mothers' time with their children should be a major determinant of children's educational outcomes. Researchers have therefore had difficulty explaining why the decrease in recent decades in mothers' time with children due to mothers' increased employment has not been matched by a parallel decline in children's academic performance. Bianchi resolves the discrepancy by arguing that the mothers' time has decreased less than is widely thought and that fathers' time has increased.) Since the research that documents positive associations between engagement and child outcomes in fact uses measures emphasizing paternal activities likely to promote development, such as play, reading, and having conversations, we earlier recommended that paternal involvement be explicitly reformulated as positive involvement (Pleck, 1997). Some scholars now use this term explicitly (Lamb, Chuang, & Cabrera, in press) and operationalize it to include both paternal time and other variables such as support and closeness (Amato & Rivera, 1999; Harris, Furstenberg, & Marmer, 1998). Another reflection of this shift in meaning is that recent research using time diaries gives more attention to subcategories of engagement time (Yeung et al., 2001) and supplements diary measures of engagement with assessments of specific activities and qualitative dimensions (Hofferth, 2003). Also consistent with this reformulation, evidence has accumulated that the amount of engagement time is significantly correlated with positive qualitative features such as warmth and closeness (Amato, 1987; Amato & Rivera, 1999; Fagan, 1998; Harris et al., 1998; Roggman & Peery, 1988; Rohner & Veneziano, 2001; Sagi, 1982; Toth & Xu, 1999) and monitoring (Toth & Xu, 1999).

Some researchers continue to use the unmodified term but explicitly operationalize it as development-promoting engagement. For example, Finley and Schwartz's (in press) Father Involvement Scale assesses engagement as fathers' instrumental, expressive, and mentoring activities. Other studies have combined engagement time and qualitative dimensions into constructs closely related to positive engagement, but using other names. For example, Amato (1987) developed a summary "paternal support" variable combining frequency of positive paternal activities with the child's report of the father being a favorite person to have talks with and the person in the family the child tells if he or she is really worried. Finley and Schwartz's (in press) Affective Quality of Fathering Scale combines reports of the amount of time spent with one's father with perceived support and closeness. Cox, Owen, Lewis, and Henderson (1989) operationalized parents' "warm, sensitive responding" to their infants as including both amount and quality of interaction. Researchers have even reinterpreted "authoritative parenting," an existing construct of long standing, to include engagement time. Marsiglio, Amato, Day, and Lamb (2000, pp. 1182–1183) used this term for the configuration of "spending time with children, providing emotional support, giving everyday assistance, monitoring children's behavior, and noncoercive disciplining." Note that the addition of parent-child time modifies Baumrind's concept of authoritativeness so substantially that using Baumrind's term may be inappropriate. However, Steinberg's work on parental style since at least the early 1990s has described authoritativeness with language potentially connoting engagement—for example, Lamborn, Mounts, Steinberg, and Dornbush's (1991, p. 1053) statement that parental style has an "acceptance/involvement" dimension.

Overall, in recent years researchers have focused more on positive paternal engagement than on engagement in its original, content-free sense. This shift is evident in researchers' implicit redefinitions of engagement, the emergence of positive engagement as an alternative construct, and in the use of other terms to describe paternal time in conjunction with qualitative characteristics of the father-child relationship. This shift is also evident in the most important recent diary study, the 1997 PSID, which reports considerable detail on specific categories of engagement and accessibility time and complements diary assessments with measures of development-promoting activities and of qualitative aspects of the father-child relationship.

OTHER METHODOLOGICAL ISSUES: ENGAGEMENT

Relationship between Fathers' and Others' Perceptions of Fathers' Engagement

The validity of fathers' self-reports about their engagement has long been a concern. Several studies using father-mother pairs, however, have found high agreement between fathers' reports of their involvement and wives' assessments (Ahmeduzzaman & Roopnarine, 1992; Beitel & Parke, 1998; Bonney, Kelley, & Levant, 1999; Coley & Morris, 2002; Deutsch, Servis, & Payne, 2001; Kelley, 1997; Levant, Slattery, & Loiselle, 1987; Roopnarine & Ahmeduzzaman, 1993; Smith & Morgan, 1994; Tulananda, Young, & Roopnarine, 1994). The father-mother correlations in these studies appear higher than those reported in past studies for father-child agreement about father acceptance, rejection, discipline, and closeness (Marsiglio, Amato, et al., 2000). When differences exist, fathers rate their participation higher than mothers do, but the differences are small (Coley & Morris, 2002; Deutsch, Lozy, & Saxon, 1993).

Fathers' and children's estimates of father's percentage of all caregiving are also significantly correlated (Deutsch et al., 1993). The father-child correlation is higher than those reported in studies of father-child agreement on many other constructs (Marsiglio, Amato, et al., 2000). Hwang and Lamb (1997) also cited, as evidence of the validity of fathers' reports of engagement, strong relationships between fathers' reports of their engagement and children's reports of which parent they prefer in situations such as when the child is hurt or when the child wants to play. In addition, fathers' reports of their involvement are unrelated to measures of social desirability response set (De Luccie, 1996b; Palkovitz, 1984). Fathers' reports of paternal engagement may differ more from mothers' and may be more influenced by social desirability in divorced families (Braver et al., 1993; but see Coley & Morris, 2000). In summary, if mothers' and children's reports are used as the criterion, fathers' reports of their engagement appear to have reasonable validity. Self-selection bias among fathers participating in research (Costigan & Cox, 2001) is likely a greater threat to validity than is self-report bias.

Stability over Time

Engagement appears unstable over time among fathers who are primary caregivers in the early years (reviewed in Hwang & Lamb, 1997). In normative samples, however, paternal engagement shows considerable stability (Aldous, Mulligan, & Bjarnason, 1998; Beitel & Parke, 1998). For fathers' caregiving at 6, 15, 24, and 36 months of age, the NICHD Early Child Care Research Network (2000) noted correlations ranging from .54 to .73, with an average of .65. Hwang and Lamb (1997) reported moderate stability over a 14-year period. Accessibility shows less stability (Lamb, Chuang, & Hwang, in press).

Solo Paternal Engagement

Fathers' amount of solo time with the child has received some attention (Barnett & Baruch, 1987; Beitel & Parke, 1998; Crouter & Crowley, 1990; Levant et al., 1987). In some studies, early solo participation in child care is associated with fathers' continued participation in child care when they were older (Aldous et al., 1998). More research is needed to determine the extent to which solo engagement has unique sources or consequences.

Secondary Activities

As illustrated in Table 9.1, time diary methods for assessing engagement often collect information about "secondary" activities, those activities reported by parents when they are asked if they were "doing anything else" during a primary activity. Although little analyzed to date, secondary engagement time is now receiving some attention. Zick and Bryant (1996) estimated that secondary engagement time comprises about one third of all parental engagement (primary and secondary activities combined). Their analyses indicate that fathers' primary and secondary engagement time generally has similar correlates. However, some differences exist; for example, living in a rural area is associated with fathers' higher levels of secondary engagement but has no association with primary engagement. Bianchi (2000) also reported levels and time trends in fathers' secondary engagement time.

Absolute versus Proportional Measures

Analyses of the correlates of paternal engagement generally employ either absolute or proportional measures of this construct. Theoretically, both could be important (e.g., the impact of paternal engagement on a child may be a function of either the absolute amount of time a father spends or how much time he spends compared to the child's mother, or both). The correlates of the two kinds of measures are often different (e.g., De Luccie, 1996b; Deutsch et al., 2001). Unfortunately, the available research results as yet provide no basis for understanding when absolute or relative engagement may be the more important variable to consider.

Typologies

Typological rather than quantitative approaches to assessing paternal engagement merit more exploration. Using cluster analysis procedures with observational data on fathers of children up to age 3 years, Belsky, Youngblood, Rovine, and Volling (1991) found three patterns: child-with-father positive, child-with-father negative, and child-with-father moderate. In a sample of fathers of 15-month-olds, Jain, Belsky, and Crnic (1996) identified four groups: caretakers, playmates-teachers, disciplinarians, and disengaged fathers.

Engagement per Child versus for All Children

Finally, assessment of paternal involvement with a specific child should be distinguished from involvement summed or averaged across all children (for fathers who have more than one child). Drawing on the distinction between shared and nonshared environmental influences in behavioral genetics (Plomin, 1989), different children of the same father receive both a shared component of paternal influence and a nonshared or unique component. One analysis estimated that 31% of the total variation in paternal behavior toward children—and 26% of the total variation in paternal affect—actually occurs between siblings (i.e., within families) rather than between families (Harris & Morgan, 1991). Future research should explore the extent to which generic versus child-specific components of paternal involvement and other paternal behaviors can be empirically distinguished and investigate how their predictors and consequences vary.

Summary

Recent research provides positive evidence on two important methodological issues concerning engagement. Fathers' reports of their engagement appear to have validity relative to mothers' and children's reports, and paternal engagement is relatively stable over time in normative samples. Several other issues, however, remain for further exploration: the meaning of secondary activities, the distinction between absolute and relative measures, typologies of engagement, and the distinction between fathers' engagement per child versus in total.

RESPONSIBILITY

Lamb et al. (1985, p. 884) defined responsibility as referring "not to the amount of time spent with or accessible to children, but to the role father takes in making sure that the child is taken care of and arranging for resources to be available for the child. For example, this might involve arranging for babysitters, making appointments with pediatricians and seeing that the child is taken to them, determining when the child needs new clothes, etc." This component of paternal involvement has been the least studied.

It has also been operationalized in more diverse ways than has engagement or accessibility (Pleck & Stueve, 2001). The reason is that Lamb et al.'s definition refers both to a *process* ("making sure the child is taken care of") and to a type of activity, *indirect care*.

Responsibility as Process

Coltrane's (1996, p. 54) observation—"in most families, husbands notice less about what needs to be done, and wait to be asked to do various chores and require explicit directions if they are to complete the tasks successfully . . . most couples continue to characterize husband's contributions to housework and child care as 'helping their wives'"—illustrates what is at issue in process responsibility. It involves taking initiative, monitoring, and planning for the child. Numerous other existing concepts capture aspects of process responsibility.

Process responsibility is analogous to the concept of *executive function* in family systems theory (Broderick, 1993). Dienhart's (2001) concept of *tag team parenting* can be interpreted as a particular mode of sharing process responsibility between parents. Erera, Minton, Pasley, and Mandel (1999; see also Masciadrelli, 2001) concept of the "child's psychological presence to the father" is related to process responsibility. Walzer's (1996) qualitative study of new parents notes three types of *mental baby care:* worrying, processing information about what to expect, and managing the division of labor. Walzer observes that "it is not only the baby's appointments and supplies that mothers tend to manage . . . but their babies' fathers as well" (p. 226). Another cognate concept is Stueve and Pleck's (2001, 2003) notion of parental arranging and planning. When asked to describe examples of their experiences in *arranging and planning* things for their children, the majority of fathers say that they defer to their wives, that they do this conjointly with their wives, or that they do so in only a limited area. It is interesting that the minority of mothers who describe arranging and planning as an activity shared with the child's father, rather than as a solo activity, have husbands who are more highly engaged with the child (Pleck & Stueve, 2003).

Responsibility as Indirect Care

Indirect care refers to activities conducted *for* the child but not *with* the child (Beitel & Parke, 1998). Examples include arranging medical appointments, arranging nonparental care, and shopping for the child. Some research labels these activities *child-related work* (Hossain, 2001; Kelley, 1997). Parke (2002) noted that parents' managerial role in fostering and arranging their children's peer relationships is a particularly important indirect care activity. Fathers' arrangement of their children's health care has also been explored (Bailey, 1991). The specific indirect care activity receiving most attention is making child care arrangements (Leslie, Anderson, & Branson, 1991; Peterson & Gerson, 1992).

Measures

Existing instruments address the two aspects of responsibility in varying and sometimes confusing ways. Two scales clearly focus on process by asking parents to rate tasks in terms of who remembers, plans, and schedules them, regardless of who actually ends up doing them. McBride and Mills (1993) use this format for a set of indirect care tasks. However, Baruch and Barnett's (1986) process-oriented responsibility combines both indirect and direct care activities (as well as housework). From one perspective, Baruch and Barnett assess responsibility across a broader domain than do McBride and Mills. From another perspective, though, by including direct care Baruch and Barnett's measure is inconsistent with Lamb et al.'s definition. At the minimum, researchers using this measure should distinguish process responsibility for the two kinds of care.

The majority of existing measures intended to assess responsibility in terms of "who usually does" activities, thus not addressing process in terms of taking initiative, monitoring, and planning. To be consistent with at least the second part of Lamb et al.'s definition, only indirect care tasks should be included, such as the executive functions subscale of C. Bruce and Fox's (1997) Paternal Involvement Scale. However, numerous other nonprocess responsibility measures also include direct care activities. Indeed, Radin's (1994) PICCI subscales labeled "child care responsibility" and "socialization responsibility" ask who usually performs lists of tasks including *only* engagement activities (e.g., feeding the child and helping children to learn).

More recent nonprocess responsibility measures concern both direct and indirect care activities. For example, Hofferth's (2003) responsibility scale asks parents to report who usually performs five indirect care tasks, plus bathing, playing with, and disciplining children (cf. Hossain, 2001; Hwang & Lamb, 1997; Sanderson & Sanders-Thompson, 2002). These scales generally have high internal reliability, raising the possibility that a parent's performance of indirect care and direct care may be empirically correlated.

Interrelationship of Process Responsibility, Indirect Care, and Direct Care

Several analyses provide further data about the empirical interrelationships among these different aspects of responsibility. McBride and Mills's (1993) process measure of responsibility for indirect care is significantly correlated with fathers' level of engagement and accessibility, but only in two-earner families. In a study of student fathers, process responsibility was correlated with indirect care as well as engagement and accessibility (Masciadrelli, 2001). In Deutsch et al.'s (2001) factor analysis of 32 parenting activities, two of the factors emerging correspond to process responsibility and indirect care: "attention" (e.g., worrying and making decisions about the child) and "logistics" (e.g., arranging child care, arranging play dates, and taking a child to the doctor or dentist). In a factor analysis of mothers' perceptions of their husbands' behavior, the first of several factors corresponds to the process responsibility (e.g., "my husband considers child care my responsibility," "I have to ask for my husband's assistance in child care") and another to indirect care (Beitel & Parke, 1998). Overall, the balance of evidence suggests that process responsibility and indirect care may be relatively independent but that indirect care and direct care are somewhat intercorrelated.

Father-Mother Agreement and Stability over Time

The correlations between fathers' and mothers' ratings of fathers' process responsibility are reported to be high (Deutsch et al., 2001; Hwang & Lamb, 1997; McBride & Mills, 1993). Beitel and Parke (1998) found high test-retest correlations over a 2-week period for mothers' perceptions of their husbands' involvement in indirect care (but stability of fathers' perceived process responsibility was not reported). However, when longer periods are observed, stability diminishes, at least with responsibility measures including performance of indirect and direct care (Hwang & Lamb, 1997; Lamb, Chuang, & Hwang, in press).

Fathers as Primary Child Care Arrangements during Mothers' Work

The father being the family's primary child care arrangement when the mother is at work has also been interpreted as reflecting responsibility. Although obviously involving direct care, the father is indeed the parent in charge during this time (Pleck, 1997). Data about fathers as primary care arrangements have been routinely collected in federal surveys for several decades, making time comparisons possible. However, because paternal arrangements are an alternative to other child care arrangements, use of paternal arrangements is influenced by the characteristics of families' child care markets and is also associated with the father and mother having nonoverlapping work hours, which in turn are related to parents' sociodemographic characteristics. There has in fact been considerable analysis of paternal child-care arrangements, especially in infancy, from the perspectives of child-care policy and work schedule policy (Averett, Gennetian, & Peters, 2000; Brayfield, 1995; Casper, 1997; Casper & O'Connell, 1998; Glass, 1998; Presser, 1989).

Summary

Existing research has conceptualized responsibility in two general and sometimes overlapping ways: as a process entailing taking initiative for care and as performing indirect care. It is important that researchers studying responsibility be clear how they interpret it. The preponderance of evidence suggests that indirect care and process responsibility are relatively independent but that direct and indirect care are somewhat intercorrelated. In addition, there has been some attention to particular forms of indirect care such as arranging health care and making child care arrangements. Fathers' being a child's primary child care arrangement during the mothers' work hours has also been interpreted as reflecting responsibility.

OVERVIEW OF MEASUREMENT AND CONCEPTUALIZATION

It is evident that the concept of paternal involvement raises many more conceptual and methodological issues than are first apparent. The influence of time diary methodology on the development and usage of the construct has been both substantial and mixed. On the one hand, time diary research initially helped promote attention to fathers' actual time expenditure with their children and provided data about it from large representative samples in the United States as well as other countries. At the same time, early diary studies obscured that the primary focus of most existing research should be—and actually has been—on "positive" paternal involvement, or those paternal activities potentially promoting development. At least for engagement, recent investigations provide relatively favorable results on core methodological questions such as potential self-report bias and stability over time, issues relatively neglected in earlier studies. Progress in research on the responsibility component of involvement has been impeded by its conceptualization in two fundamentally different ways, as taking initiative and as indirect care. Nonetheless, the two different conceptions of responsibility can at least be more clearly identified and distinguished in current research. While being mindful of the limitations of existing measures for the components of involvement, we now turn to review the available data on average levels of paternal involvement, the composition of the activities in the engagement component in relation to child age, and the sociodemographic correlates of involvement.

LEVELS OF PATERNAL INVOLVEMENT

LEVELS OF PATERNAL ENGAGEMENT AND ACCESSIBILITY

Subsequent to our earlier review (Pleck, 1997), several large-scale time diary studies conducted in the 1990s provide data concerning levels of paternal engagement and accessibility in the United States and other industrial countries. Four of these are summarized in Table 9.2. In addition, Zuzanek (2000) summarized 1970s and 1980s time diary data on paternal engagement from Finland and Norway, as did J. Bruce, Lloyd, and Leonard (1995) for the United Kingdom, Poland, Bulgaria, Venezuela, Indonesia (Java), and Nepal (see also Gershuny, 2000).

The 1997 Child Development Supplement of the PSID (Yeung et al., 2001) is particularly valuable because it reports paternal engagement on a per child basis. Table 9.2 includes another recent U.S. national diary study with a smaller sample, the 1998 Family Interaction, Social Capital, and Trends in Time Use study (hereafter the Family Interaction study). Recent Canadian and Dutch time diary studies are also included. Two of the studies report results on accessibility as well as engagement, and three provide data on important subcategories of engagement: physical care, play, and teaching. Most studies' samples are restricted to fathers in two-parent families (including unmarried and unemployed fathers), excepting the Dutch study, which included only employed fathers (whether married, living with a partner, or neither). The age ranges of the children with whom engagement and accessibility are assessed vary somewhat among these studies, and there may be other differences in study design and procedures that limit the comparability of their results.

Table 9.2 presents data on paternal engagement in two forms: in absolute terms (hours/day) and as a proportion of mothers' time (i.e., relative engagement and accessibility). In the PSID, fathers are engaged an average of 1.83 hours per day per child aged 12 or younger, and are accessible 3.56 hours per day. (For consistency with other studies in the table, accessibility was recalculated from Yeung et al.'s [2001] Tables 1 and 2 to include rather than exclude engagement time. Although Yeung et al.'s Table 3 reported data on accessibility including engagement, their Tables 1 and 2 reported accessibility as excluding engagement, requiring this recalculation.) Fathers' relative engagement is 73%, and their relative accessibility is 71%. Fathers are engaged an average of .71 hours per day per child in play and companionship, which is 39% of fathers' total engagement per child. Fathers' average of .51 hours in physical care constitutes 28% of their total engagement per child. These two activity subcategories comprise fully two thirds of fathers' total engagement. Detailed breakdowns are also available by child age as well as by activity category and subcategory (Yeung et al., 2001).

The three other studies report markedly lower levels of paternal engagement than the 1997 PSID, even though they concern engagement for all children rather than per

Table 9.2

Paternal Engagement and Accessibility in Four Time Diary Studies, 1990s

Paternal Involvement Measure	Sample	Hours/ Day	% of Mothers' Time	Study Details	Source
Engagement (total)	Fathers in two parent families with child < 13	1.83	73	USA, 1997: PSID-Child Development Supplement; N (fathers) = 1453[a]	Calculated from Yeung et al. (2001)
Physical care		.51	78		
Play		.71	93		
Teaching		.08	56		
Accessibility		3.56	71		
Engagement	Married fathers with child < 18	1.0[b]	55	USA, 1998 Family Interaction and Time Use Study; N (fathers) = 194[c]	Bianchi (2000)
Accessibility		3.8	65		
Engagement (total)	Married employed fathers with child < 18	.88	74.4	Canada, 1998, General Social Survey; N (total sample) = 10,749[c]	Zuzanek (2000)
Physical care		.41	66.8		
Play, teaching[d]		.38	93.4		
Engagement (total)	Employed fathers with child < 15	.62	44.0	Netherlands; N (total sample) = 3,227[c]	Zuzanek (2000)
Physical care		.28	39.1		
Play, teaching[d]		.25	58.9		

[a]Time reported for a target child, from child's time diary.
[b]Data available to only one decimal place in this study.
[c]Time for all the parent's children, from parent's time diary.
[d]Play and teaching are combined in Zuzanek's report.

child. The three latter studies have a higher upper limit on child age than the PSID, partially accounting for the difference because fathers' engagement time decreases with child age (Pleck, 1997). Relative paternal engagement in the PSID and the 1998 Canadian survey are closely comparable. Relative engagement is substantially lower, however, in the Family Interaction study. This has no obvious explanation, other than the possibility that this study is compromised by small sample size and low response rate compared to the other studies. (Its sample consisted of 184 fathers, compared to the 1761 children in the PSID. Hofferth et al. (2002) reported the response rate for the Family Interaction study as 56%.) Fathers' relative engagement in the 1995 Dutch study is also considerably lower than in the PSID, perhaps explained by the fact that fathers' proportional engagement is lower in families in which the mother is not employed, and that wives' employment rate in the Netherlands is markedly lower than in the other countries considered here (although the Dutch sample also includes some single fathers).

Overall, the engagement and accessibility statistics from the PSID are higher than many might expect, both in absolute terms and as proportions of mothers' levels. It should be recalled that in this study, in almost all cases mothers were the informants about whom the child spent time with, so that fathers' potential overestimation of their time with their children is not an issue.

COMPOSITION OF PATERNAL ENGAGEMENT AND ACCESSIBILITY AND ASSOCIATION WITH CHILD AGE

In the 1997 PSID, play/companionship is the largest single paternal engagement activity (39% of all engagement). Caregiving is the next largest component (28%), and the combination of the two accounts for about two thirds of all paternal engagement time. Table 9.3 provides data concerning how paternal engagement varies by age of child and also provides comparison data for maternal engagement. Total paternal engagement is somewhat lower for older than for younger children. Fathers' predominant activities are play, followed by caregiving, in both age groups presented. Play and caregiving are likely mothers' predominant activities.

In addition, fathers of children aged 3 to 5 years spend somewhat less time in play

Table 9.3
Total and Selected Engagement Time (hr/day) for Fathers and Mothers of Children Aged 3–5 and 9–12 (1997 PSID)

Engagement	Children aged 3–5		Children aged 9–12	
	Fathers	Mothers	Fathers	Mothers
Caregiving	.41	.58	.45	.50
Play/companionship	.69	.79	.57	.52
Teaching/achievement related	.07	.17	.10	.14
Total engagement	1.96	2.68	1.54	2.03

Note: In addition to the three activities shown, total engagement includes household activities, social activities, and other activities. Data are also available for children aged 0–2 and 6–8.
Source: Derived from Yeung et al. (2001).

than do mothers, and the margin by which fathers of 9- to 12-year-olds exceed mothers in play is small. It is possible that more detailed analysis of activities within play and caregiving might reveal more striking gender differences than are apparent in Table 9.3. Nonetheless, Table 9.3 suggests that the fathers' and mothers' engagement times are more similar than different in composition. In particular, the difference between fathers' and mothers' frequency of play may now be smaller than previous research has indicated. The difference between fathers' and mothers' average level of play in past research may have also obscured the recognition that play is also *mothers'* most frequent engagement activity.

The high average proportion of play in paternal involvement also bears on the critique of the involvement construct, especially engagement, as viewing fathering through a mother template, that is, defining involvement as what mothers do (Hawkins & Palkovitz, 1999). The critics' major concern is the exclusion of breadwinning, an issue that raises serious questions beyond the scope of this chapter (Pleck & Stueve, 2001). However, this argument also focuses more specifically on engagement activities with the child. The critique assumes that mothers' predominant form of engagement is physical caregiving, whereas fathers' is play. It further presumes that involvement is defined to include only the latter. For example, Palkovitz (1997, p. 210) asserted that Lamb et al. (1985) limited involvement to "direct child care and related housework" and "hands-on child care and housework," thus excluding fathers' characteristic engagement activities. In reality, Lamb et al. (p. 884) explicitly defined engagement as including "shared activities" as well as caretaking. Time diary and all other measures of total engagement explicitly include play. The concept of involvement may be limited by its exclusion of fathers' breadwinning, but it is certainly not limited by excluding fathers' play.

SOCIODEMOGRAPHIC CORRELATES OF PATERNAL ENGAGEMENT AND ACCESSIBILITY

In an earlier review (Pleck, 1997), we concluded that research finds no consistent associations between paternal involvement and either socioeconomic variables or race and ethnicity. These associations have been studied in many small convenience samples, but it is appropriate to give priority to the results of analyses using large representative samples. In recent studies, links with socioeconomic status are weak or marginal. For example, fathers' education and own income (*family* income is considered in a later section as a potential indicator of family stress) are unrelated to total engagement in the 1997 PSID (Hofferth, 2003). The only differences found in more detailed analyses are that more educated fathers spend more time in engagement and accessibility combined on weekdays, and more educated fathers also spend more time in activities coded as teaching/achievement related on both weekdays and weekend days (Yeung et al., 2001). Relationships between paternal engagement and either education or income are also weak and inconsistent in the NICHD Study of Early Childcare (NICHD Early Child Care Research Network, 2000) and in analyses of the 1987–1988 NSFH (Aldous et al., 1998; Marsiglio, 1991; Toth & Xu, 1999).

The 1997 PSID also indicates no significant association between race-ethnicity and total engagement (Hofferth, 2003). In further analyses, compared to White fathers, African American fathers spend less time in engagement and accessibility combined on weekends (although they spend significantly more time with their children in household work), but Latino fathers show significantly more time in engagement and accessibility combined (Yeung et al., 2001). Ethnicity is unrelated to paternal engagement in the NICHD study (NICHD Early Child Care Research Network, 2000). Most NSFH analyses report that Latino fathers are more frequently engaged than White fathers and that African American and White fathers do not differ (Bartkowski & Xu, 2000; Toth & Xu, 1999; Wilcox, 2002; see also Parke et al., in press). In the National Survey of Children (NSC), children report non-White fathers to be nonsignificantly higher in involvement (Harris et al., 1998).

The concept of involvement, especially engagement, has been criticized as based on the experience of White, middle-class fathers and as therefore less relevant to fathers in other sociodemographic groups (Marsiglio, Day, & Lamb, 2000). The concept arose, however, primarily from analyses of national time diary surveys in which socioeconomic status (SES) and ethnic differences in engagement and accessibility were minimal, a pattern that continues in recent large-scale studies. If the question is whether defining involvement as Lamb et al. (1985) did erroneously leads to viewing lower SES or minority-ethnic fathers in two-parent families as deficient relative to White, middle-class fathers, all available data indicate not. It is true, however, that applying Lamb et al.'s definition of involvement to *non*residential fathers, both ethnic minority and White, can inappropriately lead to a deficit interpretation. For additional discussion of critiques of the construct of paternal involvement, see Pleck and Stueve (2001).

Mothers' employment status is the sociodemographic predictor of involvement studied perhaps most frequently in both past and recent studies. Recent results are entirely consistent with earlier conclusions that fathers' proportion of the total parental time spent with children is higher when mothers are employed but that any increase in fathers' time in absolute terms (minutes per day) is small and not robust (Pleck, 1997). The variety of other sociodemographic predictors investigated in earlier research (Pleck, 1997) continues to receive attention. Several new potential sociodemographic predictors are now being studied as well: region of the United States (lower engagement in the South; see Bartkowski & Xu, 2000; Bryant & Zick, 1996), rural versus urban residence (minimal differences; Bryant & Zick, 1996), and religiosity and religious affiliation (inconsistent results; see Bartkowski & Xu, 2000; Wilcox, 2002; for qualitative studies, see Armato & Marsiglio, 2002; Auerbach, Silverstein, & Zizi, 1997; Gavanas, 2003; Lunkskow, 2002; Silverstein, Auerbach, Grieco, & Dunkel, 1999).

HAVE PATERNAL ENGAGEMENT AND ACCESSIBILITY INCREASED IN RECENT DECADES?

Whether paternal involvement has increased in recent decades has been of considerable interest (LaRossa, 1988). Lamb et al. (1985; Pleck et al., 1985) recounted data from one time use study indicating that fathers' engagement time rose between 1924 and 1977, and from three diary studies documenting increases between the mid-1960s and early 1980s. Lamb (1987) and Pleck (1985) further cited Juster's (1985) time diary comparison between 1975 and 1981 as further evidence of increasing paternal involvement. Pleck (1997) made an additional comparison suggesting an increase in paternal engagement: Averaging across 11 national or local studies collecting data about fathers' and mothers' time use between the mid-1960s and the early 1980s, fathers' engagement was about one third of mothers', and fathers' accessibility was about one half (Lamb et al., 1985); in 13 studies conducted between the mid-1980s and the early 1990s, fathers' relative engagement rose to an average of 43.3%, and their average relative accessibility increased to 65.6%.

Two recent analyses now provide even stronger evidence about change in paternal involvement over time in the United States, and good comparisons are now also available for Canada and the Netherlands. The strength of these new studies is that within each, the same investigators used exactly the same design and procedures to analyze cross-sectional data at two points in time. These four comparisons are summarized in Table 9.4.

Sandberg and Hofferth (2001) compared the time spent with parents reported in children's time diaries collected in the 1997 PSID (discussed earlier) with diaries collected in 1981. The 1981 children's diaries were collected as part of a follow-up to the 1975–1976 STU, also using a national representative sample. Earlier analysis of the 1981 data (Timmer et al., 1985) had not distinguished between engagement and accessibility (i.e., only the combined measure was analyzed), so Sandberg and Hofferth used only the summary measure of engagement and accessibility for the 1981–1997 comparison. For all fathers in two-parent families with a child under 13, the sum of engagement and accessibility time increased significantly between 1981 and 1997, with no change in relative accessibility. Because this comparison is confounded by the increase in the proportion of two-parent families with employed mothers between 1981 and 1997, the comparison is repeated within maternal employment statuses. In families with employed mothers, paternal accessibility increased significantly, and relative accessibility rose correspondingly. Fathers' accessibility time also increased nonsignificantly in families with nonemployed mothers. (Fathers' relative accessibility dropped in one-earner families. This decrease occurred because both employed *and* nonemployed mothers increased their accessibility time during this period, with nonemployed mothers doing so to an especially marked degree—perhaps the most intriguing finding in Sandberg and Hofferth's analysis.)

In the second U.S. analysis, Bianchi (2000) compared married fathers' reports of their time with their children in the 1998 Family Interaction study (discussed earlier) with the 1965–1966 Americans' Use of Time study. Significant increases were evident in fathers' engagement and accessibility, both in absolute and relative terms. The Canadian data show increases in both absolute and relative paternal engagement between 1986 and 1996. In the Netherlands, paternal engagement time increased between 1980 and 1995.

In another U.S. study using time estimate rather than time diary measures, employed fathers estimated that they spent 3.48 hours per day with their children in 1997, compared to 2.74 hours in 1977 (Bond, Galinksy, & Swanberg, 1998). Zuzanek (2000) summarized time diary data for fathers in Finland in 1979 and 1987 and in Norway in 1971–1972 and 1981–1982, likewise documenting increases in fathers' absolute and relative engagement. Overall, the data suggest that average levels of paternal engagement and accessibility have increased in the United States over the last several decades, both in absolute and relative terms. Sandberg and Hofferth's (2001) analysis is particularly strong because it controls for maternal employment status, and shows that paternal involvement has increased in two-earner families over this period. There are also good data showing increases in paternal engagement in Canada and the Netherlands between the 1980s and the 1990s and in Finland and Norway in earlier decades.

Table 9.4

Change in Paternal Engagement and Accessibility in the United States, Canada, and the Netherlands

Country: Years Compared	Paternal Involvement Measure	Sample	Earlier Date		Later Date		Study Details and Source
			Hours/ Day	% of Mothers' Time	Hours/ Day	% of Mothers' Time	
USA: 1981, 1997	Engagement/ Accessibility combined	Fathers in two parent families with child < 13	2.64	73.9	3.25*	73.6	1981 Followup to 1975–76 Study of Time Use, 1997 PSID-Child Development Supplement; Sandberg & Hofferth (2001)
		Mother not employed	2.83	76.6	3.20	69.9	
		Mother employed	2.43	75.5	3.28*	86.4	
USA: 1965–1966, 1998	Engagement	Married fathers with child < 18	0.4	24	1.0*	55	1965–66 Americans' Use of Time, 1998 Family Interaction & Time Use Study; Bianchi (2000)
	Accessibility		2.8	51	3.8*	65	
Canada: 1988, 1996	Engagement	Married employed fathers with child < 18	.51	59	.88[a]	74.4	1986 General Social Survey; 1998 General Social Survey; Zuzanek (2000)
	Accessibility		3.51	82	3.23[a]	79.9	
Netherlands: 1980, 1995	Engagement	Employed fathers with child < 15	.46	49.1	.62[a]	44.0	1980 and 1995 surveys conducted by the Netherlands Social and Cultural Planning Bureau; Zuzanek (2000)

*$p < .05$

[a] Significance test not reported in source.

PATERNAL RESPONSIBILITY: LEVELS AND CHANGE OVER TIME

Responsibility has been investigated in diverse ways, as noted earlier. Using the available indicators, fathers' average share of responsibility is substantially lower than mothers' (Leslie et al., 1991; McBride & Mills, 1993; Peterson & Gerson, 1992) and lower than mothers' share of engagement or accessibility (McBride & Mills, 1993). Questionnaire measures of responsibility have not been replicated in similar samples over time; nor have data about performance of specific tasks, including selection of nonparental child care arrangements, been collected in similar ways in comparable samples. Thus, it is difficult to assess possible change over time in levels of paternal responsibility.

Data exist over several decades, however, regarding fathers as primary child care arrangements for preschool children during mothers' hours of work, a direct indicator of responsibility. In 1996, the most recent year for which data are available, the rate is 23% (unpublished tabulations in Child Trends, 2002). About the same rate has been found for fathers' care of infants (NICHD Early Child Care Research Network, 1997). To put this percentage in context, in the 1991 data for which more detailed information is available, in two-parent families fathers were the primary arrangement (23% in that year) as often as child care centers and preschools combined (24%), as often as family day care homes (23%), and more often than grandparents (16%). In addition, 7% of *single* working mothers reported the father as the primary arrangement (O'Connell, 1993). Casper (1997) reported detailed analyses of factors associated with paternal child care arrangements, showing that most such fathers are employed, primarily full-time, and additionally that paternal arrangements are more common in families with two or more preschoolers, are most common in the Northeast and least common in the South, and are less common in families living in suburbs rather than urban or rural areas.

In the earliest data available (for 1977), 17% of fathers were reported by working mothers to be the primary arrangement (O'Connell, 1993), in contrast to 23% in 1996. Presser (1989) cited other evidence that paternal care for children during mothers' working hours increased between 1965 and 1985. Casper and O'Connell (1998), examining fathers' rates of being a primary *or* secondary arrangement, conducted analyses showing that the rate of total paternal arrangements fluctuates inversely with unemployment rates. Specifically, the total paternal arrangement rate increased from 23% to 30% between 1988 and 1991, then dropped to 25% in 1993, corresponding to a decrease in unemployment. However, increases in unemployment cannot be the only explanation for increases in paternal primary arrangements over time. O'Connell (1993) pointed out that unemployment was at similar levels in 1985 and 1991, yet primary paternal arrangements rose from 16% to 20%. Overall, the relatively high rate of primary paternal care in dual-earner families suggests that for a significant portion of the workweek, a substantial minority of fathers have a high level of responsibility. In addition, the rate of fathers' being the primary child care arrangement has gradually increased since 1977.

SOURCES OF PATERNAL INVOLVEMENT

We review selected aspects of the four factors influencing the level of paternal involvement proposed by Lamb et al. (1985, 1987; Pleck et al., 1985): motivation, skills and self-confidence, social supports, and institutional policies and practices (see

Pleck, 1997, for a more comprehensive review of earlier research; for potential bio-genetic and evolutionary factors in paternal behavior, see Fox & Bruce, 2001; Geary, 2000; Parke, 2002; Tamis-Lemonda & Cabrera, 2002). As most available research concerns engagement, the following findings refer to this component unless otherwise stated. As in the earlier section on sociodemographic predictors of involvement, we give priority here to studies using representative samples. Predictors of paternal involvement have been analyzed especially frequently using the 1987–1988 NSFH (only selected NSFH analyses will be cited for particular findings; see Eggebeen, 2002, for a review; NSFH analyses include Aldous et al., 1998; Aldous & Mulligan, 2002; Bartkowski & Xu, 2000; Blair & Hardesty, 1994; Blair et al., 1994; Cooksey & Fondell, 1996; Ishii-Kuntz & Coltrane, 1992; Marsiglio, 1991; McBride et al., in press; Toth & Xu, 1999; Wilcox, 2002; Xu, Hudspeth, & Estes, 1997). Because these analyses employ somewhat different independent variables in their models, consistency of results across different NSFH analyses indicates how robust particular predictors are.

MOTIVATION

Child's Gender

Fathers' motivation for involvement is often thought to be greater for sons than for daughters. Sons report more paternal involvement in the 1981 National Survey of Children (Harris et al., 1998). In the 1987–1988 NSFH, male children received more paternal engagement (Bartkowski & Xu, 2000; Marsiglio, 1991), and this effect was heightened when all the family's children are male (Wilcox, 2002). In the more recent 1997 PSID, however, total paternal engagement was unrelated to child gender (Hofferth, 2003); analyses of specific activity categories (engagement and accessibility combined) indicate that it was higher only for play/companionship on weekdays (Yeung et al., 2001). Recent smaller studies also found no effect for child gender (Fagan, 1996; Hossain & Roopnarine, 1993; Sanderson & Sanders-Thompson, 2002). It is possible that child gender exerts less influence on paternal involvement today than in previous decades.

Biological Relationship to the Child and Legal Relationship with the Child's Mother

These factors influence fathers' motivation, but their effect varies according to context. For children they live with, fathers are more engaged with their biological children than with other children (Blair et al., 1994; Hofferth et al., 2002; Marsiglio, 1991; Pleck & Stueve, 1997). At the same time, stepfathers are more engaged with their new partner's children than with their own biological children who live elsewhere. This initially appears inconsistent with evolutionary psychology's parental investment hypothesis that individuals maximize their genetic contribution by investing in their biological children. To explain it, evolutionary psychologists propose an alternate relationship investment hypothesis, in which remarried men gain from investing in their spouses' children from prior unions because it increases their prospect of further childbearing with their new partner (Anderson, Kaplan, Lam, & Lancaster, 1999; Anderson, Kaplan, & Lancaster, 1999; Hofferth et al., 2002). Among nonbiological fathers, those cohabiting with the mother are more engaged than are those married to the mother. This may occur because cohabiting nonbiological fathers are less likely to have biological children living elsewhere and because whether or not the child accepts the male as married to his or her mother may create tension (Hofferth et al., 2002).

Own Father's Involvement

The two plausible but opposing hypotheses are that fathers (a) *model* their own fathers' involvement (whether low or high) or (b) *compensate* for their fathers' lack of involvement (i.e., become highly involved if their own fathers' involvement was low). In studies generally using small convenience samples, prior reviews found evidence supporting both hypotheses (Parke, 2002; Pleck, 1997). In the 1997 PSID (Hofferth, 2003), the best available current analysis, fathers' perceptions of their own fathers' actual degree of involvement with them were unrelated to fathers' engagement time with their children. However, own fathers' involvement was significantly positively related to fathers' positive activity engagement, warmth, monitoring, and responsibility. (As noted earlier, Hofferth's responsibility scale assesses fathers' relative performance of five indirect child-care tasks and three types of positive engagement. For purposes of this review, it is interpreted as a measure of both positive engagement and responsibility.) The PSID also assessed from whom fathers thought they had learned the most about parenting. Reporting one's father as this person can be interpreted as fathers' self-perceived modeling after their own fathers. This variable is unrelated to engagement time and warmth but is significantly *negatively* related to paternal monitoring, positive activity engagement, and responsibility, that is, fathers who report consciously modeling after their own fathers are less involved (Hofferth, 2003). Thus, the best available test of the association between fathers' own fathers' involvement and own involvement supports the modeling hypothesis. In terms of fathers' perceptions of the degree to which they have modeled after their own father, however, results support the compensation hypothesis.

This inconsistency suggests that the effect of conscious modeling may differ markedly from the more objective modeling inferred from degree of similarity between own paternal involvement and own father's involvement. However, although the 1997 PSID provides the best current data, this study's perhaps necessary reliance on fathers' retrospective reports about their own fathers' involvement is clearly a major methodological limitation. Future investigations should explore factors promoting or inhibiting modeling. The son's affective evaluation of his father's involvement is likely to be a key moderator: The son may model his own father's level of involvement if the son's affective response to it is positive but compensate for it if his response is negative. Researchers exploring the compensation hypothesis also need to clarify conceptually whether they expect compensation to occur only when own father involvement is low or also when own father involvement is high, as these two formulations have different implications for how data are analyzed.

Early Socialization for Involvement

During childhood, boys are given dolls less frequently than girls are, and they are discouraged from playing with dolls (Parke, 2002), potentially reducing later motivation for involvement. In a study in which preschool children were asked to pose with an infant for a photograph, boys stood farther away when asked to pose as a daddy than when given no instructions; by contrast, girls stood closer when asked to pose as a mommy (Reid, Tate, & Berman, 1989). Whether fathers' involvement covaries with other early socialization experiences such as babysitting, working with children, caring for younger siblings, and even simply having younger siblings has been little studied, and results are inconsistent (Gerson, 1993; Rustia & Abbott, 1993).

Proximal Socialization

Paternal involvement is associated with more proximal socialization experiences such as reading books on child care before and during pregnancy (Russell, 1983, 1986), attending the birth (Russell, 1983, 1986; but see Palkovitz, 1985), "rehearsal" for parenthood (e.g., amount of daydreaming involving being a parent, parental feelings, reaction to quickening; Feldman et al., 1983), and taking days off from work immediately after birth (Lamb, Chuang, & Hwang, in press; Pleck, 1993). However, these associations may result from selection factors, as other studies in which background factors were controlled found no linkage between attending birth preparation classes and aspects of involvement (Beitel & Parke, 1998; Hofferth, 2003).

Gender-Role Orientation

A number of studies concern gender-role orientation, that is, the extent to which individuals report themselves as having masculine (M) and feminine (F) traits, assessed by the Bem Sex Role Inventory (BSRI) and by the Personal Attributes Questionnaire (PAQ). Most of this research conceptualizes gender-role orientation as a determinant of involvement, although it expresses cautions about causal inference (Lamb et al., 1987). Several cross-sectional comparisons find that involved fathers are more likely to be androgynous (i.e., high in both M and F; Palkovitz, 1984; Rosenwasser & Patterson, 1984–1985; Sanderson & Sanders-Thompson, 2002) or to be higher in F (Russell, 1983, 1986). However, other cross-sectional studies find no associations (DeFrain, 1979; Lamb et al., 1982; Levant et al., 1987; Radin, 1994). Longitudinal studies also yield mixed results (Grossman et al., 1988; Kurdek, 1998; Radin, 1994).

Future research should more often employ longitudinal designs that permit assessment of causal direction. Research should also formulate and test further hypotheses about the kinds of involvement that are most theoretically related to M and to F, as suggested by Radin's (1994) findings. Future studies should also make use of conceptual developments in the construct of gender-role orientation. Some researchers distinguish positive and negative forms of both M (i.e., M+, M–) and F (F+, F–; Spence et al., 1979), finding they have different correlates. For example, adolescent risk behaviors appear associated with the negative but not positive components of M and F (Pleck et al., 1994a). An obvious hypothesis is that father involvement is a function of positive F, and perhaps of positive M as well. This distinction might also figure in fathers' modeling versus compensating for the involvement of their own fathers. Modeling may occur when the male perceives his own father as high in positive M and/or F, and compensation if he perceives his own father as having negative M and/or F. Finally, future research should explore factors mediating the influence of gender-role orientation. In one study, the effect of gender-role orientation on involvement was nonsignificant when perceived parenting skill was added to the predictive model, suggesting that perceived skill is the mediator of the gender-role orientation effect (Sanderson & Sanders-Thompson, 2002).

Beliefs about Gender, Fathering, and Parenting

Numerous studies have investigated paternal attitudes about gender, mothering, fathering, and child rearing as correlates of paternal involvement. It is difficult to integrate their results. Some analyses in large representative samples such as the NSFH report that paternal involvement is higher among men with more egalitarian beliefs about women or about gender roles (Blair et al., 1994; Goldscheider & Waite, 1991; Ishii-Kuntz & Coltrane, 1992), but other analyses (including others using the NSFH) have failed to confirm this relationship (Bartkowski & Xu, 2000; Marsiglio, 1991; Pleck, 1985; Toth & Xu, 1999; Wilcox, 2000). Yet other studies find significant associations at only some of the time periods examined (Aldous et al., 1998; NICHD Early Child Care Research Network, 2000). In yet additional studies, only selected aspects of fathers' gender attitudes related to their involvement. For example, in both the NSFH (Toth & Xu, 1999) and the PSID (Hofferth, 2003), involvement was not linked to the belief that it is best if the husband supports the family and the wife takes care of the home and children, but rather to the belief that if both husband and wife are employed full-time, they should share home responsibilities equally.

Measures of attitudes specifically about masculinity appear unrelated to involvement (Barnett & Baruch, 1987; Bonney et al., 1999; for discussion of the linkages among attitudes toward women, gender roles, and masculinity, see Pleck et al., 1994b). Belief that fathers' role is important and that fathers should be involved is often associated with level of involvement (Beitel & Parke, 1998; Hofferth, 2003; Palkovitz, 1984; Rane & McBride, 2000; but see McBride & Mills, 1993). Involvement is also predicted by fathers' holding positive beliefs about men's competence with children (Russell, 1983, 1986), as well as about men's ability to be close to children (Haas, 1988). Broader values about child rearing, parenting, and family life have also been examined. Results are inconsistent regarding whether traditional child-rearing values (emphasizing that children should be obedient) are linked to paternal involvement (Bartkowski & Xu, 2000; Cowan & Cowan, 1987; Toth & Xu, 1999). The NICHD Early Child Care Research Network (2000) found this association only if the wife was not employed or was employed part-time.

Future research on the role of fathers' beliefs about gender, fathering, and parenting needs to take into account that attitudes in these three domains tend to be intercorrelated. The results found for a particular kind of belief will vary according to which other beliefs, if any, are controlled. The extent to which fathers' beliefs are intercorrelated with mothers' also needs to be considered, and this intercorrelation may vary. In one study, fathers' and mothers' beliefs in innate gender differences were highly correlated, but their beliefs about the importance of father involvement were relatively independent (Beitel & Parke, 1998). Assessing the independent association between paternal beliefs and behavior requires controlling for maternal beliefs and vice versa.

Paternal Identity

Paternal identity, framed in a symbolic interactionist perspective, can be viewed as a broader disposition that motivates involvement. In one approach, paternal identity is interpreted as broad and multidimensional, such as Ihinger-Talman, Pasley, and Buehler's (1993) operationalization of paternal identity as a composite of role satisfaction, self-perceived competence, investment (wanting to learn more about fathering), and role salience (the importance of fatherhood compared to other roles). However, these different components have differential relationships with involvement (Minton & Pasley, 1996), and paternal role satisfaction and competence are independent constructs in their own right. Thus, most research operationalizes paternal identity more narrowly as identity salience (also termed identity commitment and identity centrality), the importance of fatherhood to the individual, especially as compared to other roles. Perhaps surprisingly, the linkage between paternal identity salience and measures of paternal involvement is disconfirmed (Maurer, Pleck, & Rane, 2001; McBride & Mills, 1993; McBride & Rane, 1997; Minton & Pasley, 1996; Sanderson & Sanders-Thompson, 2002) more often than it is confirmed (Fox & Bruce, 2001; Hossain & Roopnarine, 1994).

Future research on the problematic link between paternal identity and involvement needs to address several theoretical issues. Conceptually, fathering includes a wide range of activities (e.g., caregiving, breadwinning), so that different fathers reporting that being a "father" is important to them may have different ones in mind. Using Ihinger-Tallman et al.'s (1993) language, fatherhood is a social status or position that includes many different roles. Using the more common application of "role" to fatherhood, the father role includes different domains (Maurer et al., 2001; Stueve & Pleck, 2001). When research assesses identity salience at the domain level (e.g., caregiving), associations with paternal involvement are more consistent (Maurer et al., 2003; Rane & McBride, 2000). In addition, the gender-incongruent nature of paternal involvement should have theoretical implications for its link to identity. For example, behavior in gender-incongruent domains may have stronger association to the perceived expectations of others than to identity because identity in gender-incongruent roles is less clearly established. Consistent with this hypothesis, in Maurer et al.'s (2001) multivariate models, paternal caregiving is related to the expectations for caregiving that fathers perceive from their wives but not to their own paternal caregiving identity. Additionally, cognitive approaches to paternal identity need further exploration, such as Carver and Scheier's (1998) *control theory* model of identity, distinguishing goals parents hold at a more concrete program level versus a more abstract principle level. Using this approach, Hansen (2001) found that fathers with more abstract parenting goals were less behaviorally involved, whereas mothers showed the opposite association. Finally, paternal identity needs more conceptual development as a phenomenon occurring in a father's relationship with a specific child, rather than as a generic disposition (Pasley, Futris, & Skinner, 2002).

Future research should also take several methodological issues into account. Identity measures in which respondents divide a fixed quantity into portions corresponding to the importance of fathering compared to other roles are often used, such as the Identity Pie Chart (Futris et al., 1998; Strauss & Goldberg, 1999) and the Role Penny-Sort Task (McBride & Mills, 1993). Although intuitively plausible, these divisional assessment procedures have the limitations of single-item measures. When divisional measures are compared with multi-item questionnaire scales for overall paternal identity salience, only the latter predict paternal involvement (Maurer et al., 2003). Assessing paternal identity through fathers' narratives about their fathering experiences is a promising new methodology (Pleck & Stueve, in press; Stueve & Pleck, 2001, 2003).

In summary, the bulk of the substantive research on father's motivation for involvement focuses on four of the variables just considered: own father's involvement, gender-role orientation, beliefs about gender and fathering, and paternal identity. Although there is general support for the role of these four antecedents, for none are the research results unequivocal. These mixed results may occur because of the conceptual and methodological issues we highlight for each predictor. The minimal attention that early and proximal socialization for paternal involvement has received compared to other motivational predictors is also noteworthy.

SKILLS AND SELF-CONFIDENCE

Fathers' perceptions of their own competence as fathers has received much less attention than other factors considered in this chapter, but interest is increasing. Indeed, Hawkins et al. (2002) operationalized paternal involvement with questionnaire items assessing fathers' views of how good a job they do in a broad set of parenting domains, in effect redefining involvement as self-perceived competence. Fathers' perceived competence is indeed associated with their involvement (Baruch & Barnett, 1986; Beitel & Parke, 1998; Ehrenberg, Gearing-Small, Hunter, & Small, 2001; McHale & Huston, 1984; Pleck & Stueve, 1997), although Crouter et al. (1987) observed this relationship only among sole-breadwinner fathers. In several of these studies, the association is between mothers' reports about fathers' competence and fathers' reports of involvement, or vice versa, so that the association is not due to shared method variance. A further methodological issue, however, is that when marital adjustment is controlled, the association between skill and father involvement is nonsignificant (Bonney et al., 1999; Sanderson & Sanders-Thompson, 2002). The linkages among fathers' involvement, fathers' skills, and marital processes need more exploration.

Fathers' knowledge about child development is associated with positive engagement, though not time in routine care (Bailey, 1993). Furthermore, numerous interventions designed to promote parenting skills among fathers have increased involvement (Beitel & Parke, 1986; Cowan, 1988; Cowan & Cowan, 2002; Fagan & Hawkins, 2000; Klinman & Kohl, 1984, 1986; Levant, 1988; Levant & Doyle, 1983; McBride, 1990; McBride & Lutz, this volume). In a recent example using a quasi-experimental, pretest-posttest design, traditional Head Start parent involvement activities were adapted specifically for fathers. Fathers in the treatment group showed increased confidence in their parenting (Fagan & Stevenson, 2002), and those who received a high dosage of the intervention showed significant increases in engagement and accessibility, as well as increased support of their child's learning, in an 8-month follow-up (Fagan & Iglesias, 1999).

Overall, research confirms the influence of fathers' skills and self-confidence on their involvement. These variables, however, are surprisingly understudied relative to motivational predictors. This disparity is problematic because skills and self-confidence may be important mediators of the impact of motivational factors on involvement.

SOCIAL SUPPORTS AND STRESSES

Social Support within Marriage and Other Coparental Relationships

Recent research has focused on the extent to which mothers are gatekeepers for fathers' involvement. Allen and Hawkins (1999) distinguished three components of gatekeeping: mothers' being reluctant to give up responsibility by setting rigid standards, external validation of maternal identity, and differentiated conceptions of family roles. They classified about one fifth of a sample of Utah mothers as gatekeepers and found that this subgroup performed more of the family's housework and child care. Other studies corroborate that substantial subgroups of mothers feel ambivalent about father involvement and do not want their husbands to be more involved (Dienhart & Daly, 1997; Pleck, 1985). Other evidence indirectly supporting the gatekeeping hypothesis includes the negative association between maternal breastfeeding and paternal involvement (Beitel & Parke, 1998), as well as the findings that fathers are more involved when wives had involved fathers or currently have positive relationships with their own fathers (Feldman et al., 1983; Haas, 1988; Radin, 1994; but see Beitel & Parke, 1998).

However, the most critical linkage for the gatekeeper hypothesis is between mothers' attitudes and fathers' involvement. Although this relationship is often confirmed in recent studies with small convenience samples (Beitel & Parke, 1998; Bonney et al., 1999; DeLuccie, 1995; Glass, 1998; Maurer et al., 2001; McBride & Rane, 1998), it is not confirmed in the NSFH (Aldous et al., 1998; Ishii-Kuntz & Coltrane, 1992; Marsiglio, 1991), and this relationship is also disconfirmed in two of five earlier studies (Pleck, 1997). Of course, even when found, positive associations do not necessarily mean that the direction of causality is from maternal attitudes to father involvement. Also at variance with the notion of maternal gatekeeping, paternal and maternal involvement are significantly positively correlated, even with child age controlled (Aldous et al., 1998; Amato & Rivera, 1999; Harris & Ryan, in press; Ishii-Kuntz & Coltrane, 1992). Taken together, although there is some evidence for maternal gatekeeping, it is not robust.

A second line of research concerns the influence of marital quality on paternal involvement. (Marital adjustment has also been viewed as a consequence of paternal involvement, as reviewed later.) In cross-sectional studies with large representative samples, the association is inconsistent. For example, in the NSFH Blair et al. (1994) found a positive relationship, but Aldous et al. (1998) did not. The NICHD study finds a positive relationship with mothers' reports of marital satisfaction but no linkage to fathers' reports (NICHD Early Child Care Research Network, 2000). In a Dutch national household survey, in couples with more involved fathers, husbands perceived the marriage as more stable, but wives did not (Kalmijn, 1999). Negative relationships are sometimes found in older small-sample studies, but the marital measures generally concern frequency of conflict or disagreement rather than global satisfaction (Pleck, 1997). In longitudinal analyses, so far conducted only with convenience samples, the association is more consistently positive. This includes research relating prenatal levels of marital adjustment to paternal involvement in the first year (Coysh, 1983; Feldman et al., 1983; Levy-Schiff & Israelashvili, 1988; but see Grossman et al., 1988) as well as studies explicitly relating the degree and direction of change over time in marital adjustment to change in involvement (Volling & Belsky, 1991). When marriages deteriorate in quality, paternal interaction also becomes more negative and intrusive (Belsky et al., 1991; Brody et al., 1986). There is some evidence that mothers, by contrast, become more involved with children when marriage deteriorates, in a more compensatory process (Belsky et al., 1991). Overall, in representative cross sections, relationships found between global marital adjustment and paternal involvement are positive. In longitudinal studies with less representative samples, they are also positive. On balance, high paternal involvement appears more often grounded in good marital relationships than in poor ones.

Other Social Supports

In large representative samples, fathers' social networks are generally smaller and contain a smaller proportion of kin than do mothers'. The important exception, however, is that for children aged 2 to 4 years, fathers' proportion of kin (especially female kin) temporarily increases, and mothers' network size decreases (Munch, McPherson, & Smith-Lovin, 1997). Fathers' social networks are similar to mothers' in satisfaction offered by contact (Bost, Cox, Burchinal, & Payne, 2002). However, men's networks provide them with less encouragement and fewer resources relevant to parenting (Hossain & Roopnarine, 1993; Lein, 1979). In Riley's (1990) study, fathers reported discussing child-rearing concerns with an average of five members of their social network, including roughly equal numbers of kin and nonkin. However, wide variation exists, with almost one fifth of fathers reporting that they discussed child rearing with no one. Involved fathers may even encounter hostility from acquaintances, relatives, and workmates (Hwang et al., 1984; Russell, 1983, 1986).

Having a larger social network does not predict higher involvement and in one-earner families may actually predict lower involvement (Riley, 1990), consistent with Bott's (1957) classic finding that greater involvement with kin networks is associated with more traditional marital division of labor. The degree of support for fathering provided by the network is the more important variable, but it can influence involvement in opposing ways. In Riley's (1990) study, fathers' engagement was strongly related to the number of nonkin allies, defined as those providing at least three kinds of support, in two-earner families. Frequency of communication about children with nonkin persons is correlated with positive engagement (Ahmeduzzaman & Roopnarine, 1992; Roopnarine & Ahmeduzzaman, 1993; Tulananda et al., 1994), indicating that engaged fathers may seek out supportive communication with nonkin, which in turn reinforces their engagement. At the same time, frequency of this communication is negatively correlated with accessibility, suggesting that nonkin individuals may also provide care that substitutes for fathers' time (see also Glass, 1998; Van Dijk & Siegers, 1996). Fathers' perception of the level of involvement of other fathers they know, an indirect indicator of support, is significantly associated with paternal involvement (Maurer, 2002).

Stress

Level of stress in the parent role appears unrelated to paternal involvement (McBride & Mills, 1993; McBride, Rane, Schoppe, & Ho, in press). More global but short-term stress, assessed by frequency of daily hassles, is negatively linked to involvement (Fagan, 2000; Jain, Belsky, & Crnic, 1996). More generalized stress does not predict lower involvement. However, stress may moderate its effects, as suggested by Almeida and Galambos's (1991) finding that increasing involvement with adolescents is associated with more frequent father-adolescent conflicts among stressed fathers but with less frequent conflicts among nonstressed fathers. Low family income can be viewed as a potential indicator of global family stress. This variable is unrelated to paternal involvement in the NSFH (Wilcox, 2002). In the NICHD study, family income is negatively related to engagement, but the relationship is small and becomes nonsignificant when mothers' marital satisfaction is controlled (NICHD Early Child Care Research Network, 2000), suggesting that any income effect is mediated by marital satisfaction.

Summary

Overall, research provides limited support for the maternal gatekeeping hypothesis, but several pieces of key evidence are inconsistent with it. Paternal involvement appears to be grounded in positive marital relationships more often than negative ones. Research on nonmarital social support is limited but indicates that social supports from outside the marital relationship for involved fatherhood appear to be weak. The influence of nonmarital social support for paternal involvement varies in different contexts. This support has received far less research attention than it deserves, especially because fathers may use peers rather than their own parents more often as models (Daly, 1993; Masciadrelli, Pleck, & Stueve, 2002). Except in the short term, parental stress and more global stress are unrelated to paternal involvement.

INSTITUTIONAL POLICIES AND PRACTICES

The most striking characteristic of research on institutional policies and practices is that workplace influences have been studied almost to the exclusion of all other institutions. Because workplace policies and practices have received considerable attention in their own right (Hood, 1993; O'Brien & Shemlit, 2003; Russell & Hwang, this volume; for recent data on paternity leave in Europe, see Wisensale, 2001, Table 9.2), we do not recapitulate their effects here. There is anecdotal evidence concerning other institutions (Klinman & Kohl, 1984), but current research evidence for their impact is thin. In the most relevant recent study, fathers reported receiving less support than did mothers from social institutions such as child care providers, health care providers, early childhood intervention programs, and health and social service departments (Hossain & Roopnarine, 1993). More investigation of fathers' interactions with these institutions and their consequences is clearly needed (Lamb, 1986).

OVERVIEW OF SOURCES OF PATERNAL INVOLVEMENT

Certain aspects of Lamb et al.'s (1985) motivation factor (beliefs, attitudes, identity) receive much more attention than the other three factors. This appears to reflect an assumption that involvement is more a function of fathers' psychological characteristics than of their ecology. Furthermore, the influences investigated thoroughly within the other three factors include only two: the marital relationship (in the social support factor) and workplace influences (in institutional policies). Many potential influences on paternal involvement according to Lamb et al.'s model are relatively unexplored, particularly skills and self-confidence, nonmarital social supports, and institutional practices outside the workplace.

Among the influences on paternal involvement that have been studied extensively, no single variable exerts a predominant influence. Furthermore, hardly any predictor is significantly associated with paternal involvement in every available study, suggesting that associations with involvement of even the most consistent predictors may vary in different contexts. Variables associated with paternal involvement may act together additively, paralleling the concept of cumulative risk in the study of negative developmental outcomes. That is, the presence or absence of a particular factor may be less important than the cumulative number of predisposing characteristics.

Factors promoting father involvement may also operate interactively. Indeed, part of Lamb et al.'s (1985) original conceptualization is the notion that the four factors exert influence in a specific sequence. This formulation holds that motivation must be present for skills, self-confidence, and social supports to predict involvement. Likewise, for institutional practices to be a limiting factor, the three prior factors must be in place. This aspect of Lamb et al.'s conceptualization provides a way of understanding why most fathers do not seek out fatherhood education programs (motivation for greater involvement is low), yet the fathers who do enroll increase their involvement (i.e., among the motivated, skills may be a limiting factor). Similarly, most fathers of newborns do not take formal paternity leaves (suggesting that for most fathers, job expectations are not a limiting factor). At the same time, a small minority struggles to obtain formal leave at considerable personal cost (among the subgroup with motivation, skills, and other supports, workplace demands are indeed a barrier). While conceptually appealing, this sequential or interactive feature of Lamb et al.'s model has received only limited empirical testing.

Finally, mothers' employment status has received particular attention as a critical moderator of factors influencing paternal involvement (NICHD Early Child Care Research Network, 2000). Several studies have found that predictors of paternal involvement vary in one-earner compared to two-earner families (Barnett & Baruch, 1987; Crouter et al., 1988; NICHD Early Child Care Research Network, 2000; Riley, 1990; Volling & Belsky, 1991), suggesting that these are different ecological contexts. However, their results about exactly *how* the dynamics of paternal involvement differ in these two ecologies are not consistent. This may indicate that there are further ecological differences within samples of single-earner families and within dual-earner families. Overall, future research should explore further how factors associated with paternal involvement may act as cumulative predisposing factors, how they may interact with each other, and how their influence varies in different ecological contexts.

CONSEQUENCES OF PATERNAL INVOLVEMENT

CONSEQUENCES FOR CHILDREN

Whether positive paternal involvement has desirable consequences for children is naturally of particular interest (Lamb, Chuang, & Cabrera, in press; Lamb & Lewis, this volume; Palkovitz, 2002b; Parke, 2002; Silverstein & Auerbach, 1999, and Marsiglio & Pleck, in press, address the broader question of how essential fathers are to children's development). This particular question has received much more thoughtful attention in prior reviews than the other topics we review in this chapter, so our discussion here can be more interpretive. We first briefly review studies that meet two important methodological criteria: controlling for maternal involvement and obtaining data on paternal involvement and child outcomes from different sources. Other studies not meeting these criteria but having the advantages of longitudinal design are then discussed, followed by brief consideration of intervention studies and an overview of conceptual and methodological issues to be addressed in future research.

Research with Maternal Involvement Controlled and Different-Source Data

One important limitation of most available studies of the association between positive paternal involvement and child outcomes is that maternal involvement is not taken into account (Amato & Rivera, 1999; Pleck, 1997). A second critical weakness in the majority of investigations is same-source bias: the same informant providing data about both paternal involvement and child outcomes (Amato & Rivera, 1999). Amato and Rivera's review (see also Marsiglio, Amato, et al., 2000) located nine studies satisfying both criteria. Of these nine investigations, five suggest that paternal involvement has positive child correlates, to which Parke (2002) adds a sixth: Hart et al. (1998).

Subsequent to or not cited in Amato and Rivera (1999; Marsiglio, Amato, et al., 2000), several additional studies with maternal involvement controlled and different-source data provide further evidence of positive correlates of positive paternal engagement. Two of these use longitudinal data from the NSC. Girls who reported that their fathers spent enough time with them show better mental health outcomes later as adults (Wenk, Hardesty, Morgan, & Blair, 1994). In addition, qualitative dimensions of the father-child relationship such as reporting getting enough paternal love predicted subsequent self-esteem and life satisfaction in both men and women, and boys' feeling treated as a grownup by their fathers predicted subsequent adult self-esteem. In another NSC analysis including other adult outcomes, paternal involvement in childhood was associated with adult children's higher economic-educational achievement and lower delinquency, whereas maternal involvement was not (Harris et al., 1998). When closeness to father and mother are controlled, these relationships remain significant, and lower psychological distress emerges as an additional positive consequence of paternal involvement as well. This analysis also examined the joint effect of paternal and maternal involvement. Although no significant interaction effects emerged, both fathers' and mothers' being highly involved were associated with markedly lower adult psychological distress, and both being less involved predicted lower economic-educational attainment and higher delinquency.

In another longitudinal NSFH analysis, again controlling for maternal involvement and with independent data sources, positive paternal engagement was associated with lower frequency of later behavior problems among boys, as well as among children whom parents initially reported as difficult to raise (Aldous & Mulligan, 2002). In a large sample of British adolescents, positive engagement by both fathers and mothers contributed significantly and independently to positive school attitudes (Flouri, Buchanan, & Bream, 2002). Taking these additional analyses into account, 10 of 14 studies controlling for maternal involvement and employing different-source data thus found positive correlates of paternal involvement. Furthermore, Yeung, Duncan, and Hill's (2000) longitudinal analysis using the PSID found that fathers' attitudes, church attendance, and risk avoidance when their children were young predicted their children's education, wage rate, and avoidance of nonmarital births as young adults, with mothers' characteristics and behaviors as well as sociodemographic factors controlled.

Other Longitudinal Studies

Several longitudinal studies with independent-source data, but not controlling for maternal involvement, provide further evidence for positive effects. Because child outcomes are assessed subsequent to the assessment of father involvement, the research can at least rule out the possibility that child outcomes are influencing paternal involvement. If longitudinal studies also control for sociodemographic and other initial characteristics, there is some basis for ruling out selection factors as the source of the association as well.

Among studies with shorter follow-up periods, for example, fathers' degree of positive engagement in the month following birth has an independent association with infants' cognitive functioning at 1 year (Nugent, 1991). A factor probably contributing to this effect is that fathers who are more engaged perceive their infants as more cognitively competent (Ninio & Rinnott, 1988). Gottfried et al. (1988) reported significant relationships between positive father engagement at age 6 and Wechsler Intelligence Scale for Children (WISC) IQ, academic achievement, and social maturity at age 7. In a predominantly minority urban sample, positive paternal engagement in 10th grade predicted fewer problem behaviors in 11th grade, with problem behaviors in the prior grade controlled (Zimmerman, Salem, & Notaro, 2000). In another short-term longitudinal study focusing on the father-adolescent relationship, more accessible fathers were more accepting of their adolescents, and involvement predicted increasing acceptance over time as reported by both the father and the adolescent (Almeida & Galambos, 1991).

In studies following developmental outcomes for longer periods, adolescents with positively involved fathers at age 3–5 and 7–9 hold less traditional views as adolescents about dual-earner couples and about parents sharing child care (Williams et al., 1992). Snarey (1993), studying fathers drawn from a sample initiated in the 1940s (Glueck & Glueck, 1950), coded the degree of active engagement in children's intellectual development, social development, and physical development during childhood and during adolescence in the 1950s and 1960s. With sociodemographic and other factors controlled, positive paternal engagement explained 11% to 16% of the variance in daughters' and sons' educational mobility relative to their parents, and 6% to 13% of their occupational mobility, assessed when the children were in their twenties.

Intervention Studies

An interpretive challenge in research finding associations between paternal involvement and good developmental outcomes is ruling out the possibility that paternal engagement is actually a consequence (rather than cause) of positive child characteristics. Intervention studies potentially provide the strongest sort of evidence that the association occurs at least in part because paternal involvement influences child outcomes. As reviewed in Parke (2002), several studies of interventions that increase father involvement have found these increases to be associated with positive changes in children. In addition, in Fagan and Iglesias's (1999) recent quasi-experimental intervention with Head Start fathers, children whose fathers received a high dosage of the intervention showed improved mathematics readiness scores. However, the samples used in these interventions restrict their generalizability. In addition, the available intervention studies are at best quasi-experimental. No evaluation study employing true random assignment of subjects to treatment and control conditions is yet available.

Conceptual and Methodological Issues for Future Research

The body of research supporting positive child consequences for paternal involvement is still relatively small if attention is restricted to studies controlling for maternal involvement and using different source data. Furthermore, a significant minority of studies with these two methodological strengths do not find significant effects, and uncontrolled selection factors may account for some of the association in the investigations that do. Three conceptual issues remain to be addressed in future research on child consequences.

First, future research may do well to return to Lamb et al.'s (1985) view that positive effects of paternal involvement are likely to occur primarily or only in specific contexts. It may be that the positive effects of involvement do not occur across enough different contexts that multivariate analysis will consistently demonstrate a main effect (vs. interaction effect) for involvement. Indeed, some of the supportive evidence for positive effects considered earlier is restricted to specific contexts according to child gender or other characteristics (Aldous & Mulligan, 2002; Wenk et al., 1994). Positive effects of paternal involvement may be no less important for being limited to particular contexts.

Second, as noted in prior reviews (Parke, 2002; Pleck, 1997), most research focuses on direct father-to-child effects. Because paternal and maternal behavior can influence each other, paternal involvement can also influence the child indirectly by virtue of its effects on mothers. Paternal involvement can have further indirect effects through its impact on the child's sibling relationships as well as peer relationships, thus impacting on developmental outcomes through yet additional pathways. Not taking these indirect effects into account leads to overestimation of the direct influence of paternal involvement on child outcomes. Establishing that paternal involvement has an independent association with child outcomes requires controlling for maternal involvement, as some available research does. Going a logical step further, establishing the direct effect of paternal involvement also necessitates controlling for the child's sibling relationships and peer relationships, a step not yet undertaken.

In addition, it is likely that the child outcomes currently studied as consequences of involvement also have a reciprocal influence on involvement, so that paternal involvement may have an evocative effect analogous to that studied in behavioral genetics (Plomin, 1989). That is, paternal involvement may lead to good child outcomes, which reinforce paternal involvement, which in turn further enhances child outcomes. The overall association between paternal involvement and child outcomes overestimates the direct effect of the former on the latter way if this evocative effect is not taken into account. At the same time, the potential indirect and evocative effects of paternal involvement on the child are not merely factors that need to be controlled for in estimating the direct effects of paternal involvement. From another perspective, they are the pathways comprising the total effect of paternal involvement (i.e., direct, indirect, and evocative effects combined). Thus, studies in which the association between paternal involvement and child outcomes becomes nonsignificant when maternal involvement is controlled should be interpreted as indicating only that involvement has no independent and direct effect on the child, not that it necessarily has no effect.

Third, if the effects of child outcomes on paternal involvement are to be seriously considered, it is necessary to take into account the potential dynamic that negative outcomes in the child may elicit increased paternal (and maternal) involvement, so that involvement is thus associated with negative rather than positive outcomes. Finding this initially counterintuitive association, De Luccie (1996a) suggested exactly this compensatory process. That this potential compensatory effect occurs in some subgroups while direct positive effects occur in others could account for the lack of overall association between involvement and child outcomes found in some investigations. Even more intricate compensatory processes may occur. In one longitudinal study with maternal behavior controlled and independent data sources, high levels of positive paternal behaviors and low levels of negative paternal behaviors during the second and third years predicted increased (not decreased) child inhibition at age 3, with this effect heightened among those who were rated as having negatively reactive temperaments as infants (Belsky, Hsieh, & Crnic, 1998). The authors' interpretation was that for negative infants, parental sensitivity might mean accepting and therefore inadvertently sustaining the child's worries, while negative behaviors such as intrusiveness would push the child to overcome her wariness.

Overall, in recent years more and better evidence has become available that positive paternal involvement is correlated with desirable child outcomes. At the same time, this increase in supportive evidence has been accompanied by increased awareness of the methodological and conceptual complexity of the association between paternal involvement and children's development. The research agenda has thus shifted from whether paternal involvement has positive consequences to questions about the context in which and the processes by which paternal effects occur.

CONSEQUENCES FOR MOTHERS AND FOR MARRIAGE

Almost all current research in this area focuses on effects on marital variables. A few older studies concern the impact of fathers' involvement on broader outcomes in mothers such as psychological well-being (Baruch & Barnett, 1986) and self-esteem (Russell, 1983), outcomes neglected in more recent work. There has also been some interest in the long-term effects of greater paternal involvement on womens' success in the labor force (Levine et al., 1981). However, little recent evidence exists concerning these potential influences, although they could be easily studied longitudinally in the NSFH.

As noted earlier, marital adjustment can be viewed as both a source and consequence of paternal involvement. Two opposing hypotheses are possible for marital satisfaction considered as an outcome. The concept of maternal gatekeeping (Allen & Hawkins, 1999) implies not only that mothers limit paternal involvement but also that mothers' marital satisfaction is lower if fathers are more involved. Distinct from the gatekeeping notion, if both parents are actively involved, disagreements about child rearing may be more likely to occur, and mishaps in communication and arrangements may happen more frequently. The opposing hypothesis is that greater involvement leads to better marital adjustment because wives will feel more supported and the spouses will share more in common.

Frequency of conflict or disagreement is higher when fathers are highly involved, although this has been documented primarily in older studies with small samples, and this negative association may be restricted to or at least stronger in dual-earner families (Crouter et al., 1987; Gerson, 1993; Russell, 1983). The cross-sectional research with representative samples that we reviewed earlier indicates that when significant associations are found between fathers' involvement and more global measures of marital adjustment, they are positive. In other recent studies with representative samples, low father involvement is associated with wives' anger at their husbands (Ross & Van Willigen, 1996). When fathers are less involved than mothers think is desirable, mothers perceive an unfair division of labor and report greater stress (Milkie, Bianchi, Mattingly, & Robinson, 2002). In Snarey's (1993) longitudinal study of men born in the 1930s, positive paternal engagement when their children were young accounted for 12% of the variance in fathers' marital success at midlife. Paternal engagement during adolescence contributed an additional 9%, with sociodemographic factors controlled. Other longitudinal research suggests that the fathers' self-perceived competence and satisfaction in their paternal role have positive consequences for marriage (see review in Snarey, 1993).

Overall, there is more evidence that paternal involvement has positive consequences for marriage than negative consequences. The effects of paternal involvement on marriage should of course depend on whether mothers and fathers want fathers to be involved, as confirmed by the most detailed recent analysis (Milkie et al., 2002). The failure to control for mothers' and fathers' expectations may be why some cross-sectional analyses find no significant association. At the same time, it is striking that a number of other analyses find positive effects for paternal involvement even when expectations are not taken into account.

Consequences for Fathers

The potential consequences of involvement most often studied are role conflict and satisfaction, psychological well-being, and generativity. More involved fathers feel that they lack time for their careers and that their family responsibilities interfere with their work, but they also feel less strain in their family role performance (Baruch & Barnett, 1986). In fathers of preschoolers, work-family role strain is lowest when their pattern of role commitments entails low work commitment and high parental commitment (Greenberger & O'Neil, 1990). In dual-earner families, more involved fathers experience more work-family stress, but in single-earner families they report less stress (Volling & Belsky, 1991). Also in dual-earner families, more accessible fathers are more likely to feel bothered about their having a nontraditional role (Jump & Haas, 1987). In spite of these stresses and conflicts, however, more accessible fathers do not report being less satisfied with their parental role overall (Jump & Haas, 1987). It should be recognized that low paternal involvement can lead to role strains as well (Silverstein, Auerbach, & Levant, 2002).

In the NSFH, the relationship between paternal engagement and depression is inconsistent in different analyses (Blair & Hardesty, 1994; Eggebeen & Knoester, 2001). Two longitudinal studies provide evidence about short-term and long-term consequences on men's well-being. Of the voluminous research literature on the transition to parenthood, only Hawkins and Belsky (1989) examined fathers' postnatal psychological outcomes as a function of their degree of participation in infant care. In this study, fathers of boys generally declined in self-esteem over the transition, whereas fathers of girls increased in self-esteem. Fathers showed the opposite pattern on a measure of empathy. Additionally, the more involved fathers were with children of either gender, the more they declined in self-esteem. One possible interpretation of the decline in self-esteem among fathers of boys is that boys are more difficult to care for and that fathers of boys are more involved with them. Although achieving the status of fatherhood has an overall positive effect, the difficulties that fathers experience caring for boys lower self-esteem to a greater degree. Another interpretation was that because the self-esteem measure was highly correlated with traditional masculine traits, fathers of sons are demonstrating "nontraditional development for men [i.e., decrease in masculinity, increase in femininity] and the influence of gender-linked father involvement on this development" (p. 381), which Hawkins and Belsky view as beneficial.

A new direction in research on the consequences of paternal involvement on fathers concerns *generativity*. Citing Benedek (1959), Erikson (1964, p. 130) remarked, "parenthood is, for most, the first, and for many, the prime generative encounter." Generativity is important because it is related to psychological well-being, both theoretically and empirically (e.g., Erikson, 1964; Peterson & Klohnen, 1995; Stewart, Ostrove, & Helson, 2001; Vaillant, 1977). Caregiving behavior alone does not significantly predict generativity for fathers or mothers (Bailey, 1992, 1994). Similarly, Christiansen and Palkovitz (1998) reported only small correlations between overall paternal involvement and fathers' generativity. On the other hand, studies of involvement in specific child-rearing behaviors and areas of parenting (e.g., play, taking a child on routine jobs, consulting with teachers, and supervising homework) find relationships between such involvement and generativity in fathers (Bailey, 1992; McKeering & Pakenham, 2000, including Snarey's (1993) longitudinal analysis; Snarey, 1993). Positive paternal engagement is also significantly related to civic engagement, an indicator of societal generativity, in the only study using a large representative sample (Eggebeen & Knoester, 2001; Wilcox, 2002). In the one available study, men's paternal identity predicts their generativity (Christiansen & Palkovitz, 1998). Relatively consistent associations occur between generativity and women's satisfaction in the parental role, though not with perceived parental competence (MacDermid, Franz, & DeReus, 1998; MacDermid, Heilbrun, & DeHaan, 1997). These relationships need to be examined for fathers as well.

Overall, higher paternal involvement may exact some costs for fathers in the short run in terms of increased levels of work-family conflict (in dual-earner couples) and decreased self-esteem as traditionally assessed. These costs do not appear to reduce overall satisfaction with parenthood, however. Limited longitudinal evidence suggests that in the long term, high involvement has a modest positive impact on career success and a greater positive effect on at least one personality outcome, fathers' societal generativity. These data are consistent with Hawkins et al.'s (1993) and Snarey's (1993) argument that although fathers who become highly involved may experience significant disequilibrium and stress in the short run, these experiences stimulate them ultimately to achieve higher levels of functioning. As with consequences for marriage, these effects should be contingent on mothers' and fathers' wanting fathers to be highly involved. It is noteworthy that several studies suggest long-term positive consequences for fathers themselves without taking expectations into account.

CONCLUSIONS

Research conducted since Lamb et al. (1985) proposed the construct of paternal involvement suggests several summary conclusions. Investigations in the United States have focused much more on positive paternal involvement than on involvement in its original, content-free sense. In addition, scholars have operationalized responsibility in two somewhat different though overlapping ways: as indirect care tasks and as taking initiative for the child's care, whether direct or indirect.

In the most recent data from a large representative sample, the 1997 PSID, the average child aged 12 or under living with his or her father receives an average of 1.83 hours/day of engagement from the father and 3.56 hours of accessibility. Fathers' engagement and accessibility are roughly three-quarters that of mothers'. Play/companionship and caregiving combined comprise about two thirds of fathers' engagement. Paternal engagement is generally unrelated to fathers' ethnicity and socioeconomic status. Average levels of paternal engagement and accessibility have increased in the United States during the last several decades, both in absolute and relative terms.

Lamb et al.'s (1985) model specifying motivation, skills and self-confidence, social supports, and institutional practices as the key facilitating factors for paternal involvement continues to be useful. Among motivational variables, own father's involvement, gender-role orientation, beliefs about gender and fathering, and paternal identity have received the most attention. Research confirms the influence of fathers' skills and self-confidence on their involvement. These variables, however, are surprisingly understudied relative to motivational predictors. There is limited support for the maternal gatekeeping hypothesis, but several pieces of key evidence are inconsistent with it. Paternal involvement appears to be grounded in positive marital relationships more often than negative ones. Social supports from outside the marital relationship for involved fatherhood appear to be weak, and their influence appears to vary in different contexts. In institutional policies and practices, workplace influences have been studied almost to the exclusion of all other contexts. The impacts of other institutions such as child care, health, education, and social services need more attention.

Research on the consequences of paternal involvement for children has made considerable methodological progress. In 10 of the 14 studies in which maternal involvement is controlled and different-source data are used, positive paternal engagement is associated with desirable outcomes in children, adolescents, and young adults. There is more evidence that paternal involvement has positive consequences for marriage than negative ones. Finally, although high paternal involvement exacts some costs on fathers themselves, it generally appears to have compensating benefits.

REFERENCES

Ahmeduzzaman, M., & Roopnarine, J. L. (1992). Sociodemographic factors, functioning style, social support, and fathers' involvement with preschoolers in African-American families. *Journal of Marriage and the Family, 54,* 699–707.

Aldous, J., & Mulligan, G. M. (2002). Fathers' child care and children's behavior problems. *Journal of Family Issues, 23,* 624–647.

Aldous, J., Mulligan, G. M., & Bjarnason, T. (1998). Fathering over time: What makes the difference? *Journal of Marriage and the Family, 60,* 809–820.

Allen, J., & Hawkins, A. (1999). Maternal gatekeeping: Mothers' beliefs and behaviors that inhibit greater father involvement in family work. *Journal of Marriage and the Family, 61,* 199–212.

Almeida, D. M., & Galambos, N. L. (1991). Examining father involvement and the quality of father-adolescent relations. *Journal of Research on Adolescence, 1,* 155–172.

Almeida, D. M., Wethington, E., & McDonald, D. A. (2001). Daily variation in paternal engagement and negative mood: Implications for emotionally supportive and conflictual interactions. *Journal of Marriage and Family, 63,* 417–429.

Amato, P. R. (1987). *Children in Australian families: The growth of competence.* New York: Prentice Hall.

Amato, P. R., & Rivera, F. (1999). Paternal involvement and children's behavior. *Journal of Marriage and the Family, 61,* 375–384.

Anderson, K. G., Kaplan, H., Lam, D., & Lancaster, J. (1999). Paternal care by genetic fathers and stepfathers: II. Reports by Xhosa high school students. *Evolution and Human Behavior, 20,* 433–451.

Anderson, K. G., Kaplan, H., & Lancaster, J. (1999). Paternal care by genetic fathers and stepfathers: I. Reports from Albuquerque men. *Evolution and Human Behavior, 20,* 405–431.

Armato, M., & Marsiglio, W. (2002). Self-structure, identity, and commitment: Promise Keepers' godly man project. *Symbolic Interaction, 25,* 41–65.

Auerbach, C., Silverstein, L. B., & Zizi, M. (1997). The evolving structure of fatherhood among Haitian Americans. *Journal of African-American Male Studies, 2,* 59–85.

Averett, S. L., Gennetian, L. A., & Peters, E. H. (2000). Patterns and determinants of paternal child care during a child's first three years of life. *Marriage and Family Review, 29,* 115–136.

Bailey, W. T. (1991). Fathers' involvement in their children's health care. *Journal of Genetic Psychology, 152,* 289–293.

Bailey, W. T. (1992). Psychological development in men: Generativity and involvement with young children. *Psychological Reports, 71,* 929–930.

Bailey, W. T. (1993). Fathers' knowledge of development and involvement with preschool children. *Perceptual and Motor Skills, 77,* 1032–1034.

Bailey, W. T. (1994). Fathers' involvement and responding to infants: "More" may not be "better." *Psychological Reports, 74,* 92–94.

Bailey, W. T. (1995). A longitudinal study of fathers' involvement with young children: Infancy to age 5 years. *Journal of Genetic Psychology, 155,* 331–339.

Barnett, R. C., & Baruch, G. B. (1987). Determinants of fathers' participation in family work. *Journal of Marriage and the Family, 49,* 29–40.

Bartkowski, J. P., & Xu, X. (2000). Distant patriarchs or expressive dads? The discourse and practice of fathering in conservative Protestant families. *Sociological Quarterly, 41,* 465–485.

Baruch, G. K., & Barnett, R. C. (1986). Consequences of fathers' participation in family work: Parents' role strain and well-being. *Journal of Personality and Social Psychology, 51,* 983–992.

Baumrind, D. (1966). Effects of authoritative parental control on child behavior. *Child Development, 37,* 887–907.

Beitel, A. H., & Parke, R. D. (1998). Paternal involvement in infancy: The role of maternal and paternal attitudes. *Journal of Family Psychology, 12,* 268–288.

Belsky, J., Hsieh, K., & Crnic, K. (1998). Mothering, fathering, and infant negativity as antecedents of boy's externalizing problems and inhibition at age 3 years: Differential susceptibility to rearing experience? *Development and Psychopathology, 10,* 301–319.

Belsky, J., Youngblood, L., Rovine, M., & Volling, B. (1991). Patterns of marital change and parent-child interaction. *Journal of Marriage and the Family, 53,* 487–498.

Benedek, T. (1959). Parenthood as a developmental phase: A contribution to libido theory. *Journal of the American Psychoanalytic Association, 7,* 389–417.

Berk, S. F. (Ed.). (1980). *Women and household labor.* Beverly Hills, CA: Sage.

Bianchi, S. M. (2000). Maternal employment and time with children: Dramatic change or surprising continuity? *Demography, 37,* 401–414.

Blair, S. L., & Hardesty, C. (1994). Parental involvement and the well-being of fathers and mothers of young children. *Journal of Men's Studies, 3,* 49–68.

Blair, S. L., Wenk, D., & Hardesty, C. (1994). Marital quality and paternal involvement: Interconnections of men's spousal and parental roles. *Journal of Men's Studies, 2,* 221–237.

Bond, J. T., Galinsky, E., & Swanberg, J. E. (1998). *The 1997 National Survey of the Changing Workforce.* New York: Families and Work Institute.

Bonney, J. F., Kelley, M. L., & Levant, R. F. (1999). A model of fathers' behavioral involvement in child care in dual-earner families. *Journal of Family Psychology, 13*, 401–415.

Bost, K. K., Cox, M. J., Burchinal, M. R., & Payne, C. (2002). Structural and supportive change in couples' family and friendship networks across the transition to parenthood. *Journal of Marriage and the Family, 64*, 517–531.

Bott, E. (1957). *Family and social network: Roles, norms, and external relationships in ordinary urban families.* New York: Free Press.

Braver, S. L., Wolchik, S. A., Sandler, I. N., Sheets, V., Fogas, B., & Bay, R. C. (1993). A longitudinal study of noncustodial parents: Parents without children. *Journal of Family Psychology, 7*, 9–23.

Brayfield, A. (1995). Juggling jobs and kids: The impact of employment schedules on fathers' caring for children. *Journal of Marriage and the Family, 57*, 321–332.

Broderick, C. B. (1993). *Understanding family process: Basics of family systems theory.* Thousand Oaks, CA: Sage.

Brody, G. H., Pillegrini, A. D., & Sigel, I. E. (1986). Marital quality and mother-child and father-child interactions with school-aged children. *Developmental Psychology, 22*, 291–296.

Bruce, C., & Fox, G. L. (1997). *Measuring father involvement among lower-income White and African-American populations.* Presented at the National Council on Family Relations, Crystal City, VA.

Bruce, J., Lloyd, C. B., & Leonard, A. (1995). *Families in focus.* New York: The Population Council.

Bryant, W. K., & Zick, C. D. (1996). An examination of parent-child shared time. *Journal of Marriage and the Family, 58*, 227–237.

Cabrera, N. J., Tamis-LeMonda, C. S., Bradley, R. H., Hofferth, S., & Lamb, M. E. (2000). Fatherhood in the twenty-first century. *Child Development, 71*, 127–136.

Casper, L. M. (1997). My daddy takes care of me! Fathers as care providers (P70-59). Washington, DC: U.S. Bureau of the Census.

Casper, L. M., & O'Connell, M. (1998). Work, income, the economy, and married fathers as child-care providers. *Demography, 35*, 243–250.

Carver, C., & Scheier, M. (1998). *On the self-regulation of behavior.* Cambridge, England: Cambridge University Press.

Child Trends. (2002). *Charting parenthood: A statistical portrait of fathers and mothers in America.* Washington, DC: Author.

Christiansen, S. L., & Palkovitz, R. (1998). Exploring Erikson's psychosocial theory of development: Generativity and its relationship to paternal identity, intimacy, and involvement in childcare. *Journal of Men's Studies, 7*, 133–156.

Coley, R. L., & Morris, J. E. (2002). Comparing father and mother reports of father involvement among low-income minority families. *Journal of Marriage and Family, 64*, 982–997.

Coltrane, S. (1996). *Family man.* New York: Oxford University Press.

Coltrane, S., & Adams, M. (2001). Men's family work. In R. Hertz & N. L. Marshall (Eds.), *Working families: The transformation of the American home.* Berkeley, CA: University of California Press.

Cooksey, E. C., & Fondell, M. M. (1996). Spending time with his kids: Effects of family structure on fathers' and children's lives. *Journal of Marriage and the Family, 58*, 693–707.

Costigan, C. L., & Cox, M. L. (2001). Fathers' participation in family research: Is there a self-selection bias? *Journal of Family Psychology, 15*, 706–720.

Cowan, C. P. (1988). Working with men becoming fathers: The impact of a couples group intervention. In P. Bronstein & C. P. Cowan (Eds.), *Fatherhood today: Men's changing role in the family* (pp. 276–298). New York: Wiley.

Cowan, C. P., & Cowan, P. A. (1987). Men's involvement in parenthood: Identifying the antecedent and understanding the barriers. In P. Berman & F. A. Pederson (Eds.), *Men's transitions to parenthood* (pp. 145–174). Hillsdale, NJ: Erlbaum.

Cowan, P. A., & Cowan, C. P. (2002). What an intervention design reveals about how parents affect their children's academic achievement and behavior problems. In J. Borkowski, S. L. Ramey, & M. Bristol-Power (Eds.), *Parenting and the child's world* (pp. 75–98). Mahwah, NJ: Erlbaum.

Cox, M. J., Owen, M. T., Lewis, J. M., & Henderson, V. K. (1989). Marriage, adult adjustment, and early parenting. *Child Development, 60,* 1015–1024.

Coysh, W. S. (1983, August). *Predictive and concurrent factors related to fathers' involvement in childrearing.* Paper presented to the American Psychological Association, Anaheim, CA.

Crouter, A. C., & Crowley, M. S. (1990). School-age children's time alone with fathers in single- and dual-earner families: Implications for the father-child relationship. *Journal of Early Adolescence, 10,* 296–312.

Crouter, A. C., Perry-Jenkins, M., Huston, T., & McHale, S. M. (1987). Processes underlying father involvement in dual-earner and single-earner families. *Developmental Psychology, 23,* 431–440.

Daly, K. (1993). Reshaping fatherhood: Finding the models. *Journal of Family Issues, 14,* 510–530.

Daly, K. (1996). *Families and time: Keeping pace in a hurried culture.* Thousand Oaks, CA: Sage.

Day, R., & Lamb, M. E. (Eds.). (in press). *Conceptualizing and measuring paternal involvement.* Mahwah, NJ: Erlbaum.

DeFrain, J. (1979). Androgynous parents tell who they are and what they need. *Family Coordinator, 28,* 237–243.

De Luccie, M. F. (1996a). Mothers: Influential agents in father-child relations. *Genetic, Social, and General Psychology Monographs, 122,* 287–307.

De Luccie, M. F. (1996b). Predictors of paternal involvement and satisfaction. *Psychological Reports, 79,* 1351–1359.

Deutsch, F. M., Lozy, J. L., & Saxon, S. (1993). Taking credit: Couples' reports of contributions to child care. *Journal of Family Issues, 14,* 421–437.

Deutsch, F. M., Lussier, J. B., & Servis, L. J. (1993). Husbands at home: Predictors of paternal participation in childcare and housework. *Journal of Personality and Social Psychology, 65,* 1154–1166.

Deutsch, F. M., Servis, L. J., & Payne, J. D. (2001). Paternal participation in child care and its effects on children's self-esteem and attitudes toward gendered roles. *Journal of Family Issues, 22,* 1000–1024.

Dienhart, A. (2001). Make room for daddy: The pragmatic potentials of a tag-team structure for sharing parenting. *Journal of Family Issues, 22,* 973–999.

Dienhart, A., & Daly, K. (1997). Men and women cocreating father involvement in a nongenerative culture. In A. Hawkins & D. Dollahite (Eds.), *Generative fathering* (pp. 147–164). Thousand Oaks, CA: Sage.

Eggebeen, D. J. (2002). Sociological perspectives on fatherhood: What do we know about fathers from social surveys? In C. Tamis-LeMonda & N. Cabrera (Eds.), *Handbook of father involvement* (pp. 189–209). Mahwah, NJ: Erlbaum.

Eggebeen, D. J., & Knoester, C. (2001). Does fatherhood matter for men? *Journal of Marriage and Family, 63,* 381–393.

Ehrenberg, M. F., Gearing-Small, M., Hunter, M. A., & Small, B. J. (2001). Childcare task division and shared parenting attitudes in dual-earner families with young children. *Family Relations, 50,* 143–153.

Erera, P. I., Minton, C., Pasley, K., & Mandel, S. (1999). Fathering after divorce in Israel and the U.S. *Journal of Divorce and Remarriage, 31,* 55–82.

Erikson, E. H. (1964). *Insight and responsibility.* New York: Norton.

Fagan, J. (1996). A preliminary study of low-income African American fathers' play interactions with their preschool-age children. *Journal of Black Psychology, 22,* 7–19.

Fagan, J. (1998). Correlates of low-income African American and Puerto Rican fathers' involvement with their children. *Journal of Black Psychology, 24,* 351–367.

Fagan, J. (2000). Head Start fathers' daily hassles and involvement with their children. *Journal of Family Issues, 21,* 329–346.

Fagan, J., & Hawkins, A. (Eds.). (2000). *Clinical and educational interventions with fathers.* New York: Haworth Press.

Fagan, J., & Iglesias, A. (1999). Father involvement program effects on fathers, father figures, and their Head Start children: A quasi-experimental study. *Early Childhood Research Quarterly, 14,* 243–269.

Fagan, J., & Stevenson, H. C. (2002). An experimental study of an empowerment-based intervention for African American Head Start fathers. *Family Relations, 51,* 191–198.

Fein, R. A. (1974). Men and young children. In J. H. Pleck & J. Sawyer (Eds.), *Men and masculinity* (pp. 81–84). Englewood Cliffs, NJ: Prentice Hall.

Feldman, S. S., & Aschenbrenner, B. (1983). Impact of parenthood on various aspects of masculinity and femininity: A short-term longitudinal study. *Developmental Psychology, 19,* 278–289.

Feldman, S. S., Nash, S. C., & Aschenbrenner, B. G. (1983). Antecedents of fathering. *Child Development, 54,* 1628–1636.

Finley, G. E., & Schwartz, S. J. (in press). The father involvement and nurturant fathering scales: Retrospective measures for adolescent and adult children. *Educational and Psychological Measurement.*

Flouri, E., Buchanan, A., & Bream, V. (2002). Adolescents' perceptions of their fathers' involvement: Significance to school attitudes. *Psychology in the Schools, 39,* 575–582.

Fox, G. T., & Bruce, C. (2001). Conditional fatherhood: Identity theory and parental investment theory as alternative sources of explanation of fathering. *Journal of Marriage and Family, 63,* 394–403.

Gavanas, A. (2003). *Masculinizing fatherhood.* Ann Arbor: University of Michigan Press.

Geary, D. C. (2000). Evolution and proximate expression of human paternal investment. *Psychological Bulletin, 126,* 55–77.

Gershuny, J. (2000). *Changing times: Work and leisure in postindustrial society.* Oxford, England: Oxford University Press.

Gerson, K. (1993). *No man's land: Men's changing commitments to family and work.* New York: Basic Books.

Glass, J. (1998). Gender liberation, economic squeeze, or fear of strangers: Why fathers provide infant care in dual-earner families. *Journal of Marriage and the Family, 60,* 821–834.

Glueck, S., & Glueck, E. (1950). *Unravelling juvenile delinquency.* New York: Commonwealth Fund.

Goldscheider, F. K., & Waite, L. J. (1991). *New families, no families: The transformation of the American home.* Berkeley: University of California Press.

Gottfried, A. E., Gottfried, A. W., & Bathurst, K. (1988). Maternal employment, family environment, and children's development: Infancy through the school years. In A. E. Gottfried & A. W. Gottfried (Eds.), *Maternal employment and children's development: Longitudinal research* (pp. 11–58). New York: Plenum Press.

Greenberger, E., & O'Neil, R. (1990). Parents' concerns about their child's development: Implications for fathers' and mothers' well-being and attitudes toward work. *Journal of Marriage and the Family, 52,* 621–635.

Grossman, F. K., Pollack, W. S., & Golding, E. (1988). Fathers and children: Predicting the quality and quantity of fathering. *Developmental Psychology, 24,* 82–91.

Haas, L. (1988, November). *Understanding fathers' participation in childcare: A social constructionist perspective.* Paper presented to the National Council on Family Relations, Philadelphia.

Hansen, D. M. (2001). *Parental caregiving cognitive control: A new construct for understanding parental caregiving, identity commitment, and caregiving involvement.* Unpublished doctoral dissertation, Department of Human and Community Development, University of Illinois at Urbana-Champaign.

Harris, K. H., Furstenberg, F. F., & Marmer, J. K. (1998). Paternal involvement with adolescents in intact families: The influence of fathers over the life course. *Demography, 35,* 201–216.

Harris, K. H., & Morgan, S. P. (1991). Fathers, sons, and daughters: Differential paternal involvement in parenting. *Journal of Marriage and Family, 53,* 531–544.

Harris, K. H., & Ryan, S. (in press). Father involvement and the diversity of family context. In R. Day & M. E. Lamb (Eds.), *Conceptualizing and measuring paternal involvement.* Mahwah, NJ: Erlbaum.

Hart, C. H., Nelson, D. A., Robinson, C. C., Olsen, S. F., & McNeilly-Choque, M. K. (1998). Overt and relational aggression in Russian nursery-school-age children: Parenting style and marital linkages. *Developmental Psychology, 34,* 687–697.

Hawkins, A. J., & Belsky, J. (1989). The role of father involvement in personality change in men across the transition to parenthood. *Family Relations, 38,* 378–384.

Hawkins, A. J., Bradford, K. P., Palkovitz, R., Christiansen, S. L., Day, R. D., & Call, V. R. A. (2002). The inventory of father involvement: A pilot study of a new measure of father involvement. *Journal of Men's Studies, 10,* 183–196.

Hawkins, A. J., Christiansen, S. L., Sargent, K. P., & Hill, E. J. (1993). Rethinking fathers' involvement in child care: A developmental perspective. *Journal of Family Issues, 14,* 531–549.

Hawkins, A. J., & Palkovitz, R. (1999). Beyond ticks and clicks: The need for more diverse and broader conceptualizations and measures of father involvement. *Journal of Men's Studies, 8,* 11–32.

Hochschild, A. (1989). *The second shift: Working parents and the revolution at home.* New York: Viking Press.

Hofferth, S. L. (2003). Race/ethnic differences in father involvement in two-parent families: Culture, context, or economy? *Journal of Family Issues, 24,* 185–216.

Hofferth, S. L., Pleck, J. H., Stueve, J. L., Bianchi, S., & Sayer, L. (2002). The demography of fathers: What fathers do. In C. Tamis-Lemonda & N. Cabrera (Eds.), *The handbook of father involvement* (pp. 63–90). Mahwah, NJ: Erlbaum.

Hood, J. (Ed.). (1993). *Men, work, and family.* Thousand Oaks, CA: Sage.

Hossain, Z. (2001). Division of household labor and family functioning in off-reservation Navajo Indian families. *Family Relations, 50,* 255–261.

Hossain, Z., & Roopnarine, J. L. (1993). Division of household labor and child care in dual-earner African-American families with infants. *Sex Roles, 29,* 571–583.

Hossain, Z., & Roopnarine, J. L. (1994). African-American fathers' involvement with infants: Relationship to their functioning style, support, education, and income. *Infant Behavior and Development, 17,* 175–184.

Hwang, C. P., Elden, G., & Frannson, A. (1984). *Employers' and co-workers' attitudes toward father taking parental leave* (Report 31). Sweden: University of Goteborg, Department of Psychology.

Hwang, C. P., & Lamb, M. E. (1997). Father involvement in Sweden: A longitudinal study of its stability and correlates. *International Journal of Behavioral Development, 21,* 621–632.

Ihinger-Tallman, M., Pasley, K., & Buehler, C. (1993). Developing a middle-range theory of father involvement postdivorce. *Journal of Family Issues, 14,* 550–571.

Ishii-Kuntz, M., & Coltrane, S. (1992). Predicting the sharing of household labor: Are parenting and housework distinct? *Sociological Perspectives, 35,* 629–647.

Jain, A., Belsky, J., & Crnic, K. (1996). Beyond fathering behaviors: Types of dads. *Journal of Family Psychology, 10,* 431–442.

Jump, T. L., & Haas, L. (1987). Fathers in transition: Dual-career fathers participating in child-care. In M. Kimmel (Ed.), *Changing men: New research on men and masculinity* (pp. 98–114). Beverly Hills, CA: Sage.

Juster, F. T. (1985). A note on recent changes in time use. In F. T. Juster & F. Stafford (Eds.), *Time, goods, and well-being* (pp. 313–332). Ann Arbor, MI: Institute for Social Research.

Juster, F. T., & Stafford, F. (Eds.). (1985). *Time, goods, and well-being.* Ann Arbor, MI: Institute for Social Research.

Kalmjin, M. (1999). Father involvement in childrearing and perceived stability of marriage. *Journal of Marriage and the Family, 61,* 409–421.

Kelley, M. L. (1997). The division of family work among low-income African Americans. *Journal of African American Men, 2,* 87–102.

Khaleque, A., & Rohner, R. P. (2002). Perceived parental acceptance-rejection and psychological adjustment: A meta-analysis of cross-cultural and intracultural studies. *Journal of Marriage and Family, 64,* 54–64.

Klinman, D. G. (1986). Fathers and the educational system. In M. E. Lamb (Ed.), *The father's role: Applied perspectives* (pp. 413–428). New York: Wiley.

Klinman, D. G., & Kohl, R. (1984). *Fatherhood U.S.A.* New York: Garland.

Koestner, R., Franz, C., & Weinberger, J. (1990). The family origins of empathic concern: A 26-year longitudinal study. *Journal of Personality and Social Psychology, 58,* 709–717.

Kurdeck, L. A. (1998). Prospective predictors of parenting satisfaction for fathers and mothers with young children. *Journal of Family Psychology, 12,* 56–65.

Lamb, M. E. (Ed.). (1976). *The role of the father in child development.* New York: Wiley.

Lamb, M. E. (Ed.). (1981). *The role of the father in child development* (2nd ed.). New York: Wiley.

Lamb, M. E. (Ed.). (1986). *The father's role: Applied perspectives.* New York: Wiley.

Lamb, M. E. (1987). Introduction: The emergent American father. In M. E. Lamb (Ed.), *The father's role: Cross-cultural perspectives* (pp. 3–25). Hillsdale, NJ: Erlbaum.

Lamb, M. E. (Ed.). (1997). *The role of the father in child development* (3rd ed.). New York: Wiley.

Lamb, M. E. (2000). The history of research on father involvement: An overview. *Marriage and Family Review, 29,* 23–42.

Lamb, M. E., Chuang, S. S., & Cabrera, N. (2003). Promoting child adjustment by fostering positive paternal involvement. In R. M. Lerner, F. Jacobs, & D. Wertlieb (Eds.), *Handbook of applied developmental science* (Vol. 1, pp. 211–232). Thousand Oaks, CA: Sage.

Lamb, M. E., Chuang, S. S., & Hwang, C. P. (in press). Internal reliability, temporal stability, and correlates of individual differences in paternal involvement: A 15-year longitudinal study in Sweden. In R. Day & M. E. Lamb (Eds.), *Conceptualizing and measuring paternal involvement.* Mahwah, NJ: Erlbaum.

Lamb, M. E., Frodi, A. M., Hwang, C. P., & Frodi, M. (1982). Varying degrees of paternal involvement in infant care: Attitudinal and behavioral correlates. In M. E. Lamb (Ed.), *Non-traditional families: Parenting and child development* (pp. 117–138). Hillsdale, NJ: Erlbaum.

Lamb, M. E., Pleck, J. H., Charnov, E. L., & Levine, J. A. (1985). Paternal behavior in humans. *American Zoologist, 25,* 883–894.

Lamb, M. E., Pleck, J. H., Charnov, E. L., & Levine, J. A. (1987). A biosocial perspective on paternal behavior and involvement. In J. B. Lancaster, J. Altman, & A. Rossi (Eds.), *Parenting across the lifespan: Biosocial perspectives* (pp. 11–42). New York: Academic Press.

Lamborn, S. D., Mounts, N. S., Steinberg, L., & Dornbusch, S. M. (1991). Patterns of competence and adjustment among adolescents from authoritative, authoritarian, indulgent, and neglectful families. *Child Development, 62,* 1049–1065.

LaRossa, R. (1988). Fatherhood and social change. *Family Relations, 37,* 451–457.

Larson, R. W. (1993). Finding time for fatherhood: The emotional ecology of adolescent-father interactions. *New Directions for Child Development, 62,* 7–25.

Lein, L. (1979). Male participation in home life: Impact of social supports and breadwinner responsibility on the allocation of tasks. *Family Coordinator, 28,* 489–495.

Leslie, L. A., Anderson, E. A., & Branson, M. P. (1991). Responsibility for children: The role of gender and employment. *Journal of Family Issues, 12,* 197–210.

Levant, R. F. (1988). Education for fatherhood. In P. Bronstein & C. P. Cowan (Eds.), *Fatherhood today* (pp. 253–275). New York: Wiley.

Levant, R. F., & Doyle, G. F. (1983). An evaluation of a parent education program for fathers of school-aged children. *Family Relations, 32,* 29.

Levant, R. F., Slattery, S. C., & Loiselle, J. E. (1987). Fathers' involvement in housework and child care with school-aged daughters. *Family Relations, 36,* 152–157.

Levine, J. A. (1976). *Who will raise the children? New options for fathers (and mothers).* New York: Bantam Books.

Levine, J. A., Harlan, S., Seligson, M., Pleck, J. H., & Lein, L. (1981). *Child care and equal opportunity for women.* Washington, DC: U.S. Commission on Civil Rights.

Levy-Shiff, R., & Israelashvili, R. (1988). Antecedents of fathering: Some further exploration. *Developmental Psychology, 24,* 434–440.

Lundskow, G. N. (2002). *Awakening to an uncertain future: A case study of the Promise Keepers.* New York: Peter Lang.

MacDermid, S. M., Franz, C. E., & DeReus, L. A. (1998). Generativity: At the crossroads of social roles and personality. In D. P. McAdams & E. de St. Aubin (Eds.), *Generativity and adult development: How and why we care for the next generation* (pp. 181–226). Washington, DC: American Psychological Association.

MacDermid, S. M., Heilbrun, G., & DeHaan, L. G. (1997). The generativity of employed mothers in multiple roles: 1979 and 1991. In M. E. Lachman & J. B. James (Eds.), *Multiple paths of midlife development* (pp. 207–240). Chicago: University of Chicago.

Marsiglio, W. (1991). Paternal engagement activities with minor children. *Journal of Marriage and the Family, 53,* 973–986.

Marsiglio, W., Amato, P., Day, R. D., & Lamb, M. E. (2000). Scholarship on fatherhood in the 1990s and beyond. *Journal of Marriage and the Family, 62,* 1173–1191.

Marsiglio, W., Day, R. D., & Lamb, M. E. (2000). Exploring fatherhood diversity: Implications for conceptualizing father involvement. *Marriage and Family Review, 29,* 269–293.

Marsiglio, W., & Pleck, J. H. (in press). Fatherhood and masculinities. In R. W. Connell, J. Hearn, & M. Kimmel (Eds.), *The handbook of studies of men and masculinities.* Thousand Oaks, CA: Sage.

Masciadrelli, B. P. (2001). *Academic stress and father involvement among university student fathers.* Unpublished master's thesis, Department of Human Development and Family Studies, University of Maine, Orono.

Masciadrelli, B. P., Pleck, J. H., & Stueve, J. L. (2002, November). *Fathering and role model influences.* Paper presented to the National Council on Family Relations, Houston, TX.

Maurer, T. W. (2003). *Parental caregiving and breadwinning behaviors: Multiple approaches for understanding predictors of mothers' and fathers' involvement.* Unpublished doctoral dissertation, Department of Human and Community Development, University of Illinois at Urbana-Champaign.

Maurer, T. W., Pleck, J. H., & Rane, T. R. (2001). Parental identity and reflected-appraisals: Measurement and gender dynamics. *Journal of Marriage and Family, 63,* 309–321.

Maurer, T. W., Pleck, J. H., & Rane, T. R. (2003). Methodological considerations in measuring paternal identity. *Fathering, 1,* 117–130.

McBride, B. A. (1990). The effects of a parent education/play group program on father involvement on child rearing. *Family Relations, 39,* 250–256.

McBride, B. A., & Mills, G. (1993). A comparison of mother and father involvement with their preschool age children. *Early Childhood Research Quarterly, 8,* 457–477.

McBride, B. A., & Rane, T. R. (1997). Role identity, role investments, and paternal involvement: Implications for parenting programs for men. *Early Childhood Research Quarterly, 12,* 173–197.

McBride, B. A., & Rane, T. R. (1998). Parenting alliance as a predictor of father involvement: An exploratory study. *Family Relations, 47,* 229–236.

McBride, B. A., Rane, T. R., Schoppe, S. J., & Ho, M. (in press). Multiple determinants of father involvement: An exploratory analysis using the PSID-CDS data set. In R. Day & M. E. Lamb (Eds.), *Conceptualizing and measuring paternal involvement.* Mahwah, NJ: Erlbaum.

McBride, B. A., Schoppe, S. J., & Rane, T. R. (2002). Child characteristics, parenting stress, and parental involvement: Fathers versus mothers. *Journal of Marriage and the Family, 64,* 998–1011.

McHale, S. M., & Huston, T. L. (1984). Men and women as parents: Sex role orientations, employment, and parental roles with infants. *Child Development, 55,* 1349–1361.

McKeering, H., & Pakenham, K. I. (2000). Gender and generativity issues in parenting: Do fathers benefit more than mothers from involvement in child care activities? *Sex Roles, 43,* 459–480.

McLoyd, V. C. (1989). Socialization and development in a changing economy: The effects of paternal job and income loss on children. *American Psychologist, 44,* 293–302.

Milkie, M. A., Bianchi, S. Z., Mattingly, M. J., & Robinson, J. P. (2002). Gendered division of child-rearing: Ideals, realities, and the relationship to parental well-being. *Sex Roles, 47,* 21–38.

Minton, C., & Pasley, K. (1996). Fathers' parenting role identity and father involvement: A comparison of nondivorced and divorced, nonresident fathers. *Journal of Family Issues, 17,* 26–45.

Moynihan, D. P. (1965). *The Negro family and the case for national action.* Washington, DC: U.S. Government Printing Office.

Munch, A., McPherson, J. M., & Smith-Lovin, L. (1997). Gender, children, and social contact: The effects of childrearing for men and women. *American Sociological Review, 62,* 509–520.

NICHD Early Child Care Research Network. (1997). Child care in the first year of life. *Merrill-Palmer Quarterly, 43,* 340–360.

NICHD Early Child Care Research Network. (2000). Factors associated with fathers' caregiving activities and sensitivity with young children. *Journal of Family Psychology, 14,* 200–219.

Ninio, A., & Rinott, N. (1988). Fathers' involvement in the care of their infants and their attributions of cognitive competence to infants. *Child Development, 59,* 652–663.

Nugent, J. K. (1991). Cultural and psychological influences on the father's role in infant development. *Journal of Marriage and the Family, 53,* 475–485.

O'Brien, M., & Shemlit, I. (2003). *Fathers in the workplace: Literature review and analysis.* Manchester, England: Equal Opportunities Commission.

O'Connell, M. (1993). *Where's papa? Fathers' role in child care.* Washington, DC: Population Reference Bureau.

O'Neil, R., & Greenberger, E. (1994). Patterns of commitment to work and parenting: Implications for role strain. *Journal of Marriage and the Family, 56,* 101–112.

Palkovitz, R. (1984). Parental attitudes and fathers' interactions with their 5-month-old infants. *Developmental Psychology, 20,* 1054–1060.

Palkovitz, R. (1985). Fathers' birth attendance, early contact, and extended contact with their newborns: A critical review. *Child Development, 56,* 392–406.

Palkovitz, R. (1997). Reconstructing "involvement": Expanding conceptualizations of men's caring in contemporary families. In A. J. Hawkins & D. C. Dollahite (Eds.), *Generative fathering: Beyond deficit perspectives* (pp. 200–216). Thousand Oaks, CA: Sage.

Palkovitz, R. (2002a). *Involved fathering and men's adult development.* Mahwah, NJ: Erlbaum.

Palkovitz, R. (2002b). Involved fathering and child development: Advancing our understanding of good fathering. In C. S. Tamis-LeMonda & N. Cabrera (Eds.), *Handbook of father involvement: Multidisciplinary perspectives* (pp. 119–140). Mahwah, NJ: Erlbaum.

Parke, R. D. (2002). Fathers and families. In M. H. Bornstein (Ed.), *Handbook of parenting* (2nd ed., Vol. 3, pp. 27–73). Mahwah, NJ: Erlbaum.

Parke, R. D., Coltrane, S., Fabricius, W., Powers, J., & Adams, M. (in press). Measurement of father involvement in Mexican-American families. In R. Day & M. E. Lamb (Eds.), *Conceptualizing and measuring paternal involvement.* Mahwah, NJ: Erlbaum.

Pasley, K., Futris, T. G., & Skinner, M. L. (2002). Effects of commitment and psychological centrality on fathering. *Journal of Marriage and Family, 64,* 130–138.

Peterson, B. E., & Klohnen, E. C. (1995). Realization of generativity in two samples of women at midlife. *Psychology and Aging, 10,* 20–29.

Peterson, R. R., & Gerson, K. (1992). Determinants of responsibility for child care arrangements among dual-earner couples. *Journal of Marriage and the Family, 54,* 527–536.

Pleck, J. H. (1981). *The myth of masculinity.* Cambridge, MA: MIT Press.

Pleck, J. H. (1983). Husbands' paid work and family roles: Current research issues. In H. Lopata & J. Pleck (Eds.), *Research in the interweave of social roles: Vol. 3. Families and jobs* (pp. 231–333). Greenwich, CT: JAI Press.

Pleck, J. H. (1985). *Working wives, working husbands.* Beverly Hills, CA: Sage.

Pleck, J. H. (1992). Families and work: Small changes with big implications. *Qualitative Sociology, 15,* 427–432.

Pleck, J. H. (1993). Are "family-supportive" employer policies relevant to men? In J. C. Hood (Ed.), *Men, work, and family* (pp. 217–237). Newbury Park, CA: Sage.

Pleck, J. H. (1997). Paternal involvement: Levels, sources, and consequences. In M. E. Lamb (Ed.), *The role of the father in child development* (pp. 66–103). New York: Wiley.

Pleck, J. H., Lamb, M. E., & Levine, J. A. (1985). Epilogue: Facilitating future change in men's family roles. In R. A. Lewis, & M. Sussman (Eds.), *Men's changing roles in the family* (pp. 11–16). New York: Haworth Press.

Pleck, J. H., Sonenstein, F. L., & Ku, L. C. (1994a). Problem behaviors and masculinity ideology in adolescent males. In R. Ketterlinus & M. E. Lamb, (Eds.), *Adolescent problem behaviors* (pp. 165–186). Hillsdale, NJ: Erlbaum.

Pleck, J. H., Sonenstein, F. L., & Ku, L. C. (1994b). Attitudes toward male roles among adolescent males: A discriminant validity analysis. *Sex Roles, 30,* 481–501.

Pleck, J. H., & Stueve, J. (1997, November). *Paternal engagement: Its caretaking and development-promoting components in a diverse national sample of young adult residential fathers.* Presented at the National Council on Family Relations, Crystal City, VA.

Pleck, J. H., & Stueve, J. L. (2001). Time and paternal involvement. In K. Daly (Ed.), *Minding the time in family experience: Emerging perspectives and issues* (pp. 205–226). Oxford, England: Elsevier Science.

Pleck, J. H., & Stueve, J. L. (2003). Assessing paternal identity through narratives: The importance of parental identity "conjointness." In R. Day & M. E. Lamb (Eds.), *Conceptualizing and measuring paternal involvement* (pp. 83–107). Mahwah, NJ: Erlbaum.

Plomin, R. (1989). Environment and genes: Determinants of behavior. *American Psychologist, 44,* 105–111.

Polatnick, M. (1973–1974). Why men don't rear children: A power analysis. *Berkeley Journal of Sociology, 18,* 45–86.

Presser, H. B. (1989). Can we make time for children? The economy, work schedules, and child care. *Demography, 26,* 523–543.

Radin, N. (1994). Primary-caregiving fathers in intact families. In A. E. Gottfried & A. W. Gottfried (Eds.), *Redefining families: Implications for children's development* (pp. 55–97). New York: Plenum Press.

Rane, T. R., & McBride, B. A. (2000). Identity theory as a guide to understanding fathers' involvement with their children. *Journal of Family Issues, 21,* 347–366.

Reid, P. T., Tata, C. S., & Berman, P. W. (1989). Preschool children's self-presentations in situations with infants: Effects of sex and race. *Child Development, 60,* 710–714.

Riley, D. (1990). Network influence on father involvement in childrearing. In M. Cochran, M. Larner, D. Riley, L. Gunnarsson, & C. R. Henderson Jr. (Eds.), *Extending families: The social networks of parents and their children* (pp. 131–153). Cambridge, England: Cambridge University Press.

Robinson, J. P. (1977a). *How Americans used time in 1965.* Ann Arbor, MI: Institute for Social Research.

Robinson, J. P. (1977b). *How Americans use time: A social-psychological analysis.* New York: Praeger.

Roggman, L. A., & Peery, J. C. (1998). Caregiving, emotional involvement, and parent-infant play. *Early Child Development and Care, 34,* 191–199.

Rohner, R. P., & Veneziano, R. A. (2001). The importance of father love: History and contemporary evidence. *Review of General Psychology,, 5,* 382–405.

Roopnarine, J. L., & Ahmeduzzaman, M. (1993). Puerto Rican fathers' involvement with their preschool-age children. *Hispanic Journal of Behavioral Sciences,* 96–107.

Rosenwasser, S. M., & Patterson, W. (1984–1985). Nontraditional male: Men with primary child care/household responsibilities. *Psychology and Human Development, 1,* 101–111.

Ross, C. E., & Van Willigen, M. (1996). Gender, parenthood, and anger. *Journal of Marriage and the Family, 58,* 572–584.

Russell, A., & Russell, G. (1989). Warmth in mother-child and father-child relationships in middle childhood. *British Journal of Developmental Psychology, 7,* 279–235.

Russell, G. (1983). *The changing role of fathers.* St. Lucia, Queensland: University of Queensland Press.

Russell, G. (1986). Primary caretakers and role sharing fathers. In M. E. Lamb (Ed.), *The father's role: Applied perspectives* (pp. 29–60). New York: Wiley.

Rustia, J. G., & Abbott, D. (1993). Father involvement in infant care: Two longitudinal studies. *International Journal of Nursing Studies, 30,* 467–476.

Sagi, A. (1982). Antecedents and consequences of various degrees of paternal involvement in child rearing: The Israeli project. In M. E. Lamb (Ed.), *Nontraditional families: Parenting and child development* (pp. 205–222). Hillsdale, NJ: Erlbaum.

Sandberg, J. F., & Hofferth, S. L. (2001). Changes in children's time with parents: United States, 1981–1997. *Demography, 38,* 423–436.

Sanderson, S., & Sanders-Thompson, V. L. T. (2002). Factors associated with perceived paternal involvement in childrearing. *Sex Roles, 46,* 99–111.

Silverstein, L. B., & Auerbach, C. F. (1999). Deconstructing the essential father. *American Psychologist, 54,* 397–407.

Silverstein, L. B., Auerbach, C. F., Grieco, L., & Dunkel, F. (1999). Do Promise Keepers dream of feminist sheep? *Sex Roles, 40,* 665–688.

Silverstein, L. B., Auerbach, C. F., & Levant, R. F. (2002). Contemporary fathers reconstructing masculinity: Clinical implications of gender role strain. *Professional Psychology: Research and Practice, 33,* 361–369.

Skow, J. (1989, August 7). The myth of male housework. *Time,* 62.

Smith, H. L., & Morgan, S. P. (1994). Children's closeness to father as reported by mothers, sons and daughters: Evaluating subjective assessments with the Rasch model. *Journal of Family Issues, 15,* 3–29.

Snarey, J. (1993). *How fathers care for the next generation: A four-decade study.* Cambridge, MA: Harvard University Press.

Spence, J. T., Helmreich, R. L., & Holanan, C. T. (1979). Negative and positive components of psychological masculinity and femininity and their relationships to self-reports of neurotic and acting out behaviors. *Journal of Personality and Social Psychology, 37,* 1673–1682.

Stewart, A. J., Ostrove, J. M., & Helson, R. (2001). Middle aging women: Patterns of personality change from the 30s to the 50s. *Journal of Adult Development, 8,* 23–37.

Strauss, R., & Goldberg, W. A. (1999). Self and possible selves during the transition to fatherhood. *Journal of Family Psychology, 13,* 244–259.

Stueve, J. L., & Pleck, J. H. (2001). "Parenting voices": Solo parent identity and co-parent identities in married parents' narratives of meaningful parenting experiences. *Journal of Social and Personal Relationships, 18,* 691–708.

Stueve, J. L., & Pleck, J. H. (2003). Fathers' narratives of arranging and planning: Implications for understanding paternal responsibility. *Fathering, 1,* 51–70.

Tamis-LeMonda, C. S., & Cabrera, N. (Eds.). (2002). *Handbook of father involvement: Multidisciplinary perspectives.* Mahwah, NJ: Erlbaum.

Timmer, S. G., Eccles, J., & O'Brien, K. (1985). How children use time. In F. T. Juster & F. P. Stafford (Eds.), *Time, goods, and well-being* (pp. 353–382). Ann Arbor, MI: Institute for Social Research.

Toth, J. F., & Xu, X. (1999). Ethnic and cultural diversity in fathers' involvement: A racial/ethnic comparison of African American, Hispanic, and White fathers. *Youth and Society, 31,* 76–99.

Tulananda, O., Young, D. M., & Roopnarine, J. L. (1994). Thai and American fathers' involvement with preschool-age children. *Early Child Development and Care, 97,* 123–133.

Vaillant, G. E. (1977). *Adaptation to life.* Boston: Little, Brown.

Volling, B. L., & Belsky, J. (1991). Multiple determinants of father involvement during infancy in dual-earner and single-earner families. *Journal of Marriage and the Family, 53,* 461–474.

Walzer, S. (1996). Thinking about the baby: Gender and divisions of infant care. *Social Problems, 43,* 219–234.

Wenk, D., Hardesty, C. L., Morgan, C. S., & Blair, S. L. (1994). The influence of parental involvement on the well-being of sons and daughters. *Journal of Marriage and the Family, 56,* 229–234.

Wilcox, W. B. (2002). Religion, convention, and paternal involvement. *Journal of Marriage and Family, 64,* 780–792.

Williams, E., Radin, N., & Allegro, T. (1992). Sex-role attitudes of adolescents raised primarily by their fathers. *Merrill-Palmer Quarterly, 38,* 457–476.

Wisensale, S. K. (2001). *Family leave policy: The political economy of work and family in America.* New York: M. E. Sharpe.

Xu, X., Hudspeth, C. D., & Estes, S. (1997). The effects of husbands' involvement in child rearing activities and participation in household labor on marital quality: A racial comparison. *Journal of Gender, Culture, and Health, 2,* 187–209.

Yeung, W. J., Duncan, G. J., & Hill, M. S. (2000). Putting fathers back in the picture: Parental activities and children's adult outcomes. *Marriage and Family Review, 29,* 97–113.

Yeung, W. J., Sandberg, J. F., Davis-Kean, P. E., & Hofferth, S. L. (2001). Children's time with fathers in intact families. *Journal of Marriage and Family, 63,* 136–154.

Zick, C. D., & Bryant, W. K. (1996). A new look at parents' time spent in child care: Primary and secondary time use. *Social Science Research, 25,* 260–280.

Zimmerman, M. A., Salem, D. A., & Notaro, P. C. (2000). Make room for daddy: II. The positive effects of fathers' role in adolescent development. In R. D. Taylor & M. C. Wang (Eds.), *Resilience across contexts: Family, work, culture, and community* (pp. 233–253). Mahwah, NJ: Erlbaum.

Zuzanek, J. (2000). *The effects of time use and time pressure on child-parent relationships.* Waterloo, Ontario: Otium.

CHAPTER 10

The Development and Significance of Father-Child Relationships in Two-Parent Families

MICHAEL E. LAMB and CHARLIE LEWIS

A LL ACCOUNTS OF socialization and personality development, following Freud's lead, have emphasized the crucial importance of parent-child relationships. Psychoanalytic theory was noteworthy for its emphases on the crucial formative role of early experiences; on the complex ways in which children's experiences, memories, and fantasies have enduring influences on their development; and, especially in Freud's earliest writing, on the crucial importance of father-child relationships. All of these beliefs have affected subsequent research on child development in general and on parent-child relationships in particular.

In this chapter we review current research on the nature and importance of father-child relationships. We begin by describing the factors that influence father-child interactions and relationships, noting that men's interactions with their children need to be understood within a network of family relationships. Studies of infants and young children have predominated, and these thus continue to dominate our examination, in the second section, of studies concerned with the characteristics of father-child relationships, including the amount of time that fathers spend with their children and differences between maternal and paternal styles of interaction. In the third section we examine fathers' responses to parenthood and to their infants, the processes by which infants become attached to their parents, and differences in the nature and impact of mother- and father-child relationships. Changes in the nature of relationships between children and their parents in childhood and adolescence are discussed in the final substantive section. Here, we describe the mechanisms by which parent-child relationships are gradually transformed over this period and the roles that fathers play in the lives and socialization of their adolescent sons and daughters. Throughout the chapter we discuss both normative issues and the factors that distinguish individual parent-child relationships from one another. We focus particularly on development in two-parent families because fathers in other family constellations are discussed in this volume by Amato and Sobolewski and by McLanahan and Carlson.

FATHERING WITHIN FAMILIES

MOTHERS, FATHERS, AND PARENT-CHILD RELATIONSHIPS

The emergence of fatherhood research in the 1970s in part reflected increased attention to the complexity of family relationships and the patterns of influence within the family system (Lamb, 1976d; Lewis & Weinraub, 1976; Pedersen, 1980). Over the past 30 years, researchers have shown that fathers not only influence children by interacting with them but also affect maternal behavior, just as mothers influence paternal behavior and involvement (Cummings & O'Reilly, 1997; Lamb, 1997) and children influence their parents (Bell, 1968). Indeed, the quality of marital relationships appears to be a good marker of the way that parents interact with their children from an early age. Fathers are consistently more involved in interaction with their infants when they are highly engaged in interaction with their partners (Belsky, Gilstrap, & Rovine, 1984) and when both they and their partners have supportive attitudes regarding paternal involvement (Beitel & Parke, 1998). For example, Grych and Clark (1999) reported that in the year after the birth of the first child, marital quality predicted the amount of appropriate stimulation that fathers gave their 4- and 12-month-olds, whereas Lundy (2002) reported that marital dissatisfaction adversely affected paternal synchrony and thus the security of infant-father attachment. Likewise, Goldberg and Easterbrooks (1984) found that high marital quality was associated with both more sensitive maternal and paternal behavior as well as higher levels of functioning on the part of the toddlers. By contrast, infants whose fathers abused alcohol tended to have insecure attachments to their mothers (Das Eiden & Leonard, 1996). Such patterns are not evident only in Anglo-American families. For example, Durrett, Otaki, and Richards (1984) found that the Japanese mothers of securely attached infants reported greater levels of spousal support than did the mothers of insecurely attached infants. (We discuss infant-parent attachments in the next section.)

Harmony between the parents thus seems to be a key predictor of father-child relationships. This pattern seems to hold even when the father's own psychological makeup is taken into account. After controlling for individual differences in the fathers' psychological adjustment, for example, Cox, Owen, Lewis, and Henderson (1989) reported that American men in close confiding marriages had more positive attitudes toward their 3-month-old infants and toward their roles as parents than did fathers in less successful marriages, whereas mothers in close confiding marriages were warmer and more sensitive. Similar results were obtained in Israel by Levy-Shiff and Israelashvili (1988). Meanwhile, Heinicke and Guthrie (1992) reported that couples who were well adapted to one another provided better care than did parents whose spousal adaptation was poor or declining, and similar findings were reported by researchers in a variety of cultures (Durrett, Richards, Otaki, Pennebaker, & Nyquist, 1986; Engfer, 1988; Jouriles, Pfiffner, & O'Leary, 1988; Meyer, 1988). It is interesting that both Belsky, Gilstrap, et al. (1984) and Lamb and Elster (1985) reported that American fathers' interactions with their infants were influenced by the ongoing quality of interaction with their partners much more profoundly than mothers' behavior was. The reason may be that paternal behavior and engagement are somewhat discretionary or at the behest of mothers (Allen & Hawkins, 1999), whereas maternal behavior is driven by clearer conventions and role definitions. In any event, marital conflict consistently has harmful effects on socioemotional development and child adjustment (Hetherington & Stanley-Hagen, 1999; Kelly, 2000), presumably because it adversely affects the parents' interactions with their children.

Although the connection between spousal and parent-child relationships is clear, it must be understood within a network of factors outside the home. For a start, parental employment factors influence the amount of paternal care and the closeness of father-child relationships, although sometimes in unexpected ways. For example, Crouter, Perry-Jenkins, Huston, and McHale (1987) reported that, at least in dual-earner families, increased paternal involvement in child care was often at the expense of marital happiness. In addition, fathers in dual-earner families sometimes appear less sensitive toward their 4-month-old sons, who are thus more likely to develop insecure attachments to their fathers than to their mothers (Braungart-Rieker, Courtney, & Garwood, 1999). Similarly, Grych and Clark (1999) found that fathers with wives who were unemployed or worked part-time were more sensitive when they were involved, whereas fathers whose wives were employed full-time behaved more negatively when they were more highly involved. Beyond infancy, the relationships among maternal employment, paternal involvement, and positive father-child relationships became more positive, however. Thus, maternal employment is associated with increased paternal involvement in the preschool (Berry & Rao, 1997) and school-age (Crouter, Helms-Erikson, Updegraff, & McHale, 1999) periods of development. These involved fathers also knew more about their children's daily experiences. Such findings underscore the need to view the relationships with both parents in the context of other important characteristics and experiences of the families.

FATHER-CHILD INTERACTION IN EARLY CHILDHOOD

THE EXTENT OF FATHER-CHILD INTERACTION

Many efforts have been made to determine how much time fathers spend with their young children, and this literature is reviewed in great detail by Pleck and Masciadrelli in this volume. Like other reviewers, Pleck and Masciadrelli note the considerable variability among the reported estimates and the large individual differences, both no doubt attributable to socioeconomic, cultural, and demographic differences among the populations studied and to the opportunistic sampling procedures that characterize most of this research. Maternal employment status is one possible source of variation. Men who worked fewer hours and whose wives or partners worked more hours were reliably more involved with their children in the study conducted by the NICHD Early Childcare Research Network (2000), but the association in dual-earner families between the number of hours worked and the amount of parent-child contact was not direct or straightforward in that study. Gottfried, Gottfried, and Bathurst (1988) and Crouter et al. (1987) likewise reported that fathers in dual-earner families were more involved in child care than were fathers in single-earner families, although the mothers' employment status did not affect paternal involvement in leisure activities and fathers' sex-role attitudes did not predict the types of paternal involvement (McHale & Huston, 1984).

The extent of paternal involvement may differ also depending on the amount of encouragement and support that fathers receive: Lind (1974), for example, found that Swedish fathers who were taught how to care for their newborns and were encouraged to do so were more involved with their infants three months later, while the greater burdens imposed on families by the birth of preterm babies appeared to facilitate paternal involvement (Parke & Beitel, 1986). Other paternal characteristics surely affect involvement, as well: Levy-Shiff and Israelashvili (1988) found that Israeli fathers who were rated prenatally as warm and interested played more with their 9-month-olds, whereas prenatal perceptiveness, sensitivity, and a tolerance for external intrusions were correlated with greater involvement in caretaking. McHale and Huston (1984) reported that fathers who perceived themselves as more skillful were more involved later, but knowledge affected involvement differently among Mormon and non-Mormon fathers in another study, leaving uncertainty about the association between involvement and knowledge of child development (Roggman, Benson, & Boyce, 1999). Short-term interventions for new fathers do not appear to influence paternal behavior or involvement (Belsky, 1985; Pannabecker, Emde, & Austin, 1982; Parke & Beitel, 1986), although Myers (1982) reported that fathers became more knowledgeable and were more involved when they were shown how to conduct standardized assessments of their newborns, and Israeli fathers who were more involved with their 9-month-olds perceived them as more competent (Ninio & Rinott, 1988). Apparently, perceptions of infant competence and paternal involvement reinforce one another. Grossmann and Volkmer (1984) reported that the predelivery desire of German fathers to be present during delivery had a greater impact on their reported involvement than did actual presence during childbirth. This outcome was not surprising in light of Palkovitz's (1985) conclusion that birth attendance, in and of itself, does not appear to have consistent, clear, or robust effects on paternal involvement or behavior. On the other hand, birth attendance followed by extensive postpartum father-infant interaction in the hospital may stimulate greater paternal involvement and engagement (Keller, Hildebrandt, & Richards, 1985).

The child's gender also affects the extent to which fathers interact with their infants. Many researchers have shown that fathers interact preferentially with their sons from shortly after birth (Cox et al., 1989; Gewirtz & Gewirtz, 1968; Kotelchuck, 1976; Lamb, 1977a, 1977b; NICHD Early Childhood Research Network, 2000; Parke & Sawin, 1980; Rendina & Dickerscheid, 1976; Weinraub & Frankel, 1977; West & Konner, 1976; Woollett, White, & Lyon, 1982). Beyond infancy, however, this effect appears hard to detect and relatively small (Lytton & Romney, 1991).

Whatever factors influence fathers' tendencies to be more or less involved in interactions with their children, there appears to be substantial stability, at least during the period from birth through the first 30 months (Hwang & Lamb, 1997; Lamb et al., 1988; Nugent, 1987; Pruett & Litzenburger, 1992). It is not surprising that work demands played an important role in determining how involved the Swedish fathers in Lamb et al.'s (1988) study were, just as they did in a later study conducted in the United States (Hyde, Essex, & Horton, 1993). According to Lamb, Chuang, and Hwang (in press), the amount of time that the Swedish fathers spent interacting with their children grew less as the children grew older, although the amount of time that they were accessible (both awake and in the home) grew as the children moved from infancy into childhood and adolescence. Stability over the 15-year period was quite low, however.

CHARACTERISTICS OF MOTHER- AND FATHER-CHILD INTERACTION

Even in the first trimester of their children's lives, fathers and mothers appear to engage in different types of interactions with their infants. When videotaped in face-to-face interaction with their 2- to 25-week-old infants, for example, fathers tended to provide staccato bursts of both physical and social stimulation, whereas mothers tended to be more rhythmic and containing (Yogman, 1981). Mothers addressed their babies with soft, repetitive, imitative sounds, whereas fathers touched their infants with rhythmic pats. During visits to hospitalized premature infants, mothers were responsive to social cues, fathers to gross motor cues (Marton & Minde, 1980), and although Israeli mothers visited and interacted with hospitalized preterm infants more than fathers did (Levy-Shiff, Sharir, & Mogilner, 1989), fathers were consistently more likely to stimulate and play with their infants, but less likely to engage in caretaking.

When observed with infants and toddlers, American fathers tend to engage in more physically stimulating and unpredictable play than mothers do (Clarke-Stewart, 1978; Crawley & Sherrod, 1984; Dickson, Walker, & Fogel, 1997; Lamb, 1977c; Power & Parke, 1979; Teti, Bond, & Gibbs, 1988), although rough physical play becomes less prominent as children grow older (Crawley & Sherrod, 1984). Because these types of play elicit more positive responses from infants, young children often prefer to play with their fathers when they have the choice (Clarke-Stewart, 1978; Lamb, 1977c). Mothers are more likely to hold their 7- to 13-month-old infants in the course of caretaking, whereas fathers are more likely to do so while playing or in response to the infants' requests to be held (Belsky, 1979; Lamb, 1976b, 1977c). It is thus not surprising that infants respond more positively to being held by their fathers than by their mothers (Lamb, 1976b, 1977c). On the other hand, Frascarolo-Moutinot (1994) and Labrell (1994) reported that French and Swiss fathers were also more intrusive than mothers were, and all researchers agree that most of the differences between mothers and fathers are not large. Both parents encourage visual exploration, object manipulation, and attention to relations and effects (Power, 1985; Teti et al., 1988).

Fathers and mothers do not simply play differently; play is often an especially salient component of father-infant relationships. According to Kotelchuck's (1976) informants, mothers spent an average of 85 minutes per day feeding their 6- to 21-month-olds, 55 minutes per day cleaning them, and 140 minutes playing with them. The comparable figures for fathers were 15, 9, and 72 minutes. According to parental diaries (Yarrow et al., 1984), similarly, the average father spent 6 and 7.3 hours per week playing with his 6- and 12-month-old, respectively (43% and 44% of the time spent alone with the infant) compared with 17.5 and 16.4 hours by the average mother (16% and 19%, respectively, of the time she spent alone with the infant). Clarke-Stewart (1978) and Rendina and Dickerscheid (1976) also suggested that fathers were consistently notable for their involvement in play and their lack of involvement in caretaking.

It is not only affluent Euro-American fathers who specialize in play: Middle-income African American (Hossain, Field, Pickens, Malphurs, & Del Valle, 1997; Hossain & Roopnarine, 1994) and Hispanic American (Hossain et al., 1997) fathers were also more likely to play with their infants than to feed or clean them, despite their claiming (like many Euro-American fathers) that parents should share child-care responsibilities (Hyde & Texidor, 1988). English fathers are also more likely than mothers to play with rather than care for both normal and handicapped infants and toddlers (McConachie, 1989), and similar differences are evident in India, regardless of whether mothers are employed (Roopnarine, Talukder, Jain, Joshi, & Srivastav, 1992), as well as in France, Switzerland, and Italy (Best, House, Barnard, & Spicker, 1994; Frascarolo-Moutinot, 1994; Labrell, 1996). By contrast, Taiwanese fathers reported that they rarely played with their children (Sun & Roopnarine, 1996), and fathers on Israeli kibbutzim did not play with their 8- and 16-month-olds more than mothers did, although the mothers were much more actively involved in caretaking and other forms of interaction than the fathers were (Sagi, Lamb, Shoham, Dvir, & Lewkowicz, 1985). Likewise, German (Best et al., 1994), Swedish (Frodi, Lamb, Hwang, & Frodi, 1983; Lamb, Frodi, Hwang, & Frodi, 1982, 1983), and Aka (hunter-gatherer; Hewlett, 1987) fathers are not notably more playful than mothers. In an interesting article, Zaouche-Gaudron, Ricaud, and Beaumatin (1998) argued that French fathers who differentiated between maternal and paternal roles tended to have a more positive impact on their children's development than did those whose roles were less distinctive.

Within industrial cultures, patterns of parental behavior may differ when both parents work full-time during the day (Pedersen, Cain, Zaslow, & Anderson, 1982). Working mothers stimulated their infants more than nonworking mothers did, and they were far more active than their husbands were. As expected, fathers with nonworking wives played with their infants more than mothers did, but this pattern was reversed in families with working mothers. Likewise, Field, Vega-Lahr, Goldstein, and Scafidi (1987) reported that employed mothers were much more interactive in face-to-face interactions with their infants than employed fathers were. Maternal employment does not necessarily change the nature of father-child relationships, however. The relationship between employment and the quality of child-father interaction was moderated by the fathers' attitudes and ages in the large NICHD Early Child Care Study (2000), with younger men and those committed to equal parenting more sensitive in their play styles. Such belief systems are very important. In New Delhi, for example, a strong traditional culture is maintained, and fathers in dual-earner families are indistinguishable from men in single-earner families (Suppal & Roopnarine, 1999).

What happens when fathers are highly involved in infant care? Field (1978) reported that primary caretaking fathers and mothers behaved more similarly than primary and secondary caretaking fathers, although fathers engaged in more playful and noncontaining interactions than mothers did regardless of their involvement in child care. Pruett (1985; Pruett & Litzenburger, 1992) studied only fathers who were highly involved in infant care but repeatedly remarked on the distinctive playfulness of these fathers. Frascarolo-Moutinot (1994) reported no differences in playfulness between "new fathers" and "traditional" fathers, although the wives of the new fathers were less intrusive and controlling than were the wives of traditional fathers. Lamb and his colleagues (Lamb, Frodi, Frodi, & Hwang, 1982; Lamb, Frodi, Hwang, Frodi, & Steinberg, 1982a, 1982b) reported that mothers were more likely than fathers to vocalize, display affection toward, touch, tend to, and hold their infants whether or not their partners took a month or more of paternity leave.

Overall, these findings suggest that the distinctive maternal and paternal styles are quite robust and are still evident when fathers are highly involved in child care. Fathers tend to adopt a more playful interaction style than mothers do, especially in cultures or subcultures with clear divisions of labor. These patterns are not ubiquitous, however, as noted earlier, and some cultures (e.g., Northern Thailand) have a clear division of labor in which fathers and mothers do not differ with respect to playfulness or sensitivity (Tulananda & Roopnarine, 2001).

THE DEVELOPMENT OF RELATIONSHIPS
IN EARLY CHILDHOOD

PATERNAL SENSITIVITY IN EARLY INFANCY

Even though new mothers experience more life changes and report more satisfaction from their new roles than fathers do (Dulude, Wright, & Belanger, 2000), most men in a variety of cultural settings clearly adapt positively to parenting. For example, men in many countries report being elated when their infants are born (Bader, 1995; Greenberg, 1985; Greenberg & Morris, 1974), frequently visit hospitalized newborns (Levy-Shiff et al., 1989; Marton & Minde, 1980), and continue to feel emotionally connected to their infants, such that fathers and mothers are equivalently anxious about leaving their babies and toddlers in someone else's care (Deater-Deckard, Scarr, McCartney, & Eisenberg, 1994; Hock & Lutz, 1998; but see Wille, 1998, for contrasting results). New fathers behave just as mothers do when introduced to their newborn infants (Rödholm & Larsson, 1982), and they are effective sources of heat for neonates (Christensson, 1996). The nurturant attentiveness of new fathers may reflect the fact that mothers and fathers experience similar changes in hormonal levels (increasing levels of prolactin and cortisol and decreased levels of testosterone and estradiol) around the birth of their infants (Storey, Walsh, Quinton, & Wynne-Edwards, 2000).

Men quickly learn about the uniqueness of their own newborn children, although there is evidence to suggest that they are not as perceptive as mothers. When blindfolded and denied access to olfactory cues, for example, Israeli and American fathers were able to recognize their infants by touching their hands after only 60 minutes of exposure (Bader & Phillips, 1999; Kaitz, Lapidot, Bronner, & Eidelman, 1992; Kaitz, Shiri, Danziger, Hershko, & Eidelman, 1994). Fathers could not recognize their infants by touching their faces, however, whereas mothers could do so (Kaitz, Meirov, Landman, & Eidelman, 1993; Kaitz et al., 1994), perhaps because the mothers had spent twice as much time with their infants prior to testing (12.6 hours vs. 6.8 hours, on average). It is interesting that both mothers and fathers were better at identifying their own newborns by touching their hands than by touching their faces.

Kaitz, Chriki, Bear-Scharf, Nir, and Eidelman (2000) reported that Israeli mothers soothed their newborns more effectively than new fathers did, regardless of parity, whereas American fathers and mothers both responded appropriately to infant cues when observed feeding their infants (Parke & Sawin, 1977). Fathers and mothers both adjust their speech patterns when interacting with infants—speaking more slowly, using shorter phrases, imitating, and repeating themselves more often than when talking to adults (Blount & Padgug, 1976; Dalton-Hummel, 1982; Gleason, 1975; Golinkoff & Ames, 1979; Kokkinaki & Kugiumutsakis, 2000; C. Lewis et al., 1996; Rondal, 1980). Infant-directed singing has more exaggerated features than simulated singing or normal singing (Trehub, Hill, & Kamenetsky, 1997; Trehub, Unyk, et al., 1997), and Warren-Leubecker and Bohannon (1984) reported that fathers increased their pitch and frequency range even more than mothers did when speaking to 2-year-olds. Although they can discriminate among male voices, however, 4-month-olds do not show preferences for their fathers' voices (Ward & Cooper, 1999), perhaps because their daily exposure to paternal speech is often very low (Korman & Lewis, 2001).

Some researchers have found no differences between levels of maternal and paternal sensitivity during the first year. In the face-to-face and still-face paradigms, for example, mothers and fathers were equally sensitive with their 4-month-olds while infants showed equivalent patterns of affect and self-regulation with their mothers and fathers (Braungart-Rieker, Garwood, Powers, & Notaro, 1998), although boys may behave more negatively with their fathers when their mothers are employed (Braungart-Rieker et al., 1999). Both parents are sufficiently sensitive to developmental changes in their children's abilities and preferences that they adjust their play and stimulation patterns accordingly (Crawley & Sherrod, 1984), although Israeli fathers of 6-month-olds expect cognitive maturity and social autonomy to be acquired more slowly than mothers do (Mansbach & Greenbaum, 1999). In addition, French fathers appeared highly attuned to their toddlers' interests when playing with them, although their tendencies to tease were disruptive (Labrell, 1994). Notaro and Volling (1999) reported no differences in the sensitivity and responsiveness of American mothers and fathers who were observed interacting with their 1-year-olds for 3 minutes while the parents were preoccupied completing questionnaires.

Others have reported contrasting results, however. When observed playing with their 8-month-olds, American fathers were less sensitive to cues regarding their infants' interests and activities than mothers were (Power & Parke, 1983), prohibited their infants' activities and talked more (Brachfeld-Child, 1986), and were somewhat less likely to retrieve their crying infants than mothers were (Donate-Bartfield & Passman, 1985). Likewise, Heermann, Jones, and Wikoff (1994) reported that fathers were rated lower than mothers on several multifactorial scales at every age studied. In another study, fathers of both full- and preterm infants appeared less sensitive than mothers when their infants were 3 and 12 months old (Harrison & Magill-Evans, 1996). Because most men interact with their children so much less than mothers do, we cannot distinguish biological and social causes of these differences: We need to explore individual differences as well as changes in men over time.

INDIVIDUAL DIFFERENCES IN RESPONSIVENESS

Belsky et al. (1984) reported that although fathers were less actively engaged in interaction with their 1-, 3-, and 9-month-old infants than mothers were, the differences narrowed over time. Individual differences in paternal engagement were quite stable over time, especially between 3 and 9 months, and it is obviously important to determine why fathers differ in their sensitivity and engagement. Fathers' recollections of their own childhood relationships play an important role in shaping paternal sensitivity: Researchers have shown that men who had loving and secure relationships with their parents were more sensitive, attentive, and involved than were fathers who recalled poor relationships (Cowan, Cohn, Cowan, & Pearson, 1996). Perceived psychological well-being on the part of fathers is associated with paternal sensitivity (Broom, 1994), but it is not clear whether and how symptoms of depression affect paternal sensitivity: McElwain and Volling (1999) found that depressed fathers were less intrusive when observed playing with their 12-month-olds, whereas Field, Hossain, and Malphurs (1999) reported that depressed fathers did not interact with their infants more negatively than nondepressed fathers did. Infants with depressed mothers have more positive interactions with their nondepressed fathers, however, as though either the fathers or infants were seeking to make up for less satisfying mother-infant relationships (Hossain, Field, Gonzalez, Malphurs, & Del Valle, 1994). In addition, paternal depression appeared to mediate the adverse effects of paternal alcohol abuse on paternal attitudes and behavior (Das Eiden, Chavez, & Leonard, 1999; Das Eiden &

Leonard, 2000). Paternal responsiveness also appears to vary depending on the degree to which fathers assume responsibility for infant care: caretaking experience appears to facilitate parental responsiveness (Donate-Bartfield & Passman, 1985; Zelazo, Kotelchuck, Barber, & David, 1977), and fathers who are more involved in the treatment of their medically compromised infants appear to interact with them more positively than those who are more distressed by their infants' ill-health (Darke & Goldberg, 1994). This may explain why low-income American fathers who lived with their infants appeared more sensitive than those who did not (Brophy-Herb, Gibbons, Omar, & Schiffman, 1999). There is also an intriguing association between paternal reactivity to infant signals and the magnitude of the hormonal changes experienced by new fathers (Storey et al., 2000).

As fathers interact with their infants less and assume less responsibility for child care than mothers do, we might expect paternal sensitivity to decline over time relative to that of mothers, but the available evidence does not reveal a clear developmental pattern of this sort. Variations and developmental changes notwithstanding, most fathers are sufficiently responsive to their infants that attachments should form provided that a sufficient amount of father-infant interaction takes place.

The Development of Father-Infant Attachments

The establishment of attachment relationships between children and parents constitutes one of the most important aspects of human social and emotional development, and Bowlby's attachment theory has guided most research on this topic in the last four decades. Bowlby (1969) began with the assumption that survival in the "environment of evolutionary adaptedness" depended on the infant's ability to maintain proximity to protective adults. Unlike the young of many other species, however, human infants are not ambulatory and cannot cling to adults. Instead, human infants rely on signals (e.g., cries and smiles) to entice adults to approach them. One crucial aspect of the process called *attachment formation* is that infants come to focus their bids for attention on a small number of familiar individuals. This focalization represents one aspect of a process of attachment formation that proceeds through four developmental phases: indiscriminate social responsiveness (first and second months); discriminating sociability (two to seven months); maintenance of proximity to a discriminated figure (month seven through the second year); and goal-corrected partnerships (year three on). When adults respond promptly and appropriately to infant signals, infants come to perceive them as predictable or reliable, and secure infant-parent attachments result, whereas insecure attachments may develop when adults do not respond sensitively (Ainsworth, Blehar, Waters, & Wall, 1978; DeWolff & Van IJzendoorn, 1997; Lamb, Thompson, Gardner, & Charnov, 1985; Thompson, 1998). When adults respond rarely, no attachments at all may develop, and it is thus crucially important to determine whether fathers are appropriately responsive to their infants.

An early interview study with mothers suggested that infants begin to protest separations from both parents at 7 to 9 months of age and that by 18 months of age, 71% protested separation from both parents (Schaffer & Emerson, 1964). Babies formed attachments to those with whom they interacted regularly regardless of their involvement in caretaking. Likewise, Pedersen and Robson (1969) found that 75% of the mothers reported that their infants responded positively and enthusiastically when their fathers returned from work, with the intensity of greeting by boys particularly correlated with the frequency of paternal caretaking, paternal patience with infant fussing, and the intensity of father-infant play. Among daughters, however, intensity of greeting was correlated only with reported paternal apprehension about girls' well-being.

Separation protest was the preferred measure when observational studies of father-infant attachment began in the 1970s. Kotelchuck (1976) reported that 12-, 15-, 18-, and 21-month-old infants predictably protested when left alone by either parent, explored little while the parents were absent, and greeted them positively when they returned. Few infants protested separation from either parent when the other parent remained with them. A majority of the infants were more concerned about separation from their mothers, but 25% preferred their fathers, and 20% showed no preference for either parent. Later research confirmed, not surprisingly, that infants and toddlers also protested being left by either parent in nursery school settings (Field et al., 1984). Somewhat unexpectedly, however, Guatemalan babies who experienced a great deal of interaction with their fathers started to protest separation later (not earlier) than those whose fathers were uninvolved (Lester, Kotelchuck, Spelke, Sellers, & Klein, 1974) and the phase during which protest occurred was briefer when involvement was greater (Kotelchuck, 1976; Spelke, Zelazo, Kagan, & Kotelchuck, 1973). These counterintuitive correlations suggest that the intensity of separation protest may not index the intensity of attachment. On the other hand, low paternal involvement in caretaking was associated with reduced interaction and proximity seeking in the laboratory (Spelke et al., 1973), and when paternal involvement increased at home, there was a concomitant increase in the amount of father-infant interaction in the laboratory (Zelazo et al., 1977). Measures of separation protest were unaffected.

Feldman and Ingham (1975), Lamb (1976b), and Willemsen, Flaherty, Heaton, and Ritchey (1974) all reported no preferences for either parent in different laboratory procedures focused on responses to separation and reunion by American infants. Distress did not discriminate between mothers and fathers in a study by Cohen and Campos (1974) either, but on measures such as the frequency of approach, speed of approach, time in proximity, and use of parents as secure bases from which to interact with strangers, 10-, 13-, and 16-month-old infants showed preferences for their mothers over their fathers, as well as clear preferences for fathers over strangers. Likewise, Ban and Lewis (1974) reported that 1-year-olds touched, stayed near, and vocalized to mothers more than to fathers in 15-minute free-play sessions, whereas no comparable preferences were evident among 2-year-olds.

By the mid-1970s, therefore, there was substantial evidence that most American children developed attachments to their fathers in infancy. It was unclear how early in their lives infants formed these attachments during the crucial period between 6 and 9 months of age, during which infants form attachments to their mothers (Bowlby, 1969). Lengthy home observations subsequently revealed that 7-, 8-, 12-, and 13-month-old infants in traditional Euro-American families showed no preference for either parent over the other on attachment behavior measures, although all showed preferences for the parents over relatively unfamiliar adult visitors (Lamb, 1977c). Similar patterns were evident in a later study of 8- and 16-month-old infants on Israeli kibbutzim (Sagi et al., 1985). Patterns of separation protest and greeting at home also showed no preferences for either parent in the North American study, but the situation changed during the second year of life, when many of the infants began to show preferences for their fathers.

There was controversy at this time concerning the existence of preferences for mothers over fathers, and there were no data available concerning father-infant interaction in naturalistic settings. According to attachment theory (Bowlby, 1969), preferences among attachment figures may not be evident when infants do not need comfort or protection from attachment figures, but infants should focus their attachment behavior more narrowly on primary attachment figures when distressed. When infants are distressed, the display of attachment behaviors increases, and infants organize their behavior similarly around whichever parent is present (Lamb, 1976a, 1976e). When both parents are present, however, distressed 12- and 18-month-olds turn to their mothers preferentially (Lamb, 1976a, 1976e), whereas 8- and 21-month-olds show no comparable preferences (Lamb, 1976b). Especially between 10 and 20 months of age, therefore, mothers appear to be more reliable sources of comfort and security, even though fathers are more desirable partners for playful interaction, especially with boys (Clarke-Stewart, 1978; Lamb, 1977a, 1977c).

In a longitudinal study of less involved and highly involved Swedish fathers and their partners, Lamb et al. (1983) found that 8- and 16-month-olds showed clear preferences for their mothers on measures of both attachment and affiliative behavior, regardless of the fathers' relative involvement in child care. One reason for this unexpected result may have been that these Swedish fathers were not especially active as playmates; Lamb et al. speculated that playfulness may serve to enhance the salience of fathers and that in the absence of such cues, infants develop clear-cut preferences for their primary caretakers. Frascarolo-Moutinot (1994) reported that Swiss fathers and mothers were both used as secure bases and sources of security, but only when the fathers were unusually involved in a variety of everyday activities with their infants. By contrast, Swiss infants with traditional fathers clearly obtained more comfort and security, even at home, from their mothers than from their fathers. Increased paternal involvement thus does seem to strengthen infant-father attachment, but when mothers assume primary responsibility for child care, they are likely to be the preferred attachment figures. Most infants, however, clearly form attachments to both their fathers and mothers.

THE SECURITY OF CHILD-FATHER ATTACHMENT

Attachment theorists believe that maternal sensitivity determines the security of infant-mother attachment and thus of subsequent psychological adjustment (Ainsworth et al., 1978), and it seems reasonable to assume that individual differences in paternal sensitivity influence the security of infant-father attachment. Cross-sectional studies provide contradictory results. Notaro and Volling (1999) reported no significant associations between assessments of American mother- and father-infant attachment in the Strange Situation and near contemporaneous measures of parental responsiveness in a brief (3-minute) session. These findings were consistent with an earlier report that measures of father-infant interaction at home when infants were 6 and 9 months of age were unrelated to the security of infant-father attachment in the Strange Situation (Volling & Belsky, 1992) and with Rosen and Rothbaum's (1993) observation that measures of both maternal and paternal behavior were weakly associated with Strange Situation assessments of attachment security. By contrast, Goosens and Van IJzendoorn (1990) reported that the sensitivity of fathers in a free-play session was correlated with near contemporaneous assessments of infant-father attachment in a sample of Dutch fathers, and a meta-analysis of eight studies concerned with the association between paternal sensitivity and the quality of infant-father attachment in the Strange Situation revealed a small but statistically significant association (Van IJzendoorn & DeWolff, 1997) that was significantly weaker than the modest but reliable association between maternal sensitivity and the security of infant-mother attachment.

Father-infant attachments are more likely to be insecure when fathers report high levels of stress (Jarvis & Creasey, 1991), as attachment theory would predict, and longitudinal studies also reveal some important continuities. For example, Steele, Steele, and Fonagy (1996) reported that British mothers' perceptions of their attachments to their own mothers during pregnancy predicted the security of their infants' attachments to them at age 1, and fathers' perception of their childhood attachments predicted the security of their infants' attachments to them. Consistent with this, Van IJzendoorn (1995) reported an association between the security of infant-father attachment and the Dutch fathers' representations of their own childhood attachments. The same holds for behavioral measures. Cox, Owen, Henderson, and Margand (1992) found that American fathers who were more affectionate, spent more time with their 3-month-olds, and had more positive attitudes were more likely to have securely attached infants 9 months later. Caldera, Huston, and O'Brien (1995) likewise reported that American infants were more likely to appear insecure in the Strange Situation at 18 months when their fathers appeared more detached in a semistructured laboratory setting 12 months earlier.

The effects of infant-father attachment on subsequent behavior have also been studied. In infants on Israeli kibbutzim, Sagi, Lamb, and Gardner (1986) reported that the security of both mother- and father-infant attachment was associated with indexes of the infants' sociability with strangers: Securely attached infants were more sociable than were insecure-resistant infants. Earlier, Lamb, Hwang, Frodi, and Frodi (1982) reported that Swedish infants who were securely attached to their fathers were more sociable with strangers, although there was no association between the security of infant-mother attachment and sociability in their sample. Main and Weston (1981) found that the security of both mother-infant and father-infant attachments affected American infants' responses to an unfamiliar person (dressed as a clown). Unfortunately, it was not possible to determine which relationship had the greater impact because the clown session took place at the same time as the assessment of the mother-infant attachment—6 months before assessment of the father-infant attachments. Belsky, Garduque, and Hrncir (1984), however, reported that the security of both attachment relationships, but especially the infant-mother attachment, affected executive capacity, an index of cognitive performance, in a sample of American toddlers.

The results of other studies suggest that infant-mother attachments may have greater and more consistent predictive power than infant-father attachments. Main, Kaplan, and Cassidy (1985) reported that earlier and concurrent assessments of mother-child attachment had greater impact on American children's attachment-related responses than earlier and concurrent assessments of child-father attachment. Similar results were reported by Suess, Grossmann, and Sroufe (1992), who studied associations between parent-infant attachment security and the quality of German children's later interaction with peers. It is interesting that although the parents' sensitivity toward their 12-month-olds did not predict later behavior problems in one study (Benzies, Harrison, & Magill-Evans, 1998), Verscheuren and Marcoen (1999) reported that the security of child-mother attachments had a greater effect on the positive self-perceptions of 5- and 6-year-olds than did child-father attachments, whereas child-father attachments had a greater effect on behavior problems. In both studies, secure attachments to one parent partially but not completely offset the effects of insecure attachment to the other, and we might expect the same to be true in infancy. By contrast, Steele, Steele, Croft, and Fonagy (1999) found that 6-year-olds' ability to read affective expressions in cartoons was predicted by the security of infant-mother attachments five years earlier but not by infant-father attachments at 18 months or by these British parents' feelings of attachment during pregnancy.

Most of the evidence suggests that we should take into account infants' attachments to both of their parents, however. Like Suess et al. (1992), Fagot and Kavanagh (1993) underscored the importance of considering the quality of attachment to both parents. In their study, both parents found interaction with insecurely attached infants to be less pleasant, and both tended to become less involved in interactions with insecurely attached boys, a factor that may explain the greater likelihood of behavior problems among boys. Fathers had unusually high levels of interaction with insecure-avoidant girls, who received the fewest instructions from their mothers. In a study of 20-month-olds, Easterbrooks and Goldberg (1984) found that the children's adaptation was promoted by both the amount of paternal involvement and, more important, the quality or sensitivity of their fathers' behavior. By contrast, the security of neither infant-mother nor of infant-father attachment influenced the adjustment at age 5 of infants raised on traditional kibbutzim (those with central dormitories for children) in Israel, although the security of the infant-caretaker relationship did predict later behavior (Oppenheim, Sagi, & Lamb, 1988).

Gable, Crnic, and Belsky (1994) reported robust associations among marital quality, the quality of parent-child relationships, and child outcomes in a study of American 2-year-olds. Infants characterized by negative emotionality early in the first year tended to become more positive when they had active, sensitive, and happily married mothers, whereas some infants became more negative when their fathers were dissatisfied with their marriages, insensitive, and uninvolved in their children's lives (Belsky, Fish, & Isabella, 1991). Attachments cannot be treated in isolation of other factors, particularly the relationship between the parents.

THE MOTHER-FATHER-INFANT SYSTEM AND THE CHILD'S COGNITIVE AND BEHAVIORAL SKILLS

Over time, all members of the mother-father-child triad shape and adapt to one another. In her observational study of 15- to 30-month-olds, for example, Clarke-Stewart (1978) found that intellectual competence was correlated with measures of maternal stimulation (both material and verbal), intellectual acceleration, and expressiveness, as well as with measures of the fathers' engagement in play, their positive ratings of the children, the amount they interacted, and the fathers' aspirations for the infants' independence. However, examination of the correlational patterns over time suggested that the mothers affected the children's development and that this, in turn, influenced the fathers' behavior. In other words, paternal behavior appeared to be a consequence of, not a determinant of, individual differences in child behavior. Similarly, Hunter, McCarthy, MacTurk, and Vietze (1987) reported that although the qualities of both mother- and father-infant interaction in play sessions were individually stable over time, the paternal variables were not associated with differences in the infants' cognitive competence, whereas the indexes of maternal behavior were predictively valuable. Not only do patterns of influence not always run directly from parents to children, but the impact of the two parents is often equivalent as well: In two-parent households, mothers' enhanced levels of responsibility make them more influential.

Paternal behavior appears to be influential as well, however. Yarrow et al. (1984) reported that paternal stimulation had an especially important role to play in the development of American boys' (but not girls') mastery motivation in the first year of life. Wachs, Uzgiris, and Hunt (1971) found that increased paternal involvement was associated with better performance on the Uzgiris-Hunt scales. Magill-Evans and Harrison (1999) reported that the sensitivity of both mothers and fathers to their 3- and 12-month-olds predicted individual differences in the linguistic and cognitive capacities of the children when they were 18 months old, while Yogman, Kindlon, and Earls (1995) found that infants with more involved fathers had higher IQs than those whose fathers were less involved, even after controlling for socioeconomic differences. Finnish fathers who read more often to their 14- and 24-month-old infants had children who were later more interested in books (Lyytinen, Laakso, & Poikkeus, 1998). In addition, Labrell (1990) reported that paternal scaffolding (i.e., providing indirect rather than direct help) promoted independent problem solving by French 18-month-olds. Symbolic activity by 30- and 42-month-olds was predicted by maternal but not paternal distancing strategies in a later study (Labrell, Deleau, & Juhel, 2000), however.

Although mothers and fathers both adjust their speech characteristics when speaking to young children, maternal and paternal communicative styles differ. Gleason (1975) and Rondal (1980) have suggested that because fathers use more imperatives, attention-getting utterances, and utter more complex sentences than mothers do, they contribute in unique, though still poorly understood, ways to linguistic development. Infants clearly view both parents as potential sources of information: In ambiguous settings, they look to either parent for clarification, and they are equally responsive to information from mothers and fathers (Dickstein & Parke, 1988; Hirshberg & Svejda, 1990). Nevertheless, Rondal's (1980) research suggests that the different communicative styles adopted by mothers and fathers forces children to learn a greater variety of linguistic conventions. For example, the Belgian 2-year-olds he studied addressed their mothers using the informal *tu*, whereas they addressed their fathers using the more formal *vous*.

Youngblade and Belsky (1992) found no significant associations between the security of infant-father attachment and the quality of father-child interaction when these American children were 3 years old, although those children who had more positive interactions with their fathers at age 3 interacted more positively with peers two years later. Because the security of infant-father attachment at age 1 was inversely associated with indexes of peer play at age 5, Youngblade and Belsky speculated that unsatisfying parent-child relationships led children to look outside their families for more rewarding relationships. These associations were not replicated when infant-father attachment was assessed using the Attachment Q-sort rather than the Strange Situation: Secure infant-father attachments were associated at that time with more positive interactions with peers (Youngblade, Park, & Belsky, 1993), leaving some confusion about the pattern of predictive associations.

CHILDHOOD AND ADOLESCENCE

The preschool years represent a peak in levels of father-child interaction, at least in public situations (Amato, 1989), with a slow decline in the elementary school period (Mackey, 1985). Seven areas of change—including physical and locomotor growth, language, impulse control, social-cognitive understanding, conception of the self, cognitive executive processes, and the desire for autonomy—characterize the years between infancy and school and have significant effects on the nature and quality of parent-child relationships (Maccoby, 1984).

It is important to recognize that the transition from infancy to early childhood brings dramatic changes in the roles of parents because physical, mental, and linguistic development makes new behavioral capacities possible and facilitates the comprehension of more complex parental communication. From the end of infancy, the amount of child care performed by parents also declines progressively (DeLuccie, 1996; Galinsky, 1999). Toward the end of the second year of life, therefore, parents increasingly attempt to shape their children's social lives by directly encouraging children to behave in appropriate ways and discouraging them from inappropriate and socially proscribed behavior. The ability to conceptualize symbolically facilitates another important process—observational learning—because the observer must be able to store a model's behavior in memory and then recall it for subsequent performance in order for this form of learning to be effective (Bandura, 1969, 1977). Prior to this, continuing egocentrism and the social-cognitive immaturity of preschoolers impose restraints on their interaction skills and, presumably, on the extent to which they can benefit from complex (e.g., observational) learning experiences.

CHILDHOOD

As in infancy, data from a range of cultures show that mothers continue to spend more time with their children than fathers do (Collins & Russell, 1991; Pleck & Masciadrelli, this volume). Collins and Russell's review suggested that when observed together, mothers and fathers initiated activities with equal frequency (Noller, 1980), however, with broad similarities in their reactions to their children's play and cognitive styles (Bronstein, 1984). Continuities within individual patterns of paternal closeness over time during middle childhood suggest that there are discernible parental styles in this period (Herman & McHale, 1993).

Baumrind and her colleagues began in the 1960s to examine the associations between specific child-rearing patterns and particular child outcomes (Baumrind, 1967, 1971, 1973, 1975; Baumrind & Black, 1967). These researchers distinguished four patterns of parenting, which they labeled authoritarian, authoritative, permissive, and nonconformist. According to Baumrind, authoritarian parents value obedience and recommend forceful imposition of the parents' will; permissive parents believe that they should be nonintrusive but available as resources; and nonconformist parents, although opposed to authority, are "less passive and exert more control than permissive parents" (Baumrind, 1975, p. 14). Between the extremes represented by authoritarian and permissive parents fall authoritative parents, who encourage independence and attempt to shape their preschoolers' behavior using rational explanation. According to Baumrind, authoritative parents are sensitive to and facilitate their children's changing sense of self. Furthermore, by allowing themselves to learn from their children, authoritative parents maximize their positive impact, teaching their children, as authoritarian and permissive parents do not, that social competence emerges within a context of interpersonal give-and-take. Although authoritative parents strive to foster independence, they also inculcate a value system characterized by conformity to cultural and societal norms by balancing the use of both reasoning and punishment.

COMPARISONS BETWEEN PARENTS

How do mothers and fathers differ with respect to their parenting styles and their ability to serve as role models for their children? Many researchers have examined the parents' functions as role models, but few have examined and compared their parenting styles systematically. In neither case have the results been satisfying or consistent. Beyond the infancy period, mothers and fathers appear to adopt quite similar interaction styles, although they may do so for very different reasons. Social learning theorists have long assumed that the different interactional styles of mothers and fathers must somehow help boys and girls acquire gender-appropriate behavioral repertoires (e.g., Block, 1976). Consistent differences between parents have been hard to identify, however (Lytton & Romney, 1991; Russell & Saebel, 1997; Siegal, 1987). For example, Lytton and Romney's meta-analysis of 172 studies involving over 27,000 children revealed only one consistent difference between mothers and fathers: a significant, but small, tendency for fathers to encourage the use of sex-typed toys more than mothers did. Otherwise, there were insufficient data to support the claim that mothers and fathers differentially affect their children's sex-role development. In one recent study, however, Lindsey and Mize (2001) examined parent-child and child-peer dyads in pretence and physical play sessions. Not only did mothers engage in more pretend play with their daughters while father-son dyads specialized in physical play, but patterns of parent-child pretence and physical play also predicted the amounts of the same type of play with peers. Lytton and Romney further reported that the similarities between the behavior of mothers and fathers increased beyond the preschool years. For example, Labrell et al.'s (2000) more recent research suggests that by 42 months French fathers were no longer more challenging than mothers. Similarly, each parent's language comes to resemble the other's, especially when they interact in mother-father-child triads (Pellegrini, Brody, & Stoneman, 1987), and the communicative balance between parent and child appears to be comparable for mothers and fathers (Welkowitz et al., 1990). Unfortunately, researchers typically observe mothers and fathers in the same context. Different settings impose different constraints on parents (C. Lewis & Gregory, 1987; Ross & Taylor, 1989), and most researchers do not sample contexts in such a way that different parental styles might be expressed. This tendency is likely to obscure any differences between the behavior of mothers and fathers.

Children as young as preschoolers clearly differentiate between the roles of mothers and fathers in a variety of cultures. For example, Raag and Rackliff (1998) introduced preschoolers to a laboratory playroom in which a range of sex-neutral and sex-stereotyped toys were laid out and then asked the children which toys they and their parents thought it was appropriate to play with. Many boys, particularly those who had chosen sex-stereotypical toys, stated that their fathers would consider cross-sex toy play to be "bad." Thus, fathers were believed by sons but not daughters to have more restrictive rules of conduct than mothers did. By the time of their entry into school, furthermore, children appear to have highly stereotyped views of parental roles. Domestic work is widely described as the mother's prerogative, whereas bread-winning is seen as the province of fathers throughout the school years (Hartley, 1960; Langford, Lewis, Solomon, & Warin, 2001; Williams, Bennett, & Best, 1975), and interviews with over 800 5- to 15-year-olds in four societies revealed that these beliefs persisted into middle childhood and adolescence (Goldman & Goldman, 1983).

Attempts to compare mothers' and fathers' approaches to parenting have yielded inconclusive findings. Baumrind's analysis underscores the need to study parents' philosophies of child rearing, but it has been hard to discern much about the effects of fathers' styles on child development using this general blueprint, and Baumrind's own research focused on parents rather than mothers and fathers separately. Studying the parents of 305 Australian preschoolers, Russell et al. (1998) found that mothers were more likely to identify with the authoritative style of parenting, whereas fathers were more likely to describe themselves as either authoritarian or permissive. Parents were also more often identified with the authoritarian perspective when the child under discussion was a son. Such contrasts suggest that we need to consider both the children's impact on the parents' child-rearing beliefs and the reasons why mothers and fathers may have differing philosophies, as these may well be colored by the domestic roles that they assume. Of course, this assertion needs to be explored empirically in a wide variety of cultural and subcultural settings. In addition, as Darling and Steinberg (1993) pointed out, Baumrind has yet to document the developmental processes by which authoritative parents shape their children's development.

Whatever the differences between maternal and paternal behavioral styles, there is impressive evidence that mothers and fathers may have different effects on child development. Such influences are moderated by external factors such as parental employment patterns (Gottfried, Gottfried, & Bathurst, 2002). For example, Hoffman and Youngblade (1999) found that American fathers' involvement in routine child care was associated with children's higher school grades and with less stereotypical views about adult sex-roles on the part of daughters. Such data suggest that fathers may play a special role as intermediaries between the family and the outside world. As Parke and his colleagues show in this volume, furthermore, fathers and mothers have distinct influences on the development of peer relationships. Specifically, physically playful, affectionate, and socially engaging father-son interaction predicts later popularity, just as mothers' verbal stimulation predicts popularity. Parke and his colleagues argue that father-child interactions teach children to read their partners' emotional expressions and that these skills are later displayed in interactions with peers. Similarly, fathers who are more sensitive to their 5-year-olds' emotional states have children with more competent peer relationships three years later (Gottman, Katz, & Hooven, 1997).

ADOLESCENCE

The relationships between fathers and their adolescent children have been documented empirically (e.g., Holmbeck, Paikoff, & Brooks-Gunn, 1995; Shulman & Seiffge-Krenke, 1997), although this research literature is relatively atheoretical and descriptive (Hosley & Montemayor, 1997). Research comparing mothers and fathers reveals few differences between mothers' and fathers' interactional styles (Russell & Saebel, 1997; Silverberg, Tennenbaum, & Jacob, 1992). In early adolescence, children shift their dependence first to same-sex and then to opposite-sex peers, while continuing the processes of self-differentiation and individuation that become the major themes of development in adolescence (Grotevant, 1998). The biological changes associated with puberty also foster change and promote distance between parents and children in early adolescence (Collins, 1990; Hill & Holmbeck, 1987; Steinberg, 1988, 1990), with the parent-child relationship increasingly marked by self-assertion, distance, and conflict as children develop. The effects of puberty are frequently confounded with the effects of other age-related changes, such as the transition from elementary to junior high or from junior high to high school (Collins & Russell, 1991; Simmons & Blyth, 1987), unfortunately, but whatever their relative importance, the biological, social, and cognitive changes associated with puberty all make early adolescence a critical transitional period during which youngsters are expected to consolidate their knowledge of the norms and roles of adult society and, at least in Western industrialized societies, begin to become emotionally and economically independent of their parents (Grotevant, 1998).

Steinberg (1987) found that early-maturing sons and daughters reported more conflict with their mothers than did later maturing children, although these processes may take different forms and have different meanings in mother-child and father-child relationships. Adolescents believe that their mothers know them better than their fathers do, and although they care about both mothers and fathers, daughters are more likely than sons to differ with parents regarding the degree of closeness (Hosley & Montemayor, 1997; Langford et al., 2001; Youniss & Ketterlinus, 1987). Large-scale surveys show that the vast majority of adolescents continue to rely on their parents for advice, support, and emotional intimacy (Maccoby & Martin, 1983; McGrellis, Henderson, Holland, Sharpe, & Thomson, 2000; Noller & Callan, 1986; Offer, Ostrov, & Howard, 1981), suggesting that parent-adolescent relationships are marked by increasing interdependence and mutuality rather than by detachment and conflict. However, Langford et al. (2001) explored the paradoxes and contradictions in parent-adolescent relationships as the parties strive for such mutuality.

Researchers have also described some interesting differences in the ways in which mothers and fathers relate to their adolescent sons and daughters (Collins & Russell, 1991; Steinberg, 1987, 1990). Collins and Russell focused on three dimensions of parent-child relationships in middle-class families: interactions (measured by frequency, extent, and structure), affect (indexed by the degree of positive affect, closeness, and cohesion), and cognition (indexed by discrepancies between parents' and children's perceptions of their relationships). They concluded that, as in infancy, mothers engage in more frequent interaction with children in middle childhood and adolescence (especially interactions involving caretaking and routine family tasks) than fathers do and that most father-child interactions during this developmental period involve play, recreation, and goal-oriented actions and tasks (see also Lamb, 1997; Montemayor & Brownlee, 1987; Russell & Russell, 1987). However, mothers and fathers are equivalently involved in activities related to their children's and adolescents' scholastic and extracurricular performance and achievement (Youniss & Smollar, 1985), and both parents frequently engage in nurturant caretaking in middle childhood (Russell & Russell, 1987). Nevertheless, adolescents in North America (Hosley & Montemayor, 1997) and Britain (Langford et al., 2001) consistently report being closer to their mothers than to their fathers.

When dyadic and systemic aspects of parent-adolescent relationships are examined (Larson & Richards, 1994; Steinberg, 1990), mothers appear to engage in more shared activities with daughters than with sons, although both relationships are marked by relatively high levels of both closeness and discord. Fathers, by contrast, tend to be more engaged with their sons, have less contact with daughters, and generally have more distant relationships with their children than mothers do (Hosley & Montemayor, 1997; Montemayor & Brownlee, 1987; Youniss & Ketterlinus, 1987). Such patterns are found in diverse cultural contexts. For example, Korean daughters see their fathers as distant and controlling (Rohner & Pettengill, 1985). Because fathers spend less time with and have fewer conversations with their adolescent children, one might expect them to be less influential, and the literature suggests that daughters report being relatively uninfluenced by their fathers (Larson & Richards, 1994). Even sons feel that mothers provide more support than fathers do (Youniss & Smoller, 1985). On the other hand, there is clear evidence that some fathers have positive influences on their children's academic performance (Chen, Liu, & Li, 2000) and achievement particularly in sports (Jodl, Michael, Malanchuk, Eccles, & Sameroff, 2001). In addition, Phares (1996, 1997) concluded a review of the literature on child psychopathology by noting that fathers have powerful direct and indirect effects on their children's adjustment. For example, Brennan, Hammen, Katz, and Le Brocque (2002) reported that maternal depression had a more reliable effect on adolescents when the fathers were substance abusers, whereas maternal and paternal depression had additive effects.

As in earlier years, of course, some patterns of influence in adolescence are quite complex and indirect. In an observational study, for example, Gjerde (1986) found that mother-son interactions were less stormy when fathers were present than when mothers and sons were observed alone, whereas father-son interactions were of poorer quality in triadic than in dyadic settings. Parents and adolescents may view their interaction quite differently as well. Noller and Callan (1988) videotaped 41 mother-father-adolescent triads discussing the adolescents' behavior and then had trained observers, the interactants, and members of other mother-father-child triads rate the degree of anxiety, dominance, involvement, and friendliness shown by each of the interactants. The ratings made by the experts were very similar to those made by members of other families. Interactants rated other members of their families more negatively than they rated themselves, although the ratings by participating and nonparticipating parents were more divergent than ratings by adolescents who were and were not involved.

PATERNAL INFLUENCES ON ADOLESCENT DEVELOPMENT

Because the two parents' behaviors, attributions, and attitudes are complexly interrelated, it is hard to identify paternal effects (Ogletree, Jones, & Coyl, 2002), but studies focused on adolescents' perceptions of their parents' influences and a small number of longitudinal investigations provide valuable insight into patterns of influence over time.

The evidence to date suggests that there is a long-term association between reported paternal involvement and the psychosocial adjustment of adolescents. For example, Burns and Dunlop (1998) reported that adults' feelings about their relationships and peer interactions were positively correlated with their experiences of parental care in the adolescent years. Such continuities might be important for understanding father-child relationships because earlier paternal involvement predicts their adult children's feelings of satisfaction in spousal relationships and self-reported parenting skills (Franz, McClelland, & Weinberger, 1991). Likewise, fathers' expressions of hostility toward their 16-year-olds and the extent to which they undermined their teenagers' autonomy predicted the degree of hostility and low ego resiliency reported in the 16-year-old by close friends at age 25 (Allen, Hauser, O'Connor, & Bell, 2002). Measures of teenager-mother hostility also predicted adjustment at age 25.

A few researchers have examined paternal involvement in children's lives in relation to both concurrent parent-child measures and the children's later psychosocial functioning. For example, C. Lewis, Newson, and Newson (1982) found that the reported involvement of British fathers in two-parent households at ages 7 and 11 predicted the child's performance in national examinations at age 16 as well as whether they had a criminal record by age 21. In their analyses of data from the U.K. National Child Development Study, furthermore, Flouri and Buchanan (2002a, 2002b) reported a variety of positive predictive associations between patterns of paternal involvement and later indexes (until the children were 33 years of age) of psychosocial adjustment even when possible mediating factors (e.g., gender, parental socioeconomic status, family structure, parental mental health, maternal involvement) were controlled for in the statistical analyses. Maternally reported father involvement at age 7 predicted the child's self-reported closeness to father at 16 and lower levels of police contact as reported by the child's mother and teacher (Flouri & Buchanan, 2002a). This in turn predicted marital satisfaction and diminished psychological distress at age 33 (Flouri & Buchanan, 2002b), whereas self-reported closeness to mother at age 16 predicted only marital satisfaction 17 years later. Furthermore, Koestner, Franz, and Weinberger (1990) reported significant associations between paternal involvement at age 5 and the children's feelings when they were in their early 30s (i.e., some 26 years later). Similarly, Franz, McClelland, Weinberger, and Peterson (1994) recontacted children initially studied by Sears, Maccoby, and Levin (1957) and reported that "over a period of 36 years, the children of warm, affectionate fathers, and boys with warm mothers and less stressful childhood years were more likely to be well adjusted adults who, at age 41, were mentally healthy, coping adequately, and psychosocially mature" (p. 141). Results such as these suggest that, in the long term, patterns of father-child closeness might be crucial predictors of later psychosocial adjustment, although the patterns of influence remain to be explored in depth.

These longitudinal studies relied predominantly on maternal reports of early paternal involvement and warmth, however, and we must be cautious when inferring paternal influences from these data, particularly as marital closeness is a strong predictor of psychological well-being as well (Cummings & O'Reilly, 1997; Davies & Cummings, 1994; Grych & Fincham, 1990). Maternal reports of high paternal involvement may reflect something else, such as family harmony or the mother's own psychological well-being, and this would explain why levels of paternal involvement are often unrelated to contemporaneous indexes of adjustment. For example, Israeli teenagers' academic performance was related to their descriptions of maternal, but not paternal, involvement (Feldman, Guttfreund, & Yerushalmi, 1998).

CONCLUSION

As indicated earlier, most researchers have focused on early development, particularly infancy. Studies have revealed that men develop strong attachments to their infants but that these relationships and their effects on childhood functioning have to be understood within the complexity of the child's other relationships and cultural experiences. The diverse ways in which the children's experiences and memories influence later personality is in part a reflection of the complexity of family and other interactions to which children are exposed.

Within this context, father-child relationships appear to have a significant impact on later psychosocial development. Most attempts to tease apart men's influences on their children have involved analyses of the security of attachments. While interesting, this enterprise seems to continue a long tradition (Richards, 1982) of examining men using measures that may place them in a poor light relative to mothers. Only recently have researchers attempted to establish more patricentric research themes (Palkovitz, 1997, 2002; Warin, Solomon, Lewis, & Langford, 1999). For example, Grossmann et al. (2002) explored the relative influences of early attachments and parent-child sensitivity in play—a more traditionally paternal activity in many cultures. They found that security of infant-mother attachment was a better predictor of the child's feelings of security at age 6 and 10 than was the security of infant-father attachment but that by age 10, the father's sensitivity during 10 minutes of free play at age 2 also predicted security and by 16, only this measure of father-toddler play significantly predicted adjustment. Such patterns of influence underline the need to recall the limited range of measures used in research and the strong possibility that researchers may have overlooked many paternal influences.

REFERENCES

Ainsworth, M. D. S., Blehar, M. C., Waters, E., & Wall, S. (1978). *Patterns of attachment*. Hillsdale, NJ: Erlbaum.

Allen, J. P., Hauser, S. T., O'Connor, T. G., & Bell, K. L. (2002). Prediction of peer-rated adult hostility from autonomy struggles in adolescent-family interactions. *Development and Psychopathology, 14*, 123–137.

Allen, S. M., & Hawkins, A. J. (1999). Maternal gatekeeping: Mothers' beliefs and behaviors that inhibit greater father involvement in family work. *Journal of Marriage and the Family, 61*, 199–212.

Amato, P. R. (1989). Who cares for children in public places? *Journal of Marriage and the Family, 51*, 981–990.

Bader, A. P. (1995). Engrossment revisited: Fathers are still falling in love with their newborn babies. In J. L. Shapiro, M. J. Diamond, & M. Greenberg (Eds.), *Becoming a father* (pp. 224–233). New York: Springer.

Bader, A. P., & Phillips, R. D. (1999). Fathers' proficiency at recognizing their newborns by tactile cues. *Infant Behavior and Development, 22*, 405–409.

Ban, P., & Lewis, M. (1974). Mothers and fathers, girls and boys: Attachment behavior in the one-year-old. *Merrill-Palmer Quarterly, 20*, 195–204.

Bandura, A. (1969). *Principles of behavior modification*. New York: Holt, Rinehart, and Winston.

Bandura, A. (1977). Self-efficacy: Toward a unifying theory of behavioral change. *Psychological Review, 84*, 191–215.

Baumrind, D. (1967). Child care practices anteceding three patterns of preschool behavior. *Genetic Psychology Monographs, 75*, 43–88.

Baumrind, D. (1971). Current patterns of parental authority. *Developmental Psychology Monographs, 4*, 1–103.

Baumrind, D. (1973). The development of instrumental competence through socialization. In

A. Pick (Ed.), *Minnesota symposium on child psychology* (Vol. 7, pp. 3–46). Minneapolis: University of Minnesota Press.

Baumrind, D. (1975). *Early socialization and the discipline controversy.* Morristown, NJ: General Learning Press.

Baumrind, D., & Black, A. E. (1967). Socialization practices associated with dimensions of competence in preschool boys and girls. *Child Development, 38,* 291–327.

Beitel, A. H., & Parke, R. D. (1998). Parental involvement in infancy: The role of maternal and paternal attitudes. *Journal of Family Psychology, 12,* 268–288.

Bell, R. Q. (1968). A reinterpretation of the direction of effects in studies of socialization. *Psychological Review, 75,* 81–95.

Belsky, J. (1979). Mother-father-infant interaction: A naturalistic observational study. *Developmental Psychology, 15,* 601–607.

Belsky, J. (1985). Experimenting with the family in the newborn period. *Child Development, 56,* 407–414.

Belsky, J., Fish, M., & Isabella, R. (1991). Continuity and discontinuity in infant negative and positive emotionality: Family antecedents and attachment consequences. *Developmental Psychology, 27,* 421–431.

Belsky, J., Garduque, L., & Hrncir, E. (1984). Assessing performance, competence, and executive capacity in infant play: Relation to home environment and security of attachment. *Developmental Psychology, 20,* 406–417.

Belsky, J., Gilstrap, B., & Rovine, M. (1984). The Pennsylvania Infant and Family Development Project: I. Stability and change in mother-infant and father-infant interaction in a family setting at one, three, and nine months. *Child Development, 55,* 692–705.

Benzies, K. M., Harrison, M. J., & Magill-Evans, J. (1998). Impact of marital quality and parent-infant interaction on preschool behavior problems. *Public Health Nursing, 15,* 35–43.

Berry, J. O., & Rao, J. M. (1997). Balancing employment and fatherhood: A systems perspective. *Journal of Family Issues, 18,* 386–402.

Best, D. L., House, A. S., Barnard, A. L., & Spicker, B. S. (1994). Parent-child interactions in France, Germany, and Italy: The effects of gender and culture. *Journal of Cross-Cultural Psychology, 25,* 181–193.

Block, J. (1976). Issues, problems and pitfalls in assessing sex differences: A critical review of "The Psychology of Sex Differences." *Merrill Palmer Quarterly, 22,* 283–340.

Blount, G. B., & Padgug, E. J. (1976). Mother and father speech: Distribution of parental speech features in English and Spanish. *Papers and Reports on Child Language Development, 12,* 47–59.

Bowlby, J. (1969). *Attachment and loss: Vol. 1. Attachment.* New York: Basic Books.

Brachfeld-Child, S. (1986). Parents as teachers: Comparisons of mothers' and fathers' instructional interactions with infants. *Infant Behavior and Development, 9,* 127–131.

Braungart-Rieker, J., Courtney, S., & Garwood, M. M. (1999). Mother- and father-infant attachment: Families in context. *Journal of Family Psychology, 13,* 535–553.

Braungart-Rieker, J., Garwood, M. M., Powers, B. P., & Notaro, P. C. (1998). Infant affect and affect regulation during the still-face paradigm with mothers and fathers: The role of infant characteristics and parental sensitivity. *Developmental Psychology, 34,* 1428–1437.

Brennan, P. A., Hammen, C., Katz, A. R., & Le Brocque, R. M. (2002). Maternal depression, paternal psychopathology, and adolescent diagnostic outcomes. *Journal of Consulting and Clinical Psychology, 70,* 1075–1085.

Broom, B. L. (1994). Impact of marital quality and psychological well-being on parental sensitivity. *Nursing Research, 43,* 138–143.

Bronstein, P. (1984). Differences in mothers' and fathers' behaviors toward children: A cross-cultural comparison. *Developmental Psychology, 29,* 995–1003.

Brophy-Herb, H. E., Gibbons, G., Omar, M. A., & Schiffman, R. P. (1999). Low-income fathers and their infants: Interactions during teaching episodes. *Infant Mental Health Journal, 20,* 305–321.

Burns, A., & Dunlop, R. (1998). Parental divorce, parent-child relations and early adult relationships: A longitudinal study. *Personal Relationships, 5,* 393–407.

Caldera, Y., Huston, A., & O'Brien, M. (1995, April). *Antecedents of father-infant attachment: A longitudinal study.* Paper presented to the Society for Research in Child Development, Indianapolis, IN.

Chen, X., Liu, M., & Li, D. (2000). Parental warmth, control, and indulgence and their relations to adjustment in Chinese children: A longitudinal study. *Journal of Family Psychology, 14,* 401–419.

Christensson, K. (1996). Fathers can effectively achieve heat conservation in healthy newborn infants. *Acta Paediatrica, 85,* 1354–1360.

Clarke-Stewart, K. A. (1978). And daddy makes three: The father's impact on mother and young child. *Child Development, 49,* 466–478.

Cohen, L. J., & Campos, J. J. (1974). Father, mother, and stranger as elicitors of attachment behaviors in infancy. *Developmental Psychology, 10,* 146–154.

Collins, W. A. (1990). Parent-child relationships in the transition to adolescence: Continuity and change in interactions, affect, and cognition. In R. Montemayor, G. R. Adams, & T. P. Gullotta (Eds.), *From childhood to adolescence* (pp. 103–110). Newbury Park, CA: Sage.

Collins, W. A., & Russell, G. (1991). Mother-child and father-child relationships in middle childhood and adolescence: A developmental analysis. *Developmental Review, 11,* 99–136.

Cowan, P. A., Cohn, D. A., Cowan, C. P., & Pearson, J. L. (1996). Parents' attachment histories and children's externalizing and internalizing behaviors: Exploring family systems models of linkage. *Journal of Consulting and Clinical Psychology, 64,* 53–63.

Cox, M. J., Owen, M. T., Henderson, V. K., & Margand, N. A. (1992). Prediction of infant-father and infant-mother attachment. *Developmental Psychology, 28,* 474–483.

Cox, M. J., Owen, M. T., Lewis, J. M., & Henderson, U. K. (1989). Marriage adult adjustment, and early parenting. *Child Development, 60,* 1015–1024.

Crawley, S. B., & Sherrod, R. B. (1984). Parent-infant play during the first year of life. *Infant Behavior and Development, 7,* 65–75.

Crouter, A. C., Helms-Erikson, H., Updegraff, K., & McHale, S. M. (1999). Conditions underlying parents' knowledge about children's daily lives in middle childhood: Between- and within-family comparisons. *Child Development, 70,* 246–259.

Crouter, A. C., Perry-Jenkins, M., Huston, T. L., & McHale, S. M. (1987). Processes underlying father-involvement in dual-earner and single-earner families. *Developmental Psychology, 23,* 431–440.

Cummings, E. M., & O'Reilly, A. W. (1997). Fathers in family context: Effects of marital quality on child adjustment. In M. E. Lamb (Ed.), *The role of the father in child development* (3rd ed., pp. 49–65, 318–325). New York: Wiley.

Dalton-Hummel, D. (1982). Syntatic and conversational characteristics of fathers' speech. *Journal of Psycholinguistic Research, 11,* 465–483.

Darke, P. R., & Goldberg, S. (1994). Father-infant interaction and parent stress with healthy and medically compromised infants. *Infant Behavior and Development, 17,* 3–14.

Darling, N., & Steinberg, L. (1993). Parenting style as context: An integrative model. *Psychological Bulletin, 113,* 487–496.

Das Eiden, R., Chavez, F., & Leonard, K. E. (1999). Parent-infant interactions among families with alcoholic fathers. *Development and Psychopathology, 11,* 745–762.

Das Eiden, R., & Leonard, K. E. (1996). Paternal alcohol use and the mother-infant relationship. *Development and Psychopathology, 8,* 307–323.

Das Eiden, R., & Leonard, K. E. (2000). Paternal alcoholism, parental psychopathology, and aggravation with infants. *Journal of Substance Abuse, 11,* 17–29.

Davies, P. T., & Cummings, E. M. (1994). Marital conflict and child adjustment: An emotional security hypothesis. *Psychological Bulletin, 116,* 194–208.

Deater-Deckard, K., Scarr, S., McCartney, K., & Eisenberg, M. (1994). Paternal separation anxiety: Relationships with parenting stress, child-rearing attitudes, and maternal anxieties. *Psychological Science, 5,* 341–346.

DeLuccie, M. (1996). Predictors of paternal involvement and satisfaction. *Psychological Reports, 79,* 1351–1359.

DeWolff, M. S., & Van IJzendoorn, M. H. (1997). Sensitivity and attachment: A meta-analysis on parental antecedents of infant attachment. *Child Development, 68,* 571–591.

Dickson, K. L., Walker, H., & Fogel, A. (1997). The relationship between smile type and play type during parent-infant play. *Developmental Psychology, 33,* 925–933.

Dickstein, S., & Parke, R. D. (1988). Social referencing in infancy: A glance at fathers and marriage. *Child Development, 59,* 506–511.

Donate-Bartfield, D., & Passman, R. H. (1985). Attentiveness of mothers and fathers to their baby cries. *Infant Behavior and Development, 8,* 385–393.

Dulude, D., Wright, J., & Belanger, C. (2000). The effects of pregnancy complications on the parental adaptation process. *Journal of Reproductive and Infant Psychology, 18,* 5–20.

Durrett, M. E., Otaki, M., & Richards, P. (1984). Attachment and the mothers' perception of support from the father. *International Journal of Behavioral Development, 7,* 167–176.

Durrett, M., Richards, P., Otaki, M., Pennebaker, J., & Nyquist, L. (1986). Mother's involvement with infant and her perception of spousal support, Japan and America. *Journal of Marriage and the Family, 68,* 187–194.

Easterbrooks, M. A., & Goldberg, W. A. (1984). Toddler development in the family: Impact of father involvement and parenting characteristics. *Child Development, 53,* 740–752.

Engfer, A. (1988). The interrelatedness of marriage and the mother-child relationship. In R. A. Hinde & J. Stevenson-Hinde (Eds.), *Relationships within families: Mutual influences* (pp. 104–118). New York: Oxford University Press.

Fagot, B. L., & Kavanagh, K. (1993). Parenting during the second year: Effects of children's age, sex, and attachment classification. *Child Development, 64,* 258–271.

Feldman, R., Guttfreund, D., & Yerushalmi, H. (1998). Parental care and intrusiveness as predictors of the abilities-achievement gap in adolescence. *Journal of Child Psychology and Psychiatry, 39,* 721–730.

Feldman, S. S., & Ingham, M. E. (1975). Attachment behavior: A validation study in two age groups. *Child Development, 46,* 319–330.

Field, T. (1978). Interaction behaviors of primary versus secondary caretaker fathers. *Developmental Psychology, 14,* 183–184.

Field, T., Gewirtz, J. L., Cohen, D., Garcia, R., Greenberg, R., & Collins, K. (1984). Leave-takings and reunions of infants, toddlers, preschoolers, and their parents. *Child Development, 55,* 628–635.

Field, T. M., Hossain, Z., & Malphurs, J. (1999). "Depressed" fathers' interactions with their infants. *Infant Mental Health Journal, 20,* 322–332.

Field, T., Vega-Lahr, N., Goldstein, S., & Scafidi, F. (1987). Interaction behavior of infants and their dual-career parents. *Infant Behavior and Development, 10*, 371–377.

Flouri, E., & Buchanan, A. (2002a). Father involvement in childhood and trouble with the police in adolescence: Findings from the 1958 British cohort. *Journal of Interpersonal Violence, 17*, 689–701.

Flouri, E., & Buchanan, A. (2002b). What predicts good relationships with parents in adolescence and partners in adult life: Findings from the 1958 British birth cohort. *Journal of Family Psychology, 16*, 186–198.

Franz, C. E., McClelland, D. C., & Weinberger, J. (1991). Childhood antecedents of conventional social accomplishments in mid-life adults: A 35-year prospective study. *Journal of Personality and Social Psychology, 60*, 586–595.

Franz, C. E., McClelland, D. C., Weinberger, J., & Peterson, C. (1994). Parenting antecedents of adult adjustment: A longitudinal study. In C. Perris, W. A. Arrindell, & M. Eisemann (Eds.), *Parenting and psychopathology* (pp. 127–144). New York: Wiley.

Frascarolo-Moutinot, F. (1994). *Engagement paternal quotidien et relations parents-enfant* [Daily paternal involvement and parent-child relationships]. Unpublished doctoral dissertation, Universite de Geneve, Geneva, Switzerland.

Frodi, A. M., Lamb, M. E., Hwang, C. P., & Frodi, M. (1983). Father-mother-infant interaction in traditional and nontraditional Swedish families: A longitudinal study. *Alternative Lifestyles, 5*, 142–163.

Gable, S., Crnic, K., & Belsky, J. (1994). Coparenting within the family system: Influences on children's development. *Family Relations, 43*, 380–386.

Galinsky, E. (1999). *Ask the children: What America's children really think about maternal employment.* New York: Morrow.

Gewirtz, H. B., & Gewirtz, J. L. (1968). Visiting and caretaking patterns for Kibbutz infants: Age and sex trends. *American Journal of Orthopsychiatry, 38*, 427–443.

Gjerde, P. F. (1986). The interpersonal structure of family interaction settings: Parent-adolescent relations in dyads and triads. *Developmental Psychology, 22*, 297–304.

Gleason, J. B. (1975). Fathers and other strangers: Men's speech to young children. In D. P. Dato (Ed.), *Language and linguistics* (pp. 289–297). Washington, DC: Georgetown University Press.

Goldberg, W. A., & Easterbrooks, M. A. (1984). The role of marital quality in toddler development. *Developmental Psychology, 20*, 504–514.

Goldman, J. D. G., & Goldman, R. J. (1983). Children's perceptions of parents and their roles: A cross-national study in Australia, England, North America and Sweden. *Sex Roles, 9*, 791–812.

Golinkoff, R. M., & Ames, G. J. (1979). A comparison of fathers' and mothers' speech with their young children. *Child Development, 50*, 28–32.

Goosens, F. A., & van IJzendoorn, M. H. (1990). Quality of infants' attachments to professional caregivers: Relations to infant-parent attachment and day care characteristics. *Child Development, 61*, 832–837.

Gottfried, A. E., Gottfried, A. W., & Bathurst, K. (1988). Maternal employment, family environment, and children's development: Infancy through the school years. In A. E. Gottfried & A. W. Gottfried (Eds.), *Maternal employment and children's development: Longitudinal research* (pp. 11–58). New York: Plenum.

Gottfried, A. E., Gottfried, A. W., & Bathurst, K. (2002). Maternal and dual earner employment status and parenting. In M. H. Bornstein (Ed.), *Handbook of parenting* (Vol. 2, pp. 207–230). Mahwah, NJ: Erlbaum.

Gottman, A. E., Katz, L., & Hooven, C. (1997). *Meta-emotion.* Mahwah, NJ: Erlbaum.

Greenberg, M. (1985). *The birth of a father.* New York: Continuum.

Greenberg, M., & Morris, N. (1974). Engrossment: The newborn's impact upon the father. *American Journal of Orthopsychiatry, 44*, 520–531.

Grossmann, K., Grossmann, K. E., Fremmer-Bombik, E., Kindler, H., Scheurer-Englisch, H., & Zimmermann, P. (2002). The uniqueness of the child-father attachment relationship: Fathers' sensitive and challenging play as a pivotal variable in a 16-year long study. *Social Development, 11*, 307–331.

Grossmann, K. E., & Volkmer, H. J. (1984). Fathers' presence during birth of their infants and paternal involvement. *International Journal of Behavioral Development, 7*, 157–165.

Grotevant, H. D. (1998). Adolescent development in family contexts. In W. Damon & N. Eisenberg (Eds.), *Handbook of child psychology: Vol. 3. Social, personality, and emotional development* (5th ed., pp. 1097–1149). New York: Wiley.

Grych, J. H., & Clarke, R. (1999). Maternal employment and development of the father-infant relationship in the first year. *Developmental Psychology, 35*, 893–903.

Grych, J. H., & Fincham, F. D. (1990). Marital conflict and children's adjustment: A cognitive-contextual framework. *Psychological Bulletin, 108*, 267–290.

Harrison, M. J., & Magill-Evans, J. (1996). Mother and father interactions over the first year with term and preterm infants. *Research in Nursing and Health, 19*, 451–459.

Hartley, R. (1960). Children's concepts of male and female roles. *Merrill Palmer Quarterly, 6*, 83–91.

Heermann, J. A., Jones, L. C., & Wikoff, R. L. (1994). Measurement of parent behavior during interactions with their infants. *Infant Behavior and Development, 17*, 311–321.

Heinicke, C. M., & Guthrie, D. (1992). Stability and change in husband-wife adaptation and the development of the positive parent-child relationship. *Infant Behavior and Development, 15*, 109–127.

Herman, M. A., & McHale, S. M. (1993). Coping with parental negativity: Links with parental warmth and child adjustment. *Journal of Applied Developmental Psychology, 14*, 121–130.

Hetherington, E. M., & Stanley-Hagen, M. M. (1999). The effects of divorce and custody arrangements on children's behavior, development, and adjustment. In M. E. Lamb (Ed.), *Parenting and child development in "nontraditional" families* (pp. 137–160). Mahwah, NJ: Erlbaum.

Hewlett, B. S. (1987). Intimate fathers: Patterns of paternal holding among Aka pygmies. In M. E. Lamb (Ed.), *The father's role: Cross-cultural perspectives* (pp. 295–330). Hillsdale, NJ: Erlbaum.

Hill, J., & Holmbeck, G. N. (1987). Familial adaptation to biological change during adolescence. In R. M. Lerner & T. Foch (Eds.), *Biological-psychological interactions in early adolescence: A life-span perspective* (pp. 207–223). Hillsdale, NJ: Erlbaum.

Hirshberg, L. M., & Svejda, M. (1990). When infants look to their parents: I. Infants' social referencing of mothers compared to fathers. *Child Development, 61*, 1175–1186.

Hock, E., & Lutz, W. (1998). Psychological meaning of separation anxiety in mothers and fathers. *Journal of Family Psychology, 12*, 41–55.

Hoffman, L. W., & Youngblade, L. M. (1999). *Mothers at work: Effects on children's well-being.* Cambridge, England: Cambridge University Press.

Holmbeck, G., Paikoff, R., & Brooks-Gunn, J. (1995). Parenting adolescents. In M. H. Bornstein (Ed.), *Handbook of parenting* (Vol. 1, pp. 91–118). Mahwah, NJ: Erlbaum.

Hosley, C. A., & Montemayer, R. (1997). Fathers and adolescents. In M. E. Lamb (Ed.), *The role of the father in child development* (3rd ed., pp. 162–178). New York: Wiley.

Hossain, Z., Field, T. M., Gonzalez, J., Malphurs, J., & Del Valle, C. (1994). Infants of depressed mothers interact better with their nondepressed fathers. *Infant Mental Health Journal, 15,* 348–357.

Hossain, Z., Field, T., Pickens, J., Malphurs, J., & Del Valle, C. (1997). Fathers' caregiving in low-income African-American and Hispanic American families. *Early Development and Parenting, 6,* 73–82.

Hossain, Z., & Roopnarine, J. L. (1994). African-American fathers' involvement with infants: Relationship to their functional style, support, education, and income. *Infant Behavior and Development, 17,* 175–184.

Hunter, F. T., McCarthy, M. E., MacTurk, R. H., & Vietze, P. M. (1987). Infants' social-constructive interactions with mothers and fathers. *Developmental Psychology, 23,* 249–254.

Hwang, C. P., & Lamb, M. E. (1997). Father involvement in Sweden: A longitudinal study of its stability and correlates. *International Journal of Behavioral Development, 21,* 621–632.

Hyde, J. S., Essex, M. J., & Horton, F. (1993). Fathers and parental leave: Attitudes and expectations. *Journal of Family Issues, 14,* 616–641.

Hyde, B. L., & Texidor, M. S. (1988). A description of the fathering experience among Black fathers. *Journal of Black Nurses Association, 2,* 67–78.

Jarvis, P. A., & Creasey, G. L. (1991). Parental stress, coping, and attachment in families with an 18-month-old infant. *Infant Behavior and Development, 14,* 383–395.

Jodl, K. M., Michael, A., Malanchuk, O., Eccles, J. S., & Sameroff, A. (2001). Parents' roles in shaping early adolescents' occupational aspirations. *Child Development, 72,* 1247–1265.

Jouriles, E. N., Pfiffner, L. J., & O'Leary, S. G. (1988). Marital conflict, parenting, and toddler conduct problems. *Journal of Abnormal Psychology, 16,* 197–206.

Kaitz, M., Chriki, M., Bear-Scharf, L., Nir, T., & Eidelman, A. I. (2000). Effectiveness of primiparae and multiparae at soothing their newborn infants. *Journal of Genetic Psychology, 161,* 203–215.

Kaitz, M., Lapidot, P., Bronner, R., & Eidelman, A. L. (1992). Parturient women can recognize their infants by touch. *Developmental Psychology, 28,* 35–39.

Kaitz, M., Meirov, H., Landman, I., & Eidelman, A. L. (1993). Infant recognition by tactile cues. *Infant Behavior and Development, 16,* 333–341.

Kaitz, M., Shiri, S., Danziger, S., Hershko, Z., & Eidelman, A. L. (1994). Fathers can also recognize their newborns by touch. *Infant Behavior and Development, 17,* 205–207.

Keller, W. D., Hildebrandt, K. A., & Richards, M. E. (1985). Effects of extended father-infant contact during the newborn period. *Infant Behavior and Development, 8,* 337–350.

Kelly, J. B. (2000). Children's adjustment in conflicted marriage and divorce: A decade review of research. *Journal of the American Academy of Child Psychology, 39,* 963–973.

Koestner, R., Franz, C., & Weinberger, J. (1990). The family origins of empathic concern: A 26-year longitudinal study. *Journal of Personality and Social Psychology, 58,* 709–717.

Kokkinaki, T., & Kugiumutzakis, G. (2000). Basic aspects of vocal imitation in infant-parent interaction during the first 6 months. *Journal of Reproductive and Infant Psychology, 18,* 173–187.

Korman, M., & Lewis, C. (2001). Mothers' and fathers' speech to their infants: Explorations of the complexities of context. In M. Almgren, A. Barreña, M.-J. Ezeizabarrena, I. Idiazaabal, & B. MacWhinney (Eds.), *Research on child language acquisition* (pp. 431–453). Somerville, MA: Cascadilla Press.

Kotelchuck, M. (1976). The infant's relationship to the father: Experimental evidence. In M. E. Lamb (Ed.), *The role of the father in child development* (pp. 329–344). New York: Wiley.

Labrell, F. (1990). *Educational strategies and their representations in parents of toddlers.* Paper presented at the Fourth European Conference on Developmental Psychology, Stirling, Scotland.

Labrell, F. (1994). A typical interaction behavior between fathers and toddlers: Teasing. *Early Development and Parenting, 3,* 125–130.

Labrell, F. (1996). Paternal play with toddlers: Recreation and creation. *European Journal of Psychology of Education, 11,* 43–54.

Labrell, F., Deleau, M., & Juhel, J. (2000). Fathers' and mothers' distancing strategies towards toddlers. *International Journal of Behavioral Development, 24,* 356–361.

Lamb, M. E. (1975). Fathers: Forgotten contributors to child development. *Human Development, 18,* 245–266.

Lamb, M. E. (1976a). Effects of stress and cohort on mother- and father-infant interaction. *Developmental Psychology, 12,* 435–443.

Lamb, M. E. (1976b). Interactions between eight-month-old children and their fathers and mothers. In M. E. Lamb (Ed.), *The role of the father in child development* (pp. 307–327). New York: Wiley.

Lamb, M. E. (1976c). Interactions between two-year-olds and their mothers and fathers. *Psychological Reports, 38,* 447–450.

Lamb, M. E. (Ed.). (1976d). *The role of the father in child development.* New York: Wiley.

Lamb, M. E. (1976e). Twelve-month-olds and their parents: Interaction in a laboratory playroom. *Developmental Psychology, 12,* 237–244.

Lamb, M. E. (1977a). The development of mother-infant and father-infant attachments in the second year of life. *Developmental Psychology, 13,* 637–648.

Lamb, M. E. (1977b). The development of parental preferences in the first two years of life. *Sex Roles, 3,* 495–497.

Lamb, M. E. (1977c). Father-infant and mother-infant interaction in the first year of life. *Child Development, 48,* 167–181.

Lamb, M. E. (1981). The development of social expectations in the first year of life. In M. E. Lamb & L. R. Sherrod (Eds.), *Infant social cognition: Empirical and theoretical considerations* (pp. 155–175). Hillsdale, NJ: Erlbaum.

Lamb, M. E. (1987). Predictive implications of individual differences in attachment. *Journal of Consulting and Clinical Psychology, 55,* 817–824.

Lamb, M. E. (1997). Fathers and child development: An introductory overview and guide. In M. E. Lamb (Ed.). *The role of the father in child development* (3rd ed., pp. 1–18, 309–313). New York: Wiley.

Lamb, M. E., Chuang, S. S., & Hwang, C. P. (in press). Internal reliability, temporal stability, and correlates of individual differences in paternal involvement: A 15-year longitudinal study. In R. D. Day & M. E. Lamb (Eds.), *Re-conceptualizing and measuring father involvement.* Mahwah, NJ: Erlbaum.

Lamb, M. E., & Elster, A. B. (1985). Adolescent mother-infant-father relationships. *Developmental Psychology, 21,* 768–773.

Lamb, M. E., Frodi, A. M., Frodi, M., & Hwang, C. P. (1982). Characteristics of maternal and paternal behavior in traditional and nontraditional Swedish families. *International Journal of Behavioral Development, 5,* 131–141.

Lamb, M. E., Frodi, A. M., Hwang, C. P., & Frodi, M. (1982). Varying degrees of paternal involvement in infant care: Attitudinal and behavioral correlates. In M. E. Lamb (Ed.), *Nontraditional families: Parenting and child development* (pp. 117–137). Hillsdale, NJ: Erlbaum.

Lamb, M. E., Frodi, M., Hwang, C. P., & Frodi, A. M. (1983). Effects of paternal involvement on infant preferences for mothers and fathers. *Child Development, 54,* 450–458.

Lamb, M. E., Frodi, A. M., Hwang, C. P., & Frodi, M., & Steinberg, J. (1982a). Effects of gender and caretaking role on parent-infant interaction. In R. N. Emde & R. J. Harmon (Eds.), *Development of attachment and affiliative systems* (pp. 109–118). New York: Plenum.

Lamb, M. E., Frodi, A. M., Hwang, C. P., Frodi, M., & Steinberg, J. (1982b). Mother- and father-infant interaction involving play and holding in traditional and nontraditional Swedish families. *Developmental Psychology, 18,* 215–221.

Lamb, M. E., Hwang, C. P., Broberg, A., Bookstein, F. L., Hult, G., & Frodi, M. (1988). The determinants of paternal involvement in primiparous Swedish families. *International Journal of Behavioral Development, 11,* 433–449.

Lamb, M. E., Hwang, C. P., Frodi, A. M., & Frodi, M. (1982). Security of mother- and father-infant attachment and its relation to sociability with strangers in traditional and nontraditional Swedish families. *Infant Behavior and Development, 5,* 355–367.

Lamb, M. E., Thompson, R. A., Gardner, W., & Charnov, E. L. (1985). *Infant-mother attachment: The origins and developmental significance of individual differences in Strange Situation behavior.* Hillsdale, NJ: Erlbaum.

Langford, W., Lewis, C., Solomon, Y., & Warin, J. (2001). *Family understandings: Closeness and authority in families with a teenage child.* London: Family Policy Studies Centre.

Larson, R., & Richards, M. H. (1994). *Divergent realities: The emotional lives of mothers, fathers and adolescents.* New York: Basic Books.

Lester, B. M., Kotelchuck, M., Spelke, E., Sellers, M. J., & Klein, R. E. (1974). Separation protest in Guatemalan infants: Cross-cultural and cognitive findings. *Developmental Psychology, 10,* 79–85.

Levy-Shiff, R., & Israelashvili, R. (1988). Antecedents of fathering: Some further exploration. *Developmental Psychology, 24,* 434–440.

Levy-Shiff, R., Sharir, H., & Mogilner, M. B. (1989). Mother- and father-preterm infant relationship in the hospital preterm nursery. *Child Development, 60,* 93–102.

Lewis, C. (1984, September). *Men's involvement in fatherhood: Historical and gender issues.* Paper presented at the meeting of the British Psychological Society (Developmental Section), Lancaster, England.

Lewis, C. (1986). *Becoming a father.* Milton Keynes, England: Open University Press.

Lewis, C., & Gregory, S. (1987). Parents' talk to their infants: Interpreting observed differences between mothers and fathers. *First Language, 7,* 201–216.

Lewis, C., Newson, L. J., & Newson, E. (1982). Father participation through childhood. In N. Beail & J. McGuire (Eds.), *Fathers: Psychological perspectives* (pp. 174–193). London: Junction.

Lewis, C., Kier, C., Hyder, C., Prenderville, N., Pullen, J., & Stephens, A. (1996). Observer influences on fathers and mothers: An experimental manipulation of the structure and function of parent-infant conversation. *Early Development and Parenting, 5,* 57–68.

Lewis, M., & Weinraub, M. (1974). Sex of parent × sex of child: Socioemotional development. In R. Richart, R. Friedman, & R. Vande Wiele (Eds.), *Sex differences in behavior* (pp. 165–189). New York: Wiley.

Lewis, M., & Weinraub, M. (1976). The father's role in the child's social network. In M. E. Lamb (Ed.), *The role of the father in child development* (pp. 157–184). New York: Wiley.

Lind, R. (1974, October). *Observations after delivery of communications between mother-infant-father.* Paper presented at the meeting of the International Congress of Pediatrics, Buenos Aires, Argentina.

Lindsey, E. W., & Mize, J. (2001). Contextual differences in parent-child play: Implications for children's gender role development. *Sex Roles, 44,* 155–176.

Lundy, B. L. (2002). Paternal socio-psychological factors and infant attachment: The mediating role of synchrony in father-infant interactions. *Infant Behavior and Development, 25,* 221–236.

Lytton, H., & Romney, D. M. (1991). Parents' differential socialization of boys and girls: A meta-analysis. *Psychological Bulletin, 109*, 267–296.

Lyytinen, P., Laakso, M. L., & Poikkeus, A. M. (1998). Parental contribution to child's early language and interest in books. *European Journal of Psychology of Education, 13*, 297–308.

Maccoby, E. (1984). Middle childhood in the context of the family. In W. A. Collins (Ed.), *Development during middle childhood: The years from six to twelve* (pp. 184–239). Washington, DC: National Academy of Sciences Press.

Maccoby, E. E., & Martin, J. (1983). Socialization in the context of the family: Parent-child interaction. In P. H. Mussen & C. M. Hetherington (Eds.), *Handbook of child psychology: Vol. 4. Socialization, personality, and social development* (4th ed., pp. 1–101). New York: Wiley.

Mackey, W. C. (1985). *Fathering behaviors: The dynamics of the man-child bond.* New York: Plenum.

Magill-Evans, J., & Harrison, M. J. (1999). Parent-child interactions and development of toddlers born preterm. *Western Journal of Nursing Research, 21*, 292–307.

Main, M., Kaplan, N., & Cassidy, J. (1985). Security in infancy, childhood and adulthood: A move to the level of representation. *Monographs of the Society for Research in Child Development, 50*, 66–104.

Main, M., & Weston, D. M. (1981). The quality of the toddler's relationship to mother and to father: Related to conflict behavior and the readiness to establish new relationships. *Child Development, 52*, 932–940.

Mansbach, I. K., & Greenbaum, C. (1999). Developmental maturity expectations of Israeli fathers and mothers: Effects of education, ethnic origin, and religiosity. *International Journal of Behavioral Development, 23*, 771–797.

Marton, P. L., & Minde, K. (1980, April). *Paternal and maternal behavior with premature infants.* Paper presented at the meeting of the American Orthopsychiatric Association, Toronto, Ontario.

McConachie, H. (1989). Mothers' and fathers' interaction with their young mentally handicapped children. *International Journal of Behavioral Development, 12*, 239–255.

McElwain, N. L., & Volling, B. L. (1999). Depressed mood and marital conflict: Relations to maternal and paternal intrusiveness with one-year-old infants. *Journal of Applied Developmental Psychology, 20*, 63–83.

McGrellis, S., Henderson, S., Holland, J., Sharpe, S., & Thompson, R. (2000). *Beyond the moral maze: A quantitative study of young people's values.* London: Tuffnell Press.

McHale, S. M., & Huston, T. L. (1984). Men and women as parents: Sex role orientations, employment, and parental roles with infants. *Child Development, 55*, 1349–1361.

Meyer, H. J. (1988). Marital and mother-child relationships: Developmental history, parent personality, and child difficultness. In R. A. Hinde & J. Stevenson-Hinde (Eds.), *Relationships within families: Mutual influences* (pp. 119–139). Oxford, England: Clarendon Press.

Montemayor, R., & Brownlee, J. (1987). Fathers, mothers, and adolescents: Gender-based differences in parental roles during adolescence. *Journal of Youth and Adolescence, 16*, 281–291.

Myers, B. J. (1982). Early intervention using Brazelton training with middle-class mothers and fathers of newborns. *Child Development, 53*, 462–471.

NICHD Early Child Care Research Network. (2000). Factors associated with fathers' caregiving activities and sensitivity with young children. *Journal of Family Psychology, 14*, 200–219.

Ninio, A., & Rinott, N. (1988). Fathers' involvement in the care of their infants and their attributions of cognitive competence to infants. *Child Development, 59*, 652–663.

Noller, P. (1980). Cross-gender effects in two-child families. *Developmental Psychology, 16*, 159–160.

Noller, P., & Callan, V. J. (1988). Understanding parent-adolescent interactions: Perceptions of family members and outsiders. *Developmental Psychology, 24*, 707–714.

Notaro, P. C., & Volling, B. L. (1999). Parental responsiveness and infant-parent attachment: A replication study with fathers and mothers. *Infant Behavior and Development, 22,* 345–352.

Nugent, J. K. (1987). The father's role in early Irish socialization: Historical and empirical perspectives. In M. E. Lamb (Ed.), *The father's role: Cross-cultural perspectives* (pp. 169–193). Hillsdale, NJ: Erlbaum.

Offer, D., Ostrov, E., & Howard, K. (1981). *The adolescent: A psychological self-portrait.* New York: Basic Books.

Ogletree, M. D., Jones, R. M., & Coyl, D. D. (2002). Fathers and their adolescent sons: Pubertal development and parental involvement. *Journal of Adolescent Research, 17,* 418–424.

Oppenheim, D., Sagi, A., & Lamb, M. E. (1988). Infant-adult attachments on the kibbutzim and their relation to socioemotional development 4 years later. *Developmental Psychology, 24,* 427–433.

Palkovitz, R. (1985). Fathers' birth attendance, early contact, and extended contact with their newborns: A critical review. *Child Development, 56,* 392–406.

Palkovitz, R. (1997). Reconstructing "involvement": Expanding conceptualizations of men's caring in contemporary families. In A. J. Hawkins & D. C. Dollahite (Eds.), *Generative fathering: Beyond deficit perspectives* (pp. 200–216). Thousand Oaks, CA: Sage.

Palkovitz, R. (2002). *Involved fathering and men's adult development.* Mahwah, NJ: Erlbaum.

Pannabecker, B., Emde, R. N., & Austin, B. (1982). The effect of early extended contact on father-newborn interaction. *Journal of Genetic Psychology, 141,* 7–17.

Parke, R. D., & Beitel, A. (1986). Hospital-based interventions for fathers. In M. E. Lamb (Ed.), *The father's role: Applied perspectives* (pp. 293–323). New York: Wiley.

Parke, R. D., MacDonald, K. B., Burks, V. M., Carson, J., Bhavnagri, N., Barth, J. M., et. al. (1989). Family and peer systems: In search of the linkages. In K. Kreppner & R. M. Lerner (Eds.), *Family systems and life-span development* (pp. 65–92). Hillsdale, NJ: Erlbaum.

Parke, R. D., & Sawin, D. B. (1977, March). *The family in early infancy: Social interactional and attitudinal analyses.* Paper presented at the meeting of the Society for Research in Child Development, New Orleans, LA.

Parke, R. D., & Sawin, D. B. (1980). The family in early infancy: Social interactional and attitudinal analyses. In F. A. Pedersen (Ed.), *The father-infant relationship: Observational studies in a family setting* (pp. 44–70). New York: Praeger.

Pedersen, F. A. (Ed.). (1980). *The father-infant relationship: Observational studies in a family setting.* New York: Praeger.

Pedersen, F. A., Cain, R., Zaslow, M., & Anderson, B. (1982). Variation in infant experience associated with alternative family roles. In L. Laosa & I. Sigel (Eds.), *Families as learning environments for children* (pp. 203–221). New York: Plenum.

Pedersen, F. A,. & Robson, K. (1969). Father participation in infancy. *American Journal of Orthopsychiatry, 39,* 466–472.

Pellegrini, A. D., Brody, G. H., & Stoneman, Z. (1987). Children's conversational competence with their parents. *Discourse Processes, 10,* 93–106.

Phares, V. (1996). *Fathers and developmental psychopathology.* New York: Wiley.

Phares, V. (1997). Psychological adjustment, maladjustment, and father-child relationships. In M. E. Lamb (Ed.), *The role of the father in child development* (3rd ed., pp. 261–283, 380–392). New York: Wiley.

Pleck, J. H., & Stueve, J. L. (in press). Time and paternal involvement: Reconsideration and new data. In K. Daly (Ed.), *Minding the time in family experience: Emerging perspectives and issues.* Greenwich, CT: JAI Press.

Power, T. G. (1985). Mother- and father-infant play: A developmental analysis. *Child Development, 56,* 1514–1524.

Power, T. G., & Parke, R. D. (1979, March). *Toward a taxonomy of father-infant and mother-infant play patterns.* Paper presented to the Society for Research in Child Development, San Francisco.

Power, T. G., & Parke, R. D. (1983). Patterns of mother and father play with their 8-month-old infant: A multiple analyses approach. *Infant Behavior and Development, 6,* 453–459.

Pruett, K. (1985). Oedipal configurations in young father-raised children. *Psychoanalytic Study of the Child, 40,* 435–460.

Pruett, K., & Litzenberger, B. (1992). Latency development in children of primary nurturing fathers: Eight-year follow up. *Psychoanalytic Study of the Child, 4,* 85–101.

Raag, T., & Rackliff, C. L. (1998). Preschoolers' awareness of social expectations of gender: Relationships to toy choices. *Sex Roles, 38,* 685–700.

Rendina, I., & Dickerscheid, J. D. (1976). Father involvement with first-born infants. *Family Coordinator, 25,* 373–379.

Richards, M. P. M. (1982). How should we approach the study of fathers? In L. McKee & M. O'Brien (Eds.), *The father figure* (pp. 57–71). London: Tavistock Publications.

Rödholm, M., & Larsson, K. (1982). The behavior of human male adults at their first contact with a newborn. *Infant Behavior and Development, 5,* 121–130.

Roggman, L. A., Benson, B., & Boyce, L. (1999). Fathers with infants: Knowledge and involvement in relation to psychosocial functioning and religion. *Infant Mental Health Journal, 20,* 257–277.

Rohner, R. P., & Pettengill, S. M. (1985). Perceived parental acceptance-rejection and parental control among Korean adolescents. *Child Development, 56,* 524–528.

Rondal, J. A. (1980). Fathers' and mothers' speech in early language development. *Journal of Child Language, 7,* 353–369.

Roopnarine, J. L., Talukder, E., Jain, D., Joshi, P., & Srivastav, P. (1992). Personal well-being, kinship ties, and mother-infant and father-infant interactions in single-wage and dual-wage families in New Delhi, India. *Journal of Marriage and the Family, 54,* 293–301.

Rosen, K. S., & Rothbaum, F. (1993). Quality of parental caregiving and security of attachment. *Developmental Psychology, 29,* 358–367.

Ross, H., & Taylor, H. (1989). Do boys prefer daddy or his physical style of play? *Sex Roles, 20,* 23–33.

Russell, A., Aloa, V., Feder, T., Glover, A., Miller, H., & Palmer, G. (1998). Sex-based differences in parenting styles in a sample with preschool children. *Australian Journal of Psychology, 50,* 89–99.

Russell, A., & Saebel, J. (1997). Mother-son, mother-daughter, father-son and father-daughter: Are they distinct relationships? *Developmental Review, 17,* 111–147.

Russell, G., & Russell, A. (1987). Mother-child and father-child relationship in middle childhood. *Child Development, 58,* 1573–1585.

Sagi, A., Lamb, M. E., & Gardner, W. P. (1986). Relations between Strange Situation behavior and stranger sociability among infants on Israeli kibbutzim. *Infant Behavior and Development, 9,* 271–282.

Sagi, A., Lamb, M. E., Shoham, R., Dvir, R., & Lewkowicz, K. S. (1985). Parent-infant interaction in families on Israeli kibbutzim. *International Journal of Behavioral Development, 8,* 273–284.

Schaffer, H. R., & Emerson, P. E. (1964). The development of social attachments in infancy. *Monographs of the Society for Research in Child Development, 29*(Whole No. 94).

Sears, R. R., Maccoby, E. E., & Levin, H. (1957). *Patterns of childrearing.* Evanston, IL: Row, Peterson.

Shulman, S., & Seiffge-Krenke, I. (1997). *Fathers and adolescents: Developmental and clinical perspectives.* London: Routledge.

Siegal, A. U. (1987). Are sons and daughters more differently treated by fathers than by mothers? *Developmental Review, 7,* 183–209.

Silverberg, S., Tennenbaum, D., & Jacob, T. (1992). Adolescence and family interaction. In V. van Hasselt & M. Herson (Eds.), *Handbook of social development* (pp. 347–370). New York: Plenum.

Simmons, R. G., & Blyth, D. A. (1987). *Moving into adolescence: The impact of pubertal change and school context.* Hawthorne, NY: Alders de Gruyter.

Spelke, E., Zelazo, P., Kagan, J., & Kotelchuck, M. (1973). Father interaction and separation protest. *Developmental Psychology, 9,* 83–90.

Steele, H., Steele, M., Croft, C., & Fonagy, P. (1999). Infant-mother attachment at one year predicts children's understanding of mixed emotions at six years. *Social Development, 8,* 161–178.

Steele, H., Steele, M., & Fonagy, P. (1996). Associations among attachment classification of mothers, fathers, and their infants. *Child Development, 67,* 541–555.

Steinberg, L. (1988). Reciprocal relations between parent-child distance and pubertal maturation. *Developmental Psychology, 24,* 122–128.

Steinberg, L. (1987). The impact of puberty on family relations: Effects of pubertal status and pubertal timing. *Developmental Psychology, 23,* 451–460.

Steinberg, L. (1990). Interdependence in the family: Autonomy, conflict, and harmony in the parent-adolescent relationship. In S. S. Feldman & G. Elliott (Eds.), *At the threshold: The developing adolescent* (pp. 255–276). Cambridge, MA: Harvard University Press.

Storey, A. E., Walsh, C. J., Quinton, R. L., & Wynne-Edwards, R. E. (2000). Hormonal correlates of paternal responsiveness in new and expectant fathers. *Evolution and Human Behavior, 21,* 79–95.

Suess, G. J., Grossmann, K. E., & Sroufe, L. A. (1992). Effects of infant-attachment to mother and father on quality of adaptation in preschool: From dyadic to individual organization of self. *International Journal of Behavioral Development, 15,* 43–65.

Sun, L. C., & Roopnarine, J. L. (1996). Mother-infant, father-infant interaction and involvement in childcare and household labor among Taiwanese families. *Infant Behavior and Development, 19,* 121–129.

Suppal, P., & Roopnarine, J. L. (1999). Paternal involvement in child care as a function of maternal employment in nuclear and extended families in India. *Sex Roles, 40,* 731–744.

Teti, D. M., Bond, L. A., & Gibbs, E. D. (1988). Mothers, fathers, and siblings: A comparison of play styles and their influence upon infant cognitive level. *International Journal of Behavioral Development, 11,* 415–432.

Thompson, R. A. (1998). Early sociopersonality development. In W. Damon & N. Eisenberg (Eds.), *Handbook of child psychology: Vol. 3. Social, emotional, and personality development* (5th ed., pp. 25–104). New York: Wiley.

Trehub, S. E., Hill, D. S., & Kamenetsky, S. B. (1997). Parents' sung performance for infants. *Canadian Journal of Experimental Psychology, 51,* 385–396.

Trehub, S. E., Unyk, A. M., Kamenetsky, S. B., Hill, D. S., Trainor, L. J., Henderson, J. L., et al. (1997). Mothers' and fathers' singing to infants. *Developmental Psychology, 33,* 500–507.

Tulananda, O., & Roopnarine, J. L. (2001). Mothers' and fathers' interactions with preschoolers in the home in northern Thailand: Relationships to teachers' assessments of children's social skills. *Journal of Family Psychology, 15,* 676–687.

Van IJzendoorn, M. H. (1995). Adult attachment representation, parental responsiveness, and infant attachment: A meta-analysis of the predictive validity of the Adult Attachment Interview. *Psychological Bulletin, 117,* 387–403.

Van IJzendoorn, M. H., & DeWolff, M. S. (1997). In search of the absent father—meta-analyses of infant-father attachment: A rejoinder to our discussants. *Child Development, 68,* 604–609.

Verscheuren, K., & Marcoen, A. (1999). Representation of self and socioemotional competence in kindergartners: Differential and combined effects of attachment to mother and to father. *Child Development, 70,* 183–201.

Volling, B., & Belsky, J. (1992). Infant, father, and marital antecedents of infant-father attachment security in dual-earner and single-earner families. *International Journal of Behavioral Development, 15,* 83–100.

Wachs, T., Uzgiris, I., & Hunt, J. (1971). Cognitive development in infants of different age levels and from different environmental backgrounds. *Merrill-Palmer Quarterly, 17,* 283–317.

Ward, C. D., & Cooper, R. P. (1999). A lack of evidence in 4-month-old human infants for paternal voice preference. *Developmental Psychobiology, 35,* 49–59.

Warin, J., Solomon, Y., Lewis, C., & Langford, W. (1999). *Fathers, work and family life.* London: Family Policy Research Centre.

Warren-Leubecker, A., & Bohannon, J. N., III. (1984). Intonation patterns in child-directed speech: Mother-father differences. *Child Development, 55,* 1379–1385.

Weinraub, M., & Frankel, J. (1977). Sex differences in parent-infant interaction during free play, departure, and separation. *Child Development, 48,* 1240–1249.

Welkowitz, J., Bond, R. N., Feldman, L., & Tota, M. E. (1990). Conversational time patterns and mutual influence in parent-child interactions: A time-series approach. *Journal of Psycholinguistics Research, 19,* 221–243.

West, M. M., & Konner, M. J. (1976). The role of the father: An anthropological perspective. In M. E. Lamb (Ed.), *The role of the father in child development* (pp. 185–216). New York: Wiley.

Wille, D. (1998). Longitudinal analyses of mothers' and fathers' responses on the maternal separation anxiety scale. *Merrill-Palmer Quarterly, 44,* 216–233.

Willemsen, E., Flaherty, D., Heaton, C., & Ritchey, G. (1974). Attachment behavior of one-year-olds as a function of mother vs. father, sex of child, session, and toys. *Genetic Psychology Monographs, 90,* 305–324.

Williams, J., Bennett, S., & Best, D. (1975). Awareness and expression of sex stereotypes in young children. *Developmental Psychology, 11,* 635–642.

Woollett, A., White, D., & Lyon, L. (1982). Observations of fathers at birth. In N. Beail & J. McGuire (Eds.), *Fathers: Psychological perspectives* (pp. 72–94). London: Junction.

Yarrow, L. J., MacTurk, R. H., Vietze, P. M., McCarthy, M. E., Klein, R. P., & McQuiston, S. (1984). Developmental course of parental stimulation and its relationship to mastery motivation during infancy. *Developmental Psychology, 20,* 492–503.

Yogman, M. (1981). Games fathers and mothers play with their infants. *Infant Mental Health Journal, 2,* 241–248.

Yogman, M. W., Kindlon, D., & Earls, F. (1995). Father involvement and cognitive-behavioral outcomes of preterm infants. *Journal of the American Academy of Child and Adolescent Psychiatry, 34,* 58–66.

Youngblade, L. M., & Belsky, J. (1992). Parent-child antecedents of 5-year-olds' close friendships: A longitudinal analysis. *Developmental Psychology, 28,* 700–713.

Youngblade, Y. M., Park, K. A., & Belsky, J. (1993). Measurement of young children's close friendship: A comparison of two independent assessment systems and their association with attachment security. *International Journal of Behavioral Development, 16,* 563–587.

Youniss, J., & Smoller, J. (1985). *Adolescent relations with mothers, fathers, and friends*. Chicago: University of Chicago Press.

Youniss, J., & Ketterlinus, R. D. (1987). Communication and connectedness in mother- and father-adolescent relationships. *Journal of Youth and Adolescence, 16,* 191–197.

Zaouche-Gaudron, C., Ricaud, H., & Beaumatin, A. (1998). Father-child play interaction and subjectivity. *European Journal of Psychology of Education, 13,* 447–460.

Zelazo, P. R., Kotelchuck, M., Barber, L, & David, J. (1977, March). *Fathers and sons: An experimental facilitation of attachment behaviors*. Paper presented at the meeting of the Society for Research in Child Development, New Orleans.

CHAPTER 11

Fathering and Children's Peer Relationships

ROSS D. PARKE, JESSICA DENNIS, MARY L. FLYR, KRISTIE L. MORRIS, COLLEEN KILLIAN, DAVID J. MCDOWELL, and MARGARET WILD

FATHERS ARE MAJOR but often-unrecognized members of the family who play a central role in children's socialization. At the same time, it is understood that families share the socialization role with a variety of other agents including peers. Often these two socialization agents—fathers and peers—have been viewed as independent influences and, only recently have the links between fathers and peers been examined. Our goal in this chapter is to examine the relations between fathers and peers and how they jointly influence children's social outcomes.

Several assumptions guide our review. First, we assume that fathers and mothers play unique as well as overlapping roles in the development of children's peer relationships. Second, we argue that fathers are best understood as part of a family system in which individual family members are influenced by sets of relationships among family members (fathers-children). Third, fathers are influenced by the network of relationships formed with extrafamilial sources such as friends, coworkers, and community resources. Fourth, just as families are viewed within a systems framework, peers are best understood from a social systems perspective that recognizes that children form a variety of distinctive types of relationships with age-mates such as acquaintanceships, dyadic friendships, romantic relationships, and relationships with groups of peers (Rubin, Bukowski, & Parker, 1998; Schneider, 2000). Fifth, we recognize that children's peer relationships are important for children's short- and long-term

Preparation of this chapter and of the research reported in this chapter was supported by the following grants: NSF grant BNS8919391 to R. D. Parke and NICHD grant HT 32391 to R. D. Parke and R. O'Neil. The authors would like to thank the staff and superintendents of the Fontana and Juripa School Districts for their support of the research in this chapter, and appreciation goes to Faye Harmer for typing the manuscript.

adjustment (Parker & Asher, 1987). Therefore, increasing our understanding of how families, including fathers, contribute to children's adaptation to peers is an important task because it can guide our intervention and prevention efforts.

A final set of assumptions that guide our reviews concerns the nature of the links between family and peer systems. Several perspectives on the nature of the relation between families and peers as well as the relative importance of family and peers in childhood socialization are available. In his classic formulation of this issue, Hartup (1979) noted that children's relationships with peers are viewed as either independent of family ties or interdependent social systems. Advocates of the independent view argue that family and peer systems develop separately and that each performs unique functions in the socialization process (e.g., Harlow, 1958). More recently, some writers (e.g., Harris, 1995, 1998) have extended the independence argument and proposed that parents have little influence on children's behavior beyond a biological or genetic contribution. Instead, Harris argued that the peer group is largely responsible for socialization of children's social behavior. In contrast to the independent view, others argue that family and peer systems mutually influence each other in the cause of socialization. Most recent accounts, and the viewpoint that guides this chapter, are that both families and peers play important roles in children's social development and recognize the interdependence between these two social systems (Parke et al., 2002; Vandell, 2000). Moreover, the nature of family-peer relationships varies across developmental periods as well as across different family types and ecological, historical, and cultural contexts. Our goal is to provide a contemporary perspective on the roles played by fathers as part of the family system in the development of children's peer relationships.

In the first section of this chapter we propose a tripartite model that suggests that fathers influence their children's peer relationships through three pathways. These three pathways are (a) the nature of the father-child relationship, (b) the type of direct advice or supervision provided by fathers in regard to their children's peer relationships, and (c) the type of managerial strategies that the father uses to facilitate or limit children's opportunities for contact with their peers. Several mediating processes that may account for father-peer links are examined, including children's emotion-regulatory skills, their cognitive representations of social relationships, and their attention-regulatory processes. In addition, we highlight briefly the ways in which the fathers' marital relationship influences his impact on children's peer relationships. Then we examine cross-cultural variations in father-peer relationships. Finally, we note remaining issues and unresolved problems in this area as a guide for future research.

FATHER-PEER RELATIONSHIPS: A THREE-PATHWAY MODEL

There are many ways in which fathers influence their children's relationships with peers. We propose three different paths that lead to variations in children's peer relationships. These three paths consist of lessons learned in the context of the father-child relationship, fathers' direct advice concerning peer relationships, and fathers' regulation of access to peers and peer-related activity. Although our focus is on fathers, it is important to recognize that mothers play these roles as well. To the extent that the literature permits, we note differences between mothers and fathers in how they influence their children's peer relationships.

PATHWAY ONE: THE FATHER-CHILD RELATIONSHIP AND PEER RELATIONSHIPS

In considering the first pathway, two approaches have been taken: namely, studying the effects of fathers' absence and directly assessing the father-child relationship.

Father Absence and Peer Relationships

Evidence that fathers matter for children's peer relationships came initially from studies of father absence. Although these studies have been criticized (Hetherington & Deur, 1971), they provide suggestive evidence and merit brief discussion. Stolz (1954) studied children who were infants during World War II, when many of their fathers were away at war. When the children were 4 to 8 years old, Stolz found that those whose fathers had been absent during their infancy had poorer peer relationships. Studies of the sons of Norwegian sailors, who were away for many months at a time, point to the same conclusion: The boys whose fathers were often absent were less popular and had less-satisfying peer-group relationships than did boys whose fathers were regularly available (Lynn & Sawrey, 1959). Possibly, boys who grow up without their fathers have less chance to learn the behaviors that other boys in their culture value. They may, for example, tend to be shy, timid, and reluctant to play rough games—traits that are correlated with poor peer relationships (Rubin et al., 1998).

The age at which father absence begins is important, too (Parke, 1996). In one classic study, boys who were separated from their fathers before the age of 5 years were more dependent on their peers and less assertive (Hetherington, 1966). They played fewer rough physical contact sports such as football, boxing, or soccer and focused more on nonphysical and noncompetitive activities. In contrast, when fathers were available until their sons were 6 years of age, their later departure had less effect: Boys whose fathers left when they were 6 years of age or older behaved similarly to boys in father-present homes. Later studies suggested that the effects of father absence on boys' development of social competence may be due to the inability to delay gratification. Mischel, Shoda, and Peake (1988) found that 4-year-olds who were unable to delay gratification were less socially and cognitively competent in adolescence.

More recent and more compelling evidence of the potential detrimental impact of fathers' absence on children's social adjustment comes from several nationally representatives data sets (McLanahan & Teitler, 1999). One study, the National Longitudinal Study of Youth (NLSY; Mott, 1994), involved a sample of mothers and children who were between 5 and 9 years of age when they were assessed. The data from this group of over 6,000 children and their mothers confirmed that children in homes where the father was absent were at higher risk for school and peer problems. But the gender and race of the child qualified the picture. White boys were affected by father absence more than were Black boys and White boys from homes where a father was in residence. Only 9% of the White boys from father-present homes were rated by their mothers as "not liked by their peers," whereas over 25% of the White boys from father-absent homes were unpopular with their age-mates. Similarly, there was some evidence that White girls from father-absent homes were at a behavioral disadvantage in comparison with White girls in homes with fathers. Moreover, boys and girls expressed their reactions to father absence in different ways: Boys tended to act out or externalize, whereas girls tended to display an internalizing pattern. White girls from father-absent homes had more trouble getting along with other children than did girls from father-present families. For Black boys or girls, there was little evidence of adverse behavior associated with a father's absence. The patterns for the White children were not due to the early effects of maternal and family background (e.g., a mother's education, income, or health) that were present before the father left the home. The effects were reduced, however, when factors linked with the disruption of the father's departure—such as family income or long-term maternal health—were taken into account.

Mott (1994) suggested that the reason for these racial differences may lie in the pattern of the father's absence in Black and White homes:

> Black fathers are much more likely to have been absent from the home very early in the child's life. In contrast . . . White fathers are more likely to leave in the preschool and early school ages and, in all likelihood, are more likely to keep leaving in the years ahead. For Black children, the biological father, if he is going to leave, is probably gone. For White children, the father leaving process will represent a continuing drama throughout the children's early and mid-school years. . . . the departure of parents when children are at the school ages probably represents a greater potential for ongoing psychological damage than does father leaving at very early ages. (p. 125)

In addition, although there were nearly three times as many Black children as White children without fathers or father figures present, Black fathers were more likely to continue to maintain contact with their offspring than White fathers were. The traditional reliance of Black families on extended kin networks for support may be a further factor in accounting for the lessened impact of fathers' absence on Black children. It is misleading to assume that boys alone are negatively affected by father absence. Girls suffer also, but both the timing of the effects and the domains in which father absence is evident are different. In an early classic study, Hetherington (1972) showed that studies of the impact of father absence on girls were inconclusive because they measured the wrong behaviors at the wrong time. According to Johnson's theory of reciprocal role taking, fathers are particularly important for helping girls learn to interact with males, a task that begins in adolescence (Collins, 2002). Among the fatherless girls, those whose mothers were either divorced or widowed were anxious around boys. The daughters of the widows were shy and uncomfortable, whereas the daughters of divorced mothers were more assertive and outgoing with male peers. This pattern was consistent with the finding that girls from divorced families date earlier and more often than do girls from either widowed or two-parent families. And as several researchers have found, divorce is associated with earlier onset of sexuality. For example, Furstenberg and Teitler (1994), using the National Survey of Children data set, found that more adolescents from disrupted families had initiated sex before age 17. Similarly, others (Wu, Cherlin, & Bumpass, 1997) found that age of onset of first sexual intercourse was earlier in father-absent families using the NLSY and the National Survey of Families and Households studies. It is not surprising that girls, especially among Whites and Hispanics in father-absent homes, have higher rates of premarital childbearing (Cherlin, Kiernan, & Chase-Lansdale, 1995), an effect that may be due, in part, to early onset of puberty among these girls.

In summary, father absence is linked with deficiencies in peer relationships, although the effects vary with race, gender of the child, and the domain assessed. However, these studies leave unanswered central questions about the causes of the effects of father absence on children's peer competence, such as the specific aspects of the fathers' attitudes and behaviors that may lead to poorer peer relationships. At the same time, progress is being made in eliminating alternative explanations, such as maternal stress and reduced income, which are often associated with father absence (McLanahan, 1997; McLanahan & Teitler, 1999). This recent work more clearly implicates father absence as the probable cause of these outcomes. To understand better the specific aspects of the father-child relationship that may be important in explaining these father-peer links, we examine next the evidence concerning the effects of variation in the quality of father-child relationships in father-present families on children's relationships with peers.

THE QUALITY OF THE FATHER-CHILD RELATIONSHIP

Researchers have examined the impact of the quality of the father-child relationship on children's relationships with their peers from two perspectives. First, those in the attachment tradition have explored the connection between the father's infant attachment and social adaptation in the peer group. The second tradition focuses on the links between the quality of father-child interaction, especially in play, and children's peer relationships.

Attachment and Social Adaptation

An impressive amount of research suggests that the quality of the child-mother attachment is related to children's later social and emotional development in preschool, in middle childhood, and even in adolescence. A secure attachment to the mother is likely to lead to better social and emotional adjustment. Securely attached children are better liked by others, have higher self-esteem, and are more socially skilled (Thompson, 1998). Does the quality of the infant's or child's attachment to the father matter?

Although the quality of the father-child attachment relationship is linked with peer competence, the evidence is clearly mixed. Youngblade, Park, and Belsky (1993) found that earlier secure attachment to fathers, but not mothers, was linked with positive interactions with friends among preschool-age children. Similarly, Kerns and Barth (1995) reported that secure attachment to fathers was linked with preschool children's cooperative and friendly behavior with peers; secure attachment to mothers was linked to peer popularity for boys. However, others have failed to find robust links between infant-father attachment as assessed in the Strange Situation and indexes of later social competence, such as children's understanding of mixed emotions at age 6 (Steele, Steele, Croft, & Fonagy, 1999) or preschool children's emotional regulation with a distressed sibling (Volling, 2001). Recent conceptual and empirical work by the Grossmanns (Grossmann, Grossmann, Fremmer-Bombik, et al., 2002; Grossmann, Grossmann, & Zimmerman, 1998) assists in clarifying this picture. These authors argued that father and mother attachment relationships derive from different sets of early social experiences. Specifically, mothers provide security when the child is distressed, whereas fathers "provide security through sensitive and challenging support as a companion when the child's exploratory system is aroused" (Grossmann, Grossmann, Fremmer-Bombik, et al., 2002, p. 311). In short, mothers function as distress regulators and fathers as challenging but reassuring play partners. In support of their argument, Grossmann, Grossmann, Fremmer-Bombik, et al. (2002) found that fathers' play sensitivity and quality of infant-mother attachment predicted children's internal working model of attachment at age 10. At age 16 dimensions of adolescents' attachment representation as assessed by the adult attachment interview were predicted by only fathers play sensitivity. Moreover, paternal play sensitivity leaves its mark on children's partnership representations 6 years later, at age 22, as well (Grossmann, Grossmann, Winter, & Zimmerman, 2002). Specifically, young adults whose fathers were more sensitive in their early play interactions had more secure partnership representations of their current romantic relationships. They viewed their partners as available and their relationships as warm and mutually supportive—hallmarks of healthy romantic ties. Their results supported the assumption that fathers and mothers play different roles in the attachment system and that fathers' play sensitivity rather than the security of their attachment relationship with their infants is a better predictor of the children's long-term attachment representations. In light of the links between the quality of children's attachment representations and their social competence (Cassidy, Kirsh, Scolton, & Parke, 1996), these findings are of particular importance for the understanding of the antecedents of children's peer relationships. Finally, these data suggest that the quality of the father-child relationship, especially in play contexts, is important for later peer outcomes (Parke, 1996).

Father-Child Interaction and Children's Social Adaptation

In contrast to the attachment tradition, researchers in the cognitive social learning tradition assume that face-to-face interactions between children and fathers may afford children the opportunity to learn social skills that are necessary for successful peer relationships (see Parke & O'Neil, 1997, for a fuller description). This research has shown that controlling parent interactional styles were related to negative social outcomes for children and that warm interactional styles were related to positive outcomes. In addition, these studies suggested that fathers' ability as play partners was positively linked to children's social competence with peers. In an early study, MacDonald and Parke (1984) observed fathers and their 3- and 4-year-old boys and girls in 20 minutes of structured play in their homes. Teachers ranked these children in terms of their popularity among their preschool classmates. For both boys and girls, fathers who exhibited high levels of physical play with their children and elicited high levels of positive feelings during the play sessions had children who received the highest peer popularity ratings. For boys, however, this pattern was qualified by the fathers' level of directiveness. Boys whose fathers were both highly physical and low in directiveness received the highest popularity ratings, and the boys whose fathers were highly directive received lower popularity scores. Girls whose teachers rated them as popular had physically playful and feeling-eliciting but nondirective fathers and directive mothers. Later studies in our lab have confirmed this general pattern. Popular children have fathers who were able to sustain physical play for longer periods and used less directive or coercive tactics (see Parke, Burks, Carson, Neville, & Boyum, 1994; Parke, Cassidy, Burks, Carson, & Boyum, 1992). Nor are these relations limited to single-time parents. In a longitudinal examination of these issues, Barth and Parke (1993) found that fathers who were more effective play partners had children who made a more successful transition to elementary school. Other researchers report that the style of father-child play is important as well. Mize and Pettit (1997) found that preschool children whose play with their fathers was characterized by mutuality or balance in making play suggestions and following partners' suggestions were less aggressive, more competent, and better liked by their peers. Similarly, Hart et al. (1998, 2000) found that greater playfulness, patience, and understanding with children, especially on the part of the father, were associated with less aggressive behavior with peers among Russian as well as Western children. Children's friendships are also influenced by their relationship with their fathers. Youngblade and Belsky (1992) found that a positive father-child relationship at age 3 was associated with less negative and less asynchronous friendships at age 5, whereas more negative father-child relationships forecast less satisfactory friendships.

The quality of the emotions displayed by fathers and children during play is an important predictor of social competence with other children as well. Perhaps children model their parents' emotional expressions; children rejected by their peers may have learned to settle their problems in an angry and sometimes aggressive fashion. Emulating their parents' negative and angry tactics and emotions can lead to maladaptive behavior for children with their peers and friends. Carson and Parke (1996) found that fathers of preschool-aged children who showed more anger were more likely to be rejected by their peers than were children of fathers who showed less anger. In addition, when fathers were more likely to engage in reciprocal exchanges of negative feelings with their children, teachers rated these children as more aggressive and lower in sharing. In contrast, when parents responded to children's positive expressions with positive reactions of their own, their children were more popular with their peers (Carson & Parke, 1996; Isley, O'Neil, Clatfelter, & Parke, 1999). A similar pattern was evident in observations of families at dinner. Boyum and Parke (1995) found in a study of kindergarten-aged children that fathers displayed less anger toward children who were better accepted by their peers. Finally, Isley, O'Neil, and Parke (1996) found that fathers' negative emotions expressed during play with their sons not only predicted how well their 5-year-old boys were accepted by their classmates concurrently but also was associated with their sons' social acceptance one year later as well. Although there is often overlap between mothers and fathers, this study showed that fathers make a unique contribution independent of the mothers' contribution to their children's social development. Together, these recent findings lead to a revision in traditional thinking about the ways that mothers and fathers influence their children's development. According to the sociologist Talcott Parsons (Parsons & Bales, 1955), mothers were the emotional brokers in the family, and the fathers' role was instrumental. Instead, this recent work suggests that fathers play a much larger role in the socialization of children's emotions than earlier theory suggested, and it is through the management of their own emotions and their reactions to their children's emotions that fathers may have the greatest impact on their children's social relations with peers and friends. In sum, the quality of father-child interaction patterns, including their emotional displays during these exchanges, are important antecedents of children's competence with peers.

A Cautionary Note on Interpretation of Father Effects

Our examination of the links between father involvement and children's peer relationships are consistent with other recent reviews. For example, Marsiglio, Amato, Day, and Lamb (2000) examined 72 studies published in the 1990s, the majority of which involved young children and adolescents and the remaining concerned young adults. Their review revealed moderate negative associations between authoritative paternal behavior and internalizing and externalizing problems in children, which, in turn, are associated with poorer peer relationships (Schneider, 2000). Moreover, Amato and Rivera (1999) found that the positive paternal influence on children's behavior was similar for European American, African American, and Latino fathers. However, Marsiglio et al. (2000) offer three important caveats to their conclusion that "positive father involvement is generally beneficial to their children" (p. 1183). First, most researchers rely on a single data source, which raises the problem of shared method variance. Although this is a valid concern, many studies in the father-peer area have utilized independent sources of family and peer information (e.g., MacDonald & Parke, 1984; Pettit & Mize, 1998), which lends greater confidence to the results from these studies. Second, as others have noted as well (Amato & Rivera, 1999; Parke, 1996, 2002), many researchers do not control for the quality of the mother-child relationship when examining paternal effects. Because the behavior and attitudes of mothers and fathers are often highly related (Holden, 1997), this step is critical. In fact, only 8 of the 72 studies reviewed by Marsiglio et al. (2000) controlled for the quality of the mother-child relationship; 5 of the 8 studies continued to show a father effect after taking into account mother-child effects. In the domain of interest for this chapter—father-peer relationships—there is clear evidence that fathers make a unique contribution to children's peer relationships. As noted earlier, Isley et al. (1996, 1999) found that fathers' level of affect and control predicted children's adaptation with peers both concurrently and one year later after maternal effects were controlled (see also Hart et al., 1998, 2000; Mosley & Thompson, 1995). Although there is overlap between the effects of mothers and fathers on their children's peer relationships, evidence is accumulating that fathers and mothers make separate contributions to children's peer competence (Parke, 1996; Rohner, 1998).

A third caveat concerns problems of inferring direction of causality because most studies are correlational and often cross-sectional rather than longitudinal. However, two strands of evidence suggest that the direction of effects can plausibly flow from paternal behaviors to child outcomes. First, longitudinal studies support the view that fathers influence their children (for reviews, see Amato & Rivera, 1999; Parke, 1996, 2002). Several longitudinal studies of links between paternal behavior and peer outcomes are cited in this chapter (Barth & Parke, 1994; Gottman, Katz, & Hooven, 1997; Isley et al., 1996, 1999). Moreover, the effects of fathering on developmental outcomes are not restricted to childhood; early father-child relationships forecast important variations in later empathy and marital relationship quality as well (Franz, McClelland, & Weinberger, 1991; Koestner, Franz, & Weinberger, 1990). The other strand of evidence that supports the plausibility of the father-to-child direction of effects comes from intervention studies and reports of reverse-role families (for reviews, see Fagan & Hawkins, 2000; McBride & Lutz, this volume; G. Russell, 1999). In both of these types of quasi-experimental studies, shifts in father involvement or the quality of the father-child relationship is associated with changes in children's outcomes. At the same time, it is important to underscore that children play an active role in shaping paternal behavior as well and that the mutual influence of father and child in the formation of their relationships must clearly be recognized.

POSSIBLE MEDIATORS BETWEEN FATHERING AND PEER ADJUSTMENT

A variety of processes have been hypothesized as mediators between parent-child interaction and peer outcomes. These include affect management skills such as emotion encoding and decoding, emotion-regulatory abilities, cognitive representations, attributions problem-solving skills, and attention-regulation abilities (Ladd, 1992; Parke et al., 1994). It is assumed that these abilities or beliefs are acquired in parent-child interchanges over the course of development and, in turn, guide the nature of children's behavior with their peers. It is also assumed that these styles of interacting with peers may determine children's level of acceptance by their peers. In this section we focus on the three sets of processes that seem particularly promising candidates for mediator status, namely affect management skills, cognitive representational processes, and attention-regulation skills.

Affect Management Skills

It is not only the quality of emotions that fathers display that matters to children's social development, but also how children and their fathers deal with emotional displays. What do children learn from playing with their fathers? Being able to read a play partner's emotional signals and to send clear emotional cues is critical for successfully maintaining ongoing play activities. These skills allow partners to modulate their playful behavior so that neither becomes overly aroused or too understimulated and play continues to provide an optimal level of excitement for both partners. Children learn to recognize others' emotions, improve their own emotional skills, and regulate their emotions in the context of parent-child play (Parke et al., 1992). Father-child play may be a particularly important context because its range of excitement and arousal is higher than in the more modulated play of mothers and children.

Are fathers accepting and helpful when children become distressed, angry, or sad, or are fathers dismissing and rejecting? Several researchers have found that fathers' comforting and acceptance of their children's emotional distress are linked with more positive peer relationships (Roberts, 1994). For example, Gottman et al. (1997) found that fathers' acceptance of and assistance with their children's sadness and anger at 5 years of age was related to the children's social competence with their peers three years later at age 8. Girls were less negative with friends, and boys were less aggressive. Mothers' management of children's emotions, in contrast, was generally a less significant predictor of children's later social behavior. Other findings suggest that the strategies parents employ to manage children's negative emotions are associated with children's emotional reactivity, coping, and social competence (O'Neil, Parke, Isley, & Sosa, 1997). Fathers who reported being more distressed by their child's expressions of negative affect had children who were more likely to report using anger and other negative emotions to cope with distressing events. When fathers reported using strategies to minimize distressing circumstances, children were more likely to report using reasoning to cope with a distressing situation. Fathers who reported emotion- and problem-focused reactions to the expression of negative emotions had children who were described by teachers as less aggressive and disruptive (see Parke & O'Neil, 1997, for further details about the mother's role in this process). Recently, Contreras and Kerns (2000) found that father-child attachment security was indirectly related to children's peer competence. Specifically, security with fathers was correlated with child coping, and coping was linked with behavior regulation with peers and marginally with teachers' reports of children's competence with peers. In contrast, the link between mother-child security and peer outcomes was fully mediated by children's coping strategies (Contreras, Kerns, Weimer, Gentzler, & Tomich, 2000). This work highlights the role of fathers in learning about relationships, especially in learning the emotion-regulatory aspects of relationships. Fathers provide a unique opportunity to teach children about emotion in the context of relationships due to the wide range of intensity of affect that fathers display and the unpredictable character of their playful exchanges with their children (Parke, 1995, 1996; Parke & Brott, 1999).

During early and middle childhood, children acquire and begin to use display rules for the socially appropriate expression of emotion. A few studies have examined links between knowledge of display rules and social competence. For example, Underwood, Coie, and Herbsman (1992) found that aggressive children have more difficulty understanding display rules. Recently, we explored the relations between children's use of socially appropriate rules for displaying negative emotions and social competence with peers (McDowell, O'Neil, & Parke, 2000). We employed Saarni's (1984) "disappointing gift paradigm," which enabled us to assess children's ability to mask negative emotions in the face of disappointment. Our data indicated that 4th grade children (especially girls) who displayed positive affect or behavior following the presentation of a disappointing gift (thus using display rules) were rated more socially competent by teachers and peers. Only recently have researchers begun to examine links between children's experiences with parents and their ability to use display rules. Garner and Power (1996), studying a preschool sample, found that children's negative emotional displays in a disappointment situation were inversely related to observed maternal positive emotion. More recently, McDowell and Parke (2002) found that both fathers and mothers who were highly controlling of their children's emotional expressiveness, especially boys, demonstrated less knowledge about appropriate use of display rules. However, much remains to be understood regarding the intergenerational continuity between parental socialization strategies and children's use of display rules.

Together, these studies suggest that various aspects of emotional competence—encoding, decoding, cognitive understanding, and emotion regulation—play an important role in accounting for variations in peer competence. Our argument is that these aspects of emotion may be learned in the context of family interaction, including father-child interaction, and serve as mediators between the parents and peers. Accumulating support for this view suggests that this is an important direction for future research.

Cognitive Representational Models

One of the major puzzles in the area of family-peer relations is how children transfer the strategies that they acquire in the family context to their peer relationships. A variety of theories assume that individuals possess internal mental representations that guide their social behavior. Attachment theorists offer working models (Bowlby, 1969), whereas social and cognitive psychologists have provided scripts or cognitive maps that could serve as guides for social action (Bugental & Goodnow, 1998). Researchers within the attachment tradition have examined attachment-related representations and have found support for Bowlby's argument that representations vary as a function of child-parent attachment history (Main, Kaplan, & Cassidy, 1985). For example, children who had been securely attached infants were more likely to represent their family in their drawings in a coherent manner, with a balance between individuality and connection, than were children who had been insecurely attached (Sroufe, Egeland, & Carlson, 1999). As noted earlier, securely attached children have better peer relationships as well.

Research in a social-interactional tradition has revealed links between parent and child cognitive representations of social relationships as well (Burks & Parke, 1996). Moreover, parents of children of different sociometric statuses differ in their cognitive models of social relationships. Several aspects of cognitive models, including attributions, perceptions, values, goals, and strategies, have been explored (see Bugental & Goodnow, 1998; Mills & Rubin, 1993). We recently explored the links between parent and child cognitive representations of social relationships (McDowell, Parke, & Spitzer, 2002). In this study, parents and their kindergarten-age children responded to a series of vignettes reflecting interpersonal conflict dilemmas by indicating how they might react in each situation. Open-ended responses were coded for goals, causes, strategies, and advice. The cognitive representations of social behavior of both fathers and mothers were related to their children's representations. Moreover, fathers' but not mothers' cognitive models of relationships were linked to children's social competence. Fathers' strategies that were rated high on confrontation and instrumental qualities were associated with low teacher ratings of children's social competence. Fathers with relational-prosocial goals have children who are rated as more competent by both teachers and peers. Perhaps fathers are more influential in conflict-laden domains, whereas mothers are more influential in social domains involving personal and relationship issues. In any case, these data suggest that fathers' cognitive representations of social relationships are important correlates of children's social competence with peers.

The effects are not limited to young children, however. Recently, researchers have reported that similar cognitive representational processes are important mediators between parenting and peer outcomes in adolescence as well. Paley, Conger, and Harold (2000) found that both maternal and paternal affect had significant direct and indirect effects (via adolescent cognitive representations of parents) on adolescents' negative social behavior as reported by siblings. In turn, these sibling reports were related to decreased peer acceptance as rated by teachers. Of particular interest was the finding that parental behavior and the mediating cognitive reorientations predicted adolescent behavior and peer acceptance two years later.

Fathers' recollections of their early relationships with their own mothers and fathers can help us better understand the impact of fathers on their children's overall behavior as well. As Bowlby (1973) commented, "Because children tend unwittingly to identify with parents and therefore to adopt, when they become parents, the same patterns of behavior towards children that they themselves have experienced during their own childhood, patterns of interaction are transmitted, more or less faithfully, from one generation to the next" (p. 301). Considerable work using the adult attachment interview to tap mothers' recollections of their relationships with their own mothers during infancy and childhood has documented that the mothers' patterns of memories related to the quality of their current attachment relationships with their own infants (Thompson, 1998).

Do fathers show similar relations between their early memories and their later relationships with their children? In a German longitudinal study, researchers found that a father's recollections of his own childhood relationship with his parents was indeed linked to his relationship with his own children (Grossmann & Fremmer-Bombik, 1994). Fathers who viewed their own attachment relationship with their parents as secure developed a more secure attachment relationship with their own infants, were more often present at the birth of their infant, participated more in infant care, and were more supportive of their wives than were men who recalled their attachments with their parents as insecure. Moreover, fathers who remembered their childhood attachment experiences, including both positive and negative feelings, and who were open and nondefensive about their recollections, continued to be better fathers as their children developed. They were better play partners to their toddlers; by the time their children reached 6 years of age, these fathers served as more sensitive guides during a teaching task and continued to be engaging and tender play partners. Later, when their offspring were 10, these men were more accepting of their children's daily concerns and problems. Remembering both the good and the bad aspects of his own childhood makes a father more sensitive to the needs and feelings of his own child. An American study confirmed these European observations. Cowan, Cohn, Cowan, and Pearson (1996) found that fathers who recalled an earlier attachment relationship with their parents characterized as low in loving and high in expression of anger had children who tended to be rated as more externalizing (e.g., aggressive and hyperactive) in kindergarten. To summarize briefly, fathers' recollections of their own attachment relationships are linked with their own parenting style and their relationships with their children; in turn, these parenting styles are linked with children's peer relationships.

Together, this set of studies suggests that cognitive models of relationships may be transmitted across generations, and these models may serve as mediators between family contexts and children's relationships with others outside of the family.

Attention Regulation

In concert with emotion regulation and social cognitive representations, attention-regulatory processes have come to be viewed as an additional mechanism through which familial socialization experiences might influence the development of children's social competence. These processes include the ability to attend to relevant cues, to sustain attention, to refocus attention through such processes as cognitive distraction and cognitive restructuring, and other efforts to reduce purposefully the level of emotional arousal in a situation that is appraised as stressful (Lazarus & Folkman, 1984). Attentional processes are thought to organize experience and to play a central role in cognitive and social development beginning early in infancy (Rothbart & Bates, 1998). Thus, Wilson (1999) aptly considers attention-regulatory processes as a shuttle linking emotion regulation and social cognitive processes because attentional processes organize both cognitions and emotional responses and thus influence the socialization of relationship competence. In support of the direct link between attention regulation and peer relationships, Eisenberg et al. (1993) found that children who were low in attention regulation were also low in social competence. In addition, work conducted in our laboratory (O'Neil & Parke, 2000) has suggested that attentional processes may work in tandem with emotion-regulatory abilities to enhance social functioning. Parenting style may be an important antecedent of children's ability to refocus attention away from emotionally distressing events. Data from 5th graders in our study indicated that when mothers adopted a negative, controlling parenting style in a problem-solving discussion, children were less likely to use cognitive decision making as a coping strategy. Also, children were more likely to report greater difficulty in controlling negative affect when distressed. Lower levels of cognitive decision making and higher levels of negative affect were associated with more problem behaviors and higher levels of negative interactions with classmates (as reported by teachers). Similarly, when fathers adopted a negative, controlling style, children were more likely to use avoidance as a mechanism for managing negative affect. In addition, fathers who reported expressing more negative dominant emotions such as anger and criticism in everyday interactions had children who reported greater difficulty controlling negative emotions. Avoidant coping and negative emotionality were related to higher levels of parent-reported problem behaviors. In sum, the ability to regulate attention appears to be another possible mediating mechanism between parenting and children's competence with peers.

In this section we proposed three sets of processes—emotion-regulatory skills, cognitive representations of social relationships, and attention-regulatory abilities—that may, either alone or in concert, serve as mediators between fathers and peer outcomes. More attention to the ways in which these three sets of mediators interact with others in accounting for variations in peer outcomes is needed.

PATHWAY TWO: FATHERS AS ADVISORS, SOCIAL GUIDES, AND RULE PROVIDERS

Learning about relationships through interaction with parents can be viewed as an indirect pathway because the goal is often not explicitly to influence children's social relationships with extrafamilial partners such as peers. In contrast, parents influence children's relationships directly in their roles as direct instructors, educators, or advisers. In this role, parents explicitly set out to educate their children concerning the appropriate manner of initiating and maintaining social relationships. Research that emerged over the last 10 years suggests that young children gain competence with peers when parents supervise and facilitate their peer experiences, whereas among older children, great supervision and guidance on the part of parents of children's peer relationships may function more as a remediation effort (Parke & O'Neil, 1997, 2000).

In a study of parental supervision, Bhavnagri and Parke (1991) found that children exhibited more cooperation and turn taking and had longer play bouts when assisted by an adult than when playing without assistance. Although both fathers and mothers were effective facilitators of their children's play with peers, under natural conditions mothers were more likely to play this supervisory and facilitatory role than were fathers (Bhavnagri & Parke, 1991; Ladd & Golter, 1988).

As children develop, the forms of management shift from direct involvement or supervision of the ongoing activities of children and their peers to less public forms of management, involving advice or consultation concerning appropriate ways of handling peer problems. This form of direct parental management has been termed *consultation* (Lollis, Ross, & Tate, 1992).

Much work has documented the advice-giving role of mothers (A. Russell & Finnie, 1990; see Parke & O'Neil, 2000, for a review). Other evidence offers support for the role of fathers' advice giving and the development of children's social competence with peers. In one study (O'Neil, Garcia, Zavala, & Wang, 1995), parents were asked to read to their 3rd-grade child short stories that described common social themes (e.g., group entry, ambiguous provocation, and relational aggression) and to advise the child about the best way to handle each situation. High-quality advice was considered to be advice that promoted a positive, outgoing, social orientation on the part of the child rather than avoidance or aggressive responses. The findings varied as a function of parent and child gender. Among father-son dyads and mother-daughter dyads, parental advice that was more appropriate and more structured was associated with less loneliness and greater social competence among children. It is interesting that among father-daughter and mother-son dyads, higher quality advice about how to handle social conflict was associated with poorer teacher-rated social competence. In contrast to the gender-specific findings for the content of parental advice, the quality of parent-child interactions during the advice-giving session was positively related to children's social competence. Other results from our study, based on a triadic advice-giving session in which mothers, fathers, and their 3rd grader discussed how to handle problems that their child had when interacting with peers indicated that parental style of interaction appeared to be a better predictor of children's social competence than the actual solution quality generated in the advice-giving session (Wang & McDowell, 1996). Specifically, the controlling nature of fathers' style and the warmth and support expressed by mothers during the advice-giving task were significant predictors of both teacher and peer ratings of children's social competence.

Another avenue through which parents can regulate their children's peer relationships is the provision of rules or guidelines. Rules concerning children's peer relationships include guidelines regarding what activities the children can engage in and when, with whom, and where they can play. To date, little attention has been given to the role of rules in the development and maintenance of children's peer relationships. Particularly relevant to the links between rules and peer relationships is the work of Furstenberg et al. (1999), in which the relations between parents' restrictions on the activities of their adolescents' social behavior were explored. The construct of *restrictions* included monitoring, rules, teaching good judgment, and restricting activities. Findings revealed that a higher number of restrictions was linked to fewer problem behaviors (e.g., school truancy, substance abuse) and higher social involvement with peers. However, the operationalization of the restrictions construct combined rules with several parenting skills so that the role of rules alone in the regulation of children's behavior with peers was less clear. Simpkins and Parke (2002b) explored the relations between the number of parental play rules and 6th-grade children's loneliness, depression, and friendship quality. Boys whose parents had fewer play rules reported lower levels of depression but more conflict in their best friendships. Boys' loneliness and positive qualities in their best friendships were not significantly predicted by paternal play rules, nor were girls' outcomes significantly correlated with the number of parental play rules. As in the case of other aspects of parental management, the process by which rules are jointly negotiated by children and their parents is poorly understood. Parental perception of the child's level of responsibility and self-regulatory ability and the child's perception of the fairness of the rules probably all play a role in both the negotiation process and the extent to which the rules are likely to be followed.

The direction of effects in each of these studies, of course, is difficult to determine, and future models that explain links between parental management strategies and children's social development need to incorporate bidirectional processes. Under some circumstances, parents may be making proactive efforts to guide their children's social efforts, whereas under other circumstances, parents may be providing advice in response to children's social difficulties (see also Ladd & Golter, 1988; Mize, Pettit, & Brown, 1995). Overly involved parents or those who offer highly specific advice, for example, may simply be responding to their children's poor social abilities. Moreover, high levels of control may inhibit children's efforts to develop their own strategies for dealing with peer relations (Cohen, 1989).

Nevertheless, the bulk of the evidence suggests that direct parental influence in the form of supervision, advice giving, and play rules can significantly increase the interactive competence of young children and illustrates the utility of examining direct parent strategies as a way of teaching children about social relationships. Finally, more attention needs to be given to the developmental aspects of this issue so that we have a fuller understanding of how the impact of this direct form of influence changes across development.

PATHWAY THREE: FATHERS AS MANAGERS OF CHILDREN'S SOCIAL OPPORTUNITIES

Fathers (and mothers) also play an important role in the facilitation of their children's peer relationships by initiating informal contact between their own children and potential play partners, especially among young children (Bhavnagri, 1987). A series of studies by Ladd and his colleagues suggests that parents' role as social activity arranger may play a facilitating part in the development of their children's friendships (Ladd, 1992). For example, Ladd and Golter (1988) found that children of parents who actively arranged peer contacts had a larger range of playmates and more frequent play companions outside of school than did children of parents who were less active in initiating peer contacts. When children entered kindergarten, boys, but not girls, with parents who initiated peer contacts were better liked and less rejected by their classmates than were boys with noninitiating parents.

Although the focus of past research has been on young children, recent research has shifted to examination of parental management of the social lives of adolescents. In spite of the shift toward independence, Mounts (2000) found that parents continued to play an active role in guiding and shaping adolescents' choice of friends and activities. Although this work is informative, the relative role played by mothers and fathers was not examined. Updegraff, McHale, Crouter, and Kupanoff (2001), however, addressed this issue by examining both fathers' and mothers' direct involvement in adolescent's peer relationships. Parents' direct involvement was measured by parents' reports of their peer-oriented activities (e.g., I spend time talking with my children about their friends; I talk to the parents of my children's friends—i.e., parents' knowledge about adolescents' peer experience such as everyday activities, whereabouts, companions) and parents' time spent with their adolescents and their peers (e.g., amount of time spent with the parent and one or more peers). Mothers were more knowledgeable about adolescents' peer relationships and were higher in peer-oriented activities than were fathers. Fathers and mothers spent equal amounts of time with adolescents and their friends, but mothers spent more time with their daughters and their friends and fathers with their sons and their friends. These activities were largely chauffeuring, attending sporting events, and eating meals together—leisure activities in which fathers as well as mothers are active participants (Larson & Richards, 1994; Parke & Buriel, 1998). Do these strategies matter for adolescents' friendships and peer relationships? First, even after controlling for parental acceptance, maternal time was positively related to boys' involvement with a best friend, and father involvement in peer-oriented activities predicted adolescents' peer-group involvement. As Updegraff et al. (2001) noted, these findings are "consistent with the idea that involvement with a best friend is more central to girls and women's experience and that peer group activities are more salient for boys and men" (p. 666). For girls, mothers', but not fathers', time with daughters and their peers was related to greater involvement with friends. Mothers may influence daughters' relationships by providing them with opportunities for peer contact.

Parents also influence their children's social relations by providing them with the opportunity to participate in more formal after-school activities such as team sports, Brownies, Cub Scouts, and so on. Participation in these activities can allow children access to a wider range of social experiences than can more informal play situations and can contribute to their social and cognitive development. Bryant (1985) found that participation in formal activities for 10-year-olds was associated with better perspective taking. Although some studies have found that mothers are more involved in the interface between the children and social institutions and view these settings as being more important for children's development of social skills than do fathers, few studies have investigated fathers' participation in formal after-school activities with their children (Bhavnagri, 1987). Even though many fathers may serve as coaches of their children's sports team or lead their scout groups, little is known about the effects of these interactions on either their relationships with their children or on their children's peer relationships.

Another way in which parents can affect their children's social relationships is through monitoring of their children's social activities. This form of management is particularly evident as children move into preadolescence and adolescence and is associated with the relative shift in importance of family and peers as sources of influence on social relationships. At this stage, monitoring refers to a range of activities, including the supervision of children and choice of social settings, activities, and friends. Parents of delinquent and antisocial children engaged in less monitoring and supervision of their children's activities, especially with regard to children's use of evening time, and were less in control of their sons' choice of friends than were parents of nondelinquent children (Patterson & Stouthamer-Loeber, 1984). Other researchers have found that poorly monitored children have lower academic skills, lower peer acceptance (Sandstrom & Coie, 1999), and higher rates of delinquent and externalizing behavior (Pettit et al., 1999; Xiaoming, Stanton, & Feigelman, 2000). In this section, several ways on which fathers serve as managers of children's relationships were outlined, including providing opportunities for contact with peers and monitoring their contacts. We noted how these parental strategies shift as the child develops, but we stress that parents play a role as manager even during adolescence. In the next section, we examine several pathways through which parental management is achieved, namely parental social networks and neighborhood social capital.

Parental Networks, Social Capital, and Peer Relationships

Parents' own social networks also may enhance children's social development and adjustment. Cochran and Niego (1995) suggested several ways that parents' own networks may influence children's social competence. First, the structure of parents' networks influence the exposure children have to possible social interactive partners (e.g., the offspring of adult network members). Second, the extent to which children observe the social interactions of parents with members of their networks may influence the children's own styles of social interaction. Third, parents in supportive social networks may have enhanced well-being that, in turn, may improve parents' relationships with their children.

Community networking has implications for youth development. Adolescent boys were found to have better school performance and attendance and more positive social behavior when their social networks included large numbers on nonrelated adults (Cochran & Bo, 1989). In a study by Fletcher, Darling, Steinberg, and Dornbusch (1995), nonrelated adults were found to influence the behavior of adolescents through the emotional support of the adolescents' parents as well as by their modeling of various parenting practices that encouraged and discouraged certain parenting behaviors. Moreover, children of these parents directly influenced the behaviors of their friends in a way that reflected their parents' beliefs and practices. Another way these two networks may be linked was proposed by Coleman (1988), who argued that when both parents and their children are acquainted with other parents and their children, they form network closure. When network closure exists, there are likely to be more shared values and more social control over their offspring, which, in turn, would be related to better social outcomes. Darling, Steinberg, Gringlas, and Dornbusch (1995) found that social integration (as indexed by network closure) and value consensus were related to adolescent social and academic outcomes. Adolescents who reported high degrees of contact among their parents, friends, and their friends' parents were less deviant and higher in academic achievement than were their peers who were less socially integrated.

Evidence suggests that structural characteristics of networks such as network size are associated with social adjustment in young children as well. Homel, Burns, and Goodnow (1987), for example, found that the number of friends in parents' social networks was related to social skill and social adjustment in 9- to 11-year-olds. Recently, this work was extended by showing relationships among characteristics of parents' networks, parents' relationship attitudes, and children's social competence in kindergarten and first grade (Simpkins, O'Neil, Lee, Parke, & Wang, 2002). When mothers reported more closeness and enjoyment from their networks, they reported greater efficacy in managing their own relationships and felt more efficacious in assisting their children in forming social relationships. Fathers whose networks contained more nonkin members and were a source of more age-mates for their children reported feeling more efficaciousness in their personal relationships. When mothers viewed their social networks as sources of closeness and enjoyment, teachers and peers described their children as better accepted by classmates. Similarly, when fathers described their network relationships in a more positive light, their children were rated by teachers as better accepted and less aggressive. When mothers' nonkin network provided the study child with more age-mates, children were rated by peers as better accepted. Similarly, when fathers reported a larger network of kin members and when fathers' network of nonkin afforded their children more age-mates, children tended to be rated by peers as better accepted. Although the specific mechanisms that account for these relationships remain to be determined, these findings suggest that parents' social networks may provide children with both better models of social relationships and more opportunities to interact with same-aged peers and refine developing social skills.

Finally, Simpkins and Parke (2002a) found that the quality of both maternal and paternal friendships was related to children's friendship quality. In the case of girls, different qualities of parental and maternal friendships were related to daughters' friendship qualities. The positive aspects of girls' friendships (i.e., help, resolution of conflict, validation) were largely related to their fathers' positive friendship qualities, whereas the negative aspects of girls friendships (e.g., observed and self-reported conflict) were related to maternal friendship qualities. Boys' friendship patterns were less clearly related to the quality of their friendships than in the case of girls. Perhaps girls have more exposure to parents' friends than boys—a possibility that could account for the pattern of findings. As these studies illustrate, the quality and scope of adult friendships and social networks are important correlates not just of children's peer competence but of their friendship qualities as well. Together, this work suggests that parents' social and friendship networks as well as the social capital of the community are important determinants of children's opportunities for social contact with peers as well as potentially influential forms of informal community-based control of children's social relationships.

BEYOND THE FATHER-CHILD RELATIONSHIP: THE MARITAL DYAD AS A CONTRIBUTOR TO CHILDREN'S PEER RELATIONSHIPS

Another way in which fathers influence their children's peer relationships is through their marital relationships (Parke et al., 2001). Two perspectives have been offered to explain these possible links between marital relationships and children's peer relationships. First, some propose a direct model, which means that exposure to marital conflict may directly alter children's capacity to function effectively in other social contexts (Cummings & O'Reilly, 1997). Others propose an indirect model whereby marital relationships alter parent-child relationships, consequently affecting children's outcomes (Fauber & Long, 1991).

INDIRECT MODEL

Poor parenting and poor marriages often go together, and some father effects are best understood by recognizing this link between parenting and marriage. Gottman and Katz (1989) found that a poor parenting style, characterized as cold, unresponsive, angry, and low in limit setting and structuring, led to higher levels of anger and noncompliance on the part of 5-year-old children when interacting with their parents. This style was especially likely to be seen in couples with troubled marriages. This combination led to poor peer outcomes: Children from such homes have lower levels of positive play with peers, more negative peer exchanges, and poorer physical health. Moreover, marital conflict has lasting effects on children's development. In a follow-up study, Katz and Gottman (1994) obtained teachers' ratings of internalizing (depression, withdrawal) and externalizing (aggression, disruption) behavior three years later, when the children were 8 years old. Couples who at the time of the earlier assessment used a mutually hostile style of conflict resolution—one characterized by contempt and belligerence toward each other—had children who exhibited higher levels of externalizing behavior three years later. Families in which the husband exhibited an angry and withdrawn style in resolving marital disputes had children who were higher in internalizing behavior. Not only the level of conflict in marriages matters; how conflict is managed is critical as well.

Similarly, Cowan, Cowan, Schulz, and Hemming (1994) examined the influence of marital quality on children's social adaptation to kindergarten with results suggesting evidence of both direct and indirect links to children's social adjustment. It is interesting that internalizing difficulties (e.g., shy or withdrawn qualities) were predicted by the influences of marital functioning on parenting quality, whereas externalizing difficulties (e.g., aggressive or antisocial qualities) were predicted directly by qualities of marital interaction.

Stocker and Youngblade (1999) provided further support for the role of parental behavior as a mediator between marital conflict and peer competence. These investigators found that the paternal, but not maternal, hostility directed toward their child served as a mediator between marital conflict and problematic peer relationships. A variety of possible mechanisms may account for these outcomes, including shifts in the affective interactions between fathers and children, which would impair children's affect management skills (Parke et al., 1992; Parke & McDowell, 1998).

Family systems theory suggests that marital discord not only adversely affects mother-child and father-child relationships but also may impair qualities of the mother-father-child triadic relationship by reducing the effectiveness of how well mothers and fathers work together with their child. In a study that examined the contribution of marital adjustment to the effectiveness of joint mother-father supportiveness, Westerman and Schonholtz (1993) found that fathers', but not mothers', reports of marital disharmony and disaffection were significantly related to the effectiveness of joint parental support toward their children's problem-solving efforts. Joint parental support was related to fathers' and teachers' reports of children's behavior problems. Men's lack of involvement in the triadic family process could account for these findings because women tend to engage and confront, whereas men tend to withdraw in the face of marital disharmony (Gottman, 1994).

Direct Model

Other work has focused on the specific processes by which the marital relationship itself directly influences children's immediate functioning and long-term adjustment. More frequent interparental conflict and more intense or violent forms of conflict not only disturb children but may lead to externalizing and internalizing problems (see Cummings, Goeke-Morey, & Raymond, this volume).

To date, few studies of the links between marital problems and children's outcomes have focused explicitly on children's social competence with peers. Recent work from our lab has addressed this gap in a study of 6th-grade children and their parents. O'Neil, Flyr, Wild, and Parke (1999) examined the links between marital conflict and interparental communication styles on emotion-regulatory abilities and cognitive representations of parent-child relations that, in turn, may influence peer children's relationships. Marital communication and conflict management style were observed during a problem-solving session. More negative paternal problem-solving strategies were associated with greater peer-rated avoidance and lower teacher-rated acceptance. Similarly, when mothers exhibited better problem-solving skills, adolescents were rated as less avoidant by peers. Poorer maternal problem-solving and communication strategies were linked to teacher ratings of less social engagement. These findings confirmed our anticipated link between marital conflict and children's peer relationships.

Our next step was to explore two possible mediators between parental conflict and peer competence, namely, children's perceptions of marital conflict and children's emotion-regulatory abilities. First, we examined the relation between indexes of marital conflict and children's perception of interparental conflict (Kim, Parke, &

O'Neil, 1999). Children's perceptions of marital conflict correlated with parents' reports of marital conflict in both grades 5 and 6. Moreover, mothers and fathers agreed on the amount of conflict at both assessment points. In a second set of analyses, O'Neil et al. (1999) examined the relations between observations of marital communication and of conflict management and children's perceptions of interparental conflict. Our results showed that when fathers expressed more negative affect during discussion of a marital disagreement, 6th graders reported more frequent and intense interparental conflict. When fathers used more negative problem-solving strategies (e.g., hostility, denial, disruptive process), adolescents reported more intense interparental conflict. In contrast, when fathers used better problem-solving strategies (e.g., negotiation, listener responsiveness), adolescents reported less frequent and less intense conflict. Less perceived personal threat and greater resolution were also associated with less interparental conflict. Mothers' observed communication and conflict management strategies were virtually unrelated to adolescents' perceptions of interparental conflict. Together, these two sets of analyses suggested a reliable relation between both self-report and observed indexes of parental marital conflict and children's perceptions of marital conflict.

As a next step, Kim et al. (1999) examined the relation between children's perceptions of marital conflict and children's competence with peers. Kim et al. found that the frequency of parental conflict and the content of marital conflict yielded the most reliable relations with children's social competence. Teacher ratings of disruptive behavior were associated with frequent parental conflict, and children's self-blame was associated with teacher ratings of verbal and physical aggression. Frequent parental conflict was associated with teacher ratings of shy behavior and sadness, whereas children's self-blame was related to a host of negative outcomes, including peer ratings of dislike, verbal and physical aggression, and peer and teacher ratings of excluding behavior. Children's self-blame was negatively associated with peer ratings of friendliness and peer and teacher ratings of prosocial behavior. In sum, there were clear relations among parental reports of marital conflict, children's perception of marital conflict, and children's peer competence.

Children who perceive high levels of marital conflict may, in turn, have more difficulty in their self-regulation of emotion. According to prior research, this ability is an important correlate of children's peer competence (Eisenberg & Fabes, 1994; McDowell et al., 2000; O'Neil & Parke, 2000). Moreover, Davies and Cummings (1994) suggested that emotional reactivity in response to conflict may, in fact, mediate the links between marital conflict and child outcomes. In a direct test of the model, Davies and Cummings (1998) assessed the links among children's emotional security, level of destructive and constructive marital functioning, and children's internalizing and externalizing behaviors. As predicted by the emotional security model, the links between marital discord and children's internalizing symptoms were mediated by measures of emotional security. O'Neil et al. (1999) provided a further evaluation of the relation between marital conflict and children's emotion-regulatory abilities. Children's emotion-regulatory ability was measured by a self-report index of emotional reactivity and strategies for coping with emotional upset. We found several linkages between marital communication, conflict management style, and children's regulation of emotion. The rate and tone of the mother's verbal and listening behaviors with her spouse were inversely related to children's reports of displayed anger. These analyses also revealed inverse relations between fathers' listener responsiveness, positive mood and involvement in problem solving with their spouses, and children's reports of displayed anger. In addition, a child's calm response to conflict situations was positively related to the rate of a father's verbal engagement in the marriage and to a less intrusive marital communication style by mothers.

These data are consistent with earlier work suggesting a link between marital conflict and children's emotion-regulatory abilities. As in prior studies, fathers' as well as mothers' style of dealing with marital conflict was related to children's emotion-regulatory abilities (Katz & Gottman, 1993). Several researchers have found that these emotional competence skills are linked to social competence with peers (Denham, 1998; Eisenberg & Fabes, 1994; Parke, 1994). Children who are less emotionally reactive and who respond with less anger and more positive coping strategies are more socially competent.

Conflict is inevitable in most parent relationships and is not detrimental to children's functioning under all circumstances. Disagreements that are extremely intense and involve threat to the child are likely to be more disturbing to the child. When conflict is expressed constructively, is moderate in degree, is expressed in the context of a warm and supportive family environment, and shows evidence of resolution, children may learn valuable lessons regarding how to negotiate conflict and resolve disagreements (Davies & Cummings, 1994).

PUTTING THE PIECES TOGETHER

Recollections often combine with current conditions—such as the quality of the marriage and parenting competence—to alter children's development. Although fathers' own attachment memories are important, an even better understanding of children's behavior with peers emerges when contemporary family relationships are considered as well. Fathers with poor attachment histories were often in marriages characterized by high conflict and low satisfaction, and in turn, these men were ineffective parents (low in warmth, responsiveness, and structuring; Cowan et al., 1996). In combination, these three paternal factors—prior attachment history, current marital relationship, and parenting competence—predicted externalizing behavior two years later when the children were in kindergarten nearly twice as well as did the fathers' attachment history alone. More important, this combination predicted externalizing behavior two times better than these same indexes for mothers. In contrast, mothers' poor prior attachment history predicted children's internalizing behavior in kindergarten. Again, internalizing behavior was better understood when mothers' current marriage and parenting were also considered. The combination of these factors with mothers' recollections was twice as good a predictor of children's internalizing behavior as were fathers' scores. Cowan et al. (1996) noted, "Given the fact that men are more implicated in problems of aggression and women in problems of depression, it may not be surprising that fathers and mothers make different contributions to young children's externalizing and internalizing behavior" (p. 11). Not only are both fathers and mothers important to understanding children's development, but each makes distinct contributions to children's social developmental outcomes as well. In sum, this work underscores the fact that fathers' contributions to children's peer competence are best understood as a multifactor process in which fathers' prior family history, their current parenting, and their marital relationships all need to be considered. Fathers' role in children's peer relationships is best understood as a set of packaged variables—in which a variety of aspects of fathers' current and past ties both within and outside the family all merit attention. Only by recasting the issue of father-peer linkages in this way are we going to be successful in putting the pieces together.

CULTURAL PERSPECTIVES ON FATHER-PEER LINKAGE

An issue that has generated considerable interest is the variability in children's development across cultures as well as between and within cultural subgroups within the same country. Two issues are of interest, namely, the relative influence of parents and peers in different cultures and the nature of family-peer linkages across cultures. The relative impact of parents and peers varies across cultures. In a classic study of Russian and American children, Bronfenbrenner (1970) found that Russian children were more likely to follow parental rules when with their peers than were American children, who exhibited a greater tendency to deviate from parental rules when with their peers. More recently, Chen, Greenberger, Lester, Dong, and Guo (1998) found that peer influences were stronger correlates of misconduct among European and Chinese Americans than among Chinese and Taiwanese adolescents.

In spite of overall differences in the relative contribution of peers and families to children's social outcomes, numerous researchers have reported that the parental and peer correlates of children's social competence are similar. In the Chen et al. (1998) study, for example, family relationships (parent-offspring conflict, parental warmth, and parental monitoring) as well as peer sanctions (peer approval/disapproval of misconduct) were related to child misconduct in similar ways across European, Chinese American, and Chinese groups. Others have reported similar relations between parental practices and children's peer relationships. In a study based in China, Chen and Rubin (1994) reported that authoritarian parenting and punitive disciplinary practices were linked with childhood aggression and peer rejection; on the other hand, parental warmth and authoritative parenting predicted social competence, which then predicted peer acceptance. Studies of Russian parents revealed a similar pattern. Children of punitive, authoritarian mothers in combination with less responsive fathers displayed more reactive overt and relational aggression (Hart et al., 2000).

However, it is critical to extend our examination of father-peer relationships and especially mediating processes to a wider range of cultures. In this chapter we have argued, for example, that emotion-regulatory skills that are acquired, in part, in the context of father-child physical play are central mediating processes in accounting for the links between fathers and peer interactive competence. However, over the past decade, serious challenges have confronted the assumption about the universality of paternal physical play styles. Evidence from Chinese Malaysia, Taiwan, Thailand, Sweden, and India has suggested that fathers and mothers rarely engage in physical play with their children (Lamb, 1997; Roopnarine, this volume; Sun & Roopnarine, 1996). Similarly, observations of Aka pygmies of Central Africa by Hewlett (1991, this volume) were consistent with these other cultures: Mothers and fathers rarely, if ever, engaged in vigorous or physical play. Moreover, in other cultures, such as some communities in Italy, neither mothers nor fathers, but other women in the extended family or within the community, were more likely to play physically with infants (New & Benigni, 1987). These cross-cultural variations alert us to the possibilities that other mediators may be involved for non-Western cultures or that emotion-regulatory and other aspects of emotional competence may be learned in nonphysical play contexts or in interaction with other socialization agents.

In terms of parental management, similarities and differences across cultures are evident as well (Hart et al., 1998). In Russia, China, and the United States parental initiating and arranging decreases as children develop. In all three countries, mothers who initiated more peer contacts had children who were more accepted by peers. However, Chinese children were given more autonomy in their initiating activities with peers. Mothers in all cultures were more likely to arrange peer contacts if their children were perceived by teachers as less socially competent. Parental monitoring has similar positive effects on children's misconduct in a variety of cultures, including Denmark (Arnett & Belle-Jensen, 1993), England (Belson, 1975), China (Chen et al., 1998), and Australia (Feldman, Rosenthal, Mont-Reynaud, & Leung, 1991).

In terms of the impact of marital conflict on children's peer relationships, several recent studies have found that similar links are evident for Latino as well as Euro-American families. Among Latino families (mainly Cuban American), Lindahl and Malik (1999) found that marital conflict was associated with higher levels of externalizing behavior in boys. More recently, Kim (2001) found links between marital conflict and children's social adjustment in school among Mexican Americans as well. These links were evident for parental reports of overt conflict, parental reports of marital quality, and independent observations of marital interaction and children's perceptions of marital conflict. Of interest was the finding that parental biculturalism moderated the links between children's perception of marital conflict and children's adjustment. Children of parents who were higher in biculturalism were less affected by marital conflict than were those who were less bicultural. Finally, children with high levels of social support were buffered from the effects of perceived marital conflict and of marital hostility. Children with more social support from extrafamilial kin and peers were rated lower in externalizing and internalizing problems than were children with less social support. Together, these findings underscore that similar links between marital problems and children's social adjustment are evident among Latino children as well.

Across a variety of cultures, the relative influence of families and peers on children's social behavior may differ, but the family processes (e.g., child rearing, advice giving, monitoring), marital processes (e.g., husband-wife conflict), and peer processes (e.g., association with deviant peers) by which these socialization agents achieve their influence are similar.

REMAINING ISSUES AND FUTURE TRENDS

Several issues remain to be explored in future research. In terms of historical issues, we are witnessing a clear but modest shift in the extent to which fathers are active caregivers and participants in the lives of children (Parke & Brott 1999; Pleck, 1997; Pleck & Masciadrelli, this volume), but we know much less about how these shifts, in turn, alter children's social competence. Men are becoming fathers at later ages—and not just for the first time; many men are reexperiencing fatherhood in middle or old age as a result of divorce and remarriage. The impact of this shift in timing in the onset of first-time or repeated fatherhood on their interaction patterns with their children and, consequently, on their children's social competence with peers remains unclear. Some evidence (Neville & Parke, 1997) suggests that older fathers engage in less vigorous physical play and instead focus on more cognitively oriented activities than do on-time fathers. In light of the importance of this type of playful interchange between fathers and children for their social development (Parke et al., 1992; Parke, 1994), one could speculate that more peer-related difficulties may emerge for offspring of these older fathers. Alternatively, older fathers may contribute in different but still effective ways to their children's social competence by increasing their investment in advice-giving activities and by encouraging and facilitating opportunities for peer-related interactions (Parke, 2002).

A question at the core of fatherhood research is the criticality of fathers for children's social development in light of the recent evidence that children of lesbian families are socially well adjusted (Patterson, 1995). As argued elsewhere (Parke, 2001), we need to distinguish between the behavior and experiences that fathers provide and the gender of the individual who delivers these experiences. It could be helpful to revisit the issue and ask whether it is exposure to males and/or females that is critical or whether it is exposure to the interactive style typically associated with either mothers or fathers that matters. As Ross and Taylor (1989) found, boys prefer the paternal (vs. maternal) play style—whether enacted by mothers or fathers. This work suggests that boys may not necessarily prefer their fathers but rather their physical style of play. This observation is of relevance to the issue of whether children's peer relations are different from children who are reared in households composed of two female parents. As just noted, children raised in these families do not differ in social relationships with peers (Patterson, 1995, this volume), which raises questions about the criticality of the father role. However, many questions remain. For example, do lesbian partners adopt father and mother roles and therefore provide the same set of experiences (e.g., active play) for their children? In short, there may be opportunities to experience both maternal and paternal interactive styles in same-gender households. Whether this is the case is not yet clear, but regardless of the outcome, the research addressing such a question will be helpful in informing the current debate about the necessity of fathers for children's social development (Parke, 2001; Silverstein & Auerbach, 1999). In addition, we do not know whether lesbian parents in their roles as managers of children's social environments provide opportunities for exposure to male figures or male interactive styles.

Another poorly understood issue concerns the unique contributions of fathers to children's peer relationships. Although fathers' physical play style has been suggested as a unique way in which fathers influence their children's social adaptation, this is clearly not the only way in which fathers influence their children's peer relationships. In light of the cross-cultural evidence that physical play is not a universal feature of the father-child interactive style, more detailed examination of the alternative pathways through which children learn emotional competence and that are important for successful peer relationships is warranted.

Moreover, the relative importance of fathers as interactive agents, advisors, or managers of social opportunities is not clearly understood. Similarly, the relative impact of these different influence pathways for fathers versus mothers is not well charted, although it appears that mothers play a more prominent role as social managers than do fathers. It is clear that more effort needs to be devoted to partialing out the relative contributions to different aspects of the fathers' roles as well as differences across mother and father roles. In a related vein, we need to explore the possibility of a typology of fatherhood in which different types of fathers devote various amounts of their socialization effort to each of the three pathways. Magnusson (Magnusson & Cairns, 1996) has championed the person-oriented rather than variable-oriented focus. Consistent with this perspective is the cafeteria model of socialization, in which fathers vary in terms of how large a portion of interactive, advisory, or managerial roles they choose to play in their children's lives (Parke, 1992). Some fathers may be highly involved as interactive partners but low on advice giving and arranging opportunities for peer contact. Others may be highly invested in the managerial aspects of fathering but spend little time in interaction or advising. At this point, we simply do not know the effects of different combinations of paternal socialization investment strategies on children's peer outcomes. Different combinations may produce different but equally socially competent children—in recognition of the fact that satisfactory developmental adaptations can be achieved through multiple routes. Jain, Belsky, and Crnic (1996) applied this person-oriented approach to the description of fathers in intact families and identified several types of men: caregivers, playmates, teachers, disciplinarians, and disengaged fathers. This person-oriented approach to the classification of fathering types in relation to their efforts to socialize their children for peer relationships merits more attention by researchers.

Although it is assumed that fathers' roles change across development, more specification of these shifts are needed. As other work has suggested (Collins & Russell, 1991; Larson & Richards, 1994), the direction of influence between parent and child becomes more balanced across development, as issues of autonomy become of more central importance, especially during adolescence. In support of this developmental shift, Shulman and Seiffge-Krenke (1997) found that fathers become increasingly emotionally distant during adolescence, which, in turn, may increase their offsprings' autonomy achievement and their non-family-based involvements. Detailed assessments of how changes in the father-adolescent relationship alter peer relationships would clearly be worthwhile.

Finally, the direction of effects continues to be an unresolved issue. Although it is implicitly assumed that fathers are influencing their children's peer relationships, the correlational and often cross-sectional nature of the vast majority of the data on this issue suggests that the direction of causality may flow from child to parent as well. In light of recent advances in temperament research (Putham, Sanson, & Rothbart, 2002), it is clear that children elicit different types of reactions from their caregivers, including their fathers. A transactional model (Sameroff & Chandler, 1975) in which fathers and children mutually influence each other across time will prove most useful for guiding research in this area (Kuczynski, 2003; Parke et al., in press). A related issue concerns the question of how the peer system influences fathers and families and vice-versa. The mapping of how children's increased involvement in peer activities across development alters the father-child relationship is needed. Both positive and negative effects need to be better understood; associating with deviant peers or joining a gang may cause deterioration in father-adolescent relationships, whereas developing strong ties to a high-achieving peer group may strengthen father-child bonds. For example, preschool-age children's relationships with peers and friends can influence their adjustment to a new sibling (Kramer & Gottman, 1992) and, in the case of elementary school–age children, their relationships with their parents (Repetti, 1996). We simply need to broaden our search for these bilateral links between family and peer systems.

In closing, it is clear that fathers make important contributions to the development of both positive and negative peer relationships, but more attention to the role of the child in this process will be necessary to improve our understanding in this area. If fathers are part of the problem, then they can also be part of the solution. By a more nuanced understanding of the father's role in children's peer relationships, we will be in a better position to develop more effective guidelines for preventive and interventionist efforts on behalf of children who experience peer problems.

REFERENCES

Amato, P., & Rivera, F. (1999). Paternal involvement and children's behavior. *Journal of Marriage and the Family, 61*, 375–384.

Amert, J., & Balle-Jensen, L. (1993). Cultural bases of risk behavior: Danish adolescents. *Child Development, 64*, 1842–1855.

Barth, J., & Parke, R. D. (1993). Parent-child relationship influences on children's transition to school. *Merrill Palmer Quarterly, 39*, 173–195.

Belson, W. A. (1975). *Juvenile theft: The causal factors*. London: Harper & Row.

Bhavnagri, N. (1987). *Parents as facilitators of preschool children's peer relationships*. Unpublished doctoral dissertation, University of Illinois at Champaign-Urbana.

Bhavnagri, N., & Parke, R. D. (1991). Parents as direct facilitators of children's peer relationships: Effects of age of child and sex of parent. *Journal of Personal and Social Relationships, 8*, 423–440.

Bowlby, J. (1969). *Attachment and loss*. New York: Basic Books.

Bowlby, J. (1973). *Separation and loss*. New York: Basic Books.

Boyum, L. A., & Parke, R. D. (1995). The role of family emotional expressiveness in the development of children's social competence. *Journal of Marriage and the Family, 57*, 593–608.

Bronfenbrenner, U. (1970). *Two worlds of childhood: U.S. and USSR*. New York: Russell Sage Foundation.

Bryant, B. K. (1985). The neighborhood walk: Sources of support in middle childhood. *Monographs of the Society for Research in Child Development, 50*(3, Serial No. 210).

Bugental, D., & Goodnow, J. (1998). Socialization processes. In W. Damon (Gen. Ed.) & N. Eisenberg (Vol. Ed.), *Handbook of child psychology: Vol. 3. Social, emotional and personality development* (5th ed., pp. 389–462). New York: Wiley.

Burks, V. S., & Parke, R. D. (1996). Parent and child representations of social relationships: Linkages between families and peers. *Merrill-Palmer Quarterly, 42*, 358–378.

Carson, J. L., & Parke, R. D. (1996). Reciprocal negative affect in parent-child interactions and children's peer competency. *Child Development, 67*, 2217–2226.

Cassidy, J., Kirsh, S. J., Scolton, K. L., & Parke, R. D. (1996). Attachment and representations of peer relationships. *Developmental Psychology, 32*, 892–904.

Chase-Lansdale, P., Cherlin, L., & Kierman, A. J. (1995). The long-term effects of parental divorce on the mental health of young adults: A developmental perspective. *Child Development, 6*, 1614–1634.

Chen, C., Greenberger, E., Lester J., Dong, Q., & Guo, M. (1998). A cross-cultural study of family and peer correlates of adolescent misconduct. *Developmental Psychology, 34*, 770–781.

Chen, X., & Rubin, K. H. (1994). Family conditions, parental acceptance, and social competence and aggression in Chinese children. *Social Development, 3*, 269–290.

Cochran, M., & Bo, I. (1989). The social networks, family involvement, and pro- and antisocial behavior of adolescent males in Norway. *Journal of Youth and Adolescence, 4*, 377–398.

Cochran, M., & Niegro, S. (1995). Parenting and social networks. In M. Bornstein (Ed.), *Handbook of parenting: Vol. 3. Status and social conditions of parenting* (pp. 393–418). Mahwah, NJ: Erlbaum.

Cohen, J. S. (1989). *Maternal involvement in children's peer relationships during middle childhood.* Unpublished doctoral dissertation, University of Waterloo, Ontario, Canada.

Coleman, J. (1988). Social capital in the creation of human capital. *American Journal of Sociology, 94,* 95–120.

Collins, W. A. (2002, March). *Romantic relations: Fact and fancy.* Presidential address, Society for Research in Adolescence, Chicago.

Collins, W. A., & Russell, A. (1991). Mother-child and father-child and adolescence: Relationships in middle childhood: A developmental analysis. *Developmental Review, 11,* 99–136.

Contreras, F., Kerns, K. A., Weimer, B. L., Gentzler, A. L., & Tomich, P. (2000). Emotion regulation as a mediator of associations between mother-child attachment and peer relationships in middle childhood. *Journal of Family Psychology, 14,* 111–124.

Contreras, J. M., & Kerns, K. A. (2000). Emotion regulation processes: Explaining links between parent-child attachment and peer relationships. In K. A. Kerns, J. M. Contreras, & A. M. Neal-Barnett (Eds.), *Family and peers: Linking two social worlds* (pp. 1–25). Westport, CT: Praeger.

Cowan, P. A., Cohn, D. A., Cowan, C. P., & Pearson, J. L. (1996). Parents' attachment histories and children's externalizing and internalizing behaviors: Exploring family systems models of linkage. *Journal of Consulting and Clinical Psychology, 64,* 53–63.

Cowan, P. A., Cowan, C. P., Schulz, M. S., & Hemming, G. (1994). Prebirth to preschool family factors in children's adaptation to kindergarten. In R. D. Parke & S. G. Kellam (Eds.), *Exploring family relationships with other social contexts* (pp. 75–114). Hillsdale, NJ: Erlbaum.

Cummings, E. M., & O'Reilly, A. W. (1997). Fathers in family context: Effects of marital quality on child adjustment. In M. E. Lamb (Ed.), *The father's role in child development* (3rd ed., pp. 241–260). New York: Wiley.

Darling, N. E., Steinberg, L., Gringlas, B., & Dornbush, S. (1995). *Community influences on adolescent achievement and deviance: A test of the functional community hypothesis.* Unpublished manuscript.

Davies, P. T., & Cummings, E. M. (1994). Marital conflict and child adjustment: An emotional security hypothesis. *Psychological Bulletin, 116,* 387–865.

Davies, P. T., & Cummings, E. M. (1998). Exploring children's emotional security as a mediator of the link between marital relations and child adjustment. *Child Development, 69,* 124–139.

Denham, S. A. (1998). *Emotional development in young children.* New York: Guilford Press.

Eisenberg, N., & Fabes, R. (1994). Emotion regulation and the development of social competence. In M. Clark (Ed.), *Review of personality and social psychology.* Newbury Park, CA: Sage.

Eisenberg, N., Fabes, R., Bernzweig, J., Karbon, M., Poulin, R., & Hanish, L. (1993). The relations of emotionality and regulation to preschoolers' social skills and sociometric status. *Child Development, 64,* 1418–1438.

Fagan, J., & Hawkins, A. J. (Eds.). (2000). *Clinical and educational interventions with fathers.* New York: Haworth.

Fauber, R. L., & Long, N. (1991). Children in context: The role of the family in child psychotherapy. *Journal of Consulting and Clinical Psychology, 59,* 813–820.

Feldman, S., Rosenthal, D. A., Mont-Reynaud, R., & Leung, K. (1991). Ain't misbehavin': Adolescent values and family environments as correlates of misconduct in Australia, Hong Kong and the United States. *Journal of Research on Adolescence, 1,* 109–134.

Fletcher, A. C., Darling, N. E., Steinberg, L., & Dornbusch, S. (1995). The company they keep: Relation of adolescents' adjustment and behavior to their friends' perceptions of authoritative parenting in the social network. *Developmental Psychology, 31,* 300–310.

Franz, C. E., McLelland, D., & Weinberger, J. (1991). Childhood antecedents of conventional social accomplishment in midlife adults: A 23-year prospective study. *Journal of Personality and Social Psychology, 6,* 586–595.

Furstenberg, F. F., & Teitler, J. (1994). Reconsidering the effects of marital disruption. What happens to children of divorce in early adulthood? *Journal of Family Issues, 15,* 173–190.

Furstenberg, F. F., Cook, T. D., Eccles, J., Elder, G. G., & Sameroff, A. (1999). *Managing to make it.* Chicago: University of Chicago Press.

Garner, P. W., & Power, T. G. (1996). Preschoolers' emotional control in the disappointment paradigm and its relation to temperament, emotional knowledge, and family expressiveness. *Child Development, 67,* 1406–1419.

Gottman, J. M. (1994). *What predicts divorce?* Hillsdale, NJ: Erlbaum.

Gottman, J. M., & Katz, L. F. (1989). Effects of marital discord on young children's peer interaction and health. *Developmental Psychology, 25,* 373–381.

Gottman, J. M., Katz, L. F., & Hooven, C. (1997). *Meta-emotion: How families communicate emotionally.* Mahwah, NJ: Erlbaum.

Grossmann, K., Grossmann, K. E., Fremmer-Bombik, E., Kindler, H. Scheurer-Englisch, H., & Zimmerman, P. (2002). The uniqueness of the child-father attachment relationship: Fathers' sensitive and challenging play as a pivotal variable in a 16-year longitudinal study. *Social Development, 11,* 307–331.

Grossmann, K. E., & Fremmer-Bombik, E. (1994, July). *Father attachment representations and quality of interactions with their children in infancy.* Poster presented at the meeting of the International Society for the Study of Behavioral Development, Amsterdam.

Grossmann, K. E., Grossmann, K., Winter, M., & Zimmerman, P. (2002). Attachment relationships and appraisal of partnership: From early experience of sensitive support to later relationship representation. In L. Pulkkinen & A. Caspi (Eds.), *Personality in the life course: Path to successful development* (pp. 73–105). Cambridge, England: Cambridge University Press.

Grossmann, K. E., Grossmann, K., & Zimmerman, P. (1998). A wider view of attachment and exploration: Stability and change during the years of immaturity. In J. Cassidy & P. R. Shaver (Eds.), *Handbook of attachment: Theory, research and clinical applications* (pp. 760–786). New York: Guilford Press.

Harlow, H. F. (1958). The nature of love. *American Psychologist, 13,* 673–685.

Harris, J. R. (1995). Where is the child's environment? A group socialization theory of development. *Psychological Review, 102,* 458–489.

Harris, J. R. (1998). *The nurture assumption.* New York: Free Press.

Hart, C. H., Nelson, D. A., Robinson, C. C., Olsen, S. F., McNeilly-Choque, M. K., Porter, C. L., et al. (2000). Russian parenting styles and family processes: Linkages with subtypes of victimization and aggression. In K. A. Kerns, J. M. Contreras, & A. M. Neal-Barnett (Eds.), *Family and peers: Linking two social worlds* (pp. 47–84). Westport, CT: Praeger.

Hart, C. H., Yang, C., Nelson, D. A., Jin, S., Bazarakaya, N., Nelson, L., et al. (1998). Peer contact patterns, parenting practices and preschoolers' social competence in China, Russia, and the United States. In P. T. Slee & K. Rigby (Eds.), *Children's peer relations* (pp. 3–30). London: Routledge.

Hartup, W. W. (1997). The social worlds of childhood. *American Psychologist, 34,* 944–949.

Hetherington, E. M. (1966). Effects of father absence on sex-typed behavior in Negro and White pre-adolescent males. *Journal of Personality and Social Psychology, 4,* 87–91.

Hetherington, E. M., & Deur, J. (1971). The effects of father's absence on child development. *Young Children, 26,* 233–248.

Hewlett, B. S. (1991). *Intimate fathers.* Ann Arbor: University of Michigan Press.

Holden, G. W. (1997). *Parents and the dynamics of child rearing.* Boulder, CO: Western Press.

Homel, R., & Burns, A. (1989). Environmental quality and the well being of children. *Social indicators research, 21,* 133–158.

Homel, R., Burns, A., & Goodnow, J. (1987). Parental social networks and child development. *Journal of Social and Personal Relationships, 4,* 159–177.

Isley, S., O'Neil, R., Clatfelter, D., & Parke, R. D. (1999). Parent and child expressed affect and children's social competence: Modeling direct and indirect pathways. *Developmental Psychology, 35,* 547–560.

Isley, S., O'Neil, R., & Parke, R. D. (1996). The relation of parental affect and control behaviors to children's classroom acceptance: A concurrent and predictive analysis. *Early Education and Development, 7,* 7–23.

Jain, A., Belsky, J., & Crnic, L. (1996). Beyond fathering behavior: Types of dads. *Journal of Family Psychology, 10,* 431–442.

Katz, L. F., & Gottman, J. M. (1993). Patterns of marital conflict predict children's internalizing and externalizing behavior. *Developmental Psychology, 29,* 940–950.

Katz, L. F., & Gottman, J. M. (1994). Patterns of marital interaction and children's emotional development. In R. D. Parke & S. Kellam (Eds.), *Exploring family relationships with other contexts* (pp. 49–74). Hillsdale, NJ: Erlbaum.

Kerns, K., & Barth, J. (1995). Parent-child attachment and physical play: Convergence across components of parent-child relationships and their relations to peer competence. *Journal of Social and Personal Relationships, 12,* 243–260.

Kim, M. (2001). *Marital conflict and peer outcomes in Euro and Mexican-American families.* Unpublished doctoral dissertation, University of California, Riverside.

Kim, M., Parke, R. D., & O'Neil, R. (1999, April). *Marital conflict and children's social competence: Concurrent and predictive analyses.* Poster presented at the annual meeting of the Western Psychological Association, Irvine, CA.

Koestner, R., Franz, C., & Weinberger, J. (1990). The origins of empathic concern: A 26-year longitudinal study. *Journal of Personality and Social Psychology, 58,* 709–717.

Kramer, L., & Gottman, J. M. (1992). Becoming a sibling—with a little help from my friends. *Developmental Psychology, 28,* 685–699.

Kuczynski, L. (Ed.). (2003). *Handbook of dynamics in parent-child relations.* Thousand Oaks, CA: Sage.

Ladd, G. W. (1992). Themes and theories: Perspectives on processes in family-peer relationships. In R. D. Parke & G. W. Ladd (Eds.), *Family-peer relationships: Modes of linkage* (pp. 1–17). Hillsdale, NJ: Erlbaum.

Ladd, G. W., & Golter, B. S. (1988). Parents' management of preschoolers' peer relations: Is it related to children's social competence? *Developmental Psychology, 24,* 109–117.

Lamb, M. E. (Ed.). (1997). *The role of the father in child development* (3rd ed.). New York: Wiley.

Larson, R., & Richards, M. (1994). *Divergent realities.* New York: Basic Books.

Lazarus, S., & Folkman, S. (1984). *Stress, appraisal, and coping.* New York: Springer.

Lindahl, K. M., & Malik, N. M. (1999). Marital conflict, family processes and boys' externalizing behavior in Hispanic American and European American families. *Journal of Clinical Child Psychology, 28,* 12–24.

Lollis, S. P., Ross, H. S., & Tate, E. (1992). Parents' regulation of children's peer interactions: Direct influences. In R. Parke & G. Ladd (Eds.), *Family-peer relationships: Modes of linkage* (pp. 255–281). Hillsdale, NJ: Erlbaum.

Lynn, D. B., & Sawrey, W. L. (1959). The effects of father absence on Norwegian boys and girls. *Journal of Abnormal and Social Psychology, 59,* 258–262.

MacDonald, K., & Parke, R. D. (1984). Bridging the gap: Parent-child play interaction and peer interactive competence. *Child Development, 55,* 1265–1277.

Magnusson, D., & Cairns, R. B. (1996). Developmental science: Toward a unified framework. In R. B. Cairns, G. H. Elder Jr., & J. Costello (Eds.), *Developmental science* (pp. 7–30). New York: Cambridge University Press.

Main, M., Kaplan, N., & Cassidy, J. (1985). Security in infancy, childhood and adulthood: A move to the level of representation. In I. Bretherton & E. Waters (Eds.), *Growing points in attachment theory and research. Monographs of the Society for Research in Child Develoipment, 50*(1–2, Serial No. 209).

Marsiglio, W., Amato, P., Day, R., & Lamb, M. E. (2000). Scholarship on fatherhood in the 1990's and beyond. *Journal of Marriage and the Family, 62,* 1173–1191.

McDowell, D. J., O'Neil, R., & Parke, R. D. (2000). Display rule application in a disappointing situation and children's emotional reactivity: Relations with social competence. *Merrill-Palmer Quarterly, 46,* 306–324.

McDowell, D. J., & Parke, R. D. (2002). Differential knowledge of display rules for positive and negative emotions: Influence from parents, influences on peers. *Social Development, 9,* 415–432.

McDowell, D. J., Parke, R. D., & Spitzer, S. (2002). Parent and child cognitive representations of social situations and children's social competence. *Social Development, 11,* 469–486.

McLanahan, S. (1997). Paternal absence or poverty: Which matters more? In G. Duncan & J. Brooks-Gunn (Eds.), *Consequences of growing up poor* (pp. 35–48). New York: Russell Sage Foundation.

McLanahan, S., & Teitler, J. (1999). The consequences of father absence. In M. E. Lamb (Ed.), *Parenting and child development in "nontraditional families"* (pp. 83–102). Mahwah, NJ: Erlbaum.

Mills, R. S., & Rubin, K. H. (1993). Parental ideas as influences on children's social competence. In S. Duck (Ed.), *Learning about relationships* (Vol. 2, pp. 98–117). Newbury Park, CA: Sage.

Mischel, W., Shoda, Y., & Peake, P. K. (1988). The nature of adolescent competencies predicted by preschool delay of gratification. *Journal of Personality and Social Psychology, 4,* 687–696.

Mize, J., & Pettit, G. (1997). Mothers' social coaching, mother-child relationship style, and children's peer competence: Is the medium the message? *Child Development, 68,* 312–332.

Mize, J., Pettit, G. S., & Brown, E. G. (1995). Mothers' supervisions of their children's peer play: Relations with beliefs, perceptions, and knowledge. *Developmental Psychology, 31,* 311–321.

Mosley, J., & Thompson, E. (1995). Fathering behavior and child outcomes: The role of race and poverty. In W. Marsiglio (Ed.), *Fatherhood: Contemporary theory, research, and social policy* (pp. 148–165). Thousand Oaks, CA: Sage.

Mott, F. L. (1994). Sons, daughters and fathers' absence: Differentials in father-leaving probabilities and in home environments. *Journal of Family Issues, 15,* 97–128.

Mounts, N. (2000). Parental management of adolescent peer relationships. What are its effects on friend selection? In K. A. Kerns, J. M. Contreras, & A. M. Neal-Barnett (Eds.), *Family and peers: Linking two social worlds* (pp. 169–194). Westport, CT: Praeger.

Neville, B., & Parke, R. D. (1997). Waiting for paternity: Interpersonal and contextual implications of the timing of fatherhood. *Sex Roles, 37,* 45–59.

New, R., & Benigni, L. (1987). Italian fathers and infants: Cultural constraints on paternal behavior. In M. E. Lamb (Ed.), *The father role: Cross-cultural perspectives* (pp. 139–168). New York: Wiley.

O'Neil, R., Flyr, M. L., Wild, M. N., & Parke, R. D. (1999, April). *Early adolescents' exposure to marital conflict: Links to relationships with parents and peers.* Paper presented at the biennial meeting of the Society for Research in Child Development, Albuquerque, NM.

O'Neil, R., Garcia, J., Zavala, A., & Wang, S. (1995, April). *Parental advice giving and children's competence with peers: A content and stylistic analysis.* Paper presented at the biennial meeting of the Society for Research in Child Development, Indianapolis, IN.

O'Neil, R., & Parke, R. D. (2000). Family-peer relationships: The role of emotion regulation, cognitive understanding, and attentional processes as mediating processes. In K. Kerns, J. Contreras, & A. Neal-Barnett (Eds.), *Family and peers: Linking two social worlds* (pp. 195–225). Connecticut: Praeger.

O'Neil, R., Parke, R. D., Isley, S., & Sosa, R. (1997). *Parental influences on children's emotion regulation in middle childhood.* Paper presented at the biennial meeting of the Society for Research in Child Development, Washington, DC.

Paley, B., Conger, R., & Harold, G. T. (2000). Parents' affect, adolescent cognitive representations and adolescent social development. *Journal of Marriage and the Family, 62,* 761–776.

Parke, R. D. (1992). Epilogue: Remaining issues and future trends in the study of family-peer relationships. In R. D. Parke & G. W. Ladd (Eds.), *Family-peer relationships modes of linkage* (pp. 425–438). Hillsdale, NJ: Erlbaum.

Parke, R. D. (1994). Progress, paradigms, and unresolved problems: A commentary on recent advances in our understanding of children's emotions. *Merrill-Palmer Quarterly, 40,* 157–169.

Parke, R. D. (1995). Fathers and families. In M. H. Bornstein (Ed.), *Handbook of parenting* (Vol. 3, pp. 27–63). Hillsdale, NJ: Erlbaum.

Parke, R. D. (1996). *Fatherhood.* Cambridge, MA: Harvard University Press.

Parke, R. D. (2002a). Fathers and families. In M. H. Bornstein (Ed.), *Handbook of parenting* (2nd ed., Vol. 3, pp. 27–73). Mahwah, NJ: Erlbaum.

Parke, R. D. (2002b). Parenting in the new millennium: Prospects, promises and pitfalls. In J. P. McHale & W. S. Grolnick (Eds.), *Retrospect and prospect in the psychological study of families* (pp. 65–94). Mahwah, NJ: Erlbaum.

Parke, R. D., & Brott, A. A. (1999). *Throwaway dads: The myths and barriers that keep men from being the fathers they want to be.* Boston: Houghton Mifflin.

Parke, R. D., & Buriel, R. (1998). Socialization in the family: Ecological and ethnic perspectives. In W. Damon (General Ed.) & N. Eisenberg (Vol. Ed.), *Handbook of child psychology: Vol. 3. Social, emotional, and personality development* (5th ed., pp. 463–552). New York: Wiley.

Parke, R. D., Burks, V. M., Carson, J. L., Neville, B., & Boyum, L. A. (1994). Family-peer relationships: A tripartite model. In R. D. Parke & S. G. Kellam (Eds.), *Exploring family relationships with other social contexts* (pp. 115–145). Hillsdale, NJ: Erlbaum.

Parke, R. D., Cassidy, J., Burks, V. M., Carson, J. L., & Boyum, L. (1992). Family contribution to peer competence among young children: The role of interactive and affective processes. In R. Parke & G. Ladd (Eds.), *Family-peer relationships: Modes of linkage* (pp. 107–134). Hillsdale, NJ: Erlbaum.

Parke, R. D., Killian, C., Dennis, J., Flyr, M., McDowell, D. J., Simpkins, S., et al. (in press). Managing the external environment: The parent and child as active agents in the system. In L. Kuczynski (Ed.), *Handbook of dynamics in parent-child relations.* Thousand Oaks, CA: Sage.

Parke, R. D., Kim, M., Flyr, M. L., McDowell, D. J., Simpkins, S. D., Killian, C., et al. (2001). Managing marital conflict: Links with children's peer relationships. In J. Grych & F. Fincham

(Eds.), *Child development and interparental conflict* (pp. 291–314). New York: Cambridge University Press.

Parke, R. D., & McDowell, D. J. (1998). Toward an expanded model of emotion socialization: New people, new pathways. *Psychological Inquiry, 9,* 303–307.

Parke, R. D., & O'Neil, R. (1997). The influence of significant others on learning about relationships. In S. Duck (Ed.), *The handbook of personal relationships* (2nd ed., pp. 29–60). New York: Wiley.

Parke, R. D., & O'Neil, R. (2000). The influence of significant others on learning about relationships: From family to friends. In R. Mills & S. Duck (Eds.), *The developmental psychology of personal relationships* (pp. 15–47). New York: Wiley.

Parke, R. D., Simpkins, S., McDowell, D. J., Kim, M., Killian, C., Dennis, J., et al. (2002). Relative contributions of families and peers to children's social development. In P. K. Smith & C. Hart (Eds.), *Handbook of social development* (pp. 156–177). New York: Wiley.

Parker, J. G., & Asher, S. R. (1987). Peer relations and later personal adjustment: Are low-accepted children at risk? *Psychological Bulletin, 102,* 357–389.

Parsons, T., & Bales, R. F. (1955). *Family, socialization, and interaction process.* Glencoe, IL: Free Press.

Patterson, C. (1995). Gay and lesbian parents. In M. H. Bornstein (Ed.), *Handbook of parenting* (Vol. 3, pp. 253–274). Mahwah, NJ: Erlbaum.

Patterson, G. R., & Shouthamer-Loeber, M. (1984). The correlation of family management and delinquency. *Child Development, 55,* 1299–1307.

Pettit, G., & Mize, J. (1998). Mothers' and fathers' socializing behavior in three contexts: Links with children's social competence. *Merrill-Palmer Quarterly, 44,* 173–193.

Pettit, G. S., Bates, J. E., Dodge, D. A., & Meece, D. W. (1999). The impact of afterschool peer contact on early adolescent externalizing problems is moderated by parental monitoring, perceived neighborhood safety and prior adjustment. *Child Development, 70,* 768–778.

Pleck, J. (1997). Paternal involvement: Levels, sources, and consequences. In M. Lamb (Ed.), *The role of the father in child development* (3rd ed., pp. 67–103). New York: Wiley.

Putham, S. P., Sanson, A. V., & Rothbart, M. K. (2002). Child temperament and parenting. In M. Bornstein (Ed.), *Handbook of parenting* (2nd ed., Vol. 1, pp. 225–278). Mahwah, NJ: Erlbaum.

Repetti, R. (1996). The effects of perceived social and academic failure experience on school-age children's subsequent interactions with parents. *Child Development, 67,* 1467–1482.

Roberts, W. (1994). *The socialization of emotional expression.* Paper presented at the Canadian Psychological Association, Vancouver, British Columbia.

Rohner, R. P. (1998). Father love and child development: History and current evidence. *Current Directions in Psychological Science, 1,* 157–161.

Ross, H. S., & Taylor, H. (1989). Do boys prefer daddy or his physical style of play? *Sex Roles, 20,* 23–33.

Rothbart, M., & Bates, J. (1998). Temperament. In W. Damon & N. Eisenberg (Eds.), *Handbook of child psychology: Social, emotional, and personality development* (Vol. 3, pp. 105–176). New York: Wiley.

Rubin, K., Bukowski, W., & Parker, J. (1998). Peer interaction, relationships and groups. In W. Damon & N. Eisenberg (Eds.), *Handbook of child psychology: Social, emotional, and personality development* (5th ed., Vol. 3, pp. 619–700). New York: Wiley.

Russell, A., & Finnie, V. (1990). Preschool children's social status and maternal instructions to assist group entry. *Developmental Psychology, 26,* 603–611.

Russell, G. (1999). Primary caregiving families. In M. E. Lamb (Ed.), *Parenting and child development in "nontraditional families"* (pp. 39–56). Mahwah, NJ: Erlbaum.

Saarni, C. (1984). An observational study of children's attempt to monitor their expressive behavior. *Child Development, 55,* 1504–1513.

Sameroff, A. J., & Chandler, M. J. (1975). Reproductive risk and the continuum of caretaking casualty. In F. D. Horowitz (Ed.), *Review of child development research* (Vol. 4, pp. 187–244). Chicago: University of Chicago Press.

Sandstrom, M. J., & Cole, J. D. (1999). A developmental perspective on peer rejection: Mechanisms of stability and change. *Child Development, 70,* 955–966.

Schneider, B. (2000). *Friends and enemies.* London: Arnold.

Shulman, S., & Seiffge-Krenke, I. (1997). *Fathers and adolescents.* New York: Routledge.

Silverstein, L. B., & Auerbach, C. F. (1999). Deconstructing the essential father. *American Psychologist, 54,* 397–407.

Simpkins, S., O'Neil, R., Lee, J., Parke, R. D., & Wang, S. J. (2002). *The relation between parent and children's social networks and children's peer acceptance.* Unpublished manuscript.

Simpkins, S., & Parke, R. D. (2001). The relations between parental friendships and child friendships: Self-report and observational analyses. *Child Development, 72,* 569–582.

Simpkins, S., & Parke, R. D. (2002a). Do friends and nonfriends behave differently? A social relations analysis of children's behavior. *Merrill-Palmer Quarterly, 48,* 263–283.

Simpkins, S., & Parke, R. D. (2002b). Maternal monitoring and rules as correlates of children's social adjustment. *Merrill-Palmer Quarterly, 48,* 360–377.

Sroufe, L. A., Egeland, B., & Carlson, E. A. (1999). One social world: The integrated development of parent-child and peer relationships. In W. A. Collins & B. Laursen (Eds.), *Relationships as developmental contexts* (pp. 241–262). Mahwah, NJ: Erlbaum.

Steele, E., Steele, M., Croft, C., & Fonagy, P. (1999). Infant-mother attachment at one year predicts children's understanding of mixed emotions at six years. *Social Development, 8,* 161–178.

Stocker, C. M., & Youngblade, L. (1999). Marital conflict and parental hostility: Links with children's sibling and peer relationships. *Journal of Family Psychology, 13,* 598–609.

Stolz, L. M. (1954). *Father relations of war-born children.* Stanford: Stanford University Press.

Sun, L. C., & Roopnarine, J. L. (1996). Mother-infant, father-infant interaction and involvement in childcare and household labor among Taiwanese families. *Infant Behavior and Development, 19,* 121–129.

Thompson, R. A. (1998). Early sociopersonality development. In W. Damon & N. Eisenberg (Eds.), *Handbook of child psychology: Social emotional and personality development* (5th ed., Vol. 3, pp. 25–104). New York: Wiley.

Underwood, M. K., Coie, J. D., & Herbsman, C. R. (1992). Display rules for anger and aggression in school-age children. *Child Development, 63,* 366–380.

Updegraff, K. A., McHale, S. M., Crouter, A. C., & Kupanoff, K. (2001). Parents' involvement in adolescents' peer relationships: A comparison of mothers' and fathers' roles. *Journal of Marriage and the Family, 63,* 655–668.

Vandell, D. L. (2000). Parents, peer groups, and other socializing influences. *Developmental Psychology, 36,* 699–710.

Volling, B. L. (2001). Early attachment relationships as predictors of preschool children's emotion regulation with a distressed sibling. *Early Education and Development, 12,* 185–207.

Wang, S. J., & McDowell, D. J. (1996). *Parental advice-giving: Relations to child social competence and psychosocial functioning.* Poster session presented at the annual meeting of the Western Psychological Association, San Jose, CA.

Westerman, M. A., & Schonholtz, J. (1993). Marital adjustment, joint parental support in a triadic problem-solving task, and child behavior problems. *Journal of Clinical Child Psychology, 22,* 97–106.

Wilson, B. J. (1999). Entry behavior and emotion regulation abilities of developmentally delayed boys. *Developmental Psychology, 35,* 214–223.

Wu, L., Cherlin, A., & Bumpass, L. (1997). *Family structure, early sexual behavior and premarital births* (Institute for Research in Poverty Discussion paper, DP#1125-97). Madison: University of Wisconsin.

Xiaoming, L., Stantom, B., & Feigelman, S. (2000). Impact of perceived parental monitoring on adolescent risk behavior over 4 years. *Journal of Adolescent Health, 1,* 49–56.

Youngblade, L., & Belsky, J. (1992). Parent-child antecedents of five-year-olds' close friendships: A longitudinal analysis. *Developmental Psychology, 28,* 700–713.

Youngblade, L., Park, K., & Belsky, J. (1993). Measurement of young children's close friendship: A comparison of two independent assessment systems and their associations with attachment security. *International Journal of Behavioral Development, 16,* 563–587.

CHAPTER 12

The Effects of Divorce
on Fathers and Children

Nonresidential Fathers and Stepfathers

PAUL R. AMATO and JULIE M. SOBOLEWSKI

D URING THE SECOND HALF of the 20th century, large-scale economic and cultural developments in the United States transformed the role of fathers. Prior to this century, fathers served as the instrumental leaders of their families (Parsons & Bales, 1955). Fathers determined their families' social status, provided economic support to their wives and children, and served as role models of employment and achievement for their sons. After World War II, wives and mothers moved into the paid labor force in large numbers. As dual-earner families replaced father-breadwinner families, the belief emerged that fathers should share child-rearing responsibilities with mothers (Thornton, 1989). According to this new cultural perspective, fathers should be engaged in their children's lives, not only because it relieves the burden experienced by employed mothers but also because it benefits children. Although men's behavior has changed more slowly than many people would prefer, fathers have taken on a greater share of child rearing during the last few decades (Robinson & Godbey, 1999).

At the same time that our culture was encouraging fathers to play a larger role in their children's lives, changes in family structure were undermining this process. The divorce rate in the United States doubled between the early 1960s and 1980, and demographers estimate that about one half of first marriages initiated in recent years will be disrupted voluntarily (Bramlett & Mosher, 2001). The percentage of births to unmarried mothers also increased substantially since 1970, with one third of all births in the late 1990s being to unmarried women (Terry-Humen, Manlove, & Moore, 2001). In a large proportion of these cases (about 40%), mothers are cohabiting with the fathers of their children (Smock, 2000). Consequently, these children, although born outside of marriage, live with both biological parents. Cohabiting relationships, however, are even more unstable than marriages, with the majority ending in disruption (Smock,

2000). Official divorce statistics, therefore, substantially underestimate the extent of instability among childbearing unions in the United States.

The high rate of marital disruption, combined with the increase in nonmarital births, means that about half of all children will spend some portion of their preadult years residing in single-parent households, usually with their mothers (Bumpass, 1990). Correspondingly, the percentage of men living with biological children decreased from 53% in 1965 to 35% in 1995 (Eggebeen, 2002). In the United States, about 11 million men currently reside apart from their children (Sorensen & Zibman, 2001). These changes have created a contradiction at the heart of contemporary fatherhood: Although cultural expectations for fathers are higher than ever, changes in family structure have physically (and perhaps emotionally) separated large numbers of men from their children.

Remarriage creates an additional complication for fathers. Most divorced individuals remarry, and nearly one half of all marriages involve a second (or higher order) marriage for one or both partners (U.S. Bureau of the Census, 1998, Table 157). As a result, about 15% of all children currently reside with a mother and a stepfather, and about one third of all children will live with a stepparent—usually a stepfather—prior to reaching adulthood (Bumpass, Raley, & Sweet, 1995). Because of these changes in family structure, many men today are nonresidential fathers to their biological children and residential stepfathers to their wives' children.

How are these new family realities affecting fathers and their children? To answer this question, we focus on relationships between nonresident fathers and their children following divorce, along with relationships between stepfathers and stepchildren following remarriage. Research has demonstrated that children with divorced parents score lower than children with continuously married parents on a variety of indicators of adjustment, development, and well-being (see Amato, 2000, for a review). A number of factors appear to be responsible for the problems experienced by children of divorce, with the loss of the fathers' economic and social resources playing a prominent role (Lamb, 1999). In this chapter we focus on the transmission of financial and social capital from fathers and stepfathers to children and on the extent to which biological children and stepchildren benefit from this transmission.

FATHERS' FINANCIAL AND SOCIAL CAPITAL

Following Coleman (1988), we divide parental resources into financial capital and social capital. Financial capital refers to income—or goods and experiences purchased with income—provided by fathers to their children. Examples of income-related resources include wholesome food, residence in safe neighborhoods, access to high-quality schools, commodities that facilitate children's academic success (books, computers, travel, and private lessons), adequate medical care, and support for college attendance.

Social capital, as defined by Coleman (1988), is a resource that adheres in the relationships between people, that is, in family and community relations that facilitate children's cognitive and social development. Support and monitoring are dimensions of paternal involvement that represent fundamental resources for children (Baumrind, 1968; Maccoby & Martin, 1983; Rollins & Thomas, 1979). Support is reflected in affection, responsiveness, encouragement, instruction, and everyday assistance. These behaviors facilitate children's positive development by conveying a basic sense of trust and security, reinforcing children's self-conceptions of worth and competence, and promoting the learning of practical skills. Monitoring is reflected in rule formulation, discipline, and supervision. Through monitoring, children learn that their behavior must operate within a set of socially constructed boundaries. And by explaining the reasons behind rules (induction), fathers and mothers help children to internalize rules and engage in self-regulation. As children grow into adolescence, effective parents gradually relax the extent of monitoring in line with children's growing ability to engage in self-regulation. Nevertheless, throughout the teen years, monitoring is necessary to ensure that children do well in school and do not drift into delinquent or antisocial activities (see the chapter by Lamb and Lewis in this volume).

Another aspect of social capital refers to parents' connections with other adults. In this context, Coleman (1988) discussed the importance of closure, that is, a strong link between two (or more) adults who each have a relationship with the child. For example, fathers have a positive effect on their children's development when they provide emotional support to mothers and back up mothers' authority. Fathers also can connect children to other groups and institutions in the community, such as schools, sports teams, and religious organizations. When fathers communicate with their children's teachers, involve their children in sports and other community activities, and participate with their children in religious services, fathers create a network of supportive social ties within which children can develop successfully.

The rise in divorce and nonmarital births during the last several decades, and the corresponding physical separation of men from their children, have made it difficult for fathers to provide social and financial capital to their children. When men live apart from their children, parents and children do not benefit from economies of scale, so there is less money to go around. Moreover, geographical distance makes it difficult for men to monitor their children's behavior, to provide emotional support when their children need it, and to participate in children's after-school and weekend activities. In addition, the norms regulating stepfathers' obligations to their stepchildren are unclear. Indeed, stepchildren and biological children may compete with one another for men's income and time.

In the remainder of this chapter we attempt to answer several questions about fathers and children after divorce. How much child support do nonresident, divorced fathers pay? What factors predict nonresident fathers' payment of child support? How much contact do nonresident fathers have with their children? What factors predict contact between nonresident fathers and children? And does the provision of financial and social capital by nonresident fathers benefit children? We address similar questions with respect to stepfathers: To what extent do stepfathers provide social and financial capital to their stepchildren? What factors are associated with stepfather involvement? And does the involvement of stepfathers have positive consequences for stepchildren? (The chapter by McLanahan and Carlson in this volume focuses on children and never-married fathers.)

NONRESIDENT, DIVORCED FATHERS

Social scientists have learned much about nonresident, divorced fathers and their children during the last two decades. Much of our knowledge is based on large-scale, national data sets, such as the National Longitudinal Survey of Youth (e.g., King, 1994a), the National Survey of Families and Households (e.g., Seltzer & Brandreth, 1994), the

Panel Study of Income Dynamics (e.g., Hill, 1992), the Child Health Supplement of the National Health Interview Survey (e.g., Seltzer & Bianchi, 1988), the Survey of Income and Program Participation (e.g., Bartfeld, 2000), the Current Population Surveys (e.g., Graham & Beller, 1996), and the U.S. Census (e.g., Beller & Graham, 1993). Supplementing these data sources are regional samples of divorced and separated families, such as the Wisconsin Children, Incomes, and Program Participation Survey (Seltzer, Schaeffer, & Charng, 1989), the Wisconsin Court Record Database and Parent Survey (Lin, 2000), and samples of families selected randomly from county divorce records (e.g., Maccoby & Mnookin, 1992). Although most of these studies have focused on divorced fathers, some studies also included data on never-married, nonresident fathers, and we briefly note the differences between these two groups in our discussion.

FINANCIAL CAPITAL: HOW MUCH CHILD SUPPORT DO FATHERS PAY?

Approximately 13 million children live with single mothers, which makes them potentially eligible for child support from their fathers (U.S. Bureau of the Census, 2001, Table 58). Fathers' child support payments have a significant impact on children's standard of living. In families headed by divorced single mothers, fathers' child support payments represent about one fifth of total household income (Teachman & Paasch, 1993). Bartfeld (2000) found that fathers' compliance with child support orders following divorce decreased the needs-adjusted income gap between custodial mothers' and noncustodial fathers' households by about 30%. Nord and Zill (1996) found that mothers and their children were less likely to be using public assistance when nonresident fathers paid child support. Despite the importance of child support for the economic well-being of children, however, only about 60% of custodial mothers have child support awards (U.S. Bureau of the Census, 2000). Child support awards are more common among divorced mothers than among never-married mothers, and they are more common among White mothers than among Black mothers or Hispanic mothers (Beller & Graham, 1993). The value of these awards also tends to be higher for divorced mothers than for never-married mothers (Beller & Graham, 1993; Nord & Zill, 1996; Teachman & Paasch, 1993; U.S. Bureau of the Census, 2000).

For mothers who are awarded child support, fathers' child support compliance has increased since the early 1980s, with stricter enforcement efforts helping to narrow the gap between awards and the amount received (Beller & Graham, 1993). However, studies conducted in the 1990s report that even when mothers have child support awards, between one fifth and one third of divorced fathers do not pay any child support (Beller & Graham, 1993; Knox & Bane, 1994; Maccoby & Mnookin, 1992; Meyer, 1999; Nord & Zill, 1996; Seltzer, 1991). Of those mothers who receive any support, fathers pay between two thirds and 90% of what is owed (Braver, Fitzpatrick, & Bay, 1991; Graham, Beller, & Hernandez, 1994; Teachman, 1991).

Our understanding of men's compliance with child support awards is complicated by the fact that estimates vary with the source of the report. Most of the studies cited in the preceding paragraph relied on custodial mothers' reports, which tend to be lower than noncustodial fathers' reports. In a study that included divorced fathers as well as divorced mothers, Braver, Fitzpatrick, et al. (1991) found that custodial parents (mostly mothers) reported receiving 69% of what was owed, whereas noncustodial parents (mostly fathers) reported paying 92% of what was owed. In another study based on fathers' reports, 5% paid nothing, 33% paid partial support, 42% paid close to what was owed, and 20% paid more than what was owed (Lin, 2000). Minton and Pasley (1996) found even higher levels of compliance, with virtually all fathers reporting that they paid support. Differences between the reports of mothers and fathers make it difficult to reach definitive conclusions about how much child support fathers actually pay.

Men's failure to pay child support has led to the image of the *deadbeat dad*—a term frequently invoked in the media. But even though some nonresident fathers provide little or no economic support to their children, a large proportion of fathers regularly pays the full amount of child support. Based on mothers' reports, this group ranges from one fourth to one half of all fathers (Beller & Graham, 1993; Maccoby & Mnookin, 1992; Meyer, 1999; Nord & Zill, 1996; Teachman & Paasch, 1993). Estimates based on fathers' reports are even higher. Teachman (1991) noted that fathers tend to pay no support or nearly the full amount of support. These results suggest two groups of fathers: those who generally meet their child support obligations and those who do not, although it is difficult to determine the precise size of these two groups in the population.

FACTORS ASSOCIATED WITH PAYING CHILD SUPPORT

Fathers' Characteristics

Perhaps the best predictor of whether fathers pay child support is the existence of a court order (Nord & Zill, 1996; Teachman & Paasch, 1993). Otherwise, one of the most consistent factors that predicts the payment of child support is the father's ability to pay. Studies consistently show that fathers' income, employment, and education are good predictors of child support payment (Arditti, 1992b; Beller & Graham, 1993; Braver, Fitzpatrick et al., 1992; Hill, 1992; Landale & Oropesa, 2001; Lin, 2000; Maccoby & Mnookin, 1992; Meyer, 1999; Seltzer et al., 1989; Teachman, 1991; Thompson & Laible, 1999). Correspondingly, having a large burden of support (the proportion of the father's income owed as child support) lowers the likelihood of compliance (Meyer, 1999), as does an order to pay alimony in addition to child support (Lin, 2000). Apparently, many fathers fail to provide support because they cannot afford to meet their child support obligations.

Although the ability to pay is a crucial factor, some fathers fail to provide child support even though they can afford to do so (Sorenson & Zibman, 2001). Studies indicate that such fathers often have strong, negative feelings about the divorce. Some men are angry at their ex-wives (Arendell, 1995), wish to avoid their ex-wives (Arditti, 1992b), are dissatisfied with the property division (Arditti, 1992b), or think that their child support orders are unfair (Lin, 2000). These findings indicate that hostile feelings following divorce (toward ex-wives, the courts, or the enforcement system) undermine many fathers' motivation to support their children economically. In contrast, fathers who voluntarily agree to make financial contributions to their children, compared with fathers who have child support obligations imposed on them by the courts, are more likely to pay support, pay larger amounts of support, and generally comply with the full terms of the award (Beller & Graham, 1993; Nord & Zill, 1996; Teachman, 1991; Teachman & Paasch, 1993).

Another factor associated with child support compliance is the amount of father-child contact. Fathers who maintain frequent contact with their children tend to pay child support regularly (Maccoby & Mnookin, 1992; Nord & Zill, 1996; Seltzer, 1991; Teachman, 1991; Teachman & Paasch, 1993; Thompson & Laible, 1999). Similarly, fathers who have input into everyday decisions about their children tend to pay more child support (Seltzer, 1991), as do fathers with joint legal or joint physical custody of their children (Nord & Zill, 1996). Moreover, fathers who live close to their children and hence are able to see their children regularly tend to pay more child support (Hill, 1992; Nord & Zill, 1996; Seltzer, 1991; Seltzer et al., 1989; Teachman & Paasch, 1993). Paying child support and maintaining frequent contact may be two indicators of an underlying commitment to children. Alternatively, paying child support and maintaining contact may reinforce each other. Men who see their children regularly may develop close emotional bonds with them and hence feel a strong obligation to maintain financial support, whereas men who pay child support regularly may wish to see their children frequently to ensure that their support payments are being spent appropriately.

These findings suggest two distinct strategies for increasing compliance, depending on whether fathers are poor or nonpoor (Greene & Moore, 2000). Interventions that elevate fathers' incomes (by providing education, job training, and assistance in locating suitable employment) may be more effective for poor fathers, whereas stricter enforcement strategies may be more effective among fathers whose incomes are sufficient to pay the support that they owe. Enforcement appears to be effective for at least some fathers, as reflected in the positive association between income withholding and child support receipt (Lin, 2000). Increasing fathers' stakes in child support arrangements (through mediated agreements or shared legal custody) also may facilitate payment among nonpoor men (Nord & Zill, 1996). Similarly, ensuring that fathers have generous visitation schedules is likely to increase compliance. Regardless of strategy, establishing an early pattern of child support compliance appears to be important because early compliance with support orders is a good predictor of consistent, ongoing child support payments (Thompson & Laible, 1999).

Finally, fathers who have been separated or divorced for longer periods of time are less likely to pay (Beller & Graham, 1993; Nord & Zill, 1996; Seltzer, 1991; Seltzer, Schaeffer, & Charng, 1989; Teachman, 1991; Teachman & Paasch, 1993). Fathers' contact with children also tends to decline with time (Furstenberg, Nord, Peterson, & Zill, 1983; Seltzer, 1991; Seltzer et al., 1989; Stephens, 1996; Thompson & Laible, 1999). Taken together, these findings suggest that some men's commitment to their biological children grows weaker as they spend more years living apart from their families.

Mothers' Characteristics

Maternal characteristics also bear on whether child support is paid and how much is paid. For example, White mothers are more likely than Black mothers to receive support (Braver, Fitzpatrick, et al., 1991; Graham & Beller, 1996). Presumably, this difference at least partly reflects the higher rate of employment and the higher incomes of White fathers compared with Black fathers. Other maternal factors that predict payment of support are being older (Beller & Graham, 1993), being better educated (Beller & Graham, 1993; Seltzer, 1991), and living somewhere in the United States other than the West (Beller & Graham, 1993). Also, when mothers report less preseparation conflict with the child's father, payment of child support is more regular (Kurdek, 1986).

Some studies show that maternal remarriage is associated with less child support (Beller & Graham, 1993) or with a longitudinal decrease in child support (Hill, 1992). Other research, however, fails to find an effect of maternal remarriage (Lin, 2000), and Nord and Zill (1996) found that the mother's remarriage was associated with greater payment of child support.

Children's Characteristics

Evidence on children's characteristics is mixed. Although some research reports that mothers of older children are less likely to receive support (Lin, 2000), other studies report that mothers of older children are more likely to receive support (Seltzer, 1991). Seltzer found that having sons is associated with a lower likelihood of receiving support, but this finding has not been widely replicated.

Marital Status at the Time of the Child's Birth

Although our discussion is primarily concerned with divorce, never-married mothers and divorced mothers differ with respect to the receipt of child support. Seltzer (1991) reported that 64% of divorced fathers pay support, compared with 29% of never-married fathers. She also found that the monthly average amount paid is about twice as high for divorced fathers as for never-married fathers. Meyer (1999) found that the burden of support is more of a hindrance to compliance among never-married fathers than among divorced fathers. However, at least some of the difference in support levels between divorced and never-married fathers may be related to the fact that never-married fathers are more likely to pay support informally. Greene and Moore (2000) found that nearly half of all never-married fathers paid informal support in the form of cash, groceries, and toys.

SOCIAL CAPITAL: HOW MUCH CONTACT DO NONRESIDENT FATHERS HAVE WITH CHILDREN?

In most studies, *contact* primarily refers to visitation and engaging in activities with the child, but in some studies it also includes communication by telephone or mail. A consistent finding in the literature is that many divorced fathers have little or no contact with their children (e.g., Furstenberg & Nord, 1985; Furstenberg, Nord, Peterson, & Zill, 1983; Seltzer & Bianchi, 1988; Stephens, 1996). Recent studies, however, reveal more frequent contact between divorced fathers and their children, suggesting that fathers have increased their level of involvement over the last 20 years. For example, in two studies based on national data collected in 1981, only 16% to 20% of children saw their nonresident fathers on a weekly basis (Furstenberg et al., 1983; Seltzer & Bianchi, 1988). In contrast, several studies based on national data collected between 1987 and 1994 indicate that weekly visits with resident fathers occurred for approximately 24% to 38% of children (King, 1994a; Landale & Oropesa, 2001; Nord & Zill, 1996; Stephens, 1996). Another study, conducted in Iowa in the 1990s, found that over one half of adolescents saw their nonresident fathers weekly (Simons, Whitbeck, Beaman, & Conger, 1994). Consistent with these studies, Hetherington noted an increase in father involvement between the 1970s and the 1990s in her three longitudinal studies of divorce (Hetherington & Kelly, 2002).

Despite an apparent increase in contact, a large group of children never (or almost never) sees their nonresident fathers. Depending on the study, this group ranges from approximately one quarter to almost one half of all children with divorced parents (Furstenberg & Nord, 1985; Furstenberg et al., 1983; King, 1994a; Landale & Oropesa, 2001; Maccoby & Mnookin, 1992; Seltzer, 1991; Seltzer & Bianchi, 1988; Seltzer & Brandreth, 1994; Stephens, 1996). Most studies on father-child contact have relied on mothers' reports. Some researchers have interviewed both former spouses, however, and these studies consistently find that fathers report more frequent father-child contact than do mothers (Braver, Wolchik, et al., 1991; Manning & Smock, 1999; Seltzer & Brandreth, 1994). For example, Minton and Pasley (1996) found that fathers reported at least some contact with their children in all but about 9% of families and frequent contact with their children in just under half of families. Similarly, 87% of fathers in a study by Arditti (1992b) reported that they saw their children at least once per month, although 22% of the men in this study had joint custody.

Despite the disparity between mothers' and fathers' reports of contact, it appears that at least one fourth to one third of nonresident fathers maintain frequent contact with their children and that a roughly equal proportion of fathers maintains little or no contact. These findings suggest two groups of divorced fathers: those who stay highly involved and those who are uninvolved. (These two groups overlap substantially with fathers who regularly pay the full amount of child support and those who do not, as noted earlier.) Thus, although the overall level of father contact is lower than many observers would prefer, a large (and apparently growing) number of fathers make relationships with their children following divorce a high priority.

According to Hetherington and Kelly (2002), men's predivorce involvement with their children is not a good predictor of their postdivorce involvement. In their study, some fathers who were highly engaged with their children while the marriage was intact continued to be highly engaged with their children after the marriage ended. Correspondingly, other fathers neglected their children during the marriage as well as after the divorce. Another group of men consisted of *divorce-activated fathers*. These men became more involved with their children following divorce, either because they were concerned about losing their children's affection or because conflict with the mother had faded. A fourth group consisted of *divorce-deactivated fathers* who gradually abandoned the parenting role. In some cases, involvement declined because these men were preoccupied with their new lives following divorce. But other men became less involved either because they found time with their children to be too painful or because mothers put obstacles in their way. Consistent with this conclusion, Umberson and Williams (1993) found that divorced fathers frequently complained about the emotional difficulties associated with maintaining contact: the pain of returning children after visits, feeling irrelevant because they have little influence in their children's lives, and frustration when ex-spouses deliberately create barriers to visitation.

Although many fathers see their children regularly following divorce, the time that fathers and children spend together is not always of high quality. Furstenberg and Nord (1985) pointed out that nonresident fathers' contact with children tends to be social rather than instrumental. Similarly, Lamb (1999) noted that fathers often act more like visitors than parents after divorce. One national sample found that during visits, approximately 60% of fathers engaged mostly in leisure activity with their children, and the remaining 40% mixed leisure time with activities such as helping with school and discussing problems (Stewart, 1999). This situation is not exclusive to fathers. Although nonresident mothers typically have more contact with their children than do nonresident fathers (Seltzer & Bianchi, 1988), an emphasis on leisure activities also characterizes relationships between children and nonresident mothers (Stewart, 1999). It appears that the logistics of living in separate residences leads parents (of both genders) and children to have relationships that are primarily recreational in nature. This situation is exacerbated by postdivorce visitation arrangements that often give nonresident parents insufficient time to sustain close and psychologically meaningful relationships with their children (Lamb, in press). Moreover, Wallerstein, Lewis, and Blakeslee (2000) noted that few rules (and successful models) are available to guide the behavior of nonresident parents. (We consider the implications of this point later when discussing children's well-being.)

WHAT FACTORS ARE ASSOCIATED WITH CONTACT?

Fathers' Characteristics

A key variable associated with contact is the geographical distance between the father's and the child's residence. It is not surprising that fathers have less face-to-face contact when they live far away from their children (Arditti, 1992b; Furstenberg et al., 1983; Hetherington & Kelly, 2002; Manning & Smock, 1999; McKenry, Price, Fine, & Serovich, 1992; Seltzer, 1991; Stephens, 1996; Thompson & Laible, 1999). Being geographically separated, however, does not necessarily mean that fathers and children spend little time together. Seltzer (1991) noted that children whose parents have been separated for longer periods (and hence tend to live farther apart) have fewer but more extended visits with their fathers.

Fathers' socioeconomic status is a consistent predictor of involvement, with high levels of education and income being associated with more frequent contact (Seltzer et al., 1989; Stephens, 1996; Thompson & Laible, 1999). Similarly, Landale and Oropesa (2001) found that fathers' employment was an important predictor of father-child contact among mainland Puerto Ricans. Well-educated fathers with high levels of income also are more likely to maintain consistent contact over long periods of time (Maccoby & Mnookin, 1992). In addition, the early establishment of a reliable visitation schedule—which is associated with continued contact over time—is more common among well-educated men (Thompson & Laible, 1999). It is not clear why paternal education and income are positively associated with contact, but these resources either strengthen men's emotional commitment to their children or make it easier for men to travel and see their children.

Fathers tend to have more contact with their children if they have joint legal custody or joint physical custody (Braver & O'Connell, 1998; Nord & Zill, 1996). Seltzer (1998) found that nonresident fathers with joint legal custody visited their children more often and had more overnight visits than did other nonresident fathers, even after controlling for a range of demographic characteristics and the father's level of involvement prior to divorce. Arditti and Keith (1993) reported comparable findings. Moreover, contact is more frequent when specific visitation provisions are included in the child support agreement (Nord & Zill, 1996). These findings suggest that legal arrangements following divorce have significant implications for the amount of subsequent father involvement.

Fathers' feelings also are associated with how often they have contact with their children. Fathers who feel close to their children after divorce tend to report seeing their children often (Arditti, 1992b). Similarly, satisfaction with parenting, feelings of parental competence, and perceptions of having influence over their children are associated with more father-child contact and greater involvement in child-related activities (Braver & O'Connell, 1998; McKenry et al., 1992; Minton & Pasley, 1996). The direction of causality in these studies is unclear, however, because these positive feelings also may result from high levels of involvement.

When fathers remarry after divorce, their contact with children tends to decrease (Seltzer, 1991; Stephens, 1996; Thompson & Laible, 1999). Stephens found that both new marriages and new children were negatively related to the frequency of contact between fathers and their nonresident children, whereas Manning and Smock (1999) found that remarriage decreased fathers' contact with nonresident children only if the union produced new biological children. Presumably, fathers' new unions (and the new children produced in these unions) occupy men's attention and reduce the amount of time they have to spend with their nonresident children. Mothers' feelings about the new union also are important. Custodial mothers who have misgivings about fathers' new spouses and home environments are less likely to allow their children to have overnight visits (Maccoby & Mnookin, 1992).

With respect to fathers' race and ethnicity, research findings are mixed. Some studies report that African American fathers have especially frequent visitation with their children (King, 1994b; Mott, 1990; Seltzer, 1991), but other studies find no difference (Seltzer & Bianchi, 1988). Two studies found that Hispanic fathers were most likely never to visit their children (King, 1994b; Seltzer & Bianchi, 1988), although replication of this finding is necessary before drawing firm conclusions. Overall, race and ethnicity do not appear to be strong or consistent predictors of father-child contact.

Mothers' Characteristics

Maternal characteristics and perceptions also are related to men's postdivorce contact with children. For example, maternal remarriage lowers children's contact with fathers (Furstenberg et al., 1983; Seltzer, 1991; Stephens, 1996; Thompson & Laible, 1999), as does the presence of substitute father figures or caretakers in the custodial home (Greene & Moore, 2000; Seltzer & Bianchi, 1988). Furstenberg et al. (1983) found that maternal remarriage was a stronger (negative) predictor of father-child contact than was paternal remarriage, whereas Seltzer (1991) found that mothers' and fathers' remarriages had similar consequences for the amount of time that children and nonresident fathers spent together. MacDonald and DeMaris (2002) reported that contact between children and biological fathers was lower when stepfathers reported having close relationships with their stepchildren. This finding suggests that stepfathers impede father involvement when they form close bonds with stepchildren, although it also is probable that children tend to form close bonds with stepfathers when their biological fathers are uninvolved. In contrast, other research finds no association between the quality of children's relationships with nonresident fathers and stepfathers (Buchanan, Maccoby, & Dornbusch, 1996; Furstenberg & Nord, 1985; White & Gilbreth, 2001).

Contact between fathers and children tends to be more frequent when former spouses have a cooperative, rather than a conflicted, relationship (Kurdek, 1986; Rettig, Leichtentritt, & Stanton, 1999; Thompson & Laible, 1999). Ahrons and Miller (1993) found that mothers' perceptions of the mother-father relationship—but not fathers' perceptions of the mother-father relationship—were related to the amount of contact between fathers and children. This finding suggests that custodial mothers encourage or discourage father involvement, depending on how they feel about their former husbands. Braver and O'Connell (1998) reported that one-third of divorced fathers claimed that their ex-wives had denied visitation privileges at least once. Similarly, about one-fourth of custodial mothers stated that they had denied visitation at least once. Some of these mothers blocked visitation either because their children did not want to see their fathers or because the fathers' visits tended to upset the children. Other mothers blocked visitation to avoid their ex-husbands or to minimize their ex-husbands' influence on the children. Nevertheless, although some mothers put obstacles in the way of visitation, King and Heard (1999) found that most mothers wanted their former husbands to stay involved with the children. Moreover, most mothers were satisfied with high levels of father-child contact, even if this sometimes resulted in conflict between parents. (Of course, a subset of mothers was satisfied when fathers had little or no contact.)

Children's Characteristics

Although parents' characteristics appear to be of primary importance, researchers also have considered child factors that may influence nonresident father-child contact. Research on children living with continuously married parents suggests that fathers tend to be more involved with sons than with daughters. It is not clear, however, whether nonresident fathers follow the same pattern. Some studies suggest no difference between sons and daughters in the frequency of father contact (Cooksey & Craig, 1998; Furstenberg et al., 1983; Mott, 1990; Stephens, 1996), whereas other studies find that sons enjoy longer and more frequent visits than daughters do (Hetherington, 1993; Manning & Smock, 1999). In contrast, Seltzer (1991) found that contact was slightly lower for sons than for daughters.

Evidence on the ages of children also is inconsistent. Some studies show that contact between fathers and children is more likely when children are older (Seltzer, 1991; Seltzer & Bianchi, 1988), whereas other studies show that contact is more likely when children are younger (Nord & Zill, 1996). Yet other studies find no evidence of age differences in contact (Furstenberg et al., 1983; Seltzer et al., 1989). A few studies find that fathers are more likely to have contact with older children, but given that any contact occurs, fathers tend to see younger children more frequently than they see older children (Seltzer & Bianchi, 1988; Stephens, 1996). In general, the discrepancies in this research literature may be due to variations in the age ranges of children studied, as well as to variations in the manner in which contact is measured.

Marital Status at the Time of the Child's Birth

Children born into marriage are more likely than children born outside of marriage to have at least some contact with their nonresident fathers (Nord & Zill, 1996; Seltzer & Bianchi, 1988). For example, one study reported that the percentage of children who never see their fathers was 18% for those with divorced parents and 40% for those with never-married parents (Seltzer, 1991). Seltzer pointed out that divorced fathers are more likely than never-married fathers to have lived with their children for some period of time. A period of coresidence probably strengthens emotional bonds between fathers and children and hence increases the likelihood that fathers stay involved with their children after the union is disrupted.

Effects of Father Involvement

Fathers' Financial Capital

A large number of studies have documented the harmful toll that economic hardship takes on children: Poverty is associated with poor nutrition, health problems, low school grades, an elevated risk of dropping out of school, and a higher incidence of emotional and behavioral problems, such as depression, low self-esteem, conduct disorders, and conflict with peers (Luthar, 1999; Seccombe, 2000). In married, two-parent families, fathers contribute on average about two thirds of the family income (Amato & Booth, 1997). Because men are primarily responsible for the standard of living of two-parent families, their earnings are associated with a variety of positive outcomes among children (Amato, 1998). Following divorce, however, it is not the income of nonresident fathers, but the amount of income that is transferred to children in the form of child support, that affects children's standard of living.

Does fathers' payment of child support benefit children? Several studies, using an impressive variety of large data sets, have revealed positive associations between the amount of child support paid and measures of children's well-being. Furstenberg, Morgan, and Allison (1987), using the National Survey of Children, found that fathers' child support payments were negatively related to mothers' and teachers' reports of behavior problems. McLanahan, Seltzer, Hanson, and Thomson (1994), using the National Survey of Families and Households, found that fathers' payment of child support was positively associated with mothers' reports of children's school grades and negatively associated with mothers' reports of behavior problems in school. King (1994a), using the National Longitudinal Survey of Youth, found that payment of child support was positively associated with children's reading and math scores. Similarly, Knox and Bane (1994), using the Panel Study of Income Dynamics, and Graham et al. (1994), using the Current Population Survey, found that fathers' payment of child support was positively associated with children's years of attained education. In general, these associations do not vary with the sex or race of children.

Amato and Gilbreth's (1999) meta-analysis of the literature on father involvement confirmed this conclusion. In their study, based on pooled data from 33 independent samples, fathers' payment of child support was positively and significantly associated with measures of children's academic achievement and negatively and significantly associated with measures of children's externalizing problems (but not with measures of children's internalizing problems). Overall, the evidence strongly suggests that fathers' payment of child support benefits children. Presumably, these benefits occur for the same reason that fathers' income benefits children in two-parent households. That is, regular child support payments improve children's health and nutrition, increase the amount of stimulation in the home environment, and improve children's access to educational resources. Fathers' payment of child support also may benefit children indirectly by lowering the level of stress experienced by mothers.

Fathers' Social Capital

Divorce is often followed by a decline over time in the amount of contact between fathers and children, as noted earlier. Nevertheless, our review indicates that a significant number of noncustodial fathers see their children frequently and maintain supportive relationships. If the father-child relationship is an important resource for children, then a continuation of this relationship following marital disruption should benefit children. Although this assumption seems reasonable, a large number of studies fail to find significant associations between the frequency of father contact and measures of children's adjustment and well-being (see Amato, 1998, for a review).

Why do studies suggest beneficial effects on children when nonresident fathers pay child support yet fail to suggest beneficial effects when nonresident fathers visit their children? One explanation is that father contact provides opportunities for parents to quarrel. Although contact with fathers may be beneficial, conflict between parents may cancel out, or even reverse, any benefits. Support for this interpretation comes from a study by Amato and Rezac (1994), who found that contact with nonresident fathers following divorce appeared to lower behavior problems among sons when conflict between parents was low and to increase behavior problems among sons when conflict between parents was high. Two other studies reported similar findings (Healy, Malley, & Stewart, 1990; Hetherington, 1993). Similarly, a study by King and Heard (1999) found that frequent visitation was associated with negative child outcomes (poorer adjustment and more behavior problems) when mothers were dissatisfied with the amount of father contact.

Another likely explanation for the absence of father effects focuses on the nature of the father-child relationship following divorce. As noted earlier, contact between nonresident fathers and children tends to be recreational (e.g., going out to eat and see movies) rather than instrumental. Compared with fathers in two-parent households, nonresident fathers provide less help with homework, are less likely to set and enforce rules, and provide less monitoring and supervision of their children (Amato, 1987; Furstenberg & Nord, 1985). If noncustodial fathers are no longer playing the role of authoritative parent, then mere contact—even sharing good times together—may not contribute in a positive way to children's development.

Consistent with this interpretation, studies with null results tend to be those that examine the frequency of contact only, whereas studies with significant results tend to be those that measure supportive aspects of the parent role. For example, Barber (1994) found that adolescents who frequently obtained advice from noncustodial fathers (about educational plans, employment goals, and personal problems) were less likely than other adolescents to experience symptoms of depression. Similarly, Simons et al. (1994) found that the quality of noncustodial fathers' parenting (as reflected in providing emotional support, giving reasons for decisions, providing consistent discipline, and praising children's accomplishment) was negatively related to externalizing problems among adolescent sons and daughters. Indeed, in both studies, the quality of the father-child relationship largely accounted for the significant bivariate differences in well-being between offspring in divorced single-parent households and two-parent households.

The meta-analysis of this literature by Amato and Gilbreth (1999) confirmed this explanation. Their study found that the frequency of father visitation following divorce was not generally associated with child outcomes. The extent to which fathers engaged in active, authoritative parenting, however, was significantly associated with higher academic achievement (based on 11 independent samples), fewer externalizing problems (based on 26 independent samples), and fewer internalizing problems (based on 13 independent samples). The meta-analysis also revealed a significant interaction between year of study and father contact. In studies conducted primarily in the 1990s, the associations between contact and measures of children's well-being were statistically significant, but in studies conducted in earlier years, the corresponding associations were not significant. This finding suggests that noncustodial fathers were doing a better job of parenting their children during the 1990s than in earlier decades, resulting in positive father effects in the more recent studies.

A second recent meta-analysis also is pertinent to this topic. This meta-analysis, based on 20 studies, found that children in joint physical custody arrangements were better adjusted, on average, than were children in sole-custody arrangements (Bauserman, 2002). Many studies included in this meta-analysis defined joint physical custody with reference to the amount of time children spent with fathers following divorce. (Children typically were classified as being in joint physical custody when they spent at least 25% of their time with fathers.) Consequently, the results of this meta-analysis support Amato and Gilbreth's (1999) conclusion that children benefit when fathers have opportunities to act like real parents (and not visitors) following divorce.

Our discussion of social capital also pointed out the importance of fathers in establishing closure in children's social networks. Unfortunately, few studies have examined the extent to which divorced fathers help to connect their children to other groups and institutions in the community. A number of studies, however, consider men's relationships with their former spouses following divorce, and these studies consistently show that the level of conflict and cooperation between parents is a good predictor of children's postdivorce adjustment. For example, Buchanan et al. (1996) found that the stress of feeling caught between hostile parents after divorce was linked with poor outcomes for adolescents. Similarly, Healy et al. (1990) found that children exhibited more behavior problems if parents engaged in legal conflict following marital dissolution. Guidubaldi, Cleminshaw, Perry, Nastasi, and Lightel (1986) noted that mothers' satisfaction with the postdivorce relationship with fathers was associated with a variety of independently assessed positive outcomes among sons and daughters. In addition, Heath and MacKinnon (1988) showed that parental cooperation was positively associated with social competence among children living in single-mother households. Overall, these studies suggest that fathers, as part of a cooperative parental partnership, have the potential to benefit children in single-mother households, much as they benefit children in two-parent households.

Father Involvement and the Well-Being of Adult Children of Divorce

Parental divorce appears to affect children's relationships with parents well into adulthood. Compared to adults with continuously married parents, adults with divorced parents have less frequent contact with parents, exchange less assistance with parents, and describe their relationships with parents less positively (Amato & Booth, 1997;

Aquilino, 1994; Cooney, 1994; Zill, Morrison, & Coiro, 1993). Although divorce appears to weaken children's ties with both parents, most studies indicate that the consequences of divorce are stronger for the father-child relationship than for the mother-child relationship, presumably because most children reside with their mothers following marital dissolution.

Even though problematic parent-child relationships may originate in childhood, they take on new significance as children make the transition to adulthood—a time when youth leave home, complete their educations, develop career plans, become economically independent, marry, and form their own families. During these critical years, children receive many potential benefits from parents, including emotional support; advice with educational plans, jobs, homes, and family life; practical assistance with everyday tasks, such as child care; and money for special purchases, such as a down payment on a car or home. Parents also connect children with kin (e.g., grandparents) and other adults (e.g., family friends) who can serve as sources of support or assistance. These transitional years have become more difficult in recent decades due to declining wages for young men, the rising cost of housing, and an increase in the cost of a college education (Amato & Booth, 1997). Correspondingly, the number of years that youth are economically and emotionally dependent on parents appears to be increasing (Furstenberg, 2000). For example, recent cohorts of youth have been relatively slow to leave the parental home, and among those who do, nest returning is common (Goldscheider & Goldscheider, 1994). Indeed, only when parents reach the last decade of the life course does the flow of assistance between generations shift primarily from children to parents (Rossi & Rossi, 1990). Because the early adult years present many challenges to youth and because parents represent a key resource for making the transition to adulthood, weak ties with parents may exacerbate prior psychological problems in offspring or precipitate new ones. Consistent with this reasoning, cross-sectional research consistently shows that young adults' reports of emotional closeness to parents are positively associated with psychological well-being (Amato, 1994a; Rossi & Rossi, 1990; Umberson, 1992). These studies also find independent effects of fathers even with the mother-child relationship statistically controlled.

Amato and Sobolewski (2001), in a 17-year longitudinal study, found that the quality of the father-child relationship following divorce (as reflected in trusting fathers, feeling respected by fathers, and feeling close to fathers) was associated with psychological well-being in a sample of young adult offspring (mean age = 28 years). Marital discord preceding divorce appeared to erode adult children's feelings of affection for mothers, whereas divorce (independently of marital discord) appeared to erode children's feelings of affection for fathers. Presumably, divorce had a more negative effect on father-child relationships than on mother-child relationships because most children lived with their mothers following divorce. Young adults with divorced parents also reported lower levels of psychological well-being than did young adults with continuously married parents. Consistent with studies of younger children (e.g., Barber, 1994; Simons et al., 1994), weak ties with fathers accounted for most of the gap in psychological well-being between these two groups. The Amato and Sobolewski study suggests that a poor relationship between children and fathers following divorce is a risk factor for poor psychological functioning not only in childhood, but in adulthood as well.

STEPFATHERS

Compared with the large research literature on nonresident fathers, fewer studies have focused on stepfathers. This lack of research is due partly to the complexity and variability of stepfamilies, which makes them difficult to study. Stepfather families may include the mother's children from a former relationship, the father's children from a former relationship, and biological children from the new marriage. Some stepfathers live with their stepchildren, whereas other stepfathers (those married to noncustodial mothers) live apart from their stepchildren and interact with them only during visitation. And with nonmarital cohabitation becoming increasingly common, stepfathers may be married to or cohabiting with children's mothers. Most of the research described in this section is based on samples of married stepfathers who live with their stepchildren—the most common type of stepfamily. The diversity of structural features in stepfamilies, however, means that we should be cautious in reaching general conclusions about stepfathers and their relationships with stepchildren.

Stepfathers' Financial Capital

In the majority of cases, remarriage following divorce (or the first marriage of a never-married mother) improves the economic well-being of mothers and their children. McLanahan and Sandefur (1994) pointed out that the median family income of stepfather families, although slightly lower than that of continuously married two-parent families, is more than twice that of single-mother families. Moreover, the poverty rate is about three times higher in single-mother families than in stepfather families. In a longitudinal analysis, Teachman and Paasch (1993) found that remarriage dramatically decreased the frequency of household poverty among single mothers. The extent to which stepfathers share their earnings with stepchildren, however, has received little attention from researchers. Anderson, Kaplan, and Lancaster (1999) found that stepfathers spend about as much money on their stepchildren as they do on their nonresident biological children. Stepfathers, however, do not spend as much money on stepchildren as continuously married, biological fathers spend on their resident children. Nevertheless, remarriage continues to be the quickest and most reliable way for most single mothers and their children to escape from economic hardship.

Given that parents' financial resources are associated with positive child outcomes (as noted earlier), it follows that the arrival of a stepfather (and his financial capital) should benefit children. Children in stepfamilies, however, are no better off—and in some ways are worse off—than children in single-parent households. In a meta-analysis, Amato (1994b) reported that children residing with stepparents scored lower than children with continuously married parents on measures of academic achievement, behavior problems, psychological adjustment, self-esteem, and the quality of peer relations. Moreover, children in stepfamilies scored significantly lower than children in single-parent families on measures of psychological adjustment (Amato, 1994b). Consistent with these findings, McLanahan and Sandefur (1994) found that controlling for family income did not account for any of the negative outcomes experienced by children living in stepfamilies. Although the increase in household income following remarriage undoubtedly makes children's lives better in certain respects, other problems that occur commonly in stepfather families appear to offset the positive consequences of an improved standard of living. (African American families may be an exception to this pattern, as we note later.)

STEPFATHERS' SOCIAL CAPITAL

Although the great majority of custodial mothers view remarriage as a positive event, children tend to be less enthusiastic. The remarriage of custodial mothers tends to be stressful for children because it usually involves moving (often to a new neighborhood or town), adapting to new people in the household, and learning new rules and routines. In addition, early relationships between stepfathers and stepchildren are often tense. During the time that they live with single mothers, some children become accustomed to having a substantial degree of autonomy. These children may resent the additional monitoring and supervision provided by stepfathers and may react with hostility when stepfathers attempt to exert authority. Other children experience loyalty conflicts and feel that becoming close to stepfathers is a betrayal of their biological fathers. Yet other children—especially older daughters—feel jealous because they must share maternal time and attention with stepfathers. For some children, remarriage ends any lingering hopes that the two biological parents will one day reconcile (see Hetherington & Kelly, 2002, and Wallerstein et al., 2000, for discussions of children's feelings toward new stepfathers).

Hetherington and Jodl (1994) reported that relationships between stepfathers and adolescent stepchildren are especially difficult and tend to follow a trajectory of gradual detachment and withdrawal. After remarriage, most stepfathers make a good-faith effort to gain their stepchildren's approval, trust, and respect. Adolescents, however, often rebuff stepfathers' attempts to establish positive relationships. After a while, many stepfathers stop trying to get close to their stepchildren and settle for a disengaged parenting style, characterized by low levels of involvement, affection, discipline, and monitoring. Correspondingly, some adolescent stepchildren become disengaged and spend little time at home or in family activities (Coleman, Ganong, & Fine, 2000). A significant minority of stepfathers and stepchildren do not even think of each other as belonging to the same family (Furstenberg, 1987).

It is no surprise that the bonds between stepfathers and stepchildren are not as strong as the bonds between biological fathers and children. Continuously married fathers give more time and attention to their biological children than stepfathers give to their stepchildren (Amato, 1987; Fine & Kurdek, 1994; Fine, Voydanoff, & Donnelly, 1993; Thomson, McLanahan, & Curtin, 1992). Similarly, stepfathers provide less warmth and nurturance to their stepchildren than to their own biological children, and stepfathers derive less satisfaction from their stepchildren than from their own biological children (Coleman et al., 2000; MacDonald & DeMaris, 1996). As Hetherington noted, only about one third of stepfathers exhibit an authoritative parenting style, compared with about 60% of continuously married mothers and fathers (Hetherington & Kelly, 2002). Clearly, stepfathers, as a group, do not provide the same level of social capital to their stepchildren as married, biological fathers do to their children.

Strain between stepfathers and stepchildren can spill over and affect the quality of marital relationships, and remarried parents tend to report higher levels of tension and disagreement than do spouses in first marriages (Coleman et al., 2000). Hetherington and Kelly (2002) reported that stepchildren were the most common cause of arguments between spouses in remarriages. Partly for this reason, remarriages are more likely than first marriages to end in divorce, but only if stepchildren are present in the household (White & Booth, 1985).

Relationships in stepfamilies tend to be more distant and less cohesive than relationships in never-divorced, two-parent families (Bray & Kelly, 1998; Hetherington & Jodl, 1994). Some stepchildren resolve household tension by leaving their mothers' homes to reside with their biological fathers (Buchanan et al., 1996). Alternatively, stepchildren tend to leave home and establish residential independence at earlier ages than do children living with both biological parents (Aquilino, 1991; Kiernan, 1992). Moreover, stepchildren are more likely than biological children to leave home for reasons related to family conflict. In many stepfamilies, tension is resolved only when stepfathers or stepchildren leave the household.

Factors That Promote Positive Stepfather-Stepchild Relations

Although relationships in stepfathers' households can be difficult, some stepfathers manage to establish close and supportive relationships with their stepchildren. Relatively little is known, however, about the factors that promote positive ties between stepfathers and stepchildren. Research suggests that stepchildren are especially likely to reject stepfathers who attempt to exercise authority and discipline too early in the remarriage. Correspondingly, stepchildren are more likely to accept stepfathers who leave discipline to mothers and continue to act in a friendly manner, even if stepfathers' initial attempts at friendship are rebuffed (Coleman et al., 2000). Existing research also suggests that relationships tend to be closer when stepfathers have biological children as well as stepchildren living in the household, stepfathers and mothers are happily married, mothers encourage stepfather and stepchildren to share activities, and stepfathers and mothers have similar values and beliefs about raising children (Brand & Clingempeel, 1987; Coleman et al., 2000; Hetherington & Jodl, 1994; Marsiglio, 1992; Skopin, Newman, & McKenry, 1993). Some authors report that children with weak ties to their nonresident fathers are more accepting of stepfathers (MacDonald & DeMaris, 2002; Wallerstein et al., 2000). In contrast, three studies found that the quality of the stepfather-stepchild relationship was not correlated with the quality of the father-child relationship, indicating that the two relationships are largely independent of each other (Buchanan et al., 1996; Furstenberg & Nord, 1985; White & Gilbreth, 2001).

Some evidence suggests that girls have a more difficult time than boys interacting with and accepting stepfathers (Buchanan et al., 1996; Vuchinich, Hetherington, Vuchinich, & Clingempeel, 1991). As noted earlier, adolescent children (as opposed to younger children) are more resistant to the arrival of stepfathers and are especially likely to reject the stepfather as an authority figure (Buchanan et al., 1996; Hetherington & Jodl, 1994; Wallerstein et al., 2000). Presumably, the biological, psychological, and social changes that accompany adolescent development are difficult enough to navigate without the additional stress of adjusting to life in a stepfamily. Taking these findings together, it appears that young boys are the most likely candidates to form close bonds with stepfathers.

Effects of Stepfather Involvement

Although stepfathers contribute less social capital to their stepchildren than do bio-logical, married fathers, stepfathers still have the potential to make positive contri-butions to their stepchildren's lives. Existing research suggests that children benefit when they have close relationships with stepfathers (Bronstein, Stoll, Clauson, Abrams, & Briones, 1994; Crosbie-Burnett & Giles-Sims, 1994). For example, White and Gilbreth (2001) found that a close relationship with stepfathers (as reported by children) was related to fewer internalizing and externalizing problems among chil-dren (as reported by mothers). Buchanan et al. (1996) found that acceptance of a step-father's authority was associated with positive outcomes for adolescents. Another study found that close ties with stepfathers was positively related to the psychologi-cal well-being of young adult offspring (Amato, 1994a). Hetherington (1993) reported that relationships with stepfathers are better predictors of children's adjustment in re-marriages of long duration. These studies indicate that although relations between stepfathers and stepchildren are often difficult, children benefit when these ties be-come close.

Several studies suggest that stepfathers may be particularly beneficial in African American families. McLahanan and Sandefur (1994) found that in African American families (but not European American families), children who lived with stepfathers were less likely to drop out of high school or (among daughters) have a nonmarital birth. Similarly, a recent study of African Americans living in high-poverty neighbor-hoods found that girls living with their mothers and stepfathers were less likely than girls living with single mothers to become sexually active or pregnant (Moore & Chase-Lansdale, 2001). However, the protective effect of a stepfather held only when mothers were married and not when they cohabited with a partner. Nelson, Clark, and Acs (2001) reported comparable results: Among African Americans, adolescents liv-ing with stepfathers were better off in many respects than were adolescents living with single mothers, but adolescents living with cohabiting parents were worse off than were those living with single mothers.

CONCLUSIONS

In the beginning of this chapter, we pointed out that recent social change has placed fathers in a difficult position. On the one hand, our culture expects fathers to be highly involved in their children's lives. On the other hand, changes in family structure have physically separated a large number of fathers from their children. With respect to fi-nancial provision, most divorced fathers appear to make a good-faith effort to meet their child support obligations, although a large minority does not. Similarly, most divorced fathers appear to maintain frequent contact, although, once again, a large minority does not. And even among fathers who see their children frequently, author-itative parenting appears to be relatively rare. In most families, therefore, divorce rep-resents a significant barrier to the flow of financial and social capital from fathers to children.

Following divorce, many fathers live with their new wives' children. Perhaps men provide the same level of resources to children today as in the past, but these resources are redistributed from biological children to stepchildren. Due to a lack of research, it is not clear how much of their earnings stepfathers spend on stepchildren, but stepfathers do not appear to invest as much income in their stepchildren as continuously married fathers invest in their biological children. Moreover, although some stepfathers develop close, authoritative relationships with their stepchildren, most do not. In general, it appears that men's provision of resources to stepchildren does not offset the reduction in resources that divorced men transmit to biological children. And from a child's perspective, having a stepfather usually does not make up for the loss of a biological father.

Overall, the high level of divorce in American society has not only undermined the goal of encouraging greater paternal involvement in children's lives, but also increased the risk of a variety of financial, educational, and psychological problems for children. During the last two decades, policy makers have taken a number of steps to ensure that nonresident fathers fulfill their financial obligations to children (see Garfinkel, McLanahan, Meyer, & Seltzer, 1998, for a review). Policy makers have devoted less attention, however, to steps that might facilitate the transmission of social capital from nonresident fathers to children. The research literature suggests several strategies for how this might be accomplished.

First, research suggests that the key issue is not how often nonresident fathers see children but what nonresident fathers do when they are with their children. Many fathers who see their children do not engage in authoritative parenting—an outcome that reflects the constraints of traditional visitation arrangements. Because of time limitations, most fathers want to ensure that their children enjoy themselves during visits. Consequently, many fathers take their children to restaurants or movies but do not engage in authoritative practices, such as helping with homework or talking over personal problems. In addition, nonresident fathers who maintain frequent contact tend to be relatively permissive and indulgent. Because men fear that their relationships with children are tenuous, they often are reluctant to set firm rules or discipline their children for misbehavior. The activities shared by nonresident fathers and their children may be enjoyable, but in the absence of authoritative parenting, these activities contribute little to children's development. Indeed, many nonresident fathers complain that visitation arrangements with their children are insufficient to maintain anything other than superficial relationships (Arendell, 1995; Braver & O'Connell, 1998; Umberson & Williams, 1993).

Current custody and visitation arrangements make it difficult for children to sustain and develop close ties with fathers following divorce (Lamb, 1999, in press). For example, a study of child custody in California (a relatively liberal state) found that about one fourth of all children had no court-ordered provisions for contact with their fathers and about one fifth of all children had no court-ordered provisions for overnight visits with their fathers (Maccoby & Mnookin, 1992). Similarly, a national study based on the Survey of Income and Program Participation found that one fourth of noncustodial parents with formal child support agreements (including divorced and never-married parents) did not have an explicit provision for visitation (Nord & Zill, 1996). If formal visitation arrangements are minimal, then many fathers—even fathers who had close relationships with their children during their marriages—will reduce their visits or stop seeing their children. Ensuring that visitation arrangements provide adequate amounts of time for nonresident fathers to maintain close and authoritative relationships with their children is a reasonable policy goal.

As noted earlier, a longitudinal study by Seltzer (1998) showed that nonresident fathers with joint legal custody visited their children more often and had more overnight visits than did other nonresident fathers. Moreover, a recent meta-analysis found that children with joint legal or joint physical custody arrangements tended to be better adjusted than children in sole mother–custody arrangements (Bauserman, 2002). These findings suggest that policies that encourage nonresident fathers to maintain the parental role after divorce can positively influence men's behavior and children's well-being. Of course, children and parents are not randomly allocated to custody arrangements, and it is possible that the associations between joint custody, father involvement, and child adjustment reflect the characteristics of parents who choose—and are able to maintain—cooperative custody arrangements. For example, parents with joint physical custody, compared with parents with sole custody, have higher levels of education, are less likely to be poor, and are more likely to have cooperative relationships (Arditti, 1992a; Nord & Zill, 1996; Pearson & Thoennes, 1990). Nevertheless, these findings indicate that when parents are capable of cooperating following divorce, joint custody arrangements (legal or physical) are likely to be in children's best interests.

Research consistently shows that postdivorce arrangements (child support payment and visitation schedules) work best when mothers and fathers agree on them voluntarily. This conclusion underscores the importance of providing mediation and other services to help parents reach decisions through mutual agreement rather than through litigation and court mandate. In this context, the U.S. Commission on Child and Family Welfare (1996) recommended abandoning the concepts of custody and visitation, as these terms imply that one parent wins the children and the other parent loses. Instead, the Commission recommended the adoption of parenting plans in which parents make decisions jointly about children's primary residences, the amount of time children will spend with each parent, and the types of responsibilities each parent will hold. Moving away from traditional notions of custody and visitation may be a useful step toward increasing fathers' incentives to maintain positive roles in their children's lives.

The adoption of educational programs for divorcing parents (especially programs that stress the importance of cooperative parenting) also may improve some men's ability to act in an authoritative fashion. These programs have been introduced in many courts (Kelly, 1994), and the great majority of parents (fathers as well as mothers) claim to have found them worthwhile (U.S. Commission on Child and Family Welfare, 1996). Of course, when fathers are abusive or have mental health problems, encouraging interaction between fathers and children is unlikely to be in children's best interests. Nevertheless, new demographic realities mean that we need new strategies for maintaining the social and emotional bonds between fathers and children, as well as policies that remove potential barriers to these bonds.

In conclusion, fathers' and children's lives have diverged significantly during the last few decades, and each group has much to lose. Although children benefit from fathers' financial and social capital, fathers also benefit from their relationships with children. Resolving the fundamental contradiction between the culture of fatherhood and the social organization of fatherhood will require either that we find ways to strengthen and stabilize childbearing unions or that we discover new ways of keeping fathers and children connected following the disruption of childbearing unions.

REFERENCES

Ahrons, C. R., & Miller, R. B. (1993). The effect of the postdivorce relationship on paternal involvement: A longitudinal analysis. *American Journal of Orthopsychiatry, 63,* 441–450.

Amato, P. R. (1987). Family processes in one-parent, step-parent, and intact families: The child's point of view. *Journal of Marriage and the Family, 49,* 327–337.

Amato, P. R. (1994a). Father-child relations, mother-child relations, and offspring psychological well-being in early adulthood. *Journal of Marriage and the Family, 56,* 1031–1042.

Amato, P. R. (1994b). The implications of research on children in stepfamilies. In A. Booth & J. Dunn (Eds.), *Stepfamilies: Who benefits? Who does not?* (pp. 81–88). Hillsdale, NJ: Erlbaum.

Amato, P. R. (1998). More than money? Men's contributions to their children's lives. In A. Booth & A. Crouter (Eds.), *Men in families* (pp. 241–278). Hillsdale, NJ: Erlbaum.

Amato, P. R. (2000). Consequences of divorce for adults and children. *Journal of Marriage and the Family, 62,* 1269–1287.

Amato, P. R., & Booth, A. (1997). *A generation at risk: Growing up in an era of family upheaval.* Cambridge, MA: Harvard University Press.

Amato, P. R., & Gilbreth, J. (1999). Nonresident fathers and children's well-being: A meta-analysis. *Journal of Marriage and the Family, 61,* 557–573.

Amato, P. R., & Rezac, S. (1994). Contact with nonresidential parents, interparental conflict, and children's behavior. *Journal of Family Issues, 15,* 191–207.

Amato, P. R., & Sobolewski, J. M. (2001). The effects of divorce and marital discord on adult children's psychological well-being. *American Sociological Review, 66,* 900–921.

Anderson, K. G., Kaplan, H., & Lancaster, J. (1999). Paternal care by genetic fathers and stepfathers. *Evolution and Human Behavior, 20,* 405–431.

Aquilino, W. S. (1991). Family structure and home-leaving: A further specification of the model. *Journal of Marriage and the Family, 53,* 999–1010.

Aquilino, W. S. (1994). Impact of childhood family disruption on young adults' relationships with parents. *Journal of Marriage and the Family, 56,* 295–313.

Arditti, J. A. (1992a). Differences between fathers with joint custody and noncustodial fathers. *American Journal of Orthopsychiatry, 62,* 186–195.

Arditti, J. A. (1992b). Factors related to custody, visitation, and child support for divorced fathers: An exploratory analysis. *Journal of Divorce and Remarriage, 17,* 23–42.

Arditti, J. A., & Keith, T. Z. (1993). Visitation frequency, child support payment, and the father-child relationship postdivorce. *Journal of Marriage and the Family, 55,* 699–712.

Arendell, T. (1995). *Fathers and divorce.* Thousand Oaks, CA: Sage.

Barber, B. L. (1994). Support and advice from married and divorced fathers: Linkages to adolescent adjustment. *Family Relations, 43,* 433–438.

Bartfeld, J. (2000). Child support and the postdivorce economic well-being of mothers, fathers, and children. *Demography, 37,* 203–213.

Baumrind, D. (1968). Authoritarian versus authoritative parental control. *Adolescence, 3,* 255–272.

Bauserman, R. (2002). Child adjustment in joint-custody versus sole-custody arrangements: A meta-analytic review. *Journal of Family Psychology, 16,* 91–102.

Beller, A. H., & Graham, J. W. (1993). *Small change: The economics of child support.* New Haven, CT: Yale University Press.

Bramlett, M. D., & Mosher, W. D. (2001). First marriage dissolution, divorce, and remarriage: United States. In *Advance data from Vital and Health Statistics, No. 323.* Hyattsville, MD: National Center for Health Statistics.

Brand, E., & Clingempeel, G. W. (1987). Interdependencies of marital and stepparent-stepchild relationships and children's psychological adjustment: Research findings and clinical implications. *Family Relations, 36,* 140–145.

Braver, S. L., Fitzpatrick, P. J., & Bay, R. C. (1991). Noncustodial parent's report of child support payments. *Family Relations, 40,* 180–185.

Braver, S. L., & O'Connell, E. (1998). *Divorced dads: Shattering the myths.* New York: Tarcher Putnam.

Braver, S. L., Wolchik, S. A., Sandler, I. N., Sheets, V. L., Fogas, B., & Bay, R. C. (1991). A longitudinal study of noncustodial parents: Parents without children. *Journal of Family Psychology, 7,* 9–23.

Bray, J. H., & Kelly, J. (1998). *Stepfamilies: Love, marriage, and parenting in the first decade.* New York: Broadway Books.

Bronstein, P., Stoll, M. F., Clauson, J., Abrams, C. L., & Briones, M. (1994). Fathering after separation or divorce: Factors predicting children's adjustment. *Family Relations, 43,* 469–479.

Buchanan, C. M., Maccoby, E. E., & Dornbusch, S. M. (1996). *Adolescents after divorce.* Cambridge, MA: Harvard University Press.

Bumpass, L. L. (1990). What's happening to the family? Interactions between demographic and institutional change. *Demography, 27,* 483–498.

Bumpass, L. L., Raley, K., & Sweet, J. (1995). The changing character of stepfamilies: Implications of cohabitation and nonmarital childbearing. *Demography, 32,* 425–436.

Coleman, J. (1988). Social capital in the creation of human capital. *American Journal of Sociology, 94,* 95–120.

Coleman, M., Ganong, L., & Fine, M. (2000). Reinvestigating remarriage: Another decade of progress. *Journal of Marriage and the Family, 62,* 1288–1307.

Cooksey, E. C., & Craig, P. H. (1998). Parenting from a distance: The effects of paternal characteristics on contact between nonresidential fathers and their children. *Demography, 35,* 187–201.

Cooney, T. M. (1994). Young adults' relations with parents: The influence of recent parental divorce. *Journal of Marriage and the Family, 56,* 45–56.

Crosbie-Burnett, M., & Giles-Sims, J. (1994). Adolescent adjustment and stepparenting styles. *Family Relations, 43,* 394–399.

Eggebeen, D. J. (2002). The changing course of fatherhood. *Journal of Family Issues, 23,* 486–506.

Fine, M. A., & Kurdek, L. A. (1994). Parenting cognitions in stepfamilies: Differences between parents and stepparents and relations to parenting satisfaction. *Journal of Social and Personal Relationships, 11,* 95–112.

Fine, M. A., Voydanoff, P., & Donnelly, B. W. (1993). Relations between parental control and warmth and child well-being in stepfamilies. *Journal of Family Psychology, 7,* 222–232.

Furstenberg, F. F. (1987). The new extended family: The experience of parents and children after remarriage. In K. Pasley & M. Inhinger-Tallman (Eds.), *Remarriage and stepparenting: Current research and theory* (pp. 42–61). New York: Guilford Press.

Furstenberg, F. F. (2000). The sociology of adolescents and youth in the 1990s: A critical commentary. *Journal of Marriage and the Family, 62,* 896–910.

Furstenberg, F. F., Morgan, S. P., & Allison, P. D. (1987). Paternal participation and children's well-being after marital dissolution. *American Sociological Review, 52,* 695–701.

Furstenberg, F. F,. & Nord, C. W. (1985). Parenting apart: Patterns of childrearing after marital disruption. *Journal of Marriage and the Family, 47,* 893–904.

Furstenberg, F. F., Nord, C. W., Peterson, J. L., & Zill, N. (1983). The life course of children of divorce: Marital disruption and parental contact. *American Sociological Review, 48,* 656–668.

Ganong, L., Coleman, M., Fine, M., & Martin, P. (1999). Stepparents' affinity-seeking and affinity-maintaining strategies with stepchildren. *Journal of Family Issues, 20,* 299–327.

Garfinkel, I., McLanahan, S. S., Meyer, D. R., & Seltzer, J. A. (1998). *Fathers under fire: The revolution in child support enforcement.* New York: Russell Sage Foundation.

Goldscheider, F. K., & Goldscheider, C. (1994). Leaving and returning home in 20th century America. *Population Bulletin, 48,* 1–33.

Graham, J. W., & Beller, A. H. (1996). Child support in black and white: Racial differences in the award and receipt of child support during the 1980s. *Social Science Quarterly, 77*, 528–542.

Graham, J. W., Beller, A. H., & Hernandez, P. M. (1994). The effects of child support on educational attainment. In I. Garfinkel, S. McLanahan, & P. Robins (Eds.), *Child support and well-being* (pp. 317–354). Washington, DC: Urban Institute Press.

Greene, A. D., & Moore, K. A. (2000). Nonresident father involvement and child well-being among young children in families on welfare. *Marriage and Family Review, 29*, 159–180.

Guidubaldi, J., Cleminshaw, H. K., Perry, J. D., Nastasi, B. K., & Lightel, J. (1986). The role of selected family environment factors in children's post-divorce adjustment. *Family Relations, 35*, 141–151.

Healy, J. M., Malley, J. E., & Stewart, A. J. (1990). Children and their fathers after parental separation. *American Journal of Orthopsychiatry, 60*, 531–543.

Heath, P. A., & MacKinnon, C. (1988). Factors related to the social competence of children in single-parent families. *Journal of Divorce, 11*, 49–66.

Hetherington, E. M. (1993). An overview of the Virginia Longitudinal Study of Divorce and Remarriage with a focus on early adolescence. *Journal of Family Psychology, 7*, 39–56.

Hetherington, E. M., & Jodl, K. M. (1994). Stepfamilies as settings for child development. In A. Booth & J. Dunn (Eds.), *Stepfamilies: Who benefits? Who does not?* (pp. 55–80). Hillsdale, NJ: Erlbaum.

Hetherington, E. M., & Kelly, J. (2002). *For better or for worse: Divorce reconsidered.* New York: Norton.

Hill, M. (1992). The role of economic resources and remarriage in financial assistance for children of divorce. *Journal of Family Issues, 13*, 158–178.

Kelly, J. (1994). The determination of child custody. *Future of Children, 4*, 121–142.

Kiernan, K. E. (1992). The impact of family disruption in childhood on transitions made in young adult life. *Population Studies, 46*, 213–234.

King, V. (1994a). Nonresident father involvement and child well-being: Can dads make a difference? *Journal of Family Issues, 15*, 78–96.

King, V. (1994b). Variation in the consequences of nonresident father involvement for children's well-being. *Journal of Marriage and the Family, 56*, 963–972.

King, V., & Heard, H. E. (1999). Nonresident father visitation, parental conflict, and mother's satisfaction: What's best for child well-being? *Journal of Marriage and the Family, 61*, 385–396.

Knox, V. W., & Bane, M. J. (1994). Child support and schooling. In I. Garfinkel, S. McLanahan, & P. Robins (Eds.), *Child support and well-being* (pp. 285–316). Washington, DC: Urban Institute Press.

Kurdek, L. (1986). Custodial mothers' perceptions of visitation and payment of child support by noncustodial fathers in families with low and high levels of preseparation interparental conflict. *Journal of Applied Developmental Psychology, 7*, 307–323.

Lamb, M. E. (1999). Noncustodial fathers and their impact on the children of divorce. In R. A. Thompson & P. R. Amato (Eds.), *The postdivorce family: Children, parenting, and society* (pp. 105–125). Thousand Oaks, CA: Sage.

Lamb, M. E. (2002). Child development and the law. In R. M. Lerner, M. A. Easterbrooks, & J. Mistry (Eds.), *Comprehensive handbook of psychology: Vol. 6. Developmental psychology* (pp. 559–577). New York: Wiley.

Landale, N. S., & Oropesa, R. S. (2001). Father involvement in the lives of mainland Puerto Rican children: Contributions of nonresident, cohabiting, and married fathers. *Social Forces, 79*, 945–968.

Lin, I. F. (2000). Perceived fairness and compliance with child support obligations. *Journal of Marriage and the Family, 62*, 388–398.

Luthar, S. S. (1999). *Poverty and children's adjustment.* Thousand Oaks, CA: Sage.

Maccoby, E. E., & Martin, J. (1983). Socialization in the context of the family: Parent-child interaction. In E. M. Hetherington (Ed.), *Handbook of child psychology: Vol. 4. Socialization, personality, and social development* (4th ed., pp. 1–104). New York: Wiley.

Maccoby, E. E., & Mnookin, R. H. (1992). *Dividing the child: Social and legal dilemmas of custody.* Cambridge, MA: Harvard University Press.

MacDonald, W. L., & DeMaris, A. (1996). Parenting stepchildren and biological children: The effects of stepparents' gender and new biological children. *Journal of Family Issues, 17*, 5–25.

MacDonald, W. L., & DeMaris, A. (2002). Stepfather-stepchild relationship quality: The stepfather's demand for conformity and the biological father's involvement. *Journal of Family Issues, 23*, 121–137.

Manning, W. D., & Smock, P. J. (1999). New families and nonresident father-child visitation. *Social Forces, 78*, 87–116.

Marsiglio, W. (1992). Stepfathers with minor children living at home: Parenting perceptions and relationship quality. *Journal of Family Issues, 13*, 195–214.

McKenry, P. C., Price, S. J., Fine, M. A., & Serovich, J. (1992). Predictors of single, noncustodial fathers' physical involvement with their children. *Journal of Genetic Psychology, 153*, 305–319.

McLahanan, S. S., & Sandefur, G. (1994). *Growing up with a single parent.* Cambridge, MA: Harvard University Press.

McLanahan, S. S., Seltzer, J. A., Hanson, T. L., & Thomson, E. (1994). Child support enforcement and child well-being: Greater security or greater conflict? In I. Garfinkel, S. S. McLanahan, & P. K. Robins (Eds.), *Child support and child well-being* (pp. 239–256). Washington, DC: Urban Institute.

Meyer, D. R. (1999). Compliance with child support orders in paternity and divorce cases. In R. A. Thompson & P. R. Amato (Eds.), *The postdivorce family: Children, parenting, and society* (pp. 127–157). Thousand Oaks, CA: Sage.

Minton, C., & Pasley, K. (1996). Fathers' parenting role identity and father involvement: A comparison of nondivorced and divorced, nonresident fathers. *Journal of Family Issues, 17*, 26–45.

Moore, M. R., & Chase-Lansdale, P. L. (2001). Sexual intercourse and pregnancy among African-American girls in high-poverty neighborhoods: The role of family and perceived community environment. *Journal of Marriage and the Family, 63*, 1146–1157.

Mott, F. L. (1990). When is a father really gone? Paternal-child contact in father-absent homes. *Demography, 27*, 499–517.

Nelson, S., Clark, R. L., & Acs, G. (2001). *Beyond the two-parent family: How teenagers fare in cohabiting couple and blended families* (Series B, No. B-31). Washington, DC: Urban Institute.

Nord, C. W., & Zill, N. (1996). *Non-custodial parents' participation in their children's lives: Evidence from the Survey of Income and Program Participation.* Rockville, MD: Westat.

Parsons, T., & Bales, R. F. (1955). *Family socialization and interaction process.* Glencoe, IL: Free Press.

Pearson, J., & Thoennes, N. (1990). Custody after divorce: Demographic and attitudinal patterns. *American Journal of Orthopsychiatry, 60*, 233–249.

Rettig, K. D., Leichtentritt, R. D., & Stanton, L. M. (1999). Understanding noncustodial fathers' family and life satisfaction from resource theory perspective. *Journal of Family Issues, 20*, 507–538.

Robinson, J. P., & Godbey, G. (1999). *Time for life: The surprising ways Americans use their time.* University Park, PA: Pennsylvania State University Press.

Rollins, B. C., & Thomas, D. L. (1979). Parental support, power, and control techniques in the socialization of children. In W. R. Burr, R. Hill, F. I. Nye, & I. Reiss (Eds.), *Contemporary theories about the family: Vol. 1. Research-based theories* (pp. 317–364). Glencoe, NJ: Free Press.

Rossi, A., & Rossi, P. (1990). *Of human bonding: Parent-child relations across the life course.* New York: de Gruyter.

Seccombe, K. (2000). Families in poverty in the 1990s: Trends, causes, consequences, and lessons learned. *Journal of Marriage and the Family, 62,* 1094–1113.

Seltzer, J. A. (1991). Relationships between fathers and children who live apart: The father's role after separation. *Journal of Marriage and the Family, 53,* 79–101.

Seltzer, J. A. (1998). Father by law: Effects of joint legal custody on nonresident fathers' involvement with children. *Demography, 35,* 135–146.

Seltzer, J. A., & Bianchi, S. M. (1988). Children's contact with absent parents. *Journal of Marriage and the Family, 50,* 663–677.

Seltzer, J. A., & Brandreth, Y. (1994). What fathers say about involvement with children after separation. *Journal of Family Issues, 15,* 49–77.

Seltzer, J. A., Schaeffer, N. C., & Chang, H. (1989). Family ties after divorce: The relationship between visiting and paying child support. *Journal of Marriage and the Family, 51,* 1013–1031.

Simons, R. L., Whitbeck, L. B., Beaman, J., & Conger, R. D. (1994). The impact of mothers' parenting, involvement by nonresidential fathers, and parental conflict on the adjustment of adolescent children. *Journal of Marriage and the Family, 56,* 356–374.

Skopin, A. R., Newman, B. M., & McKenry, P. (1993). Influences on the quality of stepfather-adolescent relationships: Views of both family members. *Journal of Divorce and Remarriage, 19,* 181–196.

Smock, P. J. (2000). Cohabitation in the United States: An appraisal of research themes, findings, and implications. *Annual Review of Sociology, 26,* 1–20.

Sorensen, E. & Zibman, C. (2001). Poor dads who don't pay child support: Deadbeat dads or disadvantaged? *Urban Institute,* Series B, No. B-30.

Stephens, L. S. (1996). Will Johnny see daddy this week? An empirical test of three theoretical perspectives of postdivorce contact. *Journal of Family Issues, 17,* 466–494.

Stewart, S. D. (1999). Disneyland dads, Disneyland moms? How nonresident parents spend time with absent children. *Journal of Family Issues, 20,* 539–556.

Teachman, J. D. (1991). Who pays? Receipt of child support in the United States. *Journal of Marriage and the Family, 53,* 759–772.

Teachman, J. D., & Paasch, K. (1993). The economics of parenting apart. In C. E. Depner & J. H. Bray (Eds.), *Nonresidential parenting: New vistas in family living* (pp. 61–86). Newbury Park, CA: Sage.

Terry-Humen, E., Manlove, J., & Moore, K. A. (2001). Births outside of marriage: Perceptions vs. reality (Research brief). Washington, DC: Child Trends.

Thomson, E., McLanahan, S. S., & Curtin, R. B. (1992). Family structure, gender, and parental socialization. *Journal of Marriage and the Family, 54,* 368–378.

Thompson, R. A., & Laible, D. J. (1999). Noncustodial parents. In M. E. Lamb (Ed.), *Parenting and child development in "nontraditional" families* (pp. 103–123). Mahwah, NJ: Erlbaum.

Thornton, A. (1989). Changing attitudes toward family issues in the United States. *Journal of Marriage and the Family, 51,* 873–894.

Umberson, D. (1992). Relationships between adult children and their parents: Psychological consequences for both generations. *Journal of Marriage and the Family, 54,* 664–674.

Umberson, D., & Williams, C. L. (1993). Divorced fathers: Parental role strain and psychological distress. *Journal of Family Issues, 14,* 378–400.

U.S. Bureau of the Census. (1998). *Statistical abstract of the United States* (118th ed.). Washington, DC: U.S. Government Printing Office.

U.S. Bureau of the Census. (2000). *Child support for custodial mothers and fathers* (Current Population Reports, Series P20-212). Washington, DC: U.S. Government Printing Office.

U.S. Bureau of the Census. (2001). *Statistical abstract of the United States* (121st ed.). Washington, DC: U.S. Government Printing Office.

U.S. Commission on Child and Family Welfare. (1996). *Parenting our children: In the best interest of the nation.* Washington, DC: U.S. Government Printing Office.

Vuchinich, S., Hetherington, E. M., Vuchinich, R. A., & Clingempeel, W. G. (1991). Parent-child interaction and gender differences in early adolescents' adaptation to stepfamilies. *Developmental Psychology, 27,* 618–626.

Wallerstein, J. S., Lewis, J. M., & Blakeslee, S. (2000). *The unexpected legacy of divorce: A 25 year landmark study.* New York: Hyperion.

White, L. K., & Booth, A. (1985). The quality and stability of remarriages: The role of stepchildren. *American Sociological Review, 50,* 689–698.

White, L. K., & Gilbreth, J. G. (2001). When children have two fathers: Effects of relationships with stepfathers and noncustodial fathers on adolescent outcomes. *Journal of Marriage and Family, 63,* 155–167.

Zill, N., Morrison, D. R., & Coiro, M. J. (1993). Long-term effects of parental divorce on parent-child relationships, adjustment, and achievement in young adulthood. *Journal of Family Psychology, 7,* 91–103.

CHAPTER 13

Fathers in Fragile Families

SARA MCLANAHAN and MARCIA S. CARLSON

Out-of-wedlock childbearing has increased dramatically over the past four decades, giving rise to a new family form—the *fragile family,* comprised of unmarried parents and their children. The word *family* denotes the biological tie between the parents and child, and the word *fragile* underscores the high rates of economic and relationship instability in these unions. In 1960, 6% of children in the United States were born to unmarried parents; by the year 2000, the proportion was 33% (Ventura & Bachrach, 2000).

Nonmarital childbearing is occurring with increasing frequency in nearly all Western industrialized countries. Indeed, the proportion of out-of-wedlock births is higher in the Scandinavian countries that it is in the United States (Ventura, Bachrach, & Hill, 1995). The United States may be unique, however, with respect to the (lack of) involvement of unmarried fathers in the lives of their children. Whereas in the Western

The authors are grateful to Regina Leidy for assistance with references and editing. The Fragile Families and Child Wellbeing Study is funded by grants from the National Institute of Child Health and Human Development (R01HD36916), the U.S. Department of Health and Human Services (ASPE & ACF), and a consortium of private foundations: the California Healthcare Foundation, the Commonwealth Fund, the Ford Foundation, the Foundation for Child Development, the Fund for New Jersey, the William T. Grant Foundation, the Healthcare Foundation of New Jersey, the William and Flora Hewlett Foundation, the Hogg Foundation, the Christina A. Johnson Endeavor Foundation, the Kronkosky Charitable Foundation, the Leon Lowenstein Foundation, the John D. and Catherine T. MacArthur Foundation, the A. L. Mailman Family Foundation, the Charles S. Mott Foundation, the National Science Foundation, the David and Lucille Packard Foundation, the Public Policy Institute of California, the Robert Wood Johnson Foundation, the St. David's Hospital Foundation, and the St. Vincent Hospital and Health Services.

European countries, the vast majority of unmarried fathers are living with the mother when their child is born, in the United States the proportion is much lower (Bumpass & Lu, 2000).

The increase in fragile families is of great interest to social scientists that care about the family. Marriage is one of the oldest institutions in Western society, and previous studies have documented strong associations between stable marriages and a range of positive outcomes for adults and children (McLanahan & Sandefur, 1994; Nock, 1998; Waite & Gallagher, 2000). While nagging questions remain about how much of these associations is due to marriage itself, as opposed to the characteristics of people who establish and maintain stable marriages, prudence suggests that fundamental changes in family behavior be taken very seriously.

The growth of fragile families is also of interest to researchers and policy makers who care about stratification and inequality, as related to race, ethnicity, and poverty status. African Americans and Hispanics are much more likely to live in fragile families than are other groups, and they are disproportionately affected by what happens in these families. Whereas 22% of White children today are born to unmarried parents, the numbers for African American and Hispanic children are 69% and 42%, respectively (Ventura & Bachrach, 2000). Being born to unmarried parents is also tied to social class. Whereas women in the bottom two thirds of the education distribution have experienced large increases in nonmarital childbearing since 1970, women in the top third of the distribution have experienced virtually no increase (Ellwood & Jencks, 2002).

Many people believe that children in fragile families would be better off if their parents lived together and their fathers were more involved in their upbringing. Indeed, policy makers in the United States are now attempting to enlarge the role of unwed fathers by strengthening paternity establishment and child support enforcement and by funding programs to prevent nonmarital childbearing and encourage marriage. However, the scientific basis for these policies is relatively weak. Until recently, we knew very little about the men who father children outside marriage, and we knew even less about the nature of their relationships with their children and their children's mothers. (The National Institute of Child Health and Human Development, or NICHD, cosponsored several workshops in the mid-1990s focusing on the need for better data on fatherhood and male fertility; see Greene, Emig, & Hearn, 1996; Federal Interagency Forum on Child and Family Statistics, 1998; see also *Report to Congress on Out-of–Wedlock Childbearing*, 1995.) How many of these men have steady jobs? How well do they get along with the mothers? Do some fathers provide economic support but little emotional support, or do these dimensions of parenting tend to cooccur? What factors predict different support patterns? Does a father's involvement improve the well-being of his child, or does it lead to more parental conflict, leaving the child ultimately worse off? How does father involvement affect the father? How does it affect the mother?

This chapter takes a first step toward answering some of these questions for fathers in fragile families. We begin by describing the characteristics and capabilities of unmarried fathers and by comparing these men to married fathers. We also look at the diversity among unwed fathers, including men in cohabiting and visiting relationships (defined as not cohabiting but romantically involved), as well as men who are no longer in a romantic relationship with the baby's mother. Next, we describe the range of relationships between unmarried parents around the time of their child's birth and one year later. We ask how parents view their relationships, whether they have plans to marry, and how they treat one another. Following the analysis of father-mother relationships, we focus on the relationship between fathers and children, beginning with fathers' involvement during the pregnancy and around the time of birth and then examining involvement about one year later. We end the chapter with a discussion of how public policies are likely to affect father involvement in fragile families.

Our description of the characteristics and relationships of unmarried fathers draws heavily on findings from the Fragile Families and Child Wellbeing Study, a new birth-cohort study of nearly 5,000 children born to (mostly unmarried) parents in 20 large cities throughout the United States (Austin, TX; Baltimore, MD; Boston, MA; Chicago, IL; Corpus Christi, TX; Detroit, MI; Indianapolis, IN; Jacksonville, FL; Milwaukee, WI; Nashville, TN; Newark, NJ; New York City, NY; Norfolk, VA; Oakland, CA; Philadelphia, PA; Pittsburgh, PA; Richmond, VA; San Antonio, TX; San Jose, CA; and Toledo, OH). Baseline interviews were conducted with both parents shortly after their child's birth. Mothers were interviewed in person at the hospital within 48 hours of the birth, and fathers were interviewed either at the hospital or as soon as possible thereafter. Follow-up interviews with both parents were conducted when the child was approximately 1 year old and will be conducted again when the child is about 3 years old and about 5 years old. When weighted, the data are representative of births to parents in U.S. cities of 200,000 or more people. Thus, the evidence we present can be generalized to unmarried fathers living in large cities.

FATHERS' CHARACTERISTICS AND CAPABILITIES

Prior to the Fragile Families study, the most complete information available on unmarried fathers came from the National Survey of Families and Households (NSFH). According to these data, men who fathered children outside marriage were younger, less likely to have a high school degree, and less likely to have attended college than were men who fathered children inside marriage (Garfinkel, McLanahan, & Hanson, 1998). Unmarried fathers also worked fewer hours per week and had lower hourly wages than did ever-married fathers. It is not surprising that their incomes were lower than those of married fathers and that they had more problems with disability, depression, and drug and alcohol use.

A major limitation of these data (and other nationally representative data sets) is that they miss a large number of men who live apart from their children. Garfinkel et al. (1998) estimated that approximately 40% of nonresident fathers are missing from the NSFH, either because they were not interviewed or because they did not identify themselves as fathers. The problem is even more serious for low-income fathers and men who were never married to the mothers of their children (see Rendall, Clarke, Peters, Ranjit, & Verroponlou, 1997; Sorensen, 1995). The Fragile Families study improves upon previous studies by interviewing fathers at the hospital soon after their child is born, when they are more likely to be available and willing to participate in the survey, thus leading to higher response rates. The study also asks mothers about the fathers of their children, so we have some information about *all* fathers, including those who do not participate in the study.

Recent data from the Fragile Families study confirm previous findings from the NSFH and provide additional information on the characteristics and capabilities of unmarried fathers. With respect to fathers' demographic characteristics, unmarried fathers in the Fragile Families study were about 4.5 years younger than married fathers, and the age difference between unmarried parents was slightly larger (and with greater variance) than the age difference between married couples (see Table 13.1). As noted earlier, unmarried fathers were much more likely than married fathers to be from minority backgrounds. Among married fathers, Whites were the dominant group, making up 54% of fathers with a new baby. In contrast, Blacks and Hispanics were the dominant group among unmarried fathers, accounting for 78% of new fathers. About 15% of both unmarried and married fathers were partnered with women of a different race. In an interesting finding, immigrants accounted for a substantial proportion of fathers: 16% of unmarried men and 24% of married men. Religious differences between the two groups of men were small compared with other characteristics. About three-fourths of fathers were Protestant or Catholic, regardless of their marital status. Unmarried fathers attended religious services less frequently than did married fathers. Other analyses of the Fragile Families data have confirmed that religious attendance is strongly associated with marital status: More religious parents were more likely to be married at the time of their baby's birth and to have married following a nonmarital birth (Wilcox, 2002).

Unmarried fathers in the Fragile Families study were more likely to have other children than were married fathers; about half of the married fathers were having a first birth, compared with 39% of unmarried fathers. Unmarried fathers were also more likely than married fathers to have had children with other partners: 32% compared with 15%.

Despite the increase in women's participation in the labor force, breadwinning remains a key component of the father role today, and the Fragile Families data show striking differences by marital status in fathers' earnings capabilities. Whereas only 14% of the married fathers in the study had less than a high school degree and 32% had a college degree, the pattern was reversed for unmarried fathers: 37% had no high school degree, and only 5% had a college education.

Substance abuse, poor physical or mental health, and a history of incarceration may also decrease a father's ability to obtain or retain a job. According to mothers, only a small fraction of fathers in the Fragile Families study had problems with drugs or alcohol: 6% of unmarried fathers and 2% of married fathers. Analyses of fathers' mental health (not shown in Table 13.1) indicated that about one fifth of fathers reported moderate or higher levels of depressive symptoms based on the Center for Epidemiological Studies–Depression (CES-D) scale (M. Wilson & Brooks-Gunn, 2001). Most fathers were in good physical health: 70% of unmarried fathers and 78% of married fathers described their health as "very good" or "excellent." More striking was the fact that according to mothers' reports, fully one third of unmarried fathers (and 7% of married fathers) had been incarcerated at some point in their lives. Incarceration is both a cause and a consequence of low earnings (Western & McLanahan, 2001).

Whereas nearly all fathers had worked at some point during the year prior to their child's birth, a substantial proportion of unmarried fathers (20%) were not working in the week prior to the birth (compared with 7% of married fathers). It is not surprising that unmarried fathers had lower average hourly wage rates than married fathers: $10.72 compared with $17.26 (these numbers are based on predicted wages from an equation that included fathers' age, education, race-ethnicity, immigrant status, disability, substance problem, and city of residence at the time of the baby's birth). Further analyses of fathers' earnings (not shown in Table 13.1) indicated that unmarried

Table 13.1
Characteristics and Capabilities of Fathers, by Marital Status (in percent)

	Unmarried	Married
Background/Demographics Characteristics		
Age		
Under 20	12.0	0.4
20–24	35.1	12.1
25–29	23.9	25.7
30 and older	29.0	61.8
Mean age (years)	26.88	31.57
Mean age difference w/mother	3.06 yrs (5.18)	2.34 yrs (4.49)
Race/ethnicity		
White non-Hispanic	18.5	54.1
Black non-Hispanic	45.5	13.6
Hispanic	32.4	24.4
Other	3.6	7.9
Parents are of different race	15.4	14.9
Immigrant	16.0	23.6
Religious affiliation		
Protestant	44.8	44.6
Catholic	31.6	34.0
Other religion	10.2	13.4
No religion	13.4	8.1
Frequency of religious attendance (range = 1–5)	2.62	3.29
Lived with both parents age 15	40.7	70.6
Other children		
First birth	50.2	38.5
With biological mom only	18.2	46.8
With biological mom and other woman	10.7	6.8
With other woman only	20.9	7.9
Earnings-Related Characteristics		
Education		
Less than high school	36.9	13.5
High school or the equivalent	36.6	23.1
Some college	22.0	31.5
College degree or higher	4.5	31.9
Employment status		
Worked week before baby's birth	80.5	92.7
Worked year before baby's birth	95.7	99.1
Substance problem	5.8	1.7
Self-reported health status		
Poor	0.7	0.8
Fair or good	29.3	21.6
Very good or excellent	70.0	77.6
Ever incarcerated (12-month survey)	33.4	6.7
Predicted hourly wage rate	$10.72	$17.26

(*continued*)

Table 13.1
Continued

	Unmarried	Married
Attitudes		
Positive attitudes about marriage		
Better for children if parents married (agree/strongly agree)	77.3	90.8
Better for children if parents married (agree/strongly agree)	59.2	77.8
Living together is the same as marriage (disagree/str. dis.)	51.6	81.2
Mean (range = 1–4)	2.77	3.23
Traditional gender role attitudes		
Important decisions should be made by man (agree/str. agree)	32.3	31.7
Better if man earns living/women care (agree/strongly agree)	37.8	44.5
Mean (range = 1–4)	2.33	2.38
Distrust of women		
In dating, woman out to take advantage of man (agree/str. agr.)	14.1	7.5
Women cannot be trusted to be faithful (agree/strongly agree)	13.0	3.9
Mean (range = 1–4)	1.98	1.76
Unweighted number of cases (*n*)		
All fathers	3,712	1,186
Interviewed fathers	2,780	1,050

Note: All figures are weighted by national sampling weights. Fathers' age, race, education, employment status, and substance problems are reported by mothers. All other figures are reported by fathers themselves (for the subset of fathers who were interviewed).

fathers were somewhat more likely than married fathers (29% vs. 22%) to have reported irregular earnings (defined as "activities—legal, quasi-legal and illegal—that take place outside of regular, paid employment and that generate income, goods and/or services with value"; Rich, 2001).

We also examined fathers' attitudes toward family, gender, and fathering. According to the data, a majority of both unmarried and married fathers held positive views of marriage around the time of their baby's birth: 77% of unmarried men and 91% of married men agreed that marriage is better for children. As expected, married men's attitudes were somewhat more positive than those of unmarried men. Attitudes toward gender roles were not dramatically different, however, although a higher fraction of married men believed that "it is better if the man is the primary breadwinner and the woman is the primary caregiver in the home" (45% vs. 38%). In addition, unmarried men had greater distrust of women than did married men: 13% of the unmarried men said that women could not be trusted to be faithful, compared with 4% of married men.

With respect to attitudes about fathering, we examined the proportion of fathers who "strongly agree" with three statements about the father's role. Because nearly all fathers either agree or strongly agree with these statements, we distinguish those who strongly agree, indicating that they are more strongly invested in the father role. Married men were slightly more likely than unmarried fathers to strongly agree that "Being a father and raising children is one of the most fulfilling experiences a man can have," that "I want people to know that I have a new child," and that "Not being a part of my child's life would be one of the worst things that could happen to me."

Finally, a man's relationship with his own father is likely to affect his involvement with his children (Parke, 1990, 1995). Some researchers have argued that men whose fathers were neither nurturing nor involved are likely to display similar behavior toward their children. Others claim that men who did not have strong fathers tend to compensate for their own father's shortcomings by becoming more involved with their own children. Researchers have not yet sorted out the circumstances under which modeling or compensation is likely to occur.

As shown in Table 13.1, the married fathers we studied were more likely to have had involved fathers themselves: 83% of married fathers reported that their fathers were "very involved" or "somewhat involved," compared with 65% of unmarried fathers. Four percent of married fathers reported that they never knew their father, compared with 8% of unmarried fathers.

DIVERSITY AMONG UNMARRIED FATHERS

Beyond the new information about unmarried parents overall, data from the Fragile Families study also suggest that unmarried parents are a heterogeneous group with divergent backgrounds, characteristics, and expectations for the future. Although the most significant differences in personal attributes and human capital were between married and unmarried fathers as a whole, we also found some variation *within* unmarried fathers (see Carlson & McLanahan, 2002; Carlson, McLanahan, & England, 2002). Cohabiting fathers were more likely to be older, of non-Black race, and from a two-parent family and to have had biological children by other women than were noncohabiting fathers. In terms of earnings capacity, cohabiting fathers were more advantaged than were other unmarried fathers. They had higher hourly wages, were much more likely to be working, and had higher educational attainment than did their noncohabiting counterparts.

Differences in fathers' attitudes toward marriage and gender roles, as well as frequency of church attendance, were generally small. It is not surprising that more substantial differences were noted in relationship quality across relationship status categories. The greatest distinction was between couples who had broken up by the time of the baby's birth and all other unmarried couples; mothers in such couples were more likely to report that the father had been physically violent, and both mothers and fathers were more likely to report more frequent conflict, as well as less supportiveness, than were other parents. Finally, fathers who were not romantically involved with the mothers were significantly more likely to have problems with substance abuse (according to both mothers' reports about fathers and fathers' reports about themselves); nearly one fifth of mothers who were not involved with the baby's father at birth reported that the father had a substance problem.

One of the most notable differences among unmarried parents concerns their expectations of marriage. Osborne (2002) found that nearly four fifths of cohabiting mothers reported their chances of marrying the baby's father as "pretty good" or "almost certain." Only half of mothers in visiting relationships reported such high chances. Couples with high expectations of marriage were more similar to each other—and to married parents—than were couples with low expectations. They also were more likely actually to marry by the time their child was 1 year old.

Taken together, the information from the Fragile Families study suggests that unmarried fathers differ from married fathers in ways that have important implications for their long-term economic well-being and family stability. Most striking is the low level of education among unmarried fathers, with the majority of men having only a high school degree or less. This finding suggests that many fathers are limited in their ability to find and retain well-paying jobs in the future. Further, the fact that nearly half of unmarried fathers have other children by previous partners places even greater demands on their breadwinning capabilities and increases the complexity of their family relationships and parental roles. Finally, although unmarried fathers are not very different from married fathers in terms of their attitudes toward marriage and traditional gender roles, responses to the attitude questions may be biased in a positive direction because these questions were asked only of fathers who participated in the Fragile Families study.

FATHER-MOTHER RELATIONSHIPS IN FRAGILE FAMILIES

The literature presents at least three rather different views about the nature of relationships between unmarried parents. Anderson (1989) told a story in which young, inner-city men exploit young women in order to fulfill their sexual needs, while young women play along because of misguided fantasies of a middle-class life. Willis (1996) offered an economic explanation for the same behavior: He argued that unmarried women allow men to "free ride" (in terms of supporting their children) when there is a surplus of women and when women have an alternative source of support (e.g., welfare). Other researchers present a much more cooperative picture, arguing that poor fathers are doing what they can to help the mothers of their children (Furstenberg, Sherwood, & Sullivan 1992; Stack, 1974). Edin (1994) added an important caveat to this picture by arguing that some mothers use the threat of turning fathers in to the child support officials as a way of maintaining informal payments from fathers and, thus, maximizing their total family income. Her findings are supported by other qualitative studies that describe a quasi-cooperative relationship between parents (Furstenberg et al., 1992; Waller, 1997; Waller & Plotnick, 2001). A third perspective argues that in some instances the mothers refuse to marry the fathers, either because these men are unreliable as breadwinners or because they have other more serious problems such as drug abuse or antisocial behavior (Edin, 1997; W. J. Wilson, 1987).

These three views are not necessarily incompatible with each other. Relationships between unwed parents are likely to fall along a continuum from no contact to casual contact to commitment, including cohabitation. Similarly, the quality of relationships is likely to vary from hostile to benign to extremely loving, and relationships are likely to change over time. Many unwed couples may start out with high hopes for a stable relationship, only to find that they (or their partners) cannot meet their earlier expectations. In his famous study of street-corner life, Liebow (1967) argued that men who were unable to provide economic support for their families disengaged from their biological children as a way of minimizing their feelings of inadequacy. Similarly, economic stress and arguments over child support and visitation may lead to hostility and violence.

One of the most important findings to emerge from the Fragile Families study is the close connection between unmarried fathers and mothers at the time of their child's birth. Overall, 83% of unmarried parents were romantically involved with each other: 51% were cohabiting, and another 32% were romantically involved but living apart (i.e., *visiting couples*). (We used mothers' reports about parents' relationship and father involvement, as their reports provide information about *all* unmarried fathers; only 75% of fathers were interviewed.) About 8% of parents were "just friends," and only 9% had little or no contact. The proportions in various relationship types were remarkably similar across age groups, except that teenage fathers (under age 20) were less likely to be cohabiting (46%) than were fathers ages 25 and older (68% of whom were cohabiting). These figures stand in stark contrast to the myth that nonmarital births are a product of casual relationships or that unmarried mothers do not know the name of their child's father.

Although the proportions of couples in *any* romantic relationship were similar across different racial and ethnic groups, we found considerable racial-ethnic variation in the type of relationship parents were in at the time of their baby's birth (see Figure 13.1). Assuming that there is a hierarchy of relationship statuses among unmarried parents, with cohabitation at the top and no contact at the bottom, White and Hispanic fathers were more likely to be in higher order relationships than were African American fathers. Non-Hispanic White and Hispanic fathers were more likely to be living with the mother, whereas Black fathers were much more likely to be in visiting relationships. Fathers of all racial-ethnic backgrounds were about equally likely to have little or no contact with the mother.

Most unmarried fathers had high expectations about their chances of marrying the baby's mother when asked just after the baby's birth. As shown in Table 13.2, about 74% of unmarried fathers reported their chances of marriage to the mother as "pretty good" or "almost certain." We would expect fathers in the Fragile Families sample to be somewhat more positive than fathers overall because the 75% of fathers who participated in the study represent a select group that is likely more committed to their partners and their children than the average unwed father. When we asked unmarried mothers to estimate the chances that they would marry the biological father, only 58% reported the chances as "pretty good" or "almost certain." This figure is probably a better estimate of the marriage expectations of the average unmarried father than the estimate based on the fathers who participated in the study. Cohabiting fathers were more optimistic about marriage (86%) than visiting fathers (64%); surprisingly, one fifth of fathers who were not romantically involved at the time of their baby's birth said that their chances of marrying the mother were good or almost certain. (The fathers in this category who were interviewed are particularly selective of men who are more invested in the mother and/or their baby than their nonromantic counterparts who did not participate in the study.)

These high expectations may strike some readers as unbelievable, and indeed there are good reasons to believe that parents are overly optimistic in these reports. Recall that mothers (and most fathers) were interviewed shortly after their child was born, a time when they may have felt especially happy. Moreover, although nonmarital childbearing is much less stigmatized today than it was in the past, parents may still have been inclined to tell the interviewers that they were planning to marry to avoid em-

White non-Hispanics

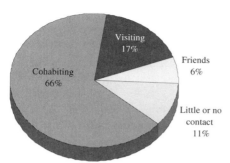

Hispanics

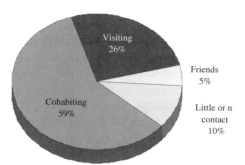

Black non-Hispanics

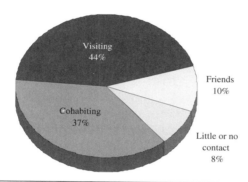

Figure 13.1 Relationship status of unmarried parents by race/ethnicity

barrassment. Fortunately, we were able to validate these responses through a series of in-depth interviews with 75 couples several months after the birth; these interviews confirmed that most parents who were romantically involved at birth had talked to each other about marriage and had plans to marry in the future (Gibson, Edin, & McLanahan, 2002).

Table 13.2 also reports information on several aspects of the quality of parents' relationships in fragile families and on the incidence of physical violence. Most parents in fragile families reported very positive relationships with their partners shortly after birth. Cohabiting fathers reported relationships that were very similar to married parents in terms of emotional supportiveness (represented by fathers' reports about mothers' affection and encouragement) and the frequency of conflict across six areas. Supportiveness was somewhat lower and frequency of conflict somewhat higher among visiting couples than among cohabiting couples. As would be expected, reported levels of supportiveness were much lower—and conflict much higher—among couples who had broken up by the time of the baby's birth (about one fifth of the sample).

Table 13.2

Fathers' Relationships with Mothers in Fragile Families (in percent)

	Unmarried				
	Total	Cohabiting	Visiting	Not Romantic	Married
Relationship quality					
Chances of marriage to mother					
No or a little chance	10.9	4.1	13.3	50.7	NA
50-50	15.2	10.2	23.2	23.1	NA
Pretty good or almost certain	73.9	85.7	63.5	26.2	NA
Supportiveness (Mother "often" . . .)					
Was fair and willing to compromise	45.8	56.6	39.2	24.3	66.5
Expressed affection or love to father	74.5	84.6	75.8	39.7	84.4
Criticized father or his ideas (coding reversed = "never")	71.4	73.9	72.4	61.7	72.7
Encouraged father to do things important to him	69.8	81.0	70.5	32.5	77.0
Mean (range = 1 to 3)[a]	2.64	2.67	2.62	2.46	2.70
Frequency of conflict ("often") about:					
Money	11.2	11.2	11.2	10.5	8.9
Spending time together	18.1	14.3	22.7	28.9	10.0
Sex	10.6	10.2	11.1	12.4	9.5
The pregnancy	6.6	3.5	9.2	20.1	3.8
Drugs	4.1	3.3	5.3	6.0	1.1
Being faithful	8.4	5.4	13.2	12.7	3.9
Mean (range = 1 to 3)[a]	1.45	1.41	1.51	1.55	1.34
Physical violence ("often" or "sometimes")					
Mother's report about father	4.0	2.2	3.1	11.7	2.7
Father's report about mother	14.1	12.0	20.2	8.0	5.6
Mother ever seriously hurt in fight with father (12-mo.)	8.1	7.7	7.5	11.2	2.7
Unweighted number of cases (*n*)	3,704[b]	1,782	1,272	650	1,186

Note: All figures are weighted by national sampling weights. All items are reported by fathers, except for mother's reports about father's violence.

[a]Possible outcomes are "never" (1), "sometimes" (2) and "often" (3).

[b]Eight of 3,712 unmarried cases had missing information on relationship status.

Rates of domestic violence were generally low among unmarried mothers; only about 4% reported at the baseline survey that the father had "sometimes" or "often" hit or slapped them. As with the other indicators of relationship quality, mothers in couples who had broken up by the time of the baby's birth reported higher rates of violence by fathers (12%) than did unmarried mothers who were still romantically involved with (2–3%) or married to (3%) their baby's father. In a surprising finding, fathers in all relationship categories reported higher levels of physical violence by the mothers than vice versa. Fourteen percent of unmarried fathers overall indicated that the baby's mother had "hit or slapped" them, with the highest proportion (20%) occurring among visiting fathers and the lowest fraction occurring among nonromantic fathers (8%). Again, the fact that the nonromantic fathers who participated in the study were very selective of the fathers in this group suggests that these results may be biased in a positive direction. Six percent of married fathers reported that the mother was violent toward them.

Reports of violence by unmarried mothers were somewhat higher one year after the child's birth. When asked at the 12-month follow-up survey if they were ever "cut, bruised, or seriously hurt in a fight" with the father, 8% of unmarried mothers responded affirmatively (compared to 4% at the baseline survey). By comparison, the fraction of married mothers who reported having ever been hurt in a fight with the father remained constant between baseline and 12 months (3%).

Table 13.3 presents information on the stability of parents' relationships over time. (Note that sampling weights were not used because the available weights do not adjust for attrition between waves. Although the figures are very similar when weighted, we present the unweighted data to focus better on changes in particular relationship types between the two survey waves.) The table shows parents' relationship status approximately one year after their baby's birth by categories of relationship status at the time of the child's birth (i.e., the percentages shown are of the row totals). Ninety-four percent of married couples were still married about one year after their baby's birth. Among unmarried couples, cohabiting relationships were much more stable than

Table 13.3
Relationship Status at Time of Birth and One Year Later (mothers' reports)

Time of Birth	12 Months after Birth of Child					
	Married	Cohabiting	Visiting	Friends	Not in Relationship	Number of Cases (*n*)
Married	94.3	1.1	0.2	0.1	4.3	1,070
Cohabiting	14.6	59.6	4.6	10.9	10.4	1,580
Visiting	5.3	32.2	14.0	25.6	23.0	1,137
Friends	1.2	9.2	3.5	44.1	42.2	261
Not in relationship	1.7	6.3	4.3	22.9	64.8	301
Unweighted number of cases (*n*)	1,307	1,363	255	648	776	4,349

Note: Figures are not weighted. Percentages shown are of row totals. Cohabitation at 12 months is defined as living together "all or most of the time" or "some of the time"; time of birth is a dichotomy (yes/no) for whether parents are living together.

other types of relationships, including those in which the parents were romantically involved but living apart. Apparently, having made the decision to cohabit by the time of the child's birth implies a certain commitment to the relationship or to raising the child together. Overall, three fourths of couples who were cohabiting when their child was born remained in a coresidential union at 12 months—15% were legally married, and 60% were still cohabiting. Being romantically involved but living apart when the child is born appears to be a very unstable status: Only 14% of couples in a visiting relationship were still in that status one year later. Nearly two fifths of visitors had increased their level of involvement—32% were cohabiting, and 5% were married. Nearly half of all visitors were no longer romantically involved—about one-quarter were "friends" and another quarter said they had no relationship. "No relationship" implies that the father is not likely to visit the child on a regular basis. Of parents who were "friends" at baseline, 44% reported still being friends one year later, 14% reported being romantically involved, 4% were visiting, 9% were cohabiting, and 1% was married. Finally, of the small number of mothers who reported no relationship when their child was born, about two thirds still had no relationship one year later, and 23% said they were friends. Surprisingly, a small but nontrivial fraction of such couples (12%) reported that they were romantically involved at one year, including 2% who were married.

To summarize, many parents in fragile families were closely connected to one another at the time of birth and had positive expectations for their future together. This finding is particularly true for cohabiting fathers who reported levels of relationship quality similar to those reported by married fathers. However, one year later, few unmarried parents had married. Although a majority of cohabiting parents were still together, more than half of visiting couples were no longer romantically involved. Given the importance of the father-mother relationship for fathers' involvement with children, the decline in the connection between unmarried parents one year following the baby's birth suggests that many fathers may lose contact with their children in the subsequent years.

WHAT ACCOUNTS FOR RELATIONSHIP STABILITY?

Researchers have developed a number of arguments for why some relationships are more stable than others and why some couples move to more committed relationships than others. Economic theory points to the role of monetary incentives in couples' decisions to enter (or remain in) cohabiting or marital unions, including shared public goods and insurance against risk. Nearly all of the empirical evidence about how earnings capacity affects union formation shows that men's earnings are positively associated with marriage (see Ellwood & Jencks, 2002, for a review) and cohabitation (Clarkberg, 1999; Smock & Manning, 1997) and negatively associated with divorce (Hoffman & Duncan, 1995; South & Lloyd, 1995). However, the evidence is less consistent with respect to women's earnings (Ellwood & Jencks, 2002; Lichter, McLaughlin, & Landry, 1992).

Beyond economic factors, culture—defined as widely shared beliefs and practices—can also affect decisions about family formation. Most researchers agree that the 1960s and 1970s were a watershed period for changes in norms and practices governing the family (Cherlin, 1992). Widespread changes in family-related behaviors—such as increases in sexual activity, childbearing, and coresidence outside marriage;

delays in marriage; and increases in divorce—were accompanied by dramatic changes in the social acceptance of all of these behaviors. Because cultural change is neither uniform nor uncontested, we would expect some groups to cling longer to traditional views and, hence, to be more likely to get and stay married than couples with less traditional values and gender roles (Clarkberg, Stolzenberg, & Waite, 1995). Cohabitation is a "looser bond" (Schoen & Weinick, 1993) or an "incomplete institution" (Nock, 1995) with roles that are less scripted by gender or family expectations, so we would expect that positive attitudes about marriage, traditional gender role attitudes, or religiosity would encourage marriage more than cohabitation. Consistent with this argument, individuals who cohabit are typically more politically liberal, less religious, and more favorable toward nontraditional family roles than are those who do not cohabit (Smock, 2000; Thornton, Axinn, & Hill, 1992).

Finally, given the growing cultural emphasis on marriage as a source of love and companionship rather than an economic exchange, we would expect the emotional quality of a couple's relationship to affect the movement from dating to cohabitation and from either dating or cohabitation to marriage. Many studies from psychology and sociology show that partners' perceptions of the emotional quality of marriages affect whether they stay together or break up (Booth, Johnson, White, & Edwards, 1985; Cowan, Cowan, Schulz, & Heming, 1994; Gottman, 1994; Karney & Bradbury, 1995; Sanchez & Gager, 2000; Sayer & Bianchi, 2000). Drug or alcohol abuse, infidelity, and violence within marriage are strongly associated with low marital quality and with divorce (Amato & Rogers, 1997; Kurtz, 1995; Sanchez & Gager, 2000; Sayer & Bianchi, 2000; White, 1990).

Research based on the Fragile Families study suggests that the earnings capacity and employment of both mothers and fathers encourage union formation (Carlson et al., 2002). Fathers' employment was important for both cohabitation and marriage, and the father's wage rate was particularly salient for marriage. Surprisingly, while mothers' education had a strong positive effect on all levels of union formation, fathers' education had no effect, net of wages. Besides economic factors, noneconomic predictors also had powerful effects on union transitions: Promarriage attitudes and church attendance increased the chances of marriage, whereas women's distrust of men reduced cohabitation and marriage and increased union dissolution. Finally, there was strong evidence that the emotional quality of parents' relationship affected union formation and stability. Feeling supported by a partner was very important for subsequent relationship status, even after controlling for parents' initial relationship status. In contrast, disagreement and conflict did not appear to be a significant factor in relationship outcomes at one year.

Incarceration is also an important factor in the formation and stability of family relationships. Western, Lopoo, and McLanahan (2002) found that after controlling for a wide range of social, psychological, and economic characteristics, fathers who had been incarcerated at some point in their lives were much less likely to be cohabiting with or married to the mother of their child one year after birth. This effect suggests that high incarceration rates among Black men of low socioeconomic status help account for low rates of marriage among this demographic group. According to Western et al. (2002), if the risk of incarceration were reduced to zero for Black fathers with less than high school education, marriage rates among this group would increase by 45%, and the Black-White gap in marriage rates would be reduced by nearly half (Western et al., 2002).

Parents' fertility history affects union formation, and multiple-partner fertility has been shown to pose particular challenges to parents' relationship stability over time (Carlson et al., 2002; Mincy, 2002). In the Fragile Families study, having children by multiple partners was more common among African Americans than among other racial-ethnic groups. Mincy (2002) found that 46% of Black fathers had one or more children by another partner (as reported by mothers), compared with 22% of White fathers and 29% of Hispanic fathers. The relatively high rates of multiple-partner fertility among African Americans may also help account for the low marriage rates among this group.

In sum, data from the Fragile Families study show that whereas many unmarried parents are optimistic about their future together at birth, their lack of human capital appears to be an important barrier to union formation. Parents' resources may be insufficient to establish an independent household or to meet their cultural norms of the financial prerequisites for marriage (Gibson et al., 2002). Further, although parents with positive and supportive relationships are more likely to stay together or move toward the marriage end of the relationship spectrum, a nontrivial number of couples struggle with personal or relationship problems such as substance use, physical violence, and frequent conflict. Finally, family formation among unmarried parents is often complicated by the fact that one or both parents may have children by a previous relationship.

FATHER-CHILD RELATIONSHIPS IN FRAGILE FAMILIES

Much of what we know about the relationship between unmarried fathers and their children comes from studies of divorced and separated nonresident fathers, and much of this research focuses on two aspects of father involvement—paying child support and father-child contact. Despite the new images of fatherhood, being the breadwinner continues to be central to the meaning of fatherhood for most men and women, and a father's ability to fulfill the breadwinner role continues to be a strong predictor of his relationship with his child. Fathers who are unable to live up to the breadwinner ideal are less likely to find the father role rewarding and more likely to withdraw from their children in order to save face. Alternatively, mothers may discourage the involvement of men who are unable to provide for their children.

The literature shows that whereas one third of divorced fathers pay support on a regular basis and maintain frequent contact with their children, another third disappear rather quickly from their child's life (Cherlin & Furstenberg, 1991; Furstenberg, Morgan, & Allison, 1987; Garfinkel, McLanahan, & Robins, 1994; Marsiglio, 1993; Seltzer, 1994; Shiono & Quinn, 1994). (Recent data from the Census Bureau and Health and Human Services ACF suggest that an increasing share of fathers is paying child support. We expect that fathers' visitation may also be increasing, although we are not aware of such data.) The picture for never-married fathers is somewhat different. Whereas formal child support agreements are even less common among never-married fathers, informal support, especially the purchase of goods and services for the child, seems to be somewhat more common (Edin & Lein, 1997; Marsiglio & Day, 1997; Waller, 1997). Recent analyses of the Fragile Families data indicate that only 13% of nonresident fathers had paid any formal child support—with an average payment of $1,543—during the year subsequent to a nonmarital birth (Nepomnyashchy, Garfinkel, & Mincy, 2002).

Father-child contact also differs between divorced fathers and unmarried fathers.

Whereas many people think of unwed fathers as being less involved with their children than divorced or separated fathers, analyses of the National Longitudinal Survey of Youth–Child Supplement (NLSY-CS) data suggest otherwise: About one third of children born to unwed mothers (over age 20) between 1984 and 1990 were living with their biological fathers at birth, and another third were seeing their fathers at least once a week (McLanahan, Garfinkel, Brooks-Gunn, & Zhao, 1997). Lerman and Sorensen (1996) reported similar results using the NLSY. Even more surprising, a large proportion of fragile families appear to be quite stable during the first few years of the child's life: McLanahan et al. (1997) found (using the NLSY) that among children who were living with their biological father at birth, 77% were still doing so two years later; similarly, 69% of children who were seeing their fathers once a week or more in the first year of life were still maintaining this level of contact two years later. Finally, McLanahan and Sandefur (1994) found high levels of contact between nonresident, never-married fathers and children of all ages, using data from the NSFH.

High levels of involvement (and low levels of formal child support) among new unmarried fathers are probably due to the fact that many of the parents in fragile families are still romantically involved when we observe them; in short, their union or "marriage" is still intact. Thus, the comparison with divorced parents is probably not appropriate. Once the relationship ends, however, fathers' involvement may drop off just as rapidly among never-married couples as it does among divorced couples. Alternatively, the informality of the tie between unwed parents may cushion these families from the shock of divorce, which, in turn, may make it easier for a father to stay involved with his child after the relationship with the mother ends.

Assuming that many unwed fathers are involved with their children, the question remains: What exactly do they do, and what images and role models do they draw upon? Historically, the father's role in family life was largely defined by breadwinning. Today, however, with dramatic changes in family behaviors and attitudes since the 1960s, fathers are now involved in childrearing in numerous ways (Cabrera, Tamis-LeMonda, Bradley, Hofferth, & Lamb, 2000; Lamb, 1997; Marsiglio, Amato, Day, & Lamb, 2000; Marsiglio, Day, & Lamb, 2000; Parke, 1995). Fathering may include providing economic support; nurturing and caregiving; engaging in leisure and play activities; providing the child's mother with financial, emotional, or practical support; providing moral guidance and discipline; ensuring the safety of the child; tying the child to his extended family; and tying the child to the community (Marsiglio & Day, 1997). The new conceptualization is very useful in helping us identify multiple domains of fathers' involvement, and it can easily be extended to research on unmarried fathers. In fact, the few ethnographic studies that have looked at unwed fathers report that many of these men describe their roles in terms similar to those used by married fathers (Furstenberg et al., 1992; Waller, 1997).

Data from the Fragile Families study (Table 13.4) show that most unwed fathers provided support to the mother during the pregnancy and were involved around the time of the child's birth. According to mothers' reports, over 80% of unwed fathers contributed financial support during the pregnancy, and more than three quarters visited the mother and baby in the hospital. Eighty percent of mothers said the baby would take the father's last name, and 84% said that the father's name would be on the baby's birth certificate. Finally, mothers reported that over 90% of the fathers said they wanted to help raise the child, and over 90% of mothers themselves said they wanted the fathers to be involved.

Table 13.4

Father Involvement at Time of Birth (in percent) (mothers' reports, baseline survey)

	Overall	Cohabiting	Visiting	Not Romantic
Gave money or bought things for baby	82.9	97.0	85.6	32.5
Helped in another way	79.8	97.5	78.6	26.1
Visited baby's mother in hospital	78.1	96.2	72.9	32.1
Child will take father's surname	79.5	93.6	76.7	41.0
Father's name is on birth certificate	83.9	95.5	82.8	50.3
Father wants to be involved	91.5	99.7	95.6	56.4
Mother wants father involved	92.8	99.6	97.6	61.7
Unweighted number of cases (n)	3,704[a]	1,782	1,272	650

[a]Eight of 3,712 unmarried cases had missing information on relationship status.
Note: All figures are weighted by national sampling weights.

As we would expect, cohabiting fathers were the most likely to be involved with their children, with mothers reporting that over 90% of cohabiting fathers were involved in each of the indicators of early father involvement examined. Visiting fathers were slightly less likely to be involved than cohabiting fathers, but the greater distinction was between romantic and nonromantic fathers. Only a third of fathers who were not romantically involved with the mother gave money or bought things for the baby during the pregnancy, although 56% of these men said they wanted to be involved (according to mothers' reports), and 62% of mothers said they welcomed the fathers' involvement.

When mothers were asked about fathers' involvement about one year after the baby's birth (Table 13.5), they reported that nearly all fathers had seen their child at least once since the baby was born. However, the quantity of father-child engagement varied notably by fathers' marital status at birth. (As only 9% of unmarried parents got married between the baseline and follow-up surveys, we used marital status at baseline to be consistent with the other tables. The substantive findings are not altered if marital status at 12 months is used instead.) Fifty-eight percent of unmarried fathers saw their child every day, compared with 96% of married fathers. Seventeen percent of unmarried fathers never saw their child, compared with only 2% of married fathers. Taking all unmarried fathers, the average number of days fathers saw their children was 20, compared with 29 days for married fathers. When asked how frequently the father spent one or more hours a day with the child in the previous month, mothers reported lower levels of daily contact among unmarried fathers (53%) compared with married fathers (82%).

For fathers who saw their children on a regular basis, mothers were asked how frequently the fathers participated in specific activities with the child. There was less variation in the frequency of engagement by marital status than there was in any or no contact. Nevertheless, involvement was still slightly higher among fathers who were married to the mother at the time of the baby's birth. Fourteen percent of unmarried— and 15% of married—fathers read stories to their child every day in the week prior to the survey, whereas 33% of unmarried (and 23% of married) fathers never read to their child. A majority of fathers helped feed or give a bottle to their children on a regular

Table 13.5
Father Involvement about One Year after Baby's Birth (in percent)
(mothers' reports, 12-month survey)

	Unmarried (at birth)	Married (at birth)
Father-child contact		
Has father seen child since birth	94.9	99.9
Number of days father saw child		
in past month		
None	16.5	1.7
1–5	12.1	0.8
6–9	2.7	0.1
10–19	5.1	1.2
20–29	5.3	0.3
Everyday	58.2	96.0
Mean (range = 1–5)	19.91(13.0)	29.02(5.0)
How often father spent 1+ hours/day		
with child in past month		
Never	21.8	2.3
1–2 times	4.5	1.4
Few times/month	6.0	3.3
Few times/week	14.4	11.3
Every day or nearly every day	53.3	81.7
Frequency of father-child activities (of those who saw child in past months)		
Read stories in past week		
Never	33.0	22.8
Once/week	13.2	14.7
2–4 times/week	32.6	38.8
5–6 times/week	7.1	8.4
Every day	14.1	15.4
Mean (range = 1–5)	2.56(1.4)	2.79(1.3)
Fed child or gave bottle in past week		
Never	9.8	5.8
Once/week	6.2	4.6

basis: 52% of unmarried fathers and 56% of married fathers reported giving help in the past week. Only 10% of unmarried—and 6% of married—fathers said they never helped feed their child.

Based on previous research, it is likely that father contact may diminish over time. However, greater human capital and a high-quality mother-father relationship—net of relationship type—appear to promote greater involvement by fathers in fragile families, at least within one year of a child's birth (Carlson & McLanahan, 2002). Ethnographic research on a subset of Fragile Families couples has shown that fathers with problem behaviors—including domestic violence and criminal activity—were less likely to see their children about 30 months after the child's birth (Waller & Bailey, 2002); the lack of contact appears to reflect mothers' taking actions to protect their children, such as ending their relationship with the baby's father and limiting his access to the child after the relationship has ended. It is important to recognize that fathers' involvement with children may not always be beneficial, particularly if the father has a history of violent or abusive behavior.

In sum, although most unmarried fathers are involved during the pregnancy and around the time of the birth, one year later a nontrivial fraction of fathers has little or no regular interaction with their child. According to the mothers, nearly half of unmarried fathers do not see their child on a daily basis, and fully one-fifth of fathers had not spent any time with their child in the month prior to the survey. Involvement is significantly higher among married fathers; nearly all children born to married fathers see their father every day. Conditional on some contact with the child, however, the frequency of reading and feeding is only slightly lower for unmarried fathers. This evidence confirms our expectations that there may be considerable divergence among unmarried fathers over time, with some fathers participating actively in their young children's lives and others disengaging. Such a finding would be consistent with prior research of divorced and separated fathers, which shows that involvement declines after the relationship with the mother ends.

IMPLICATIONS FOR PUBLIC POLICY

At the beginning of this chapter we noted that the United States differed from other Western industrialized countries in terms of its low levels of cohabitation among unmarried parents. Evidence from the Fragile Families study, however, suggests that this picture may be changing. Although unwed fathers in the United States are less likely to be living with their children than unwed fathers in other countries, over 80% of U.S. fathers are romantically involved with the mothers of their children at the time of a new child's birth (McLanahan, Garfinkel, Reichman, & Teitler, 2001). Moreover, most unmarried fathers hold positive views of marriage and expect to marry the mothers of their children, although only a small proportion have actually done so by the time their child is 1 year old. Assuming that fathers' participation in children's lives offers important benefits to children as well as society (see Lamb & Lewis, this volume), policy makers have begun to ask what can be done to increase father involvement and to introduce new policies designed to achieve these goals. Included here are income transfer programs, child support policies, fatherhood initiatives, and programs to promote marriage.

WELFARE PROGRAMS

The fact that the United States relies primarily on means-tested programs to assist low-income families (as compared with most European nations, which utilize mostly universal programs) is thought to discourage marriage and cohabitation among low-income parents. The penalty occurs because income and asset eligibility tests are based on total family income and cut points are set very low. The major welfare program in the United States is Temporary Assistance to Needy Families (TANF; formerly Aid to Families with Dependent Children, or AFDC). (See Cabrera & Evans, 2000, for a discussion of issues surrounding welfare reform and father involvement.) In both of these programs, benefits are reduced by one dollar for each additional dollar of family income. So, even if a two-parent family were able to qualify for assistance, the family's benefit level would be reduced by the amount of income a cohabiting partner (or spouse) contributed. Consequently, there is little economic incentive for unmarried parents to live together and pool household resources. In 17 states, two-parent families are subject to a different (and more stringent) set of rules than single mothers. In short, U.S. welfare policies may discourage father involvement by the structure of eligibility and benefit rules.

There is a long history of concern in the United States that cash welfare benefits may increase single parenthood, either by encouraging nonmarital births or by discouraging marriage. Economic theory (Becker, 1991) tells us that individuals take account of economic incentives in determining whether to marry and have children. Thus, providing transfer income to single mothers should increase mothers' ability to bear and rear children alone and reduce their need for marriage. A vast academic literature has investigated this topic, and several generations of findings have yielded somewhat different conclusions about the effects of welfare on family formation. Recently, however, a consensus has emerged that holds that welfare benefits have a small but significant positive effect on single parenthood. Most researchers agree with Robert Moffitt (1998), who stated that "the conventional perception of the U.S. welfare system as largely favoring single-parent families over two-parent families and childless couples and individuals is essentially correct".

Part of this consensus is based on more sophisticated analyses of the cross-state differences in welfare programs and family formation. Recent evaluations of welfare reform programs in several states provide additional information. For example an assessment of the Minnesota Family Investment Program (MFIP) found that easing the rules for two-parent families increased family formation and stability among single parents and significantly reduced divorce among two-parent married families (Knox, Miller, & Gennetian, 2000).

Welfare programs were originally designed for single mothers who had lost a partner through death, divorce, or desertion. However, the Fragile Families study shows that a large proportion of unmarried parents are still romantically involved when their child is born. The fact that so many parents are romantically involved makes them particularly sensitive to welfare incentives that discourage two-parent families. For this group of parents, negative incentives may have a large negative effect on marriage and, perhaps, even cohabitation.

CHILD SUPPORT

The federal child support enforcement (CSE) program was started in 1975 to ensure that nonresident fathers provided financial support to their children. Federal matching funds were provided to states for establishing paternity, establishing child support awards, and collecting child support payments. As initially structured, collections were used to offset welfare expenditures in the AFDC program, and child support paid by fathers to mothers on welfare was to be applied to recover welfare costs; this practice continues today. In 1980 the program was broadened to serve all children eligible for support regardless of income or welfare status, but historically and at the present time, the majority of cases in the federal CSE system involve parents and children connected to the welfare system. From its inception, the CSE system was charged solely with enforcing fathers' financial support of their children, and other aspects of fathers' involvement, including visitation and custody, were (and remain) governed by state laws. (For recent discussions of the Child Support System see *Fathers Under Fire*. For early discussions see Chambers, 1979, and Krause, 1989.)

Legislative reforms in the last two decades have increased the overall effectiveness of the child support system (Case, Lin, & McLanahan, in press). Paternity establishment rates, child support orders, and child support collections have all risen. However, some research suggests that stronger enforcement may be driving low-income fathers away (Garfinkel et al., 1998; Sorenson, 1995; Sorenson & Turner, 1996), especially fathers in fragile families. As noted earlier, fathers may disengage from their children if they are not adequately fulfilling the provider role, and CSE may be creating disincentives for fathers to provide for their children.

Strong CSE may also reduce fathers' in-kind contributions to their children. Qualitative research suggests that unmarried parents generally prefer informal support arrangements (Waller & Plotnick, 2001) because the money goes to the child rather than to the state. Moreover, unmarried fathers who are living with their child are already providing support insofar as they are sharing their incomes with their children. The CSE system was developed to meet the needs of children whose fathers were not living with the mother. However, the situation for fragile families is vastly different because nearly half of these fathers are coresiding with the mother and child, at least at the time of the child's birth.

A second way that the current CSE system may discourage fathers' involvement is that child support orders are often not appropriately linked to fathers' economic status. Because many states have minimum orders (based on the assumption that the father is working full-time regardless of his actual employment status), low-income fathers may be forced to pay a much higher proportion of their income in child support than middle-income fathers (Sorenson, 1999). This policy affects fathers in fragile families more than it affects other families because the former have lower wages and are much more likely to not work year-round. Finally, failure to pay child support is often treated as a criminal act, so fathers who are delinquent in child support may be put in jail or prison, which further diminishes their long-term earnings potential (Western, 2000).

Economic theory is ambiguous about whether stronger CSE will encourage or discourage father involvement. On the one hand, child support reduces the costs of nonmarital childbearing to women (assuming that women actually receive some of the money paid by fathers). On the other hand, it increases the costs to men. The net effect is an empirical question. The research on this topic indicates that the negative effects of stronger enforcement on men appear to dominate, with strong CSE leading to lower levels of both nonmarital childbearing (Case, 1998; Garfinkel, Gaylin, McLanahan, & Huang, 2000) and divorce (Nixon, 1997). Thus, it appears that the effects of public and private transfers may go in opposite directions, with welfare benefits slightly discouraging the formation of families and strong CSE, on balance, encouraging families to form or stay together (or couples not to have a child outside of marriage in the first place).

The effects of CSE may be more complicated for low-income families who are receiving—or are potentially eligible for—welfare. Although child support is increasingly effective, children born outside of marriage are less likely to have a child support order established than are children born within marriage. In part, this may be due to the fact (as noted earlier) that unmarried parents prefer informal support arrangements and that until recently the government has largely ignored low-income fathers (Waller & Plotnick, 2001). If unmarried parents have an informal agreement between themselves such that the father contributes money under the table or makes in-kind contributions, any welfare received by the mother is in addition to any support received by the father. Because economic stability is generally associated with marriage and family formation (a so-called income effect), in this case the additional income from welfare may *encourage* family formation because parents are better able to pool their resources (Mincy & Dupree, 2000).

Qualitative studies of low-income couples show that strict enforcement also increases tension between unmarried parents—the mother may perceive that the father is not doing enough to help her and her children (not realizing that child support is used to reimburse welfare costs), and the father may perceive that the mother is going after him (not realizing that she is required to cooperate in establishing paternity as a criterion for receiving welfare). The findings in the qualitative literature are supported by studies showing that stronger CSE is associated with high conflict among low-income couples (Seltzer, McLanahan, & Hanson, 1998).

FATHERHOOD PROGRAMS

Whereas the primary mission of the CSE system has been collecting money from non-residential parents, fatherhood programs are designed to improve fathers' labor market outcomes and to strengthen fathers' connections to their children. The primary demonstration in this area was the Parents' Fair Share (PFS) program, which was designed to increase low-income noncustodial parents' earnings and ability to pay child support. The program, which was administered in seven sites around the country, drew its clientele primarily from fathers who were divorced and unemployed, had fallen behind in their child support payments, and were disconnected from their children. Most of the men who participated in the program were ordered to do so in lieu of going to jail; therefore, their enrollment likely reflects their desire to avoid incarceration more than any intrinsic motivation to improve their labor market prospects and family relationships.

Evaluation of the program highlighted the difficulty and complexity of improving labor market outcomes for low-income men and the fact that child support and welfare programs are not adequately equipped to meet the needs of poor fathers (Johnson, Levine, & Doolittle, 1999). Although the PFS program did not increase earnings and employment for participants overall, it was able to increase earnings for men with greater barriers to employment such as low education and limited previous work experience (Martinez & Miller, 2000). In addition, the program increased the proportion of fathers who provided any formal child support and slightly increased the average support amount paid by some fathers (Knox & Redcross, 2000). PFS did not, on average, increase the frequency of noncustodial fathers' visits with their children, although some positive effects were noted in sites with particularly low initial levels of father-child contact (Knox & Redcross, 2000). The overall disappointing results from the PFS program may have been due in large part to the fact that the intervention occurred too late. The program drew its clientele from men who had *already* fallen behind in their child support obligations, who were no longer involved with the mother, and who had limited contact with their child.

More recently, numerous small-scale programs have been developed to serve divorced fathers as well as fathers in fragile families; these programs diverge in their emphases but often intend to improve both fathers' parenting skills and their employment capabilities and to increase their connection to their children (see Mincy & Pouncy, 2001, for an overview of fatherhood programs). In March 2000 the Department of Health and Human Services approved 10 new state demonstration projects to "improve the opportunities of young, unmarried fathers to support their children both financially and emotionally" (Department of Health and Human Services, 2000). These demonstration programs, which developed out of the Partners for Fragile Families (PFF) programs, sponsored by the Ford Foundation in the 1990s, focus exclusively on low-income fathers and families. Their stated objective is to encourage team parenting among unwed parents and increase the earnings capacity of low-skilled fathers. These HHS-sponsored demonstrations represent the first national effort to develop programs to meet the needs of fathers in fragile families.

Marriage Promotion Initiatives

The most recent policy initiatives affecting fragile families are programs to promote marriage. These initiatives, which are designed to improve relationship quality, are based on several different models (Garfinkel & McLanahan, in press). The first is based on a behavioral model and provides new parents with an opportunity to practice communication skills through role playing and discussion. Parents participating in this program attend workshops with other new parents to learn about and practice communication skills and ways to resolve disagreements. The curriculum for these workshops is based on a set of generic tasks, and all participants practice the same skills. An example of this approach is the PREP program developed by Howard Markman and his colleagues (Renick, Blumberg, & Markman, 1992; Stanley, Blumberg, & Markman, 1999). A second model is based on increasing intimacy and helping couples resolve their personal issues. In this program, parents meet together in small groups, under the guidance of a clinician, to discuss issues that arise around the birth of the first child. The content of these programs is partly predetermined to address issues that are common to all new parents and partly reactive to issues brought forth by the parents in the group. An example of this approach is the Parents and Partners (PAP) program developed by Cowan and Cowan (see Cowan, Powell, & Cowan, 1998). A third model provides mentoring to new parents. The idea behind this approach is to match new parents with older, more experienced couples who have strong, stable relationships and who are willing to serve as role models and confidants to new parents. In this model, new parents and mentors meet on a regular basis to discuss issues related to parenting and partnering. This model is currently being used in some churches.

Although some experimental data suggest that these programs may work, all of the experiments are based on middle-class couples (Karney & Bradbury, 1995). Indeed, there is virtually no information on whether relationship programs would increase marriage probabilities for parents in fragile families. Thus, researchers have questioned whether marriage is a viable option for some parents and whether these programmatic approaches would in fact promote marriage among this population. A large proportion of unwed parents have had children by other partners. Indeed, more than half the births in the Fragile Families study were to couples with children from other relationships. In these families, the question arises, who should marry whom

(Mincy, 2002)? More important, some fathers are violent and abusive toward their partners: As noted earlier, about 8% of mothers in the Fragile Families survey reported being seriously hurt by the fathers of their children in the first year following the non-marital birth. Arguably, none of these fathers are good candidates for a healthy marriage. Yet nearly all unwed mothers said they wanted the father involved with raising the child, including mothers who reported that their partners were violent. Thus, providing services to couples who are in a relationship may have beneficial effects in terms of improving parents' relationships and ability to cooperate in raising their child.

Data from the Fragile Families study suggest that programs targeted toward fathers or couples may have a positive effect *if* they are targeted on the right parents and if they are timed correctly. Practitioners who run employment programs for disadvantaged men say that motivation is important in determining whether these men can sustain their participation in these programs long enough to reap their benefits. Similarly, the Fragile Families data suggest that new parents are highly motivated toward marriage and family formation and would likely take advantage of the services that programs may provide. Starting at the time of a new birth may provide greater momentum for strengthening fathers' capabilities and couples' relationships, given the optimism that unmarried couples have about their future at that time.

In sum, while marriage promotion initiatives have considerable promise, and while the Fragile Families study suggests that new unmarried parents may be especially responsive to such initiatives, the promise of these problems needs to be tested through demonstrations with random assignment.

CONCLUSIONS

In this chapter we described the characteristics and family relationships of fathers in fragile families, which we define as unmarried parents who are raising their child together. We find that unmarried fathers differ notably from their counterparts who are married at the time of their child's birth, particularly in terms of their human capital and fertility histories. Most unmarried fathers have a high school education or less; one fifth are not working at the time of their baby's birth; and nearly one third have children by another partner. These factors suggest that fathers will face serious challenges in providing for their children and maintaining stable family relationships over time.

Most unmarried fathers are romantically involved with their baby's mother at the time of the birth, and most have high expectations for marrying the mother in the future. However, fewer than 10% of unmarried couples have actually married by the time their child is 1 year old. Similarly, most unmarried fathers say they intend to be involved with their children over time. Yet one year later, just over half see their children on a daily basis, and one fifth have only minimal contact.

This descriptive portrait of fathers in fragile families points to both opportunities as well as challenges for policy makers interested in strengthening family ties. Contrary to popular perception that unmarried parents are not interested in family commitment, most unmarried fathers say that they value marriage, expect to marry the baby's mother, and want to be involved in rearing their children. These hopes and positive attitudes provide an encouraging starting point from which policy could help unmarried parents strengthen their family relationships. At the same time, many unmarried parents face an uncertain economic future and complex family arrangements, which make it difficult to sustain a stable family. Thus, if these fragile families are to meet their goal of raising their child together, they will likely need both public and private support.

Insofar as most individuals believe that children would be better off if they were being raised by both biological parents, and insofar as most parents in fragile families want to marry, a restructuring of social policy to strengthen fragile families would appear to have wide bipartisan support. Indeed, there is a growing emphasis in policy making of funding programs that address exactly these aims. Of course, new initiatives to promote marriage and father involvement do not exist in a vacuum, and their success will depend in large part on how they interact with welfare and CSE policies. Ultimately, we contend that the most effective strategy for helping unmarried parents would involve a multifaceted approach that focuses on both improving parents' human capital and relationship skills while also eliminating any disincentives in our tax and transfer policies.

REFERENCES

Amato, P. R., & Rogers, S. J. (1997). A longitudinal study of marital problems and subsequent divorce. *Journal of Marriage and the Family, 59*, 612–624.

Anderson, E. (1989). Sex codes and family life among poor inner city youths. *Annals of the American Academy of Political and Social Science, 501*, 59–78.

Becker, G. (1991). *A treatise on the family.* Cambridge, MA: Harvard University Press.

Booth, A., Johnson, D. R., White, L., & Edwards, J. N. (1985). Predicting divorce and permanent separation. *Journal of Family Issues, 6*, 331–355.

Bumpass, L. L., & Lu, L. (2000). Trends in cohabitation and implications for children's family contexts in the United States. *Population Studies, 54*, 29–41.

Cabrera, N. J., & Evans, V. J. (2000). Whither fathers in welfare reform. *Poverty Research News, 4*, 3–5.

Cabrera, N. J., Tamis-LeMonda, C. S., Bradley, R. H., Hofferth, S., & Lamb, M. E. (2000). Fatherhood in the twenty-first century. *Child Development, 71*, 127–136.

Carlson, M., & McLanahan, S. (2002). *Do good partners make good parents?* Center for Research on Child Wellbeing, Working Paper No. 2002-16-FF.

Carlson, M., & McLanahan, S. (in press). Early father involvement in fragile families. In R. Day & M. Lamb (Eds.), *Conceptualizing and measuring father involvement.* Mahwah, NJ: Erlbaum.

Carlson, M., McLanahan, S., & England, P. (2002). *Union formation and dissolution in fragile families.* Center for Research on Child Wellbeing, Working Paper No. 2001-06-FF.

Case, A. (1998). The effects of stronger child support enforcement on nonmarital fertility. In Garfinkel, McLanahan, Meyer, & Seltzer (Eds.), *Fathers under fire: The revolution in child support enforcement* (pp. 67–93). New York: Russell Sage Foundation.

Case, A., Lin, I., & McLanahan, S. (in press). Understanding child support trends: Economic, demographic, and political contributions. *Demography.*

Chambers, D. L. (1979). *Making fathers pay.* Chicago: University of Chicago Press.

Cherlin, A. (1992). *Marriage, divorce and remarriage.* Cambridge, MA: Harvard University Press.

Cherlin, A., & Furstenberg, F. (1991). *Divided families.* Cambridge, MA: Harvard University Press.

Clarkberg, M. (1999). The price of partnering: The role of economic well-being in young adults' first union experiences. *Social Forces, 77*, 945–968.

Clarkberg, M., Stolzenberg, R., & Waite, L. (1995). Attitudes, values, and the entrance into co-habitational unions. *Social Forces, 74,* 609–634.

Cowan, P. A., Cowan, C. P., Schulz, M. S., & Heming, G. (1994). Prebirth to preschool family factors in children's adaptation to kindergarten. In Parke & Kellam (Eds.), *Exploring family relationships with other social contexts* (pp. 75–114). Hillsdale, NJ: Erlbaum.

Cowan, P. A., Powell, D., & Cowan, C. P. (1998). Parenting interventions: A family systems perspective. In W. Damon (Ed.), *Handbook of child psychology* (Vol. 5). New York: Wiley.

Department of Health and Human Services. (2000, March 29). *HHS awards child support waivers to help promote responsible fatherhood* [Press release]. Hyattsville, MD: Author.

Edin, K. (1994). *Single mothers and absent fathers: The possibilities and limits of child support policy.* Working Paper, Center for Urban Policy Research, Rutgers University.

Edin, K. (1997). *Why don't poor fathers and mothers get married?* Paper presented at the Urban Poverty Workshop, University of Chicago.

Edin, K., & Lein, L. (1997). *Making ends meet: How single mothers survive welfare and low-wage work.* New York: Russell Sage Foundation.

Ellwood, D., & Jencks, C. (2002). *The growing differences in family structure: What do we know? Where do we look for answers?* Unpublished Working Paper, J. F. Kennedy School of Government.

Federal Interagency Forum on Child and Family Statistics. (1998). *Nurturing fatherhood: Improving data and research on male fertility, family formation, and fatherhood.*

Furstenberg, F., Morgan, P., & Allison, P. (1987). Paternal participation and children's wellbeing after marital dissolution. *American Sociological Review, 52,* 695–701.

Furstenberg, F., Sherwood, K., & Sullivan, M. (1992). *Caring and paying: What fathers and mothers say about child support.* New York: Manpower Demonstration Research Corporation.

Garfinkel, I., Gaylin, D., McLanahan, S., & Huang, C. (2000). *The roles of child support enforcement and welfare in nonmarital childbearing.* Center for Research on Child Wellbeing Working Paper No. 2000-06.

Garfinkel, I., & McLanahan, S. (in press). Strengthening fragile families. In I. Sawhill (Ed.), *Breaking the cycle: Nine ideas for improving children's futures.* Washington, DC: Brookings Institute.

Garfinkel, I., McLanahan, S., & Hanson, T. (1998). A patchwork portrait of nonresident fathers. In Garfinkel, McLanahan, Meyer, & Seltzer (Eds.), *Fathers under fire: The revolution in child support enforcement* (pp. 31–60). New York: Russell Sage Foundation.

Garfinkel, I., McLanahan, S., & Robins, P. (Eds.). (1994). *Child support and child well-being.* Washington, DC: Urban Institute.

Gibson, C., Edin, K., & McLanahan, S. (2002). *High hopes but even higher expectations: The retreat from marriage among low-income parents.* Mimeo.

Gottman, J. M. (1994). *What predicts divorce? The relationship between marital processes and marital outcomes.* Hillsdale, NJ: Erlbaum.

Greene, A. D., Emig, C., & Hearn, G. (1996, May). *A summary of the town meeting on fathering and male fertility, March 27, 1996.* Prepared for the NICHD Family and Child Well-Being Research Network.

Hoffman, S., & Duncan, G. (1995). The effect of incomes, wages and AFDC benefits on marital disruption. *Journal of Human Resources, 30,* 19–41.

Johnson, E., Levine, A., & Doolittle, F. (1999). *Fathers' fair share: Helping poor men manage child support and fatherhood.* New York: Russell Sage Foundation.

Karney, B. R., & Bradbury, T. N. (1995). The longitudinal course of marital quality and stability: A review of theory, method, and research. *Psychological Bulletin, 118,* 3–34.

Knox, V., Miller, C., & Gennetian, L. A. (2000). *Reforming welfare and rewarding work: A summary* of the final report on the Minnesota family investment program. New York: Manpower Demonstration Research Corporation.

Knox, V., & Redcross, C. (2000). *Parenting and providing: The impact of parents' fair share on paternal involvement.* New York: Manpower Demonstration Research Corporation.

Krause, H. D. (1989). Child support reassessed: Limits of private responsibility and the public interest. *University of Illinois Law Review, 9*(2), 367–398.

Kurtz, D. (1995). *For richer, for poorer: Mothers confront divorce.* New York: Routledge Press.

Lamb, M. E. (Ed.). (1997). *The role of the father in child development.* New York: Wiley.

Lerman, R., & Sorenson, E. (1996). Father involvement with their nonmarital children: Patterns, determinants, and effects on their earnings. *Marriage and Family Review, 29,* 75–95.

Lichter, D., McLaughlin, G. K., & Landry, D. J. (1992). Race and the retreat from marriage: A shortage of marriageable men? *American Sociological Review, 57,* 781–799.

Liebow, E. (1967). *Tally's corner: A study of Negro streetcorner men.* Boston: Little, Brown, and Company.

Marsiglio, W. (1993). Contemporary scholarship on fatherhood: Culture, identity, and conduct. *Journal of Family Issues, 14,* 484–509.

Marsiglio, W., Amato, P., Day, R., & Lamb, M. (2000). Scholarship on fatherhood in the 1990s and beyond. *Journal of Marriage and Family, 62,* 1173–1191.

Marsiglio, W., & Day, R. (1997). *Social fatherhood and paternal involvement: Conceptual, data, and policymaking issues.* Presented at the NICHD-sponsored Conference on Fathering and Male Fertility: Improving Data and Research.

Marsiglio, W., Day, R., & Lamb, M. (2000). Exploring fatherhood diversity: Implications for conceptualizing father involvement. *Marriage and Family Review, 29,* 269–293.

Martinez, J., & Miller, C. (2000). *Working and earning: The impact of parents' fair share on low-income fathers' employment.* New York: Manpower Demonstration Research Corporation.

McLanahan, S., Garfinkel, I., Brooks-Gunn, J., & Zhao, H. (1997). *Fragile families.* Unpublished manuscript.

McLanahan, S., Garfinkel, I., Reichman, N., & Teitler, J. (2001). Unwed parents or fragile families? In Wu & Wolve (Eds.), *Out of wedlock: Trends, causes, and consequences of nonmarital fertility* (pp. 202–228). New York: Russell Sage Foundation.

McLanahan, S., & Sandefur, G. (1994). *Growing up with a single parent: What hurts, what helps.* Cambridge, MA: Harvard University Press.

Mincy, R. B. (2002). *Who should marry whom? Multiple partner fertility among new parents.* Center for Research on Child Wellbeing, Working Paper No. 2002-03-FF.

Mincy, R. B., & DuPree, A. T. (2000). *Can the next step in welfare reform achieve PRWORA's fourth goal? Family formation in fragile families.* Center for Research on Child Wellbeing, Working Paper No. 2000-23-FF.

Mincy, R. B., & Pouncy, H. W. (2001). The responsible fatherhood movement: Evolution and goals. In Tamis-LeMonda & Cabrera (Eds.), *Handbook of father involvement: Multidisciplinary perspectives.* Mahwah, NJ: Erlbaum.

Moffitt, R. A. (1998). The effect of welfare on marriage and fertility. In Moffitt (Ed.), *Welfare, the family, and reproductive behavior* (pp. 50–97). Washington, DC: National Academy Press.

Nepomnyashchy, L., Garfinkel, I., & Mincy, R. (2002, November 7–9). *Child support and father-child contact in fragile families.* Paper presented at the annual meetings of the Association for Public Policy Analysis and Management, Dallas, TX.

Nixon, L. (1997). The effect of child support enforcement on marital dissolution. *Journal of Human Resources, 32,* 159–181.

Nock, S. L. (1995). A comparison of marriages and cohabiting relationships. *Journal of Family Issues, 16,* 53–76.

Nock, S. L. (1998). *Marriage in men's lives.* New York: Oxford University Press.

Parke, R. D. (1990). In search of fathers. In Sigel & Brody (Eds.), *Methods of family research: Normal families.* Hillsdale, NJ: Erlbaum.

Parke, R. D. (1995). Fathers and families. In Bornstein (Ed.), *Handbook of parenting: Vol. 3. Status and social conditions of parenting.* Mahwah, NJ: Erlbaum.

Rendall, M. S., Clarke, L., Peters, H. E., Ranjit, N., & Verroponlou, G. (1997). *Incomplete reporting of male fertility in the United States and Britain.* Paper presented at the Annual Meeting of the Population Association of America, Washington, DC.

Renick, M. J., Blumberg, S. L., & Markman, H. J. (1992). The Prevention and Relationship Enhancement Program (PREP): An empirically-based preventive intervention program for couples. *Family Relations, 41,* 141–147.

Report to Congress on out-of-wedlock childbearing. (1995). Hyattsville, MD: U.S. Government Printing Office.

Rich, L. (2001). Regular and irregular earnings of unwed fathers: Implications for child support practice. *Children and Youth Services Review, 23,* 353–376.

Sanchez, L., & Gager, C. (2000). Hard living, perceived entitlement to a great marriage and marital dissolution. *Journal of Marriage and the Family, 62,* 708–722.

Sayer, L. C., & Bianchi, S. M. (2000). Women's economic independence and the probability of divorce. *Journal of Family Issues, 21,* 906–943.

Schoen, R., & Weinick, R. M. (1993). Partner choice in marriages and cohabitations. *Journal of Marriage and the Family, 55,* 408–414.

Seltzer, J. A. (1994). Consequences of marital dissolution for children. *Annual Review of Sociology, 20,* 235–266.

Seltzer, J. A., McLanahan, S., & Hanson, T. L. (1998). Will child support enforcement increase father-child contact and parental conflict after separation? In Garfinkel, McLanahan, Meyer, & Seltzer (Eds.), *Fathers under fire: The revolution in child support enforcement* (pp. 157–190). New York: Russell Sage Foundation.

Shiono, P. H., & Quinn, L. S. (1994). Epidemiology of divorce. *Future of Children, 4,* 15–28.

Smock, P. (2000). Cohabitation in the United States: An appraisal of research themes, findings, and implications. *Annual Review of Sociology, 26,* 1–20.

Smock, P., & Manning, W. (1997). Cohabiting partners' economic circumstances and marriage. *Demography, 34,* 331–341.

Sorensen, E. (1995). *Noncustodial fathers: Can they afford to pay more child support?* Washington, DC: Urban Institute.

Sorensen, E. (1999). *Obligating dads: Helping low-income noncustodial fathers do more for their children.* Washington, DC: Urban Institute.

Sorenson, E., & Turner, M. (1996). Barriers in child support policy: A review of the literature. Prepared for the System Barriers Roundtable, sponsored by the National Center of Fathers and Families, Philadelphia.

South, S., & Lloyd, K. (1995). Marriage markets and nonmarital fertility in the United States. *Demography, 29,* 247–264.

Stack, C. B. (1974). *All our kin: Strategies for survival in a Black community.* New York: Harper and Row.

Stanley, S. M., Blumberg, S. L., & Markman, H. J. (1999). Helping couples fight for their marriages: The PREP approach. In R. Berger & M. T. Hannah (Eds.), *Preventive approaches in couples therapy* (pp. 279–293). Philadelphia: Brunner/Mazel.

Thornton, A., Axinn, W. G., & Hill, D. H. (1992). Reciprocal effects of religiosity, cohabitation, and marriage. *American Journal of Sociology, 98,* 628–651.

Ventura, S. J., & Bachrach, C. A. (2000). Nonmarital childbearing in the United States, 1940–1999. *National Vital Statistics Reports, 48*(16). Hyattsville, MD: National Center for Health Statistics.

Ventura, S. J., Bachrach, C. A., Hill, L., et al. (1995). The demography of out-of-wedlock childbearing. In *Report to Congress on out-of-wedlock childbearing.* Hyattsville, MD: U.S. Government Printing Office.

Waite, L., & Gallagher, M. (2000). *The case for marriage: Why married people are happier, healthier, and better off financially.* New York: Doubleday.

Waller, M. (1997). *Redefining fatherhood: Paternal involvement, masculinity, and responsibility in the other America.* Doctoral dissertation, Princeton University, New Jersey.

Waller, M., & Plotnick, R. (2001). Effective child support policy for low-income families: Evidence from street level research. *Journal of Public Policy Analysis and Management, 20,* 89–110.

Western, B. (2000). *The impact of incarceration on earnings and inequality.* Paper presented at the Annual Meeting of the American Sociological Association, Washington, DC.

Western, B., Lopoo, L., & McLanahan, S. (2002). *Incarceration and the bonds among parents in fragile families.* Mimeo.

Western, B., & McLanahan, S. (2001). Fathers behind bars: The impact of incarceration on family formation. *Contemporary Perspectives in Family Research, 2,* 309–324.

White, L. K. (1990). Determinants of divorce: A review of research in the eighties. *Journal of Marriage and the Family, 52,* 904–912.

Willis, R. (1996). *Father involvement: Theoretical perspectives from economics.* Paper presented at Conference on Father's Involvement, NICHD Family and Child Well-Being Network, Bethesda, MD.

Wilson, M., & Brooks-Gunn, J. (2001). Health status and behaviors of unwed fathers. *Children and Youth Services Review, 23,* 377–401.

Wilson, W. J. (1987). *The truly disadvantaged: The inner city, the underclass, and public policy.* Chicago: University of Chicago Press.

CHAPTER 14

Gay Fathers

CHARLOTTE J. PATTERSON

T HE CONCEPTS OF heterosexuality and parenthood are intertwined so deeply in cultural history and in contemporary thought that, at first glance, the idea of gay fatherhood can seem surprising or even exotic. Undeniably, however, some men identify themselves as gay fathers. Most of these men have been able to avoid media attention, but some have become the subjects of intense public discussion and controversy (Campbell, 1994; Ricks, 1995). For instance, Steve Lofton and Roger Croteau, a gay couple, are foster parents to five children. One of their children is a 10-year-old named Bert, who has lived with Lofton and Croteau since he was a baby, and whom the men want to adopt (Darst, 2002). However, Florida law prohibits adoption of minor children by gay adults and requires that, if possible, permanent adoptive homes be found for foster children. Thus, state officials have begun the process of identifying heterosexual prospective adoptive parents for Bert, even though he wishes to remain with Lofton and Croteau. At the time of this writing, Lofton and Croteau's challenge to the antigay adoption statute is pending in federal court (ACLU Lesbian and Gay Rights Project, 2002). Meanwhile, the case drew considerable media attention when the television personality Rosie O'Donnell came out as a lesbian adoptive parent and spoke in public on behalf of the Lofton-Croteau family (Darst, 2002). Even though this is by no means the first case of its kind (Appell, 2001; Patterson, Fulcher, & Wainright, 2002; Patterson & Redding, 1996; Perrin & the Committee on Psychosocial Aspects of Child and Family Health, 2002; Ricks, 1995; Seligmann, 1990), the publicity surrounding the Lofton-Croteau case has brought more attention to the issue of gay parenting than ever before.

In the wake of such high-profile cases, a number of questions about gay fatherhood have emerged ever more clearly into public awareness. Who are gay fathers, and how do they become parents? What kinds of parents do gay men make, and how do their children develop? What special challenges and stresses do gay fathers and their children face in daily life, and how do they cope with them? And what can acquaintance with gay fathers and their children offer to the understanding of parenthood, child development, and family life more generally? Although the research literatures bearing on such questions are still relatively new, existing studies do allow us to begin consideration of some relevant issues raised by the existence of gay fathers.

This chapter reviews the social science literature on gay fathers and their children. The chapter begins by considering sources of heterogeneity among gay fathers and examining estimates about the prevalence of gay fatherhood in the United States today. The chapter then summarizes the results of research on gay fathers, both as individuals and in their roles as parents. Finally, findings from studies of the offspring of gay fathers are considered, and the relevance of such findings to popular stereotypes is explored. Research on these issues is just beginning to emerge, and much remains to be done; accordingly, the chapter ends with a discussion of directions for future research on gay fathers and their families.

WHO ARE GAY FATHERS, AND HOW DO THEY BECOME PARENTS?

Gay fathers are a varied group. In addition to diversity engendered by age, education, race, ethnicity, and other demographic factors, some of the issues specific to gay fathers also create important distinctions among them and among their families. To illustrate the diversity of gay father families, I begin by considering some of the ways in which a man might become a gay father. I then consider some of the ambiguities that arise in deciding whether a particular man should be considered a gay father. Finally, I discuss estimates of the prevalence of gay fatherhood in the United States today.

DIVERSITY AMONG GAY FATHERS

Most gay fathers are probably divorced (Barrett & Tasker, 2001; Bozett, 1982, 1989; Green & Bozett, 1991). For instance, in a recent study of gay fathers in the United Kingdom, most reported being either separated or divorced from a female partner (Barrett & Tasker, 2001). Such gay men had entered into a heterosexual marriage and had children before declaring a public gay identity. After coming out, these men may say that they got married because they loved their wives, because they wanted children, because they wanted a domestic, married life, or because there were social and cultural pressures to marry. Some men report that they married even though they knew that they were attracted to other men, sometimes in the hope that marriage would dispel such desires. Other men explain that they were not fully aware of their sexual desires for other men until well into their marriages. Although a few men remain married after coming out, most separate from their wives and eventually divorce (Bozett, 1982, 1989).

When couples divorce after a husband comes out as gay, custody of children is likely to be granted to the wife (ACLU Lesbian and Gay Rights Project, 2002; Barrett & Tasker, 2001; Logue, 2001; Patterson et al., 2002). If the courts have biases about which parent should be given custody of minor children, they are likely to favor mothers over fathers and heterosexual over homosexual parents (Thompson, 1983). Together, these two factors usually combine to ensure that primary physical custody of children goes to the mother in such cases. Thus, the largest group of divorced gay fathers are nonresidential parents (Barrett & Tasker, 2001; Strader, 1993). Visitation arrangements may vary across a wide range of possibilities. One divorced gay father's children may visit with him every other weekend (Fadiman, 1983), whereas another man's children may visit only rarely and be forbidden to stay in his home overnight (Campbell, 1994). A divorced gay father without primary custody is likely to encounter issues related to grieving the loss of daily contact with his children while adjusting to his new life as a gay man.

A smaller group of divorced gay fathers have custody of their children and act as their primary caregivers (Barrett & Tasker, 2001). Although heterosexual mothers tend to be preferred custodians in the eyes of the judiciary (ACLU Lesbian and Gay Rights Project, 2002; Editors of the Harvard Law Review, 1990; Logue, 2001; Rivera, 1991), extenuating circumstances may place one or more children in the father's custody. In one family, the mother felt that she could care for two of the couple's three children but believed that bearing responsibility as a single parent for the third, a 10-year-old who had been diagnosed with Down syndrome and mental retardation, would overwhelm her; this family agreed that the gay father would take custody of the 10-year-old (Fadiman, 1983). In another instance, a mother's serious illness precluded her taking custody of the couple's child during a period of chemotherapy (*Roe v. Roe,* 1985). In other cases, divorcing parents choose joint custody arrangements, so that children live part of the time in each parent's household. Divorced gay fathers with primary or partial custody of their child or children may need time to adjust to being a primary caregiver for children, often as a single parent, while also striving to accommodate to their new social circumstances as gay men.

Another group of gay fathers have become foster or adoptive parents after coming out as gay (Patterson et al., 2002; Perrin et al., 2002). At this writing, one state (Florida) forbids adoption of minor children by gay or lesbian individuals, and two (Mississippi and Utah) bar adoption by same-sex couples (ACLU Lesbian and Gay Rights Project, 2002). Foster placements with and adoptions by gay adults have taken place in many states, including California, Connecticut, Illinois, Massachusetts, New Jersey, New York, Ohio, and Vermont, as well as Washington, D.C. Even in states like Virginia, where sodomy laws and other antigay statutes are still on the books, gay men have adopted children without their sexual orientation becoming a topic of public discussion (Appell, 2001). In a recent survey of adoption agencies in the United States, many reported willingness to work with openly gay prospective adoptive parents, and many reported having completed such adoptions (Brodzinsky, Patterson, & Vaziri, 2002).

Foster or adoptive placements may involve children who are biological relatives of the adoptive father, or they may involve unrelated children (Patterson, 1995a; Patterson et al., 2002). Gay men have also legally adopted the biological children of their gay partners (Patterson, 1995a; Seligmann, 1990). Because of antigay prejudices in adoption and foster care circles as well as in the courts, gay men have often had to fight for the right to adopt or to become foster parents (Ricketts, 1991), with cases sometimes remaining in the courts for years (Appell, 2001; Patterson, 1995a); others who have been given the opportunity to become foster or adoptive parents have been offered only children who are considered difficult to place due to age, mixed ethnicity, illness, or disability. Gay foster and adoptive families may thus include older children of mixed racial backgrounds, those with illnesses or disabilities, and sibling groups. A number of gay men have also completed interracial and international adoptions (Martin, 1993). Foster and adoptive gay families themselves are thus a very diverse group.

Another way in which gay men have become parents is by fathering biological children with surrogate mothers (Martin, 1993; McPherson, 1993; Sbordone, 1993). For instance, a gay couple might make a contract with a woman to bear a child or children conceived using the sperm of one member of the couple. Upon the child's birth, the woman legally relinquishes parental rights and responsibilities, and the biological father becomes the sole legal parent. The child is then reared by the two men (McPherson, 1993; Sbordone, 1993) and may eventually be adopted by the nonbiological father (e.g., In re W. S. D., 1992).

Yet another route to parenthood taken by some gay men is to conceive and raise children jointly with a woman or women with whom the men are not sexually involved (Martin, 1993; Van Gelder, 1991). In one common scenario, a gay couple and a lesbian couple might undertake parenthood together, with sperm from one of the men being used to inseminate one of the women. In an arrangement sometimes called *quadra-parenting,* the child or children might spend part of the time in one home and part of the time in the other. Of course, gay men can undertake such arrangements with women who are heterosexual as well as lesbian or who are single as well as in relationships with partners. The details of child custody and visitation may also vary considerably from family to family, as well as over time. Contrary to stereotypes about children growing up in gay households, children in such circumstances may grow up from birth not only with two fathers but also with two mothers and two homes (Van Gelder, 1991).

There is thus considerable diversity among gay fathers and among their families. Despite the variety of family forms just described, however, there is little question about whether each of the children in such families has a gay father. In other instances, however, it can be much less clear whether a particular man should be regarded as a gay father. In these cases, the dispute can revolve around the definitions of *gay* or of *father;* in what follows, each type of dispute is considered briefly.

One ambiguity in the definition of the term *gay father* involves the term *gay.* Many men who have sexual relations with other men do not identify themselves as gay (Matteson, 1987; Ross, 1978, 1983). In a pioneering study of same-sex sexual behavior, the majority of men engaging in same-sex sexual behavior in public meeting places were married and did not regard themselves as gay or homosexual (Humphreys, 1975). In other cases, men in confined settings such as jails or prisons have sex with other men but do not define themselves as gay or homosexual. If such men have children, should they be regarded as gay fathers, regardless of their self-identification as heterosexual? Although it may be useful for purposes of public health planning to consider the behavior of such men, for purposes of this chapter, use of the term *gay* is limited to those who identify themselves as gay (or queer). For purposes of the present discussion, we thus regard *gayness* neither as a fantasy nor as an activity, but as an *identity* acknowledged at least to the self and often to others, as well. Even while acknowledging the possibilities of changes in identities over time, men are referred to as gay in this chapter only when they identify themselves in this way.

Another of the ambiguities surrounding definitions of gay fatherhood involves the degree to which genetic linkages should be regarded as central in establishing parenthood. In the context of lesbian and gay families, one issue concerns the status of sperm donors. Is a gay male sperm donor properly considered as the father of children who may be conceived through donor insemination using his sperm? In some states, when donor insemination is supervised by a medical doctor, and unless the sperm donor is the recipient's husband, the sperm donor is legally considered to have relinquished both parental rights (e.g., to child custody) and parental responsibilities (e.g., to provide economic support for the child). In some instances, however, a gay male sperm donor may be known to the prospective mother, or the insemination may not be supervised by a physician. Sperm donors who set out to be anonymous may eventually become known to the child and to the mother. In some cases, sperm donors have sought greater contact with the child or legal standing as a parent. For example, in a New York case, a gay sperm donor was granted legal standing as a child's father even though the child was 13 years old and had never lived in the man's household (Dunlap, 1994). Without attempting to resolve such disputes, discussion in this chapter is focused primarily on the participants in existing research—namely, on previously married fathers who are genetically related to their offspring and on those who adopted children after acknowledging a gay identity.

Another way in which ambiguities in the definition of parenthood may arise in gay families concerns the status of a gay father's partner. Regardless of how a gay man became a parent, he may begin a relationship with a gay partner after children are already a part of his life; what, then, is the role of the new partner, vis-à-vis the children? Some have argued that the issues of gay partners are similar in many respects to those of heterosexual stepparents (Baptiste, 1987; Crosbie-Burnett & Helmbrecht, 1993). A gay partner who moved in when a child was 12 months old and who lives in the household throughout the childhood years is probably more likely to be regarded as a parent figure than is one who joins the household when a youngster is already an adolescent. Although the first man would be more likely than the second to be considered a parent by the child and by other members of the family, neither would be likely to be granted parental standing by the courts (ACLU Lesbian and Gay Rights Project, 2002). Thus, legal and psychological definitions of parenthood may often be at odds with one another in gay and lesbian families.

PREVALENCE OF GAY FATHERHOOD

In light of the diversity of gay parenthood, it is easy to appreciate the difficulties of providing accurate estimates of the numbers of gay fathers in the United States today. In response to widespread prejudice and discrimination, many gay and lesbian individuals believe that they must conceal their sexual identities in many environments. This is especially true of gay fathers and lesbian mothers, who may fear that child custody and visitation will be curtailed or even terminated if their sexual identities become known (e.g., Campbell, 1994). For these and other reasons, many gay fathers attempt to conceal their gay identities, sometimes even from their own children (Dunne, 1987; Robinson & Barret, 1986), making an accurate count of their numbers difficult to obtain.

Recent attempts to estimate the numbers of gay fathers and lesbian mothers have drawn on representative and near-representative samples of American adults, for which information about sexual orientation and parenting status have been collected (e.g., Badgett, 1998; Patterson & Friel, 2000). For example, using the most conservative estimates from the National Health and Social Life Study (Laumann, Gagnon, Michael, & Michaels, 1994), Patterson and Friel (2000) estimated the number of lesbian and gay parents in the United States at just under one million. This estimate included only those parents who reported having children who were genetically related to them. Thus, it may be an underestimate of the true numbers, in part because it does not include adoptive, foster, or other parents who are not genetically linked with their children. Other recent estimates have run higher (e.g., Badgett, 1998) or lower (ACLU Lesbian and Gay Rights Project, 2002), and no clear consensus has emerged.

Another reason why it is difficult to make accurate estimates of the numbers of gay parents is that the numbers show signs of changing over time. For instance, in one survey of gay couples (Bryant & Demian, 1994), one third of respondents under the age of 35 were either planning to have children or considering the idea of having children. In another study, a majority of gay men who were not fathers said that they would like to rear a child, and those who said they wanted children were, on average, younger than those who did not (Sbordone, 1993). Secular trends may influence both the prevalence of gay fatherhood and characteristics of gay fathers, making any numerical estimates unstable at best.

Gay fathers are thus a diverse group whose circumstances and experiences vary in many respects. Some have been married and become fathers in the context of heterosexual marriages that ended in divorce, whereas others were never heterosexually married and have become fathers only after assuming gay identities. Some are the primary caregivers for children who live with them on a full-time basis, whereas others are nonresidential parents. Some gay fathers conceal their sexual identities in public to avoid possible discrimination against them or against their children, whereas others are entirely open about their identities. There are also some areas of controversy about which men should or should not be counted as gay or as fathers. For all these reasons, the reliability of estimates of the numbers of gay fathers in the United States today remains unknown. Whatever the correct estimates may be, however, it is clear that the numbers of gay fathers are substantial and that their visibility is on the rise (Patterson, 2002).

GAY FATHERS AS PARENTS

In this section the available social science research on gay fathers is reviewed, considering descriptive material on gay fathers themselves as well as comparisons between gay fathers and heterosexual fathers, between gay fathers and gay men who are not fathers, and between gay and lesbian parents. Research on divorced gay fathers is discussed first, then studies relevant to gay men who have become fathers after assuming gay identities. Other reviews of this literature can be found in Armesto (2002), Barret and Robinson (1990, 1994), Barrett and Tasker (2001), Bozett (1980, 1989), Patterson (1992, 1997, 2000, 2002), Perrin et al. (2002), and Stacey and Biblarz (2001).

Despite the diversity of gay fatherhood, research to date has with some exceptions been conducted with relatively homogeneous groups of participants. Samples of gay fathers have been mainly Caucasian, well-educated, affluent, and living in major urban centers. Although the available evidence suggests that self-identified gay men are much more likely to live in large cities than elsewhere (e.g., Laumann et al., 1994), the representativeness of the samples of gay fathers studied to date cannot be established. Most research has been cross-sectional in nature and has involved information provided through interviews and questionnaires by gay fathers themselves. Although valuable information has been collected in this way, the degree to which data from observational and other methodologies would converge with existing results is not known. Caution in the interpretation of findings from research in this new area of work is thus required.

DIVORCED GAY FATHERS

Research on gay fathers was initiated by two investigators, one in Canada (Miller, 1979) and one in the United States (Bozett, 1980, 1981a, 1981b, 1987), and focused on concerns about gay father identities and their transformations over time. Both Miller and Bozett sought to provide conceptualizations of the steps through which a man who considers himself to be a heterosexual father may begin to identify himself, in public as well as in private, as a gay father. Based on extensive interviews with gay fathers, these authors emphasized the centrality of identity disclosure and of the reactions to disclosure by significant people in a man's life in the process of identity acquisition. Bozett argued that by disclosing his status as a gay man to those in the heterosexual world, by disclosing his status as a father to members of the gay community, and by receiving validating responses from significant others, a gay father is gradually able to integrate these previously separate aspects of his identity.

Miller's (1979) conceptualization of the acquisition of gay father identities, based on his interviews with 50 gay fathers, consists of a four-step model. In the first step, a married man who desires sexual contact with other men engages in *covert behavior,* seeking secretive and frequently anonymous sexual encounters with men, often employing excuses such as drunkenness to explain away his behavior (Ortiz & Scott, 1994). A man engaging in covert behavior of this kind is likely, according to Miller, to see his children and family life as duties and not to see life as a gay man as a viable option.

In Miller's next step, a man may have *marginal involvement* in the gay community. Although the man continues to live with his wife and children and generally presents himself in public as heterosexual, he may have occasional contact with gay men, either sexually or in gay community meeting places or organizations. At this point, a man is likely to feel guilty about his growing need to conceal important aspects of his identity from his wife and children, perhaps compensating by showering them with gifts. A man may begin to think about living separately from his wife and children during this period.

In the third step of Miller's model, *transformed participation,* a man begins to assume a gay identity for the first time. Many move away from their wives and children and begin to disclose their sexual orientation to people outside the family. It is at this stage, Miller argues, that men begin to worry about possible interventions by the courts into their relationships with their children, as well as about the possibility that the legal system may curtail or deny their visitation with their children. With the demise of pretense, however, many men feel better, have heightened self-esteem, and experience more favorable mental health.

The fourth and final step in Miller's model is called *open endorsement.* At this point, gay fathers have solidified their identities as gay men and are often working for various gay causes, whether professionally or in volunteer capacities. Miller describes the lives of these men as organized around gay communities, very often involving a gay partner. By this time, men have disclosed their gay identities to ex-wives and to children, and these relationships are now unencumbered by the psychological distance that was once involved in keeping secrets about their sexual orientation. Concerns mentioned by gay fathers at this point revolve around the difficulties of integrating identities as gay men and as fathers in a world that values one identity but stigmatizes the other.

Some ideas about what propels a man through the steps of acknowledging an identity as a gay father, both to himself and to others, have been proposed. Miller and Bozett concur that although a number of factors such as occupational autonomy and amount of access to gay communities may affect how rapidly a man acquires a gay identity and discloses it to others, the most important of these is likely to be the experience of falling in love with another man. It is this experience, more than any other, Miller and Bozett suggested, that is likely to lead a man to integrate the otherwise compartmentalized parts of his identity as a gay father. This hypothesis is open to empirical evaluation, but to date such research has not been reported.

The contributions of Miller and Bozett to research on gay fathers have been substantial, and Miller's model is apparently an accurate compilation of the retrospective reports of men he interviewed. On the other hand, approaches of this kind do not lend themselves easily to prospective purposes. For instance, these models do not provide predictions about which married men who engage in covert sexual relations with other men will eventually divorce and identify themselves as gay fathers. Similarly, these kinds of models do not account for diversity due to race, ethnicity, geographic locale, and other variables that may be crucial to understanding the experiences of gay fathers. They also explain little about gay fathers' actual behavior in parenting and other roles. Possible problems related to sampling and selection biases should also be acknowledged.

Research on the parenting attitudes of gay versus heterosexual divorced fathers has, however, been conducted (Barret & Robinson, 1990). Bigner and Jacobsen (1989a, 1989b, 1992) compared 33 gay and 33 heterosexual divorced fathers, each of whom had at least two children. With one exception, results showed no differences between motives for parenthood among gay and heterosexual men. The single exception was the greater likelihood of gay than heterosexual fathers to cite the higher status accorded to parents as compared with nonparents in the dominant culture as a motivation for parenthood (Bigner & Jacobsen, 1989b). The best interpretation of this finding is by no means clear. One possibility is that gay fathers were more candid and hence more likely to acknowledge that their desire for children might have been driven at least in part from self-serving motives. Another possibility is that because of the stigma associated with gay identity, gay fathers were less likely to take for granted the respect accorded to parents. Further research will be necessary in order to clarify these and other possibilities.

Bigner and Jacobsen (1989a) also asked gay and heterosexual fathers in their sample to report on their own behavior with their children. Although no differences emerged in the fathers' reports of involvement or intimacy, gay fathers reported that their behavior was characterized by greater responsiveness, more reasoning, and more limit setting than did heterosexual fathers. These reports by gay fathers of greater warmth and responsiveness, on the one hand, and greater control and limit setting, on the other, are strongly reminiscent of findings from research with heterosexual families and would seem to raise the possibility that gay fathers are more likely than their heterosexual counterparts to exhibit authoritative patterns of parenting behavior such as those described by Baumrind (1967; Baumrind & Black, 1967). Caution must be exercised, however, in the interpretation of results such as these, which stem entirely from paternal reports about their own behavior.

Similar results were, however, reported in an early study by Scallen (cited in Flaks, 1994). Scallen collected self-report information from 60 gay and heterosexual fathers, all of whom were divorced. In areas of problem solving, providing recreation for children, and encouraging children's autonomy, no differences were reported as a function of sexual orientation. In concert with Bigner and Jacobsen's (1989a) findings, gay fathers placed greater emphasis than did heterosexual fathers on paternal nurturance. At the same time, gay fathers also placed less importance upon their role as economic providers for children. Although the study thus revealed many similarities in the responses of gay and heterosexual divorced fathers, the gay fathers seemed to be somewhat less traditional in their views of the paternal role.

In addition to studies comparing gay and heterosexual fathers, a few researchers have made other comparisons. For instance, Robinson and Skeen (1982) compared sex-role orientations of gay fathers with those of gay men who were not fathers and found no differences. Similarly, Skeen and Robinson (1985) found no evidence to suggest that gay men's retrospective reports about relationships with their own parents varied as a function of whether they were parents themselves. Harris and Turner (1985/1986) compared gay fathers and lesbian mothers and reported that although gay fathers had higher incomes and were more likely to report encouraging their children to play with sex-typed toys, lesbian mothers were more likely to believe that their children received positive benefits such as increased tolerance for diversity from growing up with lesbian or gay parents. Studies like these begin to suggest a number of issues for research on gender, sexual orientation, and parenting behavior, and it is clear that there are many valuable directions that future work in this area could take.

Although little research has examined the sources of individual differences within gay father families, a study by Crosbie-Burnett and Helmbrecht (1993) is notable in this regard. These authors focused on a group of 48 gay stepfamilies (i.e., families composed of a gay father, his lover or partner, and at least one child who either lives in or visits the gay father's household). In assessing the aspects of stepfamily functioning that were associated with family happiness, Crosbie-Burnett and Helmbrecht found that, both for the gay father and the child, the best predictors of family happiness were concerned with the integration and inclusion of gay stepfathers. It is interesting, however, that integration of the stepfather did not predict his own ratings of family happiness. Another finding of interest from this study was that gay fathers reported greater openness about their sexual orientation than did their children; whereas only 4% of gay fathers reported that they were not open with heterosexual friends about being gay, fully 54% of adolescents reported that their heterosexual friends did not know about the father's sexual orientation. Thus, children were more closeted than their gay fathers about their status as members of a gay family, and they reported receiving less support from nongay friends. Given negative societal attitudes toward same-sex sexual relationships, it is not surprising that some adolescent offspring of gay fathers feel the need to monitor disclosures about their fathers' gay identities.

A more recent study of 92 gay fathers in the United Kingdom (Barrett & Tasker, 2001) found that those with cohabiting same-sex partners reported feeling less stress and more support in everyday life than did those without partners. For instance, gay men with cohabiting same-sex partners reported receiving greater emotional support and feeling fewer financial stresses than did those without partners. Partnered men also reported less difficulty in arranging housing and child care. Overall, however, gay fathers in this study described themselves as successfully meeting a variety of parenting challenges.

GAY MEN CHOOSING TO BECOME PARENTS

Although for many years gay fathers were generally assumed to have become parents only in the context of previous heterosexual relationships, both men and women are believed increasingly to be undertaking parenthood in the context of already-established lesbian and gay identities (Patterson, 2000, 2002). A sizable research literature describes the transition to parenthood among heterosexual couples (e.g., Cowan & Cowan, 1992), but studies have yet to address the transition to parenthood among gay men. Many issues that arise for heterosexual individuals are also faced by lesbians and gay men (e.g., worries about how children will affect couple relationships, economic concerns about supporting children), but gay men and lesbians must cope with additional issues because of their situation as members of stigmatized minorities.

A number of interrelated issues are often faced by gay men who wish to become parents (Martin, 1993; Patterson, 1994). For gay men in particular, who cannot themselves bear children, the sheer logistics of becoming parents can seem quite daunting. One of the first needs among prospective gay parents is for accurate, up-to-date information about how they could become parents, how their children are likely to develop, and what supports are likely to be available in the community where they live. Will they seek to father children who are genetically related to them, in a coparenting or surrogacy arrangement, or will they seek to become foster or adoptive parents, and what are the likely paths through which any of these aims can be accomplished? Gay men who are seeking to parent children who are genetically related to them are also likely to encounter various health concerns, such as medical screening of prospective birth parents and assistance with techniques for donor insemination, among others. As matters progress, a number of legal concerns about the rights and responsibilities of all parties are likely to emerge. Associated with all of these will generally be financial issues; in addition to the support of a child, auxiliary costs of medical and legal assistance can be considerable. Finally, social and emotional concerns of various kinds are also likely to be significant (Patterson, 1994).

As this overview suggests, numerous questions are posed by the emergence of prospective gay parents (Patterson, 1994). What are the factors that influence gay men's inclinations to make parenthood a part of their lives? What impact does parenting have on gay men who undertake it, and how do the effects compare with those experienced by heterosexuals? How effectively do special services such as support groups serve the needs of the gay fathers and prospective gay fathers for whom they were designed? What are the elements of a social climate that is supportive for gay and lesbian parents and their children? As yet, few studies have addressed such questions.

At the time of this writing, only two studies of men who have become fathers after identifying themselves as gay have been reported. Sbordone (1993) studied 78 gay men who had become parents through adoption or through surrogacy arrangements and compared them with 83 gay men who were not fathers. Consistent with Skeen and Robinson's (1985) findings with divorced gay fathers, there were no differences between fathers and nonfathers on reports about relationships with the men's own parents. Gay fathers did, however, report higher self-esteem and fewer negative attitudes about homosexuality than did gay men who were not fathers.

An interesting result of Sbordone's (1993) study was that most gay men who were not fathers indicated that they would like to rear a child. Those who said that they wanted children were younger than those who said they did not, but the two groups did not differ on income, education, race, self-esteem, or attitudes about homosexuality. Given that fathers had higher self-esteem and fewer negative attitudes about homosexuality than either group of nonfathers, Sbordone speculated that gay fathers' higher self-esteem might have been a result, not a cause or simple correlate, of parenthood. Longitudinal research could be useful in evaluating this idea, but such work has yet to be reported.

A study of gay couples choosing parenthood was conducted by McPherson (1993), who assessed division of labor, satisfaction with division of labor, and satisfaction with couple relationships among 28 gay and 27 heterosexual parenting couples. Consistent with evidence from lesbian parenting couples (Hand, 1991; Osterweil, 1991; Patterson, 1995b), McPherson found that gay couples reported a more even division of responsibilities for household maintenance and child care than did heterosexual couples. Gay couples also reported greater satisfaction with their division of childcare tasks than did heterosexual couples. Finally, gay couples also reported greater satisfaction with their couple relationships, especially in the areas of cohesion and expression of affection.

As this brief discussion has revealed, research on gay men who have chosen to become parents has barely begun. The research to date is limited in scope, and many important issues have yet to be addressed. Existing work suggests, however, that although the source of such a difference is not well understood, gay fathers are likely to have higher self-esteem than gay men who are not parents. Results to date also suggest that gay parenting couples are more likely than heterosexual couples to share tasks involved in child care relatively evenly, as well as to be more satisfied than heterosexual couples with their arrangements. Much remains to be learned about the determinants of gay parenting, about its impact on gay parents themselves, and about its place in contemporary communities. The next section summarizes what is known about the impact of gay fatherhood on members of the gay father's family.

RESEARCH ON CHILDREN OF GAY FATHERS

Gay fathers are by definition members of families; they have children and often have wives or ex-wives as well as gay partners. Of course, gay fathers most often have other family members as well, including parents, aunts, uncles, siblings, nieces, nephews, and cousins. Because research on other family members remains scarce (for exceptions, see Buxton, 1994; Hays & Samuels, 1989), this section focuses on the children of gay fathers. I consider first the results of research on children's sexual identity, then that on other aspects of children's personal and social development. All of the research to date has focused on children of divorced gay fathers. Other reviews of this material can be found in Barrett and Tasker (2001), Bozett (1987), Gottman (1990), Green and Bozett (1991), Patterson (1992, 1997, 2000, 2002), Perrin et al. (2002), and Stacey and Biblarz (2001).

Sexual Orientation

Much research on the offspring of gay fathers has examined the development of sexual identity. In response to the popular stereotype that children of gay fathers may grow up to become gay themselves, a number of researchers have studied sexual orientation among the offspring of gay fathers. Contrary to popular belief, research has revealed that the vast majority of both sons and daughters of gay fathers grow up to become heterosexual adults.

The earliest findings about sexual orientation among children of gay fathers were reported by Miller (1979) and by Bozett (1980, 1982, 1987, 1989). Their research involved interviews with gay fathers, during which fathers were asked to report on the sexual orientation of their adolescent and young adult children. In Miller's (1979) sample, 4 of 48 children were said by their fathers to be gay or lesbian. In Bozett's two samples (1980, 1982, 1987, 1989), none of 25 and 2 of 19 children were described by their fathers as gay or lesbian. Although the precise numbers are not available in published reports, it would seem that at least some of the children in Bozett's research had not yet reached adolescence, so these figures must be interpreted with caution. In addition, small sample sizes and varied sampling procedures also suggest that interpretations should be made with care. If, however, the findings from these three studies are combined, the results reveal that 6 of 92 offspring, or 6.5%, were reported by their fathers to be gay or lesbian. In the largest study of sexual orientation among the offspring of gay fathers to date, Bailey, Bobrow, Wolfe, and Mikach (1995) studied 82 adult sons of 55 gay fathers. They obtained self-reports from the majority of sons as well as reports about the sons' sexual orientation from fathers, which allowed them to assess the reliability of fathers' reports in cases where both father and son had been interviewed. Bailey and his colleagues reported that in the 41 cases in which fathers said they were "virtually certain" or "entirely certain" of their sons' orientation, and in which sons also provided information, fathers and sons agreed in all but one case; the lone disagreement occurred when a father described his son as heterosexual and the son described himself as bisexual. Fathers' reports were thus very accurate overall, allowing the confident use of paternal reports when sons could not be contacted. Of sons whose sexual orientation could be rated with confidence, 68 of 75 were said by their fathers to be heterosexual, indicating that about 9% were reported to be gay or bisexual.

An interesting aspect of the Bailey et al. (1995) study was its assessment of environmental factors relevant to the experience of the sons. If exposure to gay fathers increases the likelihood that their sons grow up to be gay men, then sons who have lived in their gay father's households over longer periods of time might be expected to show greater likelihood of being gay. In contrast to such an expectation, Bailey et al. reported that the sexual orientation of sons was unrelated to the number of years spent living in the gay fathers' households, to the frequency of current contact with the gay fathers, or to the rated quality of current father-son relationships. For instance, gay sons had actually lived with their fathers, on average, only about 6 years, whereas heterosexual sons had lived with their fathers, on average, for about 11 years. Although this difference was not statistically significant, it was clear that no evidence for environmental transmission of sexual orientation was provided by these data. As Bailey et al. concluded, these findings suggest that any environmental contributions to sexual orientation must be small.

The available data thus suggest that whereas the great majority of children of gay fathers grow up to be heterosexual, a minority—perhaps 5% to 10%—are gay or bisexual. Appropriate interpretation of these results rests heavily on estimates of the population base rates for homosexuality, and as noted earlier, these are the subject of considerable controversy at the present time (Bailey, 1995; Bailey et al., 1995). Estimates of male homosexuality range from 1% to 2% up to approximately 5% or more, depending on the details of sampling, assessment, and other aspects of methodology

(Bailey, 1995). If the lower estimates are adopted, then the 5% to 10% rates of non-heterosexuality observed among sons of gay fathers seem to be elevated over the base rates. If, on the other hand, the higher population estimates of approximately 5% are used, then rates for the offspring of gay fathers would appear to be only slightly elevated, if at all, and probably remain within the range of chance variation. At this time, the data do not allow unambiguous interpretation on this point. What is clear on the basis of existing research, however, is that the great majority of children of gay fathers grow up to be heterosexual adults.

OTHER ASPECTS OF PERSONAL AND SOCIAL DEVELOPMENT

Many aspects of the personal and social development of children of gay fathers have gone unstudied to date, but there is some evidence about relationships between parents and their children. Harris and Turner (1985/1986) studied 10 gay fathers, 13 lesbian mothers, 2 heterosexual fathers, and 14 heterosexual mothers, most of whom had custody of their children. In all, the respondents had 39 children, who ranged from 5 to 31 years of age. Parents described relationships with their children in generally positive terms, and there were no differences among gay, lesbian, and heterosexual parents in this regard. Most gay and lesbian parents did not report that their sexual identities had created special problems for their children, and it was heterosexual parents who were more likely to report that their children's visits with the other parent presented problems for them.

One longstanding cultural stereotype about gay fathers suggests that they may be more likely than other parents to perpetrate sexual abuse on their children. In contrast to the stereotype, however, the great majority of sexual abuse can be characterized as heterosexual in nature, with an adult male abusing a young female (Jones & McFarlane, 1980). Available evidence reveals that gay men are no more likely than heterosexual men to perpetrate child sexual abuse (Groth & Birnbaum, 1978; Jenny, Roesler, & Poyer, 1994; Sarafino, 1979). For example, in a study by Jenny et al., out of 269 children seen for sexual abuse during a one-year period at a large urban hospital, only two, or fewer than 1%, of adult offenders could be identified as gay or lesbian. In particular, of the 219 sexually abused girls, one attack (0.4%) was attributed to an identifiably lesbian woman; of the 50 sexually abused boys, one attack (2%) was attributed to an identifiably gay man. In contrast, 77% of abuse against girls and 74% of abuse against boys was perpetrated by the adult male partners of the children's female family members (e.g., mothers, foster mothers, grandmothers); these perpetrators identified themselves as heterosexual and were known to their communities as heterosexual men. There was thus no evidence whatever for the belief that gay men are more likely than other men to perpetrate sexual abuse against children.

Much of what is known about the peer relations of the children of gay fathers comes from the work of Bozett (1980, 1987, 1989). From his interviews with adolescent and young adult offspring of gay fathers, Bozett concluded that although children affirmed their fathers in parental roles and generally considered their relationships with gay fathers as positive ones, they nevertheless expressed some concerns. Primary among the children's concerns was that if their fathers' sexual identities were widely known, the children might also be seen as nonheterosexual. For instance, one teenager said, "I don't tell anyone else because I'm afraid that they'll think I'm gay" (Bozett, 1988, p. 227).

To avoid problems, children reported that they employed a number of strategies. These included selective disclosure of the fathers' sexual identities, nondisclosure, and what Bozett termed *boundary control,* in which children attempted to limit their fathers' expressions of gay identity. For instance, adolescents might avoid bringing friends home when the gay father and his partner were likely to be there, or an adult son might ask his father not to bring his lover or partner to a party at the son's house. Some gay fathers were reported to have accommodated children's requests in this regard, by putting away gay publications during the visits of children's friends or by avoiding expressions of affection for a gay partner when in the company of their adolescent or adult children. Bozett suggested that these kinds of negotiations were affected by the age of the child, by the nature of the father-child relationship, by the perceived obtrusiveness of the father's sexual orientation (i.e., how visible it appeared to the child), and by a number of other factors. Systematic research on the ways in which children of gay fathers cope with the potentially stigmatizing nature of their fathers' sexual orientation could make important contributions toward the understanding of children's coping with prejudice as well as toward the understanding of gay family dynamics.

Overall, then, research on children of gay fathers, though still sparse, has produced some important information. First, contrary to popular stereotypes, there is little evidence that children of gay fathers are any more likely to encounter difficulties in the development of their own sexual identities, to be the victims of sexual abuse, or, for that matter, to be placed at any significant disadvantage relative to otherwise similar children of heterosexual fathers. Although children of gay fathers do appear to encounter some special challenges (e.g., in learning how to cope with potentially stigmatizing information about their fathers' sexual orientations), there is every indication that most children surmount these without undue difficulty. Probably the most important finding in the literature on children of gay fathers is that despite the undoubted prejudice and discrimination against their fathers, children nevertheless described relationships with their gay fathers as generally warm and supportive.

DIRECTIONS FOR FURTHER RESEARCH

As the preceding discussion makes clear, research on gay fathers and their families is relatively recent and still sparse. Many important questions remain to be addressed, and there is much for future researchers to accomplish in this area. In this section, substantive issues for future research are discussed first, followed by discussion of methodological directions. Finally, some attention is devoted to political and social issues that are relevant to research on gay fathers and their families.

In considering the substantive issues for future research on gay fathers, we distinguish between normative questions, on the one hand, and individual-differences questions, on the other. Normative questions concern the central tendencies of a population, whereas individual-differences questions concern differences among members of a population. In the present context, these include questions about gay fathers considered as a group, on the one hand, and about diversity among gay fathers, on the other. I discuss directions for research on the normative questions first and then examine avenues for research on individual differences.

One important task for research is to provide normative information about actual parenting behaviors of gay fathers with infants, children, adolescents, and adult children. As contemporary research on heterosexual families attests (Parke, 2002), relationships with fathers are significant aspects of a child's family environment. Attitudes of heterosexual adults toward gay fathers may often be negative (McLeod, Crawford, & Zechmeister, 1999), but very little is known about the qualities of children's relationships with their gay fathers or about how these may compare to those of children's relationships with heterosexual fathers at different points in the life course. Is there any correlation between fathers' sexual orientation and their involvement in parenting, or style of parenting? What effects, if any, might such differences have on children's development?

Another significant direction for future research is to identify patterns of family organization and family climate that may be characteristic of gay father families. Are there distinctive ways in which gay father families differ from heterosexual families or from lesbian families, and if so, what are they? In studies of lesbian, gay, and heterosexual couples without children, Kurdek (1995) reported that many issues for couples depend more on the length of time that a couple has been together than on the gender or sexual orientation of partners. Similar research on couples with children has not, however, been reported. A number of recent studies have suggested that gay and lesbian couples are more likely than heterosexual couples to divide the labor involved in child care evenly between the partners (Chan, Brooks, Raboy, & Patterson, 1998; Hand, 1991; McPherson, 1993; Patterson, 1995c); what impact, if any, does this egalitarian tendency have on the overall family climate in gay, lesbian, and heterosexual families?

Yet a third major direction for research involves exploration of interfaces between gay father families and major educational, religious, and cultural institutions with which they have contact (Casper & Schultz, 1999). What are the most common issues and concerns for gay father families in their contacts with settings such as children's schools or parents' work environments, and how are they usually addressed? To what degree are the issues of gay father families the same as, or different from, those of lesbian mother families or of members of other stigmatized minorities (e.g., ethnic or religious minorities)?

It will also be valuable to examine in a normative spirit the issues of subgroups of gay fathers. For instance, building on the work of Bozett (1980, 1981a, 1981b) and Miller (1979), researchers might examine the normative life trajectories of nonresidential gay fathers following divorce, focusing on the challenges and stresses of such life transitions and of noncustodial parenting. In the same vein, one might examine the issues of gay stepfathers over time, comparing them with those of both heterosexual stepfathers and lesbian stepmothers.

From an individual-differences perspective, a central concern is to identify and examine factors that add to or detract from the quality of life in gay father families. For instance, using different levels of analysis, one might examine individual, family, community, and cultural factors for evidence of their impact on the well-being of individual gay fathers as well as that of their family members. Drawing on results of research with nontraditional heterosexual families (e.g., Lamb, 1999), one would expect psychologically healthy men, living in supportive families and communities in a favorable cultural milieu, to cope in more favorable ways with the challenges of life in gay father families. The relative importance of various levels of analysis is, however, far from clear, and there is much to be done in this area.

It will also be important to examine issues of contemporary relevance to gay communities, as these may influence the experience of life in gay father families. Prejudice and discrimination against gay men and lesbians is, of course, one of the important factors that must be considered. Another is the special health concerns faced by gay men, especially those attributable to HIV disease (Paul, Hays, & Coates, 1995). More often than heterosexual families, gay father families may be faced with caretaking responsibilities for family members and friends who are managing chronic illness, and with grieving the loss of loved ones from HIV-related diseases. How do these special challenges, and the environments in which they occur, affect the experiences of those who live in gay father families?

The advent of gay father and lesbian mother families also provides an opportunity to assess the long-assumed significance both of gender and of sexual orientation in parenting (Stacey & Biblarz, 2001). It will be as interesting to compare the dynamics of gay and lesbian families as it is to compare those of gay and heterosexual families. The results of such work should clarify the significance of fundamental assumptions about the significance of gender and sexual orientation in parenting that have long been taken for granted but rarely if ever subjected to rigorous test. The results of this process should be not only a better understanding of gay families in particular, but also a better understanding of families and parenting in general (Patterson, 2000, 2002).

From a methodological perspective, a number of suggestions for future research can also be offered. The first of these concerns sampling methods. Existing research has tended to involve small, unsystematic samples of unknown representativeness. Larger, more representative samples of individuals and families would be helpful. Also valuable would be longitudinal research involving observational and other varied assessment procedures. Multisite studies that systematically assess the impact of environmental as well as personal and familial processes hold great promise. Except in the case of qualitative work, rigorous statistical procedures should be employed. Methodological directions of these kinds would maximize the likelihood that future research has a major impact on understanding in this area.

SUMMARY AND OVERVIEW

Social science research on gay fathers is a relatively recent phenomenon. Because the research has arisen in the context of widespread prejudice and discrimination against members of sexual minorities, much research has been concerned to evaluate negative stereotypes about gay father families. Although a great deal in this regard remains to be done, the results of existing research fail to provide evidence for any of the prevailing stereotypes about gay fathers or about their children. On the basis of existing research, we can conclude that there is no reason for concern about the development of children living in the custody of gay fathers; on the contrary, there is every reason to believe that gay fathers are as likely as heterosexual fathers to provide home environments in which children grow and flourish. Additional research is, however, certainly needed.

As researchers seek to expand the evidence relevant to traditional stereotypes, it will also be important to begin to examine individual differences among gay fathers and among their children. In this regard, it will be important for researchers to remember that despite widespread prejudice, many gay fathers and many of their children are competent, well-functioning members of society. Having begun to address negative assumptions embodied in psychological theory as well as in popular opinion, researchers are now in a position also to explore a broader range of issues, examining the personal, social, community, and cultural factors that affect the quality of life for gay father families. Much important work remains to be done in order to understand the structure and functioning of gay father families.

REFERENCES

ACLU Lesbian and Gay Rights Project. (2002). *Too high a price: The case against restricting gay parenting.* New York: Author.

Appell, A. R. (2001). Lesbian and gay adoption. *Adoption Quarterly, 4,* 75–86.

Armesto, J. C. (2002). Developmental and contextual factors that influence gay fathers' parental competence: A review of the literature. *Psychology of Men and Masculinity, 3,* 67–78.

Badgett, M. V. L. (1998). The economic well-being of lesbian, gay, and bisexual adults' families. In C. J. Patterson & A. R. D'Augelli (Eds.), *Lesbian, gay, and bisexual identities in families: Psychological perspectives* (pp. 231–248). New York: Oxford University Press.

Bailey, J. M. (1995). Biological perspectives on sexual orientation. In A. R. D'Augelli & C. J. Patterson (Eds.), *Lesbian, gay and bisexual identities over the lifespan: Psychological perspectives* (pp. 102–135). New York: Oxford University Press.

Bailey, J. M., Bobrow, D., Wolfe, M., & Mikach, S. (1995). Sexual orientation of adult sons of gay fathers. *Developmental Psychology, 31,* 124–129.

Baptiste, D. A. (1987). Psychotherapy with gay/lesbian couples and their children in "stepfamilies": A challenge for marriage and family therapists. In E. Coleman (Ed.), *Integrated identity for gay men and lesbians: Psychotherapeutic approaches for emotional well-being* (pp. 223–238). New York: Harrington Park Press.

Barret, R. L., & Robinson, B. E. (1990). *Gay fathers.* Lexington, MA: Lexington Books.

Barret, R. L., & Robinson, B. E. (1994). Gay dads. In A. E. Gottfried & A. W. Gottfried (Eds.), *Redefining families: Implications for children's development* (pp. 157–170). New York: Plenum Press.

Barrett, H., & Tasker, F. (2001). Growing up with a gay parent: Views of 101 gay fathers on their sons' and daughters' experiences. *Educational and Child Psychology, 18,* 62–77.

Baumrind, D. (1967). Child care practices anteceding three patterns of preschool behavior. *Genetic Psychology Monographs, 75,* 43–88.

Baumrind, D., & Black, A. E. (1967). Socialization practices associated with dimensions of competence in preschool boys and girls. *Child Development, 38,* 291–327.

Bigner, J. J., & Jacobsen, R. B. (1989a). Parenting behaviors of homosexual and heterosexual fathers. In F. W. Bozett (Ed.), *Homosexuality and the family* (pp. 173–186). New York: Harrington Park Press.

Bigner, J. J., & Jacobsen, R. B. (1989b). The value of children to gay and heterosexual fathers. In F. W. Bozett (Ed.), *Homosexuality and the family* (pp. 163–172). New York: Harrington Park Press.

Bigner, J. J., & Jacobsen, R. B. (1992). Adult responses to child behavior and attitudes toward fathering: Gay and nongay fathers. *Journal of Homosexuality, 23,* 99–112.

Bozett, F. W. (1980). Gay fathers: How and why they disclose their homosexuality to their children. *Family Relations, 29,* 173–179.

Bozett, F. W. (1981a). Gay fathers: Evolution of the gay father identity. *American Journal of Orthopsychiatry, 51,* 552–559.

Bozett, F. W. (1981b). Gay fathers: Identity conflict resolution through integrative sanctioning. *Alternative Lifestyles, 4,* 90–107.

Bozett, F. W. (1982). Heterogeneous couples in heterosexual marriages: Gay men and straight women. *Journal of Marital and Family Therapy, 8,* 81–89.

Bozett, F. W. (1987). Children of gay fathers. In F. W. Bozett (Ed.), *Gay and lesbian parents* (pp. 39–57). New York: Praeger.

Bozett, F. W. (1988). Gay fatherhood. In P. Bronstein & C. P. Cowan (Eds.), *Fatherhood today: Men's changing role in the family.* New York: Wiley.

Bozett, F. W. (1989). Gay fathers: A review of the literature. In F. W. Bozett (Ed.), *Homosexuality and the family* (pp. 137–162). New York: Harrington Park Press.

Brodzinsky, D. M., Patterson, C. J., & Vaziri, M. (2002). Adoption agency perspectives on lesbian and gay prospective parents: A national study. *Adoption Quarterly, 5,* 5–23.

Bryant, A. S., & Demian. (1994). Relationship characteristics of American gay and lesbian couples: Findings from a national survey. In L. A. Kurdek (Ed.), *Social services for gay and lesbian couples* (pp. 101–117). New York: Haworth Press.

Buxton, A. P. (1994). *The other side of the closet: The coming-out crisis for straight spouses and families* (2nd ed.). New York: Wiley.

Campbell, K. (1994, November 18). A gay father's quiet battle. *Washington Blade,* p. 5.

Casper, V., & Schultz, S. (1999). *Gay parents, straight schools: Building communication and trust.* New York: Teachers College Press.

Chan, R. W., Brooks, R. C., Raboy, B., & Patterson, C. J. (1998). Division of labor among lesbian and heterosexual parents: Associations with children's adjustment. *Journal of Family Psychology, 12,* 402–419.

Cowan, C. P., & Cowan, P. A. (1992). *When partners become parents: The big life change for couples.* New York: Basic Books.

Crosbie-Burnett, M., & Helmbrecht, L. (1993). A descriptive empirical study of gay male stepfamilies. *Family Relations, 42,* 256–262.

Darst, E. (2002, March 14). Rosie: She's proud to be a gay parent. *People Magazine.*

Dunlap, D. W. (1994, November 19). Gay sperm donor awarded standing as girl's father. *New York Times,* p. B-27.

Dunne, E. J. (1987). Helping gay fathers come out to their children. *Journal of Homosexuality, 13,* 213–222.

Editors of the Harvard Law Review. (1990). *Sexual orientation and the law.* Cambridge, MA: Harvard University Press.

Fadiman, A. (1983, May). The double closet: How two gay fathers deal with their children and ex-wives. *Life,* pp. 76–78, 82–84, 86, 92, 96, 100.

Flaks, D. (1994). Gay and lesbian families: Judicial assumptions, scientific realities. *William and Mary Bill of Rights Journal, 3,* 345–372.

Gottman, J. S. (1990). Children of lesbian and gay parents. In F. W. Bozett & M. B. Sussman (Eds.), *Homosexuality and family relations* (pp. 177–196). New York: Harrington Park Press.

Green, G. D., & Bozett, F. W. (1991). Lesbian mothers and gay fathers. In J. C. Gonsiorek & J. D. Weinrich (Eds.), *Homosexuality: Research implications for public policy* (pp. 197–214). Thousand Oaks, CA: Sage.

Groth, A. N., & Birnbaum, H. J. (1978). Adult sexual orientation and attraction to underage persons. *Archives of Sexual Behavior, 7,* 175–181.

Hand, S. I. (1991). *The lesbian parenting couple.* Unpublished doctoral dissertation, Professional School of Psychology, San Francisco.

Harris, M. B., & Turner, P. H. (1985/1986). Gay and lesbian parents. *Journal of Homosexuality, 12,* 101–113.

Hays, D., & Samuels, A. (1989). Heterosexual women's perceptions of their marriages to bisexual or homosexual men. In F. W. Bozett (Ed.), *Homosexuality and the family* (pp. 81–100). New York: Harrington Park Press.

Humphreys, L. (1975). *Tearoom trade: Impersonal sex in public places.* Chicago: de Gruyter.

In re W. S. D. (1992, April 30). No. A-308-90 (D.C. Superior Ct. Fam. Div.).

Jenny, C., Roesler, T. A., & Poyer, K. L. (1994). Are children at risk for sexual abuse by homosexuals? *Pediatrics, 94,* 41–44.

Jones, B. M., & McFarlane, K. (Eds.). (1980). *Sexual abuse of children: Selected readings.* Washington, DC: National Center on Child Abuse and Neglect.

Kurdek, L. (1995). Lesbian and gay couples. In A. R. D'Augelli & C. J. Patterson (Eds.), *Lesbian, gay and bisexual identities across the lifespan: Psychological perspectives* (pp. 243–261). New York: Oxford University Press.

Lamb, M. E. (Ed.). (1999). *Parenting and child development in 'nontraditional' families* (2nd ed.). Hillsdale, NJ: Erlbaum.

Laumann, E. O., Gagnon, J. H., Michael, R. T., & Michaels, S. (1994). *The social organization of sexuality: Sexual practices in the United States.* Chicago: University of Chicago Press.

Logue, P. M. (2001). *The rights of lesbian and gay parents and their children.* New York: Lambda Legal Defense and Education Fund.

Martin, A. (1993). *The lesbian and gay parenting handbook.* New York: HarperCollins.

Matteson, D. R. (1987). The heterosexually married gay and lesbian parent. In F. W. Bozett (Ed.), *Gay and lesbian parents* (pp. 138–161). New York: Praeger.

McLeod, A. C., Crawford, I., & Zechmeister, J. (1999). Heterosexual undergraduates' attitudes toward gay fathers and their children. *Journal of Psychology and Human Sexuality, 11,* 43–62.

McPherson, D. (1993). *Gay parenting couples: Parenting arrangements, arrangement satisfaction, and relationship satisfaction.* Unpublished doctoral dissertation, Pacific Graduate School of Psychology, San Francisco, CA.

Miller, B. (1979). Gay fathers and their children. *Family Coordinator, 28,* 544–552.

Ortiz, E. T., & Scott, P. S. (1994). Gay husbands and fathers: Reasons for marriage among homosexual men. *Journal of Gay and Lesbian Social Services, 1,* 59–71.

Osterweil, D. A. (1991). *Correlates of relationship satisfaction in lesbian couples who are parenting their first child together.* Unpublished doctoral dissertation, California School of Professional Psychology, Berkeley/Alameda.

Parke, R. D. (2002). Fathers and families. In M. H. Bornstein (Ed.), *Handbook of parenting: Vol. 3. Status and social conditions of parenting* (2nd ed., pp. 317–338). Hillsdale, NJ: Erlbaum.

Patterson, C. J. (1992). Children of lesbian and gay parents. *Child Development, 63,* 1025–1042.

Patterson, C. J. (1994). Lesbian and gay couples considering parenthood: An agenda for research, service, and advocacy. *Journal of Gay and Lesbian Social Services, 1,* 33–55.

Patterson, C. J. (1995a). Adoption of minor children by lesbian and gay adults: A social science perspective. *Duke Journal of Gender Law and Policy, 2,* 191–205.

Patterson, C. J. (1995b). Families of the lesbian baby boom: Parents' division of labor and children's adjustment. *Developmental Psychology, 31,* 115–123.

Patterson, C. J. (1995c). Lesbian mothers, gay fathers, and their children. In A. R. D'Augelli & C. J. Patterson (Eds.), *Lesbian, gay and bisexual identities over the lifespan: Psychological perspectives* (pp. 262–290). New York: Oxford University Press.

Patterson, C. J. (1997). Children of lesbian and gay parents. In T. Ollendick & R. Prinz (Eds.), *Advances in clinical child psychology* (Vol. 19, pp. 235–282). New York: Plenum Press.

Patterson, C. J. (2000). Sexual orientation and family life: A decade review. *Journal of Marriage and the Family, 62,* 1052–1069.

Patterson, C. J. (2002). Lesbian and gay parenthood. In M. H. Bornstein (Ed.), *Handbook of parenting: Vol. 3. Status and social conditions of parenting* (2nd ed., pp. 317–338). Hillsdale, NJ: Erlbaum.

Patterson, C. J., & Chan, R. W. (1999). Families headed by lesbian and gay parents. In M. E. Lamb (Ed.), *Parenting and child development in 'nontraditional' families* (2nd ed.). Hillsdale, NJ: Erlbaum.

Patterson, C. J., & Friel, L. V. (2000). Sexual orientation and fertility. In G. Bentley & N. Mascie-Taylor (Eds.), *Infertility in the modern world: Biosocial perspectives* (pp. 238–260). Cambridge, England: Cambridge University Press.

Patterson, C. J., Fulcher, M., & Wainright, J. (2002). Children of lesbian and gay parents: Research, law, and policy. In B. L. Bottoms, M. B. Kovera, & B. D. McAuliff (Eds.), *Children, social science and the law* (pp. 176–199). New York: Cambridge University Press.

Patterson, C. J., & Redding, R. (1996). Lesbian and gay families with children: Public policy implications of social science research. *Journal of Social Issues, 52,* 29–50.

Paul, J. P., Hays, R. B., & Coates, T. J. (1995). The impact of the HIV epidemic on U.S. gay male communities. In A. R. D'Augelli & C. J. Patterson (Eds.), *Lesbian, gay and bisexual identities over the lifespan: Psychological perspectives* (pp. 347–397). New York: Oxford University Press.

Perrin, E. C., & the Committee on Psychosocial Aspects of Child and Family Health (2002). Technical Report: Coparent or second-parent adoption by same-sex parents. *Pediatrics, 109,* 341–344.

Ricketts, W. (1991). *Lesbians and gay men as foster parents.* Portland: National Child Welfare Resource Center, University of Southern Maine.

Ricks, I. (1995, February 7). Fathers and son. *Advocate* (674), 27–28.

Rivera, R. (1991). Sexual orientation and the law. In J. C. Gonsiorek & J. D. Weinrich (Eds.), *Homosexuality: Research implications for public policy* (pp. 81–100). Newbury Park, CA: Sage.

Robinson, B. E., & Barret, R. L. (1986). Gay fathers. In B. E. Robinson & R. L. Barret (Eds.), *The developing father: Emerging roles in contemporary society* (pp. 145–168). New York: Guilford Press.

Robinson, B. E., & Skeen, P. (1982). Sex-role orientation of gay fathers versus gay nonfathers. *Perceptual and Motor Skills, 55,* 1055–1059.

Roe v. Roe. (1985). 324 S.E. 2d 691, 228 Va. 722.

Ross, M. W. (1978). Modes of adjustment of married homosexuals. *Social Problems, 18,* 385–393.

Ross, M. W. (1983). *The married homosexual man.* London: Routledge & Kegan Paul.

Sarafino, E. P. (1979). An estimate of nationwide incidence of sexual offenses against children. *Child Welfare, 58,* 127–134.

Sbordone, A. J. (1993). *Gay men choosing fatherhood.* Unpublished doctoral dissertation, Department of Psychology, City University of New York, New York.

Seligmann, J. (1990). Variations on a theme: Gay and lesbian couples. *Newsweek* (Special Issue on the 21st century family), pp. 38–39.

Skeen, P., & Robinson, B. (1985). Gay fathers' and gay nonfathers' relationships with their parents. *Journal of Sex Research, 21,* 86–91.

Stacey, J., & Biblarz, T. J. (2001). (How) does sexual orientation of parents matter? *American Sociological Review, 66,* 159–183.

Strader, S. C. (1993). *Non-custodial gay fathers: Considering the issues.* Paper presented at the 101st Annual Convention of the American Psychological Association, Toronto, Ontario.

Thompson, R. A. (1983). The father's case in child custody disputes: The contributions of psychological research. In M. E. Lamb & A. Sagi (Eds.), *Fatherhood and family policy* (pp. 53–100). Hillsdale, NJ: Erlbaum.

Van Gelder, L. (1991, March/April). A lesbian family revisited. *Ms. Magazine,* pp. 44–47.

CHAPTER 15

Fathers in Violent Homes

GEORGE W. HOLDEN and TED BARKER

Rᴇsᴇᴀʀᴄʜ ɪɴᴛᴏ ᴛʜᴇ problem of family violence has a bifurcated history. Initial efforts began with studies into the physical abuse of children (e.g., Kempe, Silverman, Steele, Droegemueller, & Silver, 1962). That research is now in its fifth decade and has spread into multiple manifestations of maltreatment, including sexual abuse, neglect, and psychological maltreatment. The newer branch of research on family violence focuses on female victimization and partner violence; investigations into those topics began in earnest only in the late 1970s (e.g., Gelles, 1976; Straus, 1979; Walker, 1979). However, common to both branches is that researchers have been very slow to investigate one of the central characters—fathers, which in this chapter includes biological fathers, stepfathers, and father figures, unless otherwise noted.

In the last edition of this book, Sternberg (1997) reviewed the available research on fathers in physically violent families. Based on studies published up until 1996, she argued persuasively that fathers were essentially missing as subjects in research on family violence. More evidence that fathers have been overlooked can be found in a book (Jasinski & Williams, 1999) on partner violence subtitled *A Comprehensive Review of 20 Years of Research.* Fathers were barely mentioned and not even indexed, despite a chapter on children exposed to partner violence. The bias toward ignoring the father is captured in a moniker we assign to some of the youngest victims of family violence: "children of abused women," rather than "children of abusive men" (Peled, 2000).

Our purpose in this chapter is to pick up where Sternberg (1997) left off and summarize what has been learned about fathers in relation to family violence since the mid-1990s. Toward that end, we conducted a computer literature search (PSYCINFO) in order to identify relevant studies, using the search terms "fathers" and "violence OR abuse" and "family, mothers, children." Due to space considerations and the available research, most of the chapter focuses on two types of intrafamily violence: child physical abuse and marital (or partner) abuse. As we will show, a number of studies on the topic have been published in the past seven years. Students of family violence have begun to locate the fathers.

The prior failure to investigate fathers' roles in intrafamilial violence is problematic for various reasons. Foremost, it prevents us from gaining a full understanding of the etiology, nature, and consequences of violence within the family. One cannot understand family dynamics without investigating the family's organization and hierarchical nature and the interdependence among all family members (Cox & Paley, 1997). Second, without recognizing the role of the father, it is too easy to blame the mother for the problems that children may exhibit (e.g., Walker, 1979). Third, statistical interactions between parent and child gender may be especially likely in studies of family violence. Because nonviolent fathers treat their sons differently than they treat their daughters, develop relationships that differ in quality, and have differential effects on sons and daughters (e.g., Lewis, 1997; Parke, 2002), it can be expected that these types of findings hold true also in families where at least one individual is violent.

The study of fathers and family violence is necessary also to inform contemporary social issues (Williams, Boggess, & Carter, 2001). When the presence of domestic violence (used in this chapter as a synonym for such terms as *adult domestic violence, partner violence,* and *wife battering*) is raised in divorce and child custody cases, as it is in perhaps 20% of custody cases (Jaffe, Lemon, & Poisson, 2003), additional factors should be considered. In such circumstances, issues that bear assessment include the likelihood that the parent has been or will be violent to the child, the quality of child rearing provided by each parent, and whether the violent individual represents a continued threat to the other parent. These considerations need to be informed by research.

Throughout our review, four questions with regard to fathers in homes characterized by some type of intrafamilial violence periodically recur. First, to what extent are fathers the primary perpetrators of child abuse? More specifically, in what ways do fathers differ from mothers in the frequency, type, and severity of abusive behavior directed toward their children and partners? Second, do the distinctions of biological fathers, stepfathers, and father figures make a difference for the children in homes characterized by violence? Paternal relatedness may play a role in three areas: the propensity for child abuse, the quality of parenting, and the effects on children. Third, what evidence is there that violent fathers have unique effects on their children's development? Given the cooccurrence of multiple problems in families characterized by intrafamilial violence, to what extent can children's problems be linked to paternal behavior? Fourth, does child gender interact with parent gender to yield differential parenting, patterns of abuse, or effects on children? Although none of these four questions have been systematically addressed, recent research is beginning to shed light on them.

Our discussion of fathers and intrafamilial violence is divided into five sections. We begin by identifying several common methodological problems in this research area. Then we present some recent statistics concerning the incidence of various forms of family violence. The third section provides a review of what is known about fathers who perpetrate family violence, including wife abuse and physical child abuse, whereas the section that follows addresses the problem of fathers who are victims of family violence. The fifth section addresses three issues concerning child development: the parental behavior of maritally abusive fathers, their influence on child development, and their own developmental history.

METHODOLOGICAL ISSUES

Collecting accurate data about fathers' involvement in family violence is challenging for several reasons. First, recruiting fathers to participate in research studies can be difficult. In our efforts to enroll fathers from the community in several studies (e.g., Holden, Barker, Angelelli, Appel, & Hazlewood, 2003; Holden, Miller, & Harris, 1999), we have found that fathers are more difficult to recruit and schedule than mothers because of their reported work commitments. In addition, they do not express as much interest in participating in research as do their wives. For several reasons, recruiting fathers from violent families is especially challenging. It is not surprising that fathers who are perpetrators of family violence may be reluctant to get involved in research. Typically, they are in a time of crisis, and participating in research is not high on their list of priorities (e.g., Kinard, 2001). These men may be hostile toward authorities and researchers as well as concerned about possible legal ramifications of their responses. It may also be hard to locate the fathers. Some violent men may have moved out of their homes, and others may be incarcerated.

The single greatest methodological difficulty involves ensuring the quality of the informants' reports. Because family violence almost always occurs in private, researchers commonly rely on self-reports by perpetrators or reports by partners. The veracity of violent fathers' reports has been questioned, due to the undesirable nature of their social behavior, fear of legal consequences, negative emotions related to the events, and other reasons (Barnett, Miller-Perrin, & Perrin, 1997). When batterers' reports of violence are compared with their partners' reports, perpetrators may underreport, minimize, or even deny their aggression (Dutton & Hemphill, 1992; Heckert & Gondolf, 2000; Sugarman & Hotaling, 1997). Consequently, researchers sometimes rely on partners' reports because they are easier to obtain and are assumed to be more accurate.

However, women have their own perspectives, filters, motivations, and unintentional or intentional biases; their reports should not be considered the gold standard. Discrepancies between the partners' reports can be caused by a host of factors, including different perception, categorization, or evaluation of behavior; the projection of frustrations; attempts to protect someone; reliance on third-party accounts of the behavior in question; and memory failure. To help clarify questions about the quality of reports regarding violence, several researchers have recently examined the correspondence between partners' reports.

Sternberg, Lamb, and Dawud-Noursi (1998) compared, among other things, reports of family violence and children's behavior problems from 38 mothers, fathers, and their 8- to 12-year-old children. There was surprisingly little agreement across family members. For example, in only 18% of the families was there perfect agreement about the abusive behavior of each parent. In another 50% of the families, the three informants agreed about the abusive behavior of one parent but not the other. Similarly, there was little agreement about the children's behavior problems. The highest correlation was between mothers' and fathers' reports of their children's externalizing problems ($r[84] = .30$). Sternberg et al. concluded that multiple informants are necessary to gain better understanding of violence in the home and its effects on children.

Another effort to establish the reliability of fathers' reports with mothers' and their children was somewhat more successful. Jouriles, Mehta, McDonald, and Francis (1997) compared reports of family violence on the Conflict Tactics Scale (Straus, 1979). The 72 fathers reported that they engaged in a considerable amount of physical aggression toward their wives. The three most commonly reported forms of aggression were pushing, grabbing, or shoving (73%); slapping or spanking (42%); and hitting or attempted hitting with an object (31%). When mothers' reports were compared, there was only moderately good agreement that the aggressive behaviors had occurred (78%, 36%, and 44%, respectively). In addition, fathers' reports of their own aggression did not correlate highly with their partners' reports (.30) but showed a stronger association with their 7- to 9-year-old children's reports (.46). When comparing across informants, children reported significantly less parental aggression than parents did. Like Sternberg et al. (1998), Jouriles et al. recommended collecting data from multiple informants.

A third study arrived at a different conclusion. Addressing the question of whether mothers' reports of fathers can substitute for fathers' self-reports of their antisocial behavior, Caspi et al. (2001) examined data from 67 couples. The mothers reported their partners to be significantly less delinquent and less aggressive and to have fewer externalizing problems or antisocial personality disorder symptoms than the fathers reported about themselves. Even so, the reports were found to correlate from .48 to .55, depending on the measure. Despite the moderate agreement between couples, the absolute agreement was low. Consequently, Caspi et al. concluded that it was best to collect information from multiple informants, but when that was not possible, they optimistically suggested that "women can provide highly reliable information . . . about their children's fathers" (p. 920).

Another problem unique to the study of fathers and family aggression is that researchers who investigate violence often do not report whether the men are actually the children's fathers. When investigators do report such information, fathers comprise at least half of the sample (e.g., Herron & Holtzworth-Munroe, 2002; Jouriles & Norwood, 1995; O'Keefe, 1994; Sorenson, Upchurch, & Shen, 1996). Holtzworth-Munroe, Stuart, and Hutchinson (1997) used a less precise approach to the identification of paternal status. Although the number of men who were fathers was not reported, the researchers indicated that the average batterer had 1.3 children.

Reporting on the parental status of the men is a necessary first step, but such information is insufficient. Fatherhood status needs to be broken down further by whether the men are the children's biological fathers, are related by marriage, or serve as father figures. Finally, appropriate analyses using father status as an independent variable are needed. Unfortunately, these three steps are all too rarely followed in studies of family violence.

Researchers have been slow to study and collect data from violent fathers. Part of the reason may be that they are especially challenging to recruit. Violent men may also pose problems when they are used as informants, given the finding that batterers in intervention programs underreport or deny their violent behavior. However, the reports from men's partners are also subject to biases. Because high levels of agreement about the occurrence of violence are not found within families, it is advisable to collect data from multiple family members. Finally, many samples of violent men include substantial proportions of fathers, but researchers have been largely inattentive to that variable. Consequently, valuable information about fathers and family violence has been lost.

INCIDENCE RATES OF FAMILY VIOLENCE

Gaining an accurate estimate of the extent of family violence is a challenging task. Estimates are functions of the operational definitions, the source of the information (informants, Child Protective Services records, hospital reports), the method (interview, survey), as well as the length of the time frame under consideration. Rather than attempting to provide a comprehensive summary of incidence rates, we offer a sampling of recently released statistics on domestic violence and child maltreatment. Such information provides an indication of the pervasive nature of family violence in general and fathers' involvement specifically.

DOMESTIC VIOLENCE

One of the largest efforts to estimate the prevalence of domestic violence using a nationally representative sample was the National Violence Against Women Survey (NVAWS). A total of 16,000 men and women participated in the telephone survey in 1995 and 1996 (Tjaden & Thoennes, 1998). Results were then extrapolated to estimate national incidence rates. According to that study, 1.3 million women and 835,000 men are physically assaulted by an intimate partner each year. For women, the assaults by an intimate partner represent 76% of all assaults (vs. 18% for men). Women were also significantly more likely than men to suffer injury from an assault. Unfortunately, whether the perpetrators were fathers was not reported.

Parental status and likelihood of violence were reported in the multisite Fragile Families and Child Wellbeing Study. More than 1,750 mothers were interviewed shortly after the birth of their children. Wilson and Brooks-Gunn (2001) found that the lowest rate of partner abuse was among the married couples. Only 2% of the married fathers and 3% of the unmarried men, still romantically involved, were reported to hit their wives or partners. The percent of violent men increased in groups with fathers who had unstable romantic relationships with the mothers (5%), who were just "friends" with the mothers (7%), and who had no continuing relationship with the mothers (11%).

There is some evidence that the rate of partner violence declined or at least leveled off during the 1990s. One of the best sources is the National Crime Victimization Survey (NCVS), an annual report based on a nationally representative sample of victims from about 45,000 households. Rennison and Welchans (2000) reported that women experienced lower rates of partner violence (7.6 per 1,000 women) in 1997 than in 1993 (9.8 per 1,000 women). The rate rose slightly to 7.7 in 1998. The male victimization rates of 1.6 and 1.5 per 1,000 men for 1993 and 1998, respectively, did not change appreciably over time.

CHILD MALTREATMENT

One of the most comprehensive studies designed to estimate the extent of child maltreatment in the United States was the Third National Incidence of Child Abuse and Neglect Survey (NIS-3; Sedlack & Broadhurst, 1996). In comparison with the previous incidence survey, dramatic increases in maltreatment were evident from 1986 to 1993. The number of physically abused children rose from an estimated 311.5 to 614.1 per 1,000 (a 97% increase), of sexually abused children from 133.6 to 300.2 per 1,000 (a

125% increase), of emotionally abused children from 188.1 to 532.2 per 1,000 (a 183% increase), and of physically neglected children from 507.7 to 1,335.1 per 1,000 (a 163% increase). Sedlack and Broadhurst attributed the elevated rates to both a real growth in rates of child abuse as well as increased reporting by authorities.

A somewhat lower estimate of the extent of child maltreatment comes from the National Child Abuse and Neglect Data System (NCANDS, 2002). Using data from Child Protective Services (CPS) agencies throughout the United States in 2000, an estimated 3 million referrals were made to CPS concerning the welfare of approximately 5 million children. Of those, approximately two thirds (62%) were investigated, and an estimated 879,000 children were determined to be victims of some type of child maltreatment. That database also provides some information about the perpetrators. Across all types of child maltreatment, parents or parent figures were implicated in more than 80% of the child victimizations. For child physical abuse, fathers or father figures were identified as perpetrators in 28.2% of the cases in contrast to 32.1% for mothers or mother figures. Given the fact that mothers, on average, spend much more time with their children than fathers do, this result is not unexpected.

As in the case with partner violence, there is some evidence that the rates of child maltreatment have declined or at least not increased in the past few years. The CPS-based data of confirmed child maltreatment rates have either decreased or stayed the same from 1996 to 2000 (NCANDS, 2002). For example, physical abuse declined from 3.5 to 2.3 per 1,000 children; neglect declined from 7.6 to 7.3 per 1,000; and sexual abuse remained the same at .5 per 1,000.

Additional evidence of a decrease in the rate of child abuse comes from data about filicides (parental murder of a child) provided by the U.S. Bureau of Justice Statistics (U.S. Department of Justice, 2003). They reported that the rate of "infanticide" (curiously defined as homicides of children under age 5 years) from 1990 to 2000 has been steadily decreasing. For example, in 1991, 684 children were classified as victims of infanticide. The most recent data, from 2000, reveal that 548 children under age 5 were killed by their parents.

More information about fathers' perpetration of filicide can be found in a study based on the FBI's Uniform Crime Reports. Kunz and Bahr (1996) examined characteristics of 3,459 children killed by their biological parents over a 10-year period. A majority (67%) of the child homicide victims were 2 years old or younger. Boys were slightly more likely to be victims, as they made up 55% of the deaths after the first week of life. Overall, fathers were perpetrators in 47.5% of the cases. However, paternal involvement had a curvilinear relation with the child's age. Fathers were about as likely as mothers to be the perpetrators of filicide when their children were between the ages of 1 week and 12 years. Mothers comprised 90% of the offender group for infants murdered during the first week of life. Fathers were more often responsible for the homicides than mothers after children reached 12 years of age. By the time children reached 16 to 18 years old, fathers perpetrated 80% of the murders.

Summary

These statistics underscore the widespread problem of family violence. Incidence studies indicate that well over 1 million women are victims of intimate partner violence each year in the United States and more than 850,000 children are confirmed by CPS as victims of maltreatment. Men also report being victims of intrafamilial violence. Although the statistics on domestic violence generally do not indicate whether the man is a father, according to at least one study of high-risk families, married fathers were less likely to engage in marital abuse than were other men. With regard to child physical abuse, fathers are slightly less likely than mothers to perpetrate child abuse or commit homicide. One positive trend was noted: Several studies indicate that the rate of domestic violence and child abuse has leveled off or even declined somewhat over the past five years.

FATHERS AS PERPETRATORS

The bulk of the research into fathers and intrafamilial violence has focused, not surprisingly, on questions related to characteristics of the men who engage in violence. The studies under this rubric can be divided into four topics. First, because men are most often the perpetrators of domestic violence, researchers have directed much of their attention lately to the characteristics of domestic violence perpetrators. It has become increasingly clear that perpetrators are not homogeneous with respect to such variables as type of violence or psychological health. A second, but smaller, set of studies concerns fathers who physically abuse or use harsh punishment on their children. The question guiding most of those investigations has been whether fathers engage in more punitive discipline or abusive behavior than do mothers. The third topic concerning the characteristics of perpetrators is whether stepfathers are more likely to abuse their children physically than biological fathers are. This is a controversial topic, and conflicting data are used to support opposing views. Fourth, we examine the cooccurrence of both domestic violence and physical child abuse. Researchers have begun to address systematically questions about the degree and determinants of overlapping violence.

FATHERS WHO ENGAGE IN DOMESTIC VIOLENCE

During the 1990s, researchers made a sustained effort to investigate characteristics of men who abused their wives or partners. As indicated earlier, many of these men were also fathers. Researchers have accumulated considerable information about a variety of characteristics of batterers, including emotional and mental health problems, attitudes toward women and power, and the comorbidity of alcohol and drug abuse problems (see reviews by Holtzworth-Munroe, Bates, Smutzler, & Sandin, 1997; Schumacher, Feldbau-Kohn, Smith Slep, & Heyman, 2001). Among the most prominent conclusions from the decade of research is the considerable heterogeneity found in groups of violent men. Within those groups, there is increasing recognition that distinct patterns of problems and violent behavior exist (Johnson & Ferraro, 2000).

Rather than attempting to review all of the efforts to categorize domestically violent men (e.g., Gottman et al., 1995; Johnson & Ferraro, 2000), we illustrate the research by discussing the classification scheme that has received the most attention to date. In an effort to establish a typology of male batterers, Holtzworth-Munroe and Stuart (1994) reviewed 15 previously developed batterer typologies (e.g., Gondolf, 1988). They then created a new classification scheme based on several theoretically important dimensions. These were *Family Only, Borderline/Dysphoric,* and *Generally Violent/Antisocial.* The *Family Only* batterers directed their violence only toward their partners and engaged in less violence and less verbal abuse than other types of batterers but did not have diagnosable personality disorders. *Borderline/Dysphoric* batterers demonstrated more extreme behavior. They engaged in violence both inside and outside of the home, were likely to abuse their partners psychologically and sexually, and were more likely to manifest a personality disorder. They were also characterized as having a history of unstable relationships, and when involved in romantic relationships, they tended to be distrustful of their partners. The *Generally Violent/Antisocial* batterers were characterized as the most violent, the most psychologically and sexually abusive, and the most likely to be suffering from antisocial personality disorders. These men were likely to engage in violence and criminal activity outside of the home.

Based on subsequent empirical work, Holtzworth-Munroe, Meehan, Herron, Rehman, and Stuart (2000) amended the three-group typology by adding a fourth batterer category: *Low-Level Antisocial.* These men fit in between the *Family Only* and *Generally Violent* groups but did not show the high levels of fear of abandonment, dependency, and jealousy found in the *Borderline/Dysphoric* group. In that study of 102 men, each perpetrator category was represented: *Family Only* (35% of the sample), *Low-Level Antisocial* (33%), *Generally Violent* (16%), and *Borderline/Dysphoric* (15%).

Summary

Given the heterogeneity found in groups of perpetrators, it is widely recognized that a typology is helpful in better understanding the etiology, characteristics, and effects of men who engage in domestic violence. The most prominent scheme was proposed by Holtzworth-Munroe and Stuart (1994) and is beginning to receive empirical support. Although it is too soon to judge the validity of this particular typology, the importance of typologies for understanding fathers who perpetrate domestic violence is clear. For example, antisocial men who are also fathers are likely to engage in different parenting practices and have a different impact on their children than fathers who have no discernable psychological illness and limit their violence to their partners. One implication of these efforts is the need to conduct more thorough assessments of fathers who engage in child-directed violence.

FATHERS WHO ENGAGE IN PHYSICAL PUNISHMENT OR ABUSE

Whereas there has been considerable research on men who commit domestic violence, few researchers have studied the characteristics of fathers who use harsh punishment or perpetrate physical child abuse. The research that is available can be divided into two categories: studies into parental use of physical punishment and children's reports of their fathers' abusive behavior. One characteristic of violent fathers that has received some attention is the biological relationship between the violent fathers and the abused children.

Physical Punishment

Since the 1930s, one perennial topic of interest to researchers has been parents' use of spanking as a disciplinary practice (Gershoff, 2002). Although spanking is not considered abusive behavior by most family violence experts (cf., Straus, 2001), it has been described as a subabusive behavior because it is below the point of abuse on a continuum of pain infliction but may inadvertently escalate into abuse (Graziano, 1994). With regard to fathers' use of physical punishment, the question that has received the most attention is whether fathers or mothers spank their children more often.

Despite the straightforward nature of that question, the results are somewhat conflicting. Even those who review the literature do not agree. Nobes and Smith (2000), based on a review of 20 studies published since 1980, found that similar proportions of fathers and mothers reportedly use physical punishment. In contrast, Gershoff (2002), after reviewing a total of 88 studies addressing multiple aspects of physical punishment, determined that mothers report more frequent spanking than fathers. Two empirical studies illustrate the nature of the inconsistencies.

A recent interview study conducted in England by Nobes, Smith, Upton, and Heverin (1999) provided a good test of between-parent differences in their use of physical punishment. A total of 103 fathers and 362 mothers of children who ranged in age from 1 to 11 years participated. In general, very few differences between fathers and mothers were discovered. For example, 80.6% of the fathers reported using some type of physical punishment in the past year, as did 80.4% of the mothers. The same percent of mothers and fathers (26%) reported using physical punishment at least weekly. One difference that did emerge concerned the use of physical restraint (defined as pushing, holding, or throwing). Forty-two percent of the fathers reported that they had used such a method in the past year compared with 25% of the mothers. Unexpectedly, the frequency of spanking by fathers was not associated with the amount of time they were alone with their children nor the proportion of child-care in which they engaged.

Straus (2001) arrived at a different conclusion based on his analysis of data from the 1985 National Family Violence Resurvey. Using self-reports from 1,083 fathers and 1,869 mothers, he found that mothers indeed reported hitting both young children as well as adolescents more than fathers, but the differences were small. However, when the amount of time spent with a child was controlled for, fathers hit at a higher rate than mothers.

The conflicting results of these two studies can be accounted for by such variables as sample sizes, nationality of subjects, type of self-report questions asked, and the lack of substantial differences. Based on the available research, one can conclude that fathers and mothers do not systematically differ in their use of physical punishment.

Physical Abuse

The ambiguity found when looking at differences in spanking by parent gender continues when considering severe physical punishment. According to a review of 26 studies by Nobes and Smith (2000), fathers were significantly more abusive in 14 analyses, mothers were more abusive in another 14, and in 11 analyses, no significant gender of parent differences emerged. Methodological differences including sample size, definition of abuse, location, and source of information are the most likely explanations for the conflicting results.

When results were based on victims' reports, fathers are more often implicated as perpetrators. Consider the retrospective study by Muller (1995). He collected data from more than 1,500 college students and their parents. Convergent reports between parents and children indicated that 82 parents had been physically abusive, as defined by one of the eight severe violence items on Straus's (1979) Conflict Tactics Scale (e.g., "kicked, bit, or hit with a fist," "burned," or "beat up"). Of those 82 parents who were classified as abusive, 55% were fathers. Muller also found that abusive fathers reported that they had received significantly more physically abusive behavior from their own fathers than from their mothers. Similarly, abusive mothers reported more abuse from their mothers than fathers, indicating a gender interaction between abuser and child victim.

Other researchers have also found interactions between paternal violence and children's gender. Based on mothers' and children's reports, Jouriles and Norwood (1995) determined that maritally abusive fathers physically abused their sons more often than they abused their daughters. When it comes to fathers' use of psychological abuse, the interaction with child gender may go in a different direction according to J. G. Cummings, Pepler, and Moore (1999). Based on maternal reports, they found that maritally abusive fathers directed significantly more verbal aggression to their daughters than to their sons.

Summary

Relatively little attention has been devoted to fathers and their punitive or abusive behavior. Most researchers asked only whether fathers or mothers were more likely to use physical punishment or abusive behavior. The available evidence indicates that fathers do not differ significantly from mothers with respect to the frequency of physical punishment. However, fathers may be somewhat more likely than mothers to engage in the physical abuse of their children. A gender interaction has been found in some studies indicating that fathers are more likely to physically abuse their sons, and mothers their daughters.

CHILD ABUSE AND BIOLOGICAL RELATEDNESS

One attribute of fathers who commit family violence has stirred some controversy: the father's biological relationship to the child. Daly and Wilson (e.g., 1988) took an evolutionary perspective and the notion of differential parental investment to account for data indicating that stepfathers are between 50 and 100 times more likely than biological fathers to commit fatal child abuse. However, the original data used to support their hypothesis did not differentiate between stepfathers and mothers as perpetrators (Malkin & Lamb, 1994). In a more recent report, using data from Statistics Canada, Daly and Wilson (1996) reported large differences in estimated rates of child homicides between stepfathers and genetic fathers. The most dramatic differences were found for homicides during the first two years of a child's life. They calculated that the estimated annual rate of child homicide during those two years by stepfathers was close to 500 victims per million coresident father-child dyads. In contrast, the rate of child homicide for genetic fathers was less than 20 victims per million.

Work by other investigators has produced inconsistent results. Using child maltreatment data provided to the American Humane Association from 10 states, Malkin and Lamb (1994) discovered that biological parents were more likely to perpetrate major physical and fatal child abuse than were nonbiological parents. However, children living with caregivers who were not their biological parents were at greater risk of child maltreatment than were the other children. Creighton (cited in Nobes & Smith, 2000), using child maltreatment data from 2,454 cases in England and Wales, found that the father perpetrators were about equally likely to be stepfathers, father substitutes, or biological fathers.

A recent investigation from the Longitudinal Studies of Child Abuse and Neglect (LONGSCAN) consortium provides more data about the role of biological status. Radhakrishna, Bou-Saada, Hunter, Catellier, and Kotch (2001) examined the biological status of fathers in 210 families. Results revealed that children who lived in homes with a nonbiological parent figure were at least twice as likely to have a CPS report as were children living with their biological father or no father. Between ages 6 and 8 years, nearly 27% of children who lived with nonbiological father figures had a documented CPS report, in contrast to 3.8% of the children living with a biological father and 18% of the father-absent children. However, the researchers did not report the identity of the perpetrators who could then have been father figures, mothers, or third parties.

Summary

There are conflicting results regarding whether stepfathers pose a greater risk to children than biological fathers do. Although there are several reasons why stepfathers might be less invested in child welfare than biological parents, it is premature to conclude that there is an association between paternal biological relatedness and child maltreatment. There are many more paternal characteristics, including age, involvement, psychological health, and quality of relationship with the child that merit attention (Lamb, 2001).

FATHERS WHO ENGAGE IN BOTH PARTNER VIOLENCE AND CHILD ABUSE

Are maritally abusive fathers likely physically to abuse their children as well? Although anecdotal reports of such an association began to appear in the mid-1970s, only in the past decade have researchers made more careful efforts to investigate this question empirically (e.g., McCloskey, Figuerdo, & Koss, 1995; Sternberg et al., 1993). By the late 1990s, enough empirical articles were available for literature reviews (Appel & Holden, 1998; Edleson, 1999b). Based on 31 studies from mostly clinical populations (e.g., battered women's shelters, CPS), it is clear that there is a significant risk that the two forms of abuse will cooccur. Appel and Holden (1998) determined that the median percent of cooccurring marital and child abuse was 40%. Edleson (1999b) summarized a different set of clinical studies but came to similar conclusions. He found that the majority of studies indicated a comorbidity rate of 30% to 60%. Of course, in nonclinical and representative samples the rate of cooccurrence is much lower. Based on the few available studies that computed the incidence rate, Appel and Holden estimated that 6% of children in the United States are likely to be physically abused while also being exposed to marital abuse.

Although a number of studies have now reported on the rate of cooccurrence, a number of methodological problems limit the validity of those estimates. Problems include a lack of standardized definitions, reliance on small clinical samples, use of single informants, and a failure to identify the abusers. The stereotypic view is that of the father as sole perpetrator of the cooccurring violence, but there are also reports that abused mothers physically abuse their children. As Appel and Holden (1998) pointed out, there is evidence for at least five different triadic models of cooccurring violence. These models differ in terms of which parent is the perpetrator and whether the violence is bidirectional or unidirectional.

Three recent studies have gone beyond estimating the rate of cooccurrence by examining the likelihood that certain fathers will batter both their wives and their children. Two studies used the Child Abuse Potential Inventory (Milner, 1994) as a proxy for identifying men at high risk for child abuse. This instrument accurately identifies child abusers. Herron and Holtzworth-Munroe (2002) gave the instrument to a group of batterers (about half of the sample were fathers) and to a group of nonviolent, community-based comparison men. When a stringent cutoff point was used as an index of high abuse likelihood, 40% of the batterers, in contrast to only 2% of the comparison men, scored at or above that level. Using a similar approach, Holden et al. (2003) found a somewhat lower rate of risk in a sample of fathers who were in an intervention program. Eighteen percent of the batterers scored at or above the cutoff point, compared with 3% of the maritally nonviolent fathers.

In an effort to identify a variable that mediated the relation between domestic abuse and child abuse, McGuigan, Vuchinich, and Pratt (2000) focused on fathers' perceptions of their children. Using data from a longitudinal study of 181 couples, McGuigan et al. found that if marital violence occurred in the first year of parenthood, both mothers and fathers developed more negative views of their children. These negative views (e.g., perceiving the child as difficult) mediated the relation for fathers between domestic violence and risk for child abuse. When the mediator was taken into account, the direct association between domestic violence and risk for child abuse was eliminated. More studies like this one are needed to understand and predict the linkages between domestic violence and child abuse.

Summary

Fathers as perpetrators of spouse or child abuse have received limited attention from researchers in the last seven years. Although the available studies can be faulted on various methodological grounds, researchers have begun to address some key questions about abusive fathers. One familiar finding from investigations into men who batter their wives or partners is the considerable variability in characteristics of the men. Classification schemes have begun to sort out that variation. With regard to fathers and child physical maltreatment, a central question is whether fathers provide more abusive or punitive treatment than do mothers. The available evidence indicates that although fathers and mothers engage in about equal amounts of physical discipline and abuse, fathers are somewhat more likely to harm their children. A second key question concerns the fathers' biological relatedness. The conflicting evidence to date indicates that stepfather status may be one of several risk factors. The final topic related to fathers' perpetration of violence that has received research attention since the mid-1990s is the incidence of and characteristics of fathers who abuse both their partner and their children. Cooccurrence may occur in more than half of families from clinical samples, but the most important characteristics of fathers likely to engage in both forms of violence are not yet known.

FATHERS AS VICTIMS

Although fathers are typically thought of and investigated as perpetrators of family violence, at least occasionally they may be the targets of family violence. Several reports of fathers as victims of intrafamilial violence have recently been published. We first consider abuse perpetrated by wives, followed by a review of recent work on fathers who are abused by their children.

ABUSE BY WIVES

One of the most controversial topics in family violence research concerns women's violence toward men. This topic is multifaceted and has recently generated much attention from both researchers (e.g., Johnson & Ferraro, 2000) as well as nonacademics (Pearson, 1997). As reported earlier, women are not the only victims of aggression. Depending on the study, men may be assaulted as often or even slightly more frequently than women (see review by Archer, 2000). Although a majority of the studies on this topic sample high school or college students, at least some of the studies using community samples include fathers. What is not well understood is the context of the violence and the motivation behind that aggression.

Currently, two theoretical camps, the violence-against-women researchers and the family conflict researchers, are at odds over the nature of female violence toward male partners. The violence-against-women researchers posit that women are the victims of violence and that women's use of violence is either in self-defense or perhaps an outcome of a mutually abusive relationship (Dobash, Dobash, Wilson, & Daley, 1992; Johnson, 1995). Family conflict researchers believe that women, as well as men, use violence to resolve intrafamily conflict and have claimed that women initiate and carry out physical assaults on their partners as often as men do (e.g., Gelles, 1993; Straus, 1999).

The debate has continued, in part due to the biases in the different data sets utilized. For example, researchers who believe women are the victims of patriarchal violence commonly rely on data obtained from shelters, hospitals, and police statistics. In contrast, family conflict researchers have relied primarily on national probability surveys utilizing questionnaires or interviews. Nevertheless, the available data indicate that men—presumably many of whom are fathers—are frequent targets of intimate violence.

Some of the intimate violence that is directed toward men in the absence of reciprocal male violence may be indicative of husband abuse. In 1977, Steinmetz published a controversial paper titled "The Battered Husband Syndrome." She marshaled what evidence was available to show that sometimes it was the husband who was battered. Since then, only scant attention has been devoted to husband abuse (e.g., Pagelow, 1985; Straus, Gelles, & Steinmetz, 1980).

One recent exception is the qualitative study by Migliaccio (2002). He collected 12 narratives from men who claimed to have been battered by their spouse (including one report collected posthumously from the Internet by a man who had committed suicide). Of the 12 men studied, half were husbands who were also fathers. All of the fathers reported that they had stayed in the relationship longer than they would have because of their children, echoing a finding reported by Steinmetz. According to Migliaccio, the fathers' two major motives were the desire to protect children from abusive wives (reported by three of the fathers) and the fear that departure would decrease their chances of winning custody after the divorce. As one father recognized, "It was foolish of me to stay in the relationship, except that I was afraid I would lose my kids" (Migliaccio, 2002, p. 46). His fears were well founded; neither he nor any of the other fathers were awarded custody.

Husband abuse also has a more somber manifestation—*mariticide,* or husband murder. Using data from 1988 reports of homicides in the nation's 75 largest counties, Langan and Dawson (1995) determined that of the 540 estimated spouse murders, 41% of the defendants were wives. Subsequently, most (80%) of the wives were convicted. According to the FBI's Uniform Crime Reports, there were 1,684 cases of mariticide between 1991 and 1995. This total represents 6.6% of all the forms of intrafamilial homicide (Underwood & Patch, 1999). In contrast, *uxoricide*—the murdering of a wife—is much more frequent, as it represented 32.5% of the intrafamilial homicides.

In at least some mariticide cases, the murder may occur in reaction or as a consequence of abuse, something Johnson and Ferraro (2000) labeled *violent resistance.* For example, in a study of adult domestic violence fatalities in the state of Washington, 9 of the 42 cases (21%) involved females killing males (Bullock & Cubert, 2002), and of those 9 cases, 5 were reportedly committed in self-defense. Critical information about these cases is not available. Needed information includes the number of fathers among the mariticide cases, the perpetrators' motives, and whether the fathers were also abusive.

ABUSE BY CHILDREN

Fathers may also face abuse at the hands of their children. Although this topic has been largely neglected (cf., Paulson, Coombs, & Landsverk, 1990), one recent study was found. Using medical records, Laurent and Derry (1999) discovered that parent battering was reported in 3.4% of 645 hospitalized children over a 10-year span in France. Fathers were the sole victims in 9% of the cases of parent battering and were victimized along with the mothers in another 46% of the families. Most (73%) of the perpetrators were sons; their average age was 14 years (range 10–17).

As the news media periodically reminds us, children murder fathers. Two examples of patricide are the Menendez brothers in California, who shot their parents to death in 1989, and the 2001 murder by the 12- and 13-year-old King brothers in Florida. According to the FBI's Uniform Crime Reports, over the five-year period from 1991 to 1995, there were 863 cases of patricide, which represented 6.6% of all the forms of intrafamilial homicide (Underwood & Patch, 1999). As with women who murder their husbands, the children's motivation have not been systematically documented but likely includes both cases of self-defense and reactions to ongoing abuse.

Summary

Although fathers are typically thought of as perpetrators of family violence, at least some of the time they are victims of aggression perpetrated by wives and children. To what extent battered fathers engaged in family violence is not known. In fact, researchers have devoted scant attention to this type of intrafamilial violence. Information about the motivations, circumstances surrounding, or causes of violence against fathers awaits future research.

VIOLENT FATHERS AND CHILD DEVELOPMENT

Three questions are addressed in this section. The most critical question concerns the ways in which violent fathers affect their children's behavior and psychological well-being. To help answer that question, researchers have begun to examine the child-rearing practices of violent fathers. Initial data about how these men parent are available from three types of informants: children, wives, and the fathers themselves. The second question is: How do violent fathers affect their children's development? A number of studies have appeared over the past seven years, some concerned with the impact of father presence on children, some with the relations between father violence and child behavior problems, and some with the relations between father violence and child behavior problems, and some with the intergenerational transmission of abusive behavior. The third developmental question concerns the childhood experiences of perpetrators.

The Fathering of Men Who Engage in Domestic Violence

In order to understand better the development of children in homes characterized by domestic violence, researchers have recently examined how such children are parented. Researchers have now documented some of the child-rearing practices and beliefs of battered women (e.g., Holden, Stein, Ritchie, Harris, & Jouriles, 1998; Levendosky & Graham-Bermann, 2000; Sullivan, Nguyen, Allen, Bybee, & Juras, 2000). Less attention has been devoted to assessing how maritally violent fathers rear their children. Currently, at least partial information about how these men parent is available from three types of informants: children, mothers, and fathers.

Children's Reports

Children's perceptions of their domestically violent fathers have been assessed in several interview studies. Such qualitative information has revealed that violent fathers represent a major source of distress and confusion for their children. Children temporarily residing in shelters reported high levels of terror and anxiety associated with observing or overhearing marital violence (e.g., Berman, 1999; Smith, Berthelsen, & O'Conner, 1997). A common theme was children's conflicting perceptions and loyalties about their fathers. Many children expressed feelings of love for their fathers, although they were also terrified of the violence and recognized it was wrong. According to Peled's (1998) interview study of 12 preadolescent children, the youth resolved the conflicting perceptions by adopting one opinion or the other. Either fathers were viewed as bad, or the father's violence was reframed and excused.

To date, only one quantitative study of children's perceptions of violent fathers has been published (Sternberg et al., 1994). The 8- to 12-year-old children in the study were sorted into four groups: those who had been physically abused, those exposed to marital violence, those abused and exposed, and a nonabused comparison group. Perceptions of both the perpetrating and nonperpetrating parents were assessed. It was no surprise that children who were physically abused by their fathers had negative perceptions of them; however, they also reported positive qualities of their fathers and did not mention fewer positive attributes than did the children who were exposed to marital violence or the comparison children. A child-gender effect was identified:

Sons reported more negative characteristics of their fathers than daughters did. Even so, there was a trend for the sons, compared with daughters, also to identify more positive characteristics of their fathers. Those data are suggestive of the conflicting feelings sons may have about their violent fathers.

In addition to children's perceptions of their fathers, adults' retrospective memories of their violent fathers have also been studied. For example, Haapasalo (2001) collected data from 89 young male Finnish inmates. About half of the men revealed that they had been physically abused in childhood. Perceptions of fathers centered on three dimensions: high levels of control, frequent rejection, and inconsistent discipline. Recollections of paternal rejection were associated with reports of both physical abuse and fathers' mental problems.

Mothers' Reports

The fact that few researchers have collected mothers' reports of fathers' child-rearing practices is indicative of the lack of attention devoted to fathers' role in these families. Most of the studies that included maternal reports of fathers limited those reports to paternal physical abuse (Jouriles & Norwood, 1995; O'Keefe, 1994), although some investigators did collect information about multiple forms of abuse (e.g., McCloskey et al., 1995). As could be expected, mothers frequently reported that maritally violent fathers were also physically aggressive with their children. In families characterized by more extreme wife battering, fathers reportedly aggressed more against sons than against daughters (Jouriles & Norwood, 1995; O'Keefe, 1994).

We located only one relatively early study that assessed maternal reports of other paternal child-rearing qualities. Holden and Ritchie (1991) found that shelter mothers reported that their partners were more frequently angry at their children, less involved in child care, and less likely to be affectionate or to use reasoning than were the matched community mothers. When asked about the fathers' use of physical punishment and power assertion in disciplinary situations, the mothers' reports of the fathers' behavior did not differ from the comparison mothers' reports. In fact, more than one third of the shelter mothers considered their husbands to be "average" or "better-than-average" fathers.

Fathers' Self-Reports

Over the past several years, five studies have examined violent men's self-reports about parenting. One was a qualitative interview study of eight fathers attending court-mandated counseling programs (Fox, Sayers, & Bruce, 2001). The men had been previously screened for child abuse, and some of the fathers articulated a distinction between partner violence and child abuse. As one man asserted, "I want to make one thing clear. I have abused my wife, but I've never laid a finger on my kids. I'm no child abuser!" (p. 141). One theme that emerged from the interviews was the men's regard for their paternal responsibilities. This was manifest in two ways. One facet of paternal responsibility meant providing their children with either financial support, or when that was not possible due to unemployment, they reportedly provided at least emotional support. The second type of responsibility expressed was the fathers' recognition and regret about the negative impact that domestic violence had on their children.

A study by Fox and Benson (2003) took a different approach to investigating how maritally violent fathers rear their children. Using the National Survey of Families and Households data set, they compared 145 fathers who revealed that they had engaged in marital violence with a comparison sample of 1,710 nonviolent fathers. Out of 95 variables examined, significant group differences were found on only 19 variables. Differences were found on reports of discipline and negative emotion. For example, maritally violent fathers admitted more spanking, yelling, and harsh parenting than did the other fathers. Differences were also found on such variables as arguments with their children and number of perceived child behavior problems.

In line with the view that wife batterers would experience more problems in their home lives, Baker, Perilla, and Norris (2001) investigated two other parenting variables. They hypothesized that violent fathers would experience more parental stress and enjoy lower levels of parenting competence than nonviolent fathers. Questionnaires were filled out by 26 immigrant Latino batterers attending an intervention program, along with 17 comparison men and their partners. No differences were found between the two groups of fathers on measures of either parenting stress or perceived competence. However, when compared with the parenting stress experienced by their partners, batterers reported significantly less stress. The authors suspected that this finding resulted from the fathers' lack of involvement in child care. Nevertheless, based on anecdotal reports, the fathers were both aware of and concerned about the negative effects of marital violence on their children, echoing the finding by Fox et al. (2001).

A fourth effort to assess the quality of violent men's parenting using men's self-reports was conducted by Holden et al. (2003). They conducted two studies to compare the characteristics of fathers attending batterer intervention programs with matched comparison groups. In the first study, 69 fathers of children aged 1 to 12 years anonymously reported on their use of harsh discipline. When compared with 48 community fathers, no significant differences were found. However, after the 20 comparison men who admitted to engaging in partner violence were removed from the analysis, two significant effects were found. The batterers disclosed that they engaged in more psychological aggression and more minor assaults (shook, spanked, slapped, pinched) with their children than the maritally nonviolent comparison fathers.

In their second study, Holden et al. (2003) collected self-reports concerning a range of child-rearing variables from 56 batterers who were fathers and 39 matched comparison fathers. No significant group differences were found with the full sample. As in the first study, when the 11 comparison men who admitted to engaging in marital physical abuse were removed from the analyses, significant multivariate group differences emerged. Follow-up analyses indicated that the only significant difference found was with parenting stress: Similar to the Baker et al. (2001) finding, batterers reported less stress than the nonviolent comparison men.

When the data were reanalyzed based on those fathers who scored at the elevated cutoff level on the Child Abuse Potential, a number of group differences emerged. The 11 fathers who scored above the cutoff consisted of 10 batterers and one comparison father. They differed significantly from the other men on seven variables. The fathers at high risk for abuse reported significantly more anger, child externalizing problems, parenting stress, trauma symptoms, borderline personality organization, and problems with drugs than did the other men. They also indicated that they engaged in less positive parenting activities than the other fathers did. These results reflect that groups of batterers may be heterogeneous and highlight the fact that some batterers (18% in that particular sample) are indeed at high risk for physical child abuse.

Summary

Information from three types of informants about how maritally violent fathers parent their children is beginning to accumulate. Each type of informant provides a different perspective on the fathers. According to their wives, violent fathers are physically punitive and often angry. When the male batterers report on their own parenting, the few differences found are in discipline, psychological aggression, negative emotion, and parenting stress. Children report conflicting feelings about their fathers. Having a violent father whom they also love may be a particularly taxing situation for young children to reconcile. That cognitive conflict may contribute to children's negative outcomes, which is the next topic to be considered.

VIOLENT FATHERS' INFLUENCE ON CHILDREN'S DEVELOPMENT

Psychological theory, as well as experimental research, are in accord with the view that violent fathers may have a negative effect on their children's development. Social learning theory, trauma theory, and relationships theory each provide explanations of why parental violence negatively affects children (Graham-Bermann, 1998). Specific psychological mechanisms have also been implicated. Some of these include modeling, reinforcement, reactions to stress, and social cognition processes. Experimental research documenting children's reactions to marital conflict (e.g., E. M. Cummings, 1994) provides strong evidence that it is a source of children's behavior problems. In line with the theory and experimental research, recent research has begun to document associations between violent fathers and their children's development. The research can be sorted into studies concerning violent fathers and children outcomes, the effect of fathers' presence on their children, the cycle of violence, and the newest topic—how violent fathers affect their children's beliefs.

Violent Fathers and Children's Outcomes

It is now well established that children in maritally violent homes are at high risk for developing a variety of health, social, emotional, and cognitive problems (e.g., Graham-Bermann & Edleson, 2001; Holden et al., 1998). Problems range from relatively minor acts of noncompliance to suicide. These children also are likely to show symptoms of posttraumatic stress disorder (PTSD). Although most children exposed to family violence are likely to exhibit one or more trauma symptoms, researchers have found that between 26% and 50% of child samples meet the criteria for PTSD based on the fourth edition of the *Diagnostic and Statistical Manual of Mental Disorders* (Rossman, 2001).

An elevated risk for two types of behavior problems is the most commonly documented finding about these children (Edleson, 1999a). They may exhibit externalizing problems (e.g., noncompliance, aggression, anger, or defiance), or the children may experience internalizing problems, including anxiety, depression, fear, withdrawal, or low self-esteem. Depending on the study, mothers' reports indicate that anywhere from 25% to 75% of the children may have problems that are considered severe enough to warrant clinical intervention (McDonald & Jouriles, 1991). One limitation of many of the studies is that little attention was given to assessing the violent fathers and their contributions to the problems. Two recent studies have begun to address that gap.

McDonald, Jouriles, Norwood, Ware, and Ezell (2000) investigated the contributions of paternal and maternal marital violence in the adjustment problems of clinic-referred children. In a sample of 90 two-parent families seeking help for their 4- to 7-year-old children, 48% of the fathers reported being physically violent toward their partners. After controlling for family demographic variables, parent-child aggression, and marital discord, the children of maritally violent fathers had more externalizing and internalizing problems than did the children of the nonviolent fathers. It is important that paternal marital violence, but not maternal marital violence, was related to child adjustment problems.

One recent study furthered our understanding of the development of behavior problems in reaction to marital conflict by also examining children's emotional responses. Crockenberg and Langrock (2001) used a multimethod approach, including home observations designed to provoke parent-child conflicts, in collecting data from 164 6-year-old children and their parents. They discovered that children's emotional responses were an important determinant of the children's reactions to the conflict. For example, fathers' marital aggression interacted with their sons' anger to predict boys' externalizing problems. The boys' fear interacted with reports of marital aggression to predict boys' internalizing behavior. Fathers' marital aggression had a different effect on their daughters: It was linearly related to their anger, sadness, and fear.

The differential impact of children's gender in violent homes was echoed in a study by J. G. Cummings et al. (1999), who found support for an interaction between parent and child gender in a sample of 112 shelter mothers and their children. Mothers' psychological well-being was found to be a stronger predictor of daughters' adjustment than of sons' adjustment. However, the researchers did not collect fathers' data to test the corresponding relations with sons' adjustment.

One other variable may play a role in the outcome of children from maritally violent homes. Using children's reports, Sullivan, Juras, Bybee, Nguyen, and Allen (2000) discovered that biological fathers were more emotionally available than stepfathers or other father figures but that availability did not translate into children's perceptions of greater self-competence. Children with maritally violent fathers who were either biological fathers or stepfathers reported lower self-competence than did children without father figures. This effect could be accounted for by the fact that children whose biological fathers engaged in marital abuse may be more conflicted. It is likely to be especially disturbing for children to observe their fathers physically abusing their mothers. The biological status of the fathers, as well as the quality of relationship between the maritally violent fathers and children, clearly warrants more research attention.

Effects of the Presence of Violent and Nonviolent Fathers

We next consider the question of whether fathers' involvement is associated with beneficial or negative child outcomes. Many researchers have documented positive effects of paternal presence and especially paternal involvement for their children

(Lamb, 1997, 2002; Parke, 2002). But what about families characterized by violence? The answer to this question comes from four studies, two of which were reports based on the LONGSCAN data set. This longitudinal data set includes children who are at risk for maltreatment, have been substantiated as victims, or who have a history of reports of suspected maltreatment. In one study using a subsample of the LONGSCAN data, Marshall, English, and Stewart (2001) tested the association between fathers' or father figures' presence and children's behavior problems in 182 children reported to CPS. The presence of a father or father figure was related to lower child depression scores. However, no effects for different types of father figures were found (i.e., biological fathers, stepfathers, male relatives, etc.). Absence of a father figure was associated with higher rates of child aggression, but only in African American families. In addition, a trend was found linking increased father or father figure involvement with a lower likelihood of serious health problems in the children.

A second but larger LONGSCAN report of 855 mothers and 6-year-old children at risk for maltreatment examined the question of father involvement and support from the children's perspective (Dubowitz et al., 2001). Most (79%) of the children could identify someone they considered to be a father figure. These "fathers" included biological fathers, foster fathers, the mothers' boyfriends, and others. Children functioned better if they had supportive fathers (or father figures) in their lives. This was indicated by higher cognitive test scores, better self-competence, and greater social acceptance than children who did not have a father figure. Among children who reported having a father figure, perceptions of paternal supportiveness made a difference. Perceptions of support were associated with greater competence and social acceptance but fewer depressive symptoms.

A third study also found positive effects of father involvement in a high-risk population. Black, Dubowitz, and Starr (1999) recruited 175 3-year-old African American high-risk children and their families. The children were at risk for nonorganic failure to thrive, maternal drug abuse, and poverty. A subsample of 82 of the fathers or father figures were interviewed and observed interacting with their children. The children of fathers who were satisfied with parenting, provided financial support for child rearing, and engaged in nurturant play had children with better cognitive and language competence than did the children of other fathers. Employed fathers who were satisfied with parenting also had children with fewer behavior problems. However, whether the father was the biological father of the child or played the role of father figure did not make a difference on the variables assessed.

All three of these studies indicate that paternal involvement (by either biological fathers or father figures) can have positive effects on children, but that finding appears to conflict with theoretical views and other empirical data concerning violent fathers' negative effects on children. A study that helps to resolve this apparent conflict was recently published. Using data from a large, epidemiological study, Jaffee, Moffitt, Caspi, and Taylor (2003) found support for the benefits of father involvement as indexed by children's behavior problems. A negative relation was found between the amount of time fathers lived at home with their children and the children's conduct problems. However, it was a different story for fathers who engaged in antisocial behavior. In those cases, the more time the antisocial men lived at home, the more conduct problems their children exhibited. This study shows that father involvement has positive effects, as long as the men are not antisocial or, presumably, violent with their children.

Violent Fathers and the Cycle of Violence

A long-term effect of violent fathers on children that has continued to receive research attention is the intergenerational transmission of violence (see reviews by Black et al., 2001; Schumacher et al., 2001). One recent contribution to this topic was made by Muller and Diamond (1999), who collected reports of paternal and maternal aggression as well as physical abuse from 983 college students and many of their parents. Students reported on current and childhood aggressive behavior. Multiple regressions revealed that paternal physical abuse was a significant predictor of aggression for males, both currently and when they were children. Again, there was an interaction between parent and child gender. Physical abuse by mothers predicted women's contemporaneous aggressive behavior and reports of childhood aggression, but not men's.

A second recent study found evidence for the cycle-of-violence hypothesis using data from the 1985 National Family Violence Survey. Heyman and Smith Slep (2002) examined whether exposure to different types of family violence in childhood was associated with adult perpetration or victimization. When analyzing the men's data, they found that physical child abuse or exposure to domestic violence was significantly associated with perpetrating both child abuse and partner physical abuse. But child abuse and exposure effects were not found to be additive. In contrast, fathers who experienced both types of family violence (physical abuse and interparent abuse) in their family of origin were more likely than other fathers to report being a victim of partner abuse.

Violent Fathers and Children's Beliefs

A new domain in the study of the effects of violent fathers concerns children's developing beliefs, attitudes, and mental representations of the family. Two studies provide an initial glimpse at this additional negative outcome from violent fathers. Graham-Bermann and Brescoll (2000) found that the presence of adult domestic violence affected the children's views about gender, power, and violence. Using reports from 221 children aged 6 to 12 years old, they found significant relations between violence and certain beliefs. In families with more domestic violence, both boys and girls agreed with statements reflecting paternal power ("Man is the king of the castle") and acceptance of violence ("Husbands can hit wives"). In addition, there was a gender effect: Boys had significantly higher scores than girls on statements concerning the power of males over females. Similarly, Grych, Wachsmuth-Schlaefer, and Klockow (2002) found that 3- to 7-year-old children of battered women had fewer positive views of their mothers and themselves, expected interparental conflict to escalate, and had less coherent narratives about the family than did comparison children. Both of these studies provide evidence that exposure to adult domestic violence affects children's social cognition and may set the stage for subsequent maladaptive behavior.

Summary

Paternal violence, whether it be directed to mothers, to the children, or to both, is associated with a variety of negative psychological outcomes. The outcomes most frequently documented have been internalizing and externalizing problems but also include modifying the child's developing belief system and the intergenerational transmission of violence. Recent studies have made progress in specifying the fathers' role in child adjustment problems as well as in identifying child-gender interactions. Researchers have also begun to address the important issue of violent fathers' involvement and children's outcomes. The tentative conclusion is that father involvement is associated with positive child outcomes, but the more antisocial the fathers are, the more likely it is that their children will have behavior problems.

Violent Fathers' Own Development

Another fundamental developmental issue concerns the origins of paternal violence toward wives and children. A variety of theoretical perspectives address the etiology of aggressive behavior, ranging from evolutionary and biological to cultural and clinical (Barnett et al., 1997), with most attention paid lately to social learning and trauma theories. Observational learning, reinforcement, and harsh punishment are powerful teachers. Lessons taught to young children about the effective use of physical and verbal aggression to dominate others are believed to be long lasting (Dutton et al., 1996; Simons, Wu, Johnson, & Conger, 1995). Indeed, a common finding in retrospective studies is that abusive men report a history of both physical child abuse and exposure to interparent aggression, as indicated in the section above on fathers and the cycle of violence.

Some researchers have argued that our patriarchal culture also promotes a sense of entitlement to power and male authority over women (e.g., Birns, Cascardi, & Meyer, 1994; Graham-Bermann & Brescoll, 2000). Thus, patriarchal beliefs should pass from father to son. However, the data concerning misogynistic attitudes and male abusiveness are inconsistent (Barnett et al., 1997). Similarly, Dutton (1995) observed that socialization is not sufficient to explain the findings in the batterer literature. For example, socialization is insufficient as a primary causal mechanism in male feelings of jealousy and powerlessness in intimate-abusive relationships. In addition, social learning theory does not explain the considerable heterogeneity in the characteristics of male batterers (e.g., Holtzworth-Munroe, 2000).

An alternative view that is gaining adherents posits that the etiology lies in early traumatic experiences. Van der Kolk (1987, 1988) proposed that male perpetrators who have been victimized as children suffer from a delayed-onset PTSD and suggested that these individuals live with enduring vigilance for and sensitivity to environmental threats. According to Van der Kolk, male batterers characterized by trauma symptomatology have a tendency to react to stress with an all-or-nothing response and have little capacity for intimate relationships. Individuals suffering from PTSD respond to reminders of the trauma with increased heart rates, blood pressure, and skin conductance (Van der Kolk, 1996). Other research has shown that witnessing abuse or being abused as children plays a significant role in the development of PTSD symptoms, physiological reactivity, and borderline personality symptoms in both adults and children (Dutton, 1998; Kilpatrick & Williams, 1998; Weaver & Clum, 1993).

Dutton (e.g., 1995) in particular has articulated a theory of how men develop an abusive personality. His etiological model focuses on attachment disruption stemming from chronic abuse in childhood. As children, then, these men experienced betrayal by their primary attachment figures. When they become adults, they are unable to trust others, and their violence is stimulated by fears of abandonment and jealousy (Dutton, 1998). They continue to experience trauma symptoms in adulthood, which are significantly correlated with recollections of negative parental treatment by the abuse perpetrator (Dutton et al., 1996). Thus, the environmental threat and hypervigilance postulated by Van der Kolk (1988) could stem from expectancies of betrayal based in part on childhood experiences of abuse. However, like theories concerning trauma, Dutton's explanation has little to say about discontinuity, or those cases when men survived these types of experiences but did not become violent.

Summary

A number of theories have been advanced to account for the etiology of violence in males. Building on earlier socialization accounts, more recent theoretical accounts that include trauma and attachment explanations appear particularly promising. However, these theories provide little guidance in accounting for sources of discontinuity, an essential requirement for comprehensive theories of why some individuals become violent and others do not.

CONCLUSION

Considerable progress has been made into the investigation of fathers, previously reported as missing from the research literature, and intrafamilial violence. In fact, we were able to locate more than 40 studies published since the mid-1990s that in some way addressed the subject of fathers and family violence. That work covered a range of subjects, but much of it focused on the two most important topics: the characteristics of fathers who perpetrate family violence and the effects of violent fathers on children's development.

These investigations reveal the complexities of the topic but also provide some initial answers. For example, it is increasingly clear that simple stereotypes of family violence no longer hold. Men, including fathers, who physically abuse their wives are not all alike but differ on such variables as severity of abuse, psychological problems, and targets of violence. Fathers, who have most often been investigated as perpetrators of violence, are at least in some cases victims of family violence. The effects of paternal violence on children's development may depend on a host of variables beyond the type of violence, such as the child's gender and emotional response and the father's biological status and the quality of his involvement in the child's life.

Across the topics addressed in this chapter, four issues related to fathers and violence appeared sporadically. These issues concerned differences between fathers and mothers in abusive treatment of their children, whether fathers' violence has unique effects on their children, whether fathers' biological status with the child makes a difference, and the role of child gender in terms of differential parenting, victimization, or outcomes. Unfortunately, these issues were not raised in a sufficient number of studies to draw firm conclusions. When appropriate, efforts to address each of these issues should be included in designs of future research.

Indeed, the topic of fathers and family violence is ripe for new investigations. The work summarized here, taken as a whole, represents an important stride forward. But it is only a start. All of the topics addressed in this chapter warrant further attention. It is becoming increasingly clear that comprehensive studies are most urgently needed if we are to arrive at an accurate understanding of fathers and family violence. Such studies should assess multiple forms of parental violence and child maltreatment occurring both in and out of the home, collect information from multiple informants about both violent and nonviolent behaviors, identify other problems and issues with which the family is dealing, and follow the family over time. Such studies are time-consuming and expensive but would go far in helping us to understand the relations between fathers, intrafamilial violence, and children's outcomes. That knowledge is essential for successful intervention and prevention efforts to combat the widespread problem of family violence.

REFERENCES

Appel, A. E., & Holden, G. W. (1998). The co-occurrence of spouse and physical child abuse: A review and appraisal. *Journal of Family Psychology, 12,* 578–599.

Archer, J. (2000). Sex differences in aggression between heterosexual partners: A meta-analytic review. *Psychological Bulletin, 126,* 651–680.

Baker, C. K., Perilla, J. L., & Norris, F. H. (2001). Parenting stress and parenting competence among Latino men who batter. *Journal of Interpersonal Violence, 16,* 1139–1157.

Barnett, O. W., Miller-Perrin, C. L., & Perrin, R. D. (1997). *Family violence across the lifespan: An introduction* (pp. 235–250). Thousand Oaks, CA: Sage.

Berman, H. (1999). Stories of growing up amid violence by refugee children of war and children of battered women living in Canada. *Journal of Nursing Scholarship, 31,* 57–63.

Birns, B., Cascardi, M., & Meyer, S. (1994). Sex-role socialization: Developmental influences on wife abuse. *American Journal of Orthopsychiatry, 64,* 50–59.

Black, M. M., Dubowitz, H., & Starr, R. H., Jr. (1999). African American fathers in low income, urban families: Development, behavior, and home environment of their three-year-old children. *Child Development, 70,* 967–978.

Bullock, C. F., & Cubert, J. (2002). Coverage of domestic violence fatalities by newspapers in Washington state. *Journal of Interpersonal Violence, 17,* 475–499.

Caspi, A., Taylor, A., Smart, M., Jackson, J., Tagami, S., & Moffitt, T. E. (2001). Can women provide reliable information about their children's fathers? Cross-informant agreement about men's lifetime antisocial behavior. *Journal of Child Psychology and Psychiatry, 42,* 915–920.

Cox, M. J., & Paley, B. (1997). Families as systems. *Annual Review of Psychology, 48,* 243–267.

Crockenberg, S., & Langrock, A. (2001). The role of specific emotions in children's responses to interparental conflict: A test of the model. *Journal of Family Psychology, 15,* 163–182.

Cummings, E. M. (1994). *Children and marital conflict: The impact of family dispute and resolution.* New York: Guilford Press.

Cummings, J. G., Pepler, D. J., & Moore, T. E. (1999). Behavior problems in children exposed to wife abuse: Gender differences. *Journal of Family Violence, 14,* 133–156.

Daly, M., & Wilson, M. (1988). *Homicide.* New York: de Guyter.

Daly, M., & Wilson, M. (1996). Violence against stepchildren. *Current Directions in Psychological Science, 5,* 77–81.

Dobash, R. P., Dobash, R. E., Wilson, M., & Daly, M. (1992). The myth of sexual symmetry in marital violence. *Social Problems, 39,* 71–91.

Dubowitz, H., Black, M. M., Cox, C. E., Kerr, M. A., Litrownik, A. J., Radhakrishna, A., et al. (2001). Father involvement and children's functioning at age 6 years: A multisite study. *Child Maltreatment, 6,* 300–309.

Dutton, D. G. (1995). Male abusiveness in intimate relationships. *Clinical Psychology Review, 15,* 567–581.

Dutton, D. G. (1998). *The abusive personality: Violence and control in intimate relationships*. New York: Guilford Press.

Dutton, D. G., & Hemphill, K. J. (1992). Patterns of socially desirable responding among perpetrators and victims of wife assault. *Violence and Victims, 7*, 29–39.

Dutton, D. G., Starzomski, A., & Ryan, L. (1996). Antecedents of abusive personality and abusive behavior in wife assaulters. *Journal of Family Violence, 11*, 113–132.

Edleson, J. L. (1999a). Children's witnessing of adult domestic violence. *Journal of Interpersonal Violence, 14*, 839–870.

Edleson, J. L. (1999b). The overlap between child maltreatment and woman battering. *Violence Against Women, 5*, 134–154.

Fox, G. L., & Benson, M. L. (2003). Violent men, bad dads? Fathering profiles of men involved in intimate partner violence. In R. D. Day & M. E. Lamb (Eds.), *Conceptualizing and measuring father involvement*. Mackway, NJ: Erlbaum.

Fox, G. L., Sayers, J., & Bruce, C. (2001). Beyond bravado: Redemption and rehabilitation in the fathering accounts of men who batter. *Marriage and Family Review, 32*, 137–163.

Gelles, R. J. (1976). Abused wives: Why do they stay? *Journal of Marriage and the Family, 38*, 659–668.

Gelles, R. J. (1993). Through a sociological lens: Social structure and family violence. In R. J. Gelles & D. R. Loseke (Eds.), *Current controversies on family violence* (pp. 67–87). Newbury Park, CA: Sage.

Gershoff, E. T. (2002). Corporal punishment by parents and associated child behaviors and experiences: A meta-analytic and theoretical review. *Psychological Bulletin, 128*, 539–579.

Gondolf, E. W. (1988). Who are those guys? Toward a behavioral typology of batterers. *Violence and Victims, 3*, 187–203.

Gottman, J. M., Jacobson, R. H., Rushe, R. H., Shortt, J. W., Babcock, J., La Taillade, J. J., et al. (1995). The relationship between heart rate reactivity, emotionally aggressive behavior, and general violence in batterers. *Journal of Family Psychology, 9*, 227–248.

Graham-Bermann, S. A. (1998). The impact of woman abuse on children's social development: Research and theoretical perspectives. In G. W. Holden, R. Geffner, & E. N. Jouriles (Eds.), *Children exposed to marital violence: Theory, research, and applied issues* (pp. 21–54). Washington, DC: American Psychological Association.

Graham-Bermann, S. A., & Brescoll, V. (2000). Gender, power, and violence: Assessing the family stereotypes of the children of batterers. *Journal of Family Psychology, 14*, 600–612.

Graham-Bermann, S. A., & Edleson, J. L. (2001). *Domestic violence in the lives of children: The future of research, intervention, and social policy*. Washington, DC: American Psychological Association.

Graziano, A. M. (1994). Why we should study subabusive violence against children. *Journal of Interpersonal Violence, 9*, 412–419.

Grych, J. H., Wachsmuth-Schlaefer, T., & Klockow, L. L. (2002). Interpersonal aggression and young children's representations of family relationships. *Journal of Family Psychology, 16*, 259–272.

Haapasalo, J. (2001). How do young offenders describe their parents? *Legal and Criminological Psychology, 6*, 103–120.

Heckert, D. A., & Gondolf, E. W. (2000). Predictors of underreporting of male violence by batterer program participants and their partners. *Journal of Family Violence, 15*, 423–443.

Herron, K., & Holtzworth-Munroe, A. (2002). Child abuse potential: A comparison of subtypes of maritally violent men and nonviolent men. *Journal of Family Violence, 17*, 1–21.

Heyman, R. E., & Smith Slep, A. M. (2002). Do child abuse and interparental violence lead to adulthood family violence? *Journal of Marriage and the Family, 64,* 864–870.

Holden, G. W., Barker, T., Angelelli, M., Appel, A., & Hazlewood, L. (2003). *Batterers as fathers and the risk of physical child abuse.* Manuscript submitted for publication.

Holden, G. W., Miller, P. C., & Harris, S. D. (1999). The instrumental side of corporal punishment: Parents' reported practices and outcome expectancies. *Journal of Marriage and the Family, 61,* 971–981.

Holden, G. W., & Ritchie, K. L. (1991). Linking extreme marital discord, child rearing, and child behavior problems: Evidence from battered women. *Child Development, 62,* 311–327.

Holden, G. W., Stein, J. D., Ritchie, K. L., Harris, S. D., & Jouriles, E. N. (1998). Parenting behaviors and beliefs of battered women. In G. W. Holden, R. Geffner, & E. N. Jouriles (Eds.), *Children exposed to marital violence: Theory, research, and applied issues* (pp. 289–334). Washington, DC: American Psychological Association.

Holtzworth-Munroe, A. (2000). A typology of men who are violent toward their female partners: Making sense of the heterogeneity in husband violence. *Current Directions in Psychological Science, 9,* 140–143.

Holtzworth-Munroe, A., Bates, L., Smutzler, N., & Sandin, E. (1997). A brief review of the research on husband violence: Part 1. Maritally violent versus nonviolent men. *Aggression and Violent Behavior, 2,* 65–99.

Holtzworth-Munroe, A., Meehan, J. C., Herron, K., Rehman, U., & Stuart, L. (2000). Testing the Holtzworth-Munroe and Stuart (1994) batterer typology. *Journal of Consulting and Clinical Psychology, 68,* 1000–1019.

Holtzworth-Munroe, A., & Stuart, L. (1994). The typologies of male batterers: Three subtypes and the differences among them. *Psychological Bulletin, 116,* 476–497.

Holtzworth-Munroe, A., Stuart, L., & Hutchinson, G. (1997). Violent versus nonviolent husbands: Differences in attachment patterns, dependency, and jealousy. *Journal of Family Psychology, 11,* 314–331.

Jaffe, P. G., Lemon, N. K. D., & Poisson, S. E. (2003). *Child custody and domestic violence: A call for safety and accountability.* Thousand Oaks, CA: Sage.

Jaffee, S. R., Moffitt, T. E., Caspi, A., & Taylor, A. (2003). Life with (or without) father: The benefits of living with two biological parents depend on the father's antisocial behavior. *Child Development, 74,* 109–126.

Jasinski, J. L., & Williams, L. M. (1999). *Partner violence: A comprehensive review of 20 years of research.* Thousand Oaks, CA: Sage.

Johnson, M. P. (1995). Patriarchal terrorism and common couple violence: Two forms of violence against women. *Journal of Marriage and the Family, 57,* 283–294.

Johnson, M. P., & Ferraro, K. J. (2000). Research on domestic violence in the 1990s: Making distinctions. *Journal of Marriage and the Family, 62,* 948–963.

Jouriles, E. N., Mehta, P., McDonald, R., & Francis, D. J. (1997). Psychometric properties of family members' reports of parental physical aggression toward clinic-referred children. *Journal of Consulting and Clinical Psychology, 65,* 309–318.

Jouriles, E. N., & Norwood, W. D. (1995). Physical aggression toward boys and girls in families characterized by the battering of women. *Journal of Family Psychology, 9,* 69–78.

Kempe, C. H., Silverman, F. N., Steele, B. F., Droegemueller, W., & Silver, H. K. (1962). The battered child syndrome. *Journal of the American Medical Association, 181,* 107–112.

Kilpatrick, K. L., & Williams, L. M. (1998). Potential mediators of post-traumatic stress disorder in child witnesses to domestic violence. *Child Abuse and Neglect, 22,* 31–33.

Kinard, E. M. (2001). Recruiting participants for child abuse research: What does it take? *Journal of Family Violence, 16,* 219–236.

Kunz, J., & Bahr, S. J. (1996). A profile of parental homicide against children. *Journal of Family Violence, 11,* 347–362.

Lamb, M. E. (Ed.). (1997). *The role of the father in child development* (3rd ed.). New York: Wiley.

Lamb, M. E. (2001). Male roles in families "at risk": The ecology of child maltreatment. *Child Maltreatment, 6,* 310–313.

Lamb, M. E. (2002). Infant-father attachment and their impact on child development. In C. S. Tamis-LeMonda & N. J. Cabrera (Eds.), *Handbook of father involvement: Multidisciplinary perspectives* (pp. 93–118). Mahwah, NJ: Erlbaum.

Langan, P. A., & Dawson, J. M. (1995). *Spouse murder defendants in large urban counties* (NCJ-153256). Washington, DC: U.S. Department of Justice.

Laurent, A., & Derry, A. (1999). Violence of French adolescents toward their parents: Characteristics and contexts. *Journal of Adolescent Health, 25,* 21–26.

Levendosky, A. A., & Graham-Bermann, S. A. (2000). Behavioral observations of parenting in battered women. *Journal of Family Psychology, 14,* 80–94.

Lewis, C. (1997). Fathers and preschoolers. In M. E. Lamb (Ed.), *The role of the father in child development* (3rd ed., pp. 121–142). New York: Wiley.

Malkin, C. M., & Lamb, M. E. (1994). Child maltreatment: A test of sociological theory. *Journal of Comparative Family Studies, 25,* 121–133.

Marshall, D. B., English, D. J., & Stewart, A. J. (2001). The effect of fathers or father figures on child behavioral problems in families referred to Child Protective Services. *Child Maltreatment, 6,* 290–299.

McCloskey, L. A., Figueredo, A. J., & Koss, M. P. (1995). The effects of systemic family violence on children's mental health. *Child Development, 66,* 1239–1261.

McDonald, R., & Jouriles, E. N. (1991). Marital aggression and child behavior problems: Research findings, mechanisms, and intervention strategies. *Behavior Therapist, 14,* 189–192.

McDonald, R., Jouriles, E. N., Norwood, W., Ware, H. S., & Ezell, E. (2000). Husbands' marital violence and the adjustment problems of clinic-referred children. *Behavior Therapy, 31,* 649–665.

McGuigan, W. M., Vuchinich, S., & Pratt, C. C. (2000). Domestic violence, parents' view of their infant, and risk of child abuse. *Journal of Family Psychology, 14,* 613–624.

Migliaccio, T. A. (2002). Abused husbands: A narrative analysis. *Journal of Family Issues, 23,* 26–52.

Milner, J. S. (1994). Assessing physical child abuse: The Child Abuse Potential Inventory. *Clinical Psychology Review, 14,* 547–583.

Muller, R. T. (1995). The interaction of parent and child gender in physical child maltreatment. *Canadian Journal of Behavioral Science, 27,* 450–465.

Muller, R. T., & Diamond, T. (1999). Father and mother physical abuse and child aggressive behaviour in two generations. *Canadian Journal of Behavioural Science, 31,* 221–228.

National Child Abuse and Neglect Data System (NCANDS). (2002). Summary of key findings from calendar year 2000. Retrieved December 13, 2002, from http://www.calib.com/nccanch/pubs/factsheets/canstats.cfm

Nobes, G., & Smith, M. (2000). The relative extent of physical punishment and abuse by mothers and fathers. *Trauma, Violence, and Abuse, 1,* 47–66.

Nobes, G., & Smith, M. (2002). Family structure and the physical punishment of children. *Journal of Family Issues, 23,* 349–373.

Nobes, G., Smith, M., Upton, P., & Heverin, A. (1999). Physical punishment by mothers and fathers in British homes. *Journal of Interpersonal Violence, 14*, 887–902.

O'Keefe, M. (1994). Linking marital violence, mother-child/father-child aggression, and child behavior problems. *Journal of Family Violence, 9*, 63–78.

Pagelow, M. D. (1985). The "battered husband syndrome": Social problem or much ado about nothing. In N. Johnson (Ed.), *Marital violence* (pp. 172–195). Boston, MA: Routledge Kegan Paul.

Parke, R. D. (2002). Fathers and families. In M. H. Bornstein (Ed.), *Handbook of parenting: Vol. 3. Being and becoming a parent* (2nd ed., pp. 27–73). Mahwah, NJ: Erlbaum.

Paulson, M. J., Coombs, R. H., & Landsverk, J. (1990). Youth who physically assault their parents. *Journal of Family Violence, 5*, 121–133.

Pearson, P. (1997). *When she was bad: Violent women and the myth of innocence.* New York: Viking.

Peled, E. (1998). The experience of living with violence for preadolescent children of battered women. *Youth and Society, 29*, 395–430.

Peled, E. (2000). Parenting by men who abuse women: Issues and dilemmas. *British Journal of Social Work, 30*, 25–36.

Radhakrishna, A., Bou-Saada, I. E., Hunter, W. M., Catellier, D. J., & Kotch, J. B. (2001). Are father surrogates a risk factor for child maltreatment? *Child Maltreatment, 6*, 281–289.

Rennison, C. M., & Welchans, S. (2000). *Intimate partner violence* (Bureau of Justice Statistics Special Report). Washington, DC: U.S. Department of Justice.

Rossman, B. B. R. (2001). Longer term effects of children's exposure to domestic violence. In S. A. Graham-Bermann & J. L. Edleson (Eds.), *Domestic violence in the lives of children: The future of research, intervention, and social policy* (pp. 35–65). Washington, DC: American Psychological Association.

Schumacher, J. A., Feldbau-Kohn, S., Smith Slep, A. M., & Heyman, R. E. (2001). Risk factors for male-to-female partner physical abuse. *Aggression and Violent Behavior, 6*, 281–352.

Sedlak, A., & Broadhurst, D. D. (1996). *Executive summary of the Third National Incidence Study of Child Abuse and Neglect.* Washington, DC: U.S. Department of Health and Human Services.

Simons, R. L., Wu, C. I., Johnson, C., & Conger, R. D. (1995). A test of various perspectives on the intergenerational transmission of domestic violence. *Criminology, 33*, 141–170.

Sorenson, S. B., Upchurch, D. M., & Shen, H. (1996). Violence and injury in marital arguments: Risk patterns and gender differences. *American Journal of Public Health, 86*, 35–40.

Steinmetz, S. K. (1977). The battered husband syndrome. *Victimology, 2*, 499–509.

Sternberg, K. J. (1997). Fathers, the missing parents in research on family violence. In M. E. Lamb (Ed.), *The role of the father in child development* (3rd ed., pp. 284–308). New York: Wiley.

Sternberg, K. J., Lamb, M. E., & Dawud-Noursi, S. (1998). Using multiple informants and cross-cultural research to study the effects of domestic violence on developmental psychopathology: Illustrations from research in Israel. In G. W. Holden, R. Geffner, & E. N. Jouriles (Eds.), *Children exposed to marital violence: Theory, research, and applied issues* (pp. 21–156). Washington, DC: American Psychological Association.

Sternberg, K. J., Lamb, M. E., Greenbaum, C., Cicchetti, D., Dawud, S., Cortes, R. M., et al. (1993). Effects of domestic violence on children's behavior problems and depression. *Developmental Psychology, 29*, 44–52.

Sternberg, K. J., Lamb, M. E., Greenbaum, C., Dawud, S., Cortes, R. M., & Lorey, S. (1994). The effects of domestic violence on children's perceptions of their perpetrating and nonperpetrating parents. *International Journal of Behavioral Development, 17*, 779–795.

Straus, M. A. (1979). Measuring intrafamily conflict and aggression: The Conflict Tactics Scale (CT). *Journal of Marriage and the Family, 41*, 75–88.

Straus, M. A. (1999). The controversy over domestic violence by women: A methodological, theoretical and sociology of science analysis. In X. B. Arriaga & S. Oskamp (Eds.), *Violence in intimate relationships* (pp. 17–44). Thousand Oaks, CA: Sage.

Straus, M. A. (2001). *Beating the devil out of them: Corporal punishment in American families and its effects on children.* New Brunswick, NJ: Transaction.

Straus, M. A., Gelles, R. J., & Steinmetz, S. K. (1980). *Behind closed doors: Violence in the American family.* Beverly Hills, CA: Sage.

Sugarman, D. B., & Hotaling, G. T. (1997). Intimate violence and social desirability: A meta-analytic review. *Journal of Interpersonal Violence, 12,* 275–290.

Sullivan, C. M., Juras, J., Bybee, D., Nguyen, H., & Allen, N. (2000). How children's adjustment is affected by their relationships to their mothers' abusers. *Journal of Interpersonal Violence, 15,* 587–602.

Sullivan, C. M., Nguyen, H., Allen, N., Bybee, D., & Juras, J. (2000). Beyond searching for deficits: Evidence that physically and emotionally abused women are nurturing parents. *Journal of Emotional Abuse, 2,* 51–71.

Tjaden, P., & Thoennes, N. (1998). Prevalence, incidence, and consequences of violence against women: Findings from the National Violence Against Women Survey (National Institute of Justice, Centers for Disease Control and Prevention). Retrieved December 13, 2002, from http://www.ojp.usdoj.gov/nij/pubs-sum/172837.htm

Underwood, R. C., & Patch, P. C. (1999). Siblicide: A descriptive analysis of sibling homicide. *Homicide Studies, 3,* 333–348.

U.S. Department of Justice, Bureau of Justice Statistics. (2003). Homicide trends in the United States: Infanticide. Retrieved January 10, 2003, from http://www.ojp.usdoj.gov/bjs/homicide/children.htm

Van der Kolk, B. A. (1987). *Psychological trauma.* Washington, DC: American Psychiatric Press.

Van der Kolk, B. A. (1988). Trauma in men: Effects on family life. In M. B. Straus (Ed.), *Abuse and victimization across the lifespan* (pp. 170–187). Baltimore: John Hopkins University Press.

Van der Kolk, B. A. (1996). The body keeps score: Approaches to the psychobiology of post-traumatic stress disorder. In B. A. Van der Kolk, A. C. McFarlane, & L. Weisaeth (Eds.), *Traumatic stress: The effects of overwhelming experience on mind, body, and society* (pp. 214–241). New York: Guilford Press.

Walker, L. E. (1979). *The battered woman.* New York: Harper & Row.

Weaver, T. L., & Clum, G. A. (1993). Early family environments and traumatic experiences associated with borderline personality. *Journal of Consulting and Clinical Psychology, 61,* 1068–1075.

Williams, O., Boggess, J. L., & Carter, J. (2001). Fatherhood and domestic violence: Exploring the role of men who batter in the lives of their children. In S. Graham-Bermann & J. Edleson (Eds.), *Domestic violence in the lives of children: The future of research, intervention, and social policy* (pp. 157–188). Washington, DC: American Psychological Association.

Wilson, M., & Brooks-Gunn, J. (2001). Health status and behaviors of unwed fathers. *Children and Youth Services Review, 23,* 377–401.

CHAPTER 16

Intervention

Changing the Nature and Extent of Father Involvement

BRENT A. MCBRIDE and MARY M. LUTZ

FATHERS, AS ACTIVE, involved parents, began to attract the attention of social scientists in the 1970s (e.g., Lamb, 1975). This interest was in contrast to research on fathers conducted in the prior few decades, which for the most part focused on consequences for children of father absence (Biller, 1971). The refocused interest on fathers as active parents increased dramatically in the ensuing years with considerable attention given to father involvement in direct child-rearing activities (e.g., Barnett & Baruch, 1987; Larson, 1993; Marsiglio, 1991; McBride & Rane, 1997). In the past decade, researchers were joined by policy makers and the popular media in a continued and explicit focus on fathers and fathering (e.g., Coltrane & Allen, 1994; Griswold, 1993; Lamb, 1997; LaRossa, 1997; LaRossa, Gordon, Wilson, Bairan, & Jaret, 1991; Tamis-LeMonda & Cabrera, 1999; Thomas, 1998).

As outlined in the introduction to this volume and articulated in many of the chapters, several factors have contributed to this increased interest in fathers and fatherhood (e.g., changing societal conceptions of parental roles, increases in maternal employment, a growing body of literature outlining the impact of father involvement on child development, shifts in the demographic profile of modern families, increased policy debates over the well-being of children). Accompanying this increased interest has been a rapidly expanding research literature on fathers and fatherhood, especially during the past decade (Cabrera, Tamis-LeMonda, Bradley, Hofferth, & Lamb, 2000; Marsiglio, Amato, Day, & Lamb, 2000). Given the interrelatedness of many of the factors that have influenced this research agenda and the ongoing debates and concerns over various issues, it seems certain that the focus on fathers and fathering in both the research and policy arenas will not abate any time soon.

Paralleling this increased interest of researchers in the roles of fathers has been a shift in societal expectations for fatherhood. The question is no longer one of whether men are capable of providing effective parenting as women historically have done. There is ample evidence suggesting that men can have a positive impact on their children's development when actively engaged in direct child-rearing activities (e.g., Almeida & Galambos, 1991; Lamb, 1997; Snarey, 1993; Starrels, 1994; Williams, Radin, & Allegro, 1992). With men's potential to provide competent parenting no longer being the central question in this area, societal expectations have emerged that call for men to assume a more active role in raising their young children (Griswold, 1993; Knijn, in press; LaRossa, 1997; Marsiglio, 1995; McBride & Mills, 1993; Pleck & Pleck, 1997).

Consistent with this shift in societal expectations for fatherhood, fathers are slowly beginning to increase the amount of time they spend caring for their children. For example, in two thorough analyses of previous time-use studies (Hofferth, Pleck, Stueve, Bianchi, & Sayer, 2002; Pleck, 1997), measurable increases in fathers' involvement with their children over the last three decades have been identified (see Pleck & Masciadrelli, this volume). However, these increases are small, and fathers continue to spend significantly less time than mothers caring for children. This would suggest that the gap between the culture and conduct of fatherhood, first discussed by LaRossa in 1988, continues to exist. Levine and Pitt (1995), McBride and Rane (1997, 2001), Palm (1997), and others have argued that the creation of parenting programs targeted specifically for fathers may be one way to help men more effectively live up to changing societal expectations for fatherhood, thereby reducing this gap.

The emergence of such intervention programs targeted for fathers has paralleled the interest of researchers in the topic of fatherhood during the past three decades. This movement began as a grassroots effort in response to a call for the redefinition of paternal roles in the late 1970s and early 1980s, with programs emerging in various settings across the country. With the advent in recent years of several national-, state-, and local-level initiatives focusing on fatherhood issues (e.g., National Fatherhood Initiative, National Center on Fathers and Families), parenting programs for fathers can now be found in many urban, suburban, and rural settings. Although the number of programs providing services for fathers has expanded rapidly in recent years, a great amount of diversity exists in the programs that have been developed and implemented, and little work has been done to evaluate their impact systematically (Palm, 1998). As such, much of the work being done to develop these programs remains at a grassroots level and suffers from the myriad of problems associated with local or individually developed efforts (e.g., lack of shared resources and knowledge base, duplication of effort, a trial-and-error approach to developing new initiatives, etc.).

The purpose of this chapter is to provide an overview of the current status of parenting programs developed specifically for fathers, with a particular emphasis on the diversity that can be found in such initiatives. This chapter is not meant to be an exhaustive review of all programs that are currently in existence. Such an effort is not within the scope of a single chapter. The grassroots nature of these programs also makes it difficult to compile a review that addresses the entire range of programs that have been developed. As a result, little work has been done on a systematic level to develop a literature base on programs that address fatherhood, with limited information being published in the scholarly and professional outlets. This lack of published information is problematic given the number of programs targeting fathers that we know exist across the country.

We have divided this chapter into five sections: frameworks used to develop programs, models and articulated goals of programs implemented, populations served, focus of services provided, and program evaluation. Within each section we provide an overview of the variations in how programs address the issue or topic. We end the chapter with a set of recommendations for intervention programs for fathers that will help strengthen the field in general.

FRAMEWORKS USED

RATIONALE

Every type of social program should be grounded within a theoretical or philosophical framework. A sound theoretical or philosophical framework has the potential tentatively to describe, explain, and predict behavioral phenomena as they are observed within the program model. These frameworks are essential to program development because they help guide the intervention strategy and provide a rationale for services. Throughout program implementation, evidence should be gathered to support, modify, or change the initial framework. Philosophical- and theoretical-based research helps determine which intervention methods are most effective with particular contexts and populations of fathers. This evidence is needed to help further the field of fatherhood studies by creating a larger explanatory scheme for fatherhood behavior (Monette, Sullivan, & DeJong, 1998).

MULTIPLE FRAMEWORKS APPLIED

The majority of published fatherhood programs have no clearly stated philosophical or theoretical framework (Barth, Claycomb, & Loomis, 1988; Bowling, 1999; Devlin, Brown, Beebe, & Parulis, 1992; Genisio, 1996; Harrison, 1997; Huey, 1987; Kissman, 2001; Landreth & Lobaugh, 1998; Sternbach, 1990; Stone, McKenry, & Clark, 1999; Vadasy, Fewell, Greenberg, Dermond, & Meyer, 1986). Despite this, there are a number of existing fatherhood programs that have adopted a wide variety of frameworks to explain fatherhood behavior and design programs. Theoretical frameworks that have been used to guide fatherhood programs include ecological, microstructuralist, behavioral, and social-learning theories, among others.

Ecological Theory

Among the different theories that were used to guide the development of the Head Start Father Involvement Program (Fagan & Iglesias, 1999), the ecological model (Bronfenbrenner, 1977) provided a framework for exploring how to help promote paternal involvement. Programs based on ecological theory tend to emphasize the context in which fathering takes place. This orientation focuses on the behavior of a person in relation to his or her social environment. It acknowledges that a person is involved in a variety of interrelating systems, the microsystem, mesosystem, exosystem, and macrosystem. The microsystem is the diverse set of systems in which fathers conduct their daily interactions. The mesosystem is the interaction among these microsystems. The exosystem, on the other hand, is larger and consists of the different institutions that influence an individual's personal systems. The macrosystem is the overarching subculture and cultural contexts that affect all other systems. The interaction of these systems is thought to have a substantial impact on human functioning (Bronfenbrenner, 1977). Within this theoretical framework, the Head Start Fatherhood Program (Fagan & Iglesias, 1999) focused on creating a supportive link between families and the program (i.e., mesosystem). Fagan et al. hoped that this connection would increase the amount of involvement exhibited by fathers enrolled in the program.

Microstructural Theory

A microstructuralist framework is another theory on which programs for fathers are based. This model focuses on the structural conditions in the environment that promote and encourage specific fathering behaviors (Risman & Schwartz, 1989). Based on this model, the Head Start Father Involvement Program predicted that if men were part of a program that encouraged involvement in their children's lives, this involvement would become an expectation for fathers. Such an expectation would then have the potential to promote a stronger father-child connection through paternal involvement both at home and school (Fagan & Iglesias, 1999).

Behavioral Theory

When related to fatherhood, behavioral theory states that fathering behavior is developed through a series of learning experiences. This theory focuses on observable behavior and the consequences, such as reinforcement and punishment, that influence an individual's behavior (Skinner, 1958; Watson, 1924). Few programs rely solely on this framework when creating fatherhood programs. However, many programs tend to employ components of behavioral theory within the program model. A behavioral approach to fatherhood programs stresses the fact that children's behavior is learned from others. Therefore, some programs strive to teach fathers how to use behavioral theory with their children. A prime example of this is Russell and Matson's (1998) program, which trained fathers to be intervention agents for their developmentally delayed children. In this program, fathers were instructed to use behavioral therapy concepts when managing their children's conduct. Both measurable and observable behaviors were then used to evaluate the program.

Social Learning Theory

Programs driven by a social learning framework tend to rely on group and social opportunities to promote fathering behaviors and attitudes. These natural experiences hold the potential for individuals to learn from others as a result of observation and cognitive processing (Bandura, 1977). With social-learning principles in mind, the Father-Son Project invited two or more generations of men to participate in a daylong intergenerational group experience. Through stories, games, and discussions, participants were given the opportunity to model, observe, and learn from each other (Bowman, 1993).

Psychosocial Theory

Closely related to social learning theory, Erik Erikson's (1959) psychosocial theory of development has been an increasingly popular conceptual model that has been used to explain fatherhood behavior (e.g., Hawkins & Dollahite, 1997). This model describes a series of eight stages through which an individual progresses from birth to death. Each stage results in a conflict or struggle that is presented as a result of biological forces and sociocultural expectations that are placed on an individual. Generativity versus stagnation is the seventh of Erikson's eight stages of development. When applied to fatherhood, this theory contends that in order to resolve this conflict and develop properly, a man must find ways to satisfy and support the next generation (Erikson, 1959). In his 1998 outcome study of a fathering program, Bailey used a generative fathering model to guide the development of his Dads Make a Difference program. This framework aided in the development of an educational and supportive program for noncustodial fathers (Bailey, 1998).

In contrast to the use of a theoretical orientation, some programs opt to apply a philosophical framework to program development and implementation. Examples of the philosophical frameworks that were found in our literature review included the empowerment, relationship-focused, client-centered approach, context change–relationship change philosophy, and the Lamb multidimensional model of paternal involvement.

Empowerment Philosophy

The empowerment perspective was utilized in the development of the Head Start program for African American males. This philosophy recognizes that many social and societal conditions contribute to fathers' problems and seeks to give individuals understanding and mastery over these problems. Fagan and Stevenson (1995) applied the empowerment philosophy to their work with economically disadvantaged African American men. This perspective emphasized the collective responsibility these men have to help other men serve as supports for children in their communities. In accordance with this philosophy, men with children in Head Start were trained to serve as facilitators for a support group. These men gained a sense of empowerment through learning group leadership skills. They then became respected in their community by empowering others through support groups that they facilitated (Fagan & Stevenson, 1995).

Relationship-Focused Philosophy

Fatherhood programs with a relationship-focused philosophical orientation focus primarily on the one-on-one interactions that take place between a father and his child. This framework can be effective in guiding early intervention programs for children with disabilities, and it was applied to a program aimed to increase the involvement of fathers in the lives of their children with disabilities. In small group sessions that included both fathers and children, fathers were given tools to help them enhance their ability to interact with their children (Mahoney, Wiggers, & Lash, 1996).

Client-Centered Approach

Client-centered programs tend to help fathers build self-esteem and self-awareness. They are often less directive and allow fathers to discover and learn on their own. In our review, only one program stated that a client-centered approach was used. This program (Levant & Doyle, 1983) serving fathers of school-aged children chose to focus on enhancing communication and sensitivity. Many experiential methods and components, such as role playing, were used to help fathers in this program learn and practice new skills.

Context Change–Relationship Change Philosophy

A context change–relationship change philosophy guided Braver and Griffin (2000) in their Dads for Life program. They investigated a perspective that supported the fact that the context of noncustodial fathers often leads to disengagement with their children. In their extensive study, they found that it is often the father's sense of powerlessness and inequity as well as a conflictual postdivorce relationship with the mother that may make it less likely that a father will be involved with his children. This philosophy was used in their program to help change the context of fathering for noncustodial dads. Braver and Griffin hypothesized that if this context was changed, the relationship a father had with his children would change as a result.

Lamb Multidimensional Model of Paternal Involvement

Finally, the Lamb multidimensional model of paternal involvement (Lamb, Pleck, Charnov, & Levine, 1987) was applied to help McBride guide his 1991 study of a parent education and support group for fathers. This model operationalizes the construct of father involvement by breaking it down into three categories. The first category, interaction or engagement, consists of one-on-one activities between a father and his child. The second category, accessibility, requires that the father be available to his child. The third category, responsibility, consists of paternal caretaking for the welfare of a father's children. This model served as a framework for evaluating the program on the basis of the type and amount of involvement that was affected by the intervention.

These diverse philosophical and theoretical approaches to forming and implementing interventions have helped researchers and practitioners better understand fathering behavior. Given the grassroots nature of fatherhood programs, it is important to investigate and apply a variety of models to help determine which approaches are most successful in reaching various groups of men.

MODELS AND GOALS

Programs can use a variety of models to provide services for fathers. Interventions can reach out to groups of fathers or provide services on an individual basis. They can also use a combined approach by providing services in both group and individual formats. In addition, a number of programs utilize a father-child model and provide services to the father-child dyad.

GROUP MODEL

The majority of fatherhood interventions use a group model for service delivery (e.g., Bailey, 1998; Barth et al., 1988; Bowling, 1999; Bowman, 1993; Braver & Griffin, 2000; Braver, Griffin, Cookston, Sandler, & Williams, 2002; Delvin et al., 1992; Fagan & Iglesias, 1999; Fagan & Stevenson, 1995; Genisio, 1996; Harrison, 1997; Huey, 1987; Kissman, 2001; Levant & Doyle, 1983; Sternbach, 1990; Stone et al., 1999; Vadasy et al., 1986). Such an approach is desirable for a number of reasons. First, the group format is the type of setting most familiar to men when compared to other models of support, education, and skill-building programs (e.g., individual therapy, couples therapy; Andronico, 1996; Brooks, 1996). Second, a well-run group has the potential to provide a variety of benefits such as peer feedback, mutual aid, support, reality testing, and opportunities for vicarious learning (Toseland & Rivas, 2001). Third, this approach is the most cost-effective model for men whose needs can be met in a group format. It allows practitioners to reach a number of men at one time and thus provide a timely and efficient method for service delivery (Toseland & Rivas, 2001).

Some programs choose to intervene with small groups of men (e.g., 5 to 12 participants; e.g., Braver et al., 2002; Fagan & Stevenson, 1995; Genisio, 1996; Huey, 1987; Landreth & Lobaugh, 1998; Levant & Doyle, 1983). For example, in Genisio's (1996) work with incarcerated fathers, fathers' criminal backgrounds were taken into account when composing the group, and the size was limited to 10 men. Other programs choose to work with larger groups of men (e.g., more than 12 participants; e.g., Bailey, 1998; Devlin et al., 1992; Harrison, 1997; Landreth & Lobaugh, 1998; Stone et al., 1999). In the Dads Make a Difference program (Bailey, 1998), the intervention was provided to two groups of approximately 20 fathers each. Similarly, McBride's (1990, 1991) parent education and support groups provided services to 15 men at a time in a group setting. Program size differs for a variety of reasons. The recruitment strategy, program funding and resources, program goals, and community characteristics play a role in the number of fathers that can effectively participate in group interventions.

Programs can use a variety of formats to deliver services to groups of fathers. Educational groups and workshops, skill-building groups, support and self-help groups, and group retreats are ways that practitioners have utilized the group format to provide fatherhood interventions.

Educational Groups and Workshops

Programs that employ an educational group model generally focus on increasing fathers' knowledge of child development and appropriate parenting (e.g., Barth et al., 1988; Bowling, 1999; Devlin et al., 1992; Harrison, 1997; Huey, 1987; Kissman, 2001; Levant & Doyle, 1983; Mahoney et al., 1996; McBride, 1990, 1991; Sternbach, 1990; Stone et al., 1999; Vadasy et al., 1986). Many of these programs used didactic instruction, discussion, videotapes, and sometimes manuals to instruct fathers on these issues. For example, in her program for incarcerated fathers, Harrison (1997) educated fathers about the developmental stages of children from birth to 6 years of age. Pregnancy, birth, gender differences, and physical, emotional, social, cognitive, and language development were all covered in didactic instruction and films. This information was then discussed, and fathers were asked to answer an objective question or complete a workbook question at the close of the session. A discussion group format was used in McBride's 1990 and 1991 parent education groups. This flexible format allowed fathers to share relevant problems and perceptions related to fatherhood with other group members. Some of the topics that were discussed included information about different types of paternal involvement, child development, and parenting skills.

Depending on the type of the group, some programs focus on educating fathers about their legal rights as fathers, resources within the community, contraception, and sexually transmitted diseases (e.g., Barth et al., 1988; Huey, 1987). Huey's (1987) school-based program for teenage fathers used outside resources to help educate young men on issues related to fatherhood. A representative from Planned Parenthood was invited to the high school to speak to the teenage fathers about reproductive biology. In addition, a field trip was scheduled to Planned Parenthood to help students learn about reproductive biology, contraception, and sexually transmitted diseases. To discuss legal issues, an attorney was also present at one session to answer questions regarding the legal rights of fathers. Before the program ended, students were given information about where they could find resources in the community.

Compared to educational groups, educational workshops tend to be more concrete in nature and focus solely on increasing fathers' knowledge. For example, Devlin et al. (1992) conducted six group sessions that focused on educating noncustodial, divorced fathers about issues that were unique to their situation. Similarly, the Divorce Education Program (Stone et al., 1999) used a didactic approach when teaching parents about the effect that divorce has on children, as well as helpful strategies to ease the transition.

Skill-Building Groups

A number of programs go one step beyond educating groups of fathers about issues relevant to parenting. The goal of these programs is both to educate and to train fathers on a variety of skills necessary to be an effective parent. Some programs include skill training on issues such as anger management, conflict resolution, behavior management, decision making, parenting, and communication (e.g., Bailey, 1998; Barth et al., 1988; Braver & Griffin, 2000; Genisio, 1996; Harrison, 1997; Huey, 1987; Kissman, 2001; Levant & Doyle, 1983; Mahoney et al., 1996). These programs tend to take a more hands-on approach and often use videotapes, modeling, behavioral rehearsal, feedback, and practice activities for homework. Bailey (1998) chose to work on a number of skills in his Dads Make a Difference program for noncustodial fathers. Recognizing that the relationship between parents plays a vital role in a father's ability to parent, the program provided skill training on anger management and conflict resolution when interacting with ex-spouses. Through vicarious learning experiences, the program provided fathers with these skills to use with their ex-spouse along with various parenting techniques that could be used when interacting with children. These skills were then practiced through the use of role playing and coached interactions with their child's mother. Levant and Doyle (1983) used a systematic skill-training approach when teaching fathers effective ways to communicate with their children. This original program used a variety of experiential components in addition to direct skill instruction. To help fathers listen, respond, and express themselves better, the program introduced specific skills and then demonstrated them using direct, live modeling or videotapes. Fathers then role-played the skill within the group while being videotaped. This videotape was used to provide feedback for the father. Techniques to help transfer the skill were then given through activities for fathers to complete at home. Skill-focused programs such as these are helpful because they give fathers concrete ways to utilize knowledge that is gained from the group experience.

Support and Self-Help Groups

Support groups offer mutual aid to help many men cope with the demanding and stressful role of being a parent. This type of group can be challenging for men because it requires them to share common and sometimes intimate stories and experiences openly with others (Toseland & Rivas, 2001). There are a number of programs that either take a supportive approach or have support as one of the goals of the group experience (e.g., Bailey, 1998; Bowling, 1999; Fagan & Iglesias, 1999; Fagan & Stevenson, 1995; Genisio, 1996; McBride, 1991; Vadasy et al., 1986). For example, the Minnesota Early Learning Design (MELD) Program for Young Dads (Bowling, 1999) used a supportive model to decrease the isolation that young fathers experience. In some cases, however, programs that take a supportive approach do not have goals relating to support (e.g., Bailey, 1998).

A unique type of support group that is sometimes used in programs for fathers is the self-help group model. The MELD program (Bowling, 1999) creatively utilized a peer self-help model to reach out to young fathers at a juvenile detention center. Young fathers were matched with a father from the community who served as both a role model and a group facilitator. Fagan and Stevenson (1995) also used a self-help model in their work with African American males with children involved in Head Start. By training eight men to develop and lead self-help groups for other males in the program, this group was able to provide mutual support and share common experiences and struggles that were unique to this population.

Group Retreats

The Father-Son Project (Bowman, 1993) was a one-day retreat that was established for fathers and their sons. The participants invited to this retreat were receiving counseling and were recruited from the caseloads of the program directors. The retreat focused on enrichment and provided activities to help fathers and sons reflect on their personal experiences.

INDIVIDUAL MODEL

Fatherhood interventions rarely employ a strictly individual model to deliver services. Our extensive literature review revealed only one program that worked with fathers on an individual basis. This program (Russell & Matson, 1998) was small in subject size and designed for fathers who had children with developmental delays. The researcher administered direct and individual behavioral instruction to four father-child pairs in their home. The one-on-one nature of this program allowed fathers to learn and apply specific intervention strategies in their natural setting.

MIXED MODEL

Some programs choose to combine both group and individual models when delivering services to fathers (e.g., Barth et al., 1988; Braver et al., 2002; Kissman, 2001). These programs tend to deliver more general services and use individual meetings to tailor the program content to the personal experience of a father. The Dads for Life program (Braver et al., 2002) used individual sessions to apply the material that was covered during group sessions directly to the father's situation. Kissman (2001) also integrated individual meetings with fathers into his program model for noncustodial fathers. One-on-one discussions were conducted with participants after each group session. This time was used to gain insight into the unique role that each father played in the life of his child. Specific changes that each father had to make to keep in contact with his child were also discussed.

FATHER-CHILD MODEL

As mentioned previously, a variety of interventions involve children in the program model. Two programs provided some type of father-child activity (Fagan & Iglesias, 1999; Kissman, 2001), while most involved children throughout the program model (e.g., Mahoney et al., 1996; McBride, 1990, 1991; Russell & Matson, 1998; Vadasy, et al., 1986). Fagan and Iglesias's (1999) Father Involvement Program at Head Start provided weekly opportunities for fathers to interact with their children. These activities were educational in nature and were related to the classroom curriculum. Monthly program activities were scheduled for Kissman's (2001) intervention with noncustodial fathers. To promote family activities and father involvement, Easter egg hunts, Mother's Day celebrations, spectator sporting events, bowling, and educational activities were offered for program participants and their children.

The majority of initiatives that involved children in the program model worked with either preschool-aged children or children with developmental delays. These programs often involved children throughout the model by inviting them to each group meeting. McBride's 1990 and 1991 programs included two-hour parent education and playgroups for fathers and their preschool-aged children. For the first half of each session, fathers participated in a group discussion. Children then joined them for a father-child playtime for the last half of the session. Other programs that incorporated a similar format include Mahoney et al.'s (1996), Russell and Matson's (1998), and Vadasy et al.'s (1986) work with fathers and their children with developmental delays. It is important that other programs recognize the value of having children present throughout the program. Their presence at meetings can offer vicarious learning experiences for fathers and promote positive interaction and involvement.

RELATION OF MODEL AND GOALS

It is advantageous for the models used for service delivery and the stated goals of the program to be closely related. For example, if a program utilizes an educational model, it is important that the goals include increasing knowledge. Similarly, if a group is based on a supportive model for providing services, it is beneficial to have decreases in isolation as a goal. Unfortunately, as we reviewed many fatherhood programs, we found that this was not always the case. In many of these programs there was a clear mismatch between the models used for service delivery and the stated goals of the program. For example, Bailey's (1998) Dads Make a Difference Program took a supportive approach in providing program services, yet the stated goals of this initiative were to increase child support payment, increase the amount of contact a father has with his children, improve the quality of the coparent relationship, and improve overall parenting skills. Similarly, Harrison (1997) used a skills-building group model for implementing a program for incarcerated fathers, yet these men had little or no opportunity to develop these skills through interactions with their children. Such incongruence makes it extremely difficult, if not impossible, for these programs to achieve their stated goals. Because many fatherhood programs are grassroots efforts aimed at developing more systematic and effective services for men, it would be beneficial for programs to determine the utility of different models in achieving desired goals and outcomes. To accomplish this, goals must be created based on the model that is employed. The goals can then be measured to determine if the model was successful.

POPULATIONS SERVED

Fathers

Across the United States, many programs have been developed to help diverse populations of men strengthen their commitments as fathers. Whereas some serve the general population of men, many are tailored to meet the unique needs of specific populations. Examples of these populations include noncustodial fathers, incarcerated fathers, low-income fathers, teen fathers, minority fathers, and fathers of children with developmental delays.

Fathers in General

Ted Bowman and Brent McBride have developed two of the many programs that serve the general population of men (e.g., Bowman, 1993; Levant & Doyle, 1983; McBride, 1990, 1991; Ortiz & Stile, 2002; Sternbach, 1990). In his Father-Son project, Bowman (1993) recruited men from the caseloads of therapists at a community counseling center. These men were asked to participate in a one-day intergenerational retreat and were invited to ask their own father and son to the outing. The retreat used these connections and group experiences to help build and strengthen the bond between fathers and their sons. At least two generations were required to attend the retreat, and children had to be at least 10 years of age to participate.

Brent McBride's (1990) parent education and support program recruited fathers by posting flyers at various family-based organizations in the local community. The program used both a support group and father-child playtime to increase the involvement of fathers in the lives of their preschool-aged children. It also aimed at helping change fathers' perceptions of their competence as parents. Such programs are beneficial because they allow heterogeneous groups of men with a variety of backgrounds, strengths, and experiences to come together and share the mutual goal of improving their relationships with their children.

Noncustodial Fathers

Although some programs recruit fathers without regard to race, socioeconomic status, or residential status, many programs find it desirable to focus their efforts on the unique needs and issues that confront specific groups of fathers. One group receiving an increasing amount of attention in the past 10 years is divorced and noncustodial fathers. Currently, approximately 23% of children in the United States live in single-parent homes. Of this population, only 2% reside with their fathers (Annie E.

Casey Foundation, 2000). For this reason, there has been a considerable amount of interest in and development of interventions aimed at addressing the challenges faced by noncustodial fathers. Several examples of such programs exist (e.g., Bailey, 1998; Braver & Griffin, 2000; Braver et al., 2002; Devlin et al., 1992; Kissman, 2001; Stone et al., 1999).

In a federal child development center serving impoverished families, Kissman (2001) developed a male involvement program to help divorced nonresidential fathers keep in contact with their children. This program assessed the needs of its clients and offered parenting groups, vocational assistance, and substance abuse interventions to help separated fathers maintain their roles as parents. The program focused on helping fathers stay engaged in their children's lives as well as maintain financial responsibilities to their families. Another program, Dads for Life (Braver & Griffin, 2000), was longitudinal in nature and focused on changing the context of fatherhood for divorced fathers. The aim of this program was to increase children's adjustment to divorce by promoting better fathering. Dads for Life used both individual and group experiences to help fathers prevent and address behavior problems in their children. Although these two programs recruited volunteers, other programs for noncustodial fathers are court mandated.

Court-mandated programs have been used frequently with noncustodial fathers who fail to make child support payments. As an alternative to imprisonment, these programs are seen as a way of helping fathers maintain contact with their children while also continuing viable employment necessary to make child support payments. Instead of punishing fathers for not complying with child support arrangements, this type of program helps fathers address the circumstances that have made compliance difficult (Dudley & Stone, 2001). For example, the Dads Make a Difference program (Bailey, 1998) is a 10-week court-mandated initiative that educates fathers about their responsibilities. This program supports fathers in their attempt to become more involved with their children and helps separated parents to coparent their children effectively (Dudley & Stone, 2001).

Incarcerated Fathers

In recent years, a new type of program has begun to emerge that targets an often overlooked group of men—incarcerated fathers (e.g., Genisio, 1996; Harrison, 1997; Landreth & Lobaugh, 1998). The incarcerated father faces a variety of challenges to maintaining an active role in the life of his child. An example of a unique approach to helping these fathers maintain meaningful contact with their children is the Breaking Barriers with Books program (Genisio, 1996). This program was offered to fathers at a medium-security U.S. correctional institution. It provided education, parental support, and opportunities for fathers to share literature with their children. Fathers were educated about the book-sharing experience and taught how to promote positive interaction with their children during visitation. Parental support was provided in a group format with other inmates, and interactive journal writing was used as a means of expression for fathers. Another program that focused on the needs of imprisoned fathers (Harrison, 1997) was implemented at the Jackie Brannon Correctional Center in McAlester, Oklahoma. This program offered parent education and behavior management training for fathers. The education component focused on training and encouraging fathers to strengthen their roles as parents. Visitation with children of incarcerated fathers is limited; therefore, opportunities and skills to promote worthwhile contact with their children are essential for this population.

Low-Income Fathers

A lack of income can adversely affect the opportunities and resources a father can provide for his children, as well as the way he approaches parenting tasks. Initiatives that target low-income fathers are often offered through federally run early childhood programs such as Head Start and Early Head Start (e.g., Fagan & Iglesias, 1999; Fagan & Stevenson, 2002). Head Start has taken tremendous strides in developing and implementing the Fatherhood Initiative, a concerted effort designed to strengthen the role of the father in the family. Increasing male participation in Head Start, enhancing father-child bonding, and providing opportunities for interaction are just a few of the many goals of this effort. This initiative has resulted in a large-scale study of fatherhood at multiple Head Start sites across the nation (National Head Start Association, 2002). Fagan and Iglesias (1999) are two of the many researchers who have contributed to this effort. In 1999 they studied the implementation of the Father Involvement Program at four Head Start sites. This program reached out to fathers of children in the program by offering volunteering opportunities within the program, father-child activities, and support groups. The program also helped to create a father-friendly environment by providing father sensitivity training for Head Start staff (Fagan & Iglesias, 1999).

Teen Fathers

Teenage fathers are a population that is often overlooked by many social service agencies and programs. However, concrete efforts have been made to reach out to this group of fathers (Barth et al., 1988; Bowling, 1999; Huey, 1987). For example, one juvenile detention center created a program (Bowling, 1999) for single fathers who were 15 to 18 years of age. Under the guise of the MELD initiative, this program utilized a peer self-help model that matched young men with culturally similar role models in the community. In addition to this form of support, group meetings were offered to educate fathers on important parenting topics such as behavior management, decision making, and child development. Another program reaching out to teenage fathers, the Maximizing a Life Experience (MALE) group (Huey, 1987), was based in a suburban high school. Although most school-based programs focus on the needs of the pregnant or parenting female student, this pioneering program aimed to address the needs of teenage fathers. The goals of this program were to help teenage fathers connect with local resources outside the school setting, learn more about child rearing, and understand their personal rights and responsibilities as fathers.

Minority Fathers

Like many men, minority fathers may be hesitant to utilize social or mental health programs because of the stigma that has been attached to these services. In addition to this stigma, it is difficult for some minority fathers meaningfully to fulfill their role as a parent in a society that is plagued by social challenges such as racism, discrimination, and negative societal images that surround minority fatherhood (Fagan &

Stevenson, 1995; Franklin & Davis, 2001). Therefore, it is important that programs reach out to all men and provide an atmosphere in which fathers can share experiences in a safe and supportive environment (Franklin & Davis, 2001).

One tactic to help facilitate this mutually supportive atmosphere is to create programs specifically for minority populations. For example, in a Head Start center in Philadelphia, Fagan and Stevenson (1995) created an empowerment-based program called Men as Teachers. The program was developed for African American men with children. The program interviewed active Head Start fathers to identify themes that were relevant to African American men. The program then used this information to train Head Start fathers to lead self-help groups for other African American men involved in the program.

Fathers of Children with Developmental Delays or Disabilities

There are many early intervention programs that reach out to families that have children with special needs, but few specifically address the needs of fathers whose children have developmental delays (Rodriguez, Morgan, & Geffken, 1992; Russell & Matson, 1998). Despite this, there have been some notable initiatives that focus on involving and supporting the unique concerns of these fathers (Mahoney et al., 1996; Russell & Matson, 1998; Vadasy et al., 1986). The Supporting Extended Family Members (SEFAM) Father's Program (Vadasy et al., 1986) both educated and supported fathers in their efforts to understand their personal needs as parents and the needs of their child. Through activities, discussion, and support, the fathers in this program were provided a wealth of information about the long-term needs of fathers and families of children with special needs. Another noteworthy program (Mahoney et al., 1996) focused specifically on the relationship between fathers and their young children with special needs. This program held weekly father-child sessions to teach and model effective interaction strategies. During the session fathers were educated about child development and skills to increase their ability to interact effectively with their child.

Biological Fathers versus Father Figures

Fathers fit many different profiles; therefore, these populations are by no means mutually exclusive. Socially, the definition of fatherhood is expanding. Many important men in the lives of children have the potential to act as positive influences. Because of this, a number of programs struggle to define the actual meaning of a father. While some programs limit participation strictly to biological fathers, other programs offer services to father figures such as uncles, neighbors, stepfathers, nonmarital partners, or other important males in the life of a child.

Head Start has made many efforts to encourage participation by any influential man in a child's life. Fagan and his colleagues have made two notable attempts to involve both fathers and father figures in their Head Start–based programs. Their Father Involvement Program (Fagan & Iglesias, 1999) provided the opportunity for any interested father or father figure to participate. Although the majority of men participating were biological fathers of children in the program, the open invitation resulted in 32% of the participants being someone other than a biological father. Similarly, the Men as Teachers (Fagan & Stevenson, 1995) program for African American men recruited participants by describing the workshop as "a forum for low-income African

American men to discuss parenting concerns" (p. 29). This broad and welcoming portrayal of the program population did not limit the participation of any interested male.

Although the wide range of populations being served by fatherhood initiatives makes it difficult to generalize across programs, this diversity is also one of the major strengths of this field. What men need from fatherhood programs will vary based on the context of their parenting situation (e.g., the needs of low income, noncustodial fathers will be much different from those of fathers of children with developmental delays/disabilities). In creating initiatives that target specific groups of fathers, these programs are better able to meet the unique needs these men bring to the parenting situation. While tailoring their services to specific groups of men, fatherhood programs also vary in the focus of services they provide based on the needs of the population being served.

FOCUS OF SERVICES PROVIDED

AGE OF CHILDREN

The demands of parenting vary based on the age and developmental level of the child. One population that receives little attention from fatherhood initiatives is infants. The fatherhood programs that are offered for fathers of infants tend to be specifically for children who have been identified as being at risk or who have developmental delays. For example, the Father's Program (Vadasy, Fewell, Meyer, & Greenberg, 1985) is an initiative developed for fathers of children up to 5 years of age with developmental disabilities. This program was a component of a larger initiative, the SEFAM program that helped develop a supportive network of resources for families and children with special needs.

The majority of published fatherhood programs that we reviewed are offered to fathers with preschool-aged children (Fagan & Iglesias, 1999; Kissman, 2001; Landreth & Lobaugh, 1998; McBride, 1990, 1991; Russell & Matson, 1998; Vadasy et al., 1986). This is partially due to the fact that recent federal and state initiatives have emphasized the need for family and father involvement in both early intervention and preschool programs across the nation (Ortiz, Stile, & Brown, 1999). As research continues to examine the impact of fathers on their children's developmental outcomes, children from ages 3 to 5 are highly targeted as recipients of fatherhood program services. Child development centers and early intervention program sites offer a prime location to reach fathers and their young children.

School-aged children are another population that is targeted by fatherhood programs (Genisio, 1996; Levant & Doyle, 1983; Ortiz & Stile, 2002). Although it would seem likely that initiatives for fathers of school-aged children would be run in the elementary or secondary school setting, programs for this population are often offered through universities, prisons, and mental health settings. One of these programs was Levant and Doyle's (1983) program for fathers of school-aged children. This educational program was led by doctoral students on the campus of Boston University. Although these programs tend to recruit fathers heavily from schools, it is important that programs recognize the benefit of creating partnerships with elementary and secondary schools. This collaboration has the potential to greater involve fathers in the life of their child both at home and school.

Programs supporting fathers of adolescents are greatly lacking. Few, if any, are geared toward the specific needs of fathers with adolescent children. Fathers of adolescents face challenges unique to this age level, yet their active participation in child rearing can have a significant positive impact on their offspring (Harris, 1998). One of the few evaluated programs that included fathers with adolescents (Harrison, 1997) took place at the Jackie Brannon Correctional Center in McAlester, Oklahoma. This program provided training for fathers who had children from ages 8 to 17. The program was strictly educational, and children were not directly involved in the program model. Programs that help to involve fathers in the lives of their adolescent children may have the potential to curb risky behaviors by teens such as drug use and early engagement in sexual activities.

SERVICE PROVIDERS

Not all fatherhood programs provide services directly to fathers. Two notable programs targeted service providers as part of their intervention to increase paternal involvement (McBride, Rane, & Bae, 2001; Ortiz & Stile, 2002). These programs chose to increase paternal involvement indirectly by focusing their efforts on the integral role that staff and teachers play in facilitating this involvement. McBride et al. worked with prekindergarten staff to provide technical support through individual and group discussions with teachers at an early childhood program. These discussions were used to explore teacher's conceptions of paternal involvement, plan strategies for reaching out to fathers, and develop activities to encourage father involvement in classroom activities. Another program, Project Dads as Developmental Specialists (DADS; Ortiz & Stile, 2002) uses a community-university partnership to collaborate with local schools and organizations to train staff to work with fathers. Teachers and counselors are trained to help teach fathers ways they can increase their children's literacy skills. The individuals who work with families on a daily basis are in an advantageous position to create a welcoming and supportive atmosphere for fathers. For this reason, interventions and programs that target service providers have the opportunity to create a lasting effort to increase paternal involvement.

MOTHERS

Parenting for fathers does not occur in a vacuum. Research has suggested that mothers may have an influence in determining how fathers approach their parenting roles (e.g., Allen & Hawkins, 1999; DeLucie, 1995; McBride & Rane, 1998). In spite of this consistent finding, a majority of parenting programs targeted for fathers fail to acknowledge the important role that mothers play in shaping paternal involvement. One exception to this trend has been in programs for divorced and noncustodial fathers. For example, the Dads for Life program (Braver & Griffin, 2000) does not directly involve the mother but gives noncustodial fathers skills to improve their interactions with the custodial mother. By teaching fathers conflict management skills, the program expects to make it more likely that conflicts between the divorced parents will be avoided or resolved as they occur. Similarly, the Dads Make a Difference program (Bailey, 1998) for noncustodial fathers hypothesized that an improvement in the coparent relationship would lead to both increased child support payments and time spent with children. To improve this relationship, the program required custodial mothers to attend 5 of the 10 weekly sessions that were offered.

CHILDREN

The involvement of children in fatherhood programs varies with respect to the focus of the group. Many educational groups aimed primarily at increasing father's knowledge do not include children in the program model (Bailey, 1998; Braver et al., 2002; Harrison, 1997; Kissman, 2001). A six-week parent training class for incarcerated fathers (Harrison, 1997) used family-related videotapes to educate fathers about parenting and behavior management. The program found that both viewing and discussing the videotapes as a group helped fathers to improve their attitudes toward child rearing. Similarly, the MELD program (Bowling, 1999) at the Hennepin County Home School focused on teaching teenage fathers about child development and child rearing behaviors. The peer self-help model offered 80 hours of parent education through both role models and group activities.

In contrast, programs that are focused on increasing the skills of fathers often provide a variety of father-child activities throughout the program model (Bailey, 1998; Fagan & Iglesias, 1999; Genisio, 1996; Landreth & Lobaugh, 1998). The Breaking Barriers with Books program (Genisio, 1996) for incarcerated fathers incorporated constructive and positive opportunities for fathers to interact with their children. During educational group sessions fathers learned effective ways to interact with their children and were able to apply this information at the weekly father-child book-sharing time. However, there are some programs that focus on changing the parenting skills of fathers but do not involve children in the program model (e.g., the Dads for Life program for noncustodial fathers; Braver et al., 2002). This gap between the intended goal of the program and the model for program delivery is a cause for concern. It is possible that the effect of a program will either be diluted or not generalize outside the group environment and improve the father's interaction with his child.

Programs that directly involve children throughout the model usually have goals of increasing involvement and changing father-child interaction patterns. A study investigating parent training with fathers of children with developmental delays (Russell & Matson, 1998) included four father-child pairs that received between 16 and 26 sessions of in-home training. Through modeling and guidance, fathers were trained to become intervention agents and learned to administer appropriate prompts, instructions, and consequences to their children. These behaviors helped fathers maintain compliance and manage inappropriate behavior of their children with special needs. Another program (McBride, 1991) including children was designed to increase paternal involvement of 30 father-child pairs. The program was held on Saturday mornings and involved one hour of group discussion followed by one hour of father-child playtime. By including father-child playtime, the program hoped to improve the fathers' perception of parental competence and impact the type of involvement fathers have with their children.

The diversity found in the focus of the services provided in fatherhood programs is another major strength of this field. As with the populations targeted by such efforts, in varying the focus of services being provided, these programs acknowledge that a canned approach to parenting programs will not work when trying to meet the needs of fathers. Given this diversity, it is important that intervention programs for fathers be engaged in evaluation efforts in order to identify what approaches may or may not work within the unique context of a specific program.

EVALUATION

Although most fatherhood interventions engage in some type of evaluation, the majority of these efforts are narrow in scope and are not done in a systematic or planned fashion. By approaching evaluation in such a limited way, these efforts fail to provide adequate assessments of overall program functioning. Francine Jacobs's Five Tiered Approach for program evaluation (Jacobs, 1988) and the Fathering Indicators Framework developed by Vivian Gadsden and her colleagues at the National Center on Fathers and Families (Gadsden, Fagan, Ray, & Davis, 2001) provide two extremely useful tools that can be used for determining the effectiveness of programs for fathers.

FIVE TIERED APPROACH FOR PROGRAM EVALUATION

Jacobs's Five Tiered Approach (Jacobs, 1988) for program evaluation divides the evaluation process into five levels. Although the author stresses that it is desirable for programs to engage in more than one level at a time and return to previous levels when needed, each level is described sequentially and progressively involves greater evaluation efforts. This framework for evaluation can serve as a useful tool when planning, monitoring, implementing, and operating programs for fathers.

Tier One: Pre-implementation

The first tier of this approach lays the groundwork for the program. The goal of this level is to determine the need for the program, to establish the fit between the community and the program, and to gather data to help plan the program. Three tasks are involved in this level of the approach: detailing the characteristics of the program, conducting a needs assessment, and revising the program to fit these needs.

Few of the reviewed programs published information regarding this first level of program evaluation. One notable exception was the Men as Teachers program developed by Fagan and Stevenson (1995). When the Philadelphia Parent Child Center received a Head Start grant to increase the involvement of men in the program, information was gathered for approximately one year to determine the needs of men affiliated with the program. Interviews were the primary source of data collected and used to support and design the Men as Teachers program. Interviews with men who were active in the program revealed four basic needs. These men expressed a need to discuss general issues regarding parenthood. African American men, in particular, expressed a need to discuss issues relevant to their experience with the program. The men who were interviewed also thought that men interested in serving their community should have the opportunity to assume leadership roles and that efforts should be created to involve men who are reluctant to participate in the program. These findings helped support and guide the development of the Men as Teachers program. This program addressed the specific needs of African American men by training men involved in Head Start to be group leaders. These group leaders then recruited and held meetings for other men who were less involved in the program.

Tier Two: Accountability

The second tier is more specific to the actual program services and clients. The purpose of this tier of evaluation is to document the program's utilization, entrenchment, and penetration into the targeted population. This part of the evaluation is necessary to justify expenditures and maintain accountability to funders, the community, and the program clients. Tasks associated with this level include gathering descriptive data regarding participants and services provided, as well as tabulating the cost information for the delivery of service. Again, few of the reviewed programs published information regarding this type of activity. Some programs did identify efforts to collect basic demographic data about program participants (Barth et al., 1998; Devlin et al., 1992; Huey, 1987; Kissman, 2001; Landreth & Lobaugh, 1998; McBride, 1990, 1991; Russell & Matson, 1998; Stone et al., 1999; Vadasy et al., 1986), although this information was used to compare treatment and control groups as opposed to documenting service utilization and client demographics. Beyond comparing groups, it is desirable for this type of data to be used to document the number of people served, describe the typical client, find out what portion of the target population was reached, and determine how staff members spent their time implementing program services. Barth et al.'s (1988) Fatherhood project provides a good example of how a program for fathers can be engaged in this level of evaluation. In their program for adolescent fathers, a social worker was given the responsibility of program documentation. This employee routinely collected information and recorded the age of fathers, their ethnicity, service use, school and employment status, and birth weight of their children. This database was used to describe program participants and service utilization, as well as to track changes in the educational and employment status of fathers.

Tier Three: Program Clarification

This tier focuses on improving the program operation. The goal of this level is to define and refine the mission, goals, objectives, and strategies of a program. Both client satisfaction information and staff feedback are often used to achieve these goals. Jacobs (1988) suggested that staff meetings, interviews with staff, and service data are also valuable sources of information in the program clarification tier. In our review, this level of evaluation appeared to be the most overlooked. One exception to this pattern was the MELD program (Bowling, 1999). This program used both parent and facilitator satisfaction surveys to ensure that the needs of clients were being met. This feedback was obtained every 10 weeks, and adjustments to program format, goals, and services could be made based on the findings of these surveys.

Tier Four: Progress toward Objectives

Like each tier, this one builds on the previous levels of evaluation. This level assesses the program's progress toward achieving its short-term goals and objectives. Methods such as standardized test scores, interviews, and client satisfaction data can be used to evaluate the progress clients have made toward achieving short-term objectives (Jacobs, 1988). A limited number of the reviewed programs engaged in this level of evaluation. The MELD program that was previously discussed measured progress toward objectives by using a self-constructed tool called Markers of Progress to track changes in the lives of its clients. The program was designed to support young fathers, increase their awareness of the choices they have as parents, and encourage them to be committed and involved parents. The Markers of Progress tool was used to determine the extent that fathers were achieving these goals. These markers provided continuous feedback to program staff regarding the success of their program. The Dads for Life program (Braver & Griffin, 2000) also recognized the importance of achieving immediate intervention goals. To meet the overall goal of improving the relationship a father has with his child, proximal goals of increasing a father's sense of paternal authority, motivation and skill, commitment to the parenting role, and ability to manage conflict with his ex-spouse needed to be achieved. To assess the progress fathers were making toward the overall goal, data were obtained regarding the achievement of these immediate goals.

Tier Five: Program Impact

This final tier is the most demanding level of program evaluation. At this level short- and long-term objectives are both identified and measured. Programs engaged in this level of evaluation most likely have an experimental or quasi-experimental design that involves a comparison group. Because true experimental designs are time-consuming and expensive, it is rare that any human service program uses this design when evaluating the effectiveness of a program. Despite this problem, Braver's Dads for Life program (Braver et al., 2002) used a randomized trial to identify couples from public divorce records. Once randomly selected, these couples had to agree to be assessed and were randomly placed in either the experimental or control group receiving the Dads for Life program. Of the fathers identified, only 47% agreed to participate in the randomized trial. Although this low percentage makes findings difficult to generalize to other fathers, a randomized trial is considered the most reliable and controlled form of program evaluation. This program evaluation was longitudinal in design with a pretest, immediate posttest, a four-month follow-up, and a one-year follow-up test. This examination showed that Braver's treatment group benefited from the program on a number of variables when compared to the control group. The randomization in this evaluation helped to ensure that the differences between the treatment and control or comparison group were minimal and that the results of the evaluation were most likely due to the program. For this reason, true experiments are considered the most scientifically sound form of research. Jacobs's (1988) model suggests that these types of quantifiable and longitudinal data are helpful in this final level of evaluation.

The majority of evaluations are performed on existing fatherhood programs in applied-practice settings. Therefore, many programs used a more feasible form of evaluation: the quasi-experimental design. Similar to a true experiment, this design involves both a control and a treatment group (i.e., Devlin et al., 1992; Fagan & Iglesias, 1999; Harrison, 1997; Landreth & Lobaugh, 1998; Levant & Doyle, 1983; McBride, 1990, 1991). However, the major difference is that fathers were not randomly assigned to these groups. In order to avoid denying fathers potentially beneficial services, many of these programs chose to use a waiting-list control group. Although it is desirable to provide the intervention for as many fathers as possible, this lack of randomization leads to greater threats to the internal validity of the research (Upshur, 1988).

Other programs chose simply to evaluate the effect the program had on participants by using a pretest-posttest evaluation with the group of fathers who participated in the program (Barth et al., 1988; Bowling, 1999; Huey, 1987; Kissman, 2001; Mahoney et al., 1996; Russell & Matson, 1998; Vadasy et al., 1986). This form of evaluation is useful in determining if the goals and objectives of the program were met. Unfortunately, because this form of evaluation does not involve a comparison group, it is more difficult for researchers to determine if the changes were a result of the program or of other factors in the environment (Monette et al., 1998).

There are also a number of programs that use qualitative or informal means of evaluation such as direct observation, content analysis, and responses from journal writing (Fagan & Stevenson, 1995; Genisio, 1996). Jacobs (1988) suggested that qualitative data from record reviews or client interviews can add another dimension of evaluation that is helpful at this level. Such data provide the researcher with rich and descriptive information that is difficult to capture when using only standardized, quantitative measures (Monette et al., 1998). In the Breaking Barriers with Books program (Genisio, 1996) only qualitative data were used to determine the effect of the program on incarcerated fathers. Although it is beneficial to use multiple methods of evaluation, this program uniquely utilized qualitative measures to determine the program's effects on participants. Interactive journal writing, direct observation, and documentation of continued program activities were three types of qualitative measures used to evaluate this program.

PROGRAM IMPACT

The field of intervention programs that target fathers has been expanding rapidly in recent years, yet little is known about the effectiveness of these initiatives and the impact they may have on fathering behaviors (Lamb, Chuang, & Cabrera, 2002; Palm, 1998). It is only through efforts at the Tier 5 (program impact) of the Jacobs model of evaluation that we can truly understand the potential of these programs for changing the ways in which men approach parenting. Unfortunately, most interventions for fathers have been unable or unwilling to engage in this level of program evaluation.

Although there are examples of programs that have utilized quasi-experimental research designs in their efforts to document the impact of their efforts (e.g., Devlin et al., 1992; Fagan & Iglesias, 1999; Fagan & Stevenson, 2002; Harrison, 1997; Levant & Doyle, 1983; McBride, 1990, 1991), these evaluations tend to be narrow in focus and are limited in their ability to inform the field as to the effectiveness of interventions for fathers. The most common outcome examined in these efforts has been fathers' attitudes toward and perceptions of their parental roles. Fagan and Stevenson (2002) found a significant improvement in fathers' attitudes about their ability to teach their preschool children after completing six 90-minute sessions on parenting. Similarly, Harrison (1997) found a significant improvement in incarcerated fathers' attitudes regarding parenting their adolescents after participating in six weeks of parent training classes, although few of these men had the opportunity to apply these changes in attitudes to interactions with their adolescent children. Along these lines, Devlin et al. (1992), Fagan and Stevenson (2002), and McBride (1990, 1991) all found significant program effects on fathers' sense of competence and parental satisfaction after completing intervention programs, although each of these initiatives targeted different groups of men and utilized different models for implementing program services. In terms of actual parenting behaviors, Devlin et al. (1992) and Levant and Doyle (1983) reported that fathers' communication skills with their children improved after participating in their respective intervention programs. Similarly, McBride (1990, 1991) and Fagan and Iglesias (1995) reported significant program effects on fathers' involvement in child-rearing activities in the home.

Although the findings from the few studies just discussed that have empirically evaluated fatherhood initiatives using experimental or quasi-experimental designs (Tier 5 in the Jacobs model) are encouraging, they tell us very little about the impact that such programs can have on parenting behaviors. All of these evaluation studies suffer from two major limitations: (a) a reliance on self-reports of parenting and attitudes toward parenting versus direct observations and assessments of parenting behavior, and (b) the use of pretest-posttest designs that fail to examine long-term program impacts. Beyond these few studies, most of what we know about the impact of intervention programs for fathers is based on anecdotal evidence. As a result of these shortcomings in the literature, we know very little about the impact that intervention programs for fathers can have on parenting behavior, how this impact may vary based on the models being used in the interventions and the populations being served, and what components of program services are contributing to program effects. This serious gap in the research and program development literature limits this field's ability to move beyond its grassroots orientation and makes it difficult for new initiatives to receive the financial and programmatic support needed to get started.

FATHERING INDICATORS FRAMEWORK

The Fathering Indicators Framework (FIF) developed at the National Center on Fathers and Families is a tool that can be used in combination with the Jacobs model to provide a valuable paradigm for researchers and practitioners interested in evaluating programs for fathers. The FIF is based on a comprehensive review of what the field considers to be important aspects of father involvement and behavior, and it consists of six indicator categories: father presence, caregiving, children's social competence and academic achievement, cooperative parenting, fathers' healthy living, and material and financial contributions (Gadsden et al., 2001). In framing these indicators, Gadsden et al. also identified how the FIF overcomes many of the constraints that in the past have prevented researchers and practitioners from developing theoretically and empirically informed views of the roles played by fathers and of the impact that their involvement has on child development.

The Jacobs (1988) model provides a framework for program evaluation that can be used in a variety of settings and contexts and is not specific in outlining the content and focus of data to be gathered at each level of the evaluation. The FIF can provide the content needed for evaluation efforts at each level of the Jacobs model, thus making it amenable for use in guiding the development, implementation, and evaluation of fatherhood programs. For example, the six indicators outlined in the FIF can be used as a framework for conducting a needs assessment (Tier 1 in the Jacobs model of evaluation) to determine what dimensions of father involvement in a local community are most in need of being addressed by a program being planned (e.g., increasing the interaction of noncustodial fathers with their children—father presence indicator; improving the nature and quality of father-child interactions—caregiving indicator). Similarly, programs can use the FIF to guide data collection in order to document the services being provided (Tier 2 in the Jacobs model of evaluation) for program accountability (e.g., number of sessions attended to learn about effective parenting skills—children's social competence and academic achievement indicator; number of parent-child play sessions attended by fathers—caregiving indicator). The six indicators outlined in the FIF can also be used to provide the content at each of the remaining levels outlined in the Jacobs model of program evaluation. Taken together, the Jacobs and FIF models for evaluation provide a powerful paradigm for those interested in evaluating the effectiveness of programs for fathers.

CONCLUSIONS

The purpose of this chapter has been to provide an overview of the current status of parenting programs developed specifically for fathers. As can be seen in this overview, intervention programs that focus on changing the nature and extent of father involvement approach this process from a wide variety of orientations and contexts and provide services to fathers from diverse backgrounds and family settings. Unlike parenting programs that have historically targeted their services for mothers, such programs for fathers are in an infancy stage of their development and evolution. Because of the emerging nature of this field, much of the work that is being done to develop and implement programs for fathers is being conducted on a local level. Although the grassroots nature of these efforts has allowed the diversity in approaches that is evident in the review to emerge, it also acts as a barrier to the dissemination and replication of programs that are effective in altering the way men approach their parenting roles. Although this chapter is not an exhaustive review of all programs for fathers that have been developed, it does provide a glimpse into the richness that is evident in initiatives being developed and implemented across the country. At the same time, the review underscores many of the strengths that can be found in programs for fathers (e.g., tailoring program services to meet the unique needs of specific groups of fathers), while highlighting many of the shortcomings that hamper the growth of this field (e.g., little emphasis on program evaluation). We end this chapter with a set of five recommendations that are aimed at identifying ways in which researchers and practitioners can combine their efforts as they seek to expand the availability and effectiveness of parenting programs that focus on changing the nature and extent of father involvement.

INCREASE THE EMPHASIS ON PROGRAM EVALUATION

In recent years there has been a rapid expansion in the development and implementation of parenting programs that target fathers. Although these programs can be found in many areas of the country, we know very little about how they are structured within the diverse settings and contexts in which they are implemented and what impact they may be having on fathering behaviors. For many practitioners engaged in the development and implementation of initiatives for fathers, the concept of program evaluation is often viewed as an ominous process that is better left in the hands of university researchers, and one that has little relevance to what they are trying to achieve in their local communities. Practitioners engaged in these grassroots efforts have a high level of commitment to providing services to as many fathers and families as possible and are reluctant to draw resources (both financial and human) away from these efforts in order to do program evaluation. As a result of this lack of emphasis on evaluation, many of these locally developed programs suffer from the same types of problems (e.g., lack of shared resources and a common knowledge base on how to develop programs for fathers, a trial-and-error approach to developing new programs for fathers, etc.), and the field in general has been slow to move beyond its grassroots orientation.

Although many of the programs reviewed in this chapter have touched on some aspects of evaluation, it is clear that a concerted effort to make this process a central part of their focus is lacking. Program evaluation should be viewed as the systematic collection and analysis of program-related data that can be used to understand how a program delivers services and what the consequences of its services are for participants (Jacobs, 1988). Under this perspective, program evaluation should guide every step of the program development process, regardless of the size, nature, and history of the initiative. The failure to take this perspective has limited the dissemination and replication of programs for fathers that have been successful in local communities, and it prevents these initiatives from moving beyond a grassroots orientation. Jacobs's (1988) five-tiered approach to program evaluation combined with the FIF (Gadsden et al., 2001) provides an effective paradigm that can guide practitioners in exploring how evaluation can become a core component of their efforts to provide services to fathers. By using these models as a guide for evaluation efforts, practitioners working with these programs will be better able to meet the needs of fathers, document the services delivered for program accountability, and have useful information for program improvement and replication and possible information on the impact of their programs on fathering behaviors.

DEVELOP CLEARLY ARTICULATED FRAMEWORKS TO GUIDE PROGRAM DEVELOPMENT

The majority of the fatherhood programs reviewed had no clearly stated philosophical or theoretical frameworks on which their programs were based. There are a number of potential problems with initiatives that do not use such frameworks to guide their program development and implementation efforts. Programs that are not grounded within a framework tend to lack a clear focus. This makes it difficult for the practitioner to guide and direct attention at important phenomena that are relevant to the study of fatherhood. This guidance is needed to determine what aspects of fatherhood will be the focus of the program, what type of information is necessary to gather in order to develop the program, and what intervention strategy can be most effective in addressing the dimensions of fatherhood that are of interest. In addition, without a clearly defined framework, it is less likely that the program goals will be consistent with the structure and model of services being provided for fathers.

There are also related problems in evaluating programs without a clearly articulated philosophical or theoretical foundation. Without such a foundation it is difficult to identify appropriate evaluation tools to use in determining the effectiveness of a program, as well as what program components need to be modified if the evaluation indicates that the identified goals and outcomes are not being achieved. Finally, it is challenging to disseminate and replicate a program that is not based on a clearly articulated framework. As with evaluation, an emphasis on using clearly articulated theoretical or philosophical frameworks to guide program development efforts is crucial in order to move the field of parenting programs for fathers beyond its grassroots orientation.

INCREASE PROGRAMMING FOR FATHERS OF ADOLESCENTS

As described in the review, very few programs target the specific needs of fathers with adolescent children. Adolescence is a critical time period that presents a wide variety of challenges for both teens and their parents. Because some of the most complex and rapid changes in development take place during adolescence, teenagers are vulnerable to serious problems such as depression, persistent antisocial behavior, premarital sex, experimentation with drugs and alcohol, and so on (Berk, 2002). For fathers, it can often be a very frustrating and bewildering time, as they see their teenage children pulling away as they assert their autonomy, defy parental authority, seek independence and control over their lives, and struggle with their own sense of identity. The need for programs that focus on fathers of adolescents is no less pressing than the demand for similar programs targeted for fathers of infants, preschoolers, and school-aged children. When fathers are actively and positively engaged in the lives of their adolescent children, they can play an important role in helping them overcome risk factors that are associated with adolescent development (Harris, 1998). A concerted effort is needed to develop, implement, and evaluate programs that can help fathers be better prepared to face the challenges that they will be confronted with as their children go through their teenage years.

DEVELOP TRAINING PROGRAMS FOR SERVICE PROVIDERS

Although parenting programs that target their services specifically for fathers can be effective in changing the nature and extent of how men approach their parenting roles, their impact is limited to those participating in the programs. Most programs for fathers serve small numbers of participants, ranging from 1 to 15 fathers. In addition, many of these programs are developed on a local level, with highly motivated individuals providing leadership for their implementation. This grassroots, individually developed focus limits the potential impact the field of parenting programs for fathers can have on children and families in our society.

Professionals from a variety of disciplines (e.g., teachers, social workers, developmental specialists, nurses, occupational and physical therapists, counselors, etc.) provide services on a regular basis to children and families. As seen in this review, parenting programs that target fathers can also be found in a variety of disciplinary settings (e.g., schools, social service agencies, medical settings, religious organizations, etc.). Unfortunately, the majority of professionals working in these different settings have not received training that would allow them to focus their services on the unique needs that men bring to the parenting situation (McBride & Rane, 2001). In order to broaden the impact that parenting programs targeting fathers can have, the field in general must move beyond its grassroots, individually focused orientation. Efforts must be made to provide training and support services for professionals who work with children and families on a daily basis in order to enable them to address the unique needs that men bring to their parental roles. Providing these professionals with staff development and in-service training experiences that give them a knowledge base from which to design and implement specific initiatives that focus on changing the nature and extent of father involvement is an important first step in moving the field beyond its grassroots orientation.

DEVELOP A LITERATURE BASE ON PARENTING PROGRAMS FOR FATHERS

As mentioned at the beginning of this chapter, very little work has been done on a systematic level to develop a literature base on programs that address fatherhood, with limited information being published in the scholarly and professional outlets. Our last recommendation is for those professionals who are actively engaged in developing and implementing parenting programs for fathers to focus their attention on ways to address this problem. From our work with colleagues around the country, we know that there are a lot of exciting new programs for fathers that are being implemented in local communities, yet the current status of the literature base is not reflective of these efforts. If we truly want the field of parenting programs for fathers to move beyond its grassroots orientation, professionals at all levels (i.e., practitioners, researchers, policy makers, etc.) who are engaged in these initiatives need to document their efforts in published outlets. In doing so, they can share their collective expertise and experiences with others interested in developing similar programs. These new initiatives can then build on and extend previous efforts rather than taking a trial-and-error approach to developing and implementing programs for fathers.

REFERENCES

Allen, S. M., & Hawkins, A. J. (1999). Maternal gatekeeping: Mothers' beliefs and behaviors that inhibit greater father involvement in family work. *Journal of Marriage and Family, 61,* 199–212.

Almeida, D. M., & Galambos, N. L. (1991). Examining father involvement and the quality of father-adolescent relations. *Journal of Research on Adolescence, 1,* 155–172.

Annie E. Casey Foundation, Kids Count. (2000). *2000 Census Data: Living arrangements profile for United States: Table 4.* Retrieved May 24, 2002, from http://www.aecf.org/cgi-bin/aeccensus2.cgi?action=profileresults&area=1&printerfriendly=0&section=4

Annie E. Casey Foundation, Kids Count. (2000). *2000 Census Data: Living arrangements profile for the United States: Table 4.* Retrieved May 24, 2002, from http://www.aecf.org/kidscount/census/

Andronico, M. P. (1996). *Men in groups: Insights, interventions, and psychoeducational work.* Washington, DC: American Psychological Association.

Bailey, C. E. (1998). An outcome study of a program for noncustodial fathers: Program impact on child support payments, and the coparenting relationships (Doctoral Dissertation, Purdue University, 1998). *Dissertation Abstracts International, 60*(07), 2691.

Bandura, A. (1977). *Social learning.* Englewood Cliffs, NJ: Prentice Hall.

Barnett, R. C., & Baruch, G. K. (1987). Determinants of fathers' participation in family work. *Journal of Marriage and the Family, 49,* 29–40.

Barth, R. P., Claycomb, M., & Loomis, A. (1988). Services to adolescent fathers. *Health and Social Work, 13,* 277–287.

Berk, L. E. (2002). *Infants, children, and adolescents.* Boston: Allyn & Bacon.

Biller, H. B. (1971). *Father, child and sex role.* Lexington, MA: Heath.

Bowling, G. (1999). The MELD for young dads program. *Family and Correction Network Report, 20,* 10–11.

Bowman, T. (1993). The father-son project. *Families in Society, 74,* 22–27.

Braver, S. L., & Griffin, W. A. (2000). Engaging fathers in the post-divorce family. *Marriage and Family Review, 29,* 247–267.

Braver, S. L., Griffin, W., Cookston, J. T., Sandler, I. N., & Williams, J. (2002, April). *Promoting better fathering among divorced nonresident fathers.* Paper presented at the Family Psychology Research Conference, Northwestern University, Evanston, IL.

Bronfenbrenner, U. (1977). Toward an experimental ecology of human development. *American Psychologist, 32,* 513–531.

Brooks, G. R. (1996). Treatment for therapy resistant men. In M. P. Andronico (Ed.), *Men in groups: Insights, interventions, and psychoeducational work* (pp. 7–19). Washington, DC: American Psychological Association.

Cabrera, N. J., Tamis-LeMonda, C. S., Bradley, R. H., Hofferth, S., & Lamb, M. E. (2000). Fatherhood in the twenty-first century. *Child Development, 71,* 127–136.

Coltrane, S., & Allan, K. (1994). "New" fathers and old stereotypes: Representations of masculinity in 1980's television advertising. *Masculinities, 2,* 1–25.

DeLucie, M. F. (1995). Mothers as gatekeepers: A mode of maternal mediators of father involvement. *Journal of Genetic Psychology, 156,* 115–131.

Devlin, A. S., Brown, E. H., Beebe, J., & Parulis, E. (1992). Parent education for divorced fathers. *Family Relations, 41,* 290–296.

Dudley, J. R., & Stone, G. (2001). *Fathering at risk: Helping nonresidential fathers.* New York: Springer.

Erikson, E. (1959). Identity in the life cycle [monograph 1]. *Psychological Issues, 1.*

Fagan, J., & Iglesias, A. (1999). Father involvement program effects on fathers, father figures, and their Head Start children: A quasi-experimental study. *Early Childhood Research Quarterly, 14,* 243–269.

Fagan, J., & Stevenson, H. (1995). Men as teachers: A self-help program on parenting for African American men. *Social Work with Groups, 17,* 29–42.

Fagan, J., & Stevenson, H. (2002). An experimental study of an empowerment-based intervention for African American Head Start fathers. *Family Relations, 51,* 191–198.

Franklin, A. J., & Davis, T., III. (2001). Therapeutic support groups for primary intervention for issues of fatherhood with African American men. In J. Fagan & A. Hawkins (Eds.), *Clinical and educational interventions with fathers* (pp. 45–66). Binghamton, NY: Haworth.

Gadsden, V., Fagan, J., Ray, A., & Davis, J. E. (2001). *The Fathering Indicators Framework: A tool for quantitative and qualitative analysis.* Retrieved June 18, 2002, from http://www.ncof.gse.upenn.edu

Genisio, M. H. (1996). Breaking barriers with books: A fathers' book sharing program from prison. *Journal of Adolescent and Adult Literacy, 40,* 92–100.

Griswold, R. L. (1993). *Fatherhood in America.* New York: Basic Books.

Harris, K. M. (1998). *The impact of family structure and father involvement on risk behavior among adolescents.* Retrieved June 6, 2002, from http://www.cpc.unc.edu/projects/addhealth/abs4.html

Harrison, K. (1997). Parental training for incarcerated fathers: Effects on attitudes, self-esteem, and children's self-perceptions. *Journal of Social Psychology, 137,* 588–593.

Hawkins, A. J., & Dollahite, D. C. (1997). *Generative fathering: Beyond deficit perspectives.* Thousand Oaks, CA: Sage.

Hofferth, S. L., Pleck, J. H., Stueve, J. L., Bianchi, S., & Sayer, L. (2002). The demography of fathers: What fathers do. In N. Cabrera & C. Tamis-LeMonda (Eds.), *The handbook of father involvement* (pp. 63–90). Hillsdale, NJ: Erlbaum.

Huey, W. C. (1987). Counseling teenage fathers: The "Maximizing a Life Experience" group. *School Counselor, 35,* 40–47.

Jacobs, F. H. (1988). The five-tiered approach to evaluation: Context and implementation. In

H. B. Weiss & F. H. Jacobs (Eds.), *Evaluating family programs* (pp. 37–68). New York: de Gruyter.

Kissman, K. (2001). Interventions to strengthen noncustodial father involvement in the lives of their children. *Journal of Divorce and Remarriage, 35,* 135–146.

Knijn, T., & van Well, F. (2001). The labor market orientation of single mothers on welfare in the Netherlands. *Journal of Marriage and Family, 63,* 804–815.

Lamb, M. E. (1975). Fathers: Forgotten contributors to child development. *Human Development, 18,* 254–266.

Lamb, M. E. (Ed.). (1997). *The role of the father in child development* (3rd ed.). New York: Wiley.

Lamb, M. E., Chuang, S. S., & Cabrera, N. (2002). Promoting child adjustment by fostering positive paternal involvement. In R. M. Lerner, F. Jacobs, & D. Wertlieb (Eds.), *Handbook of applied developmental science* (Vol. 1, pp. 211-232). Thousand Oaks, CA: Sage.

Lamb, M. E., Pleck, J. H., Charnov, E. L., & Levine, J. A. (1987). A biosocial perspective on paternal behavior and involvement. In J. Lancaster, J. Altmann, A. Rossi, & L. Sherrod (Eds.), *Parenting across the lifespan: Biosocial dimensions* (pp. 111–142). New York: de Gruyter.

Landreth, G. L., & Lobaugh, A. F. (1998). Filial therapy with incarcerated fathers: Effects on parental acceptance of child, parental stress, and child adjustment. *Journal of Counseling and Development, 76,* 157–165.

LaRossa, R. (1988). Fatherhood and social change. *Family Relations, 36,* 451–458.

LaRossa, R. (1997). *The modernization of fatherhood: A social and political history.* Chicago: University of Chicago Press.

LaRossa, R., Gordon, B. A., Wilson, R. J., Bairan, A., & Jaret, C. (1991). The fluctuating image of the 20th century American father. *Journal of Marriage and the Family, 53,* 987–997.

Larson, R. W. (1993). Finding time for fatherhood: The emotional ecology of adolescent-father interactions. *New Directions for Child Development, 62,* 7–25.

Levant, R. F., & Doyle, G. F. (1983). An evaluation of a parent education program for fathers of school-aged children. *Family Relations, 32,* 29–37.

Levine, J. A., & Pitt, E. W. (1995). *New expectations: Community strategies for responsible fatherhood.* New York: Families and Work Institute.

Mahoney, G., Wiggers, B., & Lash, S. (1996). Using a relationship-focused intervention program to enhance father involvement. *Infant-Toddler Intervention, 6,* 295–308.

Marsiglio, W. (1991). Paternal engagement activities with minor children. *Journal of Marriage and the Family, 53,* 973–986.

Marsiglio, W. (1995). *Fatherhood: Contemporary theory, research, and social policy.* Thousand Oaks, CA: Sage.

Marsiglio, W., Amato, P., Day, R. D., & Lamb, M. E. (2000). Scholarship on fatherhood in the 1990s and beyond. *Journal of Marriage and the Family, 62,* 1173–1191.

McBride, B. A. (1990). The effect of a parent education/play group program on father involvement in child rearing. *Family Relations: Journal of Applied Family and Child Studies, 39,* 250–256.

McBride, B. A. (1991). Parent education and support programs for fathers: Outcome effects on paternal involvement. *Early Child Development and Care, 67,* 73–85.

McBride, B. A., & Rane, T. R. (1997). Role identity, role investments, and paternal involvement: Implications for parenting programs for men. *Early Childhood Research Quarterly, 12,* 173–197.

McBride, B. A., & Rane, T. R. (1998). Parenting alliance as a predictor of father involvement: An exploratory study. *Family Relations, 47,* 229–236.

McBride, B. A., & Rane, T. R. (2001). Father involvement in early childhood programs: Training staff to work with fathers. In J. Fagan & A. Hawkins (Eds.), *Clinical and educational interventions with fathers* (pp. 171–189). New York: Haworth Press.

McBride, B. A., Rane, T. R., & Bae, J. (2001). Intervening with teachers to encourage father/male involvement in early childhood programs. *Early Childhood Research Quarterly, 16,* 77–93.

Monette, D. R., Sullivan, T. J., & DeJong, C. R. (1998). *Applied social research: Tool for the human services* (4th ed.). Fort Worth, TX: Harcourt Brace College Publishers.

National Head Start Association. (2002). *Introduction to the male and father involvement initiative.* Retrieved May 24, 2002, from http://www.nhsa.org/parents/index.htm

Ortiz, R. W., & Stile, S. (2002). Project DADS: Training fathers in early literacy skills through community-university partnerships. *School Community Journal, 12,* 91–106.

Ortiz, R. W., Stile, S., & Brown, C. (1999). Early literacy activities of fathers: Reading and writing with young children. *Young Children, 54,* 16–18.

Palm, G. F. (1997). Promoting generative fathering through parent and family education. In A. J. Hakins & D. C. Dollahite (Eds.), *Generative fathering: Beyond deficit perspectives* (pp. 167–182). Thousand Oaks, CA: Sage.

Palm, G. F. (1998). *Developing a model of reflective practice for improving fathering programs.* Philadelphia: University of Pennsylvania, National Center on Fathers and Families.

Pleck, J. H. (1997). Paternal involvement: Levels, sources, and consequences. In M. E. Lamb (Ed.), *The role of the father in child development* (3rd ed., pp. 66–103, 325–332). New York: Wiley.

Pleck, E. H., & Pleck, J. H. (1997). Fatherhood ideals in the United States: Historical dimensions. In M. E. Lamb (Ed.), *The role of the father in child development* (3rd ed., pp. 33–48, 314–318). New York: Wiley.

Risman, B. J., & Schwartz, P. (1989). Being gendered: A microstructural view of intimate relationships. In B. J. Risman & P. Schwartz (Eds.), *Gender in intimate relationships* (pp. 1–9). Belmont, CA: Wadsworth.

Rodriguez, J., Morgan, S., & Geffken, G. (1992). Psychosocial adaptation of fathers of children with autism, Down syndrome, and normal development. *Journal of Autism and Developmental Disorders, 22,* 249–263.

Russell, D. W., & Matson, J. (1998). Fathers as intervention agents for their children with developmental disabilities. *Child and Family Behavior Therapy, 20,* 29–49.

Sandall, S. R. (1993). Curricula for early intervention. In W. Brown, S. K. Thurman, & L. F. Pearl (Eds.), *Family-centered early intervention with infants and toddlers: Innovative cross-disciplinary approaches* (pp. 129–172). Baltimore, MD: Brookes.

Skinner, B. F. (1958). *Science and human behavior.* New York: MacMillan.

Snarey, J. (1993). *How fathers care for the next generation: A four-decade study.* Cambridge, MA: Harvard University Press.

Starrels, M. E. (1994). Gender differences in parent-child relations. *Journal of Family Issues, 15,* 148–165.

Sternbach, J. (1990). The men's seminar: An educational and support group for men. *Social Work with Groups, 13,* 23–29.

Stone, G., McKenry, P., & Clark, K. (1999). Fathers' participation in a divorce education program: A qualitative evaluation. *Journal of Divorce and Remarriage, 30,* 99–115.

Tamis-LeMonda, C., & Cabrera, N. (1999). Perspectives on father involvement: Research and policy. *Social Policy Report: Society For Research in Child Development, 13*(2), 1–26.

Thomas, N. G. (Ed.). (1998). U.S. policy initiative on fathering. *Social Policy Report: Society For Research in Child Development, 12*(1), 22–23.

Toseland, R. W., & Rivas, R. F. (2001). *An introduction to group work practice* (4th ed.). Boston: Allyn & Bacon.

Upshur, C. C. (1988). Appendix B: Glossary of research and program evaluation terms. In H. B. Weiss & F. H. Jacobs (Eds.), *Evaluating family programs* (pp. 521–542). New York: de Gruyter.

Vadasy, P. F., Fewell, R. R., Greenberg, M. T., Dermond, N. L., & Meyer, D. J. (1985). Follow-up evaluation of the effects of involvement in the fathers program. *Topics in Early Childhood Special Education, 6,* 16–31.

Vadasy, P. F., Fewell, R. R., Greenberg, M. T., Dermond, N. L., & Meyer, D. J. (1986). Follow-up evaluation of the effects of involvement in the fathers program. *Topics in Early Childhood Special Education, 6,* 16–31.

Watson, J. B. (1924). *Behaviorism.* New York: Norton.

Williams, E., Radin, N., & Allegro, T. (1992). Sex-role attitudes of adolescents raised primarily by their fathers. *Merrill-Palmer Quarterly, 38,* 457–476.

CHAPTER 17

The Impact of Workplace Practices on Father Involvement

GRAEME RUSSELL and CARL PHILIP HWANG

T HE CONTRIBUTION OF the workplace—as both a barrier and an enabler—to men being involved as parents has been a central component of the fatherhood literature over the past 30 years. Many of the early analyses focused on employment and working hours as the major barrier to men being involved in child care, with time spent on child care being the major dependent variable. Other analyses examined the impact of societal assumptions about men being the economic provider or breadwinner and extended the consideration of father involvement to the emotional dimension. Common themes in subsequent research have included the impact of alternative working schedules (e.g., flexible hours, job sharing) on involvement and accessibility, the incidence of fathers taking paid parental leave to be the caregivers of their children, the experiences fathers have of work-family conflict, and the impact this has on the practice of fatherhood—both time spent and the nature of the interaction with children.

Emerging themes include (a) the contribution workplace culture plays (see Haas, Allard, & Hwang, 2002; Haas & Hwang, 1995) on whether (and how much) men take advantage of particular workplace initiatives (e.g., paid parental leave) that are aimed at facilitating father involvement (especially during the early stages of a child's life); (b) the investigation of links between workplace experiences (more specifically, work and family conflict) and the nature of the engagement fathers have with their children (e.g., Repetti, 1994); and (c) the workplace as a context for providing education, information, and support for fathers (e.g., Levine & Pittinsky, 1997).

What is evident in the theoretical and empirical analyses conducted over the past 20 years (e.g., Pleck, 1986, 1997) is that the relationship between workplace policies and practices and father involvement is highly complex. For example, early analyses demonstrated that the empirical relationship between workplace demands (e.g., number of hours worked) and father involvement is relatively weak and that men have much more control over both work hours and their level of involvement as a father than many of the theoretical models implied (cf. Gerson, 1993; Pleck, 1997). Although men often describe the workplace as the major barrier to their being as involved as they would like (see Russell et al., 1999), it is evident that they are not passive bystanders in this process. Indeed, it may also be that men who are highly motivated to be involved as fathers actively reduce their work hours to be more involved with their children. It is also clear that the workplace can be a key enabler to the level of involvement a father has in family life (e.g., if senior mangers provide a highly visible positive role model by taking parental leave themselves).

There are seven major sections to this chapter. First, the broad theoretical framework is described, noting in particular the relative absence of the development of perspectives that link workplace policies and practices with father involvement. The focus of the second section is on workplace policies and practices and how they influence the practice of fatherhood. The third section involves a review of our knowledge of leave provisions for fathers and how this functions to support or enable the direct involvement of fathers. The links between father involvement and flexible work practices, on the one hand, and workplace demands and expectations (e.g., hours of work, work pressure), on the other, provide the focus for the next two sections. Our limited knowledge of the provision of and impact of education and support programs is reviewed in the sixth section. Conclusions and directions for future research are covered in the final section.

THE BROAD THEORETICAL AND ANALYTIC FRAMEWORK

Our first step is to consider where the current analysis fits in relation to the broader theoretical and empirical framework that has developed for father involvement. Of particular concern here is the discussion of what is meant by father involvement and what are the possible sources or determinants of father involvement.

CONCEPTUALIZING FATHER INVOLVEMENT

For the purposes of this analysis, father involvement can be defined in terms of three dimensions (Lamb, Pleck, Charnov, & Levine, 1987): (a) engagement, which involves both time spent in *direct interaction* with children (e.g., bathing, reading a book, teaching a child how to drive a car) and the *affective* nature of the interaction; (b) accessibility, which covers being available to the child in close proximity, but not actually interacting on a one-on-one basis (e.g., being in the house while a child is doing homework); and (c) responsibility, which covers having responsibility for the day-to-day care of a child, taking time off work to care for a sick child, and the extent to which the parent takes direct or sole responsibility for decisions and activities related to the child (e.g., deciding about child care options, setting boundaries for an adolescent).

Consideration of the affective nature of parental involvement, including responsiveness to a child's needs and the quality of the father-child relationship, is particularly relevant when considering the impact of workplace policies and practices. The workplace has the potential to influence both the physical and emotional well-being of fathers, which in turn would be expected to influence the qualitative or affective nature of their involvement with their children. For example, a father who returns home after having had a demanding workday involving high levels of physical and emotional stress would be expected to have a reduced capacity to be emotionally responsive to his children.

Most analyses of workplace policies and practices have focused on accessibility or availability (see Pleck, 1997). There has been very little emphasis on exploring the links between workplace factors and the quality of parenting. Very little research, for example, examines the potential positive impact that workplace support for fatherhood—both by way of organizational policies (e.g., paid parental leave) and the support given by work colleagues and immediate managers, supervisors, and team leaders—can have on (a) perceived effectiveness as a father (e.g., feeling competent and effective as a father), (b) satisfaction with involvement in family life (e.g., being able to attend a child's school activities), and (c) the quality of father-child relationships (both perceived and actual).

SOURCES OF FATHER INVOLVEMENT

The work of Lamb, Pleck, and Levine (1985) and Pleck (1986, 1997) has highlighted the need to incorporate analyses of workplace factors into the more general four-factor model of father involvement. These authors have argued that the variations in the different types of father involvement can be explained primarily by (a) the extent to which a father wants to, or is *motivated*, to be involved; (b) how *self-confident* and *skillful* the man is as a parent; (c) the level of *support* a father receives, especially from his partners or spouse (the mother of the child); and (d) *institutional policies and practices*, especially workplace policies and practices. Even though this argument was developed in the fatherhood literature quite some time ago, there is an absence of research that has systematically investigated the separate and combined impact of these factors on the level or nature of father involvement. This is especially the case for workplace policies and practices. Haas, Allard, and Hwang (2002) provide an exception to this.

Lamb (1997, p. 6) argued that motivation, skills and self-confidence, support, and institutional practices can be conceived of as a hierarchy of factors that influence paternal behavior. Further, he argued that favorable conditions must exist at each level if increased paternal involvement and broadened paternal behavior are to be possible and beneficial.

For the purpose of the current chapter, this framework is modified slightly. For our conceptualization, motivation, skills and self-confidence, and involvement are considered to be directly linked and to be the core of what constitutes the practice of fatherhood.

THE POTENTIAL INFLUENCE
OF WORKPLACE POLICIES AND PRACTICES

Before considering the potential influence of workplace policies and practices, we first need to review the nature of the workplace and the particular factors that are likely to influence the practice of fatherhood. A man's experience of the workplace and the impact this has on him, however, occur within his individual and family context and the broader social and political system. These factors, which interact with workplace influences in complex ways, are also considered in this section.

WORKPLACE FACTORS

As was noted earlier, the workplace has traditionally been defined as a barrier to father involvement. Yet as others have pointed out (e.g., Gerson, 1993), many fathers have a great deal of flexibility in when and where they do their work. In their national workforce study in the United States, Galinsky and Swanberg (2000) reported that 63% of fathers found it relatively easy to take time off during the workday to address family or personal matters. However, only 50% said that they had been able to take a few days off to care for sick children without losing pay, forfeiting vacation time, or fabricating some excuse for missing work. Further, as we know from a history of research in those countries that offer paid parental leave, the take-up rates by fathers have not been as high as many had expected given changed expectations about father involvement and given the responses by men to survey questions about their intention to take parental leave (cf. Haas, 2002). It also seems that too much emphasis has been given to parental leave as a potential *single* enabler of father involvement. The situation is much more complex than this. To understand the potential contribution of the workplace, at least five aspects need to be considered.

The Father's Employment Characteristics

The particular employment characteristics of a father will have an impact on the extent to which he is able (or, indeed, feels entitled) to use various workplace options to facilitate his involvement with his children. For example, a father whose job requires that he work standard hours from nine to five doing project work with defined outputs in a large organization will clearly have greater opportunities to utilize available flexibility options than will a father who is employed in a customer-facing job in a small business firm. Factors to consider include (a) the nature of his employment contract (full-time, part-time, casual, short-term); (b) hours worked each week (including scheduled, expected, and variations in demand across the year); (c) work schedule (fixed hours, shift work, overtime, expectations about accessibility after regular hours); (d) work location, including whether the job involves either short- or long-term travel; (e) nature of work (e.g., sales, customer service, production, project based); (f) level of responsibility for other staff and for business outcomes (e.g., team leader, CEO); and (g) nature of the organization both in terms of business focus (demands, competitiveness, etc.) and size (e.g., small, medium, or large).

Workplace Policies

This area has received the most attention in relation to workplace influences on father involvement, although this has been somewhat limited to the consideration of parental leave, as was noted earlier. Workplace policies that have the potential to facilitate father involvement include the following:

1. *Parental leave.* This involves being the primary caregiver of a child. Needs to be considered include whether it is paid or unpaid, options in the timing of taking the leave (e.g., in first 12 months after the birth or adoption), options in structuring the leave (e.g., five hours a day vs. all day), and whether the leave is optional for either the father or the mother or whether there is a designated father period.

2. *Paternity leave.* This is the option to take leave during the period immediately after the birth or adoption (e.g., for a two-week period).
3. *Family leave.* This involves some designated period for an employee to take leave when family needs arise (e.g., a sick child needing to be cared for, attending a child's activity at school).
4. *Flexible work practices.* This involves a range of options covering flexibility in starting and finishing times (flextime), working from home, compressed workweeks, annualized hours, part-time work, and job sharing.
5. *Family support programs.* This includes Employee Assistance Programs that are primarily aimed at supporting employees who have workplace or family-based difficulties (few of these, however, would be expected to address the specific needs of fathers).
6. *Fatherhood education programs.* This includes work-based programs aimed at providing information and support for men to be more effective in their fathering role.

Work and Career Design

A possible enabler of involved fatherhood relates to the fundamental design of work and careers (cf. Bailyn, Rapoport, & Fletcher, 2000):

1. *Work design.* Factors to consider here cover whether performance is measured in terms of inputs (e.g., hours and attendance) or outputs (e.g., work completed to a certain standard), whether work is organized on a team basis, and whether the team is at one location or at different locations (e.g., a virtual team).
2. *Career design.* This includes the extent to which there is a standard career pathway linked to generally accepted time frames and organizational experiences (e.g., the need to have a standard set of experiences before being considered for management positions).

Workplace Culture

Organizational culture is usually defined as the basic pattern of shared assumptions, values, and beliefs considered to be the correct way of thinking about and acting on problems and opportunities facing an organization. The extent to which the workplace culture provides support for father involvement and for men utilizing the various workplace policies will obviously have a significant influence on the behavior of fathers. This issue has been a focus of the work of Haas and Hwang (discussed in more detail later). Particular elements of the workplace culture to consider in this context include the following:

1. *Senior management demographics and behavior.* For example, are senior managers fathers, and if so, do they demonstrate their commitment to fatherhood by taking relevant leave and using flexibility options? Do they speak openly about being a father and their level of commitment to this aspect of their life?
2. *Support from the immediate supervisor.* It is widely recognized that the effectiveness of a workplace's work-family policies is very much dependent on the behavior and commitment of immediate supervisors. In many workplaces supervisors

have significant discretion in the application of organizational policies and practices. What is relevant here is the extent to which immediate supervisors are supportive of involved fatherhood and the extent to which they are willing to support workplace policies that enable father involvement (e.g., allowing fathers to take family leave to attend a child's activity at school).

3. *Workgroup support.* This is the extent to which workgroups are flexible and supportive in relation to a man's involvement with his children.

4. *Rules, rewards, and punishments.* In many workplaces there are unwritten but widely accepted rules in relation to work attendance, expectations about adjusting personal lives to facilitate workplace demands (e.g., to work late, to travel when the demand arises). In many workplaces employees are expected to be flexible and to make adjustments to family and personal lives to satisfy work requirements. Not to do this is regarded as showing a lower than acceptable level of commitment.

Most commentators (e.g., Bankert & Googins, 1996; Cooper & Lewis, 1995; Haas & Hwang, 1995; Haas, Hwang, & Russell, 2000; Lewis, 1996; Russell, James, & Watson, 1988) agree that there are two major limitations to organizational work-family approaches adopted up to now. These limitations will especially impact the extent to which fathers use the various workplace flexibility initiatives. The first is that many policies have been targeted mainly at mothers with young children. "In the early 80's, the explanation for why work/family was becoming such a visible issue was focused mostly on the increase of women in the work force" (Bankert & Googins, 1996, p. 47). This is despite evidence that men also are seeking solutions to their need to balance work and family roles and the knowledge that workers need flexible employment conditions throughout their children's lives.

The second limitation is that work-family programs are offered and regarded as employee fringe benefits designed to facilitate individual solutions to work-family conflicts. As such, they can be offered and then taken away as economic circumstances change. Fathers may feel that taking benefits marks them as less committed to the workplace, and indeed they might not feel entitled to use them. The emphasis on individual solutions to work-family conflict also keeps work organizations from considering how work-family issues should receive more attention as part of strategic business concerns.

Business Integration

The focus here is on whether fatherhood and work-life balance for men are integrated into mainstream business strategies. As Russell and Edgar (2000) argued, this would involve fatherhood being included as part of a company-wide strategic planning process involving managers and supervisors, fatherhood being included with targets and measure (e.g., number of men who take parental leave and family leave to care for children; demographic profile of the senior management group in terms of fatherhood status), senior managers being seen as accountable for the level of active fatherhood, involved fatherhood being included in recruitment and retention strategies, and competencies being developed for managers to enable them to manage fatherhood issues raised by their employees. It would also involve organizations conducting fatherhood impact audits to determine the extent to which current or planned workplace demands impact the opportunities for fathers to be actively involved (as is discussed later, increased demands for travel have an impact on father involvement).

THE INFLUENCE OF WORKPLACE POLICIES AND PRACTICES

Workplace policies and practices have the potential to have an impact on a father's motivation to be involved, his self-confidence and skill level, and his quantitative and qualitative levels of direct involvement. This could occur in the following ways.

Motivation

By presenting an alternative model of fatherhood—one that challenges a traditional and narrow notion of a father's contributing to family life primarily through being an economic provider and having a successful career—the workplace could influence a man's motivation to be involved as a father and influence both his views about the nature of father involvement and his beliefs about the value of involved fatherhood (e.g., about the influence fathers can have on children). This process could occur in the following ways: by demonstrating a strong commitment to the value of fatherhood by integrating this into day-to-day business practices and arguments, such as identifying the business case for father involvement, taking fatherhood into account in workplace expectations about careers and work patterns (e.g., travel and work hours), presenting supportive role models of involved fatherhood at the senior management level, and having a workplace culture (including supervisors and work teams) that supports involved fatherhood.

Self-Confidence and Skills

By providing training and education courses both on interpersonal relationships (e.g., to enhance workplace teams) and the practice of fatherhood (e.g., parent education classes), the workplace could operate to enhance a man's skills and self-confidence as a father. This process could also function to increase a man's motivation to be involved as a father (e.g., by a focus on the contribution that fathers make to a child's development).

Involvement Opportunities

By providing father-friendly workplace policies and practices (e.g., paternity leave, flexible work practices, manageable work demands in terms of hours and workload), the opportunities for fathers to engage with or be involved with their children (both more frequently and in a more responsive manner) could be increased. Recent research has tended to focus on this process, but particularly in relation to parental leave during the early years of a child's life.

The Process of Influence

Another important consideration is the conceptualization of the pathway of influence of workplace factors. This could occur in several ways (cf. Voydanoff, 2002).

First, the workplace could operate directly as either a barrier or enabler to the practice of fatherhood. That is, workplace policies and practices could make a unique and separate contribution to a father's level of motivation, his self-confidence and skills, and his quantitative and qualitative involvement with his children.

Second, workplace policies and practices could moderate the relationship between individual and family characteristics and father involvement. For this pattern of influence, supportive workplace policies and practices (e.g., flexible work practices) could enable the level of involvement of an already motivated father and increase the relationship between these two factors. It could also be that a father who is highly motivated to be involved has the self-confidence and skills, has support from his family and social context, and chooses a particular workplace because it provides him with the opportunity to be involved (e.g., by having flexible work practices or paid parental leave, or a supportive workplace culture).

A third possibility is that workplace policies and practices could function to mediate the level of direct father involvement. Fathers who have a strong identity with traditional masculinity and whose primary identity is with paid work (including assumptions about the need to have a full-time job, that personal fulfillment is derived from success at work and by working long hours) would be less likely to access flexible work options to facilitate their involvement in family life. Further, fathers who lack knowledge and skills as parents might also be less likely to respond positively to workplace initiatives. On the other hand, those who have high parental self-efficacy and skills would be more likely to use these options. Another possibility is that a father who has a more supportive spouse and who lives in a culture that advocates gender equity in both work and in family life would be more likely to utilize workplace policies such as parental leave that would in turn lead to a higher level of involvement with children. This also highlights the potential influence of a father's individual and family context and the broader social-cultural context in which he lives. These factors are considered next.

The Contribution of Family Factors

The particular family context would also be expected to operate as a barrier or an enabler to the utilization of workplace options. A father in a dual worker-career family would be expected to have a higher need to use workplace policies and practices. The number and ages of children would also have an impact. Utilization would also be expected to vary according to whether the father lives in a two-parent household, he is a single parent, or he is a parent not living with his children but with access or visitation rights.

One critical argument that needs to be considered here is the gender contract (Haas & Hwang, 2000). This emphasizes the complex interaction between workplace and family investment and behavior. There are three key assumptions: (a) Men should have more power than women; (b) the roles of men and women are different (and in some societies this is associated with a belief that mothers should be the primary caregivers of young children); and (c) men's roles and ways of thinking should have greater value than women's (supporting gender differences in pay rates for jobs dominated by one sex or the other). It was argued that these assumptions influence decision making within families and can operate as barriers to men's utilizing workplace policies and practices. Partners would be expected to negotiate their particular work-family arrangements based on the assumption that it is more important for women to combine work with child care and that it is more important for men to be continuously employed and pursue job advancement. As Haas et al. (2000) noted, reducing the gender gap in decision making and child care responsibilities in the family is a necessary condition to achieve equality in the workplace. At the same time, however, it is obvious that substantial changes need to be made in assumptions in the workplace to enable both women and men to participate actively in family life.

THE SOCIAL-CULTURAL-POLITICAL CONTEXT

Workplace policies and practices operate within broader social, cultural, and political contexts. It would be expected that the extent to which fathers utilize workplace policies and practices will be influenced both by the broad social policy framework (e.g., whether leave is mandated and who provides the financial resources for the leave), cultural expectations (e.g., support for fatherhood), and relevant social and policy support systems (e.g., availability of child care, tax systems).

The relationship between fatherhood and social policy has been a topic of concern for academics, policy makers, and practitioners for quite some time (e.g., Lamb & Sagi, 1983; Levine, 1977; Levine & Pittinsky, 1997; Russell, 1983), as it has been in Scandinavian countries (e.g., Haas, 1992; Haas & Hwang, 2000). What has changed in recent years, however, is the increased involvement of governments and employers, as well as the consideration of the diversity of the needs of fathers.

Tamis-LeMonda and Cabrera (1999) provided a useful beginning framework for an analysis of approaches to the support of fathers. They identified two key areas of public policies: (a) *legislative policies* which include paternity establishment and child support, custody laws, welfare reform, and parental leave, and (b) *public education and programs,* which include public education and intervention programs funded by state and federal governments. What needs to be added to this is privately funded (e.g., Ford Foundation in the United States and the Bernard Van Leer Foundation and Joseph Roundtree Foundation in the United Kingdom) and workplace support programs (see Levine & Pittinsky, 1997; Russell, 1998).

Scandinavian countries have a long history of government interest in supporting the active involvement of fathers in family life and in recognizing the positive contribution they can make to child outcomes (see Haas, 1992; Haas & Hwang, 2000). Sweden is more advanced than other countries in the extent to which the government has mandated family-friendly policies and programs and demonstrated a commitment to the goal of gender equity and involved fatherhood. It is interesting, however, that work-families policies (e.g., providing subsidized high-quality child care) have been partly driven by a strong concern for the well-being of children. Another differentiating feature of Sweden is the emphasis placed on changing men's roles to facilitate gender equity in both breadwinning and caregiving responsibilities.

Many other national governments have begun to show an interest in evaluating their approach to fathering and have become more active in influencing practice by developing support programs. The Japanese government in its review of the issues associated with Declining Birth Rates (1977) considered factors that might lead to a greater involvement by men in parenting. The United States has the Fatherhood Initiative, whose purpose is to "examine how fathers are conceptualized in social policies and how research and policy can jointly strengthen the father's role in the family"

(Tamis-LeMonda & Cabrera, 1999, p. 5).

This concern for fathers has been the impetus for thousands of state and federally funded programs in the United States (Tamis-LeMonda & Cabrera, 1999, p. 13). The major intention of these is to help fathers, "especially unmarried and adolescent males, through job training/search and employment, parent training, and school involvement." A key theme in the program development is encouraging responsible fatherhood, a theme that is also reflected in aspects of social debate in the United States (e.g., Promise Keepers, Million Man March, etc.).

The federal government of Australia has implemented the Men and Family Relationships Initiative to fund a range of family-relationship support services through community-based organizations. A major goal is to help men deal with the emotional effects associated with marriage relationship breakdown so that they can manage relationship difficulties (e.g., with children and ex-partners) and reestablish positive relationships. The initiative also funds service organizations to develop more sensitive and responsive approaches to working with men both in the community and the workplace in order to be attractive to men and to take men's particular help-seeking strategies into account.

In the United Kingdom, the government has been active in funding initiatives to encourage a more responsive approach by employers to work-life balance (e.g., the Challenge Fund and Partnership Fund). The government has also recently funded several fatherhood initiatives. Fathers Direct, for example, has been given grants by the home office to support its work on fatherhood. A major goal of Fathers Direct is to encourage workplaces to be more father friendly.

While most reviews of national initiatives observe that fathers have been largely ignored in policy deliberations and in social support services, or that the emphasis has been on fathers as breadwinners and ensuring that they fulfill their financial responsibilities in the context of family separation, it is clear that this is in a process of rapid change in many countries. As Haas (2002) argued, government-mandated parental leave with a focus on equal parenthood has the potential to change employers' treatment of men who want to be involved fathers both directly (e.g., ensuring that employment conditions enable fathers to take parental leave) and indirectly (e.g., involved fatherhood and men taking parental leave become part of a normative workplace climate).

Conclusions

This section provided an outline of the potential workplace policies and practices that could influence the men's motivation to be involved as fathers, their level of self-confidence and skills as fathers, and their opportunities to be involved with and be responsive to their children. As was noted, the process of influence can be conceptualized to occur in three ways: direct, through a moderating process, and through mediation. It was also argued that factors beyond the workplace, particularly family and social-cultural factors, have the potential to impact the influence of the workplace. Even though the workplace has been widely recognized as a potential significant barrier and enabler of father involvement and even though workplace factors need to be considered as potential influencers along with individual, family, and social factors, surprisingly little research has adopted a comprehensive framework. Indeed, most of the research has focused narrowly on the potential influence of family leave policies and flexibility in hours (see Pleck, 1997). These issues are covered in the next two sections, followed by the consideration of the impact of work demands and stress on father involvement and a brief analysis of an emerging trend to offer workplace education and support programs for fathers.

PARENTAL LEAVE AND FATHER INVOLVEMENT

Whereas mandatory unpaid paternity leave is now widely available in many countries (see Burghes, Clarke, & Cronin, 1997; Haas et al., 2000; Wilkinson, Radley, Christie, Lawson, & Sainsbury, 1997), mandatory paid paternity leave is much less common. Deven and Moss (2002) conducted a comprehensive review of statutory leave arrangements—maternity, paternity, and parental leave—in the European Union (15 countries), Norway, Central Europe (4 countries), Australia, Canada, New Zealand, and the United States. The authors argued that the most striking trend in recent developments is the emerging emphasis on fatherhood and increased flexibility in taking leave (e.g., working part-time and extending the period of leave, having a choice about when the leave is taken in relation to the age of the child). In terms of fatherhood, this has involved either the introduction or enhancement of paternity leave or the provision of inducements to fathers to take parental leave (Sweden, Italy, and Norway). Ten of the 24 countries have entitlements for paternity leave (for 8 the leave is paid), ranging from two days to three weeks. All countries included in the study provide some form of parental leave that theoretically could be taken by fathers, and in 17 of these there is some form of payment. In Italy the total period of parental leave is extended from 10 to 11 months if the father takes at least 3 months of the leave; in Sweden 2 months are specifically designated for fathers, and in Norway (where 1 month is designated for fathers) fathers have an independent right to obtain a financial benefit if they take parental leave, regardless of the mother's employment status.

In countries where paid paternity leave is not mandated, very few organizations offer it to their employees. For example, in the United States only 1% of fathers in either the public or private sector are eligible for at least some paid paternity leave (Tamis-LeMonda & Cabrera, 1999), and in Australia the figure recently reported was 18% (Morehead, Steele, Alexander, Stephen, & Duffin, 1997).

In the United States, the 1993 Family and Medical Leave Act (FMLA) requires that organizations with 50 or more employees provide up to 12 weeks of unpaid, job-protected leave for eligible employees. This leave covers the following reasons: to care for a newborn, a newly adopted child, or a new foster child; to care for a child, spouse, or parent who has a serious health condition; and to treat one's own serious health condition. Data from the 1997 National Changing Workforce Survey (Galinsky & Swanberg, 2000) indicate that in 80% of organizations men are able to take some time off when they become fathers. In another survey ($n = 2,558$ employed persons) of the FMLA's impact conducted in 2000 (Waldfogel, 2001), it was found that while a significant number of employees who had young children took some leave, women were more likely to do this than men were (75.8% vs. 45.1%). Gender differences were quite small for those who took leave to care for a newborn or a newly adopted or a newly placed foster child: women, 35.8%; men, 34.1%. Unfortunately, data are not presented for the amount of leave taken by either women or men. Further, given the analysis provided by Cunningham (2001) for the operation of the FMLA in law firms, it might be expected that the number of days taken by fathers would be low. He pointed out that although most large law firms have adopted formal policies to meet the FMLA's minimum guidelines, these policies are not gender neutral. Specifically, he argued that whereas women can take paid leave, male attorneys are required to meet a primary-caregiver benchmark in order to take the leave. Policies in Scandinavian countries appear to be more gender neutral, and for many there are recent data available on utilization rates.

PARENTAL LEAVE IN SCANDINAVIAN COUNTRIES

Since the 1960s, the Swedish government has been the major force in helping parents combine paid employment with raising children (Haas & Hwang, 2000) by ensuring equal employment opportunity for women, subsidizing child care, and mandating paid parental leave for both fathers and mothers (funded by employers' payroll taxes, with pay compensated to 80%). It was also declared that women and men should have equal rights, responsibilities, and opportunities in the areas of breadwinning, child care, household work, and participation in public life (Haas, 1992; Haas & Hwang, 2000). The intention was for fathers to share parental leave with mothers, and two months are reserved for each parent (the remaining 10 months can be taken by either parent). As a way of encouraging more fathers to take parental leave, as of 1994 it was not possible to allocate the reserved months to the other parent. If fathers did not use their period, couples lost it.

Swedish parents are also able to access temporary paid parental leave. This compensates working parents when they stay home with sick children, care for children when their caretakers are sick, accompany children to receive health care, or visit day care centers or schools. Parents may take up to 60 days of temporary leave per child per year until children reach age 12; in 2003 they received 80% of their wages in compensation. Included in temporary parental leave are 10 "daddy days" that fathers can take within two months of childbirth.

In Denmark fathers are allowed two weeks of paid paternity leave and have the option of 32 weeks of paid parental leave. In Norway fathers have the option of two weeks of unpaid paternity leave and 12 months of paid parental leave. There is also a quota of one month designated for fathers. In her analysis of the different approaches to leave in three countries, Rostgaard (2002) argued that the ideology and social construction of mothers and fathers differ. Fatherhood and the modern father are seen as important in Sweden's leave policies, but in contrast, parenthood is emphasized in Denmark's and motherhood in Norway's leave policies.

Men's Use of Parental Leave

The rate of Swedish fathers taking parental leave is much higher than in any country that offers men this option (Haas & Hwang, 2000). The percentage of fathers who took regular parental leave was 3% in 1974, and it reached 55% for children born in 1990 but then dropped back to 51% in 1994. In a recent study of children born in 1995, however, it was found that 70% of fathers had taken parental leave, for an average of two months. Haas (2002) argued that the shift to nontransferable rights likely accounts for the increased percentage of fathers who take leave. Nevertheless, it is still the case that fathers take much less leave than mothers: Only 12% of all parental leave is taken by fathers.

Swedish fathers also take a much higher proportion of temporary parental leave days than they do regular parental leave, typically to care for sick children. However, this percentage has also declined recently. The decline has been attributed to declining levels of compensation brought on by budget cuts (Haas, 2002).

Haas (2002) also argued that the gender contract controlling social relations at work also influences men's interest in taking parental leave and men's expectations of themselves as fathers. Haas reported findings that indicate that companies do understand that they should not deny men the legal right to take parental leave. The equality law, however, insists that employers must develop active measures to encourage men to take parental leave. Further, Haas and Hwang (2000) also argued that although most unions have made some efforts to inform men of their legal rights, they seem to have done little actively to encourage men to take parental leave.

Variations in Companies' Responses to Men's Interest in Parental Leave

Despite a lack of support from the workplace, Swedish men's interest and involvement in active parenthood has grown in response to partner pressure and government encouragement (see Björnberg, 2000). Haas and Hwang's (1995) survey of the largest 200 Swedish companies, along with 48 interviews with personnel officers and fathers from nine of these companies, revealed that men's growing interest in fatherhood is an important force slowly transforming company culture. Fathers' growing interest in children, women's growing commitment to employment, and governmental campaigns and legislation supporting men's taking parental leave have all led to change in companies' response to men as fathers.

Haas and Hwang (1995) developed three heuristic categories or stages that distinguish Swedish companies' responses to men's interest in taking parental leave. Although companies do not fit perfectly within these stages, the stages provide a useful framework for conceptualizing company responses toward father involvement in the early period of a child's life.

Stage I: Passive Opposition.   Thirty-one percent of the large private sector companies were classified as being in this stage. These companies were not negative toward men's participation in family, but they expected men's involvement with children to be limited mostly to the weekends. They were willing to cope with a temporary crisis in family arrangements (e.g., a sick child) but frowned on men taking extended parental leave or working reduced hours. No special programs or policies helped employees manage family responsibilities because the company took for granted that employees' wives would be primarily responsible for children, based on the so-called natural order of things.

Stage II: Conditional Support.   Most of the companies (two thirds) were classified into this stage. In this stage, companies accepted men's interest in being together with their children and had developed some concrete father-friendly policies, including having someone in higher management assuming responsibility for work-family balance. Companies' support for men's taking parental leave, however, was almost always conditional. The first precondition for men's taking parental leave was that no other arrangements for children's care could reasonably be made. Another condition for men's leave-taking was that they were valuable employees, worth going to the trouble for. On the other hand, they also reported that companies found it difficult to allow employees who were indispensable to go on parental leave.

Stage III: Active Support. Very few companies in Haas and Hwang's (1995) study of large private companies (3%) had made the transition to this stage. In these companies the corporate culture was seen as actively supportive of men in their fathering roles, and the company and not the individual father took responsibility for working out ways for men to take parental leave. Stage III companies typically had developed written policies and formal programs to facilitate men's involvement in parental leave.

In Stage III companies, leadership on this issue came from the top, often from young managers who were fathers themselves or from older men who wanted young men to have more chances to be together with their children than they had. The active support shown toward fathers had typically an ideological and an economic base. Ideologically, companies were concerned about the welfare of children, already an important value in Swedish culture. Economically, companies recognized that there were productivity gains in having men take parental leave. Fathers' leave taking was also labeled a merit, an experience that helped men develop skills and self-confidence that in turn enhanced their work productivity.

The Impact of Organizational Culture on Men's Use of Parental Leave

Haas et al. (2002) reported on a study of 317 Swedish fathers from six companies (included in their earlier study reported earlier). The aim was to examine the impact of organizational culture on men's use of parental leave. The authors argued that organizations have a major stake in preserving the gender-based division of labor in the family and that parental leave policies that actively encourage or enable fathers to take parental leave could operate "to challenge the traditional boundaries between work and family and the basis of discrimination practices towards working mothers" (p. 320). A particular strength of the study is that data on organizational culture were obtained four years prior to the data being collected from fathers.

Another strength is the conceptualization of organizational culture in terms of "masculine ethic," "caring ethic," "father friendliness," "equal employment opportunity ethic," and "top management's attitudes toward men's participation in child care." Organizational culture was also assessed at the workgroup level in terms of "supervisors' support for men's participation in childcare," "workgroup support," and "workgroup norms." The following individual and family factors were also assessed: education level, men's attitudes toward shared parenting, partners' education, partners' willingness to share leave, and absence of economic constraints. Analyses were conducted both for whether the father took parental leave and for the number of days he took. Although it was found that individual- and family-level factors had a greater impact than organizational culture on the leave-taking behavior of the men, organizational culture variables did make a significant contribution. Organizational factors that made the greatest difference were company values based on an ethic of caring, father-friendly policies and practices, an emphasis on equal employment opportunity for women, and workgroups that are flexible and adaptive in responding to a father's desire to take time off to care for his children. Of note was the finding that perceived supervisor support had little impact on whether the man took leave or the number of days leave he took.

CONCLUSIONS

In her expansive analysis of parental leave in EU countries, Haas (2002) provided a useful summary of what workplace factors make a difference to men's accessing parental leave. Haas argued that men will be more likely to access parental leave if:

- It is a universal, individual nontransferable right of fathers, thus increasing the possibility that employers will actively enable the men who want to take leave to do so.
- It involves job protection, full benefits, and substantial pay.
- Fathers' rights to take leave are promoted in the workplace.
- The business case for supporting fathers' rights to paid leave is studied, articulated, and disseminated. This includes a systematic analysis of the potential individual performance benefits through the development of additional skills while caring for children.
- It is flexibly administered to enable parents to take turns taking leave so that leave can be taken on a part-time basis.

Workplace policies and practices with regard to parental leave, of course, are limited in their application to father involvement in the early stages of a child's life. It is ongoing flexible work practices and policies that provide the greatest opportunities to enable father involvement over the entire period of a child's life. These policies are reviewed in the next section.

FLEXIBLE WORK PRACTICES AND FATHER INVOLVEMENT

Unlike parental leave, the provision of flexible work practices (described earlier) is most often optional and varies widely from one organization to another. Large-scale studies demonstrating either the impact of specific practices or their possible role in enabling motivated fathers to be involved are therefore rare. Research data are more readily available on the types of options available to fathers, how satisfied they are with these, and how often they use them. In a more recent emerging approach, however, government policies have been developed to require organizations to offer flexible work options to enable employees—both men and women—to meet their caring responsibilities.

The critical issue of cause and effect also needs to be considered here. It is very difficult to establish whether the availability and utilization of flexible working arrangements is a cause or an effect of father involvement. Early research (reviewed later) focused on analyzing links between father involvement and the introduction of flexible working arrangements. Given the current widespread availability of flexible work practices, however, it could be that many fathers are making work decisions based on their motivation to be a more involved father. Indeed, the findings of Russell et al. (1999) support this argument: 64% of fathers said that in the past five years they had made changes in their work lives to improve the quality of their family life. The most commonly mentioned changes were reduced hours, increased flexibility, and change to a less demanding job. Nevertheless, from whichever perspective it is viewed, it can be argued that flexible work practices have the potential to be an enabler of father involvement—but we also need to take account of the fact that personal motivation provides a complex interactive component.

Another argument that is of interest here is that of Lewis (1996). She argued that the sense of entitlement employees have about workplace work-family options has a significant influence on their willingness to utilize these options. Sense of entitlement is used to denote a set of beliefs and feelings about work, family, and gender roles, as well as the extent to which it is justifiable to challenge conceptions of these roles. Thus, if fathers have a low sense of entitlement, they would be less likely to use flexible work options; conversely, if they had a high sense of entitlement, they would be more likely to use the options. Research reviewed by Lewis (1996) also indicates that informal flexibility for family reasons is often greater in female- than in male-dominated organizations. Further, she argues that men feel much less entitled than women do to employer support for family responsibilities.

FATHERS' ACCESS TO FLEXIBLE WORK PRACTICES

Several national studies indicate that a significant number of fathers report that they have access to flexible work options that theoretically could enable them to be involved with their children. Bond, Galinsky, and Swanberg (1998) reported data from the U.S. National Study indicating that 43% had access to flextime (the option to vary beginning and ending times); 63% said it was relatively easy to take time off during the workday to address family or personal matters; employed fathers in dual-earner couples who had this option were more likely than fathers without this option to take time off to attend to their children's needs; and over 90% said that their supervisor accommodates them when they have a family matter to take care of.

In another U.S. study of 70 working-class dual-earner families who were first-time parents (data collected both before and after the birth), Haley, Perry-Jenkins, and Armenia (2001) investigated both the availability and the utilization of flexible work practices (assessed one month after the wife had returned to full-time work after the birth of the baby). Significant differences were found between availability and utilization for a range of workplace practices: For flexible daily work schedule, availability was 46.6%, and utilization was 29.4%; for leave for family responsibilities, availability was 67.1%, and utilization was 32.4%.

Data collected by the Australian Bureau of Statistics (ABS) indicate that of those fathers with a child under 12 years of age: 41% had flexible start and finish times; 41% were able to work extra hours in order to take time off; and 7% worked part-time. In another study of 18,866 employees (data collected in 1995), 96% of men indicated that they are able to take time off to care for a sick family member, and 30% of these said that they had to take the leave without pay (Morehead et al., 1997). Russell et al. (1999) also reported that 33% of fathers find it hard to take time off during the day to care for family matters.

LINKS BETWEEN FLEXIBLE WORK PRACTICES AND FATHER INVOLVEMENT

Pleck (1997) reviewed the limited research data available on the links between flexible work practices and father involvement. Most of this research was conducted in a period when flexible work practices were relatively rare and in an emerging phase of development. Several of the studies therefore were conducted using a pre- and post-flexible work practices design. At the time, Pleck concluded that the findings showed that fathers were just as likely as mothers to change their schedules when flexible work practices (flextime and compressed workweeks) were introduced and that fathers who changed their schedules spent more time with their children.

Since that review, very little research has addressed this specific issue. Berry and Rao (1997), in their study of 198 full-time employed fathers in dual-earner couples with one child under 12 years of age, found that fathers who had workplace flexibility reported that they more frequently engaged in general child care activities (e.g., feeding, bathing, reading, playing). In a rare study conducted by Gerstel and Gallagher (2001), the hypothesis that men whose work is flexible will be more involved in family caregiving (including care of children, spouse, and own parents) was examined. A seven-item scale of job flexibility was developed for this study (e.g., "The time I start work is flexible," "If I need a personal day off, it is easy to take one"). The sample included 188 married couples, with 51% having children under 18 years living at home. As expected, women provided significantly more care for their children than men did. Contrary to predictions and to previous research, however, job flexibility was not a significant predictor of the amount of time men spent helping their children. Further, when analyzing specifically for providing child care, men whose jobs were more flexible were *less* likely to provide child care than were men whose jobs were less flexible.

WORKPLACE SUPPORT FOR FATHERS UTILIZING FLEXIBLE WORK OPTIONS

A common argument in the work and family literature is that access to and utilization of flexible work practices are highly dependent on the responsiveness of individual managers or supervisors. For many organizations, policies have been developed on the basis that they are discretionary and dependent on the approval of the immediate manager, often on the basis that business needs are met. Very little research has directly linked these aspects.

Barham, Gottlieb, and Kelloway (1998) examined this issue in an indirect way. They examined the variables that affect managers' willingness to grant alternative work arrangements, defined as flextime, compressed workweeks, work-at-home, part-time work, job sharing, and leave options. The study included 184 managers in a large financial services company in Canada (66% were female, and 32% were male). In terms of gender, it was found that managers were significantly less likely to grant reduced-hours flexible arrangements to men than to women. Gender differences were not found either for subordinates for any of the analyses or for managers for full-time flexible options. It is interesting, however, that they were also more likely to agree to flexible options for those with children than for those with older dependents.

EMERGING TRENDS: FLEXIBILITY AND CARING RESPONSIBILITIES

Discrimination and industrial laws in Australia compel employers to ensure that work practices do not discriminate against employees on the basis of their family responsibilities or caring status. Much of this legislation has been interpreted to protect women with child-care responsibilities; however, legislation introduced in early 2001 in one state (New South Wales) protects men and women with a wide range of caring responsibilities. The outcome of this legislative platform has been a series of cases around employees' access to flexible work practices, including part-time/job-share arrangements (even in supervisory positions) and working from home.

The Anti-Discrimination Amendment (Carers' Responsibilities) Act of 2000 (New South Wales) amended the Anti-Discrimination Act of 1977 (New South Wales) to prohibit direct and indirect discrimination against employees who are responsible for providing care to immediate family members (including a child, spouse, parent, grandchild, or sibling). This legislation provides that employers *must* accommodate an employee's request for flexibility to facilitate their caring responsibilities unless the employee is unable to carry out the inherent requirements of the position or the provision of accommodation would be unreasonable in the circumstances of the case or would cause an organization an unjustifiable hardship.

As to what constitutes reasonable accommodation in terms of working hours, flexible work practices and caring responsibilities, antidiscrimination and industrial tribunals have provided guidance. It has become increasingly difficult to argue successfully that flexible work practices are unsuitable for mainstream and senior positions and should not even be trialed. The onus appears to have shifted to the employer to justify an inflexible approach to adjusting working conditions or locations.

A similar approach was planned in the United Kingdom for 2003 in which employers will have a legal duty to consider requests for flexible working arrangements from employees who are parents with responsibility for children under 6 years (or under 18 in the case of disabled children) and who have worked for an organization for six months or more.

WORKPLACE DEMANDS AND STRESS AND THEIR IMPACT ON FATHER INVOLVEMENT

WORKPLACE DEMANDS

In many industrialized countries, the norm of a 35- to 44-hour workweek has given way to either a part-time workweek or longer hours in the full-time workweek. Fathers who are not so threatened by the possibility of job insecurity, unemployment, or underemployment might experience difficulties on another front—that of negative impacts from working intensively for longer hours. Working smarter (continually looking for new ways of doing tasks to be more productive or efficient) and longer hours against a background of high unemployment means that for many fathers the need to earn an adequate income takes an overwhelming priority in their lives. In a large study undertaken by Galinsky and Swanberg (2000) in the United States, it was found that American mothers and fathers are working longer hours and report being under greater pressure to work harder.

The demise of standard working hours for full-time work—working harder and longer—is likely to have an impact on the opportunities for employed fathers to be involved in family life. Many children therefore are likely to see less and less of their fathers in daylight hours and the weekends. The time demands of the workplace cut across all job sectors and indeed may be most keenly felt at the highly skilled end of the job market. While providing much needed flexibility for many fathers (e.g., telecommuting), advances in information technology also have the potential to increase the number of hours worked (especially for managers and professionals) by enabling them more easily to conduct work from home and to be more independent of traditional support staff (e.g., e-mails and memos can be typed from home late at night). In a study by Duxbury, Higgins, and Thomas (1996), comparisons were made of the work, family, and work-family environments of adopters and nonadopters of computer-supported supplementary work at home (e.g., work done at home, after regular hours, using computer technology). It was found that the adopters had higher levels of role overload, interference, and stress, yet there were no differences in marital or family satisfaction.

Results from the Australian Workplace Industrial Relations Survey conducted nationally with employers and employees across 2001 workplaces (staffed with more than 20 people) include data about employees' satisfaction with the balance between family in relation to the total weekly hours worked in 1995 (Morehead et al., 1997). This study also computed a work intensification index using answers to questions about perceived increases in the effort workers put into their job, the stress they had in their job, and the pace at which they worked. A decline in satisfaction with family-work balance was found to be related to longer working hours and to a high score on the work intensification index. Full-time employees were more likely than part-time employees to report a decline in satisfaction with work and family balance, and males were overall more likely than females to report a decline in satisfaction.

Working Hours

Probably the most obvious hypothesis in relation to links between the workplace and father involvement is that hours of work will be associated with fathers spending less time being available to, and providing care and support to, their children. Despite this, evidence in relation to the impact that workplace hours have on father involvement is quite mixed.

Bonney, Kelley, and Levant (1999) examined the link between work hours and the percentage of time a father spent as his child's primary caregiver (relative to the mother) and the number of child-care tasks performed (relative to the mother) for a sample of 120 fathers of preschool-aged children in southeastern Virginia. Analyses revealed that fathers who worked more hours were less involved (relative to the mother) in being the primary caregiver and in performing child-care tasks.

In a much more comprehensive study, Yeung, Sandberg, Davis-Kean, & Hofferth (2001) examined links between the weekly work hours of fathers and absolute measures of father involvement provided from time diaries of activities for a designated target child for a weekday and for a weekend day. Diaries were completed primarily by mothers alone or by mothers and the target child together. The sample was 1,761 children aged 0 to 12 (a nationally representative sample of U.S. families). Father involvement was measured in several ways: (a) engagement, the amount of time the child interacted directly with the father; (b) accessibility, the time the father was available to the child but not directly involved in interaction; (c) six major activity categories (e.g., personal care activities, play and companionship activities). It was found that for every hour a father worked, there was an associated 1 minute decrease in the time the target child spent with the father on weekdays—this was mostly associated with a reduction in play and companionship activities. Interestingly, though, this effect is not evident for fathers' involvement on weekends, and indeed other data presented in the paper indicate that fathers are more equal partners in caring for children on the weekends. Berry and Rao (1997) found that fathers who worked fewer hours reported that they were more frequently engaged in general child care activities (e.g., feeding, bathing, reading, playing).

Kaufman and Uhlenberg (2000) found an interaction between hours worked and attitudes to parenting responsibilities. This study was based on the responses of 1,667 men who participated in the 1992–1993 U.S. National Survey of Families and Households. In support of previous research, they found that men with children were more likely to work more hours than were married men without children. However, they also found that men with modern attitudes toward child-care arrangements worked significantly fewer hours than did men with traditional attitudes. Further, they found that this interaction effect was significant for men under 35 years but not for men over 35 years. The expectation here was that men in the younger cohort would be more likely to translate egalitarian child-care attitudes into behavior consistent with those attitudes.

Job Demands

A limited number of studies have examined the impact of job demands on father involvement, both in terms of qualitative and quantitative involvement. In probably the most cited study, Repetti (1994) examined the impact of daily job stressors on parent-child interaction for a sample of 15 air traffic controllers (in a major international airport in the United States) who had school-aged children. The fathers described their job stressors (e.g., workload, negative workplace social interactions) and parent-child interactions (emotional tone and quality of interactions and their parenting behavior and state of mind during these interactions) on three consecutive days. Objective measures of daily workload were also obtained from the workplace. Repetti reported that after a demanding day at work fathers were more behaviorally and emotionally withdrawn during their interactions with their children. She also reported evidence for direct spillover from negative feelings associated with distressing experiences at work to fathers' expressions of anger and greater use of discipline.

In a more comprehensive study with a random sample of 189 fathers, Stewart and Barling (1996) found significant indirect effects of father's employment experiences—namely, job decision latitude, interrole conflict, job insecurity, and job demands—on teachers' ratings of children's acting-out behaviors, shyness, and school competencies in a sample of 102 boys and 85 girls. The study found that workplace variables impacted directly on job-related affect (job satisfaction, negative mood, and job-related tension), which in turn impacted on parenting behavior (authoritative parenting, punishing behaviors, and rejecting behaviors), which in turn impacted on children's behavior (school competencies, acting out, and shyness).

Crouter, Bumpus, Head, and McHale (2001) examined the implications of men's long work hours and role overload (feelings of being overwhelmed by multiple work commitments and not having enough time for themselves) for the quality of their relationships with both their firstborn and second-born adolescents. The study included 190 dual-earner families from the central region of a Northeastern state of the United States (both working and middle-class families were included). Data were collected from both face-to-face family interviews and telephone interviews of parents and adolescents conducted on seven different evenings, asking about how family members spent their time. In contrast with previous findings, work hours and role overload did not have an effect on fathers' temporal involvement with either their firstborn or second-born adolescent. The authors suggested that this finding might be attributed to the fact that "adolescents typically share so few activities with their fathers that even fathers' very long work hours do not make an impact on the amount of time they share, a sobering thought" (Crouter et al., 2001, p. 414). In contrast, it was found that the combination of working long hours and feeling overloaded predicted the quality of the relationships that fathers had with both children. Fathers were seen as being less accepting, and the relationship was characterized by less effective perspective taking when fathers both worked long hours and felt overloaded.

GLOBALIZATION: A CONFLICT FOR FATHERHOOD?

The globalization process has resulted in increased and intense competition for talented employees and for market share based on higher product quality and lower prices. A consequence has also been significant changes in the job demands experienced by many employees and especially managers, most of whom are fathers. Demands have increased for employees to travel and to be accessible during 24 hours of operations (either in person or via video links, telephone, or e-mail).

Organizational factors that potentially could impact on a man's ability to be an involved father include, first, the structure of the organization, especially reporting systems. In many global organizations it is common to report to more than one person, and these people are often at different locations. Second, career path expectations include expectations about the nature of work experiences (e.g., in different parts of the business) and the location of assignments. The timing of these (e.g., in early- vs. midcareer phases) will also have an impact on fatherhood opportunities (including whether or not to become a father!). A third factor is expectations about overseas assignments, including the specific location and for how long. How a company plans for this and supports a father and his spouse or partner and children will have a major impact on employee well-being and organizational outcomes. Expectations about access or availability are a fourth factor. Many organizations now require people to be available outside of local business times.

These globalization expectations could have an impact on fathers by limiting their psychological and physical availability to their children; limiting their opportunities to be available at critical and salient times (e.g., when a child has an accident, when a child has an important school function); and reducing a man's positive self-image as a father and reducing his sense of self-efficacy as a parent. It could additionally impact the quality of his relationships with his children by reducing his opportunities to spend focused and hanging-out time with them. With men themselves, their partners, their children, and the community expecting more of fathers, increased work demands within a global environment will necessarily lead to higher levels of conflict and provide new challenges for men seeking to establish an identity as an involved and committed father.

WORKPLACE EDUCATION AND SUPPORT PROGRAMS

In the recent study of a national random sample of 1,000 Australian fathers (Russell et al., 1999) participants were asked what they thought were the major barriers to men becoming involved as fathers. Of the responses given, 57% were workplace factors (e.g., work demands, hours). Further, when asked what support and information they needed as fathers, the two most common responses were greater workplace flexibility and support and better access to advice and education. Delivering advice and education programs in the workplace has the potential for engaging fathers and for being an effective enabler of father involvement, especially by increasing levels of self-confidence and skill.

Supporting men in their roles as fathers is now quite clearly positioned in the corporate arena. Levine and Pittinsky (1997) is based on 20 years of research and consulting on fatherhood in the corporate world. They define father friendliness in the following way: "The father-friendly company is one that maintains a culture and programmatic mix that supports working fathers in both responsive and proactive ways. . . . Even more, they foster an understanding that it makes good business sense to enable men to be good fathers" (p. 62).

In their review of strategies that help to create a father-friendly workplace, Levine and Pittinsky (1997) highlighted several companies where workplace education and support programs have been implemented for fathers. These include Texas Instruments, Eastman Kodak, the Los Angeles Department of Water, and the U.S. Army. Although anecdotal, all programs are reported to be highly successful in terms of both the numbers attending and the level of engagement of the fathers.

Russell (1998) described both the pathways to getting fatherhood onto the corporate agenda and the different contexts in which fatherhood issues can be addressed. These pathways include (a) conducting fatherhood workshops as part of a broader and more inclusive approach to advancing equal employment opportunity and diversity agendas, (b) developing fatherhood education programs in response to needs identified either as part of counseling conducted by an Employee Assistance Program or findings from employee surveys, and (c) addressing the work-life balance issues for senior managers and their partners or spouses (a focus on parenting and fatherhood will be an inevitable outcome of this process). Russell provided several examples of the nature of corporate work with fathers (e.g., workshops for fathers, workshops for senior managers and their partners or spouses).

As Russell and Llewellyn-Smith (2001) reported, a high percentage of the fathers who attended the program felt that they did not spend enough time with their children (77%), and 61% did not consider themselves to be either highly competent or confident in their parenting role. Nonetheless, 87% said they were highly committed to being effective parents. As a result of having participated in the program, a higher percentage said they had the skills and information to be effective fathers (34% vs. 49%), and 74% indicated they had changed their behavior to improve their relationships with their children.

CONCLUSIONS

The assumption that workplace demands, a lack of workplace flexibility (particularly in terms of leave provisions), and men's strong identification with paid work and career success are the major barriers to active father involvement, and especially the involvement in child care of young children, has been a dominant theme in discourses about fatherhood. Yet, as is evident from the review conducted for this chapter, surprisingly little systematic research has been conducted on the possible contribution the workplace makes to father involvement. Further, it is clear from the analysis presented earlier that the impact of workplace practices and policies on father involvement is highly complex. In this final section we summarize the key findings and provide suggestions for approaches to future research.

SUMMARY OF KEY FINDINGS

Our review covered four workplace practices and policies: parental leave, flexible work practices, workplace demands and stress, and work-based education and support programs. In terms of the quantity and sophistication of the research, studies of parental leave and workplace demands and stress feature much more in the literature. It is these two areas as well that have dominated the public discourse about workplace factors and father involvement. Most Western countries have a recent history of public debate and policy about parental and paternity leave as well as the increasing workplace demands in terms of work hours and the intensity of work (see, e.g., Bond et al., 1998). Providing leave that men can access has been assumed to be a key enabler of men's being more involved with young children, and workplace demands and stressors have been assumed to be major barriers to men's being involved as fathers. The findings, as would be expected, are not always consistent with these hypotheses. Further, as will be argued in a moment, we need to adopt much more sophisticated models in our research approach.

In terms of parental leave, there are three noteworthy trends. First, as was identified by Deven and Moss (2002) in their review of paternity and parental leave provisions in 24 Western countries, there is an emerging emphasis on fatherhood. Paternity leave is an entitlement in 10 of the countries, and all countries provide some form of leave that in theory could be taken by fathers. In three countries (Italy, Sweden, and Norway) there are incentives in place to encourage men to take part of the parental leave entitlement. A second trend is that all analyses show a gap between fathers having access to leave and their actual utilization of this leave, even in countries where there are active campaigns and incentives to encourage men to take the leave.

The third trend therefore is the emerging analysis of the individual and workplace factors that facilitate men's taking the leave to which they are entitled. Two studies reviewed earlier have involved systematic analyses of this issue within the Swedish context. In the first, Haas and Hwang (1995) reported that part of the explanation involves the different responses that companies have to men's interest in parental leave. In their study of the top 200 Swedish companies, they found that only 3% were actively supportive of men in their fathering roles. In the second of the studies, Haas, Allard, and Hwang (2002) investigated both why individual fathers choose not to take the leave they are entitled to and the social conditions that might "discourage fathers as a group from sharing leave more equitably with mothers" (p. 322). They found that individual factors, especially men's parenting attitudes, and family-level factors, especially the partner's willingness to share parenting, had a greater impact than did organizational culture factors (e.g., father friendliness, top management support). Nevertheless, organizational factors did explain a small but significant proportion of the variance (e.g., the extent of workgroup support for men taking leave), suggesting that this should provide a fruitful avenue for future research. These authors argued that future research should continue to focus on individual, family, and organizational factors using longitudinal research designs. They also suggested that organizational factors might have less influence in Sweden because companies are required by law to provide leave. Research of this type is especially needed in other countries to help identify the process of change within organizations to support parental leave for fathers.

There has been very limited research into the impact that the availability of flexible work practices has on father involvement. Studies indicate that fathers report a high level of availability of flexible work practices but relatively low levels of utilization. Findings are not clear-cut in showing that higher levels of job flexibility are associated with higher levels of father involvement. The studies conducted to date, however, have employed very different measures of father involvement and job flexibility and have not examined possible direct links between the utilization of flexible work options and father involvement. As is the case with parental leave, there is also the question of the extent to which organizational culture and supervisory support impact on fathers' utilization of flexible work options. However, this has not yet been the subject of systematic research. An emerging trend in this area (in Australia and the United Kingdom) is legislation that compels employers to consider requests from employees (both men and women) for flexible work practices in order to fulfill caring responsibilities.

Research on the impact of workplace demands and stress on father involvement has generally focused on working hours and job demands. Findings for the relationship between working hours and father involvement are mixed. Studies vary, however, on the ages of children included and measures of father involvement (e.g., relative vs. absolute, data reported by the father vs. data reported by mothers and children). Two particularly interesting findings have emerged from this research. First, fathers who work longer hours are less involved on weekdays (particularly in relation to play and companionship activities) but not on weekends—when fathers are more equal partners in caring for children. Second, there is an interaction between hours worked and attitudes to parenting responsibilities. Men with more modern attitudes toward childcare arrangements work fewer hours than do men with traditional attitudes, particularly if they are under 35 years of age. Kaufman and Uhlengerg (2000) argued that the younger cohort of fathers is more likely to translate egalitarian attitudes toward parenting into behavior that is consistent with the attitudes. Given Haas et al.'s (2002) previous finding that men's parenting attitudes are a significant predictor of the number of days of parental leave taken by fathers in Sweden, it would seem worthwhile to include this variable in future studies as a possible mediator of the impact that workplace policies and practices have on father involvement.

Studies of the impact of job demands on father involvement differ quite markedly in terms of the samples (e.g., ages of children) and methodologies (e.g., measures of workplace demands and father involvement) employed. Nevertheless, findings are generally consistent in showing that higher levels of workplace demands or role overload are associated with a reduction of the quality of father-child interactions (e.g., fathers' being less accepting of their children, having higher levels of anger expression, being more emotionally withdrawn). It is also worth noting that studies in this area have some particular strengths in relation to identifying pathways of influence. Repetti's (1994) study, for example, included objective workplace measures of workloads, and Crouter et al. (2001) involved the temporal separation of data collection and several sources of data (parents and adolescents).

Probably the least well-developed area of workplace research is that of workplace education and support programs. Programs of this type have the potential to increase the level of skill and self-confidence of fathers, which would then be expected to have an impact on the quantity and quality of father involvement. The literature addressing this issue indicates that some governments and organizations have begun to support these programs and that where they have been conducted, fathers have been engaged successfully. Longitudinal studies are clearly needed to conduct a systematic investigation of the potential impact of these programs.

FUTURE DIRECTIONS

Given the central nature of paid work in the lives of the majority of fathers, workplace demands and expectations will continue to have an impact on the practice of fatherhood—as both a potential enabler and a barrier. As this review has shown, however, our level of understanding of the specific nature of the influence of workplace factors is quite rudimentary. Advancements in our knowledge in this area depend in part on two critical changes in approaches: expanding and refining workplace measures employed and developing more sophisticated conceptual models of the potential influence of workplace factors. These arguments were presented in detail earlier and therefore are summarized here in relation to current approaches to research.

Expanding and Refining Workplace Measures

In our initial analysis, we conceptualized work in terms of four dimensions: employment characteristics, workplace policies, work and career design, and workplace culture. Most studies to date have focused on the availability of workplace policies (e.g., parental leave), workplace culture, and aspects of the father's employment characteristics (e.g., hours of work, workplace demands). It should be noted too that the work of Haas et al. (2002) provides a comprehensive analysis of factors associated with workplace culture. What is particularly needed here is the inclusion of measures that are able to identify the extent to which the employment characteristics (e.g., level of customer contact, level of responsibility) provide the opportunity for fathers to utilize available leave or flexibility options. Future research would also benefit from the inclusion of variables associated with work design (e.g., team-based work, measurement of performance) and career design (e.g., whether men at different career stages are likely to access leave options differently).

Conceptualizing the Influence of Workplace Factors

There are two issues here: first, the conceptualization of what aspects of fatherhood practice the workplace has the potential to influence and second, the process of influence. As was argued earlier, the workplace has the potential to influence the practice of fatherhood at three levels: motivation, self-confidence and skills, and provision of enhanced opportunities for fathers to be involved, sensitive, and responsive. Most of the research to date has focused on examining assumed direct links between workplace policies (e.g., parental leave) or work demands (e.g., work hours) and father involvement. Yet, it may be that the workplace, by providing alternative career options and alternative role models of success (that include work-family balance), could function to increase the level of motivation for a father to be involved with his children. On the other hand, the workplace could provide self-development opportunities that enhance communication and interpersonal skills that will increase a father's self-confidence as a parent.

In terms of the process of influence, our analysis highlighted several ways this could function (cf. Voydanoff, 2002). Three pathways were considered. First, the workplace makes a unique and separate contribution to the nature and level of father involvement. This is the model adopted by most researchers. Second, it was argued that the workplace could moderate the relationship between individual and family characteristics and father involvement. Thus, it could be that supportive workplace policies and practices (e.g., parental leave specifically identified for fathers) could enable the level of involvement of an already motivated father and increase the relationship between these two factors. Third, it was argued that workplace policies and practices could function to mediate the level of direct father involvement. Thus, fathers who have a strong identity with traditional masculinity might be less likely to access flexible work options to facilitate their involvement in family life. Or, a father who has egalitarian attitudes to parenting and who lives in a culture where the public discourse supports gender equity would be expected to have higher utilization rates for parental leave. This in turn could lead to a higher level of involvement in child care. This is a possible interpretation of the findings of the Haas et al. (2002) study, which found that individual and family factors were significant predictors of the number of days parental leave a father took.

Findings from Haas et al. (2002) draw attention also to the need to consider the potential influence of a father's individual and family context and the broader social-cultural context within which he lives. The majority of the research reviewed for this chapter has been conducted either in Sweden or the United States. Clearly, there is a need to broaden our conceptualization and research models to include the range of employment and policy contexts experienced in different cultures and subcultures.

REFERENCES

Bailyn, L., Rapoport, R., & Fletcher, J. K. (2000). Moving corporations in the United States toward gender equity: A cautionary tale. In L. Haas, C. P. Hwang, & G. Russell (Eds.), *Organizational change and gender equity: International perspectives on fathers and mothers at the workplace* (pp. 167–180). Thousand Oaks, CA: Sage.

Bankert, E., & Googins, B. (1996, July/August). Family-friendly—says who? *Across the Board,* 45–49.

Barham, L. J., Gottlieb, B. H., & Kelloway, E. K. (1998). Variables affecting managers' willingness to grant alternative work arrangements. *Journal of Social Psychology, 138*(3), 291–302.

Berry, J. O., & Rao, J. M. (1997). Balancing employment and fatherhood. *Journal of Family Issues, 18,* 386–403.

Björnberg, U. (2000). Equality and backlash: Family, gender and social policy in Sweden. In L. Haas, C. P. Hwang, & G. Russell (Eds.), *Organizational change and gender equity: International perspectives on fathers and mothers at the workplace* (pp. 57–76). Thousand Oaks, CA: Sage.

Bond, J., Galinsky, E., & Swanberg, J. (1998). *The 1997 national study of the changing workforce.* New York: Families and Work Institute.

Bonney, J. F., Kelley, M. L., & Levant, R. F. (1999). A model of fathers' behavioral involvement in child care in dual-earner families. *Journal of Family Psychology, 13*(3), 401–415.

Burghes, L., Clarke, L., & Cronin, N. (1997). Fathers and Fatherhood in Britain. London: Family Policies Centre (Occasional Paper 23).

Cooper, C., & Lewis, S. (1995). *Beyond family friendly organisations.* London: Demos.

Crouter, A. C., Bumpus, M. E., Head, M. R., & McHale, S. M. (2001). Implications of overwork and overload for the quality of men's family relationships. *Journal of Marriage and the Family, 63*, 404–417.

Cunningham, K. (2001). Father time: Flexible work arrangements and the law firm's failure of the family. *Stanford Law Review, 53*, 967–1008.

Deven, F., & Moss, P. (2002). Leave arrangements for parents: Overview and future outlook. *Community, Work and Family, 5*, 237–256.

Duxbury, L. E., Higgins, C. A., & Thomas, D. R. (1996). Work and family environments and the adoption of computer-supported supplemental work-at-home. *Journal of Vocational Behavior, 49*, 1–23.

Galinsky, E., & Swanberg, J. E. (2000). Employed mothers and fathers in the United States: Understanding how work and family life fit together. In L. Haas, C. P. Hwang, & G. Russell (Eds.), *Organizational change and gender equity: International perspectives on fathers and mothers at the workplace* (pp. 15–28). Thousand Oaks, CA: Sage.

Gerson, K. (1993). *No man's land: Men's changing commitments to family and work*. New York: Basic Books.

Gerstel, N., & Gallagher, S. K. (2001). Men's caregiving: Gender and the contingent character of care. *Gender and Society, 15*, 197–217.

Haas, L. (1992). *Equal parenthood and social policy*. Albany: State University of New York Press.

Haas, L. (2002). Parental leave and gender equality: What can the US learn from the European Union? *Review of Policy Research, 20*, 89–114.

Haas, L., Allard, K., & Hwang, P. (2002). The impact of organizational culture on men's use of parental leave in Sweden. *Community, Work and Family, 5*(2), 319–342.

Haas, L., & Hwang, C. P. (1995). Company culture and men's usage of family leave benefits in Sweden. *Family Relations, 44*, 28–36.

Haas, L., & Hwang, C. P. (2000). Programs and policies promoting women's economic equality and men's sharing of child care in Sweden. In L. Haas, C. P. Hwang, & G. Russell (Eds.), *Organizational change and gender equity: International perspectives on fathers and mothers at the workplace* (pp. 133–162). Thousand Oaks, CA: Sage.

Haas, L., Hwang, C. P., & Russell, G. (Eds.). (2000). *Organizational change and gender equity: International perspectives on fathers and mothers at the workplace*. Thousand Oaks, CA: Sage.

Haley, H.-L., Perry-Jenkins, M., & Armenia, A. (2001). Workplace policies and the psychological well-being of first-time parents. In R. Hertz (Ed.), *Working families*. California: University of California Press.

Kaufman, G., & Uhlenberg, P. (2000). The influence of parenthood on the work effort of married men and women. *Social Forces, 78*, 931–947.

Lamb, M. E., Pleck, J. H., Charnov, E. L., & Levine, J. A. (1987). A biosocial perspective on paternal behavior and involvement. In J. B. Lancaster, J. Altmann, A. Rossi, & L. R. Sherrod (Eds.), *Parenting across the life span: Biosocial perspectives* (pp. 111–142). Hawthorne, NY: de Gruyter.

Lamb, M. E., Pleck, J. H., & Levine, J. A. (1985). The role of the father in child development: The effects of increased paternal involvement. In B. B. Lahey & A. E. Kazdin (Eds.), *Advances in clinical child psychology* (Vol. 8, pp. 229–266). New York: Plenum.

Lamb, M. E., & Sagi, A. (Eds.). (1983). *Fatherhood and social policy*. Hillsdale, NJ: Erlbaum.

Levine, J. A. (1997). *Who will raise the children? New options for fathers (and mothers)*. New York: Bantam.

Levine, J. A., & Pittinsky, T. (1997). *Working fathers: New strategies for balancing work and family*. San Diego, CA: Harvest Books.

Lewis, S. (1996). Sense of entitlement, family friendly policies, and gender. In H. Holt & I. Thaulow (Eds.), *The role of companies in reconciling working life and family life* (pp. 17–42). Copenhagen, Denmark: Danish National Institute of Social Research.

Morehead, A., Steele, M., Alexander, M., Stephen, K., & Duffin, L. (1977). *Changes at work: The 1995 Australian Workplace Industrial Relations Survey.* Canberra Department of Industrial Relations and Small Business.

Pleck, J. H. (1986). Employment and fatherhood: Issues and innovative policies. In M. E. Lamb (Ed.), *The father's role: Applied perspectives* (pp. 385–412). New York: Wiley.

Pleck, J. H. (1997). Paternal involvement: Levels, sources, and consequences. In M. E. Lamb (Ed.), *The role of the father in child development* (3rd ed., pp. 66–103, 325–332). New York: Wiley.

Repetti, R. L. (1994). Short-term and long-term processes linking job stressors to father-child interaction. *Social Development, 3*, 1–15.

Rostgaard, T. (2002). Setting time aside for the father: Father's leave in Scandinavia. *Community, Work and Family, 5*, 343–364.

Russell, G. (1983). *The changing role of fathers?* Brisbane, Australia: University of Queensland Press.

Russell, G., Barclay, L., Edgecombe, G., Donovan, J., Habib, G., Callaghan, H., & Pawson, Q. (1999). *Fitting fathers into families.* Canberra, Australia: Department of Family and Community Services.

Russell, G., & Edgar, D. (2000). Organizational change and gender equity: An Australian case study. In L. Haas, C. P. Hwang, & G. Russell (Eds.), *Organizational change and gender equity: International perspectives on fathers and mothers at the workplace* (pp. 197–212). Thousand Oaks, CA: Sage.

Russell, G., James, D., & Watson, J. (1988). Work/family policies: The changing role of fathers and the presumption of shared responsibility for parenting. *Australian Journal of Social Issues, 23*, 249–267.

Russell, G., & Llewellyn-Smith, P. (2001, December). *Working with fathers where they are: Learnings from the workplace.* Paper presented to the Family Strengths Conference, University of Newcastle.

Stewart, W., & Barling, J. (1996). Fathers' work experiences effect children's behaviours via job-related affect and parenting behaviours. *Journal of Organizational Behaviour, 17*, 221–232.

Tamis-LeMonda, C. S., & Cabrera, N. (1999). Perspectives on father involvement: Research and policy. *Social Policy Report: Society for Research in Child Development, 13*(2), 1–26.

Voydanoff, P. (2002). Linkages between the work-family interface and work, family, and individual outcomes. *Journal of Family Issues, 23*, 138–164.

Waldfogel, J. (2001). Family and medical leave: Evidence from the 2000 Surveys. *Monthly Labor Review,* September, pp. 17–23.

Wilkinson, H., Radley, S., Christie, I., Lawson, G., & Sainsbury, J. (1997). *Time out: The costs and benefits of paid parental leave.* London: Demos.

Yeung, W. J., Sandberg, J. F., Davis-Kean, E. D., & Hofferth, S. L. (2001). Children's time with fathers in intact families. *Journal of Marriage and Family, 63*, 136–154.

Author Index

Subject Index